Optimal Redistributive Taxation

Optimal Redistributive Taxation

Matti Tuomala

OXFORD
UNIVERSITY PRESS

OXFORD
UNIVERSITY PRESS

Great Clarendon Street, Oxford, OX2 6DP,
United Kingdom

Oxford University Press is a department of the University of Oxford.
It furthers the University's objective of excellence in research, scholarship,
and education by publishing worldwide. Oxford is a registered trade mark of
Oxford University Press in the UK and in certain other countries

First Edition published in 2016

Published in the United States of America by Oxford University Press
198 Madison Avenue, New York, NY 10016, United States of America

British Library Cataloguing in Publication Data
Data available

Library of Congress Control Number: 2015942941

ISBN 978–0–19–875341–4

ACKNOWLEDGEMENTS

This book draws liberally on joint work with my co-authors. My special thanks go to my co-authors Vidar Christiansen, Jeremy Edwards, Ravi Kanbur, Mick Keen, Jukka Pirttilä, Terhi Ravaska, Marja Riihelä, Risto Sullström, Ilpo Suoniemi, Hannu Tanninen, Ritva Tarkiainen, Sanna Tenhunen, and Tuuli Ylinen. I am especially grateful to Vidar, Ravi and Jukka for ongoing discussions, collaboration, and stimulation of the ideas in this book. Of course, everyone who has worked in this area owes the greatest intellectual debt to the Nobel laureate James Mirrlees, whose influence is reflected throughout the book. I am also grateful to a large number of people and colleagues who have helped in the course of my work on this book. For their comments, advice, and assistance, I would like to thank: Rolf Aaberge, Thomas Aronsson, Tony Atkinson, Alessandro Balestrino, Spencer Bastani, Marcus Berliant, Sören Blomquist, Tomer Blumkin, Robin Boadway, Francois Bourguignon, Lans Bovenberg, Craig Brett, Steve Coate, Ugo Colombino, Helmuth Cremer, Leonardo Felli, Thomas Gaube, Bas Jacobs, Laurent Jacquet, Engbert Jongen, Kaisa Kotakorpi, Hamish Low, Nicholas Marceau, Luca Micheletto, John Moore, Hisahiro Naito, Sören Bo Nielsen, Andrew Oswald, Pierre Pestieau, Martin Ravallion, Kevin Roberts, Santiago Rubio, Emmanuel Saez, Agnar Sandmo, Saikat Sarkar, Motohiro Sato, Fred Schroyen, Amartya Sen, Eytan Sheshinski, Tomas Sjögren, Peter Birch Sörensen, Richard Sturn, Kari Takala, Tuomas Takalo, Lari-Matti Tuomala, Markku Tuomala, Elina Tuominen, Jouko Vilmunen and my colleagues in our economics team at University of Tampere.

I am also grateful to the editorial and production team of OUP—Vaishnavi Ananthasubramanyam, Kristy Barker, Rebecca Bryant, Lowri Ribbons, Adam Swallow, and Aimee Wright—for their excellent work. Two anonymous reviewers have given me much useful advice for the final version of the book. Last but not least, I thank my home team: Maija-Riitta and Lari-Matti. They have provided support throughout this project.

Matti Tuomala

September 2015

TABLE OF CONTENTS

LIST OF FIGURES

LIST OF TABLES

1 Introduction

In modern societies, tax systems raise large amounts of revenue for funding public sector activities.[1] Alongside transfer systems, they also redistribute income and alleviate poverty. Although all components of public action may play a role in reducing poverty and inequality, it is nevertheless the case that tax/transfer policy and public provision of education, health care and social services together have a crucial role to play in treating the symptoms and also the causes of poverty. Not surprisingly, the setting of tax rates and the generosity and structure of transfer programmes generate heated controversy among politicians, social scientists, and the general public. Normative analysis is crucial for tax/transfer design because it makes it possible to assess separately how changes in the redistributive criteria of the government and changes in the size of the behavioural responses to taxes and transfers affect the optimal tax/transfer system. Optimal tax theory provides a way of thinking rigorously about these trade-offs. It provides a methodology for designing tax/transfer systems to achieve the best outcome given the constraints. The seminal theoretical work in this area was carried out by James Mirrlees (1971).[2] Practical tax policy debate is also influenced by the modern optimal tax theory literature, the most notable example of which is the Mirrlees Review (2011). The Review says that optimal tax theory 'is nevertheless a powerful tool and, throughout this volume, the conclusions of optimal tax theory will inform the way in which we discuss policy' (*Tax by Design: The Mirrlees Review*, p. 39).

The theory of optimal taxation begins by clarifying the objectives of policy and identifying the constraints upon policy. The tax system that best achieves the objectives while satisfying the constraints is identified as the optimum one. There are four main elements in determining the optimal income tax schedule in the Mirrlees model: the social welfare function; the distribution of earning abilities; the individual supply or behavioural response function; and the production structure. Together, these four components produce the degree of optimal after-tax/transfer distribution. Hence, the optimal tax literature combines two rather different origins of economics: the ethics-related tradition and the engineering-related tradition.

The social welfare function embodies society's values about issues of equity and fairness. It is increasing in each individual's utility, so that it fully embodies the Pareto

[1] The OECD Revenue Statistics shows that there are large differences in the share of taxes in GDP in developed countries varying in 2012 from 48 per cent in Denmark to 24.3 per cent in the US.

[2] Vickrey (1945) is an early formalization of the optimal income tax problem. But he does not solve the optimal tax formula.

principle. At the same time, it may incorporate aversion to inequality, or a degree of priority to the worse off. Under a sum-utilitarian social welfare function, the government seeks to maximize aggregate utility. This implies a case for redistribution from the rich to the poor when there is diminishing marginal utility of income. An extreme case is the utility-based version of the Rawlsian difference principle—maximin—which attaches no weight at all to anybody's well-being apart from that of the worst-off individual. Hence the government seeks to maximize the utility of the worst-off person in the society. This yields a case for redistribution, even if there is not diminishing marginal utility of income. The optimal tax theory focuses on the consequences of any form of taxation and public expenditure for the distribution of well-being, without any particular ethical concern for the values emerging from the market. In other words, pre-tax income has no independent moral significance.[3]

Social welfare can embody value judgements other than those associated with the distribution of utility. Optimal tax theory and public economics more generally have remained rooted (too rooted) in utilitarianism. Outcomes can also be assessed in different ways. We may decide to focus on individual well-being, but this does not necessarily mean experienced utility.[4] Governments may also take a non-welfaristic approach, attaching weight to objectives that do not reflect individual preferences. There are several examples of this that are relevant when considering optimal tax policy. An example of a non-welfaristic objective is poverty alleviation, where the objective may be to remove as many people as possible from below some poverty line in consumption or income.[5] Since poverty alleviation typically ignores the value of leisure to those in poverty, it is necessarily non-welfaristic. For many years (and most recently in Sen 2009), Amartya Sen has been arguing for a non-welfarist approach and notably for individual capabilities, defined broadly as the freedom that people have to function in key dimensions. Social welfare may be a function of individual well-being, but well-being assessed in terms of capabilities may lead to different conclusions.

The skill of an individual, broadly understood, is what determines his or her ability to produce income. Since factors affecting earnings ability (for example intelligence, inheritance, family background, motivation, luck) are not equally distributed, pre-tax income distribution is far from equal. In the standard optimal income tax model it is assumed that the labour services supplied by different individuals differ in productivity according to their different skills. A common efficiency unit is therefore used, and it is assumed that an individual with skill n works y hours and supplies labour services at the amount of ny, as measured in efficiency units.

The taxpayer can alter his or her behaviour according to the tax system he faces. In particular, the taxpayer chooses how much labour to supply. The labour supply function

[3] Their book *The Myth of Ownership* (Murphy and Nagel 2002) has the same starting point.

[4] Kaplow (2008a) in turn argues strongly that policy prescription should be based solely on a welfaristic social welfare function, taking account of no other considerations.

[5] See Kanbur, Keen, and Tuomala, 1994a, b.

provides essential information about the costs of a redistributive tax system. The Mirrlees model considers labour supply changes in continuous variables such as working hours (on its intensive margin). However, much of labour supply consists of the decision to work or not to work, such as the labour force participation of parents with small children, retirement decisions, and responses to disability.

The standard model uses a production structure with one basic input—labour in efficiency units—with a fixed wage. In much of the literature it is assumed that the elasticity of substitution between individuals of different productivities is constant and infinite. Consequently, the ratio of the wages of any two groups of individuals with different skills is completely independent of the number of hours supplied by these groups. This ensures that redistribution occurs only through the fiscal system. If the wages earned by the various groups of individuals also depend on their labour supply, then there is a second route by which the tax system can bring about some redistribution.

First Mirrlees (1971) examines the optimal tax problem in general terms, without assuming a specific form of utility and of the distribution of skills. A striking feature of the optimal income tax literature is that there are only very few purely analytical results concerning the marginal tax structure. Roughly speaking there are, in the Mirrlees model, two analytical results: the marginal tax rates lies between 0 per cent and 100 per cent; and it is zero at both ends of the distribution. The lower endpoint result (Seade 1977), in particular, has been taken as suggestive in arguing against very high effective marginal rates on the poor. How relevant is it? The result says that, if no one earns zero income at the optimum, then the optimal marginal tax rate faced by the lowest income earner is zero. An important requirement for this result is boundedness away from zero.[6]

It can be said that the very basic nature of income tax problems requires quantitative results. Mere general principles are not of much value. Thus, our natural aim is to find in the optimal income tax models how to connect empirical measurements to specific numerical proposals. This is also one of our main aims in this book.

How should we tax and support low-income people? In fact, characterizing optimal income transfers was one of the motivations offered by Mirrlees (1971) for his exploration of the optimal non-linear income tax, and he remarked on the inability to address transfers without regard to the rest of the income tax schedule. This idea is aptly described by Mirrlees (1971, p. 208):

> It was a major intention of the present study to provide methods for estimating desirable tax rates at the lowest income levels, and a surprise that these tax rates are the most difficult to determine, in a sense. They cannot be determined without at the same time determining the whole optimum income tax schedule. To put things another way, no such proposal can be valid out of the context of the rest of the income tax schedule.

Hence, it would be better to speak about tax/transfer schedules.

[6] As shown by Ebert (1992), if there is an atom of non-workers, there is a positive marginal tax rate at the level where earnings begin.

Transfer programmes for the poor should be distinguished from social insurance programmes such as a publicly provided pension system, medical insurance, and unemployment insurance. Social insurance has been widely regarded as the cornerstone of modern income support policy. In most developed countries, social insurance accounts for the largest share of the social security budget, and it is seen as fundamental to the prevention of poverty. Yet social insurance has been permanently under attack during recent decades. Some people see the existing systems of income maintenance as failing to provide adequate support to those with low incomes. It is argued that social insurance should be replaced by a basic income guarantee which provides benefits without any links to age or past earnings history. This view is often linked to a desire to integrate income tax and social security systems. Second, attacks have come from those who are aiming to reduce state expenditure on income maintenance. Supporters of this view argue that if there is a constraint on total government spending, then more finely targeting the payments using means-tested transfers to those most in need is the most efficient way to alleviate poverty. Finer targeting of programmes to alleviate poverty appears an attractive option in an era of greatly constrained expenditure budgets. It seems as though policy-makers could achieve greater poverty reduction with fewer resources if only they would resort to the magic of targeting. But fine targeting is not without its costs. The administrative costs of ensuring that benefits from a programme reach the target group can be high.

There is a vast literature on programmes for low-income people, both theoretical and empirical. In the normative literature on the subject, the following questions are basic ones. Why should the government be in the role of helping the poor? How should cash assistance programmes be optimally designed? What is the role of in-kind transfers or publicly provided private goods? What are the implications of behavioural economics for the programme design?

Different approaches to the role of the government can be distinguished. Government provision of transfers to the poor can be seen as necessary to correct the market failure created by the situation in which the rich are altruistic toward the poor and the welfare of the poor is a public good. Because the welfare of the poor is a public good, private charity can be expected to under-provide transfer to the poor. Then the publicly provided transfer has the potential to make all individuals better off. Governments may also take a paternalistic approach in the sense of giving weight to the well-being of persons, but judging that well-being not according to the preferences revealed by individuals themselves, but according to preferences chosen by the government. The distributive justice approach in turn views support for the poor as a moral responsibility of the government even if the rich do not care about the poor.

There are two basic approaches to thinking about the design of low-income support programmes. The integrated approach embeds the problem of designing low-income support into the general problem of choosing an optimal tax/transfer system. Thus, as suggested in the quotation from Mirrlees (1971) above, the transfer programme is designed as part of an optimal income tax system. If the social welfare weight on the poor is sufficiently large, the poor end up paying negative taxes, which can then be interpreted as transfers. We focus on this approach here. The partial equilibrium approach in turn considers the problem of minimizing the fiscal cost of providing the poor with some minimum utility or income level. For normative work, the minimum utility constraint makes the most sense. However, as a positive matter, it often seems to be that politicians do not value the leisure of the poor, and hence the minimum income constraint is an interesting one to adopt if the goal is to explain programme design. A minimum income constraint is an example of a non-welfarist objective.[7] The advantage of this approach is that it does not require the modelling of an entire economy and hence permits a sharper focus on the problem of programme design. At the same time this approach may be misleading in its avoidance of the whole tax/transfer system.

How to tax top incomes is also very topical after several decades of increasing top income share. The increasing share of total income of the top income earners has been a notable feature of changes in income inequality in English-speaking countries, while in Europe, the Netherlands, France, and Switzerland—and, elsewhere, Japan—display hardly any change in top income share (see Atkinson and Piketty 2007, 2010).[8] This trend toward income concentration has also taken place in the Nordic countries, traditionally low-inequality countries. For example, the top percentile income (disposable)[9] share in Finland doubled in the latter part of the 1990s. At the same time, top tax rates on upper-income earners have declined significantly in many OECD countries, again particularly in English-speaking countries. Piketty et al (2014) investigate the link between skyrocketing inequality and top tax rates in OECD countries and find a strong correlation between tax cuts for the highest earners and increases in the income share of the top 1 per cent since 1975.[10] Economists have formulated several hypotheses about the causes of increasing inequality, but there is not a fully compelling explanation. For example, Atkinson et al (2011) emphasize that it is very difficult to account for these figures on inequality with the standard labour supply/labour demand explanation. Hence we really have to think about things such as social policies and progressive taxation.

As mentioned above, the optimal income tax literature also provides a striking result on a top marginal tax rate. The optimal marginal tax rate for the highest-waged person is zero. Sadka (1976) says that the highest income should be subject to a zero marginal tax rate but, strictly speaking, this result applies only to a single person at the very top of the income distribution, suggesting it is a mere theoretical curiosity. Moreover, it is unclear that a 'top earner' even exists. For example, Saez (2001, p. 206) argues that 'unbounded distributions are of much more interest than bounded distributions to address the high income optimal tax rate problem'. Without a top earner, the intuition for the zero top

[7] See e.g. Besley and Coate (1995) and Moffitt (2006).

[8] The more recent estimates of Camille Landais (2007) show a rise in recent years in France.

[9] Finland is one of those few countries for which we have data on disposable (after tax/transfer) top income.

[10] Moreover, they also find that top tax rate cuts are not associated with higher economic growth.

marginal rate does not apply, and marginal rates near the top of the income distribution may be positive and even large. Calculations in Tuomala (1984) show that the zero rate is not a good approximation for high incomes.

In Mirrlees (1971) all wage distributions were unbounded above and therefore he did not have a zero rate result. He, in turn, presented precise conjectures about optimal assymptotic tax rates in the case of utility functions separable in consumption and labour. One of the least well-known features of Mirrlees' (1971) paper is the demonstration (on page 189) that the optimal marginal tax rate converges to a positive value when the upper tail of the skill distribution is of Paretian form, with this value being a function of the Pareto parameter and the characteristics of the utility function. It appears that the role of the latter depends solely on their appearance in the constraints, and does not depend on them entering the government's objective function. The key assumptions behind these results are that either the marginal utility of consumption or the social marginal valuation of utility goes to zero when the wage rates tend to infinity (see also Dahan and Strawczynski, 2012). In this situation we need only information on labour supply elasticities and the shape of the skill distribution to determine the optimal top marginal income tax rate.

Optimal income tax research, particularly recent work, has mainly focused on the upper and lower parts of the income distribution—in other words, how to tax high-income earners and low-income people. There are many good reasons for this focus. It is clear, however, that it is equally important to understand how to tax those taxpayers in between. In many advanced countries poverty rates are 10–15 per cent or even higher. Hence the group in between amounts to around 80–85 per cent of all taxpayers.

Because one of the key factors explaining the shape of an optimal income tax schedule is the assumed family of distributions of earning abilities, it is interesting to look at distributions other than the lognormal and Pareto distributions. Saez (2001, p. 226), building on the work of Diamond (1998), carried out numerical simulations and concluded, in dramatic contrast to earlier results, that marginal rates should rise between middle- and high-income earners, and that rates at high incomes should 'not be lower than 50% and may be as high as 80%'. These results are more consistent with existing tax systems. The key difference between these findings and earlier studies is in the underlying assumptions about the shape of the distribution of wages. Mirrlees (1971), Atkinson (1972), and Tuomala (1984) assumed a lognormal distribution, whereas Diamond (1998) and Saez (2001) argued that the right tail is better described by a Pareto distribution.

As is commonly known, lognormal distribution fits reasonably well over a large part of the income range, but diverges markedly at both tails. Pareto distribution, in turn, fits well at the upper tail. When James Mirrlees came to do his numerical calculations for the shape of optimal non-linear tax schedules, he used lognormal distribution. This distribution perhaps seemed a natural one for him to use, given that lognormal distribution was by then already the functional form of choice for the graduation of income distributions; however, its use by Mirrlees (1971) effectively sealed its dominance as the optimal non-linear income taxation literature exploded, and virtually every paper on the topic in the coming decades used lognormal distribution for numerical calculations.

Champernowne (1952) proposes a model in which individual incomes are assumed to follow a random walk in the logarithmic scale. In this book we replace lognormal distribution with Champernowne distribution.[11] Specifically, we use the two-parameter version of the Champernowne distribution. This distribution approaches asymptotically a form of Pareto distribution for large values of wages, but it also has an interior maximum. Without assuming constant labour supply elasticity, as in Diamond (1998) and Saez (2001), the numerical simulations in Chapter 5 of this book show that: (a) it is difficult to find the U-shaped pattern of the marginal income tax rates over the entire distribution of wages; (b) it is either sufficiently high pre-tax inequality or a combination of sufficiently high pre-tax inequality and sufficiently low revenue requirement that leads to a pattern of optimally increasing marginal tax rates.

A key question in numerical simulations is how the distribution of skill is chosen. In Saez (2001), the skill distribution is 'backed out' from the empirical distribution of income. Moreover, in order to do so, it is assumed that the tax function is linear. This does not of course match the highly non-linear tax functions observed in practice, and seems particularly inappropriate in an optimal non-linear framework. Furthermore, it has to be assumed that the elasticity of labour supply is constant. An alternative approach, one introduced in Kanbur and Tuomala (1994), is to accept the non-linearities that characterize income tax schedules, and furthermore to allow for utility functions which imply non-constant labour elasticity. They select a skill distribution which, through the model, produces an earnings distribution that matches empirical earnings distributions.

Even if the shape of the ability distribution were known, other uncertainties remain. For example, the question of what appropriate social welfare function to use—and, in particular, how much concern there should be over inequality—is a normative question that cannot be answered with data. In addition, characteristics of the individual's utility function can affect the pattern of optimal income tax rates. Dahan and Strawczynski (2001) study the importance of income effects (equivalently, declining marginal utility of consumption) for the pattern of marginal tax rates. They argue that concave utility lowers optimal tax rates at high incomes and that marginal tax rates may be declining even for a Pareto distribution of wages. Tuomala (2010) replaces the utility functions used in previous simulations with a quadratic utility of consumption with a bliss point. This greatly reduces the curvature of the utility function over consumption. This utility function with upper bound on consumption necessarily implies a concave budget constraint in Mirrlees' (1971) model. In other words, the marginal tax rates are increasing in income, at least in the utilitarian case. The simulations in Tuomala (2010) and in section 2.4 demonstrate this.

The relevant elasticities are crucial for optimal marginal tax rates. Saez (2001) used a constant labour supply elasticity formulation not because there was strong empirical

[11] It is often referred to as the Fisk distribution (see Fisk, 1961a, b). See also Bevan (2005).

evidence for it, but because there was not strong evidence against it. However, since the Saez (2001) paper, a survey by Röed and Ström (2002) has provided some evidence for labour supply elasticity declining with income for Norway. Röed and Ström (2002) (tables 1 and 2) offer a review of the evidence. They conclude that the limited evidence indicates that labour supply elasticities are declining with household income. High labour supply elasticities among low-wage workers are also confirmed by empirical evaluations of various in-work benefit schemes operating in the US, the UK, and some other countries. By contrast, there is empirical evidence on the elasticity of taxable income showing that higher elasticities are present among high-income individuals. Feldstein (1995) estimated large elasticities of taxable income with respect to tax rates among high earners. Gruber and Saez (2002) and subsequent research (see a recent survey by Saez, Slemrod, and Giertz 2012) generated much smaller elasticities. The estimates in Gruber and Saez (2002) also support the hypothesis that elasticity increases with income. If high-income workers are particularly elastic in how their taxable income decreases with higher tax rates, this would imply lower optimal marginal tax rates on high incomes, all else being the same. But, as with the distribution of abilities and the social welfare function, there is much debate over the true pattern of elasticities by income. For example, Diamond (2003, p. 13) writes: 'there is a major issue of interpreting of the elasticity given that high earners probably have more ability to do intertemporal substitution of realized income. It is the intertemporal government budget constraint that is relevant, not the annual one'. All this leaves us in an uncomfortable position.

The standard optimal tax models assume a very simple utility function which is uniform across all individuals, increases in consumption, and decreases in work effort. There is an increasing acceptance that the welfare of individuals is not solely determined by material circumstances but also depends heavily on their relative position in society. As shown by behavioural economics and happiness research, among others, utilities may be interdependent because of relative consumption or status or positional concerns. One way to explain this would be to assume that people care about the consumption or utility level of others; that people have 'social preferences'. Relative consumption (income) concern or status-seeking creates negative externalities because gains in one's status reduce someone else's. If these externalities are as important as a growing body of empirical studies seems to suggest, taxing consumption externalities might be welfare-enhancing in just the same way as any other Pigouvian tax. This simple intuition does not tell us anything about the effects of relative income concerns on the tax schedule. Is income tax an effective tool for reducing inequalities and attenuating possible externalities arising from relative income concerns? There are some papers which ask these questions in an optimal non-linear tax framework. Do people make comparisons between or among individuals of similar incomes? Or is the lifestyle of the upper middle class and the rich a more salient point of reference for people throughout the income distribution? One can also argue that rich people are largely motivated by status goods and by relative status. If so, they can be just as happy with less money, so long as other rich folk have less money too. If that is true, then taxing the rich is a free lunch. Surely the government, even a wasteful government, could use this money for something. High tax rates are also not a worry if rich people are motivated by intrinsic rewards. Chapter 7 examines the impact of redistributive non-linear income taxation in a model with relative consumption concern.

It is now well understood that while universal benefits are costly means of poverty alleviation, the other extreme of fine means-testing through income-related transfers and benefits is not without its problems either. Thus, for example, proposals such as a negative income tax or social dividend scheme have built-in conflicts between a sufficiently high income guarantee to the poor and sufficiently low marginal tax rates on the population to maintain incentives. Transfers can be made contingent upon different characteristics. This is often called 'tagging'. Categorical or contingent benefits, which make transfers conditional not upon income but upon characteristics such as old age, gender, region, unemployment, disability, etc., can be used to target resources to the poor, making benefits vary with poverty in the group as a whole. Of course, if there is variation of incomes within a group, then there will continue to be some leakage to rich individuals within groups that are poor on average, and relative neglect of poor individuals within groups that are rich on average. For these reasons, some income testing within groups may be appropriate, although the incentive effects of such income testing will again be relevant.[12] Given these developments in understanding, Atkinson (1992, quoted in Immonen et al 1998, p. 179) writes: 'the issue of policy design is not therefore a confrontation between fully universal benefits and pure income testing; rather the question is that of the appropriate balance of categorical and income tests'.

Akerlof (1978)[13] was among the first to recognize that the use of contingent information to implement several tax/transfer schedules, one for each group, was bound to be superior to being restricted to a single schedule for the whole population. However, he did not say much about the quantitative gain from such differentiation, nor about the shapes of the schedules for the different groups. The tagging literature has thus grown, and is still growing. However, its central assumption is still that the groupings available to the government are given and fixed. The government cannot rearrange these groupings—it cannot increase or decrease the number of groups, nor can it choose one type of grouping over another. Thus the assumption is on the one hand that the groupings are available to the government without cost, yet on the other hand that it is too costly for the government to deviate from the groupings specified by the analyst. However, if the implementation of tagging is itself costly, and if the costs are a function of the number and type of groupings available, the question arises: how many and which types of groups should the government choose to tag? This is the question addressed in Kanbur and Tuomala (2013).

[12] There are of course many other considerations that also arise in comparing categorical and means-tested benefits, not the least of which is the possibility of incomplete take-up of the latter as a consequence of stigma and/or hassle: see, e.g., Atkinson (1992), Besley (1990), and Cowell (1986).

[13] In fact a two-tier social dividend system, as in the Meade report (1978) pp. 271–6, is a very similar idea.

The welfarist approach ranks social outcomes solely according to how they affect individual utilities. Utility also plays a dual role in the welfarist literature on optimal taxation. It is the same utility function employed by individuals in their decision that enters the social welfare function. Both of these are open to question. The modelling of individual decision-making has been particularly questioned in the recent literature on behavioural public economics. As we mentioned earlier, the government can also take a non-welfaristic approach, attaching weight to social objectives that do not reflect individual preferences. Much of the attention of non-welfarist approaches has focused on a particular form of non-welfarism, namely poverty reduction. Policy discussion on poverty alleviation and the targeting of social policy often concentrates almost exclusively on income. Little weight is typically given to issues like the disutility the poor experience when working. Indeed, sometimes work requirements are seen in a positive light, as is often the case with 'workfare'. This is in marked contrast with conventional, utility-based objectives in optimal income taxation literature. Therefore it is worthwhile to examine the implications of poverty reduction objectives on optimal income tax rules. It must also be remembered that the dividing line between welfarism and non-welfarism is not very clear. Conventional tax analysis utilizes social welfare functions with inequality aversion, which already implies a deviation of assessing individual welfare with the same function which the individual uses himself. In some sense, the social objective functions form a continuum in the welfarism–non-welfarism scale. Kanbur et al (1994a) examine the properties of the Mirrlees-type optimal income tax model when the government objective is alleviation of income poverty. Instead of social welfare maximization, the government aims to minimize an income-based poverty index of the general additively separable form. This specification captures a number of widely used poverty measures, such as the headcount ratio and the Gini-based measure of Sen (1976). Note that while it bears similarity with a Rawlsian social welfare function (focusing on the poor), the poverty index depends only on income. In the Rawlsian difference principle, an individual's well-being is judged according to an index of primary goods. Chapter 9 examines optimal non-linear income taxation in a model with non-welfarist social objectives.

The Mirrlees model generally assumes that individuals have the same preferences, so that the same utility function can be used to represent their interests in the social welfare function. It is quite plausible to assume that in reality, for all sorts of reasons, individuals differ in both skill and preferences. Multidimensional heterogeneity in individuals' characteristics is a realistic assumption, but it complicates the analysis notably. In fact, differences in tastes raising 'different kinds of problems' is precisely the reason Mirrlees gave in 1971 for taking identical individual utility functions to determine income tax.[14] The problem of heterogeneous preferences is not just about incentives. It is also

[14] Pigou (1968, p. 58) offered a similar reasoning when he wrote 'But, since it is impossible in practice to take account of variations between different people's capacity for enjoyment, this consideration must be ignored, and the assumption made, for want of a better, that temperamentally all taxpayers are alike'.

normative, because the social objective must then involve interpersonal comparisons of individuals with diverse preferences. In the welfarist tradition of welfare economics, there is no principle on which such comparisons can be grounded. This tradition always assumes that the relevant utility functions are provided by some impartial authority. When heterogeneity emanates from preferences, comparison of the groups with different utilities is no longer clear, as was pointed out by Sandmo (1993). In this context, using a utilitarian social objective function may entail some ethical objections.

In the Mirrlees (1971) model of optimal income taxation, there is no uncertainty. Once skill type is revealed, individual effort controls income perfectly. In practice, there is considerable uncertainty in income. Income is partly due to individual effort and partly due to luck, but the government can only observe realized income, not effort. In this case, a redistributive tax system can be interpreted as a form of social insurance against the possible bad fortune of being endowed with low abilities. The optimal redistribution scheme is a balance between providing workers with adequate incentives to acquire skills and with sufficient insurance. A well-known problem in the design of optimal income tax under uncertainty, or any insurance mechanism, is asymmetric information between government and individuals. The design of optimal redistributive taxation with ability differences and with earnings uncertainty has largely been studied separately. The literature on optimal income taxation with income uncertainty is much more limited, and has generally assumed away ability differences. Mirrlees (1974) was the first to examine the design of optimal redistributive income tax under income uncertainty. Mirrlees (1974), as Tuomala (1984) and Low and Maldoom (2004), assume that all individuals are ex ante identical, so supply the same amount of labour, but differ in earnings because of some innate idiosyncratic uncertainty that is resolved after labour is supplied.

There has been relatively little attention devoted to studying optimal income taxation when both ability differences and earnings uncertainty are present. Eaton and Rosen (1980b) considered the choice of a linear progressive income tax in a model with two ability-types and uncertain earnings. Given the difficulty of obtaining analytical results in even this simple setting, they solved some numerical examples. Depending on the parameters chosen, such as the degree of risk aversion, adding uncertainty to the standard optimal redistribution problem with two ability-types could either increase or decrease the optimal linear tax rate. Tuomala (1979, 1990) considers optimal income taxation when individuals do not fully know their productivity skills in making labour supply decisions. Again, given the complexity of the problem, numerical solutions are needed. So the income tax has both a redistributive role and an insurance role.

The theory of optimal income taxation under uncertainty has been developed under the assumption that individuals maximize expected utility. However, prospect theory has now been established as an alternative model of individual behaviour, with empirical support. Kanbur et al (2008) explore the theory of optimal income taxation under uncertainty when individuals behave according to the tenets of prospect theory. It is seen that many of the standard results are modified in interesting ways. The first-order approach for solving the optimization problem is not valid over the domain of losses, and the marginal tax schedule offers full insurance around the reference consumption level.

There are various extensions to the optimal non-linear labour income tax model using other tax instruments. The most important one is commodity taxation or indirect taxation. These extensions retain the supply-side characterization of the labour market. The Mirrlees (1971) model assumes consumption is aggregated into a single composite commodity. Once multiple goods are recognized alongside leisure, commodity taxation becomes relevant. There are two important results in optimal tax theory related to commodity taxation. Diamond and Mirrlees (1971) showed that if commodity taxes were imposed optimally and pure profits were taxed, production should be efficient. Another result is the Atkinson–Stiglitz (1976) theorem (AS hereafter). It says that if utility is weakly separable in goods and leisure, and if the optimal non-linear income tax is in place, differential commodity taxation is not required. It implies that redistribution is better achieved through income tax than by taxing necessities preferentially. There has been a large literature on the AS Theorem, recently excellently summarized in Boadway (2012). If preferences are not weakly separable, higher commodity taxes should be imposed on goods that are more complementary with leisure (Christiansen 1984; Edwards, Keen, and Tuomala 1994). There are several other cases that support differential commodity taxation with non-linear income taxation. When individuals differ not only in skills but also, among others, in preferences, wealth, and needs, differential commodity taxation becomes desirable.

As in the case of commodity taxation, publicly provided private goods and pure public goods, when these goods are financed by non-linear income taxation, can be seen as additional instruments for redistribution policy. Much of the activities of the modern welfare state are related to provision of private goods (education, health care, childcare and care of the elderly, etc.). In some developed countries the share of GDP would be as much as 15–20 per cent, whereas the share of pure public goods (general administration, defence, etc.) is quite small. Redistribution is one, although not the only, reason why these intrinsically private goods are publicly provided. Introducing additional distortion policies, which would not be used in a first-best world without asymmetric information, can be useful in a second-best situation, if they help mitigate the distortions stemming from the income taxation. Such policies include, among others, provision of public goods (Boadway and Keen 1993) and public provision of private goods, such as education or day-care (e.g. Blomquist and Christiansen 1995, Boadway and Marchand 1995, Cremer and Gahvari 1997, Blomquist, Christiansen, and Micheletto 2010).[15] In more detail, this literature uses the self-selection approach to optimal non-linear taxation, along the lines of e.g. Stiglitz (1982) and Stern (1982), with two types of households that differ in their income-earning abilities. Long ago Pigou (1947, pp. 33–4) claimed that the existence of

[15] Currie and Gahvari (2008) offer a survey on public provision of private goods.

distortionary taxes was a reason for not 'carrying public expenditures as far' as would be done if we could apply the rule of equating marginal cost to marginal benefit of individuals. Pigou's claim has also often been employed in political debate on the size of the public sector. Actual economies should thus attain a lower level of public expenditure than in the situation where lump-sum taxes are assumed to be available. The validity of Pigou's reasoning, however, is usually justified in the Ramsey economy, where linear taxes and a representative consumer are assumed. This issue was analysed by Atkinson and Stern (1974) in the Ramsey tax model, following Stiglitz and Dasgupta (1971), who had noticed that Pigou's argument is not necessarily correct in an optimal tax framework. Wilson (1991) and Mirrlees (1994) consider an economy with heterogeneous individuals and point out that the government's informational constraints allow for the introduction of a lump-sum tax in addition to linear consumption taxes. These papers show that in this setting the second-best optimal level of provision can be greater than the first-best level. Gaube (2005) studies the validity of Pigou's claim within the two-type version of non-linear income taxation employed by Boadway and Keen (1993), where the lump-sum taxes are ruled out. Gaube (2005) expands the results of Boadway and Keen, providing sufficient conditions for both under- and over-provision of the public good in the income tax optimum.

How to tax capital incomes is also very topical after several decades of growing wealth/income ratios in many advanced countries (see Piketty and Zucman 2014). Two lines of thought in the tax literature rationalize the zero tax on capital. First the Atkinson–Stiglitz theorem, under special assumptions on preferences, implies zero tax on income from capital. The second line of thought supporting zero capital taxation is that of Chamley and Judd. In their case, any positive tax on capital income compounds into a high implicit tax rate on forward consumption. When individuals differ not only in productivity (wage), as in the standard model, but also, say, in inherited wealth, discount factor, longevity, we have a good case for taxing capital income. In a four-types model (two wage rates and two discount factors) of work and retirement, Tenhunen and Tuomala (2010) find implicit marginal taxation of savings for one high-skilled person and implicit marginal subsidization of savings for one low-skilled person for all but the highest correlations. Diamond and Spinnewijn (2011) use a model with jobs rather than choice of hours by workers facing a given wage rate. In a four-type model they show that, starting with the optimal earnings tax, introduction of a small tax on the savings of high earners raises social welfare, as does the introduction of a small subsidy to the savings of low earners. This is similar within the rules for tax-favoured retirement saving.[16]

There are other reasons to undermine zero capital income tax results. These are the implications of large uncertainty about future earnings and the difficulties in practice in

[16] Kocherlakota (2005) provides an argument for regressive earnings-varying wealth taxation. He analyses a model with asymmetric information about stochastically evolving skills, which is not present in Diamond and Spinnewijn (2009). On the other hand, see Nielsen and Sørensen (1997) on the optimality of the Nordic dual income tax.

distinguishing between labour and capital incomes. In the so-called new dynamic public finance literature, the emphasis is on uncertainty in an intertemporal setting (Golosov et al 2007; Kocherlakota 2010). Ability is heterogeneous, but evolves in a stochastic manner period-by-period. In each period, individuals choose their labour supply and their saving knowing their current skills, but having only expectations of their future skills. Much of the emphasis in this literature is on the implications for the taxation of capital income, with the typical finding that capital income should face positive taxation. Christiansen and Tuomala (2008) examine a model with costly (but legal) conversion of labour income into capital income. Despite preferences that would result in a zero tax on capital income in the absence of the ability to shift income, they find a positive tax on capital income.

In the real world it is very likely that inheritance affects, in particular, the income levels of the very rich. Hence, taxes on labour income alone are not able to limit inequality. Piketty and Saez (2013) develop a theory of optimal capital taxation in which they emphasize three different rationales for capital taxation. Their analysis implies that the ideal tax system should combine a progressive inheritance tax, in addition to progressive income and wealth taxes.

Should capital income be taxed more or less heavily than labour income? What is the appropriate relationship between the marginal taxation of capital income and the marginal taxation of labour income? The Nordic dual income tax features linear taxation of capital income and non-linear taxation of earnings. In principle, the capital income tax rate can be set at the highest or lowest positive tax rates, or something in between. In the background paper for the Mirrlees Review, Banks and Diamond (2010) do not conclude that labour and capital should be taxed at the same rates; however, they do suggest that the marginal tax rates on capital and labour incomes should be related to each other in some way to discourage the conversion of labour income into capital income, as opposed to the Nordic system. However, they note that without extensive calibrated calculations, it is unclear how strong the relationship between labour and capital income taxes should be. In sum, the difficulty in distinguishing, in practice, labour and capital income provides support for a so-called comprehensive income tax (i.e. taxing the sum of labour and capital income)—or, at least, for taxing capital and labour income at rates that are not too different.

The structure of this book is as follows. Chapter 2 begins with historical and international background on taxes, transfers, and redistribution in actual economies. Chapter 2 also provides some background material on different ethical positions in optimal redistributive tax literature. It briefly discusses obstacles to the employment of lump-sum taxation and introduces a simple two-type model for a first step to optimal income tax modelling. Chapter 3 provides the most direct application of results on optimal linear income taxation. Chapter 4 sets up the basic Mirrlees (1971) model and highlights the role of different elements of the model in determining the shape of the optimal non-linear tax schedule. We first consider what we can say on the basis of the first-order conditions of the problem. However, analytical characterization does not lead far. Using numerical simulations, in Chapter 5 we study the role of different elements of the model in determining the pattern of optimal non-linear tax/transfer. Chapter 6 analyses optimal redistribution in the so-called extensive margin case and briefly discusses optimal redistribution and involuntary unemployment. Chapter 7 analyses how concern for consumption relative to others ('relativity') affects the structure of optimal non-linear income taxation. The main focus of Chapter 7 is the interplay of relativity and inequality in determining the optimal structure of income taxes. Chapter 8 examines targeted programmes not only based on income information, as in previous chapters, but able to use information on characteristics that are immutable, such as age. Chapter 9 provides a general non-welfarist formulation of the income tax/transfer problem, which unifies special cases that have been studied in non-welfarist tax literature. Chapter 10 considers optimal redistribution when individuals differ not only in productivities but also in working preferences. Chapter 11 first reviews the standard benchmark model of optimal taxation with moral hazard under income uncertainty and then characterizes optimal tax rules when individual behaviour is described by prospect theory. Chapters 12 and 13 extend the optimal labour income tax with commodity taxes and public provision. In these chapters the key question is: can the government design a better redistribution system combining income taxation, commodity taxation, and public provision? In other words, can it meet the same distributional objectives but with smaller efficiency costs? Chapter 14 asks the question of how capital income should be taxed. One of the limitations of the standard income tax model is that it does not address intertemporal problems. In an intertemporal setting, capital income taxation becomes relevant. The theoretical case for capital income taxation is also discussed in Chapter 14. Finally, Chapter 15 provides concluding remarks and discussion on the policy relevance of optimal tax literature.

2 Optimal labour income taxation: background

2.1 Taxes, transfers, and redistribution in actual economies

The modern progressive income tax was created at the beginning of the twentieth century.[1] In every country, at the time of adoption, the income tax was applied to a tiny group of wealthy people, typically the top 1–2 per cent of the population. Over the past century the progressive income tax transformed from an elite tax to a mass tax, then was gradually extended to the entire population (or at least to the majority of the population). This made tax revenues much more significant. This evolution to mass income tax is an important part of the rise of the modern welfare or social state. As seen in Figure 2.1, tax revenue relative to national income has grown dramatically over the process of development. Without doubt, this remarkable growth of tax revenue is one of the most striking economic phenomena of the past two centuries. In rich countries the ratio between tax revenue and national income was less than 10 per cent in the early twentieth century, rose enormously between 1950 and 1980, and then stabilized at around 30–50 per cent in most advanced economies.[2] There is, however, a quite large range among rich countries; the tax is highest in Sweden, at around 50 per cent. Madisson (2001) documents that, on average, France, Germany, the Netherlands, and the UK raised around 12 per cent of GDP in tax revenue around 1910 (financing army, police, basic infrastructure, and general administration), rising to around 46 per cent by the turn of the millennium. The corresponding US figures are 8 per cent and 30 per cent. When looking at the current cross-section of countries' (see Table A2.1 in appendix 2.1) tax burdens relative to GDP,[3] it can be seen that in 2013 the most advanced economies in OECD countries raised between 35 per cent and 50 per cent of GDP in taxes. The United States, in turn, raised 26 per cent of GDP in taxes. Among OECD countries, only Mexico, Chile, and Turkey had lower taxes than the United States as a percentage of GDP.

[1] For example, 1909 in the UK, 1913 in the US, 1914 in France, and 1920 in Finland.

[2] It is of some interest to note that Figure 2.1 implies that Wagner's law (the tendency for public expenditure to grow faster than GDP) or the Baumol effect (stagnating productivity in services and especially in the government sector) cannot explain stability during the past three decades in those countries.

[3] National income is equal to GDP–capital depreciation + net foreign factor income. Roughly, national income is about 85–90% of GDP.

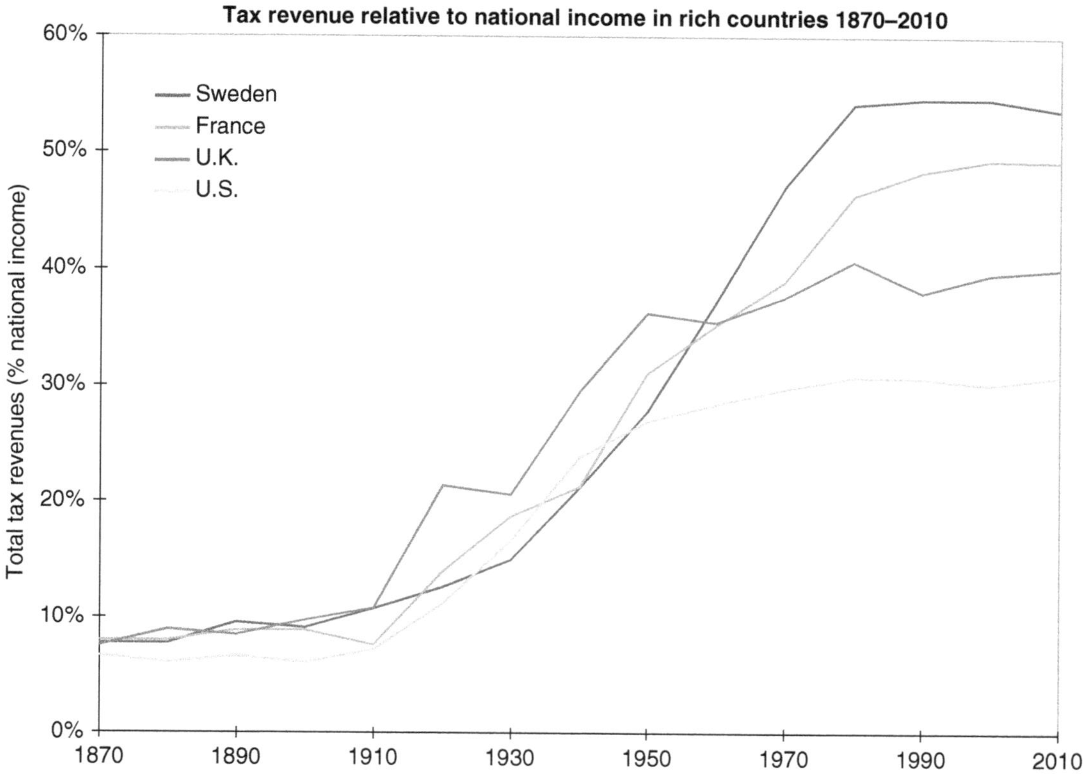

Figure 2.1 Tax revenues in rich countries 1870–2010

Source: Total tax revenues were less than 10% of national income in rich countries until 1900–1910; they represent between 30% and 55% of national income in 2000–2010. Sources and series: see Piketty.pse.ens.fr/capital21c.

How can we explain this transition from elite to mass tax? Can we see this evolution happening also in developing countries? Tax-to-national income ratios are in turn much smaller in less developed countries. Higher-income countries today raise much higher taxes than poorer countries, indicating that they have made larger investments in fiscal capacity. As noted by Besley and Persson (2013), the tax share in GDP of today's developing countries does not look very different from the tax share in GDP 100 years ago in what are now advanced countries.

2.2 **Tax structures in the OECD area**

Tax structures in Table 2.1a are measured by the share of major taxes in total tax revenue. While, on average, tax levels generally rose in the 1960s and 1970s, the share of main taxes in total revenues—the tax structure—has been remarkably stable over time. Nevertheless, several trends have emerged up to 2012, the latest year for which data is available for all thirty-four OECD countries.[4] Based on the following assumptions[5] (all

[4] Based on the individual OECD country data, the share of taxes falling on capital income has declined slightly in Europe and has been approximately stable in the United States.

[5] These assumptions are not necessarily justified.

Table 2.1a Tax structure in OECD countries[1]

	1965	1975	1985	1995	2005	2010	2012
Personal income tax	26	30	30	26	24	24	25
Corporate income tax	9	8	8	8	10	9	9
Social security contributions[2]	18	22	22	25	25	26	26
(employee)	(6)	(7)	(7)	(9)	(9)	(9)	(10)
(employer)	(10)	(14)	(13)	(14)	(14)	(15)	(15)
Payroll taxes	1	1	1	1	1	1	1
Property taxes	8	6	5	5	6	5	5
General consumption taxes	12	13	16	19	20	20	20
Specific consumption taxes	24	18	16	13	11	11	11
Other taxes[3]	2	2	2	3	3	3	3
Total	**100**	**100**	**100**	**100**	**100**	**100**	**100**

Source: OECD Revenue Statistics: 1. Percentage share of major tax categories in total tax revenue. Data are included from 1965 onwards for Australia, Austria, Belgium, Canada, Denmark, Finland, France, Germany, Greece, Iceland, Ireland, Italy, Japan, Luxembourg, the Netherlands, New Zealand, Norway, Portugal, Spain, Sweden, Switzerland, Turkey, the United Kingdom, and the United States; from 1972 for Korea; from 1980 for Mexico; from 1990 for Chile; from 1991 for Hungary and Poland; from 1993 for the Czech Republic; and from 1995 for Estonia, Israel, the Slovak Republic, and Slovenia. 2. Including social security contributions paid by the self-employed and benefit recipients (heading 2300) that are not shown in the breakdown over employees and employers. 3. Including certain taxes on goods and services (heading 5200) and stamp taxes.

labour taxes are paid by labour; all capital taxes, including corporate tax, are paid by capital and consumption taxes are paid by consumers as a rough approximation, the share of the total tax burden falling on capital income roughly corresponds to the share of capital income in national income (i.e. about 25 per cent). The remaining 75 per cent of taxes falls on labour income. Decomposing total taxes into labour taxes (including all social contributions, employer and employee), capital taxes, and consumption taxes, the share of labour taxes over the period of the past two decades has been slightly less than 40 per cent, the share of capital taxes slightly less than 30 per cent, and the share of consumption taxes slightly less than 25 per cent. In general, actual tax systems achieve some tax progressivity, i.e. tax rates rising with income, through the individual income tax. In most OECD countries, individual income tax systems have brackets with increasing marginal tax rates. Social security or payroll taxes and consumption taxes in turn are proportional or flat rates. After World War II up to the end of the 1970s, most OECD countries had very progressive individual income taxes, with a large number of tax brackets and high top tax rates (see e.g. OECD 1986). Over the past two or three decades, this has changed. For example, Landais, Piketty, and Saez (2011) found clear regressivity in the top centiles in France. An important reason for this is that capital income is largely exempt from progressive taxation. There are also doubts that the inverted U-shaped tax curve can be found in many other developed countries. In the United States as well, income tax rates decline at the very top due to the preferential treatment of realized capital gains, which constitute a large fraction of top incomes (Piketty and Saez 2013).

Due to income shifting from labour income to capital income, even in Finland the average tax rate schedule has been declining over the two or three top percentiles since 1994. In the sense of both marginal and average tax rates, the income tax is regressive in the top centiles in Finland.

Besley and Persson (2013, in figure 4) give at least a partial picture of how fiscal capacity has evolved over time, based on a sample of eighteen countries using data from Mitchell (2007). Their figure plots the distribution of three kinds of changes in tax systems since 1850. It illustrates the key changes in tax systems over time. The graph shows that income taxes began appearing in the mid-nineteenth century, and direct withholding follows somewhat later. VAT is a more modern phenomenon. In the Besley–Persson sample of eighteen countries, only the US has not introduced a form of value-added tax by the end of the year 2000.

2.3 **Inequality and redistributive policy**

The OECD's post-war history of income inequality can be divided, at least roughly, into two phases.[6] From 1945 to about the mid-1980s, pre-tax inequality, or the inequality of market incomes (incomes from earnings and capital), decreased because of a reduction in skilled/unskilled wage differentials and asset inequality. The second phase occurred from the mid-1980s onwards, when pre-tax inequality reversed course and increased. For this latter period we have evidence from the Luxembourg Income Study (LIS) database. This database provides both market (pre-tax) and disposable income distributions for a number of OECD countries over the past three decades. Table 2.1b, based on Immervoll and Richardson (2011), shows inequality trends for market or pre-tax incomes (G_m, including any private transfers) and disposable incomes (G_d, market incomes plus cash benefits minus income taxes).

Table 2.1b Redistribution in the tax-benefit systems as a whole: inequality before and after taxes and transfers, countries with full tax-benefit information for mid-80s, mid-90s, and mid-00s

	Pre-tax income		Disposable income		Redistribution	
	G_m (1)	Change. % of base period (2)	G_d (3)	$(G_m-G_d)/G_m$ % (4)	Change.% of base period G_m (5)	(5)/(2) (6)
mid-80s	36.2		26.7	26.4		
mid-90s	39.2	8.2	27.4	29.9	6	73
mid-00s	39.8	9.8	28.3	28.7	5	53

Source: Immervoll and Richardson (2013).

6 See Tanninen and Tuomala (2005).

According to LIS data over the periods considered, market incomes in working-age households have become more unequal everywhere except the Netherlands and Switzerland. In most cases, market-income inequality rose more strongly between the mid-1980s and the mid-1990s. In addition, most of the countries with data going back further than this time saw large increases in market-income Ginis before the mid-1980s (for example in the United Kingdom they rose by almost 10 points between 1979 and 1986). It is not only these large changes in market-income inequality that explain increasing trends in inequality of disposable incomes; redistribution policies had a substantial effect as well, especially since the mid-1990s. The difference between the Gini values for market incomes and disposable incomes is a much-used measure of the overall redistributive effect of taxes and transfers (column 4 in Table 2.1b). On average, across countries for which the data are available, inequality increased both before and after taxes and transfers. Between the mid-1980s and the mid-1990s, redistribution systems offset around three quarters of the increase in market-income inequality (column 6). Using the LIS database, Tanninen and Tuomala (2005) also find that redistribution in these countries is positively associated with inherent inequality up to the mid-1990s. The upwards trend in market-income inequality then continued after the mid-1990s, but at a much slower pace in most countries. Yet inequality of household disposable income (column 3) rose more rapidly in the second decade. Although the rise in market-income inequality slowed significantly, government redistribution became less effective in compensating growing inequalities. In relative terms, redistribution decreased (column 4) despite continually growing market-income inequality (column 1). Over the two decades as a whole, market-income inequality rose by about twice as much as redistribution (column 6). Taxes and transfers now reduce inequality by about 29 per cent (column 4)—more than in the mid-1980s, but less than in the mid-1990s.

Similar results for each country are presented in Immervoll and Richardson (2011) in Table 5. There is, however, a quite large range among rich countries in the extent of redistribution measured by $(G_m - G_d)/G_m$; it is highest in Sweden, at 48 per cent in 1995, and lowest in the US, at 17 per cent in 2000. Among the countries shown, tax-benefit systems in the Nordic countries, the Czech Republic, and Poland achieve the greatest reduction in inequality, lowering the Gini value by 13 points or more in the mid-2000s (this corresponds to about 40 per cent of market-income inequality in Denmark, Finland, and Sweden, and a third or less in the other countries), while the smallest redistributive effect is seen in Switzerland (5.5 points, or 18 per cent), the US (8.1. 18 per cent), and Canada (8.8. 22 per cent).

The extent of pre-tax inequality mitigation was strongest in Canada, Denmark, Finland, and Sweden, where government redistribution offset more than 70 per cent of the rise in market-income inequality up until the mid-1990s. In Denmark, redistribution increased twice as much as market-income inequality. As in other countries, on average, redistribution in these countries has become less effective in offsetting growing pre-tax inequality since then. For instance, in Finland, redistribution through taxes and benefits offset more than three quarters of the 23 per cent increase in pre-tax or market-income inequality up until 1995, but by 2004 this had dropped to 50 per cent. In a majority of the countries shown in Immervoll and Richardson (2011; Table 5), redistribution has declined since the mid-1990s. Tax-benefit systems in Canada, Finland, and Israel have become less redistributive since the mid-1990s, despite a continuing rise in market-income inequality.

Inequality can be measured in various different ways. The Gini coefficient used above is the most popular measure. However, the Gini index is not without its critics; for example, it has been criticized for not taking the shape of the distribution into account. An alternative way to study inequality is by focusing on the top income share. An important reason for this is that the top income earners' increasing share of total income over the past three decades has been a notable feature of the changes in income inequality in Anglo-Saxon countries (see Fig 2.2), including the US, UK, and Canada (see Atkinson 2002; Piketty and Saez 2003), while in Europe the Netherlands, France, and Switzerland display hardly any change in top income shares[7] (see Fig 2.3). This trend toward income concentration has also been seen in the Nordic countries (see Fig 2.4), which are traditionally low-inequality countries. The top percentile disposable income share in Finland doubled in the latter part of the 1990s. At the same time, top tax rates on upper income earners have declined significantly in many OECD countries, again particularly in English-speaking countries.[8] Economists have formulated several hypotheses about the causes of increasing inequality, but there is no fully compelling explanation. For example, Atkinson et al (2011) emphasize that it is very difficult to account for

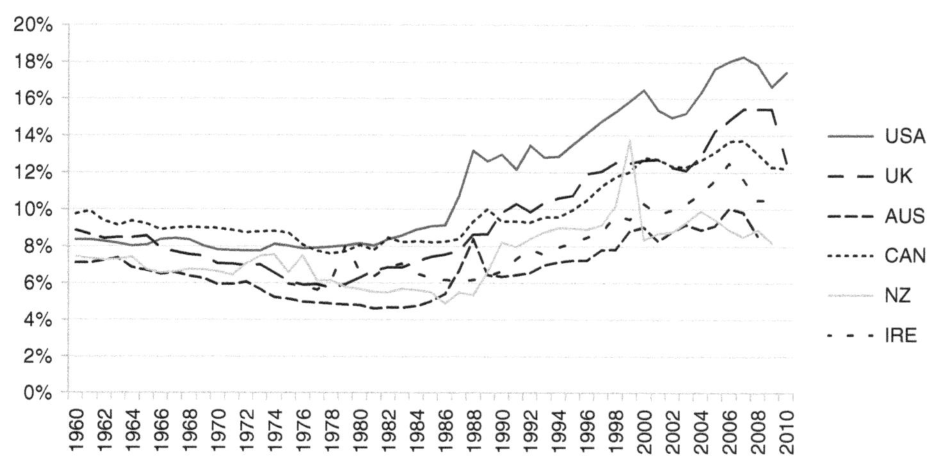

Figure 2.2 Top 1% share: English-speaking countries, 1960–2010

Source: World Top Incomes Database.

[7] The more recent estimates of Landais (2007) show a rise in recent years in France.

[8] Piketty et al (2014) investigate the link between skyrocketing inequality and top tax rates in OECD countries. They find a strong correlation between tax cuts for the highest earners and increases in the income share of the top 1 per cent since 1975.

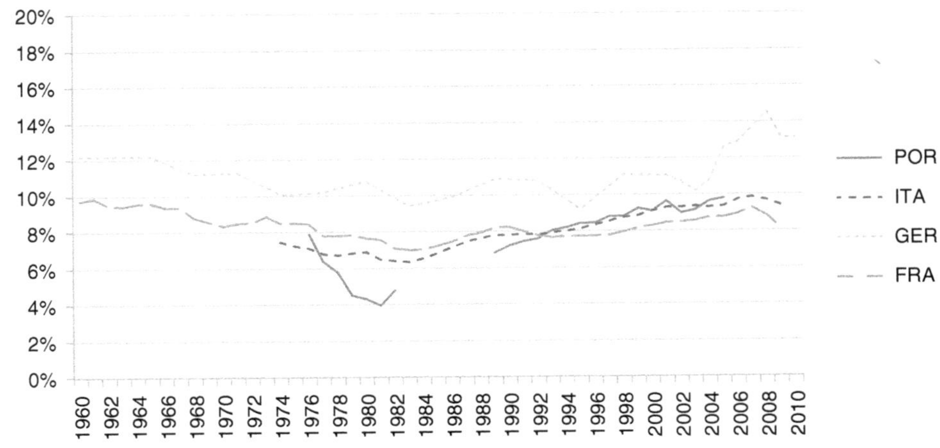

Figure 2.3 Top 1% share: Middle Europe, 1960–2010

Source: World Top Incomes Database.

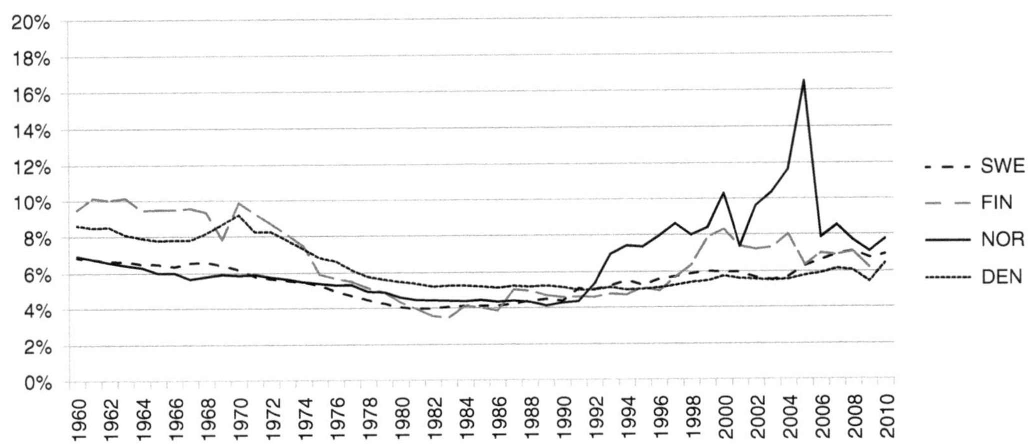

Figure 2.4 Top 1% share: Nordic Europe, 1960–2010

Source: World Top Incomes Database.

these figures using the standard labour supply/labour demand explanation. Hence we really have to think about things such as social policies and progressive taxation.

In their discussion of the United States' top income shares, Piketty and Saez (2003) argue that top capital incomes were reduced by several major events, including the Great Depression, the two World Wars, and periods of high inflation. They also argue that top tax rates played an important role, with high taxes on capital lowering the rate of capital accumulation. Following Piketty and Saez (2003), most authors have argued that the dramatic increase in tax progressivity that took place in the inter-war period in many countries studied, and which remained in place at least until recent decades, has been the main factor preventing top income shares from coming back to the very high levels observed at the beginning of the preceding century.

Piketty-Saez (2013, Figure 1) depicts the top marginal income tax rates (marginal tax rate applying to the highest incomes) in the United States, the United Kingdom, France, and Germany since 1900. During the twentieth century, top income tax rates followed an inverse U-shaped time-path in many countries. Top rates were very small around the period 1900–20 in those countries. They rose very rapidly in the 1920s–40s, particularly in the US and in the UK. Since the end of the 1970s, top tax rates on upper income earners have declined significantly in many OECD countries, again mainly in English-speaking countries. For example, the US top marginal federal individual tax rate was remarkably high—91 per cent—in the 1950s–60s, but is only 35 per cent nowadays. At the same time, a substantial fraction of capital income receives preferential tax treatment under most income tax rules. In other advanced countries, such as the Nordic countries, top tax rates on upper income have declined dramatically since the beginning of the 1990s.

Piketty, Saez, and Stantcheva (2014) find a very strong correlation between the decrease in top marginal tax rates and the surge in top income shares since 1960. In other words, the countries with the largest decrease in their top marginal tax rates are also the countries with the largest increase in top income shares. They also find no evidence of a correlation between growth in real GDP per capita and the drop in the top marginal tax rate in the period between 1960 and the present. It is important to note there has been large growth in top income shares in several advanced countries over the past few decades, at the same time as a shift in the burden of taxation from top to further down in the income distribution. Hence knowledge of average tax rates is very relevant for redistributive purposes.

2.4 Redistribution through public expenditure

In many European countries taxes exceed 40 per cent of GDP, but those countries, especially Nordic countries, generally provide much more extensive transfers and government services to their citizens than the US does. Much of the activities of the modern welfare state are related to provision of private goods or in-kind transfers (education, health care, childcare and care of the elderly, public housing, and so on) (see Table 2.1c). In practice, a large share of public expenditure is allocated to the provision of those goods. In some advanced countries the share of GDP is as much as 15–20 per cent—especially in Nordic countries—whereas the share of pure public or collective goods (general administration, police, defence, etc) is quite small. Hence much redistribution takes place through the provision of goods and services, rather than the tax-transfer system. The differences in government growth are due to a different kind of expansion of the welfare state, including publicly provided education, retirement benefits, health and other care, social insurance, and income support programmes. Unfortunately our empirical estimates on the extent of redistribution through public provision are not as strong as those on transfers in cash (in Table 2.1b).

Table 2.1c Public spending on individual goods in kind and in cash (average 2005–2009, % GDP)

	Individual goods in kind	Health	Non-market recreation and culture	Education	Social services	Market subsidies	Individual goods in cash
Austria	15.6	5.5	0.8	4.9	1.0	3.3	18.4
Finland	18.8	6.8	0.9	5.9	3.7	1.3	16.1
Germany	12.2	6.1	0.5	3.7	0.7	1.2	18.5
Greece	8.9	4.6	0.3	3.6	0.3	0.1	15.9
Ireland	13.7	6.9	0.6	4.7	1.0	0.5	11.2
Italy	13.4	6.7	0.6	4.3	0.8	0.9	17.1
Norway	17.9	6.9	0.6	5.3	3.1	1.9	12.5
Poland	13.3	4.8	1.1	5.5	1.3	0.6	14.9
Portugal	14.5	6.4	0.8	5.8	0.8	0.8	13.8
Spain	13.0	5.7	1.0	4.2	1.0	1.0	12.2
Sweden	20.4	6.3	1.0	6.5	5.3	1.4	15.5
UK	16.3	6.9	0.8	5.6	2.4	0.6	12.4

Source: Stats: OECD.org; dataset: Public Finance and Employment: Expenditures according to COFOG.

In many European countries, since around 1950 inequality was initially reduced, as they had a tax system that paid for the social or welfare state. However, we have to remember that in measuring income inequality (see Table 2.1b), we should include things like the value of health care and the value of education. Many European countries introduced a free health service and free schooling during the period of declining inequality and increased tax revenue to national income. From studies based on LIS data we know that throughout Europe, countries with higher tax rates have lower inequality.

In most OECD countries, social insurance accounts for a greater part of government spending on social security. Social insurance is seen as an important device to prevent poverty, yet since the 1980s it has come increasingly under attack. One line of attack has come from those, such as the Thatcher government in the UK in the 1980s, aiming to reduce expenditure on income maintenance. Supporters of this view argue that by using income-tested benefits, income maintenance programmes direct help to those in need with lower fiscal and incentive costs. Income or means-tested programmes provide the largest benefits to those with no income, and those benefits are then phased out at high rates for those with low earnings. Another line of attack came from the supporters of a basic income scheme, who believe what is needed is the replacement of social insurance with a basic benefit which would be independent of income and differentiated according to only a small number of categories.

In more recent years, income-tested benefits have been to some extent replaced by in-work benefits. This is particularly the case in the US and UK, and less so in other advanced countries. In-work benefits, in turn, are nil for those with no earnings and concentrated among low earners before being phased out. The weakness of these programmes is that they provide no support to those with no earnings, i.e. those most in need of support.

2.5 Defences of different ethical positions

The role of the state is evidently the starting point for the study of optimal taxation and public economics in general. What rationale may be given for the existence of the state and the power it possesses in taxation and public spending? Any normative theory such as optimal tax theory must have a view of the proper functions of the government. We can distinguish different views of the role of the government throughout the history of political philosophy. In particular, our interest here is to bring out their implications for the redistributive policy. The views vary, roughly speaking, from support for no redistribution (libertarianism) to support for relatively large redistribution (egalitarianism). The view that there would be no case for moving from the no-tax position is associated in modern political philosophy with Robert Nozick. The basic axiom of Nozick's analysis (1974) is the principle which states that each individual has the right to consume that which he or she produces. There are three principles in Nozick's analysis which test the fairness of procedure: (i) fairness in the original acquisition of wealth; (ii) fair transfer of wealth; and (iii) rectification injustice in wealth. According to Nozick, redistribution is unjust except as retribution for past entitlement injustice. Nozick's theory accepts only minimal intervention by the government—the so-called night-watchman state. Nozick writes that 'a minimal state, limited to the narrow function of protecting against force, theft, fraud, enforcement of contracts, and so on, is justified; that any more extensive state will violate persons' rights not to be forced to do certain things, and is unjustified' (1974, p. ixy). The minimal state may not impose taxes, for example, for any purposes other than to support the operations of the night-watchman state, such as the police. Nozick distinguishes between two kinds of theory concerning what he calls 'justice in distribution'. First, justice in holdings (wealth) is historical and time-slice principles of justices are invalid. Hence he is saying that the common analogy between the fair division of the cake and the just distribution of income is meaningless, because the economy per se has no income to distribute. Optimal tax policy is thus concerned not with distribution but with redistribution. Redistribution is just only when it rectifies the improper holding of wealth and thus never as a means of redistributing labour income. According to Nozick, 'taxation of earnings from labour is on a par with forced labour' (1974, p. 169).

Kenneth Arrow (1978) has strong doubts about this. He writes:

> There are large gains to social integration above and beyond what the individuals and subgroups could achieve on their own. The owners of scarce personal assets do not have a private use of

these assets which is considerable, it is only their value in a large system which makes these assets valuable, hence, there is a surplus created by the existence of society as such which is available for redistribution' (Arrow 1978, pp. 278–9).

However, even if taxes are not to be used to redistribute income, there is still the question of how they should be levied to finance the operations of the minimal state. Second, Nozick's analysis does not attempt to find a good social objective function, but rather a good set of rules for a given society's operations. The question is how to evaluate social processes and how to do this independently of the result generated. If a good set of rules consistently generates outcomes that are disastrous, how can the rules be considered good? As Sen (1984, p. 312) put it, 'there is something deeply implausible in the affirmative answer. Why should it be the case that rules of ownership, etc., should have such absolute priority...?

How does Nozick's position relate to the so-called welfare theorems? The first welfare theorem says—given some pre-conditions; no externalities, perfect competition, perfect information, rational individuals—that the results of the market mechanism are Pareto-efficient, so that the outcomes are not improvable in ways that would enhance everyone's utility (enhance someone's utility without reducing the utility of anybody else). This result is often taken—rightly or wrongly—as an argument for minimal state intervention. The market ensures a desirable outcome in the sense of Pareto efficiency. The structure of argument in the first theorem differs from that of Nozick's analysis. If the initial situation and the process—a perfectly competitive market—are fair, this is enough for Nozick. The third element—Pareto-efficient allocation—is irrelevant. There is no need for intervention. The first welfare theorem in turn takes that the outcome is the basis. It is just this focus on outcomes which distinguishes the other views from that of Nozick. In welfare economics, a Pareto-improving change means that it is unanimously preferred. This can lead to quite different conclusions about the role of the government's redistributive functions. It may be so when there is a utility interdependence so that the consumption of the poor enters the utility function of the rich. This leads to an individual interest in redistribution. It may be a form of social insurance or reflect paternalist motives. The utility interdependence, or, in other words, externality, implies that the conditions for welfare theorems do not hold. Figure 2.2a illustrates this: at the point a in the absence of transfers the rich are much better off than the poor; now the rich, however, care about the poor, and would be actually better off if there is a transfer. In Figure 2.2a we move from a to b. This would be Pareto-improving, so that both would be better off. Libertarians such as Nozick would accept this transfer if it is voluntary and involves no coercion. How can we be sure that there is a move from a to b? Namely there may be no private transfers at all, or it is too small. The reason is the well-known problem of free-riding, a possibility that was clearly expressed by Milton Friedman in his book *Capitalism and Freedom*: 'It can be argued that private charity is insufficient because the benefits from it accrue to people other than those who make the gifts...we might all of us be willing to contribute to the

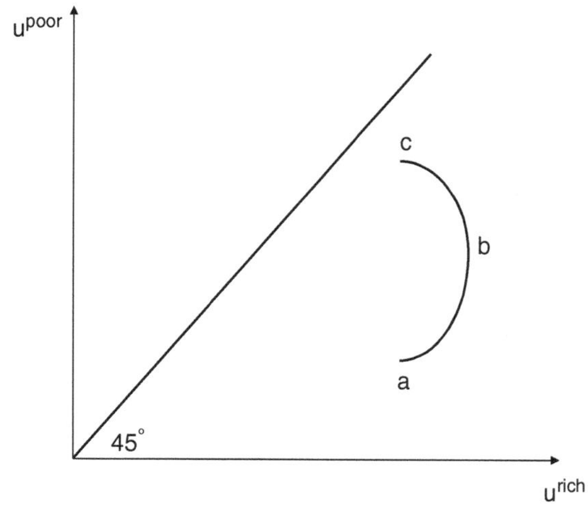

Figure 2.2a Utility interdependence

relief of poverty, providing everyone else did. We might not be willing to contribute the same amount without such assurance' (p. 191).

How to choose between Pareto-efficient allocations without a utility interdependence? How to choose the point between b and c? One way is to appeal to the notion of ethical preferences, as in Harsanyi (1955). Such preferences may lead to people supporting the government pursuing distributional policies which maximize a social welfare function in which their own interest is only one component. This gives a rationale for the Bergson–Samuelson social welfare function which expresses social states as a function of individual utilities $W = W(u^1, ..., u^N)$. Optimal tax theory generally incorporates equity concerns by taking the object of policy to be the maximization of some Bergson–Samuelson social welfare functions. This approach has come to be known as welfarism, after Sen. A central ingredient of welfarism implicit in the social welfare function W is a willingness to make interpersonal comparisons. The nature of the interpersonal comparison one is willing to make may influence the form of the W.

The next question is: what form should the social function take? A utilitarian social welfare function takes the form: $W = u^1 + ..., + u^N$. Utilitarianism implies in a two-person world that the utility of person 1 is a perfect substitute for the utility of person 2. How can we justify this form? One of the best-known modern defences of the utilitarian social welfare function was provided by Harsanyi (1955). Following Vickrey (1945), Harsanyi also made the original position assumption. In this position, the veil of ignorance prevents anyone from knowing who exactly he or she is going to be. They start from the position that choice under risky conditions can be described as a maximization of expected utility. The expected utility theorem itself does not establish any welfare implications for the so-called von Neumann–Morgenstern utility function. The Vickrey–Harsanyi argument puts matters in a different perspective. The reasoning can be understood as a mental experiment in which people are making decisions behind a veil, and they do not know which of the people 1 to N they will be. On the basis of the principle of insufficient reason the individual assigns a probability 1/N to each possible outcome; after further assumptions, Harsanayi (1955) concludes that in this situation individuals' choices will made according to the expected utility, where the utility function is defined by the von Neumann–Morgenstern utility function.[9]

A pure or classical utilitarian social welfare function is indifferent to the distribution of utilities. A natural way to introduce concern about distribution is to make the social welfare function quasi-concave in individual utilities. One example yielding quite a rich class of social welfare function is the following iso-elastic form: $W = \frac{1}{1-\beta}\sum_{i=1}^{N}(u^i)^{1-\beta},\ ui > 0$. This gives us the utilitarian case where $\beta = 0$ and it is strictly convex where $\beta > 0$.

Rawls (1971) proposed an alternative form of social welfare criterion to maximize the well-being of the least advantaged in society. The Rawlsian approach has been taken as the main alternative to utilitarianism, and this is also true in optimal tax theory. A central postulate of both the Rawlsian approach and of utilitarianism was referred to as asset egalitarianism by Arrow (1971). The natural endowments of individuals are treated as common or collective assets. Natural advantages, superiority in intelligence, or strength do not in themselves create any claim to greater rewards. The principles of justice are 'an agreement to regard the distribution of natural talents as a common asset and to share in the benefits of the distribution' (Rawls 1971, p. 101). One justification for this position is that the distribution of personal skills is morally arbitrary. Like Vickrey (1945) and Harsanyi (1955), Rawls (1971) bases his theory of justice on a similar construction. He also considers choices made in an initial position in which people have no knowledge of their social position and preferences. The 'veil of ignorance' is assumed to ensure that the choice of moral principles is impartial or just. Rawls (1971) derives in the original position the statement for maximin—the distributional formula prioritizing the interest of the worst-off. The quality of an entire life is at a stake in the original position; it implies a high degree of risk-aversion. Rawls (1971) argues that probabilities are ill-defined and should not be used in calculations. He argues that in this situation people will reveal a very high degree of risk-aversion. Consequently they will be concerned with the worst possible outcome. Society should organize in such a way that guarantees the best outcome for the least advantaged. Taxes should be raised to help the poorest, although it is important to note that Rawls' theory of justice involves much more than this one principle. In fact, there is a prior principle which attaches first importance to liberty as an objective, so that the pursuit of distributional justice takes second place to the requirement that 'each person has an equal right to the most extensive scheme of equal basic liberties compatible with a similar scheme of liberties for all' (Rawls 1971, p. 60).

Utilitarianism requires one to be willing to compare changes in utility to evaluate reforms, whereas maximin requires one to compare levels. Maximizing the utility of the worst-off person in society is not the original version of Rawlsian thought; it is a kind of

[9] Here Rawls (1971) makes a mistake when he argues that average utilitarianism assumes risk neutrality (p. 165). In fact, the degree of risk aversion is taken into account in the utility function.

welfarist version of Rawls. Arrow (1973) argues that Rawls' formulation of the objective may be seen as a limiting case of the iso-elastic function. as β tends to infinity. Hence W takes the form: $min_i u^i$ i.e. maximin. Rawls (1974) objects to this interpretation. For him, it is wrong to suggest that we can 'shift smoothly from the moral conception to another simply by varying the parameter (β)' (Rawls 1974, p. 664). Rawls (1974. p. 143) suggests that an important feature of a distributive criterion is that it should serve as a public principle: 'citizens generally should be able to understand it and have some confidence that it is realized'. He claims that the maximin, unlike utilitarianism, satisfies this criterion of sharpness or transparency. Hence a change in tax policy that benefits the least advantaged should be easily observable.

Does the assumption of the original position really imply the highly specific, indeed unique, form—maximin—as argued by Rawls (1971)? It is not at all clear what would be chosen in that kind of impartial aggregation. Vickrey and Harsanyi arrive at the utilitarian formula of maximizing the sum of utilities of all precisely from the same premises. There are also other claimants to a solution, e.g. maximizing an equity-adjusted sum-total of utilities (Mirrlees 1971). This implies that there may not exist any perfectly just social arrangement on which impartial agreement would emerge. How useful is it for the world in which we live to characterize an ideal (transcendental in Sen 2009) state justice? So is a veil of ignorance method really needed? However, as Pogge (1989) argues, one can accept Rawls' principles of justice without accepting his rationale in terms of a social contract.

2.6 **The Edgeworth model**

Edgeworth (1987) has justly become the basic reference for the original roots of modern redistribution tax theory. His analysis provides the most natural starting point for our discussion on income redistribution models because his basic approach has been used in most subsequent analyses about the theory of optimal income taxation.

Edgeworth (1987) considers the case where income is fixed. In other words, labour supply is perfectly inelastic. The gross or before-tax income of individual i is denoted by $z^i.i = 1, \dots, N$ and the tax paid by $T(z^i)$. Let us assume that all individuals have the same utility function $u(x)$ increasing and concave in disposable income x (since there is only one period, disposable income is equal to consumption). Disposable income is pre-tax earnings minus taxes on earnings, so that $x^i = z^i - T(z^i)$. The government's problem as formalized by Edgeworth (1897) chooses the tax function $T(z^i)$ to maximize the utilitarian social welfare function $W = \sum u(z^i - T(z^i))$ subject to revenue constraint $\sum T(z^i) = 0$ (pure redistributive taxation). The first-order condition of this problem yields $u'(x^i) = \lambda.i = 1, ..., N$, where λ is the multiplier associated to the government's revenue constraint. This implies that $x^i = z^i - T(z^i)$ is constant across i = $1, \dots, N$ i.e. 100 per cent tax rate. Hence, utilitarianism with fixed labour income and concave utility (marginal utility $u'(z - T)$) is decreasing with z – T produces full redistribution of incomes. This is what Edgeworth called the principle of minimum sacrifice, or the equal marginal sacrifice rule. Edgeworth only considered the utilitarian case. The result also holds for the other social welfare function. The limiting case is the maximin criterion where the government's objective is to maximize the utility of the most disadvantaged person, i.e. to maximize the minimum utility (maximin). This outcome is also very sensitive to the form of individual utilities. Namely, linear utility implies no taxes at all,[10] while introducing just a bit of concavity leads to full redistribution. The Edgeworth result, at least to some extent, created the ill-deserved reputation of utilitarianism as a radical distributive criterion. Sen (1973, p. 16) argues that

> maximising the sum of individual utilities is supremely unconcerned with the distribution of that sum... Interestingly enough, however, not only has utilitarianism been fairly widely used for distributional judgements, it has—somewhat amazingly—even developed the reputation of being an egalitarian criterion.

Lerner (1944) in turn extends the Edgeworth result to the situation in which individuals' utility functions differ and the government cannot observe utility functions (i.e. who has which utility function). Sen (1973) generalizes Lerner's result for any concave social welfare function.

In fact, there is nothing intrinsic to the utilitarian objective which leads to this outcome in the Edgeworth model. It reflects the set of opportunities which are assumed to be available. In a two-individual diagram (Figure 2.2b), the utility possibility frontier becomes symmetric. We could transfer income so that one euro taken from the rich meant one euro for the poor person. Hence maximizing the sum of their utilities gives social indifference curves which are straight lines at the 45-degree line. Both have equal levels of welfare. In this case one is led naturally to the 45-degree line. But we also note that in this example the maximin gives just the same answer as the utilitarian principle.

It is not perhaps surprising that Edgeworth, as a very conservative economist, had his own doubts: he wrote, 'the acme of socialism is thus for a moment sighted; but it is immediately clouded over by doubts and reservations' (Edgeworth 1897, p. 104).[11] It was not surprising that these conclusions raised a number of doubts and reservations. Sidgwick was one of the first to take up the so-called 'incentive question', to use modern terminology. He wrote: 'it is conceivable that a greater equality in the distribution of products would lead ultimately to a reduction in the total amount to be distributed in consequence of a general preference of leisure to the results of labour' (quoted in Edgeworth 1925). Following John Stuart Mill, Sidgwick also saw that if 'a dull equality' was imposed on liberty and diversity of opinions and tastes, the progress of knowledge and culture would be threatened. It is interesting to note that the nineteenth-century

[10] In the libertarian case we have the same outcome.

[11] It is of some interest to note that, in their ten-point programme called the Communist Manifesto, and with hardly any connection to Edgeworth's result, Marx and Engels put strong progressive income taxation in second place only to the abolition of private land ownership.

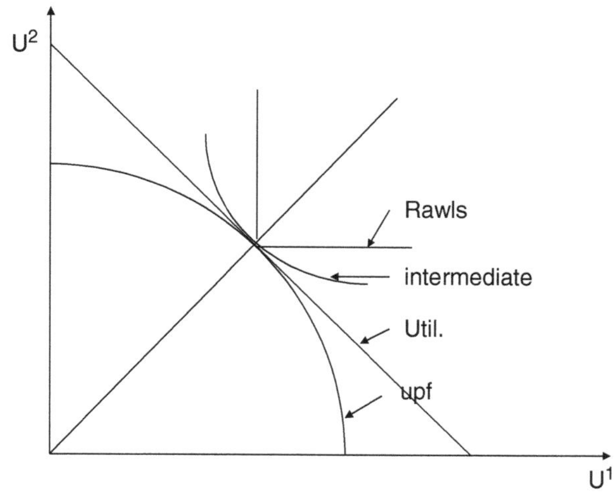

Figure 2.2b The symmetric utility possibility frontier

utilitarians were ready to sacrifice a welfarist approach, to use the term introduced by Sen. In fact, Mill and Sidgwick pointed out the importance of incorporating non-utility information in social judgements.

It is clear that a fully egalitarian result depends on the strong assumption that labour supply is perfectly inelastic. Starting with Mirrlees (1971), one of the main achievements of modern optimal tax theory has been to fill the gap which had arisen due to neglect of the incentive considerations and to derive optimal tax schedules, taking into account the effects of taxation on labour effort. A key difficulty with Edgeworth's solution is that the government cannot observe productivities of individuals (wage rates). It observes income, which is a function of productivity and effort. Other doubts and reservations have also received some attention, but clearly not enough.

As mentioned in the introduction, some ethical objections may be entailed in the use of a utilitarian social welfare objective when, because of different needs for certain consumption goods, individuals differ in their ability to generate utility. As shown by Sen (1973), the utilitarian approach cannot easily handle heterogeneity in individual utility functions. Consumption is no longer necessarily equal across individuals, and is higher for individuals more able to enjoy consumption. Namely, if individuals have the same utility functions, equal marginal utilities of all coincide with equal total utilities. Sen (1973) pointed out that, given the diversity of human beings in generating utility from consumption, the two may pull in opposite directions. To use an example given by Sen (1973), suppose two persons of equal productivity differ in the amount of utility they obtain from a given amount of income. Some are more 'efficient' at generating utility from income than others. If aversion to inequality is high, one would want to redistribute from those who are more efficient utility-generators to those who are less so. On the other hand, if aversion to inequality is low, so what matters is the sum of utilities rather than its distribution, one might want to redistribute from those who are less efficient at generating utility to the more efficient ones. The analogy would be with education or health expenditures (Arrow 1971). Should educational resources be concentrated on those who are most able to use them, or should they be allocated so that difficult learners are favoured? Similarly, how should health expenditures be allocated among persons with afflictions that are more easy versus more difficult to treat?

When individuals have heterogeneous preferences, comparing welfare across populations becomes conceptually problematic. In terms of the social welfare function, there is no well-defined comparable measure of real income across individuals when individual preference orderings are heterogeneous. Over the past several decades, the growing body of work in social philosophy, welfare economics, and social choice theory has investigated problems of responsibility. A theory of individual responsibility is often connected with a popular ideal, equality of opportunity. All conceptions of equal opportunity draw on some distinction between morally justified and unjustified inequalities. The key starting point of the literature on equality of opportunity is the idea that inequalities in outcomes can be partitioned into justifiable sources of inequality and unjustifiable (or illegitimate) sources. Roemer makes the following distinction: 'separate the influences on the outcome a person experiences into circumstances and effort: the former are attributes of a person's environment for which he should not be held responsible, and effort is the choice variable for which he should be held responsible' (Roemer 1998, p. 24). Roemer's (1998, 2008) contribution relates to an earlier philosophical debate which was launched by Dworkin (1981a, 1981b), who argued that certain types of preferences should not be accepted as a legitimate rationale for egalitarian redistribution. For example, if a person would be very unhappy were he or she unable to drive fast cars, this should not justify any claim to transfer resources to this person. On the other hand, if a person was born with low inherent abilities to succeed in the labour market, this might be a acceptable basis for redistribution.

As pointed out by Kanbur and Wagstaff (2014, p. 4), 'everything rests on coming to a separation of legitimate and illegitimate differences for the egalitarian impulse.... If preferences are themselves determined by resources, say parental resources, then a clean separation may not be possible, certainly empirically and perhaps even conceptually'.

According to Fleurbaey (2008), the concept of responsibility itself suggests different kinds of reward principles. For example Cohen (1989, p. 914) writes: 'We should... compensate only for those welfare deficits which are not in some way traceable to the individual's choices'. Fleurbaey (2008, p. 10) calls this kind of approach a liberal one[12] 'because the absence of intervention may be viewed as a hallmark of neutrality toward different ways to exercising responsibility'. Fleurbaey (2008) also pointed out that this reward principle can be connected to libertarianism: namely, if the circumstances are the same, individuals are fully responsible for their differences.

Economics literature on this question has developed in two directions. The liberal reward principle has been adopted by Fleurbaey (2008), and Fleurbaey and Maniquet

[12] Based on writings by Arneson and Cohen.

(2011) provide one conceptual way of approaching this problem. They consider optimal income tax models where individuals differ in skills and in preferences for work. The problem of redistribution becomes complex when pre-tax income inequality is determined jointly by unequal abilities and incentives in the context of multidimensionality. (We return to this problem in Chapters 10 and 14.) If one supposes that individuals are responsible for their own preferences, while they are not responsible for their productivity, the principles of compensation and responsibility suggest that they should be compensated for differences in their productivity, but should be neither penalized nor rewarded for differences in their preferences. In other words, their theory develops social objective criteria that trade off the Equal Preferences Transfer Principle (with the same preferences, redistribution across unequal skills is desirable) and the Equal Skills Transfer Principle (at a given level of skill, redistribution across different preferences is not desirable). A trade-off arises because it is impossible to satisfy both principles simultaneously (Fleurbaey 1994). Boadway et al (2002) provide a general analysis of this situation and demonstrate how the tax structure depends on weights placed on different types of households in the social welfare function. A plausible case is, e.g., where the weight given to the utility of a hard-working low-skilled worker is higher than that of a lazy high-skilled agent.

Roemer (1998) and Van de Gaer (1993) propose a compromise between the principle of compensation and the principle of responsibility. They propose combinations of the maximin and utilitarian social welfare functions, so that a high-inequality aversion is applied along the dimension of circumstances, whereas a zero-inequality aversion is applied in the dimension of responsibility. Applying these principles in practice is not easy, although some attempts have been made (see Roemer 1998; Roemer et al 2003; Schokkaert et al 2004; Aaberge and Colombino 2006). We will apply this principle in Chapter 14 in the context of capital income taxation.

For those who prefer to think of the justification for redistribution as being based on the inequality of opportunity, differences in preferences may provide a suitable basis for distinguishing economic rewards but differences in skills, in turn, do not. Following either the Roemer–Van de Gaer or Fleurbaey–Maniquet approaches, in a society consisting of individuals with the same productivity but different working preferences, there should be no redistribution. Equality of opportunities would be achieved in such a society. This point of view raises questions on the nature of preferences. In fact, there is a very fine dividing line between differences in preferences that are due on the one hand to physiological characteristics and those due on the other hand to psychological attitudes to work. It may be argued that both skills and preferences are 'circumstances of birth'. Or: how appealing are equality of opportunity principles inherently? The fairness of redistribution needs to be carefully evaluated: is it justified to redistribute income from a person who likes to consume expensive goods and is willing to work hard for that purpose to people who hate working but are also satisfied with the low income resulting from their choices? This problem has been widely discussed in the literature of social choice. A low preference for work may mean two different things: taste for leisure and difficulty to work. As Banks and Diamond (2010, p. 667) observe, 'viewing a worker as lazy (liking leisure) is very different from viewing a worker as having difficulty working longer, perhaps for physical reasons'.

2.7 Non-welfarism and paternalism

The literature of optimal redistributive taxation has so far mainly concentrated on the social welfare functions with a non-decreasing function of individual's utilities. There are good reasons to suppose that many people have different notions of welfare or distributional justice with regard to redistribution. Society may not always prefer a change which leaves everyone at least as well-off as they were before that change. For example, consider a change which has no effect on anyone except the richest individual in this society, whose wealth or income doubles. No one is worse off (ruling out envy), but it is not inconceivable that society may judge that the increased inequality in itself makes the change undesirable. It means that society may have non-Paretian objectives. For example, Simons (1938) states the ultimate case for tax progressivity in a single sentence: 'the case for drastic progression in taxation must be rested on the case against inequality—on the ethical or aesthetical judgement that the prevailing distribution of wealth and income reveals a degree (and/or kind) of inequality'. Plato in turn made the following judgement:

> We maintain that if a state is to avoid the greatest plague of all—I mean civil war—though civil integration would be a better term—extreme poverty and wealth must not be allowed to arise in any section of the citizen body, because both lead to both these disasters. That is why the legislator must now announce the acceptable limits of wealth and poverty. The lower limit of poverty must be the value of the holding. The legislator will use the holding as his unit of measure and allow a man to possess twice, thrice, and up to four times its value (quoted in Cowell 1977, p. 26).

Hence, according to Plato, no one in society should be more than four times richer than its poorest member.

Policy recommendations on redistribution, or more generally on taxation, are typically reached after balancing different considerations. They are not the product of a single optimization exercise. Hence it is necessary to distinguish outcomes and process. Outcomes appear in the social welfare function, but process often features in debates about redistribution or taxation in general. Outcomes can be assessed in different ways. We may focus only on individual well-being, but this does not necessarily mean experienced utility. We may adopt welfarism as typical in optimal tax theory. Then only utility information matters, implying that individuals are the best judges of their own welfare and their welfare is all that matters, e.g. neither liberty, rights, etc. enter into considerations, nor do quantities of particular goods consumed. This may miss aspects of social policy that are, in practice, of some concern, such as merit goods (or bads) such as hard drugs, but also such as hours worked. In the standard setting we do not care whether someone reaches given utility through transfer or through work, but it seems in practice that many people do. Any such concerns can be called paternalistic. The notion that individuals may not make the best choices for themselves raises difficult issues. In fact, individuals may want the government to intervene, to induce behaviour that is closer to what individuals wish they were doing. Myopia, procrastination, consumption of addictive goods are examples of behaviour that lead to the so-called new paternalism and that imply non-welfarist objective functions (see Kanbur, Pirttilä, and Tuomala 2006).

Much of the attention of non-welfarist approaches has focused on a particular form of non-welfarism, namely poverty alleviation. Policy discussion on poverty alleviation and the targeting of social policy often concentrates almost exclusively on income. Little weight is typically given to issues such as the disutility the poor experience when working. Indeed, sometimes work requirements are seen in a positive light, as is often the case with workfare. This is in marked contrast with conventional, utility-based objectives in optimal income taxation literature. Therefore it is worthwhile to examine the implications of poverty redistribution policy. Besley and Coate (1992) and Kanbur, Keen, and Tuomala (1994) start from the fairness principle, that everyone should be entitled to a minimal level of consumption. This approach resembles well the tone of much of policy discussion in developing countries, including the MDGs (United Nations Millennium Development Goals, one being to halve the extreme poverty rate), where the objective is explicitly to reduce poverty rather than maximize well-being. Similarly, the discussion regarding cash transfer systems is often couched especially in terms of poverty alleviation.

The principle of 'fair equality of opportunity' is one of three principles of John Rawls' 'justice as fairness'. Rawls (1971) assessed opportunity in terms of primary goods such as income, wealth, and so on. As mentioned above, for many years Amartya Sen has been arguing for the consideration of alternative evaluative bases, notably individual capabilities, defined broadly as the freedom that people have to function in key dimensions. Sen (1980) took issue with Rawls' concept of primary goods, arguing that this idea does not adequately reflect the freedoms that people have to pursue their goals. Sen (1980) pointed out the heterogeneity in people's ability to transform primary goods into freedoms. This critique led to Sen's (1985) conceptualization of well-being in terms of primary 'functionings'—'what people are able to be and do (rather than in terms of the means they possess)' (Sen 2000, p. 74). Social welfare may be a function of individual well-being, but well-being assessed in terms of capabilities may lead to different conclusions. The central element in Sen's analysis is the concept of well-being. Welfarist analysis such as classical utilitarianism equates well-being with happiness. This may often be misleading. Similarly, if we interpret well-being as a utility, we face a number of problems. In economic theory, utility is often interpreted as a kind of calibration system which reflects choices. If an individual's choice between x and y is x, then we say that he or she derives from x more utility than from y. Even if utilities are well defined, it does not necessarily reflect individual well-being. Preferences may have been formed endogenously, by a process of cognitive dissonance, so that people learn to like what is available to them (Elster 1982). Neither does equating well-being with utility take into account the diversity of motivation behind a person's choice. Sen argues that the right focus is not on utilities, or commodities, or characteristics—in the sense of Gorman (1956) and Lancaster (1971)—but rather on something that he calls a person's capability. The bike example used by Sen (1982) illustrates. There is a sequence from a commodity (a bike), to a characteristic (transportation), to a capability to function (the ability to move), to a utility (pleasure from moving). Sen argues that the third category—that of capability to function—comes closest to the notion of well-being. Sen defines functioning as 'achievements of a person; what he or she manages to do or to be'. He emphasizes that the capability approach is very flexible: 'It can be used in many different ways, since an informational format (base on capabilities) for ethical analysis does not provide a specific moral formula' (Sen 1984, p. 27).

We can see a parallel between the above discussion of fair redistribution when individuals differ in working preferences and Sen's capability approach. Namely, there is an important general problem of interpersonal variations in converting incomes into the actual capabilities of an individual to do this or be that. This could be rephrased to refer to work preferences in this kind of model. Attempts to allow for heterogeneous preferences in the population have generally involved arbitrary weights for each type of utility function featuring in the social welfare function, and therefore no specific result about the desirable direction of redistribution.

It is typical, as the Mirrlees review did, to start the discussion of a 'good tax system' with the four maxims from Adam Smith's *The Wealth of Nations*. The first of these maxims says: '(i) The subjects of every state ought to contribute towards the support of the government, as nearly as possible in proportion to their respective abilities . . . ' (2012, p. 470).

Smith interprets the 'abilities' of citizens as their revenue or income. Unlike Smith, Mill has doubts regarding the principle of taxation according to which taxpayers should contribute to the government's revenue in accordance with ability to pay. It was not obvious to Mill that this principle leads to progressive taxation in the sense of increasing average tax rate with income. As a general rule, he recommended a proportional tax. But on the other hand, as explained by Sandmo (2011), Mill recommended that income below a certain limit (in his case 50 pounds) should be exempt from taxes. In fact, this tax-exempt area, combined with proportional tax on income above 50 pounds, implies progressive taxation. In other words, average tax rates are increasing with income. We could also interpret 'abilities' as capabilities.[13] This alternative interpretation could lead us in a different direction in tax policy recommendations. For example, if we take a capabilities interpretation, the natural tax unit is the individual, rather than the household or family. How should we modify the public policy rules? For example, how do the

[13] In fact, some tax deductions can be justified in advancing capabilities.

rules of public provision of private and public goods with optimal taxation change if we make 'a fundamental shift in the focus of attention from the means of living to the actual opportunities a person has' (Sen 2009, p. 253)? We will come back to these questions in Chapter 13.

Optimal tax theory and welfare economics in general can be criticized on the basis that they do not recognize the plurality and diversity of values. Sen (2009) illustrates this by the 'three children and a flute' example, where we have to decide which of three children should be given the flute: Anne, who can play; Bob, who is poor; or Carla, who made the flute. There are 'plural and competing reasons for justice, all of which have claims to impartiality' (Sen 2009, p. 12). Hence, Sen argues that 'theorists of different persuasions, such as utilitarians, or economic egalitarians, or labour right theorists, no-nonsense libertarians... almost certainly they would each argue for totally different resolutions' (Sen 2009, p. 13). It is also the case that theorists may recognize there is some appeal to different claims. We may have some sympathy both with Bob (who is poor) and with Carla (who made the flute). It has been common practice in optimal tax theory that the optimal choice of tax and spending can indeed be parameterized in terms of the degree of inequality aversion, with the Rawlsian principle (maximin) emerging as a limiting case. As we mentioned above, Rawls did not accept Arrow's interpretation to 'shift smoothly from the moral conception to another simply by varying the parameter (β)'; it is also the case that the different views about the flute cannot be represented by varying one parameter. It is our aim to extend the optimal income tax model in the spirit of the flute example, allowing for diversity of objectives (see especially section 2.4). A number of earlier scholars in the area of public finance were aware of the diversity of social objectives. For example, Musgrave (1959, p. 5) writes: 'There is no simple set of principles, no uniform rule of normative behaviour that may be applied to the conduct of public economy. Rather we are confronted with a number of separate, though interrelated, functions that requires distinct solutions'. Musgrave followed along these lines analysing each aspect of public finance in terms of those objectives that seemed most appropriate, such as merit wants, utilities, and aggregate level of activity. There are also some examples along these lines in modern writings on tax theory, for example Feldstein (1976) on tax reform and Atkinson (1995). More recently, Weinzierl (2012, p. 1) provides an explanation for a limited use of tagging in the actual income tax system. He argues that 'this puzzle is a symptom of a more fundamental problem. Conventional theory neglects the diverse normative criteria with which, as extensive evidence has shown, most people evaluate policy. In particular if the classic principle of Equal Sacrifice augments the standard utilitarian criterion, optimal tagging is limited'. Weinzierl's (2012) approach has its own weaknesses. Namely, it is not obvious how to guarantee commensurability between two very different ethical frameworks. Utilitarianism is based on the end-state principle, libertarianism ('equal sacrifice')[14] not. Rawls (1974) objects to

[14] Liam Murphy and Thomas Nagel (2002, p. 28) have argued: 'If (and only if) that (libertarianism) is the theory of distributive justice we accept, the principle of equal sacrifice does make sense'.

this as an example of 'intuitionist' ethics—that is, an ambiguous ethical norm that requires each individual to apply his moral intuition to balance libertarian and utilitarian views (Rawls 1971, section 1).

2.8 Obstacles to optimal lump-sum taxation

If the government is unconstrained in ability to deploy lump-sum taxes it can move around the first best utility possibility frontier at will, achieving distributional objectives and financing public goods. Lump-sum tax has no effect on behaviour at margin. It is like money taken from the wallet overnight. It does have an intra-marginal effect, but no substitution effect. It also does not interfere with the necessary conditions for the first best optimum to correspond to redistribution endowment in the second welfare theorem. More specifically, the second welfare theorem says that, under certain assumptions (the absence of economics of large scale and externalities, and people are rational), every Pareto-efficient state of affairs could be achieved as a competitive equilibrium with zero tax on commodities and the appropriate lump-sum tax imposed on each individual, provided that initial endowments were distributed appropriately. It is not hard in principle to conceive of lump-sum taxes, e.g. a genuine poll tax would be one, or tax on age or sex, nearly. But most observed taxes in practice, however, are not lump-sum, and do distort, i.e. prevent the attainment of some necessary conditions for the first-best Pareto efficiency. Why do we not observe in real life many lump-sum taxes? As the examples above suggest, this is something to do with equity.[15] While there are no theoretical barriers to lump-sum taxation per se—such as a poll tax, or a tax on sex—there are therefore presumably some barriers to optimal lump-sum taxation. Indeed there are: public economics has recognized for a long time that, with asymmetric information about earnings ability, the government simply cannot finance its activities without using distorting taxes. Even without redistribution concerns, the inability to fully cover needed government expenditures with a poll tax that is low enough that everyone can (and will) pay it implies a need for distorting taxes to raise sufficient revenue, for public goods and other public expenditure, for example. And moreover, some degree of concern about income distribution is widely accepted as a government role that affects both tax-setting and other programmes that require financing.

To see the barriers to optimal lump-sum taxation, we bring this out in a model much used in optimal income tax literature: namely, the two-type model, where we have two individuals, 1 and 2. They differ only in ability or skill, described by pre-tax wage n_i (i=1,2) and have identical preferences $u = U(x) - \psi\left(\frac{z}{n}\right)$, where x is consumption, $U(x)$

[15] The community charge (poll tax) introduced by the Thatcher Conservative government in the UK, in effect from 1989/1990 to 1993, is a good example of this. The tax proved deeply unpopular. Even before the tax became law in England, the protests quickly became a national issue, with large-scale riots in London and other big cities in the UK.

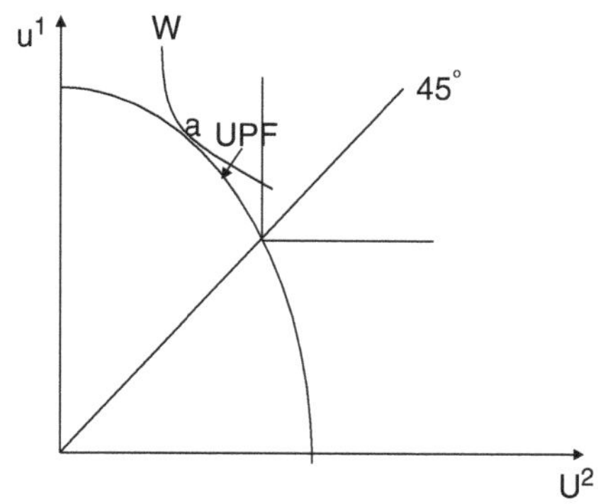

Figure 2.2c The 1.best optimum

increasing and strictly concave and y is labour supply (y could be interpreted as number of hours worked by the individual or equally well as being effort), $z = ny$ is before-tax income, and $\psi\left(\frac{z}{n}\right)$ is increasing and strictly convex. Further, we assume constant returns to scale and perfect competition in the production sector. Individual i pays t_i a lump-sum tax (i=1, 2), regardless of z and x. t_i depends on i, i.e. the government can tell which individual is which; that is, the tax authority can observe productivity. Hence taxes can be based on productivity. So $x_i = z_i - t_i$. By varying t_i (i=1, 2) the government can achieve the first best allocation it wants. Which will it choose? It depends on the social objectives. Suppose a utilitarian social welfare function.

The government maximizes $W(u^1, u^2) = u(x^1) - \psi\left(\frac{z^1}{n^1}\right) + u(x^2) - \psi\left(\frac{z^2}{n^2}\right)$ s.t. $x^1 + x^2 \leq z^1 + z^2$(linear technology) with respect to x and z. The first order conditions imply $x^1 = x^2$ and $\psi'(z^1/n^1) < \psi'(z^2/n^2)$. Because ψ is strictly convex and preferences are identical, $z^1/n^1 < z^2/n^2$, i.e. labour supply of type 1 is smaller than that of type 2. The two have the same level of consumption but the high-ability one works harder, meaning that $u^1 > u^2$. Utility is decreasing with n. This is like point a in Figure 2.2c. Mirrlees (1974) showed in the continuum case that utilitarian first-best has utility decreasing with n, $\frac{dU}{dn} < 0$, so long as leisure is normal and $u = u(x, z/n)$. (See proof in appendix 2.2.). Hence, utilitarianism is consistent with Marx's dictum from 'The Critique of the Gotha Program': 'from each according to his ability, to each according to his needs'.

The high-ability types are naturally upset! This is not a problem if the government really can observe wage rates. But suppose realistically wage rates are unobserved. The government knows one of each ability, but not which is which. The first-best optimum cannot be implemented; high-ability will pretend to be or mimic low-ability. To prove this we define $V(x, z; n) = U(x, \frac{z}{n})$. So $V(x, z, n^2) > V(x, z, n^1)$ (*). Suppose a quasi-concave social welfare function giving a point like a in Figure 2.2c, at which $u^1 = V(x^1, z^1, n^1) \geq V(x^2, z^2, n^2) = u^2$. Then we see from (*), $V(x^1, z^1, n^2) > V(x^2, z^2, n^1)$ and the high skill type will mimic the low. Hence in Figure 2.2c the points above the 45-degree line are not incentive-compatible; or, to put it another way, they violate the self-selection constraint.

So we have to put up with distorting taxes in practice. The result that the low-skill type does better than the high one at the optimum is striking and emphasizes the problem of implementing the first-best optimum when we cannot observe individual types. Hence self-selection rules out lump-sum taxation other than a poll tax. This implies that we need to use distorting taxes.

In summary: it must be in the individual's interests to choose the income–consumption pair that the government intends. Intended z and x must increase with ability (skill or productivity). If it is not so, it is better to pretend to be a low-ability type. This is the essential content of self-selection or incentive compatibility constraint. Formally for any pair i and j, using their utility functions $u(x^i, y^i) \geq u\left(x^j, \frac{n^j}{n^i} y^j\right)$.

So we face a constraint additional to technology and endowment: the situation then known as 'one of second-best'. Now our opportunities are more limited. We face a trade-off between equity and efficiency. Then we will typically want to use other tax devices to redistribute, even though they distort. We may want to introduce distortions/inefficiency in pursuit of distributional objectives. Note we need to be careful here on the meaning of 'inefficiency': the optimum is Pareto-efficient relative to constraints, but violates conditions for the first best Pareto efficient.

Optimal tax theory is concerned with the conditions for taxes that do optimize a social welfare function given asymmetric information, and how those taxes vary with both economic circumstances and alternative normative concerns. Distortionary taxation arises as an optimal form of policy in the world of imperfect information, not imposed as an exogenous constraint.

The issue of design is fundamental to public economics. We move from what we would like to achieve to what we can actually implement. Optimal taxation is only one example; others include regulation, social insurance, public provision (public good, publicly provided private goods). The government must work with imperfect information. Information imposes specific constraints on tax design, as seen above. There are two main types of information: about individuals—income, expenditure, age, marital status, etc.—and about transactions—input and output quantities, expenditure by product category. There are in turn two key types of information problem—hidden action (moral hazard), and hidden information (adverse selection).

The central element in optimal tax theory is information. Tax policies apply to the individual only on the basis of what is known about him or her. We saw above that when government can't observe wages, it may not be able to induce individuals to behave as it would like. It is no longer in the first best world. Neither n nor y is separately observable, but z=ny, the individual's income, is. It could be argued that it is inconsistent to suppose that the government can observe before-tax income and know the relationship between labour supply and ability, but not be able to base tax on ability (wage). Atkinson (1982, p. 23) makes an important point when he writes, 'The apparent inconsistency may however be due to the different status of different types of information. Most importantly, the calculated relation between y and n may be based on statistical evidence which is not acceptable in the calculation of individual taxes'.

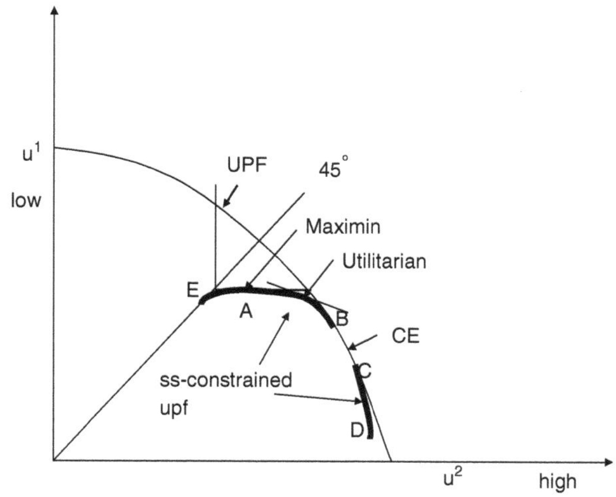

Figure 2.2d The 2.best utility possibility frontier

Atkinson also finds support from Adam Smith, who writes that 'the quantity to be paid ought to be clear and plain to the contributor, and to every other person' (2012, p. 652).

In the two-person context implementation requires $V(x^2, z^2, n^2) \geq V(x^1, z^1, n^2)$, i.e. the self-selection constraint on the high-productivity type, and $V(x^1, z^1, n^1) \geq V(x^2, z^2, n^1)$, i.e. the self-selection constraint on the low-productivity type. We might expect what is shown in Figure 2.2d, where the so-called second-best utility possibility frontier ABCD lies inside that for the first best, except at the no redistribution point.

On the segment AB, the self-selection constraint on the high-productivity type bites. Here we can find both the maximin and utilitarian solutions; at the interval BC neither self-selection constraint bites and there is no redistribution here. Competitive equilibrium lies between B and C and satisfies both self-selection constraints. Between C and D the self-selection constraint on the low-productivity type bites. The Figure suggests an interesting case in which the self-selection constraint on the high-ability type bites. On the AB segment, redistribution is from high type to low type. The optimal tax literature has focused on this case. This is an important point to note, since the Rawlsian position is often seen as very egalitarian—namely, maximizing the position of the least well-off may be consistent with quite wide inequalities. For example, we could justify cutting the tax of top income earners if that yields more revenue to redistribute to the poor. Rawls himself (as many others) believed that his position is 'strongly egalitarian' (p.76). Okun (1975), in his book *Equality and Efficiency*, contrasts Rawls with Friedman. According to Okun (1975), Friedman gives priority to efficiency and Rawls in turn to equality. As we see in Figure 2.2d, this is not quite right. From Figure 2.2d we see that the Rawlsian or maximin point A does not coincide with that for utilitarian, and neither coincides with the 45-degree line. The points from B to A are Pareto-efficient. But the points from A to E on the 45-degree line are Pareto-inefficient, making both worse off.

2.9 Pareto-efficient income taxation in the two-person case

To make things simpler, we consider the discrete-type model with individuals of two skill levels or abilities and government facing the self-selection constraint. Within these models the seminal contributions are Guesnerie and Seade (1982), Stern (1982), and Stiglitz (1982). Stern (1982) and Stiglitz (1982) focused on a model with two types of individuals. The appeal in using this approach is the simplicity of analytics and, more importantly, easily interpretable results. At the heart of the non-linear income tax analysis are the self-selection constraints or the incentive compatibility constraints restricting redistributive policy. Perhaps the most prominent advantage in this approach is its capability to address the incentive issue explicitly through analysis of the self-selection constraint. The advantage of the two-type model or, more generally, the discrete model is to clarify the mimicking issues—to prevent more able from mimicking less able—behind taxation that were not completely transparent in the continuous model, where they were expressed in terms of differential equations. However, some caution is in order. The two-type model is too simple to say something useful on the issue of progressivity. As we shall see in Chapters 12 and 13, it is useful as an ingredient when we analyse supplementary instruments to income taxation.

There are two individuals, 1 and 2. They differ only in productivity or ability, described by pre-tax wage n^i (i=1.2) and $n^2 > n^1$. They have identical preferences with respect to consumption and income. The information structure is such that the government only knows the statistical distribution of people, but does not have information on who is who. The government is assumed to design a menu of net and gross incomes (x,z) implicitly defining the tax schedule $(T=z-x)$ and letting the taxpayers self-select income points by choosing their labour supply and, hence, income (for fixed wage rates, n). What are characterizations of the Pareto-efficient structure when the self-selection constraint bites on high ability? The tax policy is determined subject to the government budget constraint and the self-selection constraint that no type of individual should choose the income point intended for the other type. It means that the binding constraint is that the skilled type should not mimic the unskilled. As seen in Figure 2.2e, both '(x,z) contracts' lie on the same indifference curve for the type 2s, and type 2's contract has more consumption, x, and more gross income, z. The utility can now be expressed as a function of disposable income and the gross income, which for a fixed wage rate can be taken as a measure of the labour supply. Since for a given skill level utility $U(x, z/n) = V(x, z, n)$ is increasing in x and decreasing in z, the indifference curves are upward-sloping. Higher utility levels correspond to lower z or higher x. Hence the indifference curve corresponds to a higher utility level as we move to the north-west in the (x,z) plane. Assumption B of Mirrlees (1971) and the Agent Monotonicity assumption (AM) of Seade (1982) imply that indifference curves in consumption–gross income space become flatter

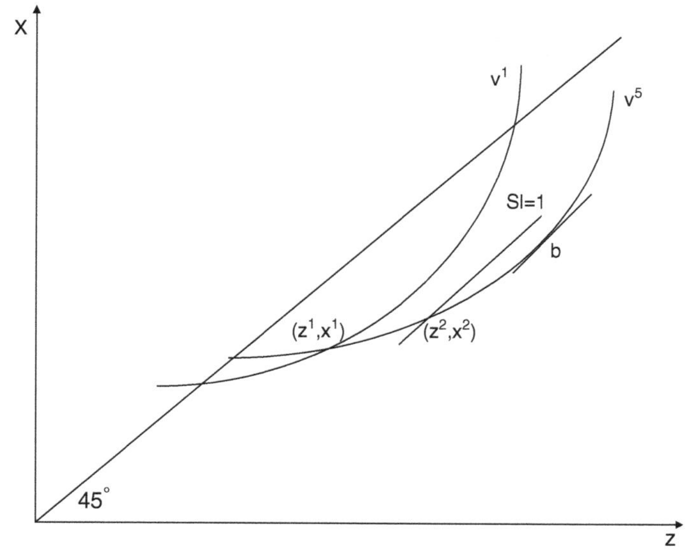

Figure 2.2e The two-type model and marginal tax rates

the higher an individual's wage rate, which in turn ensures that both consumption and gross earnings increase with the wage rate. Hence we do not need an incentive compatibility constraint for the type 1s. In other words, low-productivity workers strictly prefer their allocation.

It is useful to illustrate the marginal tax structure geometrically in the following figures 2e, f, and g (see formalities in appendix 2.3). First, we have to ask: can it be optimal to 'pool' (offer single (x.z)-pair) or is it always optimal to separate? Stiglitz (1982) shows that in the two-person case, it is always optimal to separate (see proof in appendix 2.3). Note, however, this is a rather special case. It is no longer true in the three-person case.

We have two results on marginal tax rates:

(i) No distortion at the top, i.e. the marginal tax rate (MTR) of the type 2s (high-productivity workers) is zero: $\text{MTR}^2 = 0$ (point b in Figure 2.2e and 2.2f). To see this suppose $\text{MTR}^2 > 0$. Then we replace (x^2, z^2) by b in Figure 2.2e. This leaves the indifference curves I^1 and I^2 unchanged but increases revenue. Note that generally this is just Pareto-efficient. Even with the maximin case we still want $\text{MTR}^2 = 0$.

(ii) The marginal tax rate of the type 1s (low-productivity workers) is positive: $\text{MTR}^1 > 0$. We cannot have $\text{MTR}^1 = 0$; if we could we would have both MTRs $= 0$ and be looking at a first-best situation, so the self-selection constraint on the high-skilled one would not be binding. So suppose $\text{MTR}^1 < 0$ (a point on the left from (x^1, z^1)), then replace (x^{1*}, z^{1*}) by (x^1, z^1) in which MTR is positive. This move raises more revenue from type 1.

Intuitively, the use of distortionary taxation allows the government to relax the self-selection constraint on type 2s in the following way. Let's start with the lump-sum allocation where the self-selection constraint just binds with lump-sum taxes (in Figure 2.2g points $a^1$and a^2). In those points it is possible to achieve incentive

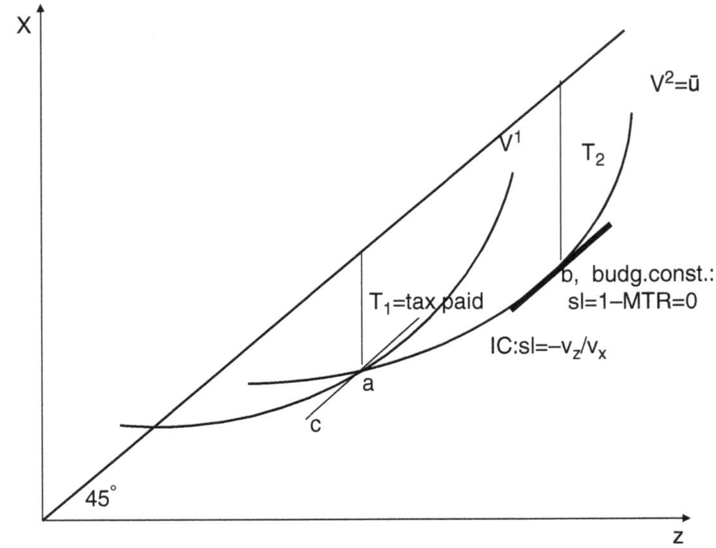

Figure 2.2f The two-type model and marginal tax rates

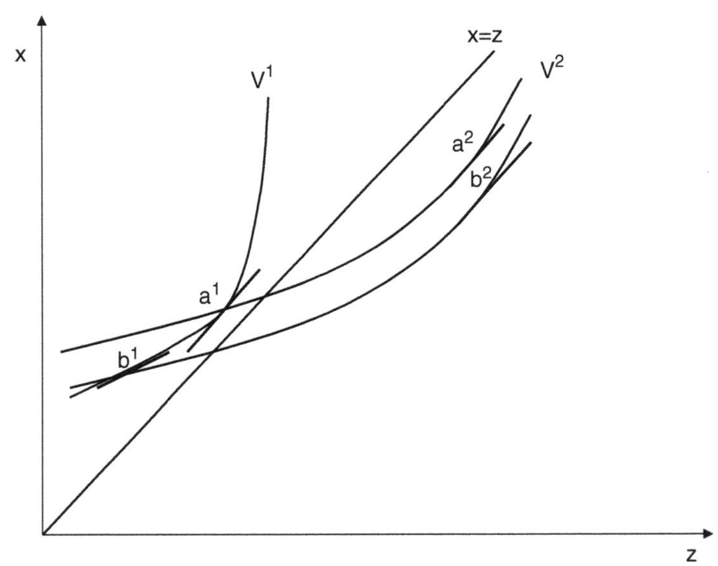

Figure 2.2g The two-type model and marginal tax rates

compatibility, while not distorting the choice of the type 1s as in Figure 2.2g. In Figure 2.2g we pass the type 2s' indifference curve through a point a^1 at which the slope of the type 1s' indifference curve is 1, i.e. the marginal tax rate is zero. Yet this allocation ($a^1$and a^2) is not optimal. Since the opportunity cost of additional income is higher for type 1s than type 2s (reflecting the higher labour supply required to generate a given income), distorting income slightly downwards for type 1s (from Figure 2.2g, by moving a very small distance leftwards along the type 1 indifference curve) by imposing a positive marginal tax rate, a point b^1, but reducing their after-tax income so their utility does not change, makes the mimicking individual worse off. Moreover, this also leaves unchanged revenue from type 1s. This reform relaxes the incentive compatibility constraint, making it possible to shift the indifference curve of type 2s and hence allowing an increase in tax revenue from them. This is possible because we can increase z^2, or decrease x^2, or both. With help from an increase of revenue from the type 2s we can increase x and/or reduce z of the type 1s. And consequently, their utility increases. Hence we can increase the extent of redistribution from the type 2s to the type 1s with such a change. As shown in Figure 2.2g, we can continue to move leftwards along the indifference curve I^1 and pushing down the indifference curve I^2. We can continue this until the marginal gain of redistribution is zero—in Figure 2.2g, point b^2.

Optimal allocation can be implemented by many tax structures. In the optimum: $x^2 > x^1$, $z^2 > z^1$, $V^2 > V^1$, $T(z^2) > T(z^1)$ but $\frac{T(z^2)}{z^2} \geq (\leq) \frac{T(z^1)}{z^1}$. Hence a tax system can be progressive or regressive.

The principle—the incentive compatibility or self-selection constraint is relaxed and redistribution can be pushed further—can be extended to more than two types. Guesnerie and Seade (1982)[16] introduced the so-called chain property and considered an arbitrary, but finite, number of types. In order to push further redistribution from higher to lower productivity workers, the income of all but the highest productive worker must be distorted downwards. Let's look at the case for more than two skill types: $n^3 > n^2 > n^1$.

An optimal tax solution can have the following properties. Figure A2.2 (in appendix 2.3) illustrates the case in which individuals are fully separated by skill type. The incentive constraint may be binding on the next lowest type only. The lowest skill types may not work. The equilibrium may be partial pooling or bunching as in Figure A2.3 (in appendix 2.3). It may be optimal that one or more skill types at the bottom are not working. They are bunched and receive the same consumption x with gross income z=0 as in Figure A2.3 (in appendix 2.3). In all these cases of multiple skill types, the marginal tax rate is zero at the top. Marginal tax rates for i = 1. 2 are between 0 and 1. Optimal allocation satisfies: $x^i > x^{i-1}$, $z^i > z^{i-1}$, $V^i > V^{i-1}$, $T(z^i) > T(z^{i-1})$. Again, the tax system can be progressive or regressive.

The lesson we take from this simple model is that distortionary taxation arises as an optimal form of policy in the world of imperfect information, not imposed as an exogenous constraint. This approach has not been without its critics. Piketty and Saez (2013. p. 15) argue

> that informational concerns and observability is not the overwhelming reason for basing taxes and transfers almost exclusively on income.... It seems more fruitful practically to assume instead exogenously that the government can only use a limited set of tax tools, precisely those that are used in practice, and consider the optimum within the set of real tax systems actually used.

[16] See also Weymark (1986) and Simula (2010), who further developed the discrete model in the quasi-linear case.

Endogenous wages: In the basic optimal income tax model, labour supplied by workers of different skills is a perfect substitute, so relative wage rates are constant. If labour supplies are imperfect substitutes, relative wages vary inversely with relative labour supplies, following classical general equilibrium modelling. The consequence, as shown by Stern (1982) and Stiglitz (1982), is that the tax system should encourage labour supply of high-skilled workers. In this two-type model (type 2s are higher skilled than type 1s), the relative wage rate of type $\frac{w^1}{w^2}$, determined on the market, is a decreasing function of y^1/y^2, so imposing a negative marginal income tax rate on the high-skilled will redistribute indirectly to the low-skilled and improve welfare (see appendix 2.3). This does not necessarily mean that the average tax rate should be reduced. Namely, if leisure is a normal good, the income effect of higher tax payments will likely also encourage high-skilled labour supply.

APPENDIX 2.1 TOTAL REVENUE AS % OF GDP IN OECD COUNTRIES

Table A2.1 Total revenue as % of GDP

Year	1965	1975	1985	1995	2005	2013
Country						
Australia	20.6	25.4	27.7	28.2	29.9	..
Austria	33.6	36.4	40.5	41	40.8	42.5
Belgium	30.6	38.8	43.5	42.8	43.4	44.6
Canada	25.2	31.4	31.9	34.9	32.3	30.6
Chile	..	..	..	18.4	20.7	20.2
Czech Republic	..	..	..	34.9	34.5	34.1
Denmark	29.5	37.8	45.4	48	49.5	48.6
Estonia	..	..	..	36.2	30.4	31.8
Finland	30	36.1	39.1	44.5	42.1	44
France	33.6	34.9	41.9	41.9	42.8	45
Germany	31.6	34.3	36.1	36.2	33.9	36.7
Greece	17	18.6	24.4	27.6	31.3	33.5
Hungary	..	..	..	41	36.8	38.9
Iceland	25.5	29.2	27.4	30.4	39.4	35.5
Ireland	24.5	27.9	33.7	31.8	29.5	28.3
Israel	..	..	..	35.2	34.3	30.5
Italy	24.7	24.5	32.5	38.6	39.1	42.6
Japan	17.8	20.4	26.7	26.4	27.3	..
Korea	..	14.2	15.3	19	22.5	24.3
Luxembourg	26.4	31.2	37.5	35.3	38.2	39.3
Mexico	..	..	15.2	14.9	17.7	19.7
Netherlands	30.9	38.4	39.9	39	36.4	..
New Zealand	23.6	28	30.6	35.8	36.4	32.1
Norway	29.6	39.2	42.6	40.9	43.2	40.8
Poland	..	..	..	36.1	32.9	..

Portugal	15.7	18.9	24.1	28.9	30.2	33.4
Slovak Republic	..	..	..	39.6	30.8	29.6
Slovenia	..	..	..	38.4	38	36.8
Spain	14.3	18	26.8	31.3	35.2	32.6
Sweden	31.4	38.9	44.8	45.6	46.6	42.8
Switzerland	16.6	22.5	23.9	25.5	26.5	27.1
Turkey	10.6	11.9	11.5	16.8	24.3	29.3
United Kingdom	29.3	33.6	35.6	32.1	33.8	32.9
United States	23.5	24.6	24.6	26.7	26.1	25.4
OECD—Average	24.8	28.6	31.7	33.6	34	34.1

APPENDIX 2.2 'UTILITARIAN COMMUNISM'

Proof utilitarian first-best has utility decreasing with n so long as leisure is normal.
Note $u=u(x,y)$
The first-order conditions of government's problem

$$u_x(x(n), y(n)) = \lambda \tag{1}$$

$$u_L(x(n), y(n)) = -\lambda n \tag{2}$$

Differentiating (1) and (2)

$$\begin{pmatrix} u_{xx} & u_{xy} \\ u_{yx} & u_{yy} \end{pmatrix} \begin{pmatrix} dx/dn \\ dy/dn \end{pmatrix} = \begin{pmatrix} 0 \\ -\lambda \end{pmatrix}$$

implies

$$\begin{pmatrix} dx/dn \\ dy/dn \end{pmatrix} = \frac{1}{\Delta} \begin{pmatrix} u_{yy} & -u_{xy} \\ -u_{yx} & u_{xx} \end{pmatrix} \begin{pmatrix} 0 \\ -\lambda \end{pmatrix} \tag{3}$$

$$= \left(\frac{\lambda}{\Delta}\right) \begin{bmatrix} u_{xy} \\ -u_{xx} \end{bmatrix}$$

where $\Delta = u_{xx}u_{yy} - (u_{yx})^2$ by concavity.
From (3):

$$\frac{du}{dn} = u_x \frac{dx}{dn} + u_y \frac{dy}{dn} = \left(\frac{\lambda}{\Delta}\right) \left[u_x u_{xy} - u_y u_{xx}\right] \Delta$$

$$= \left(\frac{\lambda}{\Delta}\right) u_y \left[u_{xy}\left(\frac{u_x}{u_y}\right) - u_{xx}\right] < 0$$

$$= (+)(-)[+]$$

latter plus if leisure is normal.

APPENDIX 2.3 FORMALITIES OF PARETO-EFFICIENT TAXATION IN THE TWO-TYPE CASE

There are two individuals, 1 and 2, or two groups with equal sizes. They differ only in ability, described by pre-tax wage n^i (i=1.2). They have identical preferences with regard to consumption and income, where x is consumption and y is labour supply. z=ny is before-tax income. This assumes constant returns to scale and perfect competition in the production sector.

$T(z^i)$ is taxes paid by type i, and $x^i = z^i - T(z^i)$.

Indirect utility function

$$V(x^i, z^i, n^i) = max_y\{U^i(x^i, y^i); z^i = n^i y^i, x^i = z^i - T(z^i)\}.$$

What are characterizations of PE structure when the self-selection constraint bites on high ability?

We know both contracts lie on the same IC for 2 (since $\lambda_2 > 0$) and 2's contract has more x and more z (from AM)

Max $V = V(x^1, z^1, n^1)$

s.t

Pareto-constraint $(\delta) V(x^2, z^2, n^2) = \bar{V}^2$,

Self-selection constraint (μ) $V(x^2, z^2, n^2) = \hat{V}(x^1, z^1, n^2)$ and

Revenue constraint (λ) $z^1 + z^2 = x^1 + x^2$ (the 'pure redistribution' case)

The Lagrangean function

$$\begin{aligned} L = {} & V(x^1, z^1, n^1) - \delta\left(V(x^2, z^2, n^2) - \bar{V}^2\right) \\ & -\mu\left(V(x^2, z^2, n^2) - \hat{V}(x^1, z^1, n^2)\right) - \lambda(z^1 + z^2 - x^1 - x^2). \end{aligned} \tag{1}$$

Differentiating with respect to z^i and x^i:(i=1, 2)

$$x^1 : V_x^1 + \mu\hat{V}_x + \lambda = 0 \tag{2}$$

$$x^2 : -(\delta + \mu)V_x^2 + \lambda = 0 \tag{3}$$

$$z^1 : V_z^1 + \mu\hat{V}_z - \lambda = 0 \tag{4}$$

$$z^2 : -(\delta + \mu)V_z^2 - \lambda = 0 \tag{5}$$

Combining (3) and (5) we have MTR for type 2:

$$-(\delta + \mu)V_x^2 - (\delta + \mu)V_z^2 = 0 \Rightarrow -\frac{V_z^2}{V_x^2} = 1 \tag{6}$$

From (6) $MTR^2=0$.

From (2) and (4) we obtain MTR for type 1.

$$\frac{V_z^1}{V_x^1} = \frac{\mu \hat{V}_z - \lambda}{\mu \hat{V}_x + \lambda} \tag{7}$$

Multiply by $\frac{\mu \hat{V}_x + \lambda}{\hat{V}_x}$ (7) we have:

$$\left(\mu + \frac{\lambda}{\hat{V}_x}\right)\frac{V_z^1}{V_x^1} = \frac{\mu \hat{V}_z}{\hat{V}_x} - \frac{\lambda}{\hat{V}_x} \Rightarrow \tag{8}$$

$$\frac{\lambda}{\hat{V}_x}\left(\frac{V_z^1}{V_x^1} + 1\right) = \mu\left(\frac{\hat{V}_z}{\hat{V}_x} - \frac{V_z^1}{V_x^1}\right) \Rightarrow \tag{9}$$

$$MTR^1 = \frac{\mu \hat{V}_x}{\lambda}\left(\frac{\hat{V}_z}{\hat{V}_x} - \frac{V_z^1}{V_x^1}\right) \tag{10}$$

$\frac{\mu \hat{V}_x}{\lambda}$ is positive and the mimicker is more able than type 1. Now in (10) both terms on the right-hand side are positive. The latter term $\left(\frac{\hat{V}_z}{\hat{V}_x} - \frac{V_z^1}{V_x^1}\right)$ is positive by the AM condition.

$$-\frac{\hat{V}_z}{\hat{V}_x} < -\frac{V_z^1}{V_x^1} \Leftrightarrow \frac{\hat{V}_z}{\hat{V}_x} > \frac{V_z^1}{V_x^1}.$$

So $MTR^1 > 0$. A positive marginal tax rate is possible only insofar as type 2 has a greater willingness to supply income than type 1 at the point (x^1, z^1).

It is always optimal to separate in a two-type model.

Proof: At a, $slope(V^1) > slope(V^2)$, see Fig A1, so either (i) $slope(V^2) < 1 (\Rightarrow MTR^2 > 0)$ in which case offer b (b has to be near enough V^2 to be the below 45-degree line through a), or (ii) $slope(V^1) > 1 (\Rightarrow MTR^1 \leq 0)$ in which case offer c (similarly c must be near enough V^1).

Note that inefficiency of pooling is not an attribute of the AM condition. Figure A2.1 uses only local properties. What AM does give us, given inefficiency of pooling, is that it cannot be the case that both self-selection constraints bind at the optimum.

Proof: Suppose not. Then the two bundles would both have to be on both indifference curves. Since pooling is inefficient, they must be different bundles. But then the indifference curves must cross more than once, violating AM. So one or other self-selection can bind.

Optimal income taxation and endogenous wages: The production side of the economy is modelled using an aggregate, constant returns to scale, production function $F(y^1, y^2)$. First, the wage rates are endogenous in a similar way as in Stern (1982) or Stiglitz (1982). In the following, $\Omega = \frac{w^1}{w^2}$ depicts the relative wage of the low-skilled type. Assuming a competitive labour market, Ω is a function of y^1/y^2, $\frac{w^1}{w^2} = \frac{F_1(y^1, y^2)}{F_2(y^1, y^2)}$. It captures the idea that the relative wage rate of type 1, determined at the market, is a decreasing function of y^1/y^2. Hence, if the government uses its policy instruments so that the

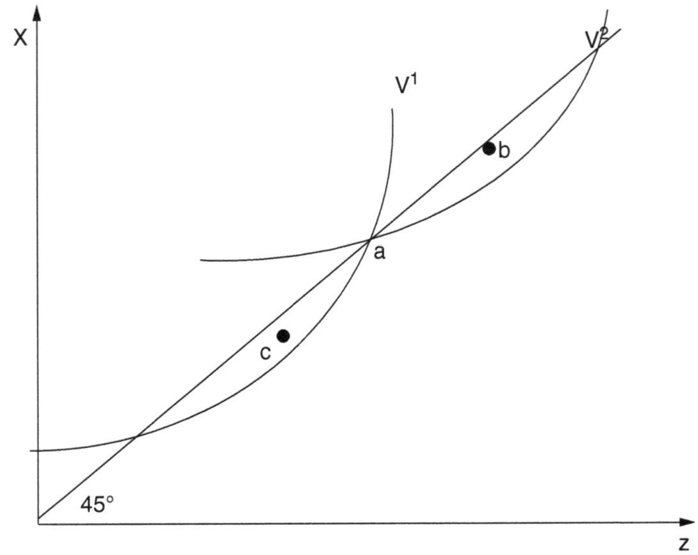

Figure A2.1 No pooling

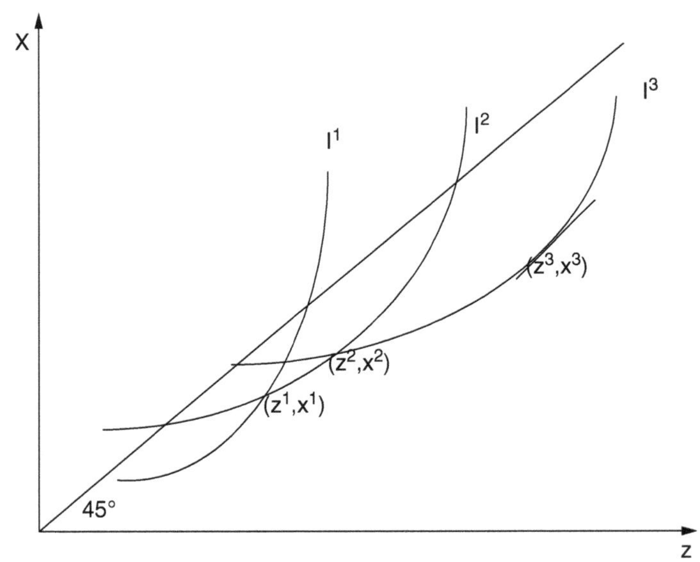

Figure A2.2 Three types and individual fully separated by skill type

relative labour supply of type 2 household rises, it carries a redistributive benefit through an increase in the relative wage of the low-skilled household. So $\frac{\partial\Omega}{\partial y^1} < 0$ and $\frac{\partial\Omega}{\partial y^2} > 0$.

Max $V(x^1, y^1)$

s.t. $V(x^2, y^2) = \bar{V}^2$ and self-selection constraint $V(x^2, y^2) \geq V(x^1, \Omega y^1)$. And production constraint $F(y^1, y^2) = x^1 + x^2$

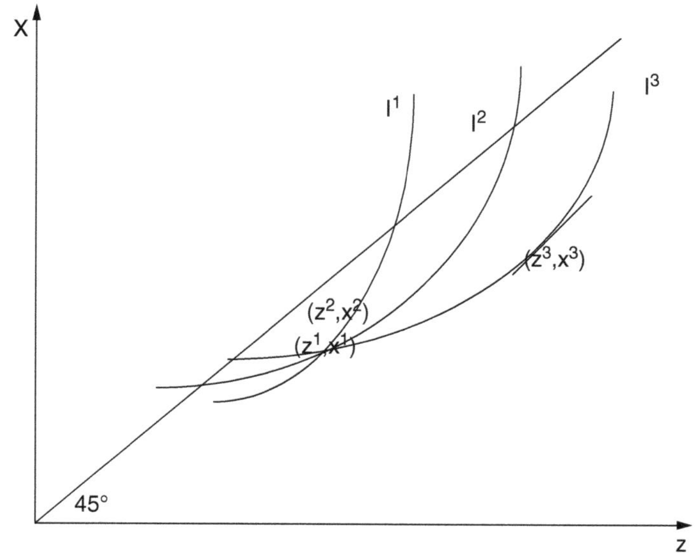

Figure A2.3 Three types and bunching

The Lagrangean

$$L = V^1(x^1, y^1) + \delta[V^2(x^2, y^2) - \bar{V}^2] + \mu[V^2(x^2, y^2) - \hat{V}(x^1, \Omega y^1)] + \lambda[F(y^1, y^2) - x^1 - x^2]. \quad (1)$$

The first order conditions:

$$x^1 : V_x^1 - \mu \hat{V}_x - \lambda = 0 \quad (2)$$

$$x^2 : (\delta + \mu) V_x^2 - \lambda = 0 \quad (3)$$

$$y^1 : V_y^1 - \mu \hat{V}_y \left(\frac{\partial \Omega}{\partial y^1} y^1 + \Omega \right) + \lambda F_{y^1} = 0 \quad (4)$$

$$y^2 : (\delta + \mu) V_y^2 - \lambda \hat{V}_y \frac{\partial \Omega}{\partial y^2} y^1 + \lambda F_{y^2} = 0. \quad (5)$$

Dividing (5) by (3) and using $MTR(wy) = 1 + \frac{V_y}{wV_x}$ $MTR^2 = \frac{\mu \hat{V}_y}{\lambda w^2} \frac{\partial \Omega}{\partial y^2} y^1$.

Find MTR^2 <0, since $\frac{\partial \Omega}{\partial y^2}$ >0 (1 and 2 are not perfect substitutes) and $\hat{V}_y < 0$.

In taking into account the general equilibrium effect on wage determination, government should be induced to lower the marginal tax rate on the more productive individuals. By doing so, the government increases their labour supply. But by increasing their use in production, this reduces the before-tax wage differential and thus relaxes the self-selection. Because of general equilibrium effects, taxation affects both factor incomes and disposable incomes, whereas only the latter effect was present in the Mirrlees model.

y^1/y^2 decreases and $\frac{w^1}{w^2}$ increases. The mimicker has to work more to get the same income as type 1. So self-selection constraint can be relaxed.

Dividing (4) by (2) and rearranging terms, we have:

$$MTR^1 = \frac{\mu \hat{V}_x}{\lambda w^1}\left(\frac{\hat{V}_y}{\hat{V}_y}\Omega - \frac{V_y^1}{V_x^1}\right) + \frac{\lambda \hat{V}_y}{\lambda w^1}\frac{\partial \Omega}{\partial y^1}y^1 > 0.$$

MTR^1 is positive: the first term is positive by AM and the second term is positive since $\frac{\partial \Omega}{\partial y^1} < 0$.

3 Optimal linear income taxation

3.1 The basic model

Analysis of the optimal non-linear income tax problem poses considerable technical difficulties[1] because the government has to choose the entire income tax function. Realizing fully the nature of this complication, it is clear that the income tax problem is considerably simplified if attention is confined to a linear tax schedule.[2] Linear income tax is the simplest redistributive programme that the government is likely to consider employing. In the linear income tax system the tax is characterized by a lump-sum income or a basic income b paid to each individual and a proportional tax on each euro earned at a rate t (the flat rate). Hence the linear income tax model provides no scope for comment on the question of progressivity in the marginal tax-rate sense. If $t > 0$ and $b > 0$ the linear income tax is progressive, in the sense that the average tax rate rises over the entire income range (see Fig 3.1a, b). The linear income tax schedule provides a minimum guaranteed income to individuals whose income falls short of the critical level. This is the feature of the linear income tax system which leads us to refer to the section of the tax schedule below z* in Figure 3.1b as a negative income tax. The negative income tax system, or the social dividend system, as it was called by Lady Rhys Williams in 1943, has been proposed, supported, and widely discussed by several distinguished economists, such as Meade, Friedman, Tobin, and Atkinson.[3] In particular, in a developing country context, a redistributive linear income tax system, which combines a lump-sum transfer with a proportional income tax and which can be implemented by withholding at source, provides a feasible and comprehensive tax-benefit system.

Individuals face a linear income tax schedule $T(z) = -b + tz$, where b = lump-sum income (basic income) and t=tax rate (constant). Every individual in this model faces a budget constraint $x(n) = az(n) + b$, where $a = (1-t)$ the net of tax rate. The revenue requirement of the government, R, to be used for expenditure on public goods is taken as given. The government's budget constraint is

$$t\sum z^i = Nb + R. \tag{1}$$

[1] From the technical point of view, it is not necessary to introduce the incentive compatibility constraints in the optimal income tax problem explicitly.

[2] This simplified problem was examined in a number of papers by Sheshinski (1972), Atkinson (1995), Itsumi (1974), Romer (1976), Stern (1976), Dixit and Sandmo (1977), Helpman and Sadka (1978), Deaton (1983), and Tuomala (1985), among others. Extensive numerical results have been provided by Stern (1976).

[3] For some history on negative income tax and related proposals, see Kesselman and Garfinkel (1978).

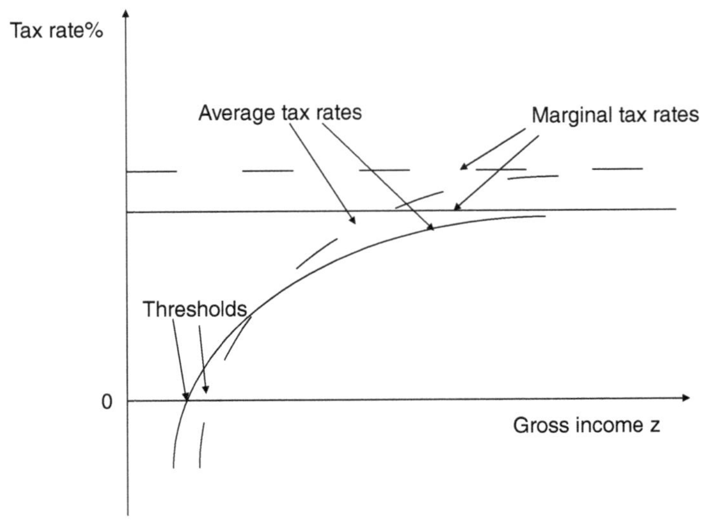

Figure 3.1a Linear income tax: average and marginal rate

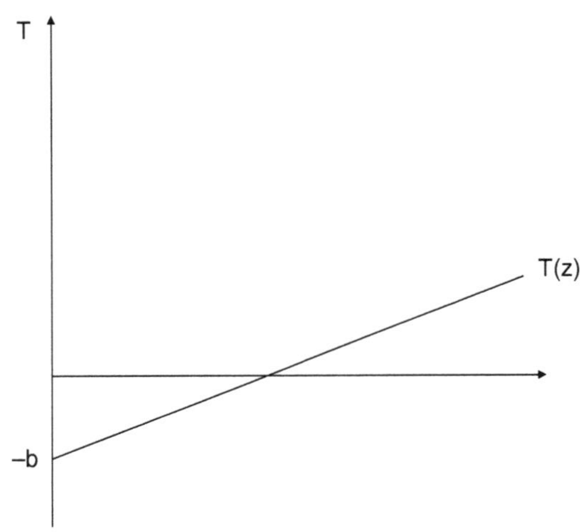

Figure 3.1b Linear income tax

The central issue considered in the analysis of the optimal linear income tax is that of choosing between the basic income and the associated tax rate. Therefore it is plausible to express individuals' preferences in terms of the indirect utility function, denoted $V(a,b)$. In making this choice, the government is assumed to be constrained by a government budget constraint and by the responses of taxpayers. The taxpayers are assumed to adjust their labour supply in response to changes in taxation.

The government's problem is to choose b and t so as to maximize the social welfare function

$$\sum W(V^i(1-t,b)) \tag{2}$$

under the budget constraint $t\sum z^i = Nb + R$.

From the first-order condition of this problem we arrive at the condition (see the derivation in appendix 2.2.1)

$$\frac{t}{1-t} = \frac{1}{e}\left[1 - \frac{z(\beta)}{\bar{z}}\right], \tag{3}$$

where $e = \frac{d\bar{z}(1-t)}{d(1-t)\bar{z}}$ (the elasticity of earnings with respect 1−t, net of tax), $\beta = W_V V_b$ is the social marginal utility of income, and $\Upsilon = \frac{z(\beta)}{\bar{z}}$. Denote $I = 1 - \Upsilon$ as a normative measure of inequality or equivalently of the relative distortion arising from the second best tax system. Clearly Υ should vary between zero and unity. One would expect it to be a decreasing function of t (given $g = \frac{R}{N}$). There is a minimum feasible level of t for any given positive g and of course g must not be too large or no equilibrium is possible. Hence any solution must also satisfy $t > t_{\min}$ if the tax system is to be progressive. That is, if the tax does not raise sufficient revenue to finance the non-transfer expenditure, R, the shortfall must be made up by imposing a poll tax (a negative b) on each individual. One would expect the elasticity of labour supply with respect to the net of tax rate e to be an increasing function of t (it need not be).

Rewriting (3) in turn, we have:

$$t = \frac{1-\Upsilon}{1-\Upsilon+e}. \tag{4}$$

This formula gives the rate of the optimal linear income tax. Given $e \geq 0$ and because $0 \leq I < 1$, then both the numerator and the denominator are nonnegative. Thus the rate of the optimal tax is between zero and one. Formula (4) captures neatly the efficiency-equity trade off. t decreases with e and Υ.

(i) In the extreme case where $\Upsilon = \frac{z(\beta)}{\bar{z}} = 1$, i.e. the government does not value redistribution at all, t = 0 is optimal. We can call this case libertarian. Libertarianism in the sense of Nozick (1974) opposes all redistribution. According to the libertarian view, the level of disposable income is irrelevant (ruling out both basic income, b, and other public expenditures, g, funded by the government).

(ii) If there is no inequality, then again $\Upsilon = 1$ and t = 0. There is no intervention by the government. The inherent inequality will be fully reflected in the disposable income. Furthermore, lump-sum tax is optimal; b = −g or T = −b.

(iii) When $\Upsilon = 0$, we call this case 'Rawlsian' or maximin. The government maximizes the basic income b (assuming the worst-off individual has zero labour income). In fact, maximizing b can be regarded as a non-welfarist case.

When the government is 'Rawlsian' or revenue maximizing, we get:[4]

$$t = \frac{1}{1+e}. \tag{5}$$

For example, if $e = 0.25$, $t = 80\%$. This is clearly much higher than tax rates in any of the actual countries with the highest tax to net national income (typically slightly over 50 per cent). Formula (5) also gives the top tax rate of the so-called Laffer curve. In popular American discourse, the tax rate–tax revenue relationship is labelled the Laffer curve.[5] It is, however, known that long ago, in 1844, Jules Dupuit gave a very clear description of this relationship. He wrote,

> if a tax is gradually increased from zero up to the point where it becomes prohibitive, its yield is at first nil, then increases by small stages until it reaches a maximum, after which it gradually declines until it becomes zero again. It follows that when the state requires to raise a given sum by means of taxation, there are always two rates of taxes which will fulfil the requirement, one above and one below that which would yield the maximum. There may be a very great difference between the amounts of utility lost through these two taxes which yield the same revenue. (Translation in Arrow and Scitowsky 1969, p. 278)

To illustrate formula (4) further, we concentrate on a special case where there are no income effects on labour supply and the elasticity of labour supply with respect to the net-of-tax wage rate is constant. If e denotes this elasticity, the quasi-linear indirect utility function is given by:

$$v(n(1-t), b) = b + \frac{[n(1-t)]^{1+\varepsilon}}{1+\varepsilon} \tag{6}$$

so that e is constant.

The inequality measure, $I = 1 - \frac{z(\beta)}{\bar{z}}$, depends on the welfare weights. These weights strictly depend on utility V(n) and hence on the tax rate and of the basic income, b. To simplify, we assume that the social marginal valuation depends only on n and not on the level of utility. We adopt a constant relative inequality aversion form of the welfare function: the contribution to social welfare of the ith individual is $\frac{n_i^{1-\beta}}{1-\beta}$, where β is the constant relative inequality aversion coefficient. Hence the social marginal value of income to an individual with wage rate n is proportional to $n^{-\beta}$. As noted by Atkinson (1995), this assumption may be described as non-welfarist. We assume, also for simplicity, that the n-distribution is a unbounded Pareto distribution $f(n) = \frac{1}{n^{1+a}}$ for $a > 0$, i.e. a Pareto tail with the coefficient α, and the utility function is (5) (see appendix 3.1). The Pareto density has a polynomial right tail. It is varying at infinity with index

[4] We can derive (5) as follows. If we want to increase the tax rate from t to t+dt then tax revenues go from R to R+dR, and dR = zdt +tdz and further dR = zdt−tez dt/(1−t). dR = 0 if and only if t/(1−t) = (1/e).

[5] 'It has been said that the virtue of the Laffer curve is that you can explain it to a congressman in half an hour and he can talk about it for six months'. Hal Varian, *Intermediate Microeconomics*. 3rd edn, p. 278.

$-\alpha-1$. Thus, the right tail is thicker as α is smaller, implying that only low-order moments exist. Using the property of the Pareto distribution:

$$E(n^j) = \frac{\alpha n_0^j}{\alpha - j} \tag{7}$$

in (4) we can calculate the values of the optimal tax rate and of the basic income from the following formula (see Table 3.1).

$$\frac{t}{1-t}e = 1 - \left[\frac{1 - \frac{1+\varepsilon}{\alpha}}{1 - \frac{1+\varepsilon}{\alpha+\beta}}\right] \tag{8}$$

Substituting the labour supply function:

$$y = [n(1-t)]^{\varepsilon} \tag{9}$$

to the revenue constraint (1), we can express the basic income and the revenue constraint relative to the average earnings and re-write the revenue constraints as follows:

$$b = t(1-t)^{\varepsilon} - g \tag{10}$$

The above analysis assumes away income effects. Including them, we have to rely on numerical simulations. The most comprehensive optimal linear income taxation simulations are those of Stern (1976). He takes a labour supply function that allows for different values of elasticity of substitution between leisure and consumption. In his central case, he takes elasticity of substitution of 0.4, a government revenue requirement of approximately 20 per cent of national income. Stern (1976) assumes that the net social marginal valuation of income decreases with the square of income, then the optimal tax rate is 54 per cent and individuals' lump-sum grant or basic income in turn equals 34 per cent of average income. In this central case, an extremely low labour-supply elasticity implies an optimal tax rate of 49 per cent, and an elasticity as high as had been used in Mirrlees (1971) implies an optimal tax rate of 35 per cent. In the absence of the need to finance government expenditures, the optimal tax rate is 48 per cent. Stern comments that 'The utilitarian approach therefore gives taxation rates which are rather high without any appeal to extreme social welfare functions, and need only invoke labour supply functions of the type which are commonly observed' (1976, p. 151).

Table 3.1 Tax rates t and b: Pareto distribution, $\alpha=2$, $g=0$

e	$\beta=1.0$	$\beta=1.0$	$\beta=2.0$	$\beta=2.0$
	t	b	t	b
0.25	58.8	47.1	64.0	49.6
0.5	50.0	35.4	54.5	46.8

How useful is the linear income tax model for the purposes of understanding the degree of redistribution in actual economies? Would it be a rough approximation of an actual tax/transfer system? This depends on the extent to which all transfers are independent of income. If they are, then the activities of the government are to be described by three elements of the linear income tax model: the total of taxes less subsidies, T, which varies with income and expenditure; the total of lump-sum transfers or subsidies, b; and the total expenditure of government on public good, R. In fact, Mirrlees (1979) relates the actual UK economy to linear income tax by classifying public expenditure into categories used in the model. This means that all transfers taken together are fairly close to a lump-sum grant, that is are about constant with income. Doing some interpolations[6] in Stern's (1976) calculations, Mirrlees (1979) finds that the optimal t was 46 per cent in 1976 in the UK if the net social marginal valuation of income decreases with the square of income and the elasticity of substitution is 0.5 and 32 per cent in the case of the Cobb–Douglas preferences. Correspondingly, lump-sum transfers b should be 36 per cent or 21 per cent of national income, compared with the marginal rate of 45 per cent and lump-sum rate of 35 per cent in the UK in 1976.

Although it is possible to examine the implications of using any type of social welfare function, a convenient approach for present purposes is to specify welfare in terms of each individual's income, rather than utility. The term $z(\beta)$ can thus be replaced by the equally distributed equivalent level of income, z_e, defined as the level of income which, if obtained by everyone, produces the same social welfare as the actual distribution. Hence, the term I can be replaced by Atkinson's inequality measure, since it is the proportional difference between arithmetic mean income and the equally distributed equivalent level. The inequality measure I depends on the distribution of z. Assume that the distribution is well approximated by a Champernowne distribution. Harrison (1974) shows that in the case of a Champernowne distribution and inequality aversion parameter approaching unity the equally distributed equivalent income corresponds to median income so that the Atkinson's measure of inequality becomes $I = 1 - \frac{z(\beta)}{\bar{z}}$.

In fact, this is exactly the measure i that Champernowne (1952, p. 609) proposes as an alternative indicator of inequality to Pareto's constant coefficient. He justifies this as follows:

> under very simplifying assumptions i, so defined, would be the proportion of total income that is absorbed in compensating for the loss aggregate satisfaction due to inequality.

The assumptions he makes are:

> (1) That pre-tax income determined satisfaction and (2) that median satisfaction was equal to arithmetic mean satisfaction.

[6] Interpolations are needed because Stern (1976) gives only the optimal marginal tax rate and not the subsidy rate. Moreover, he computed solutions only with a rather large interval of R.

Hence, Champernowne is suggesting a very specific case of Atkinson's concept of the equally distributed equivalent income where his assumption (2) holds. A great advantage of this measure is that it is easy to compute.

3.2 The optimal provision of public goods

In the model so far discussed, there has been no dependence of individual utilities on public expenditure; that is, there is no role for public good. To include the public good we write $V(1-t, b, G)$ and subtract a term λrG from the Lagrangean where r is the producer price of the public good. The producer price of private consumption is normalized to 1. Let us now define the marginal willingness to pay for the public good by the expression $\sigma = \frac{v_G}{v_b}$. The Lagrangean is then maximized with respect to G. From this condition (see appendix 3.1) we have the following rule for the supply of public good:

$$\sigma^{\star}(1 - t\bar{z}_b) = r - t\bar{z}_G \tag{11}$$

where $\sigma^{\star} = \frac{\sum \beta^i \sigma^i}{\sum \beta^i}$ is the welfare-weighted average marginal rate of substitution between public good and income for the individual. The latter term at the right-hand side is the revenue effects. They can be very important in practice. A revenue gain arising from provision of the public good strengthens the case for it. (11) can be rewritten as:

$$r = \sigma^{\star} - t(\sigma^{\star}\bar{z}_b - \bar{z}_G) \tag{11'}$$

if, for example, labour supply is independent of the level of public good provision, $\bar{z}_G = 0$, and $\bar{z}_b < 0$ if σ^* is positive. Therefore the second term in (11') would make r less than the welfare-weighted aggregate marginal rate of substitution. In Chapter 13 we return to the question of provision of public goods under optimal taxation.

3.3 Majority choice of the tax rate

It may be of some interest to consider the connection between the optimal tax rate and the tax rate chosen by the median voter. The implications of majority voting tax rates have been studied in the context of the linear income tax by Roberts (1977), who provides a number of interesting results on the conditions under which a voting equilibrium exists. Single-peaked preferences guarantee a voting equilibrium in which the median voter dominates. With single-peaked preferences, the median voter preferred tax rate is a Condorcet winner, i.e. wins in majority voting against any other alternative tax rate. Single-peakedness arises if the relationship between V and t is concave, so that $\frac{d^2V}{dt^2} > 0$. With positive marginal utility and a concave relationship between b and t, single-peakedness is guaranteed if the individual always works. Hence, the median voter is the voter with median income z (median). In fact, Roberts (1977) shows that in the case of linear income tax, it is sufficient that preferences be such that we can order people by income independently of the tax schedule.[7]

We see from formula (12) that we have the tax rate of the median voter where social welfare weights are concentrated at the median so that $z(\beta) = z(median)$. This shows that there is a close connection between optimal tax theory and political economy. Although the tax-rate formula is the same as in the optimal linear income tax model, the welfare weights are generated by the political process and not from marginal utility of consumption as in the standard utilitarian tax theory.

Median voter optimal tax rate:

$$\frac{t}{1-t} = \frac{1}{e}\left[1 - \frac{z(median)}{\bar{z}}\right] \tag{12}$$

The formula implies that when the median z approaches the mean z, the tax rate should be low, because a linear tax rate achieves little redistribution (towards the median) and hence a lump-sum tax is more efficient. On the other hand, when the median z recedes from the mean income, the tax rate approaches the revenue-maximizing tax rate $t = \frac{1}{1+e}$. If the median voter has income z (median), equal to 75 per cent of the mean income and $e = 0.25$, then the tax rate is 50 per cent. This voting theory is not very realistic in that it takes no account of the representative nature of democracy and of the possibility that individuals may have other reasons for their voting behaviour than immediate self-interest.

3.4 A two-bracket income tax

Before returning to the general optimal non-linear income tax problem, it is helpful to consider briefly a simpler extension. A two-bracket income tax applies a constant rate t_1 to all income up to some specified level z^*, and another constant rate t_2 to all income over the specified level z^*.

The government now chooses t_1,t_2, z^*, and b to maximize social welfare. This problem has been examined by Sheshinski (1989) and Slemrod et al (1994). Sheshinski (1989) shows that, under standard assumptions, marginal tax rates are increasing in income (i.e. tax schedule is convex). Slemrod et al (1994) noticed that Sheshinski's proof does not hold in general. They perform numerical simulations for an optimal two-bracket income tax using functional forms and parameters similar to those used in earlier numerical work (e.g. Stern (1976)) and show that the optimal upper bracket marginal tax rate is less than the optimal lower-bracket rate (tax schedule non-convex: see Figure 3.1c).[8] Nevertheless, in all simulations in which the optimal transfer, b, is positive, the overall income

[7] See also Creedy and Francois (1993).

[8] In the context of the two-bracket income tax with income uncertainty, Strawczynski (1998) derived the opposite result. Chapter 7 analyses income taxation under income uncertainty.

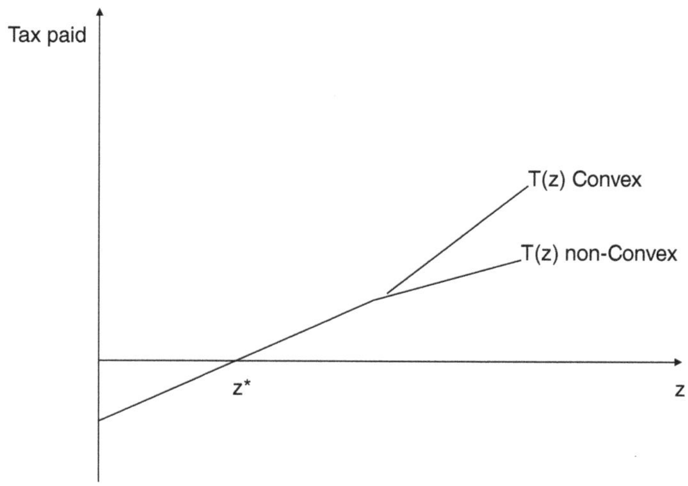

Figure 3.1c A two-bracket income tax

tax schedule is progressive in the sense that average tax rates are rising in income. In the case closest to Stern's central case (elasticity of substitution of 0.4, a government revenue requirement of approximately 20 per cent of national income, and the net social marginal valuation of income that decreases with the square of income), the optimal two-bracket tax has a marginal rate of 60 per cent on low incomes and 52 per cent for the top 23 per cent of taxpayers. The intuition behind their results is that the lower rate on high-income individuals encourages harder work and thus generation of more tax revenue. Apps et al (2013) in turn argue that Slemrod et al's (1994) simulation results depend heavily on assumption of the lognormal distribution of wages. As is well known, the lognormal distribution fits reasonably well over a large part of the income range but diverges markedly at the upper tail. The Pareto distribution in turn fits well at the upper tail. Replacing the lognormal distribution with the Pareto distribution and using reasonable elasticities, Apps et al (2013) find rising marginal tax rates in their numerical simulations.

APPENDIX 3.1 OPTIMAL LINEAR INCOME TAXATION

The government has redistributive objectives represented by a Bergson–Samuelson functional $W(V^1, ..., V^N)$ with $W' > 0$, $W'' < 0$. The government's problem is to choose b and t so as to maximize the social welfare function

$$\sum W(V^i(1-t, b)) \tag{1}$$

under budget constraint (1) in the text.

Let λ denote the multiplier associated to the budget constraint. The Lagrangian of this problem is:

$$L = \sum W(V^i(a,b)) + \lambda\Big((1-a)\sum z^i - Nb - R\Big) \tag{2}$$

Using Roy's theorem, $V_a^i = V_b^i z^i$. Then the first-order conditions with respect to b and a are:

$$\sum \beta^i z^i = \lambda\Big(\sum z^i - (1-a)\sum z_a^i\Big) \tag{3}$$

$$\sum \beta^i = \lambda\Big(N - (1-a)\sum z_b^i\Big) \tag{4}$$

where $\beta^i = W_V V_b^i$ is the social marginal utility of income.

Denote g = R / N and

$$\bar{z} = \sum_i z^i / N. \tag{5}$$

(5) Divide (3) by (4)

$$\frac{\sum \beta^i z^i}{\sum \beta^i} = \frac{\bar{z} - (1-a)\bar{z}_a}{1-(1-a)\bar{z}_b} \tag{6}$$

Denote $z(\beta) = \sum \beta^i z^i / \sum \beta^i$, welfare-weighted average labour income.

Total differentiation of revenue constraint:

$$\frac{db}{da_{gconst.}} = \frac{-\bar{z} + (1-a)\bar{z}_a}{1-(1-a)\bar{z}_b} \tag{7}$$

From (6) and (7) we note that

$$z(\beta) = -\frac{db}{da_{gconst.}} \tag{8}$$

This tells us that welfare-weighted labour supply should be equal to the constant revenue effect of tax-rate changes in b.

By total differentiation (5) and using (8) we have:

$$\frac{d\bar{z}}{da_{gconst.}} = \bar{z}_a + \bar{z}_b \frac{db}{da_{gconst.}} = \bar{z}_a - \bar{z}_b z(\beta) \tag{9}$$

When we impose g as a constant we have to give up one of our degrees of freedom. Now the interpretation of $\frac{d\bar{z}}{da_{gconst.}}$ is the effect on labour supply when a is changed, as is b, in order to keep tax revenue constant.

Using (9A) we can write (6A)

$$z(\beta) - \bar{z} = (1-a)\frac{d\bar{z}}{da_{gconst}} = -t\frac{d\bar{z}(1-t)\bar{z}}{d(1-t)(1-t)\bar{z}} \tag{10}$$

This gives (3) in the text.

The first-order condition with respect to G gives:

$$\sum W_V^i V_G^1 = \lambda\left(\sum r - (1-a)\sum z_G^i\right) \tag{11}$$

Dividing (11) by (4) we obtain:

$$\frac{\sum \beta^i \sigma^i}{\sum \beta^i} = \frac{r - (1-a)\bar{z_G}}{1-(1-a)\bar{z_b}} \tag{12}$$

Rewriting (12), we have (11') in the text.

4 The optimal non-linear labour income tax problem

The optimal non-linear tax problem is the same as the linear income tax problem, except that the tax designer has to choose any non-linear income tax schedule $T(z)$ instead of an affine function (see figure 4.1b). The pioneering work by Mirrlees (1971) addresses the optimal design of non-linear income taxes in a welfarist setting. The issue of incentives for supplying labour is tackled directly by modelling individuals as choosing between work and leisure given the tax-transfer schedule they face. There are assumed to be a large number of individuals, differing only in the pre-tax wage they can earn. Mirrlees (1971) focused on a single characteristic of individuals for simplicity, that is, their skill or ability as reflected in the wage rate or pre-tax wage. The government then chooses a schedule that maximizes a social welfare function defined on individuals' welfare, that is, on the utility they derive from their consumption–leisure bundles. There is a continuum of individuals, each having the same preference ordering, which is represented by a utility function $u=u(x,1-y)$ defined over consumption x and hours worked y, with $u_x > 0$ and $u_y < 0$ (subscripts indicating partial derivatives). The utility function is assumed to be continuously differentiable and concave. It offers a positive marginal utility of consumption and a negative marginal utility of labour. All individuals are assumed to be perfect substitutes for one another, that is, they differ only in their number of efficiency units of labour. An ability level n corresponds to each individual such that, if the individual works for y hours, he or she supplies $z=ny$ unit labour. There is a distribution of n on the interval $[0, \infty)$ represented by the density function f(n).

Suppose that the aim of policy can be expressed as maximizing the following social welfare criterion:

$$W = \int_0^\infty W(u(n))f(n)dn, \tag{1}$$

where W(.) is increasing in each individual's utility, so that it fully embodies the Pareto principle. At the same time, it may incorporate aversion to inequality, or a degree of priority to the worse-off. The government cannot observe individuals' productivities or abilities and thus is restricted to setting taxes and transfers as a function only of earnings, $T(z(n))$. The government maximizes W subject to the revenue constraint:

$$\int_0^\infty T(z(n))f(n)dn = R \tag{2}$$

where R can be interpreted as the required revenue for essential public goods. The more non-tax revenue a government receives from external sources, the lower R is. In addition to the revenue constraint, the government faces incentive-compatibility constraints. These in turn state that each n-individual maximizes utility by choice of hour or labour effort. Hence:

$$u[ny - T(ny(n)), 1 - y(n)] \geq u[n'y(n') - T(n'y(n')), \\ 1 - n'y(n')/n)] \text{ for all n and n'}. \quad (3)$$

It means that an individual of type n has to work n'/n times that of type n' to get the same income.

Incentive compatibility required that each taxpayer/consumer would choose from a set of available consumption/income pairs. That set is defined by the allocation of consumption and income among consumers. The curve c(z) in Figure 4.1a describes that allocation, showing consumption at different income levels. Each taxpayer/consumer chooses from that curve: each has an indifference curve tangential to the allocation curve, such as I^1 and I^2 in Figure 4.1a. Ruling out corners, the curve must be a lower envelope to a collection of individual indifference curves—one for each type of consumer. As a consequence, utility increased as the wage increased, at a rate equal to the derivative of utility with respect to the wage, holding consumption and income constant.

Income was also an increasing function of the consumer's wage rate. Furthermore, we have to assume that people with higher wage rates always found it easier to produce more income (by working) than those with smaller wages. Of course this assumption is restrictive but, broadly understood, quite plausible in this setting. In Figure 4.1a, the assumption means that different people's indifference curves cross one another once only. The condition is known as the single-crossing property (or sometimes the Mirrlees–Spence condition; see appendix 4.1). With that assumption, one has a full characterization of incentive-compatible allocations.

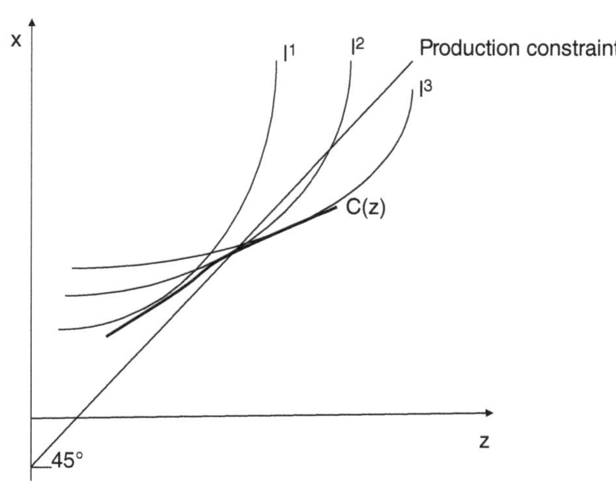

Figure 4.1a Incentive compatible

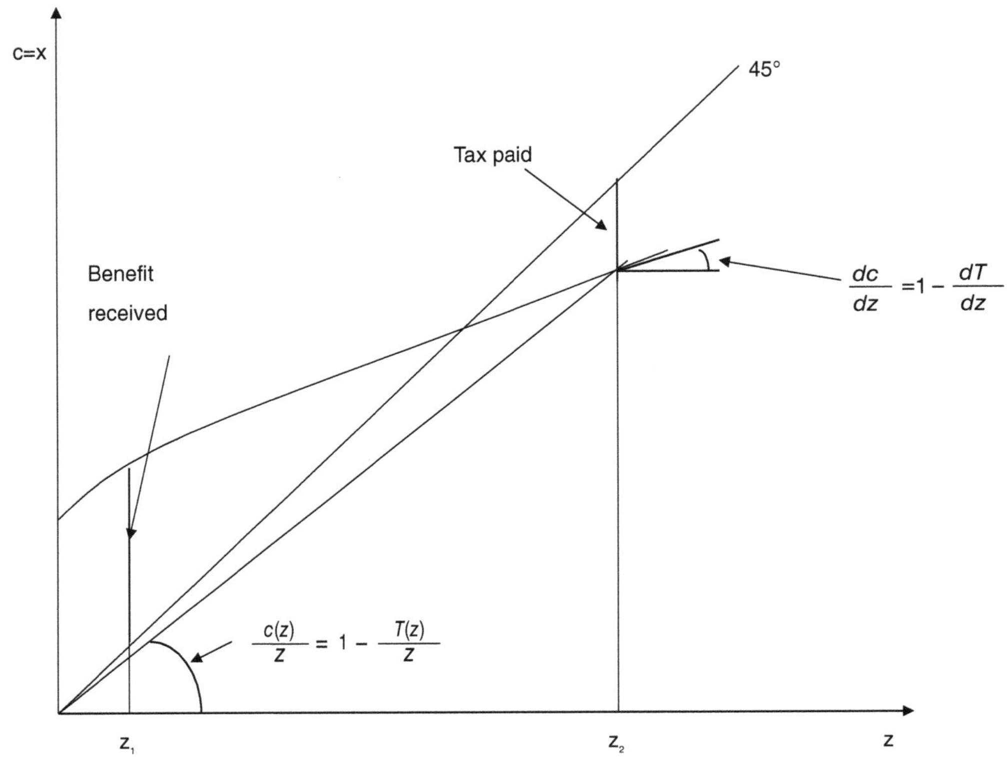

Figure 4.1b Tax schedule

Since $T(z)=ny-x$, we can think of government as choosing schedules $y(n)$ and $x(n)$[1]. In fact, it is easier to think of it choosing a pair of functions, $u(n)$ and $y(n)$, which maximize welfare index (1) subject to the incentive-compatibility condition, (3) (written in a more manageable form as $\frac{du}{dn} = -\frac{yV_y}{n} = u_n(x, z, n)$[2]; see appendix 4.1) and the revenue requirement (2). Hence the optimal income tax problem could now be converted into something very like a standard control-theory problem, with utility as the state variable and income the control variable. The envelope condition just described was essentially equivalent to a statement that the rate at which utility increased in the population, with respect to the wage rate, was equal to the partial derivative of the individual's utility with respect to the wage rate—just a known function of that individual's consumption, income, and wage.

[1] Figure 4.1b illustrates average and marginal tax rates.

[2] Totally differentiating utility with respect to n, and making use of workers' utility maximization condition, we obtain the incentive compatibility constraint. The first order condition of individuals' optimization problem is only a necessary condition for the individual's choice to be optimal, but we assume here that it is sufficient as well. Assumptions that assure sufficiency are provided by Mirrlees (1976a). Note also that while we here presume an internal solution for y, the incentive compatibility condition remains valid even if individuals were bunched at y=0 since, for them, du/dn=0.

Mirrlees (1971) first examines the optimal tax problem in general terms, without assuming a specific form of utility and of the distribution of skills. Next we recall the main analytical results from the welfarist literature on optimal non-linear income taxation (we have gathered the proofs in appendix 4.1). Four general qualitative conclusions emerge:

(1) The marginal tax rate should be non-negative everywhere. In other words, consumption never rises more rapidly than income.
(2) The marginal tax rate on the lowest earner should be zero so long as everyone supplies some labour at the optimum (Seade 1977).
(3) The marginal tax rate on the highest earner should be zero so long as wages in the population are bounded above (Sadka 1976).
(4) If there is bunching at the lower part of distribution, the marginal tax rate is positive at the end of the bunching interval.

The first result is more striking than is commonly recognized.[3] Although it may well be optimal for the average tax rate (the ratio between tax paid and income earned) on the least well-off to be negative, it cannot be desirable to subsidize their earnings at the margin.[4] Intuitively this means that it is cheaper to get people to a given indifference curve by reducing the average tax rate rather than by exacerbating deadweight loss through distorting their labour supply decisions. The limitations of the second and third results concerning the endpoints are well known: simulations suggest that zero is a bad approximation to optimal marginal tax rates in the tails of the distribution. The marginal tax rate equal to zero at the top only holds for the person with the very highest income level, and must be able to identify that person (see numerical results in Chapter 5). It does not hold elsewhere because of interdependence between marginal tax rates for lower-income people and the average tax rates for people higher up the income scale. Note the amount of revenue raised depends on the average tax, not the marginal tax rate.[5] The important assumption behind the zero marginal tax rate at the top result is that there is some upper bound to the skill distribution, as opposed to the support just being $[0,\infty)$. Mirrlees (1971) only considers, realistically, an unbounded wage(skill) distribution, and therefore he did not get the zero tax rate result. Although the marginal tax rate is zero, the average tax rates can be high.

Mirrlees (2006) noticed a further result from his 1971 model. He sketches a model in which top marginal tax rates of 100 per cent or nearly 100 per cent may be justified. He assumes high substitutability between consumption and labour, and furthermore an upper bound on labour supply in efficiency units. The government is utilitarian and an

[3] Seade (1982) clarified the conditions under which this result holds.

[4] An exception to this conclusion may occur in cases where people do not vary their hours of work continuously (on the intensive margin), but can only choose between alternative occupations (including non-work) working hours fixed (on the extensive margin). A subsidy to low-skilled work may be optimal (Diamond 1980; Saez 2002). Note that no participation decision is given in Mirrlees (1971).

[5] Although the marginal tax rate is zero, average tax rates can be high.

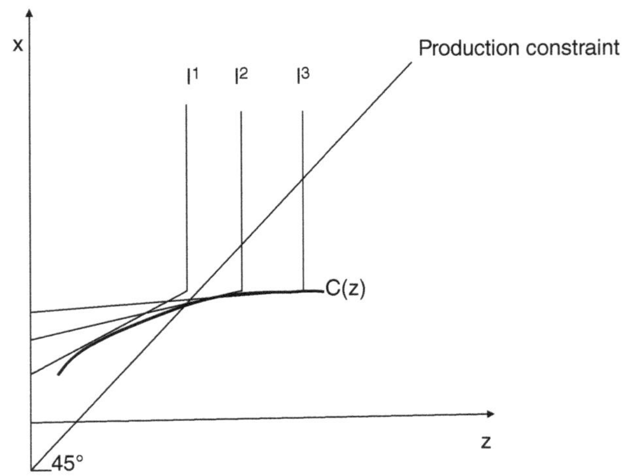

Figure 4.1c Marginal tax rates on the high incomes

individual's utility function is a concave function of consumption minus labour (e.g. log-function). This situation, with realistic wage (productivity, skill) distribution, yields marginal tax rates approaching 100 per cent on the highest incomes. The reason for this result can be seen as follows. With this utility function, the indifference curves (see Figure 4.1c) are straight lines between zero labour and upper bound. For the incentive compatibility the c(z) curve is a lower envelope of the straight lines, one line for each type of taxpayer. The single-crossing condition implies that the indifference curves become flatter when the wage rate (productivity) increases. The budget constraint is necessarily concave. The slope of c(z) curve converges to zero. In other words, the marginal tax rate converges to 100 per cent. Hence the optimal income tax is strictly increasing all the way to the top. This finding also shows how misleading the result is that the marginal tax should be zero at the top. It is very special and not particularly robust. Notwithstanding the extreme assumptions behind this result, Mirrlees (2006, p. viii) makes an important point in commenting on earlier simulation results of declining marginal tax rates with income: 'though it may be right for realistic models, [it] is not certainly a general truth.'

There is also one further extreme case in which the optimum marginal tax rate is 100 per cent (see Stern 1976). This is a case in which there is no substitutability between consumption and work. In other words, consumption and leisure are consumed in fixed proportions (reverse L-shaped indifference curves). Formally, $u = \min(x, 1-y)$. This means that there are no welfare losses from income taxation. This does not mean that the first-best optimum can be achieved, however: zero elasticity of substitution does not imply inelastic labour supply. Although the substitution effect of a wage change is zero, we still have the income effect, which gives a backward-bending supply curve.

It can also be shown that if it is optimal for some not to work, then the optimal marginal tax rate at the bottom of the income distribution is strictly positive. It is not possible to use a similar argument here as in the case of those paying the top rate of tax. The difficulty lies in the fact that if the marginal tax rates from any point downwards in the scale are lowered, this increases the tax burden of the people affected, whereas at the upper end of the income distribution, reductions in marginal tax rates mean reductions in tax payments by those involved. The essential point about the zero marginal tax rate at the lowest income level is that there is no one lower in the distribution of income, and it is therefore possible to reduce the marginal tax rate without compromising distributional objectives. Thus only efficiency considerations apply in the case of the lowest income. Nevertheless, these results continue to colour professional thinking on issues of rate structure. The lower endpoint result, in particular, has been taken as suggestive in arguing against very high effective marginal rates on the poor.

Based on the first-order conditions, optimal tax theory suggests that marginal income tax rates should be higher (i) the less responsive particular individuals are to tax rates, (ii) the more the government wishes to redistribute from rich to poor, and (iii) at points in the earnings distribution where the number of individuals is small relative to the number of taxpayers with earnings exceeding this amount.

Because of difficulties in determining the shape of the optimal income tax schedule by mere inspection of the first-order condition, following the lead of Mirrlees (1971), numerical calculations have proven useful in generating results. It can be said that the very basic nature of income tax problems requires quantitative results. Mere general results are not of much value. Numerical simulations can help join the theoretical analysis with empirical estimates of labour supply elasticities and of the distribution of skills or income in order to provide further illumination. To get any further, one has to simulate. One of our main focuses in this book is numerical simulations. Before moving to numerical simulations, we consider some simplified special cases.

4.1 Quasi-linear preferences

For simplicity and transparency we first present, following Atkinson (1990, 1995) and Diamond (1998), the special case in which preferences are quasi-linear in consumption (as earlier in linear income taxation).[6] There are no income effects in labour supply. This special case is extensively used in both theoretical and applied optimal tax literature. The quasi-linear assumption is also restrictive because it eliminates declining marginal utility of consumption (utility is linear in x), which is a key motivation for redistribution.

[6] Following Lollivier and Rochet (1983), many papers have focused on the polar case in which all income effects are absorbed by labour supply, i.e. on preferences over consumption and leisure which are separable and linear in leisure. In this case the tax schedule is independent of the labour response because the disutility of labour is constant, a fact which seems to be incompatible with the empirical findings.

Preferences are represented by a utility function:

$$u = x - \frac{y^{1+\frac{1}{\varepsilon}}}{1+\frac{1}{\varepsilon}}, \tag{4}$$

where x is a composite consumption good and hours worked are y, with $U_x = 1$ and $V_y < 0$ (subscripts indicating partial derivatives) and where V(.) is convex. Equation (4) implies a labour supply function $y = ((1 - T'(z))n)^{\varepsilon}$ with a constant elasticity ε. With these preferences we note from the first-order condition, $[((1 - T'(z))n]^{\varepsilon}$, that everybody with n>0 works. The optimal marginal taxes, denoted by $t(z(n)) = T'(z(n))$, for a type n must satisfy (see the derivation of (5) in appendix 4.2):

$$\frac{t}{1-t} = \underbrace{\left[1 + \frac{yV_{yy}}{V_y}\right]}_{A_n} \underbrace{\left[\frac{[1 - F(n)]}{nf(n)}\right]}_{B_n} \underbrace{\left[\frac{\int_n^x [1 - \phi] f(p)dp}{(1 - F(n))}\right]}_{C_n} \tag{5}$$

The marginal tax rate in (5) is depicted as $\frac{t(z)}{1-t(z)}$ instead of just $t(z)$. The reason is that the tax here is applied to the tax-inclusive tax base z or after-tax income.[7]

The elasticity in the A-term is not the conventional one. Denoting by λ the multiplier of the government budget constraint, we define the social marginal welfare weight on taxpayer n as $\phi(n) = \frac{W'(u)}{\lambda}$, where $\lambda = \int_0^{\infty} W'[u(x)]f(p)dp$. In other words, the Lagrange multiplier λ is equal to the population average of $W'[u(n)]$.[8]

The welfare weights ϕ(n) measure the social value of giving a unit of income to an individual with income n, relative to the social value of dividing it equally among all individuals. In the classical utilitarian case ϕ is constant for all n, then the marginal tax rates are uniformly zero. There is complete distributional indifference (given the quasi-linearity in preferences), then there is no taxation.

Since $W'[u(n)]$ is decreasing in n (concave function), the equity effect in C_n is increasing in n. The denominator in B_n will also be increasing in n below the mode (since nf(n) is increasing), and A_n will be larger the more elastic labour supply is. The pattern of optimal marginal tax rates is unclear, except at the very top and the very bottom, where t(z)=0 (unless there is bunching; see appendix 4.2).

[7] To see this, $dx = dz - dT$, so $\frac{dx}{dT} = \frac{dz}{dT} - 1$. Since $\frac{dz}{dT} = \frac{1}{T'(z)}$, this yields $\frac{dT}{dx} = \frac{t(z)}{1-t(z)}$ where $T'(z) = t(z)$.

[8] If the minimum income is zero, then this is not true.

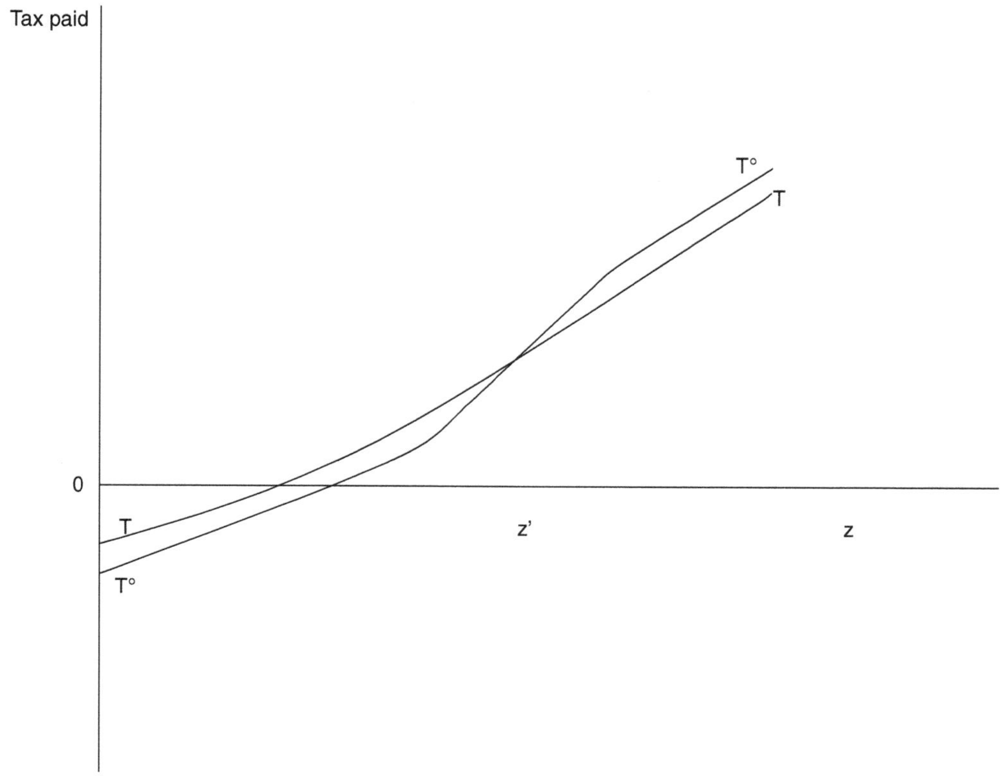

Figure 4.1d The relationship between average tax rate and marginal tax rate

To understand intuitively the marginal tax formula (5) we consider the following perturbation or tax reform: raise the marginal tax rate for individuals with income z' (say, in a small interval z' to z'+Δ where Δ is infinitesimal), leaving all other marginal tax rates unchanged (see Figure 4.1d). There are two effects of the perturbation. First, individuals with income levels in the treated interval will have their labour supply further distorted. The higher the marginal tax rate, the higher the distortion. Second, individuals with income levels above z'+Δ will pay higher taxes, but they will face no additional distortion because their marginal tax rates are the same. The first effect is a cost and the second effect is a benefit because the social welfare function values redistribution. All individuals above income level z' will pay more tax, but these individuals face no new marginal distortion. That is, the higher marginal rate at z' is inframarginal for them. Since those thus giving up income are an above-average slice of the population (the part of the population with income above z'), there tends to be a redistributive gain. Roughly speaking, the higher the benefit from the second effect relative to the cost of the first effect, the higher should be the marginal tax rate at z(n).

The formula for the optimal marginal tax rates reflects this logic. The higher the ratio $\frac{(1-F(n))}{nf(n)}$, the higher is benefit relative to cost, because the distorted group is smaller relative to the group who pays more taxes. The smaller the labour supply elasticity, the lower is the cost, because the lower is the distortion. The higher $1 - \frac{W'}{\lambda}$ is, the higher is the benefit, because the average value of W' on the interval $[n,\infty)$ is lower.

4.2 Alternative social objectives and quasi-linear preferences

The maximin or Rawlsian case: If we assume the Rawlsian social objective then the factor C_n in (5) is constant. Then the pattern of marginal tax rates depends only on B, that is, on the shape of the n-distribution. If the upper part of the n-distribution is the unbounded Pareto distribution, and the utility function is (4), then (5) takes the form $\frac{t}{1-t} = \left[1 + \frac{1}{\varepsilon}\right]\frac{1}{a}$. Hence, using the Rawlsian social welfare function, we do not obtain the rising part of the U-shaped marginal tax rates as in Diamond (1998).[9]

Poverty radicalism: The 'smoothly falling welfare weights' class of social welfare functions has long dominated analysis of optimal income taxation. However, alternatives have been suggested as capturing better certain classes of value judgements. The first of these is to be found in the literature on poverty indices. Starting with Sen (1976), the literature consciously gives a zero social marginal utility to incomes above a critical level ('the poverty line'), thus allowing a focus on incomes below this level. Sen (1976) codified this as the 'focus axiom', and it is formalized in terms of welfare weights by Atkinson (1990). Forcing welfare weights to fall to zero well before the highest incomes are reached may indeed be considered extreme relative to the standard inequality aversion. Kanbur and Tuomala (2011) refer to it as 'poverty radicalism' (see Figure 4.2a). This alternative has not been without its critics. Stern (1987), in a defence of standard parameterizations, expresses dissatisfaction with poverty indices because welfare weights fall to zero (and may do so discontinuously for some indices) at the poverty line. It is argued that this is too extreme; it can be avoided by using standard parameterizations and letting the degree of inequality aversion increase, which gives greater and greater weight to the poor, while ensuring that (i) weights fall smoothly and (ii) they do not fall to zero at a finite value of income.

If the weight is only positive on the poorest person, and is zero on everybody else, then we arrive at the Rawlsian maximin objective function, which is usually derived as a limit of a standard social welfare function where inequality aversion goes to infinity. Hence we have a version of the Rawlsian social welfare function, where the maximand is the

[9] In the general additive case with maximin, C is $\int (f(p)/U_x)dp$. It is declining with n since u(x) is concave and the integral term declines in n. This might suggest declining marginal rates.

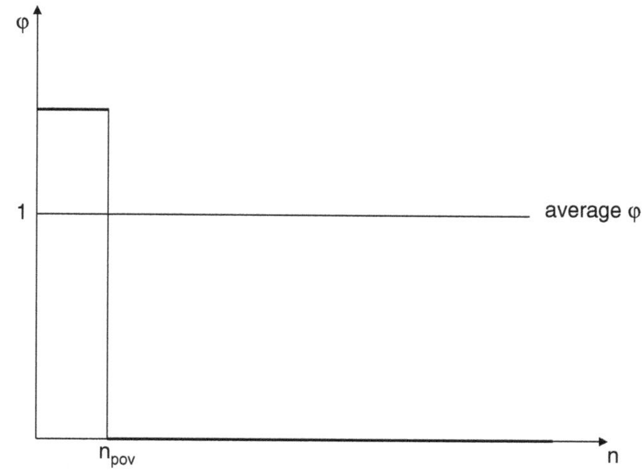

Figure 4.2a Poverty radicalism

welfare of the worst-off individual. This is a very standard interpretation in public economics. We could, however, adopt a different version. Indeed, it is interesting that Rawls (1971, p. 98) himself suggested an extension of this type:

> One possibility is to choose a particular social position, say that of the unskilled worker, and then to count the least advantaged of those with the average income and wealth of this group, or less. The expectation of the lowest representative man is defined as the average taken over this whole class. Another alternative is a definition solely in terms of relative income and wealth with no reference to social position. Thus all persons with less than half of the median income and wealth may be taken as the least advantaged segment.

Viewed in this way, poverty radicalism as depicted in Figure 4.2a can be seen as a generalization of the Rawlsian maximin to include a larger set of persons at the bottom of the distribution.

It is of some interest to note that if the Pareto distribution applies over the whole range of n and the maximand of the Rawlsian social welfare function is the welfare of those below the poverty line, the optimal marginal tax rate is increasing up to the poverty line. The importance of this observation undermines the fact that the fit of Pareto distribution over the whole range of income turns out to be quite poor. For Pareto distributions, $\frac{(1-F(n))}{nf(n)}$ is constant and equal to the Pareto parameter. However, the empirical income distribution is not a Pareto distribution at lower income levels. Therefore we apply Champernowne distribution (appendix 4.5 provides exposition of the Champernowne distribution).

If we take poverty radicalism for a social objective, the optimal tax formula becomes (see the derivation in appendix 4.2):

$$\frac{t}{1-t} = \underbrace{\left[1+\frac{1}{\varepsilon}\right]}_{A_n} \underbrace{\left[\frac{1-F(n)}{nf(n)}\right]}_{B_n} \qquad n>n^{*} \tag{6a}$$

$$\frac{t}{1-t} = \underbrace{\left[1+\frac{1}{\varepsilon}\right]}_{A_n} \underbrace{\left[\frac{F(n)}{nf(n)}\right]}_{B_n} \underbrace{[(\phi-1)]}_{C_n} \qquad n \leq n^{*} \tag{6b}$$

Hence the marginal tax rate above n* is the same as in the maximin case. Table 4.1 illustrates numerically. It shows the marginal tax rates in the case of ε=0.25 and 0.5, and the distribution of n is Champernowne with the shape parameter θ=2.5 and 3.0. From Table 4.1 we see that the marginal tax rates increase in income up the poverty line.

Charitable conservatism: Another case for extending the optimal income tax model in the spirit of the flute example in Sen (2009), allowing for the diversity of objectives, is charitable conservatism. This alternative to the standard view has been discussed by Atkinson (1990)—this time an alternative not in the radical but in the conservative direction. Atkinson (1990, 1995) considers the charitable conservative position, where the marginal welfare weight of consumption takes on two values—a high one for poor people and a low one for non-poor people. Atkinson (1990) reasons as follows (p. 241):

> It may be that complete distributional indifference characterizes the social welfare function of some Conservative governments, but there is a more charitable position, which believes that the government should be concerned with poverty but not with redistribution. This charitable conservative position exhibits a degree of concern for the poor, but this is the limit of the redistributional concern and there is indifference with respect to transfers between those above the poverty line.

Table 4.1 Optimal marginal tax rates with social objectives with poverty radicalism

	t%			
	θ = 3.0		θ = 2.5	
F(n)	ε=0.25	ε=0.5	ε=0.25	ε=0.5
0.01	90.0	85.0	90.0	82.0
0.05	90.9	85.5	90.3	82.6
0.10	91.3	86.4	91.0	83.3
0.15*	91.7	86.9	91.3	84.0
0.50	76.9	66.6	76.1	61.4
0.90	64.9	52.6	64.0	47.1
0.99	62.9	50.5	61.8	44.8

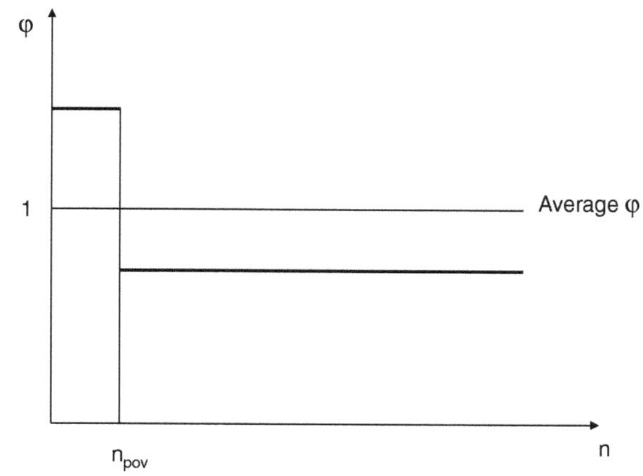

Figure 4.2b Charitable conservatism

The weights characterizing charitable conservatism as specified by Atkinson (1990, Fig 4.2b) fall discontinuously at the poverty line and are constant thereafter at a positive level. The only difference between poverty radicalism and charitable conservatism seems to be the magnitude of the weight given to above the poverty line incomes—the pattern of the weights above the poverty line (constancy) is the same for both. If we take a charitable conservative position, the last term in (5) is equal to $(1-\phi_c)$. Suppose now that there is a critical value of income, n_{pov}, known as the poverty line. The reason why this value of income is critical depends on the behaviour of the valuation function, and therefore the welfare weights. Atkinson's (1990) representation of charitable conservatism[10] is shown in Figure 4.2b. As can be seen, the weights jump to a lower value at n_{pov}.. Formally, we can write:

$$(1-N_{pov})\phi_c + N_{pov}\frac{\phi_c}{\kappa} = 1, \tag{7}$$

where N_{pov} is a fraction of people who are below the poverty line. It can be calculated when we know κ and N_{pov}.

Table 4.2 presents marginal tax rates for the Rawlsian, poverty radicalism, and charitable conservatism objective functions. The optimal marginal tax rates rise when, holding mean constant, overall inequality of the pre-tax inequality increases (from θ=3 to θ=2). (i) As might be expected, marginal tax rates are lower for charitable conservatism than for poverty radicalism. Marginal tax rates decline much faster for charitable conservatism than for poverty radicalism. (ii) The Rawlsian maximin objective function produces a very similar pattern of marginal tax rates compared to poverty radicalism—this supports the argument earlier that poverty radicalism might be thought of as a generalization of Rawlsian maximin.

[10] In the general additive case with maximin, C is $\int (f(p)/U_x)dp$. It is declining with n since u(x) is concave and the integral term declines in n. This might suggest declining marginal rates.

Table 4.2 Optimal marginal tax rates with social objectives (Rawlsian, charitable conservatism, poverty radicalism) and Champernowne distribution (N_{pov}=0.15, ε=0.3)

F(n) Θ	Maximin θ=2	Maximin θ=3	Ch.con $\kappa = 0.5$ θ=2	Ch.con $\kappa = 0.5$ θ=3	Povrad θ=2	Povrad θ=3
0.10	95.7	93.2	74.5	63.9	93.0	90.0
0.15	94.7	90.1	63.5	54.5	93.3	90.5
0.50	81.2	74.1	35.9	27.1	81.2	74.1
0.90	70.4	61.4	23.6	17.1	70.4	61.4
0.99	67.0	58.2	21.0	15.3	67.0	58.2
0.999	58.7	52.2	15.6	12.4	58.7	52.2

The intuitions behind the pattern of marginal tax in cases of maximin—that the social welfare weight is concentrated on the least advantaged—and poverty radicalism—that social welfare weights are concentrated among those living in poverty—is that since the poor are now poorer and require greater support, higher marginal tax rates are in turn necessary to meet the budget constraints. These higher marginal tax rates will of course have incentive effects on the poor, but this is traded off against the need for finer targeting to support the very poorest, when an increase in pre-tax inequality has made them even poorer. The argument runs in reverse if inequality falls. Due to the C term in (5), things are more complicated in the charitable conservatism case.

Tax perturbation approach: Saez (2001) derives an optimal tax formula by using a tax perturbation[11] approach. He also translates the analysis from n-space to z-space. If one begins with some tax schedule T(z), assumed to be optimal, it must be that no slight adjustment to the schedule will change the level of social welfare. Consider an adjustment that slightly raises the marginal tax rate at some income level, z (say, in a small interval from z to z+dz), leaving all other marginal tax rates unaltered. This has the following effects. Figure 4.3, taken from Diamond and Saez (2011), further illustrates this approach.

(1) Let H(z) be the distribution function of individuals by income z (which equals ny and so is endogenous), with density h(z). To the first order, the tax paid by everyone whose income is larger than z increases by *dtdz*; if these individuals are *(1−H(z))* in number, tax revenue increases by *(1−H(z))dtdz*.

(2) The response to the small tax increase dt of an individual earning z is equal to $dz = -z\varepsilon dt/(1-t)$. Now the income supply or gross income in case of (4) can be written $z = ny = ((1-t(z))n)^{\varepsilon} n^{\varepsilon+1}$. Hence the elasticity of labour income with

[11] There are some earlier contributions using the tax perturbation method. Christiansen (1981) introduces the tax perturbation approach, but his main interest is the conditions under which the Samuelson rule is valid when non-linear income tax and linear commodity taxes are available to finance the supply of public goods. Using a tax perturbation method, Piketty (1997) derives the optimal non-linear income tax schedule under maximin without income effects. Roberts (2001) derives it also under a utilitarian case. A kind of perturbation is discussed in Diamond (1968).

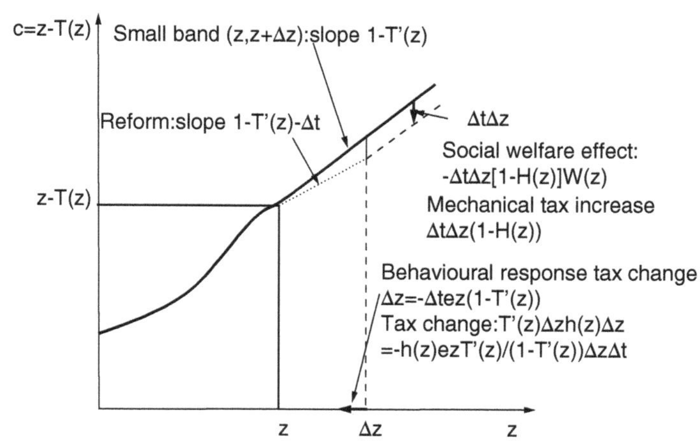

Figure 4.3 Tax perturbation approach

respect to (1−t(z)) is $\varepsilon = \frac{dz(1-t(z))}{d(1-t(z))z}$. The reduction in income dz implies a reduction in tax revenue equal to tdz (no income effects here). So we have $h(z)dztz\varepsilon dt/(1-t)$.

(3) This tax increase also creates a social welfare cost of $-dtdz[1-H(z)]W'(z)$. W'(z) is defined as the average social marginal welfare weight for individuals with income above z.

At the optimum, effects (1), (2), and (3) must exactly cancel out, so that $(1-H(z))dtdz - h(z)dztz\varepsilon dt/(1-t) - dtdz[1-H(z)]W'(z) = 0$. This implies:

$$\frac{t}{1-t} = \frac{1}{\varepsilon}\frac{(1-H(z))}{zh(z)}(1-W') \tag{8}$$

which is the equivalent of (5). The marginal tax rate is decreasing in the elasticity of taxable income ε and W'(z), as expected. It is increasing in *(1−H(z))*, the number of persons whose tax payments go up when the marginal tax rate on z rises, and decreasing in zh(z), which is the total output of those at income level z. Of course, (5) is derived under some restrictions, including quasi-linearity of preferences and a constant labour supply elasticity.

4.3 **Optimal top marginal tax rates: unbounded distribution and quasi-linear preferences**

As discussed above, the famous zero top rate result applies only to the top income-earners. If there is no upper bound of the skill distribution, the marginal tax rate at the top is no longer zero. Now we make an empirically plausible assumption that there is no upper bound.

Diamond (1998) shows that when preferences satisfy (4) and labour supply elasticity ε is constant, the optimal marginal taxes must satisfy (5). For any social welfare function W with a property that $\lim_{u\to\infty} W'(u) = 0$, and individual preferences represented by (4), then the integral in (5) asymptotically converges to 1 and $\frac{t(n)}{1-t(n)}$ converges to $\frac{t(n)}{1-t(n)} = \left[1 + \frac{1}{\varepsilon}\right] \frac{1-F(n)}{nf(n)}$ from below.

In the case of the unbounded Pareto distribution of skills above the modal skill $f(n) = \frac{1}{n^{1+a}}$ for a > 0, $\frac{1-F(n)}{nf(n)} = \frac{1}{\alpha}$, the asymptotic optimal marginal tax rate is given by:

$$\lim_{n\to\infty} \frac{t(n)}{1-t(n)} = \left[1 + \frac{1}{\varepsilon}\right] \frac{1}{\alpha}, \tag{9}$$

where α is the Pareto coefficient. Hence:

$$t = \frac{1}{1 + a\xi} \tag{10}$$

where $\xi = \left[1 + \frac{1}{\varepsilon}\right]$. Formula (10) is an explicit formula for the optimal top income tax rate. It shows that the optimal top tax rate is independent of the cut-off income z* within the top tail (see Figure 4.4). It is also the asymptotic optimal marginal tax rate coming out of the standard non-linear optimal tax model of Mirrlees (1971). That is, the optimal marginal tax rate is approximately the same over the range of very high incomes where

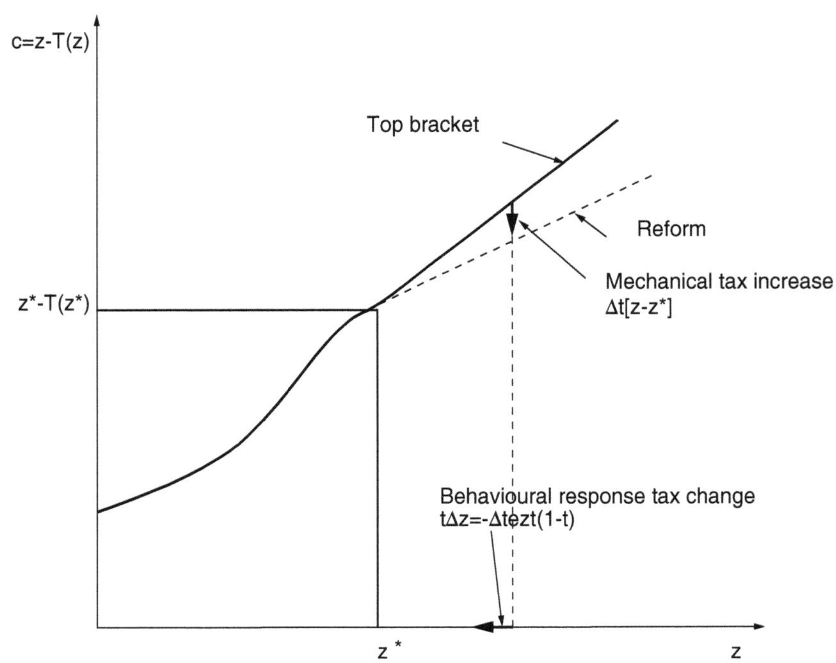

Figure 4.4 Optimal top tax rate

the distribution is Pareto and the social welfare function has curvature so that $W'[u(n)]$ tends to zero when u tends to infinity. This will, hence, approximately be true for large n or z. Assuming that the average social marginal welfare weight among top bracket income earners is zero allows us to obtain an upper bound on the optimal top tax rate. Hence (23) gives a revenue-maximizing tax rate. If we assume the maximin social objective,[12] Pareto distribution, and quasi-linear preferences, then the pattern of marginal tax rates depends only on $\frac{1-F(n)}{nf(n)}$; that is, on the shape of the n-distribution. We have the same formula as in (10).

Saez (2001) provides a simple derivation of the top income tax rate in terms of gross income z based on approximation. The government chooses t to maximize tax revenue R from the top bracket (as the government puts no marginal social welfare weight on top bracket earners);[13] $R = t(z_m(1-t)-z^*)$. z^* is a threshold and z_m is the mean income of those with incomes above z^* (in other words, if z^* is a threshold above which a hypothetical top rate of tax applies, then the mean income of those affected is z_m, and z_m-z^* is the amount of income over which the new tax rate applies). The first-order condition is $t\frac{dz_m}{d(1-t)} = z_m - z^*$.

Dividing by z_m we have: $\frac{tdz_m(1-t)}{(1-t)z_m d(1-t)} = 1 - \frac{z^*}{z_m}$ (*), where at the left-hand side we have the aggregate elasticity of income in the top bracket with respect to the net-of-tax rate 1−t. The formula (*) is essentially the same formula as formula (14) in Tuomala (1985) in the linear optimal income tax model (and formula (3) in Chapter 3). The revenue-maximizing top rate that applies above the threshold z^* is given by $\frac{t}{1-t}\varepsilon = 1 - \frac{z^*}{z_m}$ or $t = \frac{1}{1+\varepsilon/I}$, where $I = 1 - \frac{z^*}{z_m}$ is a measure of inequality. But if the distribution of top incomes has a Pareto distribution then this is equivalent to formula (10) and independent of the threshold z^*. The Pareto distribution has an important connection with van der Wijk's law. The average income z_m above the level z^* is proportional to z^* itself, i.e. or $\frac{z_*}{z_m} = \frac{\alpha-1}{\alpha}$ (see for example the discussion in Cowell 1977). Hence we have $t = \frac{1}{1+\varepsilon\alpha}$. Note that this formula is in fact the same as (5) in the optimal linear income tax in Chapter 3.[14] When $z^* = 0$, $a = 1 = \frac{z}{z-z^*}$, we have (5) in the linear income case.

Alternative social preferences and top tax rates: One may argue that it is too extreme to put zero asymptotic welfare weight on the top earners. For example, Feldstein (2012) argues that it is repugnant to set weights in this way. Alternatively we might assume that ϕ has a positive lower bound which is approached as n rises without limit. Of course this

[12] Maximizing utility of the worst-off person in the society is not the original version of Rawls (1971). It is a kind of welfarist version of Rawlsian thought. 'To interpret the difference principle as the principle of maximin utility (the principle to maximize the well-being of the least advantaged person) is a serious misunderstanding from a philosophical standpoint': Rawls, 1982).

[13] Alternatively, assume one wants to increase the marginal tax rate from t to t+dt over some income bracket [z; z+dz]. Then tax revenues go from R to R+dR, with:dR = (1−H(z)) dtdz−h(z)dzt'ez dt/(1−t) (h(y) the density function for labour income, and H(y) the distribution function). dR = 0 if and only if t/(1−t) = (1−(z))/zh(z)(1/e).

[14] When $z^* = 0$, $a = 1 = \frac{z}{z-z^*}$, we have the linear income case.

is not obvious how to determine a positive lower bound. Given the lower point of ϕ, the optimal rate is now:

$$t = \frac{1-\phi}{1-\phi+\varepsilon/I}. \tag{11}$$

The optimal top marginal tax rate is decreasing with elasticity e and the social marginal welfare weight on top earner ϕ, and increasing in the inequality parameter I. This rate is also less than the revenue-maximizing rate with the same inequality parameter and elasticity.

Atkinson (2012, p. 747) writes:

> Economists tend to assume that it is e (the elasticity) that is the core of their subject, but equally central should be a (the distribution). This is particularly the case where the distribution of top incomes is becoming more concentrated in the form of a lower value for a Pareto parameter, implying a higher optimal top tax rate.

The excellent Pareto fit of the top tail of the distribution has been well known for over a century, since the pioneering work of Pareto (1896), and has been verified in many countries and many periods, as summarized in Atkinson et al (2011). In those twenty-four countries reported in Atkinson et al (2011), the Pareto parameter typically varies between 3.0 and 1.67. The top tail of the income distribution is closely approximated by a Pareto distribution characterized by a power law density of the form $h(z) = (1/z^{1+\alpha})$, where $\alpha>1$ is the Pareto parameter.[15] Such distributions have the key property that the ratio z_m/z^* is the same for all z^* in the top tail and equal to $\alpha/(\alpha-1)$. z^* is the top x per cent threshold income and z_m is the average income of top x per cent. Higher α i.e. lower coefficient $\alpha/(\alpha-1)$, (i.e. less fat upper tail) implies lower inequality. A lower coefficient means larger top income shares and higher income inequality. In Finland in the period 1990–2009, the Pareto parameter (taxable income) varied between 3.7 (1992) and 1.79 (2004; see Figure 4.5 and also appendix 4.5).

Empirical work on the incentive effects of labour income taxation generally identified quite low labour supply elasticities. Much of this research viewed labour supply in terms of hours. It has long been recognized that behavioural responses of taxation are not confined to participation and hours worked. Feldstein (1995) proposed that we should examine the response of taxable income to changes in tax rates. Taxable income is determined not only by hours and participation; individuals can respond to other taxation margins such as job choice, intensity of work, timing of compensation, tax avoidance, and tax evasion. Feldstein (1995) found very high elasticities exceeding 1. Slemrod (1996) pointed out that many of those dramatic responses were actually

[15] It is still the case that the original purpose of the Pareto function is its most fruitful application. This view is nicely expressed by Cowell (1977, p. 88) when he writes: 'Although the Pareto formulation has proved to be extremely versatile in the social sciences, in my view the purpose for which it has originally been employed is still its most useful application—an approximate description of the distribution of income and wealth among the rich and the moderately rich'.

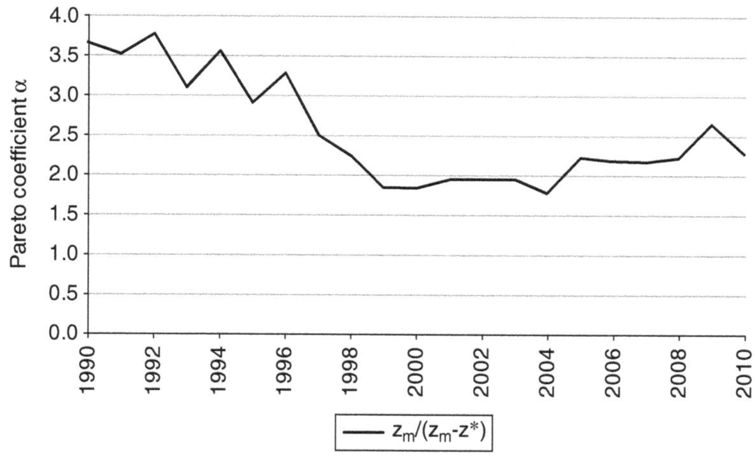

Figure 4.5 Empirical Pareto coefficient, α, in Finland 1990–2010. z* is the top 1% threshold income and z_m is the average income of top 1%.

Source: Riihelä et al (2013).

primarily due to tax avoidance rather than real economic behaviour. Subsequent research generated considerable smaller estimates. In a recent survey on taxable income elasticities, Saez et al (2012, p. 42) conclude: 'The most reliable longer-run elasticity estimates range from 0.1 to 0.4, suggesting that the U.S. top marginal rate is far from the top of the Laffer curve, but greater than one would calculate if the sole behavioural response was labour supply.'

Much attention has been devoted to the effects of top marginal tax rates on the earnings distribution. As pointed out by Atkinson et al (2010), higher top marginal tax rates can reduce top reported earnings through different channels. In particular, it has long been shown that the bulk of the elasticity response for top incomes comes from income-shifting between various tax bases. For instance, lower capital income tax rates might lead to a rise in top taxable incomes reported as capital income, but this rise can be almost entirely offset by a corresponding decline in taxable earned income reported to the labour income tax (see more on this in the context of optimal capital income taxation).

Most of the behavioural response of top incomes to top tax rates seems to be due not to a real change in economic activity and output, but simply to a re-labelling of income outlays over various tax bases. Using the terminology introduced by Saez et al (2012) in their survey, the behavioural response of top incomes involves substantial tax externalities which, like all externalities, have an impact on welfare and policy analysis. In general, the literature estimates this elasticity based on the sum of labour and capital income. Top income shares together with information on marginal tax rates by income group can be used to test theory and estimate the taxable elasticity.

We employ the property of (10) to calculate optimal top income tax rates using reduced-form estimates of the taxable income elasticity for high incomes and a Pareto parameter of Figure 4.5 from the Finnish income distribution. Figure 4.6 displays our

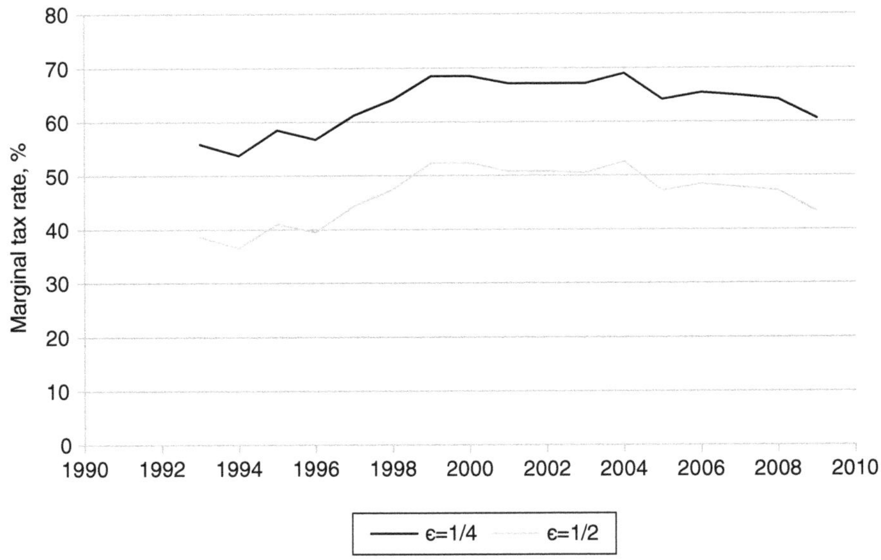

Figure 4.6 Optimal revenue-maximizing top marginal tax rates % (ε=1/4,1/2) 1993–2010

Source: Riihelä et al (2013).

Table 4.3a Utilitarian top marginal tax rates (%) ϕ=1/3

	α=1.5	α=2	α=2.5	α=3
ε=0.25	64.1	57.3	51.7	47.2
ε=0.50	47.2	40.1	34.9	30.9

Table 4.3b Utilitarian top marginal tax rates (%) ϕ=1/2

	α=1.5	α=2	α=2.5	α=3
ε=0.25	57.1	50.0	44.4	40.0
ε=0.50	40.0	33.3	28.6	25.0

Table 4.3c Rawlsian (maximizing revenue on the high earner) top marginal tax rates (%) ϕ=0

	α=1.5	α=2	α=2.5	α=3
ε=0.25	72.7	66.7	61.5	57.1
ε=0.50	57.1	50.0	44.4	40.0

simple calculations for two different values of elasticity over the period 1990–2010. The value ε=0.25 is a mid-range estimate in Table A3.1 (see appendix 4.3) and also in the recent survey by Saez et al (2012).

Tables 4.3a, b, and c illustrate with some parameter values top marginal rates with different social objectives (utilitarian and revenue-maximizing). As mentioned earlier, since the end of the 1970s, top tax rates on upper income earners have declined significantly in many OECD countries, again mainly in English-speaking countries. For example, the US top marginal federal individual tax rate was a remarkably high 91 per cent in the 1950s–60s, but is only 35 per cent nowadays. In other advanced countries, e.g. Nordic countries, top tax rates on upper income have declined dramatically since the beginning of the 1990s. The top tax rate in Finland was 44.3 per cent in 2010. The corresponding top tax rate was 62.7 per cent in 1990. The tax rates in Table 4.3a and b are based on the approximation formulas (10) and (11). They give smaller values than the asymptotic rates. For example, in the revenue-maximizing case with α=2 and ε=0.5, we have t=50 per cent, but the asymptotic rate with the same parameter values is 60 per cent (from formula (10)).

Responses to tax rates can also take the form of tax avoidance. Tax avoidance can be defined as changes in reported income due to changes in the form of compensation but not in the total level of compensation. In the Finnish tax system, tax-avoidance opportunities arise when taxpayers can shift part of their taxable labour income into capital income. Income-shifting is possible in practice for the top 1 per cent of taxpayers, i.e. for wealthy owners of closely held companies. Piketty et al (2014) extend the revenue-maximizing top tax-rate formula with the elasticity of tax avoidance. The formula takes the following form: $t = (1 + \tau a \varepsilon_A)/(1 + a\varepsilon)$ (see Piketty et al 2014 for a derivation), where $\varepsilon_A = \frac{(1-t)dA}{zd(t-\tau)}$ is the tax-avoidance elasticity and A is shifted income so that ordinary taxable income is a difference between real income and A and shifted income is taxed at a constant and uniform marginal tax rate τ lower than t. For given τ = 25 per cent[16], we assume ϵ = 0.5 (0.7)[17], ϵ^* = 0.3 (0.1), ϵ_A = 0.2 (0.6),[18] α = 2 and τ = 25 per cent, then we obtain a revenue-maximizing top rate t = 55 per cent (54.2 per cent). What are the tax policy implications of top tax rates based on this formula? They simply reflect weaknesses of the tax system. In fact, the optimal tax system should minimize the income-shifting channels. In other words: what fraction of the tax-avoidance elasticity can be eliminated by better tax design and tax enforcement?

4.4 **Additive utility and income effects**

We now move to the more general case with income effects. To make things simpler we assume that the utility function is additive:

$$u = U(x) + V(1 - y) \tag{12}$$

[16] It was capital income tax rate in the 1993 reform.

[17] $e=(d/z)e^*+e_A$ where e^* is the real labour supply elasticity, and the ordinary taxable income z=d−A (d=real income).

[18] We chose the values of elasticities assuming that in Table 1 the elasticity based on the 1993 reform also reflects income shifting, but not the estimate of elasticity based on the 1989 reform.

defined over consumption x and hours worked y, with $U_x>0$ and $Vy<0$ (subscripts indicating partial derivatives). Omitting details (see appendix 4.4) from the first-order conditions of government's maximization, we obtain the condition for the optimal marginal tax rate. It is useful to write the ABC formula for marginal rates[19,20], denoted by $t(z) = T''(z)$, in terms of traditional labour supply elasticities[21], E^u (uncompensated labour supply elasticity), and E^c (compensated labour supply elasticity):

$$\frac{t}{1-t} = \underbrace{\left[\frac{1+E^u}{E^c}\right]}_{A_n} \underbrace{\left[\frac{[1-F(n)]}{nf(n)}\right]}_{B_n} \underbrace{\left[\frac{U_x \int_n^{\infty} (1 - \frac{W' U_x^{(m)}}{\lambda})(1/U_x^m) f(m) dm}{1-F(n)}\right]}_{C_n} \tag{13}$$

Although formula (13) is more complicated than in the case without income effects, it does however provide several insights (see the derivation of (13) in appendix 4.3). There are three elements on the right-hand side of (13) that determine optimum marginal tax rates. We now consider what formula (13) tells us about optimal marginal rates at the lower part of the income distribution.

(1) First, the term on the right-hand side of (13), A_n, expressing labour supply responses in uncompensated and compensated elasticities, represents the standard efficiency effect, reflecting also conventional wisdom. It says that, other things being equal, the marginal tax rate is decreasing in E^c. It is also important to note that, for a given compensated elasticity E^c, the decomposition into uncompensated and income effects matters. The higher are income effects (in absolute terms) relative to uncompensated effect, the higher is the marginal tax rate. The higher the compensated elasticity is, the lower the optimal marginal tax rate. What is also important here is that the elasticity may vary across population. This means that we need to know how the elasticity varies with the wage rate. Is it higher at the lower end of the income distribution than at the upper part? This is an empirical question. We shall return to this in the simulations.

[19] Revesz (1989), Atkinson (1995), Diamond (1998), Piketty (1997), and Saez (2001) have formulated the Mirrlees first order conditions in terms of elasticities.

[20] There is an important difference between (13) and the formulation in Saez (2001, p. 215). Taking into account that the tax rules and other parameters will determine the relationship between the ability distribution and the resulting income distribution, Saez (2001) translates the results from those in terms of the distribution of abilities to those in terms of the distribution of income. In other words, Saez (2001) took a step forward by deriving an optimal tax formula by expressing his optimal tax formula in terms of the notion of virtual earnings distribution and verifying the consistency of his solution with Mirrlees'. Saez (2001, p. 215) defines the virtual density at earnings level z as 'the density of incomes that would take place at z if the tax schedule T (:) were replaced by the linear tax schedule tangent to T (:) at level z'.

[21] See also Wilson (1993) in the context of non-linear pricing. See appendix 4.4 for the derivation.

(2) The second term, B_n, tells us that the shape of the wage distribution affects the optimal marginal tax rate at the wage level n through the ratio $\frac{1-F(n)}{nf(n)}$. This ratio is the inverse hazard rate (or the Mills ratio) divided by n. When we increase the marginal tax rate at some n (n is low), we collect more revenue on more productive individuals, who are $1-F(n)$ in number. In other words, an increase in marginal rate depends on the proportion of the population above n. The purpose of higher marginal rate is to increase the average tax rate higher up the scale. Hence $1-F(n)$ is in the numerator. We distort only the behaviour of the marginal type, which explains why $f(n)$ in turn is in the denominator.

The marginal tax rate is higher when n is lower in the distribution ($\frac{1-F(n)}{n}$ is decreasing in n) and when nf(n), an indicator of the extent of earnings at the wage level n, is smaller. Hence, raising marginal rates on very low incomes, say z*, raises substantial revenue because most of the taxpayers have income higher than this level. Moreover, higher marginal rates at the bottom are inframarginal for this large group. In other words, the high marginal rates act as a lump-sum tax on higher earnings. Secondly, in the denominator f is not very large and n in turn is low, so there is little lost revenue. These considerations explain why several simulations produce high marginal rates at the bottom of the distribution. In particular, this is the case when the labour supply elasticity is constant. It must be remembered that our story above is based on *ceteris paribus* assumptions.

Formula (13) also suggests that, other things being equal, the marginal tax rate should be lower the denser the population is at that point, i.e. higher $f(n)$. In other words, the larger the fraction of the taxpayers paying more tax, the smaller is the group being distorted. On the other hand, for the typical distribution, the density weighted by n is likely to decline with n above some point suggesting a higher marginal tax rate on high earners. From Figures 5.1a, b, and c in Chapter 5 we see that at the lower part of n-distribution, the B-term is lower for the Champernowne distribution (defined in appendix 4.5) than in the case of lognormal distribution (see footnote 4 in Chapter 5). The component *1-F* in the numerator is smaller and the *f* component in the denominator will be larger. This suggests that the optimal marginal tax rate at a low level of income might be smaller in the Champernowne case than in the lognormal case. Our numerical simulations support this.

(3) The third term, C_n, reflects income effects and incorporates distributional concerns. U_x has also a central role in the term C; the effect itself is in the front of the integral and in the integral itself we need to know $W'U_x$[22], where W' is the social weighting of an individual and U_x is their marginal utility from consumption. There is a distinction between the concavity of individual utility functions, U_x, and concavity that might exist

[22] It can be shown that $W'U_x$ is decreasing in n* (n* is the skill level at which $W'(u(n^*))$ $U_x(x(n^*), y(n^*)) = \lambda$) so long as $W(u)$ is concave and leisure is normal. $W'(u(n^*))u_x(x, y)$ is decreasing in n*. See proof in appendix 2.3.1.

in the social welfare function, W'. While the latter involves a value judgement, the former is a representation of individual utility that in principle might be measurable. The integrand term measures the social welfare gain from slightly increasing the marginal tax rate at n and distributing as a poll subsidy to those below n the revenue raised from the consequent increase in average tax rates above n. To put it another way, the integrand in the numerator is the difference between the marginal euro that is raised and the euro equivalent of the loss in welfare for those taxpayers paying more tax above n*. $W'U_x$ indicates the impact of changes in social utility of income, and division by λ,[23] the shadow price on revenue constraint, converts this welfare measure into euros. Dividing by $1-F(n)$ gives an average for the affected population. Altogether, the C term tends to favour rising marginal rates.

The income effects enter through the terms A and C. In the term A it affects how elasticities vary with skill.[24] Income effects are related to the concavity of the utility of consumption, as people are willing to work more when after-tax income is lower. In the utilitarian case this might mean that $W'U_x$ is decreasing more sharply in the presence of income effects. This suggests that income effect should lead to a greater extent of redistribution. This effect through $W'U_x$ does not yet imply that the marginal rates are increasing in income. In fact, this effect is missing in many simulations.

A concave utility of consumption means that income effects are weaker for high-income earners. This pushes marginal tax rates down at high levels of income. On the other hand, when U_x decreases with n, its impact on inequality aversion pushes in the opposite direction. The interaction of these two forces determines the optimal tax-rate schedule. But this is about as far as we can get at this level of generality.[25] In the tradition of the non-linear taxation literature, we can provide a better understanding of the form of optimal policy through numerical simulations. We can compute post-tax income at each level of n and thus calculate inequality of pre and post-tax income as well as total income for different values of key parameters. Section 2.4 takes up this task.

[23] Note λ is itself a function of the overall distribution, $\lambda = 1/(\int_0^\infty (1/U_x)f(p)dp)$ (the social welfare function is utilitarian, i.e. W'=1).

[24] As shown by Chetty (2006), there is a relationship between risk aversion and the labour supply. Or, to put it another way, there is the connection between the coefficient of relative risk aversion (r) and the ratio of income wage elasticities. We can see this link by differentiating the FOC of individual's problem and using again the Slutzky equation:

$$\frac{\partial y/\partial b}{\partial y^c/\partial n} = \frac{U_{xx}n}{U_x} \qquad (*)$$

where y^c is compensated labour supply. As seen from (*), the curvature of the utility function with respect to consumption (the coefficient of relative risk aversion) is important because the labour supply response to an increase in income is related to how much the marginal utility of consumption changes as income changes. If U_{xx} is large, the marginal utility of consumption falls sharply as income rises, so that the taxpayer will reduce labour supply when his or her earnings rise.

[25] There are also a number of asymptotic results for the unbounded case. For example, Mirrlees (1971) demonstrates that the marginal tax rate can converge to 100 per cent under some conditions. See also Diamond (1998) and Saez (2001).

4.5 The non-linear utility of consumption and asymptotic rate

The quasi-linear cases considered above yield insights, but within the framework of the assumptions made. How robust are these insights? What happens when we move away from quasi-linearity? Saez (2001) also shows that the main results of Diamond (1998) can be generalized to preferences with income effect. Saez (2001) presents a formula for the optimal asymptotic tax rate for a more general setting based on an approximation. The welfare-maximizing top rate in the highest tax bracket equals $t = (1 - \phi)/(1 - \phi + \alpha\varepsilon^c - \eta)$, where $\phi < 1$ is the social marginal welfare weight for top income earners (it measures the social value in euros of transferring a marginal euro to an income earner in the top tax bracket) and ε^c is the compensated elasticity of taxable income, η is the income elasticity, and a is the Pareto parameter of the earnings distribution. The equation is therefore an explicit formula for the optimal asymptotic top income tax rate if the social welfare weight is taken as exogenous.

As in Diamond (1998), Dahan and Strawczynski (2012) rely on the direct limit argument, i.e. the limit of optimal non-linear marginal tax rates when the wage tends to infinity.[26] They show that Diamond's asymptotic tax formula is not limited to the linear case and can be used for the non-linear utility of consumption as well. Dahan and Strawczynski (2012) also replicate the optimal asymptotic tax of Mirrlees (1971, equation 66), but in terms of labour supply elasticities instead of marginal utilities.

As noted by Mirrlees (1971), the asymptotic marginal tax rates are sensitive to the non-linearity utility of consumption. Above in (22) we assume that utility of consumption is linear. If the marginal utility of consumption takes the form of $u_x = x^{-\gamma}$, then the asymptotic marginal tax rates are sensitive to the value of γ in the neighbourhood of 1. For example, with constant labour supply elasticity and $u_x = x^{-2}$, formula (9) in Saez (2001) yields the optimal asymptotic rate equal to 100 per cent. Mirrlees (1971) devoted much attention to the case where the utility function is of the Cobb–Douglas form, $u = \log x + \log(1-y)$, the social welfare function is isoelastic, and skills are lognormally distributed or according to the Pareto distribution. Marginal tax rate with the Pareto distribution tends asymptotically as n tends to infinity to $\frac{2}{1+\theta}$, where θ is the shape parameter or Pareto parameter. This is also true for the Champernowne distribution.

We can give a fuller description of the solution than is provided in Mirrlees (1971 case ii, pp. 196–200) in the case of Champernowne distribution (see the derivation in appendix 4.5). When the path to the singular solution starts from labour supply y=0, this implies that the marginal tax rates increase monotonically from $\tau = \frac{1}{(1+\theta)}$ to $\tau = \frac{2}{1+\theta}$ (see appendix 4.5 for the derivation). It is also important to note that these asymptotic results are independent of the net revenue requirement. Interestingly, the same

[26] Most relevant cases of asymptotic tax rates were already analysed by Mirrlees (1971, pp. 188–93).

Table 4.4 Asymptotic and numerical top marginal tax rates, f(n)=Champernowne $u=\ln x+\ln(1-y)$

	$\theta=2$	$\theta=2.5$	$\theta=3$	F(n)
Asymptotic rate	67	57	50	
Numerical rate	50.1	40.4	33.8	99

asymptotic value holds—for the current skill distribution and preferences[27]—both in the Rawlsian or maximin and utilitarian cases as long as the marginal utility of consumption goes to zero as wage goes to infinity. In other words, although the shapes of the respective marginal tax schedules differ radically in the maximin and utilitarian cases at the lower end of the income distribution, they converge at the upper end.[28] In fact, this is not surprising. In the utilitarian case the weight attached to the top incomes tend to zero when n goes to infinity. This is also true in the case where the government minimizes some well-behaved poverty index. Of course, this convergence may not be apparent over the income range of practical interest. Whether this is the case will emerge in the numerical simulations provided below.

In Table 4.4 we compare asymptotic rate with the optimum non-linear tax rate at the upper part of n-distribution. A number of interesting points emerge from the patterns in Table 4.4. There are quite big differences between the numerical and asymptotic rates. The asymptotic solution is not a very accurate approximation for even the top 1 per cent, with $\theta=2$, 2.5, and $\theta=3$. But this difference is much smaller than in Mirrlees (1971). The reason is that here we are using distribution with a much thicker upper tail than that used in Mirrlees (1971). Both asymptotic and numerical rates are in line with the top rates we find in many advanced countries. It is perhaps slightly surprising to find rather high tax rates with the Cobb–Douglas preferences where the labour elasticity is rather high, around 0.5, at the income level of top one per cent. In the case $\theta=2$ the asymptotic rate is 67. The asymptotic tax of Mirrlees (1971, equation 66) is 60 per cent: his formula is not in terms of labour supply elasticities but in terms of marginal utilities.

The current (2010) top marginal rate for the top 1 per cent in Finland is 44.3 per cent. The corresponding top tax rate was 62.7 per cent in 1990. With the Pareto parameter $\alpha = 2.5$, (2.0) the labour supply elasticity $\varepsilon = 0.25$ yields revenue-maximizing top marginal tax rate t of 61.5 per cent (66.7 per cent) and utilitarian with positive welfare weight (0.5) yields t of 52.6 per cent. The more general case with the Cobb–Douglas preferences and $a = 2.5$ gives the top rate of 57 per cent. It is clear that this kind of calculation of the optimal tax rate needs to recognize explicitly that there is much uncertainty particularly related to supply elasticities, and not only to rely on one estimate. Notwithstanding this, one conclusion we can draw from our application

[27] Mirrlees (1971) notes this in a footnote on page 200.

[28] In fact this is also true in numerical simulations. In Chapter 5 we see that both in maximin and utilitarian cases, the marginal tax rates are almost the same at the 99 per cent point of the skill distribution.

without any uncertainty is that the current top marginal tax rate in Finland is not close to the top of the Dupuit–Laffer curve.

How we assess our results for the top marginal tax rate depends also on whether elements left out of the model change them. There are good reasons to suspect that the labour market of top income earners deviates from the standard competitive model in a number of important respects.[29] Persson and Sandmo (2005) investigate optimal income taxation in a 'tournament' model where wages are determined not by productivity but by one's productivity relative to other workers. As they note, such a model might be particularly relevant to the salaries of top executives. Would it therefore be a more suitable framework within which to examine the optimal top tax rate? There are problems with the tournament explanation, however, and there is no real evidence that it applies to executive pay. For example, tournaments might provide poor incentives when it is apparent that one player is likely to win and others likely to lose the competition (due to differences in skills or other qualities; see Eriksson 1999). Finally, if the economic activity at high income levels is primarily socially unproductive rent-seeking, then it would be plausible to impose high marginal rates at top income levels.

One element left out of the above theoretical analysis is capital income. As long as capital income is taxed less heavily than labour income (as in the Nordic dual income tax), there is an incentive to convert some labour income into capital income. Narrowing the difference between tax rates of labour and capital income is one way to limit the extent of income-shifting. We come back to these questions in Chapter 14.

Taxes and transfers might affect migration in or out of the country. For example, high top tax rates might induce highly skilled workers to emigrate to low top tax-rate countries. Mirrlees (1971) assumes that migrations are impossible but emphasizes that 'since the threat of migration is a major influence on the degree of progression in actual tax systems, at any rate outside the United States, this is an assumption one would rather not make' (Mirrlees, 1971, p. 176). Mirrlees (1982) studies income taxation and migration mainly from the perspective of developing countries. As suggested by Simula and Trannoy (2010), taking into account potential losses in the tax base due to migration can significantly reduce the level of the optimal top marginal tax rate. In a simple case this can be seen by extending formula (10), adding migration effects using migration elasticity η. It is the elasticity of numbers with respect to after-tax income, x. We have the following formula: $t = \frac{1}{1+ae+\eta}$.

From Table 4.3b we see that when a=2 and e=0.25, t=2/3. If there is migration with elasticity η=0.4, then the revenue-maximizing tax rate decreases to 52.6. Thus, large migration elasticities could indeed significantly decrease countries' ability to tax high incomes. We should emphasize that this is a single-country optimum. A single country

[29] There are quite few studies in optimal taxation where workers are not paid their marginal product (see a survey by Sörensen 1999). There are models with labour market imperfections such as trade unions (e.g. Aronsson and Sjögren 2004, 2010) and search models (e.g. Hungerbuhler 2010). Stantcheva (2012) analyses models in which firms cannot perfectly observe the productivity of their workers.

does not recognize the external effects it might impose on other countries by cutting its top tax rate. From a global welfare perspective and with complete fiscal co-ordination, migration elasticity is not that relevant for optimal tax policy.

4.6 Optimal bottom marginal tax rate

The result that there will usually be a group of people in the lower end of the ability distribution 'who ought to work only if they enjoy it' (Mirrlees 1971, p. 186) has also been regarded as qualitative. The optimum is typically characterized by a certain fraction of individuals, at the bottom end, choosing not to work (where we have $\frac{dx}{dn} = \frac{dz}{dn} = 0$, there is bunching of individuals of different n). The requirement for the endpoint results is boundedness of income, boundedness away from zero, and infinite. To be specific, we have to consider more closely the zero marginal tax-rate result at the bottom end of distribution. This result needs some comments, however. Seade (1977) has noticed that the result depends on the value of $-V_y/nU_x$, the marginal rate of substitution of consumption for labour, when y=0. Two cases can be distinguished here. In the 'bunching' case, if the marginal rate of substitution remains strictly positive as $y>0$, then there will be a group of people ($0-n_0$) who do not work provided that they face a non-negative marginal tax rate. In the 'no-bunching' case, $-V_y/nU_x = 0$ for any n>0, so that if the marginal tax rates are less than one (100 per cent), then all individuals with n>0 prefer to work. In the 'bunching' case the marginal tax rate is in general not zero at the lower end of n-distribution. In fact, the utility function used in the numerical simulations does not fulfil the 'no-bunching' condition. Therefore, preferences generating bunching at the bottom must arise whenever the distribution of wages goes down to zero, provided we restrict attention to non-negative marginal tax functions. This result was noticed by Mirrlees (1971, p. 185, footnote 1) who, however, was implicitly making an assumption on individual preferences: that even when no work is done, (y = 0). Hence individuals have a strict marginal dislike for work, and so behave as if they would like to work even less, as in Figure 4.7a (corner solution). We can now express the marginal tax rate at $n=n_0$:

In the utilitarian case:

$$t(n_0) = \frac{\phi_0 - 1}{\phi_0 - 1 + \frac{n_0 f(n_0)}{F(n_0)}} \tag{14}$$

where $\phi_0 = \frac{W' U_x(x_0, 0)}{\lambda}$ is the welfare weight on non-workers.

In the maximin case:

$$t(n_0) = \frac{1}{1 + \frac{F(n_0)}{n_0 f(n_0)}} \tag{15}$$

(see the derivation in appendix 4.3).

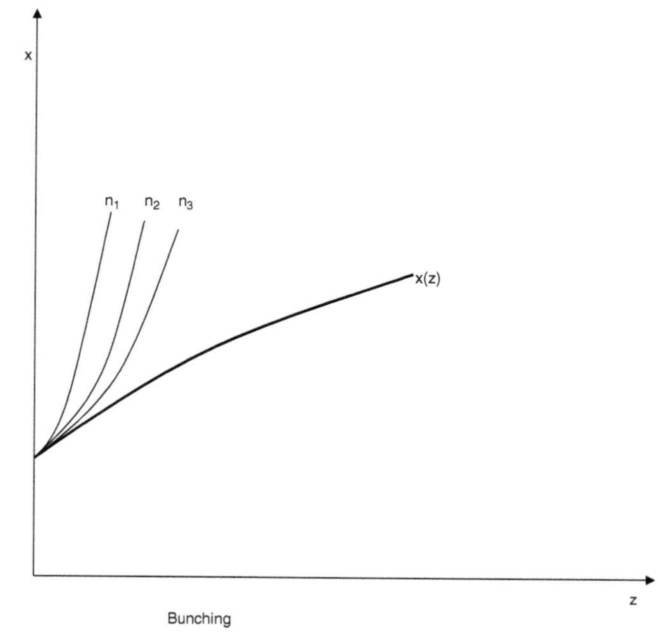

Figure 4.7a Bunching

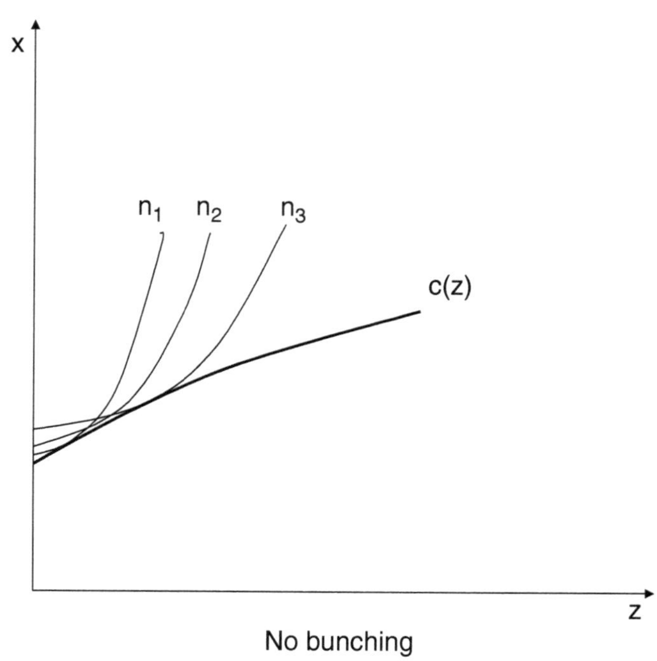

Figure 4.7b No bunching

APPENDIX 4.1 OPTIMAL NON-LINEAR INCOME TAX MODEL

There is a continuum of individuals, each having the same preference ordering, which is represented by a utility function $u=u(x,y)$ over consumption x and hours worked y. The function u is strictly increasing in x, strictly decreasing in y, defined for $x\geq 0$, i.e. the consumption is unbounded, while $0\leq y\leq 1$, with $u_x > 0$ and $u_y < 0$. Also, $u(x,y)$ is assumed to be strictly concave. Individuals are otherwise identical, but they differ in their income-earning ability, or in the pre-tax wage n they can earn. There is a distribution of n on the interval $(0,\infty)$ represented by the density function $f(n)$. The cumulative skill distribution in the population is F(n). Therefore the number of persons with labour parameter n or less is F(n). The function F(n) is assumed to be differentiable and strictly positive, giving the probability density function for skill: $f(n) = F'(n)$. The gross income of the n-individual is $z=ny$. Thus the total labour available for use in the economy is $Z = \int_0^\infty z(n)f(n)dn$.[30] The demand for consumer goods (total consumption in the society) is $X = \int_0^\infty x(n)f(n)dn$.

Individuals maximize utility subject to the budget constraint:

$$\max_{x,y} u(x,y) \text{ subject to } x = ny - T(ny), \tag{1}$$

where T depicts the non-linear tax schedule set by the government. The necessary condition of (1) is given by

$$u_x n(1 - T') + u_y = 0, \tag{2}$$

where $T'=t$ depicts the marginal tax schedule. For later use inverting utility we have $x = h(u,y)$ and calculating the derivatives

$$h_y = -\frac{u_y}{u_x}, \quad h_u = \frac{1}{u_x}, \tag{3}$$

It is usual in optimal tax theory to assume an additively separable individualistic welfare function. One can of course allow for any increasing transformation of individual utilities here, so as to capture a greater or lesser concern with inequality on the part of the government. Suppose, therefore, that the aim of policy can be expressed as maximizing the following social welfare criterion

$$W = \int_0^\infty W(u(n))f(n)dn \tag{4}$$

[30] Considering finite labour supply, we have $\int_0^\infty nf(n)dn < \infty$.

where W(.) is an increasing and concave function of utility. The government cannot observe individuals' productivities and thus is restricted to setting taxes and transfers as a function only of earnings, *T(z(n))* . The government maximizes S subject to the revenue constraint

$$\int_0^\infty T(z(n))f(n)dn = R \tag{5}$$

where R is interpreted as the required revenue for essential public goods. The more non-tax revenue a government receives from external sources, the lower R is. In addition to the revenue constraint, the government faces incentive-compatibility constraints. These in turn state that each n-individual maximizes utility by choice of hour.

$$u\{ny - T(ny(n)), y(n)\} \geq u\{n'y(n') - T(n'y(n')), n'y(n')/n\} \text{ for all n and n'}. \tag{6}$$

It means that an individual of type n has to work n'/n times that of type n' to get the same income.

Following Mirrlees (1971), it is useful to use the following 'trick'. Totally differentiating utility with respect to n, and making use of workers' utility maximization condition, (2), we obtain the incentive-compatibility constraint. This individual-optimization condition gives the self-selection constraint for the government-optimization problem. The government cannot observe individuals' productivities and thus is restricted to setting taxes and transfers as a function only of earnings, *T(z(n))*.

Differentiating $u = u(ny - T(ny), z/n)$ with respect to n gives

$$\frac{du}{dn} = u_x(1-t)y + [u_x n(1-t) + u_y]\frac{dy}{dn} \tag{7}$$

and making use of workers' utility-maximization condition, (2), we obtain the incentive-compatibility constraint,

$$\frac{du}{dn} = u_n(h(u,y),y,n) = -\frac{yu_y}{n}, \tag{8}$$ [31]

Preferences are taken to satisfy the further restriction that $\frac{\partial s}{\partial n} < 0$, where we have defined the variable $s = -u_y(x, z/n)/nu_x(x, z/n)$ to denote the marginal rate of substitution between x and y.

This is assumption B of Mirrlees (1971) and the agent monotonicity assumption of Seade (1982). It implies that indifference curves in consumption-gross income space become flatter the higher an individual's wage rate is, which in turn ensures that both

[31] The first-order condition of individuals' optimization problem is only a necessary condition for the individual's choice to be optimal, but we assume here that it is sufficient as well. Assumptions that assure sufficiency are provided by Mirrlees (1976a). Note also that while we here presume an internal solution for y, (8) remains valid even if individuals were bunched at y = 0 since, for them, $du/dn = 0$.

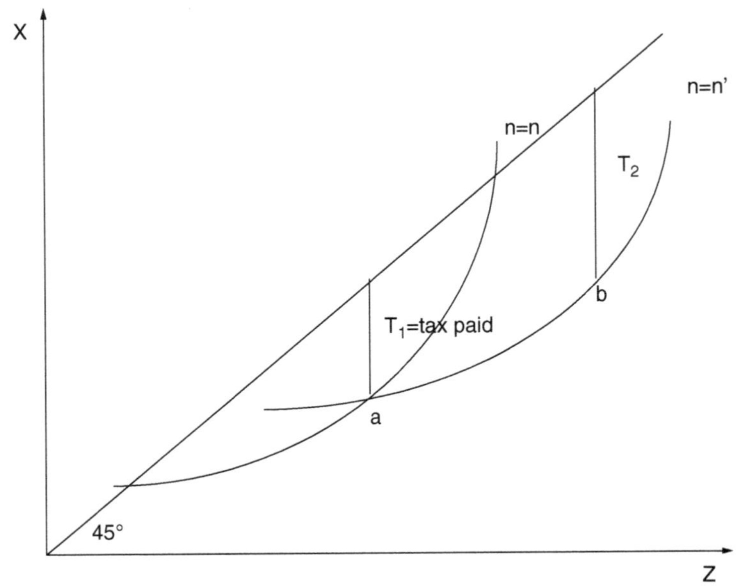

Figure A4.1.1 Single crossing condition

consumption and gross earnings increase with the wage rate. AM or the assumption B or a single-crossing condition[32] implies that for any income tax schedule the more able individual will choose to earn a higher income than the less qualified (if the marginal tax rate is less than 100 per cent) (see Figure A4.1.1). It also ensures that redistribution goes from high to low incomes.

A sufficient condition for agent monotonicity—given identical preferences—is that consumption is normal.

Proof: writing $u(x, y) = u(x, z/n)$, y being labour supplied. The slope of indifference curves in (x,z)-space is

$$\varpi(n) = \frac{-u_y\left(\frac{z}{n^2}\right)}{u_x} = \frac{-u_y y}{n u_x} \tag{9}$$

$$\varpi'(n) = \frac{1}{(nu_x)^2}\left[nu_x\left(-yu_{yy}\left(\frac{-z}{n^2}\right)\right)\right] + u_y y u_x + u_y y n u_{xy}\left(\frac{-y}{n^2}\right)$$

$$= \frac{n}{(nu_x)^2}\left\{[u_x y u_{yy} y] + u_y y u_x - u_y y u_{xy}\right\}$$

$$= \frac{n}{(nu_x)^2}\left\{y^2\left[u_{yy} - u_{xy}\left(\frac{u_y}{u_x}\right)\right]u_x + u_y y u_x\right\} \tag{10}$$

[32] It is also called the Mirrlees–Spence condition.

In (10), $\left[u_{yy} - u_{xy}\left(\frac{u_y}{u_x}\right)\right] < 0$ if and only if consumption is normal and

$$u_y y u_x < 0. \tag{11}$$

Hence it is sufficient[33] for the AM condition—given identical preferences—that consumption is normal.

Figure A4.1.1 illustrates the AM or single-crossing condition. As seen in Figure A4.1.1, the slope of the indifference curve of n is steeper than that of m at the point where they cross. The figure also implies that x(n')<x(n) and z(n')<z(n). This simply means that more productive individuals have higher consumption and gross income. To prove it more rigorously:

Define

$$v(n) = \max_{x(n),z(n)} u(x, z, n) \tag{12}$$

subject to *(x,z)* ∈ *B* and B is assumed not to depend on n.

Denote $x(n), z(n) = \arg\max_{x(n),z(n)} u(x, z, n)$
subject to *(x,z)* ∈ *B*
So

$$v(n) = u(x(n), z(n), n) \tag{13}$$

where v depends on efficiency units of labour and on the characteristic n explicitly. Following Mirrlees (1976a), note that

$$v(n) - u(x(n), z(n), n) = 0 \leq v(n') - u(x(n'), z(n'), n) \text{ for all n'} \tag{14}$$

where v is the utility level of an-individual who claims to be of type n'.

Hence n'=n minimizes $v(n') - u(x(n'), z(n'), n)$. Assuming differentiability yields the incentive constraint

$$v'(n) = u_n(x(n), z(n), n) \tag{15}$$

and the second-order condition

$$v''(n) \geq u_{nn}(x(n), z(n), n),$$

(14), (15) and $v'(n) = u_n + u_x x' + u_z z'$ imply

$$u_x x'(n) + u_z z'(n) = 0.$$

Since

$$v''(n) = u_{nn} + u_{nx}x'(n) + u_{nz}z'(n)$$

[33] Note it is not a necessary condition.

$$u_{nx}x'(n) + u_{nz}z'(n) \geq 0$$

$$-u_{nx}z'(n)\frac{u_z}{u_x} + u_{nz}z'(n) \geq 0$$

$$u_x z'(n)[\frac{u_{nz}u_x}{u_x^2} - \frac{u_{nx}u_z}{u_x^2}] \geq 0.$$

By assumption $u_x > 0$, the single-crossing condition hence implies, by differentiating the marginal rate of substitution with respect to n: $-\frac{u_{nz}}{u_x} + \frac{u_{nx}u_z}{u_x^2} \leq 0$. Hence, $z'(n) \geq 0$, gross income, z, increases with ability, and furthermore, since from $x'(n) = -\frac{u_z}{u_x}z'(n)$, consumption also increases with n.

Assuming a single-crossing condition, one only has to make sure $v'(n) = u_n(x(n), z(n), n)$ and $z'(n) \geq 0$. If $z'(n) \geq 0$ is binding, some low-ability types would be bunched at the bottom, not working, and only receiving a transfer. With such bunching, the marginal tax rate at the bottom will be positive (Seade 1977), and the income tax system will be a non-linear negative income tax.

Derivation of the marginal tax rate

Since $T = ny-x$, we can think of government as choosing schedules y(n) and x(n). In fact, it is easier to think of it choosing a pair of functions, u(n) (the state variable) and y(n) (the control variable), which maximizes index (4) subject to the incentive-compatibility condition (8) and the revenue requirement $\int[z(n)-x(n)]f(n)dn=R$. Introducing multipliers λ and $\mu(n)$ for the budget constraint and incentive-compatibility constraint, and integrating by parts, the Lagrangean becomes

$$L = \int_0^\infty ((W(u) + \lambda(ny - x))f(n) - \mu' u - \mu\Psi)dn + \mu(\infty)u(\infty) - \mu(0)u(0), \quad (16)$$

Differentiating with respect to u and y gives the first-order conditions

$$L_u = (W' - \lambda)h_u f(n) - \mu'(n) - \mu(n)\frac{u_{nx}}{u_x} = 0, \quad (17)$$

$$L_y = \lambda(n - h_y)f(n) + \mu(n)nu_x\varpi_n = 0, \quad (18)$$

Defining $\Psi(u, y, n) = u_n(h(u, y), y, n)$ too, it is straightforward to check that

$$\Psi_y = -nu_x\varpi_n, \Psi_u = \frac{u_{nx}}{u_x}.$$

Dividing (18) by λf, using (2), (3), and (9) and rearranging, (18) becomes

$$t(z(n)) = -\mu(n)u_x\varpi_n/\lambda f, \tag{19}$$

where

$$\mu(n) = \int_n^\infty (\frac{\lambda}{u_x} - W')\exp(-\int_n^{n'} u_{nx}/nu_x)f(n')dn', \tag{20}$$

is the multiplier on the incentive-compatibility constraint. This latter satisfies the transversality condition

$$\mu(0) = \mu(\infty) = 0 \tag{21}$$

and

$$\mu(n)>0, \text{ for } n \in (0, \infty). \tag{22}$$

It should be clear from (19) that the variation of the optimal marginal tax rate with the level of income is a complex matter. There are few general results on the marginal tax rates T'=t.

1. $t(z(n))\geq 0$ proof:

The idea of the proof, due to Werning (2002), is as follows. Manipulating the first-order conditions, we show that if marginal tax rates are not positive then there exist two ability or productivity levels $n^0 < n^1$, such that: (i) marginal tax rates are zero at n^0 and n^1; (ii) marginal utility of consumption is lower at n^0. These two properties together with normality of leisure imply that utility must be higher at n^0 than at n^1. However, this violates a necessary condition for incentive compatibility: more productive agents must be better off! Hence we can conclude that negative marginal tax rates cannot be optimal.

The marginal tax rate for an agent with productivity n has the same sign as the Lagrangian multiplier on the incentive constraint μ(n). We will prove that this multiplier $\mu(n) > 0$, for $n \in (0,\infty)$ as long as output y(n) is strictly positive. Optimality requires that the multiplier must be zero at the boundaries, $\mu(\underline{n}) = \mu(\bar{n}) = 0$. If $\mu(n) < 0$, for some $n \in (0,\infty)$, then there must be some 'maximal interval' $[n^0,n^1]$ with $n^0 < n^1$ such that $\mu(n) \leq 0$ for n $\in[n\in[n^0, n^1]]$, with $\mu(n^0) = \mu(n^1) = 0$ and $\mu'(n^0) \leq 0$ and $\mu x(n^1) \geq 0$. Define the expenditure function (without distortions) for individual n by:

$$E(v, n) = \min_{c,(1-y)}(n(1 - y) + x) \text{ s.t. } u(x, 1 - y) = v$$

since at n^0 and n^1 μ=0, x(n), (1−y(n) at n^0, n^1 solve this problem. The applying envelope theorem is: $E_v(v, n) = 1/U_x = 1/u_x = h_v$.

Combining (23) with these facts, we obtain:

$$E_v^0 = \frac{1 - \mu'^0/f^0}{\lambda} \geq \frac{1}{\lambda} \geq \frac{1 - \mu'^1/f^1}{\lambda} = E_v^1.$$

or $E_v(v(n^0), n^0) \geq E_v(v(n^1), n^1)$.

More explicitly: $E_v(v(n^0), n^0) \geq E_v(v(n^1), n^1)$ with $n^0 < n^1$. We now show that implies that $v(n^0) \geq v(n^1)$. Toward a contradiction, assume instead that $v(n^0) < v(n^1)$. Strict concavity of U(x,1−y) implies that $E_{vv} > 0$ and normality of leisure implies that $E_{vn} = E_{nv} = (1-y)_v \geq 0$. Thus, $n^0 < n^1$ and $v(n^0) < v(n^1)$ imply the opposite inequality, $E_v(v(n^0), n^0) < E_v(v(n^1), n^1)$, a contradiction.

Thus, $v(n^0) \geq v(n^1)$. Finally, $v(n^0) \geq v(n^1)$ violates incentive-compatibility constraints—since output is positive, more productive agents must be better off! It follows that $\mu(n) < 0$ is not possible and thus that marginal tax rates are non-negative.

2. We can also show (more trivially) that t≤100 per cent: no one would ever locate in a range where t>100 (at least in theory).

Proof. From the first-order condition for an individual choice $u_x n(1-t) + u_y = 0$, we can see that at an interior solution x'>0, $1 + \frac{u_y}{nu_x} > 1$.

3. $t(z(\bar{n})) = 0$ ($\bar{n}$ highest n, f(n) bounded above) (Sadka, 1976).

Proof. This follows from transversality conditions and (19).

4. $t(z(\underline{n})) = 0$ $\underline{n} : y(\underline{n}$ ($\underline{n}$ lowest n) (Seade, 1977).

Proof. If there is no bunching transversality condition and (19) imply the result:

If there is bunching at the lowest n, the marginal tax rate is positive at the end of bunching interval.

The two latter results assume that there are some upper and lower bounds to the ability distribution, as opposed to the support just being [0,∞). If some individuals have zero ability, they will not work and the zero marginal tax-rate result does not hold. To get any further one has to simulate.

APPENDIX 4.2 QUASI-LINEAR PREFERENCES

We assume, as in Atkinson (1990) and Diamond (1998), quasi-linear preferences $U_x = 1$ with constant the elasticity of labour.

$$u = x + V(1-y) \tag{1}$$

Each n-individual maximizes utility by choice of hours worked, solving $\max_{x,y} u = x - V(y)$ subject to the budget constraint $x = ny - T(ny)$. (2)

The first-order condition at the individual level is:

$$V_y = (1-t)n, \ \ t \equiv T' \tag{3}$$

where V_y is the first derivative of V. From the first-order conditions of government's maximization, we obtain the following condition for optimal marginal tax rate *t(z)*: [Note now: $\frac{t}{1-t} = \frac{1}{1-t} - 1 = \frac{n}{V_Y} - 1$]

The quasi-linear utility function $u = x+V(1-y)$ is defined over consumption x and hours worked y, with $u_x = 1$ and $V_y < 0$ (subscripts indicating partial derivatives). Introducing multipliers λ and $\mu(n)$ for the budget constraint (3) and incentive-compatibility constraint $\frac{du}{dn} = -\frac{yV_y}{n} = \Psi$ and integrating by parts, the Lagrangean becomes

$$L = \int_0^{\infty} ((W(u) + \lambda(ny - x))f(n) - \mu' u - \mu\Psi)dn + \mu(\infty)u(\infty) - \mu(0)u(0). \quad (4)$$

With quasi-linear preferences differentiating of the Lagrangean (20) with respect to u and y gives the first-order conditions

$$L_u = [W' - \lambda)]f(n) - \mu'(n) = 0 \quad (5)$$

$$L_y = \lambda(n + V_y)f(n) + \mu(n)(V_y + yV_{yy})/n = 0 \quad (6)$$

(5) satisfies the transversality conditions

$$\frac{\partial L}{\partial u(0)} = \mu(0) = 0; \frac{\partial L}{\partial u(\infty)} = \mu(\infty) = 0.$$

Integrating (5),

$$\mu(n) = \int_n^{\infty} [\lambda - W']f(m)dm. \quad (7)$$

This latter satisfies the transversality conditions $\mu(0)=\mu(\infty)=0$

[Integrating (5), $\int_n^{\infty} \frac{d\mu}{dn} dn = \mu(\infty) - \mu(n)$].

The transversality conditions and (6) imply

$$\mu(n) > 0, \quad \text{for } n \in (0, \infty).$$

The tranversality condition $\mu(0) = 0$ yields $\lambda = \int_0^{\infty} W'[U(x)]f(p)dp$.

From the first-order conditions of government's maximization, we obtain the following condition for optimal relative marginal tax rate $t(z)$:

$$\frac{t}{1-t} = (1 + \frac{yV_{yy}}{V_y}) \frac{1}{\lambda nf(n)} \int_n^{\infty} [\lambda - W']f(m)dm. \quad (8)$$

Multiplying and dividing (6) by $(1-F(n))$ and with $u = x - y^{1+\frac{1}{\varepsilon}}/(1 + 1/\varepsilon)$, we obtain the formula (17) in the text.

The marginal tax-rate formula is:

$$\frac{t}{1-t} = \underbrace{[1+\zeta]}_{A_n} \underbrace{\left[\frac{[1-F(n)]}{nf(n)}\right]}_{B_n} \underbrace{\left[\frac{\int_n^{\infty}[1-\phi]f(n')dn'}{(1-F(n))}\right]}_{C_n} \tag{9}$$

where a welfare weight for unit change in income is simply:

$$\phi(n) = \frac{W'(u)}{\lambda} \tag{10}$$

where $\lambda = \int_0^{\infty} W'[u]f(n')dn'$. The Lagrange multiplier λ on the government budget constraint is equal to the population average of $W'[u]$. ($W'[u(n)]$ is decreasing in n (concave function)).

Interpretation: uniform transfer to all individuals leaves labour supply unchanged and just boosts consumption, and thus utility. Hence, λ is the average of the marginal social utilities. The interpretation is that a unit increment in n leads to an increase in social valuation of W'. But to get the value of this in terms of income requires normalization. One natural procedure is to normalize by the average of W' in the population. Put another way, ϕ(n) measures the social value of giving a unit of income to an individual with income n, relative to the social value of dividing it equally among all individuals. In the classical utilitarian case ϕ is constant for all n, then the marginal tax rates are uniformly zero.

Since C is the average of $[\lambda - W']$ from n to the top of the n-distribution, C(n) is increasing in n. Formally,

$$\begin{aligned} C'(n) &= \frac{-[1-F(n)](\lambda - W')f(n) + \lambda[1-F(n)]C(n)f(n)}{\lambda[1-F(n)]^2} \\ &= [\lambda C(n) - (\lambda - W')]\frac{f(n)}{\lambda[1-F(n)]} > 0 \end{aligned} \tag{11}$$

where the sign follows from the fact that $W'[u]$ is decreasing in n. This implies that $\lambda C(n) > \lambda - W'$.

Poverty radicalism and marginal tax rates

$$n^2 f(n)\frac{1+V_y/n}{V_y + yV_{yy}} = \int_0^{n^*}((W'/\lambda) - 1)f(n)dn$$

$$\left(1+\frac{V_y(y)}{n}\right) = -\frac{V_y(y)}{ne}\frac{F(n)}{nf(n)}\left[\frac{W'}{\lambda}-1\right] \qquad n \leq n^*$$

where $e = (1 + yV_{yy}/V_y)$

$$t(n) = (1-t(n))\frac{F(n)}{enf(n)}\left[\frac{W'}{\lambda}-1\right] \qquad n \leq n^*$$

$$\frac{t(n)}{1-t(n)} = \frac{F(n)}{enf(n)}\left[\frac{W'}{\lambda}-1\right] \qquad n \leq n^*$$

$$t(n) = \frac{\frac{W'}{\lambda}-1}{\frac{W'}{\lambda}-1+\frac{enf(n)}{F(n)}} \qquad n \leq n^*$$

APPENDIX 4.3 THE TAXABLE INCOME ELASTICITY AT THE TOP

Using the Finnish data Riihelä et al (2013) estimate the elasticity of taxable income around a tax reform episode taking place between pre-reform year and post-reform year as follows:

$$\varepsilon = \frac{(\log S_1 - \log S_0)}{\log(1-t_1) - \log(1-t_0)} \tag{1}$$

where S_1 is the top 1 per cent income share after reform and S_0 before reform, t_0 is the marginal tax rate of the top 1 per cent before reform and t_1 is the marginal rate after reform. t is the net-of-tax rate (1-MTR). Absent tax changes S_0=S_1.

Applying this simple method around the 1989/90 tax reform by comparing 1989 and 1991 generates an elasticity of 0.13 for the top 1 per cent (Table A4.3.1, column 2).[34] Column 3 in Table A4.3.1 shows the elasticities for the next 4 per cent. Comparing 1992 and 1995 around the tax reform 1993 gives a much larger elasticity of 0.69 for the top 1 per cent. It shows that the elasticity estimates obtained in this way are sensitive to a specific reform.

They also estimate the elasticity using the full time-series evidence and estimate the elasticity e with a log-form regression specification of the form:

$$\log(\text{Top Income Share}) = \alpha + \text{e} \log(1-\text{t}) + \text{u}. \tag{2}$$

Such a regression without time trend yields a very high estimate of the elasticity of 0.65 for the top *1 per cent.* For the next 4 per cent the estimated elasticity is rather small 0.06. It is quite possible that inequality has also changed for some reason not related to taxation. To take into account these other considerations we could add some controls.

[34] The elasticity estimates in Pirttilä and Selin (2011) for the mean income fall in the range 0.2–0.4.

Table A4.3.1 Elasticity estimates using top income shares time-series and tax reforms (source: Riihelä et al, 2013)

	Top 1 per cent DD using the next 4% as control (1)	Top 1% Simple difference (2)	Top 95–99% Simple difference (3)
The tax reform episodes			
1989 vs. 1991 (Tax reform 1989/90)	0.32	0.13	0.01
1992 vs. 1995 (Tax reform 1993)	0.49	0.69	

This is not an easy task. We added time trends to (2). A combination of linear, square, and cube time trends did not improve the model (see Riihelä et al 2013). As pointed out by Saez et al (2012), the problem with time-trend specification is that we do not know what time trend specifications are necessary for non-tax related changes.[35]

Difference-in-differences estimates are presented in column (1) of Table 4.1. For that it is assumed, absent the tax change, the top 1 per cent share would have increased as much as the next 4 per cent.[36] These estimates are rather high for the full time-series regression and do not change with different time trends.

However, there is a great deal of uncertainty around these numbers. The elasticity is estimated using changes to top incomes that happened during the 1990s, a period when the top rate of income tax was falling and when income inequality was increasing. This approach may then confuse responses to the policy with any underlying factor (e.g. income-shifting[37]) increasing inequality.[38] Hence it is clear that our elasticity estimates are too high. This is especially true for the DD full time-series regression. Namely, income-shifting was possible in practice for the top 1 per cent taxpayers. Finally, we should also bear in mind that the taxable income elasticity is not derived from immutable preferences, but is affected by the structure of the tax system (see Kopczuk and Slemrod, 2002).

Kleven and Schultz (2014) use the full population of tax returns in Denmark since 1980 (large sample size, panel structure, many demographic variables, stable inequality). There are a number of reforms changing tax rates differentially across three income

[35] See also Piketty, Saez, and Stantcheva (2014).

[36] $\varepsilon = \frac{\log(S_1/S_1^k)-\log(S_0/S_0^k)}{\log[(1-t_1)/(1-t_1^k)]-\log[(1-t_0)/(1-t_0^k)]}$, where t^k and S^k are the marginal tax rate and the income share for the control group, top 95–99 percentiles. And a log-form regression specification of the form:

$$\log(S_1/S_1^k) - \log(S_0/S_0^k) = a + e\log[(1-t_1)/(1-t_1^k)] - \log[(1-t_0)/(1-t_0^k)] + u$$

[37] Figure 4.2 provides indirect evidence on income-shifting within the top 1%.

[38] By utilizing Norwegian micro-data on individuals, firms, and firms' owners in the period 1993–2003, Thoresen and Alstadsæter (2010) find that the interaction between business characteristics and features of the dual income tax system motivate organizational shifts that result in substantial income gains for the owners.

brackets and across tax bases (capital income taxed separately from labour income). They define treatment and control group in the year 1986 (pre-reform) and follow the same group in years before and years after the reform (panel analysis). Their key findings are: (a) small labour income elasticity (0.1) and (b) greater capital income elasticities (0.2–0.3).

APPENDIX 4.4 ADDITIVE PREFERENCES

For simplicity we assume that the utility function is additive:

$$u = U(x) + V(1 - y) \tag{1}$$

defined over consumption x and hours worked y, with $U_x > 0$ and $V_y < 0$ (subscripts indicating partial derivatives). Individuals differ only in the pre-tax wage n they can earn. Additive preferences differentiating of the Lagrangean (16) in appendix 2.3.1 with respect to u and y give the first-order conditions

$$L_u = [W' - h_u \lambda] f(n) - \mu'(n) = 0 \tag{2}$$

$$L_y = \lambda(n - h_y) f(n) - \mu(n)(V_y + yV_{yy}) = 0 \tag{3}$$

(2) satisfies the transversality conditions

$$\frac{\partial L}{\partial u(0)} = \mu(0) = 0; \frac{\partial L}{\partial u(\infty)} = \mu(\infty) = 0$$

Integrating (2),

$$\mu(n) = \int_n^\infty \left[\frac{\lambda}{U_x} - W'\right] f(n')dn'. \tag{4}$$

This latter satisfies the transversality conditions $\mu(0)=\mu(\infty)=0$

[Integrating (2), $\int_n^\infty \frac{d\mu}{dn} dn = \mu(\infty) - \mu(n)$].

The transversality conditions and (3) imply

$$\mu(n) > 0, \text{ for } n \in (0, \infty).$$

Using (4), we obtain from (3) the following condition for the optimal relative marginal tax rate *t(z)*; [Note: $\frac{t}{1-t} = \frac{1}{1-t} - 1 = \frac{U_x n}{V_Y} - 1$]

$$\frac{t}{1 - t} = \left(1 + \frac{yV_{yy}}{V_y}\right) \frac{U_x}{\lambda n f(n)} \int_n^\infty \left[\frac{\lambda}{U_x} - W'\right] f(n')dn'. \tag{5}$$

Differentiating the FOC of the individual maximization, $U_x n(1-t)+V_y=0$, with respect to net wage, labour supply, and virtual income, b, we have, after some manipulation, elasticity formulas: $E^u=\frac{(V_y/y)-(V_y/U_x)^2U_{xx}}{V_{yy}+(V_y/U_x)^2U_{xx}}$, (income effect parameter) $\xi=\frac{-(V_y/U_x)^2U_{xx}}{V_{yy}+(V_y/U_x)^2U_{xx}}$, and from the Slutsky equation $E^c=E^u-\xi$, then $E^c=\frac{(V_y/y)}{V_{yy}+(V_y/U_x)^2U_{xx}}$. Using formulas for E^{u} (=uncompensated wage elasticity) and E^{c} (=compensated wage elasticity), we have $(1+\frac{yV_{yy}}{V_y})=(1+E^u)/E^c$.

Multiplying and dividing (5) by $(1-F(n))$ we can write the formula (27 in the text) for marginal rates:

$$\frac{t}{1-t}=\underbrace{\left[\frac{1+E^u}{E^c}\right]}_{A_n}\underbrace{\left[\frac{[1-F(n)]}{nf(n)}\right]}_{B_n}\underbrace{\left[\frac{U_x\int_n^\infty(1-\frac{W'U_x^{(n')}}{\lambda})(1/U_x^{n'})f(n')dn'}{1-F(n)}\right]}_{C_n} \qquad (6)$$

The term C_n reflects income effects and incorporates distributional concerns. It measures the social welfare gain from slightly increasing the marginal tax rate at n and distributing as a poll subsidy to those below n the revenue raised from the consequent increase in average tax rates above n. From the transversality conditions we can deduce that $\mu(n)$ increases with n for low n (their social utility of income, $W'U_x$, exceeds the marginal social cost of public funds, λ) and decreases with n for high n. The turning point depends on λ.[39] The lower λ is, the higher is the n at which the turning point occurs. Thus as the revenue requirement falls, and hence λ falls, the range over which $\mu(n)$ increases stretches further. It can be shown that $W'U_x$ is decreasing in n* (n* is the skill level at which $W'(u(n^*))U_x(x(n^*),y(n^*))=\lambda$) so long as $W(u)$ is concave and leisure is normal. $W'(u(n^*))u_x(x,y)$ is decreasing in n*

Proof: We prove this in case of a general utility function u=u(x,y).
Differentiating $W'(u(n^*))u_x(x,y)$ we have

$$W''u_xu'+W'(u_{xx}x'+u_{xy}y')\ (*)$$

So long as W is concave, the first term of (*) is negative. Hence it suffices to show that $\Xi=(u_{xx}x'+u_{xy}y')<0$

Since $x(n)=ny(n)-T(ny(n))$, we have

[39] Note λ is itself a function of the overall distribution, since from (4) $\lambda=1/(\int_0^\infty(1/U_x)f(p)dp)$ (the social welfare function is utilitarian, i.e. W'=1).

$$x' = (1-t)(ny' + y)$$

so that $\Xi = (u_{xx}(1-t)y + (u_{xx}(1-t)n + u_{xy})y')$.

Using the first-order conditions of individual's utility maximization, we have

$$\Xi = (u_{xx}(1-t)y - (\frac{u_y}{u_x})(u_{xx} - u_{xy}(\frac{u_x}{u_y}))y') \quad .$$

Define leisure $s = 1-y$ and $\varsigma(x,s) = u(x, 1-s)$. So $\varsigma_s = -u_y$ and $\varsigma_{sx} = -u_{yx}$.

Now

$$\Xi = (u_{xx}(1-t)y - (\frac{\varsigma_l}{\varsigma_x})(\varsigma_{xx} - \varsigma_{xs}(\frac{\varsigma_x}{\varsigma_s}))y') < 0$$

if leisure is normal. Above we assume that y>0. For those n for which $y(n)$=0, $W'u_x$ is constant.

Since $\mu(n)$ affects the marginal tax rate positively, this means that the range over which the latter increases also stretches further—at least for this reason. In this sense, therefore, more tax revenue leads to a less progressive tax structure. The intuition, put crudely, is that the lower the revenue requirement is, the more the government can afford to support the poor with a generous poll subsidy, recouping at least part of this by a pattern of rising marginal tax rates on the better-off (see Table 4.2).

As should be obvious from the above discussion, the exact pattern this term in (6) follows as n rises depends on the social welfare function and the shape of the wage distribution. So the shape of the wage distribution is also important here. Moreover, it is obvious in the integral term in (6) that the functional form of U_x has an important role in determining the shape of the schedule.

Maximin

We can distinguish two cases:
(i) $\underline{n} \leq n_o$ and (ii) $\underline{n} > n_o$ the whole population is at work in the optimal solution.

In the case (i)

$$L = u(\underline{n}) + \int_{\underline{n}}^{\infty} \lambda(ny - x))f(n) - \lambda F(n_o)x(n_o) - \mu' u - \mu\Psi)dn + \mu(\infty)u(\infty) - \mu(\underline{n})u(\underline{n})$$

$$L_u = -\lambda h_u f(n) - \mu'(n) = 0$$

$$L_{u(no)} = 1 - \lambda h_u F(n_o) - \mu'(n) = 0$$

$Ly = 0$ implies

$$\frac{t_i}{1-t_i} = \underbrace{\left[\frac{1+E_i{}^u}{E_i{}^c}\right]}_{A_n} \underbrace{\left[\frac{1-F_i(n)}{n_i f_i(n)}\right]}_{B_n} \underbrace{\left[\frac{\int_n^\infty (\lambda/U_x^i) f_i(n')dn'}{1-F_i(n)}\right]}_{C_n}$$

at n=n$_o$;

$$(1+\frac{u_y^0(x_0,0)}{n_0 u_x^0(x_0,0)}) = -\frac{u_y^0(x_0,0)}{n_0 u_x^0(x_0,0)} \frac{\lambda F(n_0)}{n_0 f(n_0)}$$

$$t(n_0) = \frac{1}{1+\frac{\lambda F(n_0)}{n_0 f(n_0)}}$$

Optimal marginal tax rates at the bottom

Utilitarian case

From (4) and (5) we can write at n$_o$.

$$\lambda n_o f(n_o)\left(1+\frac{V_y^0(x_0,0)}{n_0 u_x^0(x_0,0)}\right) = \frac{\mu(n_o) V_y^0(x_0,0)}{n_o}$$

$$\left(1+\frac{V_y^0(x_0,0)}{n_0 u_x^0}\right) = \Psi_y(u_0,0)\frac{F(n_0)}{n_0^2 f(n_0)}\left[\frac{W'}{\lambda} - \frac{1}{u_x(x_0,0)}\right]$$

where $\Psi_y = -(V_y(n_0) + y(n_0)V_{yy}(n_0))$.

And further

$$\left(1+\frac{V_y^0(x_0,0)}{n_0 u_x^0(x_0,0)}\right) = -\frac{V_y^0(x_0,0)}{n_0 u_x^0(x_0,0)} \frac{F(n_0)}{n_0 f(n_0)}\left[\frac{W' u_x(x_0,0)}{\lambda} - 1\right]$$

and noting at $n = n_O$, y=0 and $1+\frac{V_y}{n_0 u_x} = t(n_0)$, then we have

$$t(n_0) = (1-t(n_0))\frac{F(n_0)}{n_0 f(n_0)}\left[\frac{W' u_x(x_0,0)}{\lambda} - 1\right] \text{ or}$$

$$t(n_0) = \frac{\frac{W' u_x(x_0,0)}{\lambda} - 1}{\frac{W' u_x(x_0,0)}{\lambda} - 1 + \frac{n_0 f(n_0)}{F(n_0)}}$$

Maximin case:

$$\left(1+\frac{V_y^0(x_0,0)}{n_0u_x^0(x_0,0)}\right)=-\frac{V_y^0(x_0,0)}{n_0u_x^0(x_0,0)}\frac{\lambda F(n_0)}{n_0f(n_0)}\quad \text{or}$$

$$t(n_0)=\frac{1}{1+\frac{\lambda F(n_0)}{n_0f(n_0)}}.$$

APPENDIX 4.5 PARETO DISTRIBUTION, CHAMPERNOWNE DISTRIBUTION, AND AN ASYMPTOTIC SOLUTION OF THE OPTIMAL TAX PROBLEM

There are a number of mathematical distribution functions extensively used in describing wage, income, and wealth distributions, such as lognormal, Pareto, and Gamma. Empirical evidence is not conclusive about the quality of each in fitting actual distributions. Specifically, Pareto distributions are found to fit reasonably well at the upper tail of distributions, but the fit over the whole range of income turns out to be quite poor. As for other functions such as lognormal and Gamma, while providing a good fit over a large part of the income range, they differ markedly at the upper tail. The explanation for this different performance seems to be that these functions are defined so as to reach a maximum in the interior of the interval definition, thereby giving a better fit over the values around the mode. These functions have the drawback, however, that their elasticity $\frac{nf'}{f}$ increases unboundedly after the mode has been attained, thus contradicting the large evidence of a constant elasticity at the upper tail, which is precisely what characterizes Pareto distribution. To avoid this, we adopt Champernowne distribution. Here we use the two-parameter version of Champernowne distribution also known as Fisk distribution.[40] The parameter m is the median value and θ is a constant corresponding to Pareto's constant for high incomes. Champernowne distribution approaches asymptotically a form of Pareto distribution for large values of n, but it also has an interior maximum. As the lognormal, Champernowne distribution exhibits the following features: asymmetry, a left humpback, and a long right-hand tail. It has a thicker upper tail than in the lognormal case.

Pareto distribution

Statistical study of personal income distributions originated with Pareto's formulation of income distribution in his famous *Cours d'economie politique* (1897). Pareto was well

[40] See Champernowne and Cowell (1999).

aware of the imperfections of statistical data; however, he succeeded in showing that there is a relation between the number of taxpayers with personal income greater or equal to z, N_z and the value of the income z given by a downward sloping income. It has long been well known that the original Pareto function describes only a portion of the reported income distribution. This was recognized by Pareto, but later this point was under-emphasized. Pareto (1897) specified $\log N_Z = A - \alpha \log z$ or $N_Z = e^{\gamma} z^{-\alpha}$. Normalizing by the number of income receivers, we have $\frac{N_z}{N} = 1 - H(z) = \left(\frac{z}{z_0}\right)^{-\alpha}$ where F is cumulative distribution function, α is a Pareto or a shape parameter (also measuring the thickness of the upper tail), and z_0 is a scale parameter. The density is

$$h(z) = \frac{\alpha z_0^{\alpha}}{z^{1+\alpha}}, z \geq z_0 > 0 \qquad .$$

Pareto density is always decreasing while empirical distributions are in general unimodal (first increasing and then decreasing). Therefore, Pareto distributions are useful to approximate empirical distribution above the mode.

There is an interesting link between the hazard rate and the excess mean function. Define the excess mean function

$$\varsigma(z) = E(\tilde{z} - z : \tilde{z} > z) = \frac{\int_z^{\infty} (\mathrm{w} - z) dH(\mathrm{w})}{\int_z^{\infty} dH(\mathrm{w})}, z \geq 0.$$

Integrating by parts, we can write in the form

$$\varsigma(z) = \frac{1}{1 - H} \int_z^{\infty} (1 - H(\mathrm{w})) dw, \; z_0 \geq z.$$

The mean excess function arises in connection with van der Wijk's (1939) law. It says the average income of everybody above a certain income level z is proportional to z itself. Formally,

$$\frac{\int_z^{\infty} wh(\mathrm{w}) dw}{\int_z^{\infty} h(\mathrm{w}) dw} = \eta z \text{ for some } \eta > 0.$$

The hazard rate of a Pareto distribution is given by

$$\rho(z) = \frac{\alpha}{z}, \; z > z_0.$$

For the mean excess function, a straightforward calculation gives

$$\varsigma(z^*) = \frac{z}{\alpha - 1}, \quad z > z_0.$$

Hence, Pareto distribution obeys van der Wijk's law.

In other words, $\rho(z)\varsigma(z) = \frac{\alpha}{\alpha-1}$ for all z.

We can also express Pareto distribution in the terms of elasticity with respect to z as follows:

$$\rho(z) = \frac{zh(z)}{(1 - H(z))} = -\alpha \text{ or } \frac{zh'}{h} = -(1 + \alpha).$$

It says that if income z increases by 1 per cent, the portion of income-receiving units having income greater than or equal to z declines by α per cent. The vast amount of empirical work done so far confirms that the Pareto distribution fits rather well toward the upper tail of the income distribution. This empirical evidence led Mandelbrot (1960) to introduce a weak Pareto law. Mandelbrot referred to relation $\frac{1-H(z)}{z^{-\alpha}} = 1$ for all z as the strong Pareto law. *H(z)* follows an exact Pareto distribution. If this property is to be retained for top incomes, an appropriate condition appears to be $\lim_{z\to\infty} \frac{1-H(z)}{z^{-\alpha}} = 1$. This is Mandelbrot's weak Pareto law.

Estimation of the Pareto coefficient

Figure A4.5.1 depicts the ratio $z_m/(z_m - z^*)$, with z^* ranging from zero to €300,000 annual incomes in 2000, 2005, and 2010. The ratios in different years show that top tail of the distribution is very well approximated by a Pareto distribution. The top 1 per cent threshold z^* was €99,398 and z_m was €175,680 in 2010.

Another method: assuming that *F(Z)* within the top group is such that $1-F$ is proportional to $z^{-\alpha}$, then within-group share of the top 1 per cent within the top 10

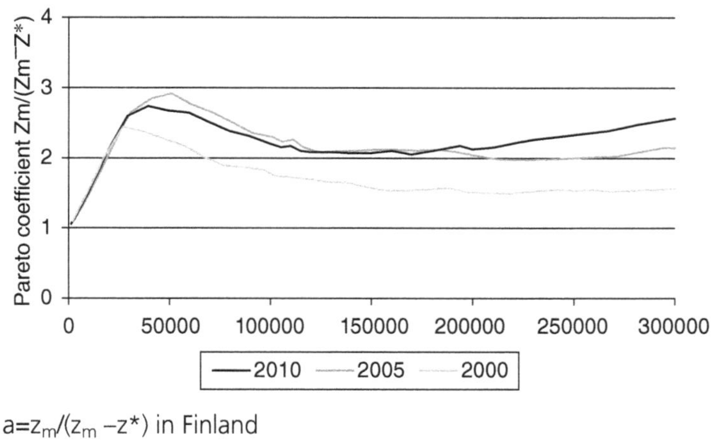

Figure A4.5.1 $a = z_m/(z_m - z^*)$ in Finland

Source: Riihelä et al (2013).

per cent, denoted by $\frac{S_1}{S_{10}}$, is given by $(0.1)^{(\alpha-1/\alpha)}$. The relation can be expressed: $\alpha = \frac{1}{1+\log_{10}(S_1/S_{10})}$

The Champernowne distribution

$$f(n) = \theta\left(\frac{m^\theta n^{\theta-1}}{(m^\theta + n^\theta)^2}\right)$$

in which θ is a shape parameter and μ is a scale parameter. The cumulative distribution function is

$$F(n) = 1 - \frac{m^\theta}{(m^\theta + n^\theta)}$$

For the inverse hazard rate

$$\lim_{n\to\infty}\frac{1-F(n)}{nf(n)} = \lim_{n\to\infty}\frac{m^\theta + n^\theta}{\theta n^\theta} \to \frac{1}{\theta}.$$

and in the elasticity form

$$\frac{nf'}{f} = \frac{\theta\left(\frac{m^\theta}{n^\theta} - 1\right)}{\left(\frac{m^\theta}{n^\theta} + 1\right)} - 1$$

and for later use

$$\left(2 + \frac{nf'}{f}\right) = 1 - \frac{\theta\left(1 - \left(\frac{m}{n}\right)^\theta\right)}{\left(1 + \left(\frac{m}{n}\right)^\theta\right)}.$$

An asymptotic solution of optimal tax problem

Now we consider a case with $u = U(x) + V(1-y)$. Define

$$v = \frac{1 + V_y/nU_x}{V_y + yV_{yy}}, \quad (1)$$

and rewrite $L_y = \lambda(n - h_y)f(n) - \mu(n)(V_y + yV_{yy}) = 0$

$$n^2 fv = \int_n^\infty ((1/U_x) - W'/\lambda)f(n)dn \quad (2)$$

Differentiating (2) with respect to n, we have

$$\frac{dv}{dn} = -\frac{v}{n}(2 + \frac{nf'}{f}) + \frac{1}{n^2}(\frac{W'}{\lambda} - \frac{1}{U_x}) \tag{3}$$

and the incentive-compatibility constraint

$$\frac{du}{dn} = -\frac{yV_y}{n} \tag{4}$$

Two differential equations in u and v provide the solution to the optimal income tax problem, together with the condition (2) and at $n=n_o$[41];

$$n_o{}^2 f(n_o)v_o = \int_0^{n_0} (1/U_x - W'/\lambda)f(n)dn \tag{5}$$

and the transversality condition $\mu(\infty)=0$ and (2) require that

$$\lambda n^2 fv \to 0(n \to \infty.) \tag{6}$$

Condition (6) guarantees an accurate value for n_o.
We analyse asymptotic marginal tax rates in the following case:
The utility function is $u = \log x + \log(1-y)$. We denote $s=1-y$ and put $w = \log n$. Now we can write:

$$v = s(s - \frac{x}{n}). \tag{7}$$

For any social welfare function W with a property that $\lim_{u\to\infty} W'(u) = 0$ we can simplify (3),[42] and if f(n) is the Champernowne distribution, then (3) becomes

$$\frac{dv}{dt} = -v(1 - \frac{\theta\left(1 - \left(\frac{m}{n}\right)^{\theta}\right)}{\left(1 + \left(\frac{m}{n}\right)^{\theta}\right)}) - s(1 - \frac{v}{s^2}). \tag{8}$$

Since

$$\lim_{n\to\infty} \frac{nf'}{f} = -(1 + \theta) \tag{9}$$

[41] n_o, largest n for which $y(n)=0$, may be in some cases rather large. In the interval $[0, n_o]$, $y=0$, and $x=x_0$ and then $u=U(x_o)-V(0)$ (*). (*) and (13) are needed for starting values in numerical solutions of (11) and (3) conditional on a trial value for n_o.

[42] Equivalently we have a maximin case.

we can rewrite

$$\frac{dv}{dw} = v(\theta - 1) - s(1 - \frac{v}{s^2}). \tag{10}$$

Hence from (4) and noting that $u = \log n + \log(s - \frac{v}{s}) + \log s$,
we have:

$$\frac{du}{dw} = \frac{du}{dn}\frac{dn}{dw} = 1 - \frac{1}{s}\frac{ds}{dw} + \frac{[(1 + v/s^2)\frac{ds}{dw} - \frac{1}{s}\frac{dv}{dw}]}{(s - v/s)} = \frac{1-s}{s} \tag{11}$$

Using (11), we can write:

$$\frac{ds}{dw} = \frac{v(1+\theta) - 2s^2}{2s} \tag{12}$$

Denote $\frac{v}{s^2} = t$, i.e the marginal tax rate.
It follows that

$$\frac{ds}{dw} = \frac{s}{2}\Big(t(1+\theta) - 2\Big) \tag{13}$$

Differentiating $t = \frac{v}{s^2}$ with respect to w and substituting $\frac{dv}{dw}$ from (10), we obtain

$$\frac{dt}{dw} = t\theta - t - \frac{1}{s}(1 - t) - 2t\frac{ds}{dw}\frac{1}{s} \tag{14}$$

Substituting (12) to (14) we have

$$\frac{dt}{dw} = (1 - t)\left[t(1+\theta) - \frac{1}{s}\right] \tag{15}$$

The solution to equation (13) and (15) is shown in Figure A4.5.2. The equations are autonomous in the sense that the evolution of t and s or (1−y) is independent of n_o.

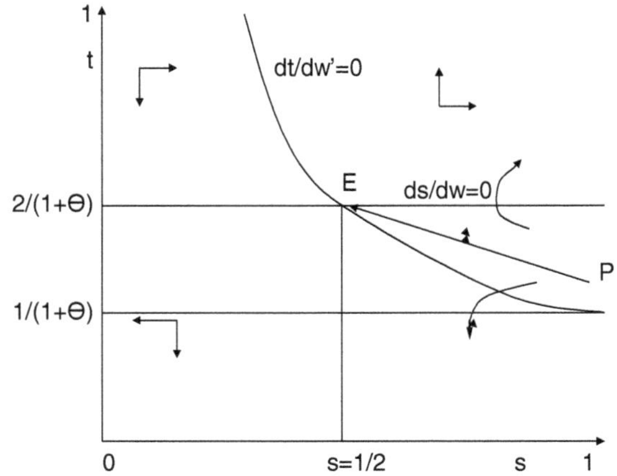

Figure A4.5.2 The solution of (14) and (15)

Hence the solution of t is determined solely from (13) and (15). For $\frac{dt}{dw} = 0$, it has to be $t = \frac{1}{(1+\theta)s}$ and for $\frac{ds}{dw} = 0$ in turn $t = \frac{2}{1+\theta}$.

Hence we have a complete description of the solution in the case of Champernowne distribution. When the path to the singular solution starts from s=1, this implies that the marginal tax rates increase monotonically from $t = \frac{1}{(1+\theta)}$ to $t = \frac{2}{1+\theta}$.

5 The shape of optimal income tax schedule: numerical simulations with income effects

The special cases considered in Chapter 4 yield insights, but within the framework of the assumptions made. How robust are these insights? What happens when we move away from quasi-linearity? On the basis of the first-order conditions it is possible to say relatively little about the general shape of the tax schedule. The optimal marginal tax rates in more general cases become considerably more difficult to interpret, because labour supply can vary with skill and because of income effects. This section presents optimal tax schedules with alternative assumptions. Therefore, numerical calculations have proved useful in generating useful results (appendix 5.4.1 gives details of the computational procedure and the FORTRAN program used). Moreover, it can be said that the very basic nature of income tax/transfer problems requires quantitative results. Mere general principles are not of much value.

What did emerge from numerical calculations in Mirrlees's (1971) pioneering contribution was that marginal tax rates are more or less constant. The suggested optimality of a constant marginal tax rate schedule was questioned by Atkinson (1972) and Tuomala (1984), who argued that the result was special to the specific functional forms used by Mirrlees (1971). For example, Atkinson (1972) showed that using a maximin objective function, as opposed to the Mirrlees utilitarian formulation, led to considerable non-linearity in the pattern of marginal tax rates. Tuomala (1984) showed that significant non-linearity occurred when a different preference structure was chosen than that used in Mirrlees (1971) (Cobb–Douglas or log–log formulation). In the numerical calculations that followed Mirrlees (1971), marginal tax rates decrease with income for the vast majority of the population. This picture is at odds with observed patterns in most advanced countries. There are, however, some counter-examples in the optimal income tax literature.[1,2] Kanbur and Tuomala (1994) show that increases in inherent inequality

[1] Increasing marginal rates may be optimal under non-standard assumptions, e.g when people care about relative levels of consumption (Tuomala 1990 and Chapter 7), when there is significant wage uncertainty (Tuomala 1990, Low and Maldoom 2004) (see Chapter 11 for more on this), and when earnings are allowed to be less than perfectly correlated with productivity (Bevan 2002).

[2] Boadway et al (2000) provide a full characterization of the solution when preferences are quasi-linear in leisure.

can alter the qualitative pattern of optimal marginal tax rates. The optimal graduation can indeed be such that marginal tax rates increase for the majority of the population, but there continues to exist a significant income range at the top where marginal tax rates decline. Diamond (1998) assumes a Pareto distribution of skills rather than the lognormal distribution that Mirrlees (1971) and others have assumed. Using quasi-linear preferences, he finds rising marginal tax rates on those above the modal skill level to be optimal.[3] Saez (2001), in a more general treatment, showed that the optimal income tax schedule would be U-shaped. Like Diamond (1998), Saez (2001) assumes that the elasticity of labour supply is constant at all productivity levels. He simulates with US data a marginal tax rate schedule that slopes upwards around a fairly high income level.

There are four key elements in the optimal non-linear income tax model which we have to specify to solve it numerically. Next we consider each of them in turn.

5.1 **Distribution**

Following Mirrlees (1971), most work on optimal non-linear and linear income taxation used the lognormal distribution[4] to describe the distribution of productivities (e.g. Atkinson 1972; Stern 1976; Tuomala 1984, 1990; Kanbur and Tuomala 1994; Immonen, Kanbur, Keen, and Tuomala 1998; Creedy 2001, 2009; Mankiw et al 2009, etc.). As is well known, the lognormal distribution fits reasonably well over a large part of income range but diverges markedly at both tails. The Pareto distribution in turn fits well at the upper tail. However, our concerns about the lognormal distribution as an adequate descriptor for observed distributions, and some problematic features of optimal non-linear income tax schedules with the lognormal distribution, have led us to look for an alternative.

Champernowne (1952) introduced a distribution which now carries his name (see appendix 4.5). In fact, the distribution had been introduced much earlier by Champernowne (1937), but that work is even less well known. In Champernowne (1952) and Champernowne (1953) it was argued that this distribution fitted observed distributions well, and a process generating the distribution was also proposed. However, it is striking how little the Champernowne distribution is used today in income distribution analysis, especially compared to the lognormal distribution. This imbalance is remarkable, especially given the well-known failure of the lognormal distribution to describe income distributions in their upper tail and the capacity of the Champernowne distribution to do just that, while at the same time doing equally well, for example, in capturing unimodality of the income density function. The Champernowne distribution

[3] See also Atkinson (1990, 1995).

[4] $ln(n; m, \sigma^2)$ with support $[0,\infty)$ with parameters m and σ (see Aitchison and Brown 1957). The first parameter m is log of the median and the second parameter is the variance of log wage. The latter is itself an inequality measure.

is unimodal and approximates a Pareto distribution in the upper tail, allowing us to represent key features of observed income distributions.

What accounts for this imbalance of treatment in the income distribution literature between the Champernowne distribution and the lognormal distribution? One reason might be the appeal of the underlying Gibrat process which leads to a lognormal distribution, but this needs to be compared closely, then, to the Champernowne process to see which comes closest to reality. A second reason is undoubtedly the convenient properties of the lognormal distribution, for example the closed-form expressions that obtain for expectations of constant elasticity functions. These properties are well laid out in Aitchison and Brown (1957), and this tract on the lognormal distribution surely contributed to its high visibility and use in applied economics generally, including in income distribution analysis.

There is, however, a third reason. When James Mirrlees came to do his numerical calculations for the shape of optimal non-linear tax schedules in his classic Nobel prize-winning paper, Mirrlees (1971), he used the lognormal distribution. This distribution perhaps seemed a natural one for him to use, given that the lognormal distribution was by then already the functional form of choice for the graduation of income distributions. However, its use by Mirrlees (1971) effectively sealed its dominance as the optimal non-linear income taxation literature exploded, and virtually every paper on the topic in the coming decades used the lognormal distribution for numerical calculations.

Champernowne (1952) proposes a model in which individual incomes are assumed to follow a random walk in the logarithmic scale. Here we use the two-parameter version of the Champernowne distribution (known also as the Fisk distribution). This distribution approaches asymptotically a form of Pareto distribution for large values of wages, but it also has an interior maximum.

The probability density function and the cumulative distribution function of the Champernowne distribution are:

$$f(n) = \theta\left(\frac{m^{\theta}n^{\theta-1}}{(m^{\theta}+n^{\theta})^{2}}\right) \text{ and } F(n) = 1-\left(\frac{m^{\theta}}{(m^{\theta}+n^{\theta})}\right) \tag{1}$$

where θ is a shape parameter and m is a scale parameter. For the distribution ratio:

$$\lim_{n\to\infty}\frac{1-F(n)}{nf(n)} = \lim_{n\to\infty}\frac{m^{\theta}+n^{\theta}}{\theta n^{\theta}} \to \frac{1}{\theta}. \tag{2}$$

confirms that the Champernowne distribution approaches asymptotically a form of Pareto distribution for large values of wages.

Before presenting the results, it may be useful to review some features of the simulation methodology, in particular in comparison to the method in Saez (2001). A key question is how the distribution of n is chosen. Ideally we would like to use empirical earnings distributions in numerical simulations. This cannot apply directly, because the distribution of z is affected by income taxation. This means that when we change utility

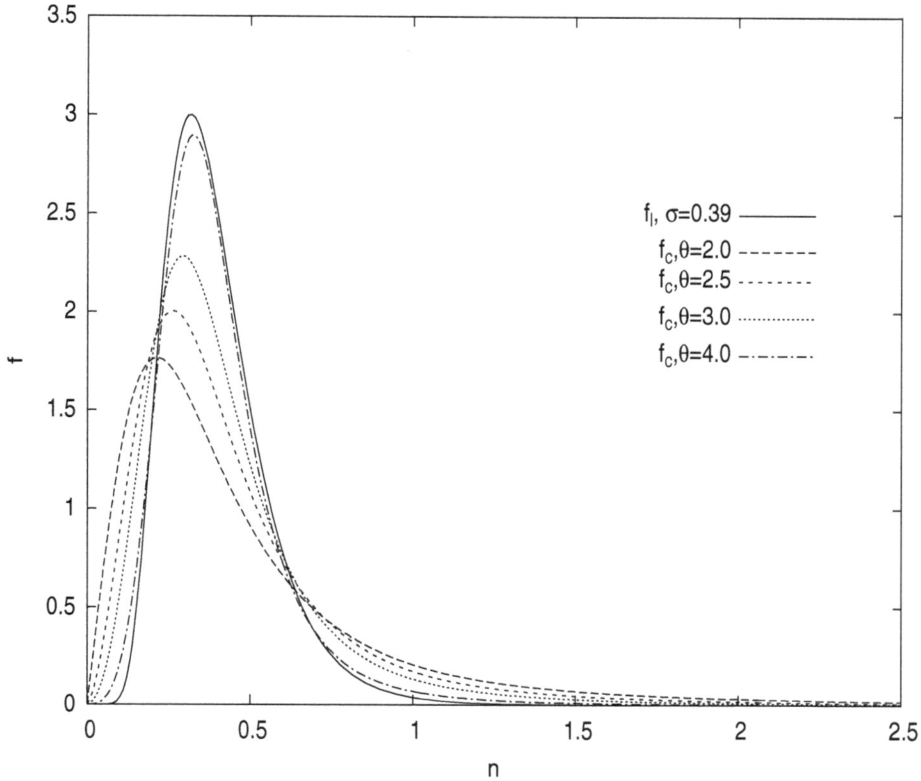

Figure 5.1a f_c = Champernowne distribution, f_l = lognormal distribution, $m = e^{-1}$

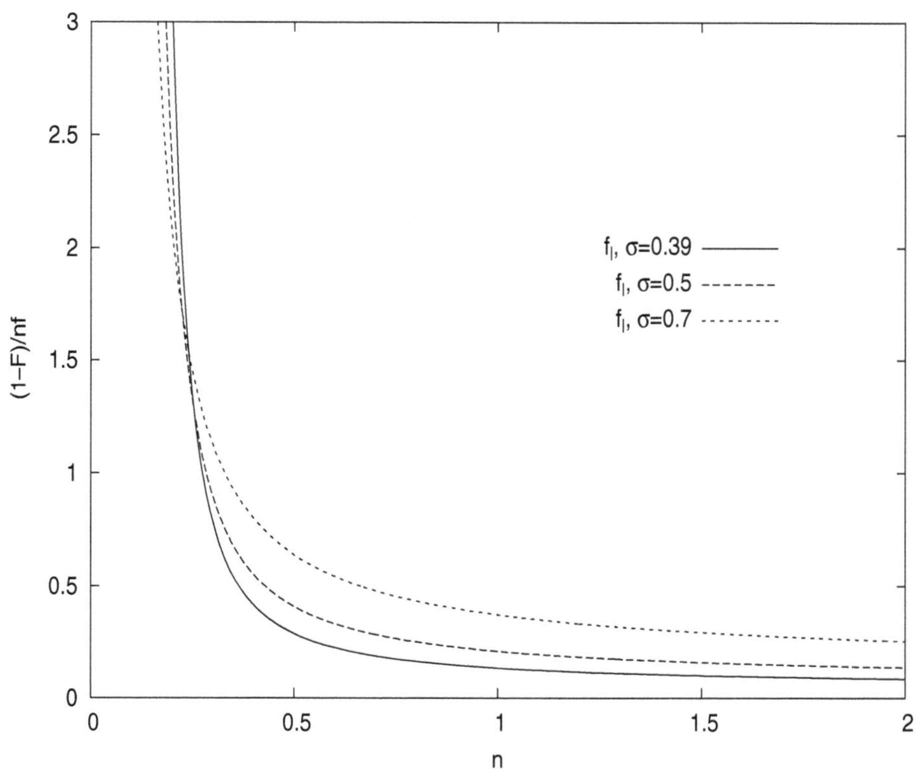

Figure 5.1b $(1-F)/nf$ f_l = lognormal distribution, $m = e^{-1}$

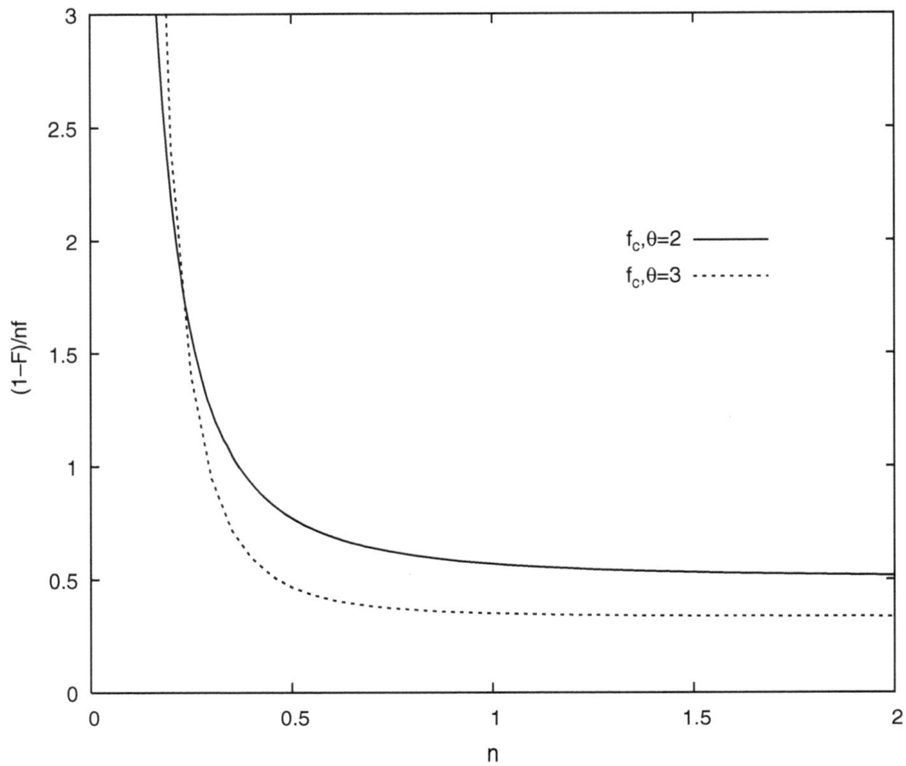

Figure 5.1c (1−F)/nf f_c = Champernowne distribution, m = e^{-1}

function or its parameters, we also change the distribution of n so that resulting distribution of z (absent the tax) remains the same. Otherwise, we get an effect through the changes in utility functions, but also through a change in the distribution of z. Inference of parameters from observed empirical earnings distributions is a long-standing issue in the optimal income taxation literature. A number of methods have been proposed, each with its own weaknesses. The Saez (2001) method is no exception. In Saez (2001), the skill distribution is 'backed out' from the empirical distribution of income. To calculate the optimal tax schedule, Saez makes additional assumptions about the model structure. He calibrates the exogenous ability distribution such that actual T(.) yields empirical income distribution and assumes that labour supply elasticity is constant (which implies a restricted form for the utility function). This assumption is contradicted by a growing body of evidence.[5,6] He further assumes a linear tax schedule in inferring

[5] Röed and Ström (2002) (table 1 and 2) offer a review of the evidence. They conclude that the limited evidence indicates that labour supply elasticities are declining with household income. Using Norwegian data, Aaberge and Colombino (2006) provide support for declining elasticities. High labour supply elasticities among low-wage workers are also confirmed by empirical evaluations of various in-work benefit schemes operating in the US, UK, and some other countries. By contrast, there is empirical evidence on the elasticity of taxable income that higher elasticities are found among high-income individuals. See e.g. Gruber and Saez (2002).

[6] The method of Kanbur and Tuomala (1994) is acknowledged by Saez (2001), footnote 4.

the skill distribution from the earnings distribution. This is contradicted by tax schedules the world over, and seems particularly inappropriate in optimal non-linear taxation. The strong assumptions required for structural identification of the model reduce the confidence of the optimal tax schedule calculations.[7] An alternative approach, one introduced in Kanbur and Tuomala (1994), is to accept the non-linearities that characterize income tax schedules, and furthermore to allow for utility functions which imply non-constant labour elasticities. We cannot now 'back out' the skill distribution, as in Saez (2001). Rather, we should select a skill distribution which, through the model, produces an earnings distribution that matches empirical earnings distributions. In other words, the income distribution inferred from the skill distribution matches the actual distribution. This is the method followed in this book.

Based on the Finnish income distribution data (cross section), Riihelä et al (2013) estimated, by using maximum likelihood methods, several two and three-parameter distributions with corresponding measures of goodness of fit (several of them plus the log-likelihood value for estimated model). Among two-parameter distributions, Champernowne is the best fitting for pre-tax income distribution in Finland (1990–2010).[8] The θ-parameter varies from 2.78 to 2.4. Over the period from the latter part of the 1990s to 2010, the θ-parameter was almost constant, at around 2.5. Hence $\theta = 2$ reflects a low range estimate (high inequality) and $\theta = 3$ in turn a high range estimate (low inequality). The Gini coefficients estimated by this distribution (Gini $= 1/\theta$) are quite close to those calculated from the data. Interestingly, the location parameter m in our notations (median) in the Champernowne distribution is quite close to that calculated from the data.

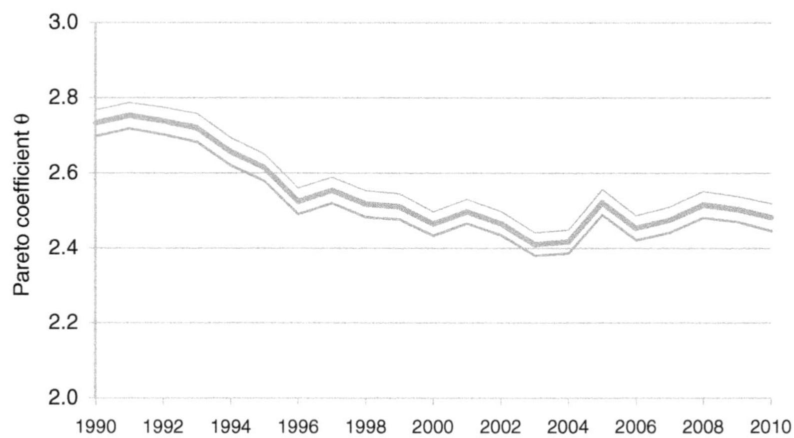

Figure 5.1d Shape or Pareto parameter θ (with confidence interval) in Finland 1990–2010: Champernowne-Fisk distribution (Riihelä et al 2013)

[7] It is very appropriate in calculating top marginal rates.

[8] See Kleiber and Kotz (2003) pp. 238–9 on empirical applications of the Champernowne–Fisk distribution.

5.2 Preferences

Labour supply responses to taxation are of central importance for income tax policy. If most of us work only for financial reward, this undoubtedly limits the possibilities of redistribution. It raises the question of necessity to provide incentives to work. What is meant by incentives to work? Many people may think that taxes have very little to do with the number of hours worked: in most jobs, the number of hours worked is fixed; furthermore, the number of hours worked in different jobs is a consequence of technological and institutional considerations, including unions and government regulation. There are labour supply responses along many dimensions. The incentive issue is not so much about hours worked but more about intensity of work. People may also be affected in their occupational choice (including education). From economic history we know that, in many countries, a continuing rise in the real wage rate over the twentieth century was associated with continuing reduction in annual hours worked. With the exception of Japan, there was a general downward trend in hours worked until the early 1980s; thereafter the trend stabilized in most of the nine OECD countries (see Tanninen and Tuomala 2009). At the beginning of the twenty-first century countries could be roughly grouped into two: in Australia, Canada, Japan, New Zealand, and the US, average annual hours of work are around 1,800 hours; in France, Germany, the Netherlands, and Sweden the average was less than 1,600 hours. Only Finland and the UK seemed to be somewhere in between.

The standard textbook model considers an individual who must allocate a unit of time (a day, a week, a month, a year) between paid work and the various non-paid activities that economists traditionally call leisure. In the standard model, labour supply arises from a balancing act between after-tax income and leisure. There are two forces at play: the income and substitution effects (Slutzky equation). Which way the combination works out depends upon preferences. With a higher wage and unchanged working hours, the individual can consume more and enjoy the same leisure. To the extent that leisure is a normal good—consumption increases when income increases, and vice versa—higher wages lead to higher consumption and leisure and less work. The substitution effect, on the other hand, makes leisure more expensive in terms of consumption forgone, and leads to less leisure and more work. The two effects operate in different directions and, in the case of a backward-sloping supply curve, the income effect dominates (see appendix 5.1).

We use in simulations the following special cases of the constant elasticity of substitution form:

$$u(x, y) = [x^{-a} + (1-y)^{-a}]^{-1/a} \tag{3}$$

where the elasticity of substitution between consumption and leisure, $\delta = 1/(1+a)$, has been used in numerical simulations:

Case u1:

$\delta = 1$ (log–log or Cobb–Douglas case)

$$u = \log x + \log(1-y) \tag{4}$$

and **case u2**:

$\delta = 0.5$ (a=1)

$$u = -\frac{1}{x} - \frac{1}{(1-y)}. \tag{5}$$

In the absence of taxation both in the case of $\delta = 1$ and $\delta = 0.5$, the labour supply function is backward-bending. From careful analysis of the econometric evidence then available, Stern (1976) derives the central estimate of $\delta = 0.408$. The relationship to the estimated coefficients is not straightforward, but some indication is given by the fact that a two-standard error range in the substitution effect would lead, by interpolating from Stern (1976, Table 2), to an interval of around 0.2–0.6 for δ. The resulting difference in the optimum (linear) tax rate in the utilitarian case is between 36 per cent and 18 per cent (interpolating from Stern 1976, Table 3a).

Other preferences yield more complex relationships between net wage and labour supply. A comprehensive review article by Stern (1986) describes many possibilities, discussing the quadratic specification and other alternatives. In fact, in the empirical labour supply studies, e.g. Keane and Moffitt (1998), preferences over working time and net income are given by a utility function that is quadratic in hours and net income.

We also solve numerically cases in which utility function is quadratic in consumption (quadratic approximation) with a bliss point;

case u12

$$u = (x-1) - a(x-1)^2 - (1-y)^{-1}; x \in (0,1) \tag{6}$$

As displayed in Figure 5.2, the utility of consumption in (6) is essentially less curved than that used in the previous simulations.

5.3 Social objectives

Based on its use of a social welfare function, the optimal tax approach is often accused of assuming a benevolent government. Is this criticism justified? Calculation of what a benevolent government should do is not the same as assuming that there is a benevolent government. Rather, we should ask what policies one would want to see a benevolent

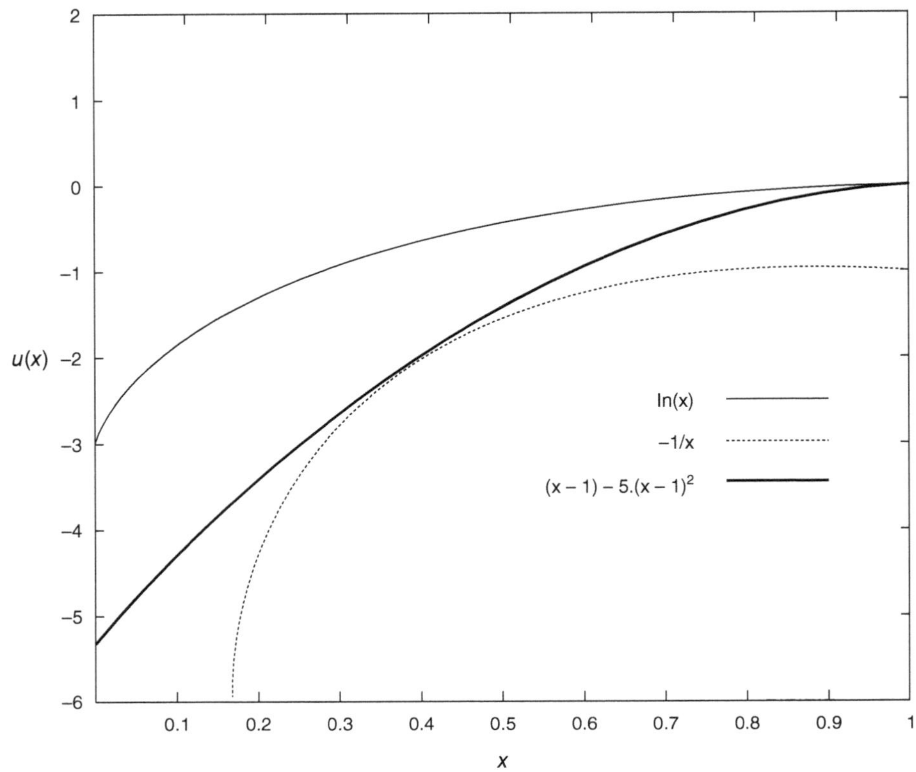

Figure 5.2 The utility of consumption

government follow. The answer to such a question can help inform a democratic debate about government policies. As Buchanan and Musgrave (1999, p. 35) wrote:

> Just as homo economicus or a competitive Walrasian system are useful fictions to model an ideal market, so it is helpful to visualize how a correctly functioning public sector would perform.... Unless 'correct' solutions are established to serve as standards, defects and failures of actual performance cannot even be identified.

The optimal tax literature mainly works with a social welfare function in which individual utility depends on both consumption and the disutility of labour. Another approach is to focus on income distribution, using a social income evaluation function as developed by Atkinson (1970) or income poverty minimization as in Kanbur et al (1994a). This approach has been criticized for giving too much weight to encouraging work, particularly by low earners. The Bergson–Samuelson social welfare function, expressing social welfare as a function of individual utilities, has been the workhorse of welfare economics since its introduction. Its special parametrizations have proved particularly fruitful in the analysis of optimal taxation. For example, much use has been made of functional forms where the social marginal utility of income falls smoothly as income rises. Indeed, choice of this pattern of welfare weights, capturing 'inequality aversion', may be described as the currently accepted practice. Of course, the rate at which welfare

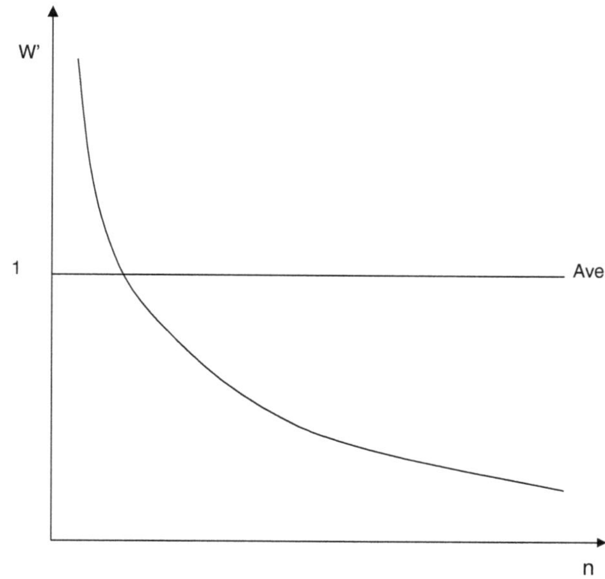

Figure 5.3a The smoothly falling welfare weights

weights fall, the magnitude of inequality aversion, is still a matter of choice. Several parameterizations exist which permit convenient representation of the degree of inequality aversion,[9] for example the 'constant elasticity' class of functions, and these have been used extensively (see Figure 5.3a).

A constant absolute utility–inequality aversion form: the social welfare function of the government is:

$$W = -\frac{1}{\beta}e^{-\beta u} \tag{7}$$

where β measures the degree of inequality aversion in the social welfare function of the government (in the case of $\beta = 0$, we define $W = u$). If we write $W^{-\beta} = \int e^{-\beta u} f(n)dn$ then the limit as $\beta \rightarrow \infty$ is given by $W = \min_n[e^u]$.

The curvature in the utility of consumption modifies social marginal weights $W'U_x$ and makes the government preferences (implicit) more redistributive. Hence the overall curvature for (7) with (4) is $1 + \beta$. Overcoming possible philosophical problems, we may take a view that ß is an observable variable, not a social judgement (see Kaplow 2008a).

The 'smoothly falling welfare weights' class of social welfare functions has long dominated the analysis of optimal taxation (see Figure 5.3a). It has to be said that the conventional inequality-aversion view has certain advantages. It avoids the discomfort of discontinuous changes in weights. It has a pleasing unity and flexibility, as captured by the inequality-aversion parameter. In spite of these properties, and its popularity, the

[9] This is called a prioritarian social welfare function by Adler (2012), who provides an excellent and comprehensive exposition on social welfare functions used in applied welfare economics.

assumption of a constant elasticity is not without problems. As noted by Little and Mirrlees (1974, p. 240), 'there is no particular reason why social marginal valuation should fall at the same proportional rate at all consumption levels. Why should twice as much consumption deserve a quarter of the weight, whether consumption is low or high?'

As we mentioned above, the optimal income tax theory has taken into account differences in social objectives. Formula (7) reflects this. It is also important to recognize the diversity of social objectives. In Chapter 4 we analysed two different positions: charitable conservatism and poverty radicalism. Next we take up new positions.

Rank-order social preferences: An alternative social weighting function is that where the social marginal valuation declines according to the ranking in the n-distribution. In other words, we have the rank-order social welfare function. Rank-order weights represent society's aversion to inequality. This social welfare function first weights individual utilities according to the rank of the individual's utility in the population, with greater weight given to individuals with lower utility, and then adds the weighted utilities. An example of the rank-order social welfare criterion is the Gini or Sen social welfare function. For example, the social marginal valuation implicit in the Gini coefficient depends on the income rank order and is bounded above by 2 and below by 0. Initially the social marginal valuation falls slowly with income, but then the decline accelerates. The ethical justification behind this rank-order social welfare function is at least equally convincing as the justification behind the traditional 'constant elasticity' class of welfare functions.[10]

Aaberge (2000) provides a parametric variant for rank-order social preferences. The weighting function $W_k(n)$ is a weighting function defined by:

$$W_k = \begin{cases} -\log F, k = 1 \\ \dfrac{k}{k-1}(1-F^{k-1}), k = 2, 3, \ldots \end{cases} \tag{8}$$

when $k \to \infty$ $W_k(n)$ approaches the utilitarian case. Then there is no concern of inequality. When k = 2, then $W_2 = 2(1-F)$. This is in effect the weighting underlying the Gini coefficient, as shown by Sen (1974), who provided an axiomatic justification for such a social welfare function. The social marginal valuation declines linearly with F, from twice the average for the lowest paid taxpayer to approaching zero when n goes to infinity (see Figure 5.3b). In the case of k = 1, the weighting function takes the form

[10] As noted by Aaberge and Flood (2008), the differences between these two approaches for measuring social welfare arise from the so-called independence axioms. 'Whilst the expected utility independence axiom requires that the ordering of distributions of individual welfare is invariant with respect to identical mixing of the distributions being compared, the rank-dependent independence axiom requires that the ordering is invariant with respect to identical mixing of the inverses of the distributions being compared' (Aaberge and Flood 2008, p. 16).

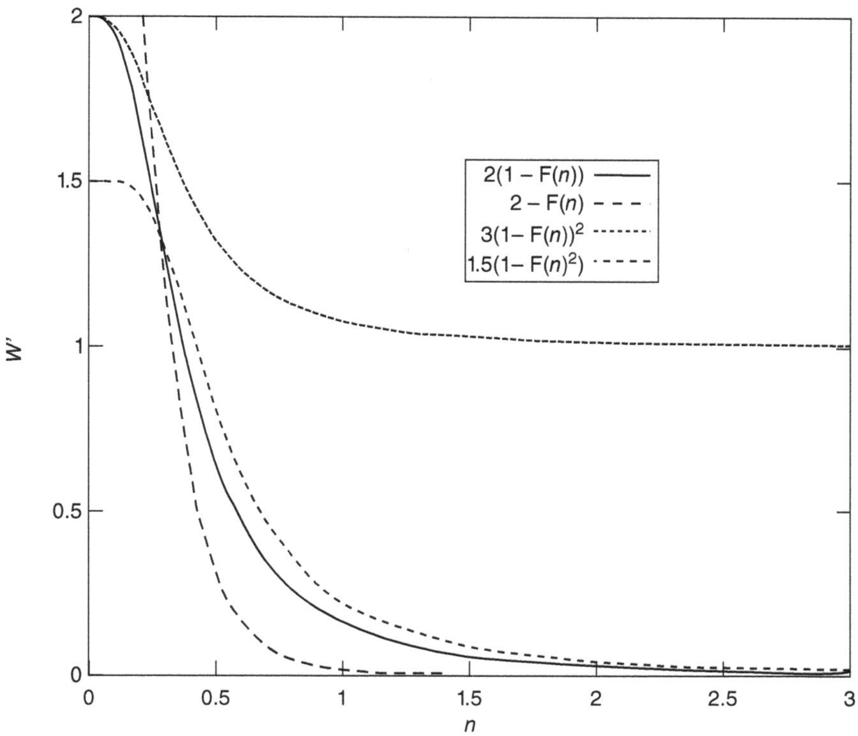

Figure 5.3b Rank order social preferences

$W_1 = -\log F$. As noted by Aaberge (2000), this is in turn the weighting underlying a measure of inequality that was proposed by Bonferroni (1930).

Yitzhaki (1979) provides another parametric variant for rank-order social objectives. The social marginal weighting function can be written now as follows: $W_\upsilon = \upsilon(1-F)^{\upsilon-1}$, where the role of the parameter υ is similar to that of the inequality-aversion parameter. When $\upsilon = 2$, we have the weighting underlying the Gini coefficient. With $\upsilon = 3$, $W_\upsilon = 3(1-F)^2$.

There are also problems with the rank-order preferences based on those weighting functions presented above. Namely some people do not accept that the weights do tend to zero very fast at the very top of the income scale, as can be seen from Figure 5.3b. We may want to allow for the possibility that the social marginal valuation remains strictly above a positive value as income tends to infinity. The following specification of the social weighting function allows for this: $W = 2 - F$. This is bounded above by 2 and tends to 1 when income increases.

Equal opportunities: An egalitarian redistribution policy should instead seek to equalize those income differentials arising from factors beyond the control of the individual. Thus, not only the outcome matters, but also its origin and how it was obtained. This is the essential idea behind Roemer's (1998) theory of equality of opportunity, where people are supposed to differ with respect to circumstances, which are attributes of the individual's environment that influence her earning potential and which are 'beyond her control'. The wage rate depends in part on their own effort (say acquiring education and training, etc.) and in part on social background. For individuals with the same effort but different background types, the maximin criterion is applied. Thus we have a social ordering over each effort group. Then we can apply the utilitarian criterion over such minimum numbers.[11] Roemer's methodology can be translated into the social welfare function framework (this topic was discussed in Chapter 2 and will be discussed further in Chapter 14).

The equality of opportunity principle developed by Roemer (1998) and Roemer et al (2003) concentrates weights uniformly on those coming from a disadvantaged background. Hence, if the likelihood of coming from a disadvantaged social background decreases with income, the weights also decrease with income. The justification for weights decreasing with income is here completely different from that in a constant elastic case; or, as in the above quotation from Little and Mirrlees (1974, p. 240), there is no justification (or it is missing) in a constant elasticity case.

We simplify things so that there are two types of social backgrounds (say parental education or incomes (wealth)). Now the social marginal welfare weights can be constructed as follows: $W'(n) = \frac{f_L(n)}{f_L(n)+f_H(n)}$, where $f_L(n)$ is the proportion of individuals at each n with a bad social background and $f_H(n)$ is the proportion of those individuals who have a better social background. The social welfare weights are zero for those coming from a better social background and one for those with a worse social background. Now, simplifying further, suppose at polar cases $W'(n=0)=1$ and $W'(n=n_{\max})=0$. Hence W'(n) decreases with n and at the top there are only those with a better social background; at the bottom only those coming from a worse social background. W' is decreasing here but for quite different reasons than in the generalized utilitarian case. One possible functional form is the complementary cumulative distribution function or simply the tail distribution, and is defined as $W'=(1-F(n))$ (see Figure 5.3c).

Revealed social preferences: What are the social welfare weights that are implied by the current tax/benefit systems if these systems would indeed have been optimized? There are a growing number of studies trying to reveal social or distributional preferences behind tax/transfer policy. Those studies start from the existing tax and transfers system and reverse-engineer it to obtain the underlying social preferences. An explicit use of interpersonal comparisons to evaluate public policy was introduced by Christiansen and Jansen (1978). They assumed that, over the period of time for which they had data, the Norwegian government had been using the indirect tax system to maximize an additive

[11] The Roemer SWF seems to be close to the leximin SWF. The Roemer SWF can be revised to incorporate the continuous formula. Aaberge and Colombino (2006) introduce a generalized version of Roemer's (1998) Equality of Opportunity (EOp) framework, which they call extended EOp. Unlike the pure EOp criterion of Roemer (1998), the extended EOp criterion allows for alternative weighting profiles in the treatment of income differentials between and within types when types are defined by (observable) circumstances that are beyond people's control.

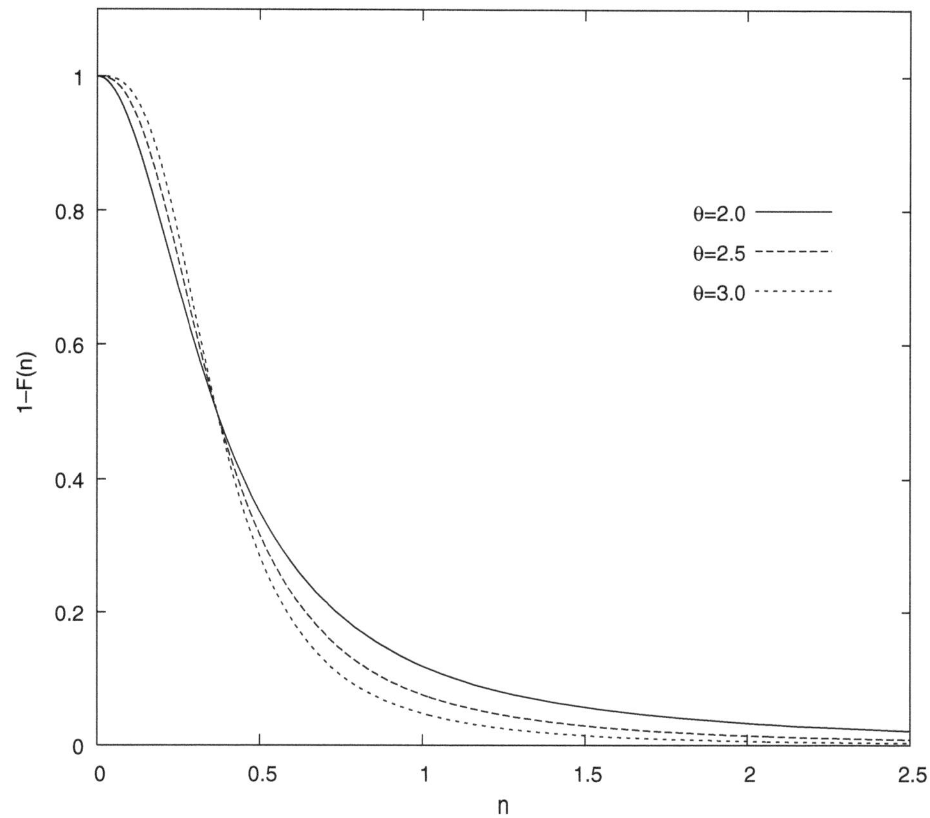

Figure 5.3c Equal opportunity social welfare function

symmetric social welfare function which depends upon a single parameter called the inequality-aversion parameter. They found that the inequality-aversion parameter was quite far from the utilitarian value, thus confirming what many would have guessed, that Norway acts so as to give more social weight to low-income people. A similar study was carried out in India by Ahmad and Stern (1984); they found a similar outcome, namely that there was substantial inequality aversion.[12] By calculating the implied social welfare weights we are able to uncover which social preferences apparently underlie current tax/benefit policy. This provides useful information to policy makers so as to improve the current tax-benefit systems. When welfare weights are increasing with income or when they are negative, the current tax system does not redistribute income in the most efficient way. Hence, welfare improvements can be achieved by reforming the tax system.

However, recently rather detailed micro-data on incomes and corresponding marginal tax rates have become available in order to study the social preferences implicit in tax-benefit systems. One of the first studies using micro-data was by Bourguignon and

[12] See also Decoster and Schokkaert (1989).

Spadaro (2012). They considered the revealed social preferences of the French tax-benefit system, considering the inverse optimal problem. Zoutman, Jacobs, and Jongen (2012) used this method to find the redistributive preferences of political parties implicit in reform proposals, combining the reform proposals with micro-data on the income distribution and elasticity of the tax base in the Netherlands. They find that all parties gave a higher social weight to the poor than the rich and that the differences between social welfare weights were rather small. Bargain et al (2011) estimate labour supply elasticities on micro-data and characterize the redistributive preferences embodied in the welfare systems of seventeen EU countries and the US, under the assumption of optimality. They find that social welfare weights are always positive, though they are not monotonically declining for low-income groups, in line with the findings from the studies just considered. They further find that there are only significant differences in social welfare weights over income between groups of countries (the US vs. continental/Nordic Europe vs. southern Europe), with rather similar social welfare weights over income within groups of countries.

Using a simple online survey with more than 1,000 participants, Saez and Stantcheva (2013) illustrate how the public preferences can be mapped into generalized social marginal welfare weights. Their results suggest that the public views on redistribution are inconsistent with standard utilitarianism.

5.4 Revenue requirement

$R = 1 - X/Z = 1 - \int x(n) f(n) dn / \int z(n) f(n) dn$ is specified as a fraction of national income varying between $X/Z = 1.1$ and $X/Z = 0.8$. If $X/Z = 1$, then taxation is purely redistributive. If $X/Z > 1$, then we have outside resources available (e.g. foreign aid; state-owned firms make positive profits).

The results of the simulations are summarized in Figures 5.4–5.14. and Tables 5.1–5.4. Tables 5.1–5.4 give labour supply,y; gross income, z; net income, x (also x at the point n_0, denoted by x_0 and F at the point n_0, denoted by F_0);[13] and optimal average (ATR) and marginal tax rates (MTR) at various percentiles of the ability distribution, when $X/Z = 0.9$ or $R = 0.1$. Tables also provide the decile ratio (P90/P10) for net income and gross income. Unlike the scalar inequality measures, the use of fractile measures such as the decile ratio allows us to consider changes in inequality at various different points in the distribution. Since marginal tax rates may be a poor indication of the redistribution powers of an optimal tax structure, we measure the extent of redistribution, denoted by RD, as the proportional reduction between the decile ratio for market income, z, and the decile ratio for disposable income, x. To relate these results to empirical labour supply

[13] $y(n_0)=0$. The range of n was n_0 to 1.5, at which point the integrated value of f(n) was more than 0.9999.

Table 5.1 (case u1)

β= 0	θ=3.3	X/Z=0.9					
F(n)	y	z	x	ATR%	MTR%	E^u	ξ
0.10	0.32	0.06	0.08	−35	38	0.58	−0.5
0.50	0.43	0.16	0.15	−7	30	0.16	−0.5
0.90	0.46	0.33	0.27	19	32	0.09	−0.5
0.97	0.47	0.49	0.37	23	33	0.07	−0.5
0.99	0.47	0.69	0.50	27	33	0.05	−0.5
P90/P10		5.44	3.26				
RD(%)			40				
n_0=0.08	x_0=0.046	F_0=0.01					

Table 5.2a (case u2)

β= 0	θ=3.3	X/Z=0.9					
F(n)	y	z	x	ATR%	MTR%	E^u	ξ
0.10	0.50	0.09	0.14	−50	58	0.18	−0.22
0.50	0.55	0.20	0.19	6	52	−0.003	−0.30
0.90	0.53	0.38	0.28	27	52	−0.09	−0.37
0.97	0.51	0.54	0.35	33	53	−0.13	−0.41
0.99	0.49	0.72	0.44	39	51	−0.18	−0.46
P90/P10		4.22	2.0				
RD(%)			52.6				

studies we give the values of the uncompensated elasticity, E^u, and income effect parameter, ξ.

5.5 **The level of marginal tax rates**

Let us consider first the level of the marginal tax rates. As expected, the marginal tax rates are higher when inequality aversion in the constant elasticity or rank-order sense is higher. The levels of marginal tax rates increase when β increases or k goes from utilitarian case $k=\infty$ to the case of $k=1$. The levels of marginal tax rates also increase with revenue (see Figs 5.9a, b, c) and decrease with the elasticity of substitution or larger labour supply responses. Increasing pre-tax inequality increases the level of marginal tax rates. These numerical results confirm our discussion in the context of marginal tax formula (13) in Chapter 4.

Table 5.2b (case u2)

β= 0	θ=2.5						
F(n)	y	z	x	ATR%	MTR%	E^u	ξ
0.10	0.41	0.06	0.14	−133	62	0.38	−0.19
0.50	0.50	0.18	0.19	3	61	0.08	−0.28
0.90	0.50	0.44	0.29	35	63	−0.04	−0.36
0.97	0.47	0.73	0.39	45	64	−0.1	−0.43
0.99	0.45	1.05	0.50	52	64	−0.16	−0.48
P90/P10		7.33	2.07				
RD(%)			71.8				
n_0=0.03	x_0=0.12	F_0=0.001					

Table 5.2c (case u2)

β= 0	θ=2	X/Z=0.9					
F(n)	y	z	x	ATR%	MTR%	E^u	ξ
0.10	0.30	0.04	0.15	−100	62	0.82	−0.17
0.50	0.45	0.17	0.19	−18	66	0.19	−0.26
0.90	0.47	0.51	0.30	41	71	0.002	−0.36
0.97	0.45	0.95	0.43	55	71	−0.1	−0.44
0.99	0.44	1.58	0.63	60	68	−0.22	−0.53
P90/P10		12.75	1.96				
RD(%)			84.6				
n_0=0.02	x_0=0.13	F_0=0.0					

5.6 Pre-tax inequality and increasing marginal tax rates

Kanbur and Tuomala (1994) show with lognormal distribution that when holding mean constant higher values of inherent inequality (higher σ) are used, optimal marginal tax rates increase with the income over the majority of the population (see Figure 5.4).

Mirrlees (1971) justified his choice of $\sigma = 0.39$ for the distribution of n from the work of Lydall (1968) on earnings distributions in the UK. Kanbur and Tuomala (1994) find some support for higher σ values in a US study by Slemrod (1992). He calculates that the Gini coefficient of wages and salaries increased from 0.489 to 0.578 in the US between 1972 and 1988. We know (see Aitchison and Brown, Theorem 2.7 and Table A1) that if σ = 0.7 and 1.0, then the Gini coefficients are 0.379 and 0.52. Moreover, the figures reported for developing countries (for example Anand and Kanbur 1993) suggest

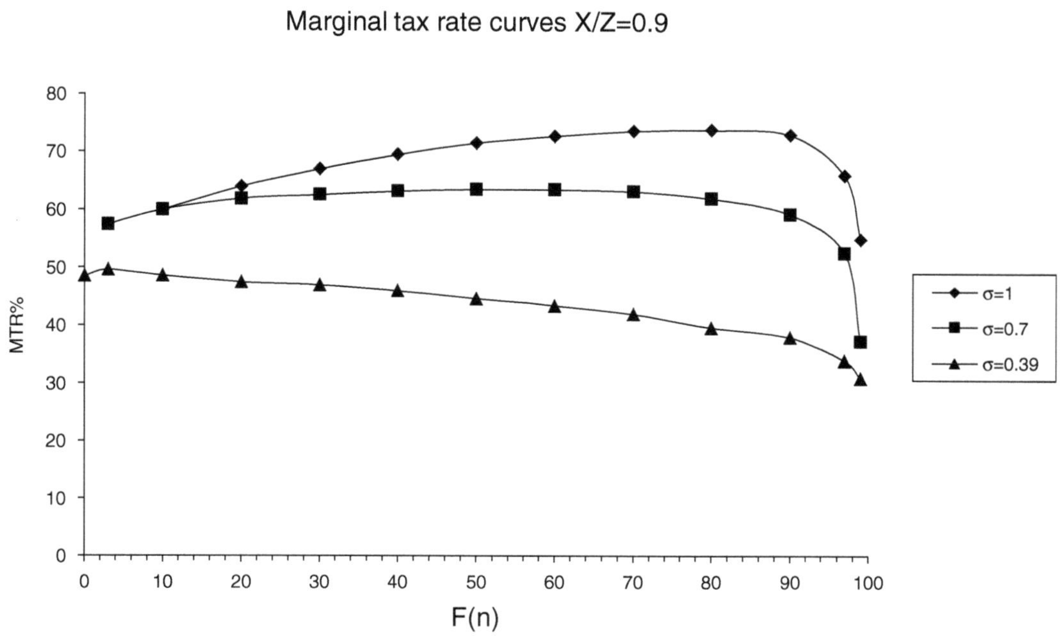

Figure 5.4 f(n) = lognormal distribution, holding mean constant $m = e^{-1}$ (Kanbur and Tuomala 1994)

inequality values in this range. Thus it seems to us that our computations with σ = .7 and 1. are not based on empirically implausible estimates. On the other hand we know (see Kleiber and Kotz 2003, p. 224) that the Gini coefficient for the Champernowne distribution is $G = 1/\theta$.[14] So if θ= 2.0 and 3.3, then the Gini coefficients are 0.5 and 0.303, respectively. To study further the degree of sensitivity of the shape of the tax schedule to the choice of parameter θ in the Champernowne distribution, we computed solutions when θ varies from 1.5 to 3.3 with different utility functions. In case of the Champernowne distribution a scale parameter m is as in Mirrlees (1971) with lognormal distribution; $e^{-1} = .36788$.[15] (See Figure 5.1d for the θ estimates in Finland.) Figures 5.5a, b, and c depict these cases. When $\theta = 2.5$, the marginal tax rates increase for the lowest decile and then remain constant. When θ is less than 2.5 the marginal tax rate is increasing with income up to around $F(n) = 0.98$.[16] These results reinforce the

[14] In Finland over the period 1987–2007 the Gini coefficient of factor income varied from 0.38 to 0.47. The corresponding values for the θ parameter are 2.6 and 2.14.

[15] Based on British income distribution data by the Royal Commission on the Distribution of Income and Wealth 1971 $\theta = 3.37$. Many distributions are fit by McDonald (1984) to US income distribution data. One of them is a distribution called a Fisk distribution, which is a special case of Champernowne distribution. The parameter θ varies in this study from 2.5 (1970) to 2.27 (1980). In Harrison's (1974) study for the British data based on data from 1952–1970, the parameter θ varies between 1.9 and 2.5. His results also depended on the estimation technique used.

[16] In the case u1 with θ lower than 2.2 the marginal tax rate increases with income.

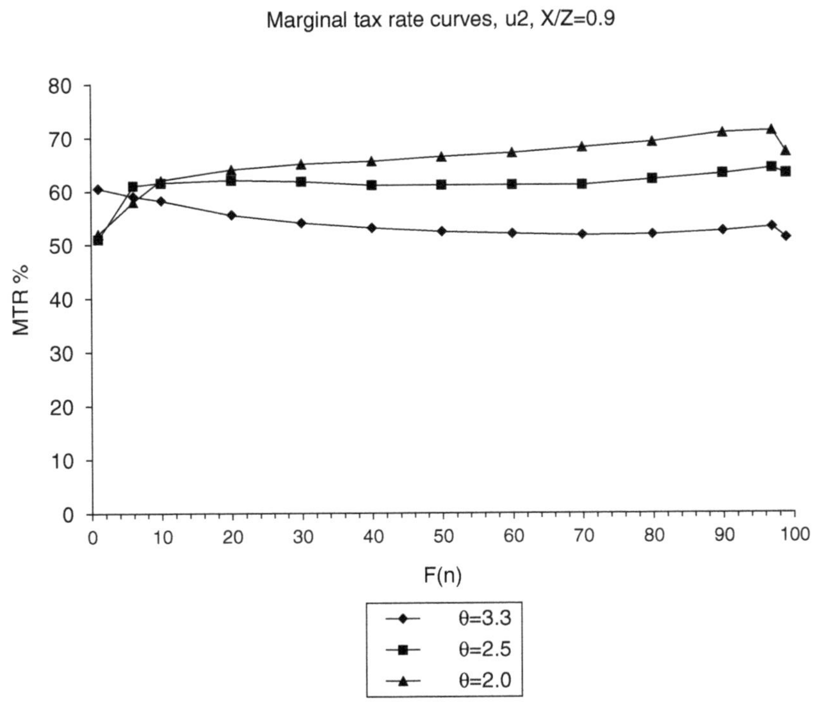

Figure 5.5a f(n)=Champernowne distribution holding mean constant $m = e^{-1}$

findings of Kanbur and Tuomala (1994) with lognormal distribution. Unlike in Kanbur and Tuomala (1994) with lognormal distribution, we have here—practically speaking—a progressive marginal rate structure throughout when θ is less than 2.5 and the case u2. In the case u1, the elasticities are decreasing in income; in the case u2 the compensated elasticities decrease until the median income and then remain constant (see Tables 5.1–5.4).

In Figure 5.4 we see that in the lognormal case the marginal tax rates increase at the bottom with higher pre-tax inequality. But as we in turn see in Figures 5.5a and b, this is not the case with the Champernowne case. When $\theta = 1.5$ and 2.0, marginal tax rates are lower at the lower part of distribution. At least partially, the explanation is that the population is denser at the lower part when θ is smaller, i.e. higher $f(n)$ (see Figure 5.1a).

5.7 Top income shares and average tax rates

As is well known, there has been large growth in top income shares over the past few decades in several advanced countries. At the same time there has been a shift in the burden of taxation in many advanced countries, from the top to further down in the income distribution. Earlier in the chapter there was a lot of emphasis on top marginal tax rates. Also, our discussion of tax structures so far has been entirely about marginal

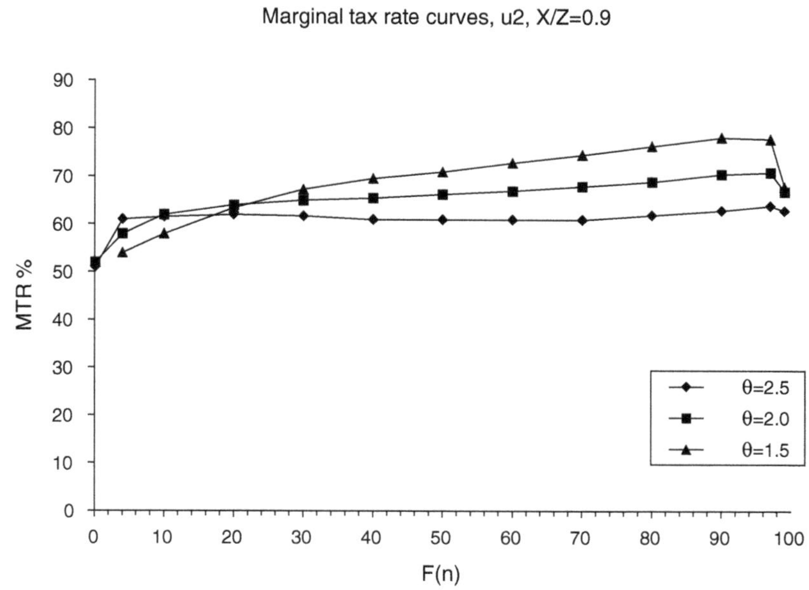

Figure 5.5b f(n) = Champernowne distribution holding mean constant m = e^{-1}

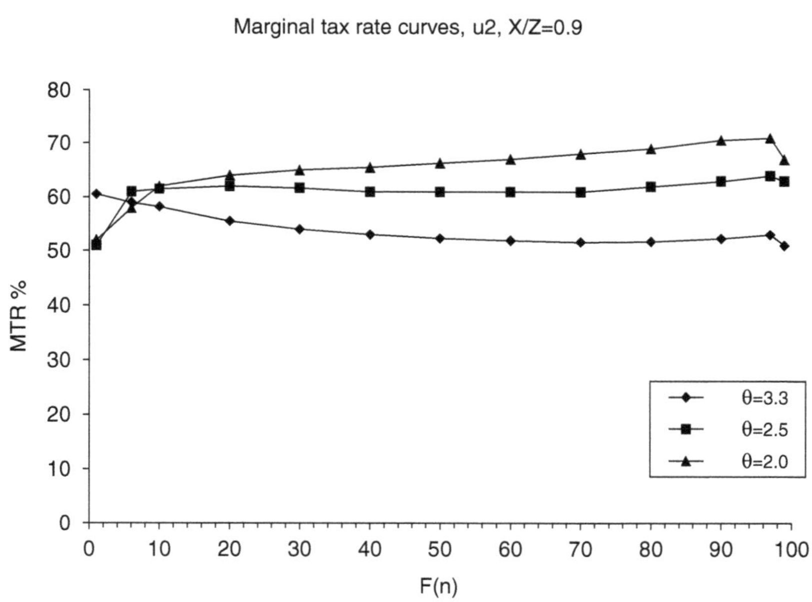

Figure 5.5c f(n) = Champernowne distribution holding mean constant m = e^{-1}

tax rates. It is true that much of the literature has focused on marginal tax rates, but computational techniques can be used to say something about average rates. Now we consider: how does optimal income tax schedule change when top income inequality increases? Our numerical results suggest that this shift in tax burden cannot be justified in the standard Mirrlees model, which embodies conventional assumptions about

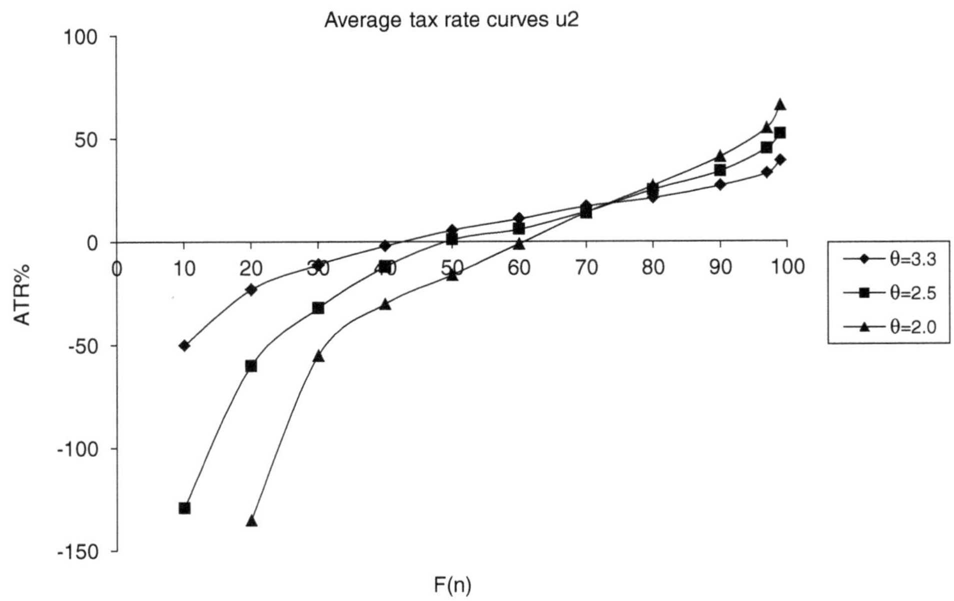

Figure 5.5d Utilitarian, f(n) = Champernowne distribution holding mean constant $m = e^{-1}$

inequality aversion and the trade-off between equity and efficiency. As we see in Figure 5.5d (utilitarian) and Figure 5.5e (maximin), an appropriate response to rising inequality is a shift towards a more progressive income tax system. The shape parameter θ in itself is an appropriate measure for increasing top income shares. Recall lower θ means greater inequality. From Figure 5.5b we see that the marginal tax rates in turn increase except in the bottom 10–20 per cent. The more relevant tax rates for redistributive purposes are average tax rates. Therefore we show in Figures 5.5d and e how average tax rates decline among the bottom 75 per cent when pre-tax income inequality increases. This is so with other specifications employed on preferences, social objectives, and revenue requirement. In fact, there is a sizeable literature on measuring progressivity, which is largely based on average tax rates (see Kakwani 1980, Lambert 1989).

5.8 The curvature of utility over consumption and increasing marginal tax rates

It is slightly surprising to notice that essentially only two utility functions—a Cobb–Douglas (or log–log) and a CES with the elasticity of substitution between consumption and leisure being 0.5[17]—are employed in these simulations. In particular, the role of the assumed form of utility of consumption in determining the shape of the tax schedule is

[17] Saez (2001) also uses utility functions with constant compensated elasticity.

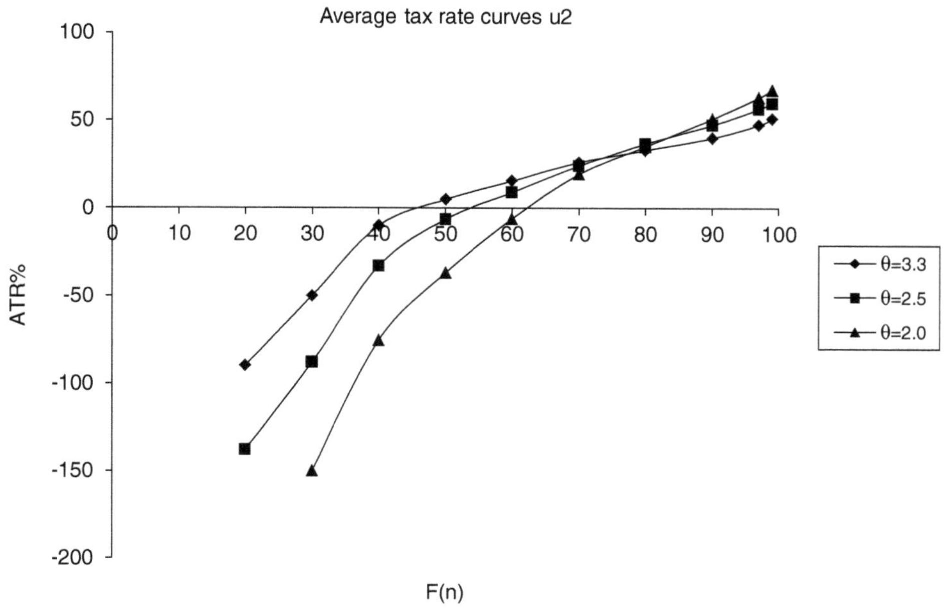

Figure 5.5e Maximin, f(n) = Champernowne distribution holding mean constant $m = e^{-1}$

not clear. Dahan and Strawczynski (2001) show, however, that rising marginal tax rates at high incomes, as presented by Diamond (1998), depend on the assumption of utility of consumption. Their simulations focus only on high levels of income, not the whole schedule. Tuomala (2010) shows numerically the sensitivity of the marginal tax rate structure to the assumed form of utility of consumption. He replaces the assumptions of utility of consumption used in previous simulations to quadratic utility of consumption with a bliss point. This form is essentially less curved than those used in previous simulations. In addition, it is important to note that there is a close link between a taxpayer's labour supply and the curvature in utility of consumption.

The utility function that is quadratic in consumption (quadratic approximation) with a bliss point,[18](6), implies that the distribution of consumption is bounded upward by $1 + \frac{1}{2a}$. For the same reason, the distribution of earnings is also bounded upward. This might limit the applicability of the model at the very upper tail of distribution. It turns out, however, to be the case that with those parameter values used in calculations in Tuomala (2010), the highest values of consumption are clearly smaller than the upper bound (= 1.1 when a = 5)—for instance, when $\sigma = 0.7$ consumption is 0.94 at the 99.9 percentile point of the ability distribution.

Previous simulations (see e.g. Mirrlees 1971; Atkinson 1972; Tuomala 1990; Kanbur and Tuomala 1994) have used either the logarithmic utility of consumption or

[18] Stern (1986) discusses the quadratic specification and other alternatives. In fact, in the recent empirical labour supply studies—see Blundell and Macurdy (1999) and Keane and Moffitt (1998)—preferences over working time and net income are given by the utility function that is quadratic in hours and net of income.

$U(x) = -1/x$. The important property of both these functions is that the coefficient of relative risk aversion (r) (the curvature of utility over consumption) is constant (r=1 and 2 with fixed labour supply). In the light of Table 1 in Chetty (2006), those values of r may be too high. The coefficient of relative risk aversion in the utility function (6) (case u12) in turn varies at different points of the function. With parameterization used in our computations, the values of r are more in line with empirical labour supply literature.[19] The utility of consumption in (6) is a kind of 'mixture' of these two forms. The utility of consumption in (6) is essentially less curved than those used in the previous simulations. Now the elasticity-based marginal tax formulation turns out to be useful because we can calculate traditional labour supply elasticities at each point of the distribution.

Much of this research viewed labour supply in terms of hours. Available evidence indicates that there is an enormous variation in elasticities of labour supply (see appendix 5.1). Estimates of uncompensated wage elasticity are typically negative, but close to zero for male workers. For females, married women, and lone parents, they vary from small negative to large positive. In the survey of the international literature by Blundell and Macurdy (1999), the estimates for males range from around 0 to 0.25 and for females from around 0 to 2.03. The income elasticities are generally small (negative) and of a magnitude such that the compensated elasticities measuring the substitution effect are positive. Empirical work on the incentive effects of labour income taxation generally identified quite low labour supply elasticities. Meghir and Phillips (2010) survey the elasticity of hours worked with respect to the wage. For men, they conclude that 'although one can start discussing the relative merits of the approaches taken, existing research will lead to the conclusion that the wage elasticity is zero' (p. 234). For women, the elasticity of weekly hours worked is 'in the range of approximately 0.0 to 0.3' (p. 230). Their preferred estimate is a value of 0.13 for all married women except those with young children. They also say that 'the results of annual labour supply show greater responsiveness to wages'. The reason for this, they argue, is probably that variations in annual hours worked are a combination of participation responses and intensive responses. Compensated elasticities were often found in other surveys to be near 0.1 or 0.2, which implies that the elasticity of substitution between leisure and consumption is around 0.5 in the CES utility function (see appendix 5.1).

The striking thing in the numerical results shown in Figures 5.6–5.8 is that, once we assume that preferences are given by the utility function that is quadratic in consumption, the shape of optimum tax schedules may be altered drastically. The marginal tax rates rise with income, practically speaking, over the whole range. The reason for this can be found in Figure 4.1c in Chapter 4. This utility function with upper bound on consumption necessarily implies a concave budget constraint in Mirrlees' (1971) model. The optimal income tax rate schedule features marginal tax rate progressivity, except that in cases ($\beta = 1$) and ($\beta = 2$) rates decline slightly at the very top of wage distribution. In fact

[19] Using thirty-three sets of estimates of income and wage elasticities, the mean value of r calculated by Chetty (2006) is 0.71 in the additive utility case.

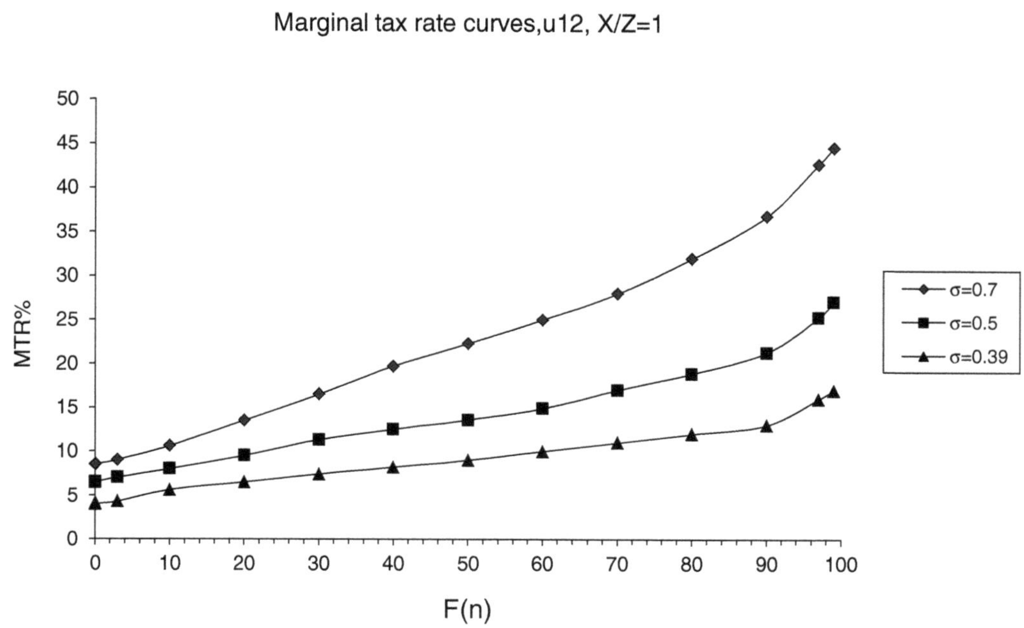

Figure 5.6 f(n) = lognormal distribution holding mean constant $m = e^{-1}$

the marginal rate rises after the 99th percentile point. The marginal tax rate increases with income up to the 99.7 percentile point.

Unfortunately, there is little evidence regarding the relationship between labour supply elasticities and wage rates.[20] Analysing data from an earlier labour supply study, Sadka, Garfinkel, and Moreland (1982) computed the compensated wage elasticity for each quintile of income distribution and found that it decreases as income increases. Röed and Ström (2002) (Tables 1 and 2) offer a review of the more recent existing evidence. They conclude that the limited evidence indicates that labour supply elasticities are declining with household income. Using Norwegian data, Aaberge and Colombino (2006) provide support for declining elasticities.[21] High labour supply elasticities among low-wage workers are also confirmed by empirical evaluations of various in-work benefit schemes operating in many countries. By contrast, there is empirical evidence that the elasticities of taxable income are higher among high-income individuals. (See e.g. Gruber and Saez 2002).

In all cases considered in Tuomala (2010), income effects were negative and relatively small at all income levels. This is compatible with empirical labour supply studies summarized by Meghir and Phillips (2010). Both compensated and uncompensated wage elasticities decline with income. This in turn is compatible with the results in Aaberge and Colombino (2006). The striking thing in the numerical results in Tuomala

[20] Empirically, we also need estimates as to how the elasticity varies with the wage rate. It is quite surprising to note that Blundell and Macurdy (1999) do not say anything about this.

[21] Aaberge and Flood (2008) find this same pattern for Sweden, too.

(2010) is that I and E^u are quite similar, as in Aaberge and Colombino (2006) (see their table 3.3). Figure 5.6 provides a graphical presentation of the marginal tax rate structure with lognormal distribution. Figures 5.7 and 5.8a, b display the marginal tax rates when f(n) is the Champernowne distribution. We see how sensitive tax rates and the shape of tax schedules are to the choice of the standard deviation, σ or θ, and the distributional parameter, β or k. As expected on the basis of the previous simulations, the levels of the marginal tax rates and the shape of the schedules are fairly sensitive to the choice of the standard deviation of n, σ (see Figure 5.4), and the distributional parameter, β (see Figure 5.7 and 5.8a,b).[22]

It is important to note that the extent of redistribution and a rising marginal tax rate may be two quite different things. Numerical results in Tuomala (2010) show that the extent of redistribution is much larger with higher β, but the marginal tax schedule is much steeper in the case of $\beta=0$. In fact, there is a slightly declining portion at top incomes with higher β. Moreover, the level of the lump-sum transfer component x_0 is fairly sensitive to the specification of the model. In particular, the level of x_0 is very sensitive to the choice of β (distributional parameter).

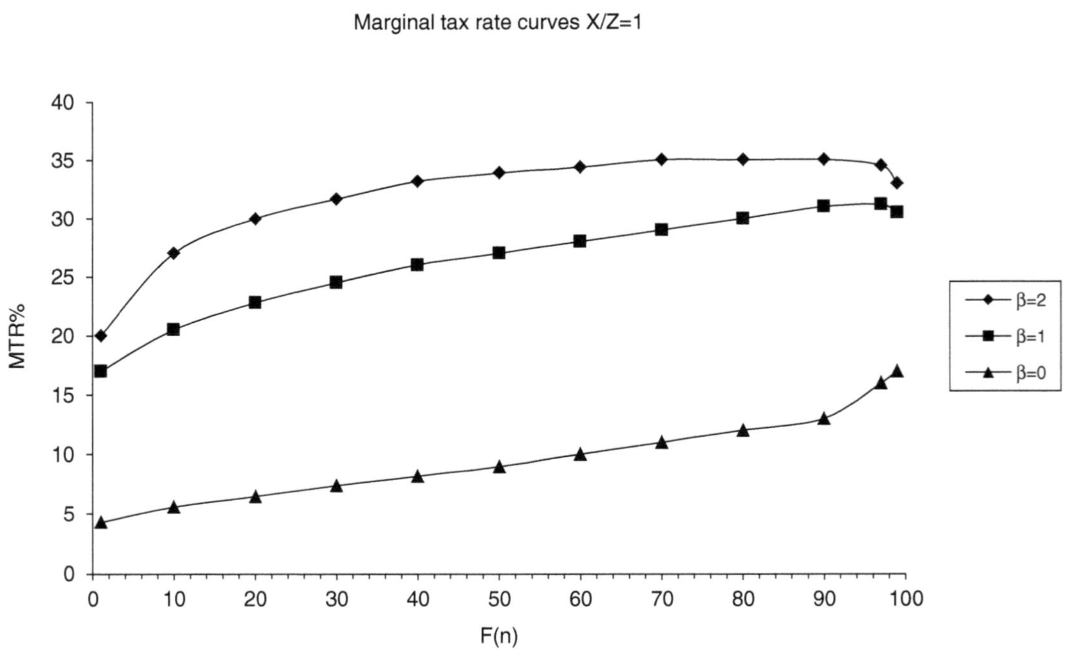

Figure 5.7 Marginal tax rates with different β, lognormal distribution with $\sigma=0.39$ and $m=e^{-1}$and $X/Z=1$

[22] Of course, when we change the parameters of the model we should also calibrate the n-distribution indirectly so that the distribution of z remains the same. In practice this is rather laborious to do.

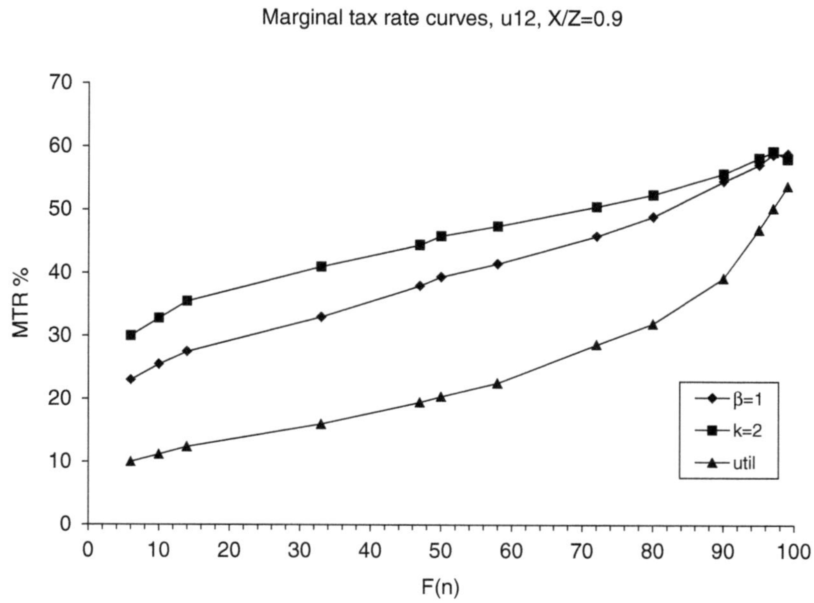

Figure 5.8a f(n) = Champernowne distribution with $\theta = 2.5$ and $m = e^{-1}$

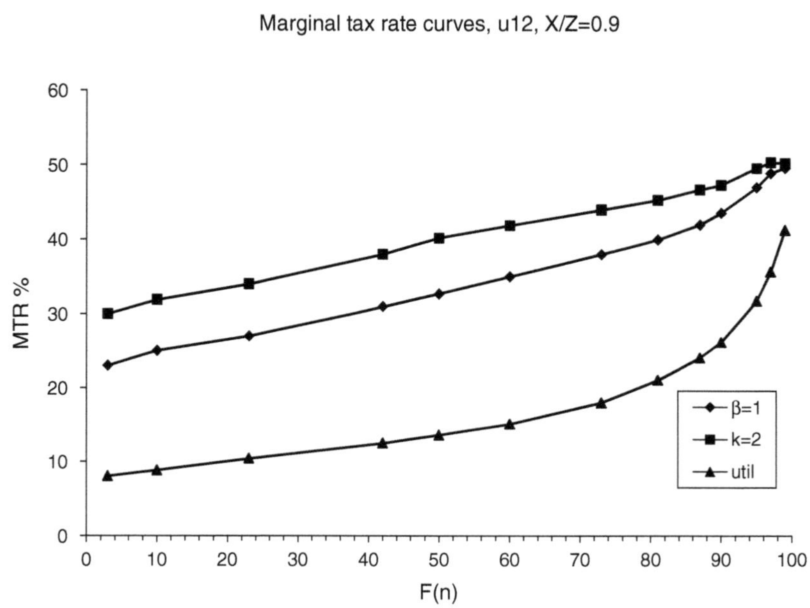

Figure 5.8b Champernowne distribution with $\theta = 3.3$ and $m = e^{-1}$

Table 5.3 (case u12)

β=0	θ=2.5	X/Z=0.9					
F(n)	y	z	x	ATR%	MTR%	E^{u}	ξ
0.10	0.16	0.03	0.05	−95	11	2.35	−0.05
0.50	0.40	0.15	0.15	−3	20	0.60	−0.08
0.90	0.50	0.44	0.35	19	39	0.27	−0.15
0.97	0.51	0.75	0.52	30	50	0.13	−0.23
0.99	0.51	1.07	0.67	37	54	−0.05	−0.36
P90/P10		14.7	7.0				
RD(%)			52.3				
n_0=0.10	x_0=0.03	F_0=0.04					

5.9 Is there a U-shaped marginal tax/transfer rate curve?

The U-shape of tax schedules in Saez (2001) was a direct consequence of the U-shaped pattern of distribution ratio. Unlike in Saez (2001), the distribution ratio in our calculations is, roughly speaking, the L-shape in all specifications considered (see Figure 5.1c). Moreover, in all cases we calculated, the elasticity of labour supply is not constant. Hence, the shape of the tax schedule is determined by the interplay between all factors discussed in the context of formula (13) in Chapter 4. In calculations displayed here, the distribution ratio is roughly speaking L-shaped in all specifications considered (see Figure 5.1c). Hence, the shape of the tax schedule is determined by the interplay between all factors discussed in the context of formula (13) in Chapter 4. The results displayed in Figures 5.7–5.8 show that it is not possible to get a U-shaped pattern in the case of quadratic utility function. In the case u1, when the pre-tax inequality is rather low we have a U-shaped marginal tax rate structure and the marginal rates are rather high at the bottom of the distribution.[23] Figure 5.9a displays the case with θ=3.3 and lower (X/Z=1.1) and higher (X/Z=0.8) revenue requirements.[24] The marginal tax rate curves decrease from the bottom to middle incomes (around median). The marginal tax rate curves slope upward starting at around the range of 60–70 percentile of wage distribution and then rise until income level is at the 99th percentile (see Figure 5.9a). Figure 5.9b shows that when θ=2.0 we do not have a U-shaped curve in either revenue requirement case. In the case of u2 (utility function (5)),[25] in turn, the marginal rates are declining

[23] Bevan (2005) also computes a U-shaped pattern with the log-log utility function.

[24] Revenue=1-X//Z.

[25] Saez (2001, p.225) criticizes CES specification because the income effects are unrealistically large, around—1. Saez's statement is not always correct and should have been qualified to that income effect is around—1 asymptotically in the case δ <1. Using (32) and denoting $\xi = n\frac{dy}{db}$, where $x = ny + b$ (b=the virtual income). We have $\xi = -\frac{1}{(1+n^{(\delta-1)})}$. Now we see that in the case δ =1 (case u1) ξ =–0.5. When δ < 1,

with income when the θ parameter is higher than 2.5. The marginal tax rates increase, however, for the lowest percentile and then fall, and above-middle incomes are roughly constant and finally rise again, although not to the height of the rates applied to lower-income individuals. In this case the marginal tax rate curves slope upward starting at around the 70–80 percentile range of the wage distribution, and then rise until income level is at the 97th percentile point. The point in which the marginal tax rate curve slopes upwards is much higher in Saez (2001)—around 80,000 dollars/year—than in our cases.[26]

As shown in Figures 5.9a and b with different utility functions and revenue requirement (X/Z-ratios), only in the case of the log–log utility function (the u1 case) and when the pre-tax inequality is low enough are the marginal rate curves clearly U-shaped, and even more so with lower revenue requirement (higher X/Z). In other words, with lower revenue requirement (higher X/Z), the tax schedule is more progressive, in the sense that the range of rising marginal rates increases. This is just what our discussion suggested in the context of the marginal tax formula (13) in Chapter 4. Some intuition for this might be developed as follows. First, it may be useful to describe the income tax schedule so that it consists of two elements: the guaranteed income—an individual with no income would get the lump-sum subsidy or the guaranteed income $x(no) = x_o = 0 - T(z=0) = -T(0)$. ($T(0)$ is negative if the government has redistributive goals)—and the pattern of marginal

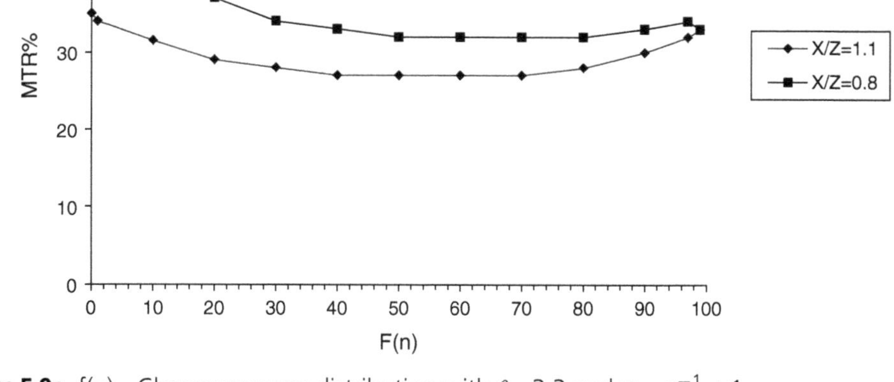

Figure 5.9a f(n) = Champernowne distribution with $\theta = 3.3$ and $m = e^{-1}$, u1

then ξ converges to -1 as n goes to infinity. As seen in Tables 5.2a $\xi = -0.46$ at the 99 percentile point of the n-distribution. It is very far from -1.

[26] See also Brewer et al (2008), who perform simulations using data from the UK.

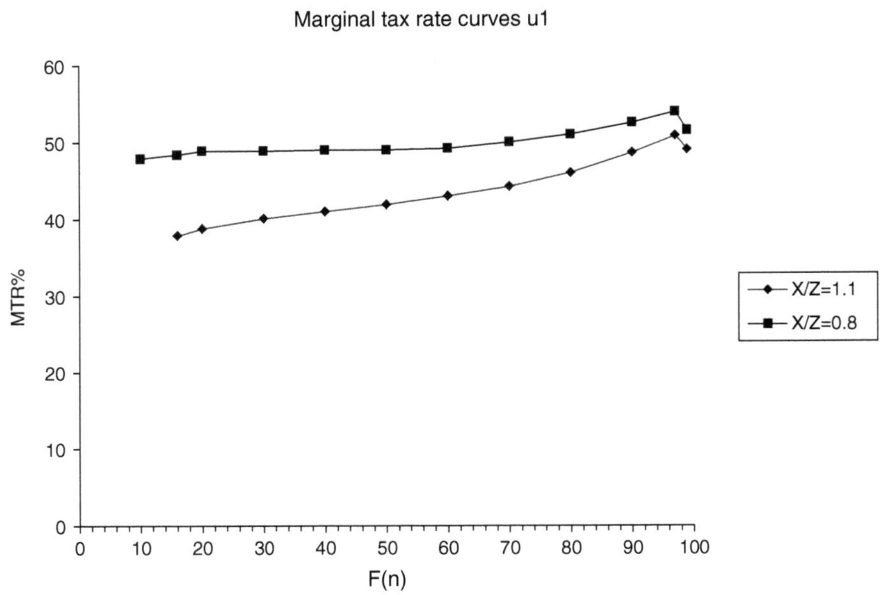

Figure 5.9b f(n) = Champernowne distribution with $\theta = 2.0$ and $m = e^{-1}$, u1

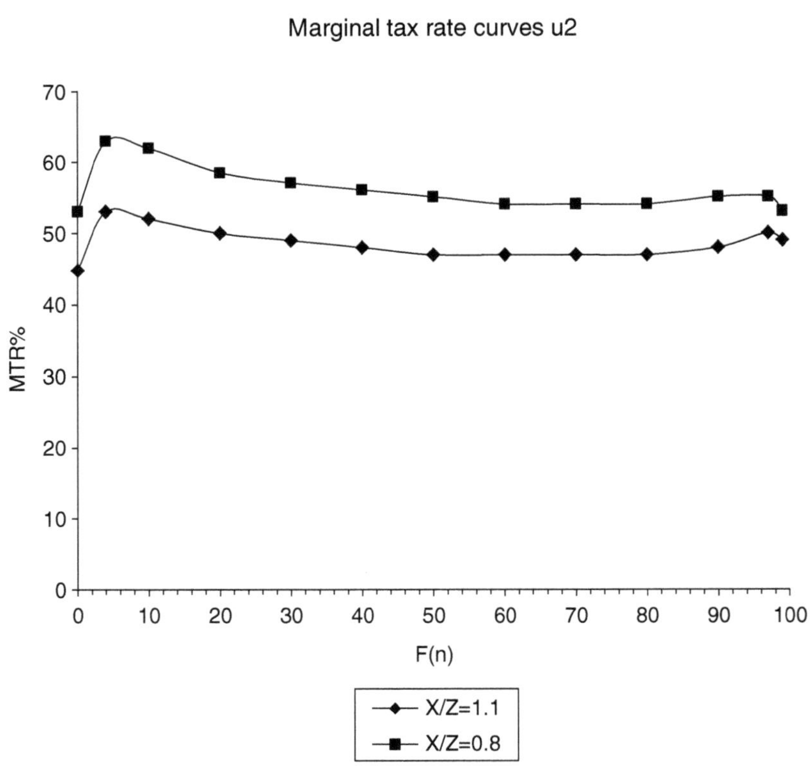

Figure 5.9c f(n) = Champernowne distribution with $\theta = 3.3$, $m = e^{-1}$ and u2

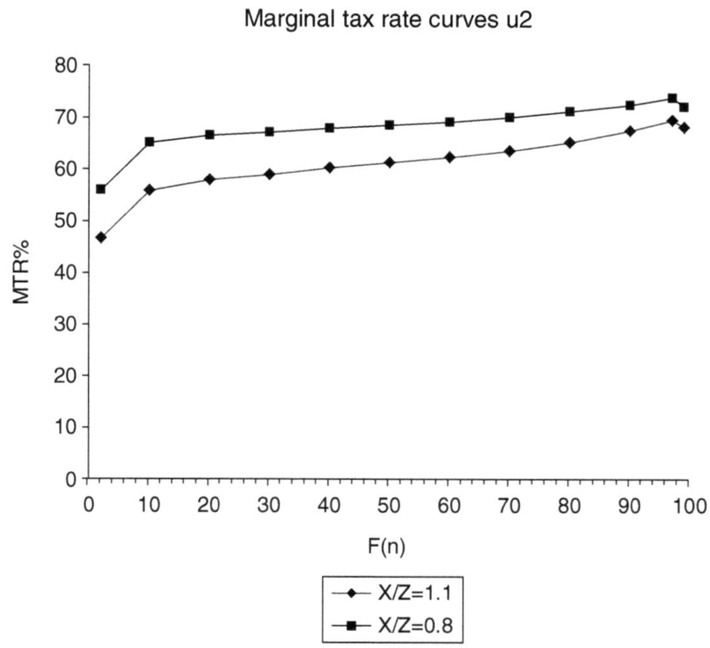

Figure 5.9d f(n) = Champernowne distribution with θ=2.0, m = e^{-1} and u2

tax rates $t(z)$. The latter element describes both how the guaranteed element is clawed back or taxed away and how the tax burden increases with income. Consider the case where revenue requirement is positive but there is high concern for the poor. In this case it is likely that there will be a high guaranteed income but also high marginal tax rates on low-income people to claw back revenue. As the revenue requirement falls, and in fact as it becomes negative so that outside resources are available, the minimum income requirement for the poor can be met easily without having to claw back revenue with high marginal tax rates. Thus we should expect to see low marginal tax rates on the poor.

5.10 Alternative social preferences: maximin and marginal tax rates

Numerical results seem to suggest that marginal tax rates tend to increase for all taxpayers with increasing inequality aversion (see Figures 5.7, 5.8 and 5.10a). The shape of the tax schedule seems to change for lower values of β in quite a similar way as with increasing revenue requirement. But if we adopt the maximin ('Rawlsian') social welfare function, things change quite dramatically, as our remarks earlier in some simplifying cases suggested. Namely, when $\beta=\infty$, we find that marginal tax rates decline continuously with income. It seems, therefore, that it is a sufficiently high inequality aversion that leads to a pattern of optimally declining marginal tax rates. It may appear

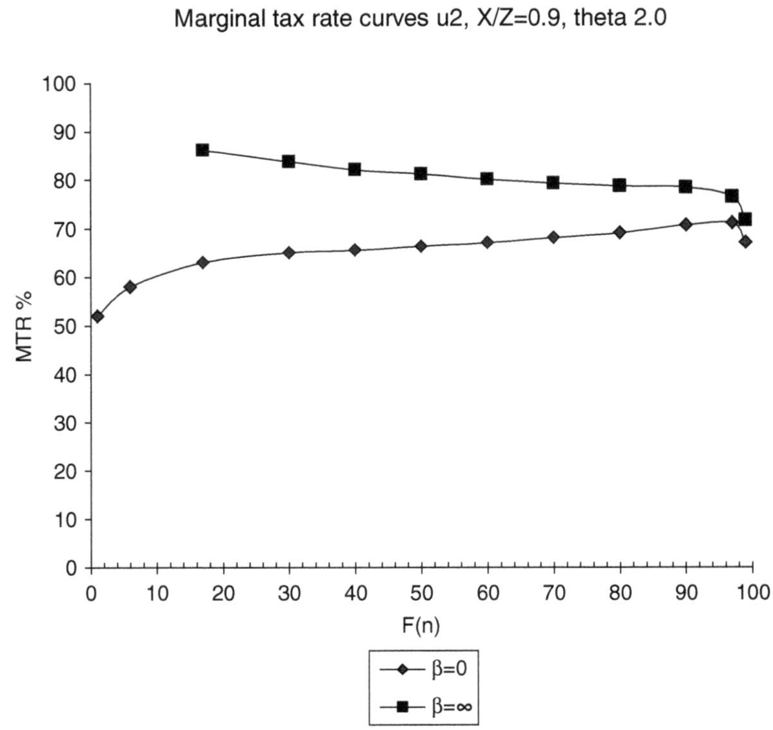

Figure 5.10a f(n) = Champernowne distribution, u2, utilitarian $\beta = 0$, X/Z = 0.9 and maximin $\beta = \infty$

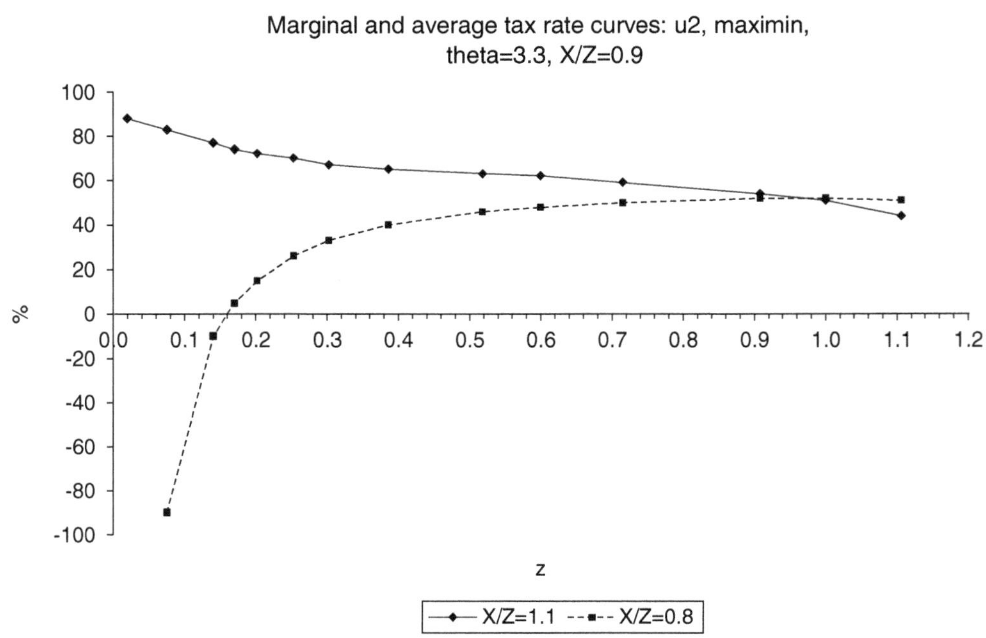

Figure 5.10b f(n) = Champernowne distribution, u2, X/Z = 0.9 and maximin $\beta = \infty$

Table 5.4 Maximin

F(n)	θ=2.5 y	z	x	ATR%	MTR%	E^u	ξ
0.11	0.005	0.001	0.14	−139	88		−0.12
0.50	0.42	0.15	0.18	−6	79	0.33	−0.22
0.90	0.52	0.45	0.23	47	72	−0.01	−0.33
0.97	0.51	0.74	0.32	57	70	−0.11	−0.40
0.99	0.51	1.08	0.43	60	63	−0.21	−0.47
P90/P50		3	1.64				
RD(%)			45.3				
n_0=0.16	x_0=0.137	F_0=0.11					

surprising that the Rawlsian objective does not lead to graduated tax rates, but it follows from the fact that this objective is not concerned with inequality among those not in the 'least fortunate group'. It is important to note that average tax rates rise with income much more steeply in the Rawlsian case than other cases considered in our simulations (see Figure 5.10b and Table 5.4). The marginal tax rate curve crosses the average tax rate curve at the income level of F(n) = 0.995. Moreover, there is more redistribution in the maximin case (see Table 5.4) than in other cases. Altogether the numerical results suggest that differences in distributional objectives have important implications for optimal tax design. In fact, in all cases shown in Tables 5.1–5.3, average tax rates are increasing in income. Analytically it is difficult to establish this. Boadway and Jacquet (2008) show that in the maximin case, assuming additive preferences in consumption and labour, single-peaked f (n), and constant elasticity labour supply, then marginal tax rates decline with n and the average tax rate $T(z)/z$ will be single-peaked in income if $T(z) < 0$ at the lowest income. Figure 5.10b confirms these patterns without assuming constant elasticity.

5.11 Other alternative social preferences: rank-order preferences, equal opportunities, poverty radicalism, and charitable conservatism

The optimal tax schedule with the Gini-weighted social preferences departs considerably from those with the linear utilitarian social welfare function. In all cases considered, the marginal tax rates increase for the two lowest deciles. With rank-order preferences k = 2 (the Gini weights) and k = 3 (and v = 3), in all cases considered, the marginal tax rates increase for the two lowest deciles. In other words, we do not obtain the U-shaped marginal tax rate curve with k = 2 and 3. Fig 5.11a displays the case with relative small pre-tax inequality (θ = 3.0) and Fig 5.11b in turn the case with large pre-tax inequality (θ = 2.0).

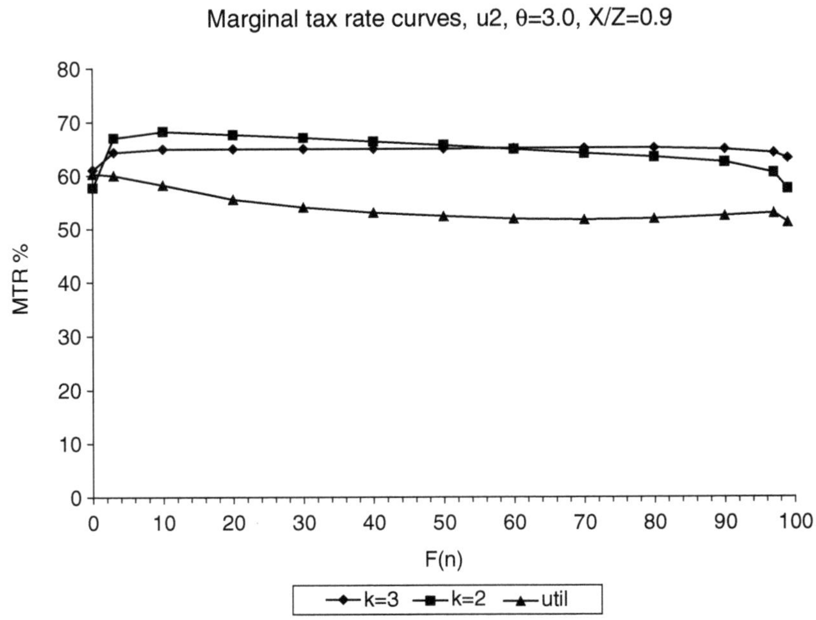

Figure 5.11a Rank-order preferences

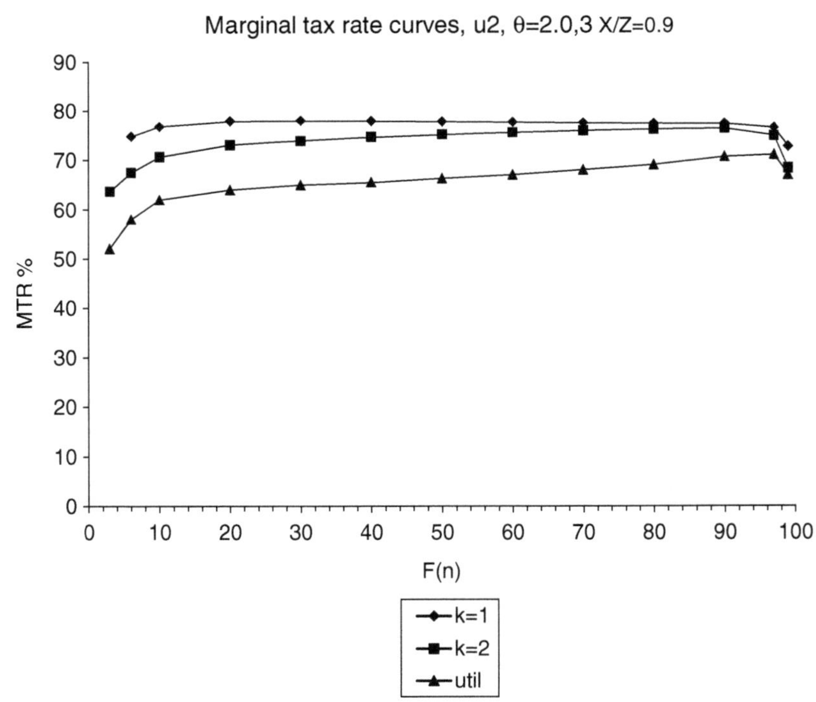

Figure 5.11b Rank-order preferences

Figure 5.11a, b displays the marginal tax rate with a different pattern of rank-order welfare weights (k=1,2,3,∞(utilitarian)), pre-tax inequality and revenue requirement R=0.1 (X/Z=0.9). Let us consider first the level of the marginal tax rate schedule. The level of marginal tax rates increases when k goes from utilitarian case k=∞ to the case of k=1. As expected, the marginal tax rates are higher when inequality aversion in the rank-order sense is higher. In all cases with the social marginal weighting underlying the Gini coefficient, and in most cases in other specifications, the marginal tax profile has the bandy-stick profile in skill and income. When k=1 or 2, in all cases considered, the marginal tax rates coincide at the upper part of the distribution. In the cases with rank order preferences k=2,3, in all cases considered, the marginal tax rates increase for the two lowest deciles. The behaviour of the social marginal valuation function is an important determinant of the pattern of optimal income taxation. The optimal tax schedule with rank-dependent social preferences departs considerably from those with the utilitarian social welfare function. Marginal tax rates are higher at all income levels for the rank-order cases than for the utilitarian case. Marginal tax rates decline much faster for the utilitarian case than for the rank-order cases when pre-tax inequality is relatively low (θ is greater than 2.5). With rank-order preferences k=2 (the Gini weights) and k=3 (and v=3), in all cases considered, the marginal tax rates are increasing for the two lowest deciles. In other words, we do not obtain the U-shaped marginal tax rate curve with k=2 and 3. When k=1 or 2, again in all cases considered, the marginal tax rates coincide at the upper part of the distribution. In other words, the marginal tax rates at the two or three highest deciles are, practically speaking, the same.

The shape of optimal tax rates in Figure 5.12 with equal opportunity social preferences is quite similar to the case of rank order with Gini weights. The justification for weights decreasing with income is here, however, completely different from that in a rank-order or a constant elastic case.[27]

Figure 5.13 displays marginal tax rates for the poverty radicalism case with F(n_{pov} = 0.15). The marginal tax rates increase up to around the poverty line. As expected, the marginal tax curve in this case resembles the maximin case except that there is an increasing part up to the poverty line. Hence, there is a kink in the optimal tax schedule with bunching at the poverty threshold. The marginal tax rate is Rawlsian above the poverty threshold.

Figure 5.14 displays marginal tax rates for the charitable conservative position in the case with k=1/3 and n_{pov} = 0.25 (see equation (7) in Chapter 4). Now things are more complicated in this more general setting with income effects than was the case in Chapter 4. As noted in the context of (13) in Chapter 4, the C-term tends to favour rising marginal rates when income is low. U_x has also a central role in the term C. Income effects

[27] Starting from the empirical finding that when poor parents have more disposable income, their children's cognitive performance improves, Gelber and Weinzierl (2014) find that the optimal welfarist policy in this context leads to more progressive taxation. In other words this would mean more redistributive policy toward low-income parents than is the existing US tax policy.

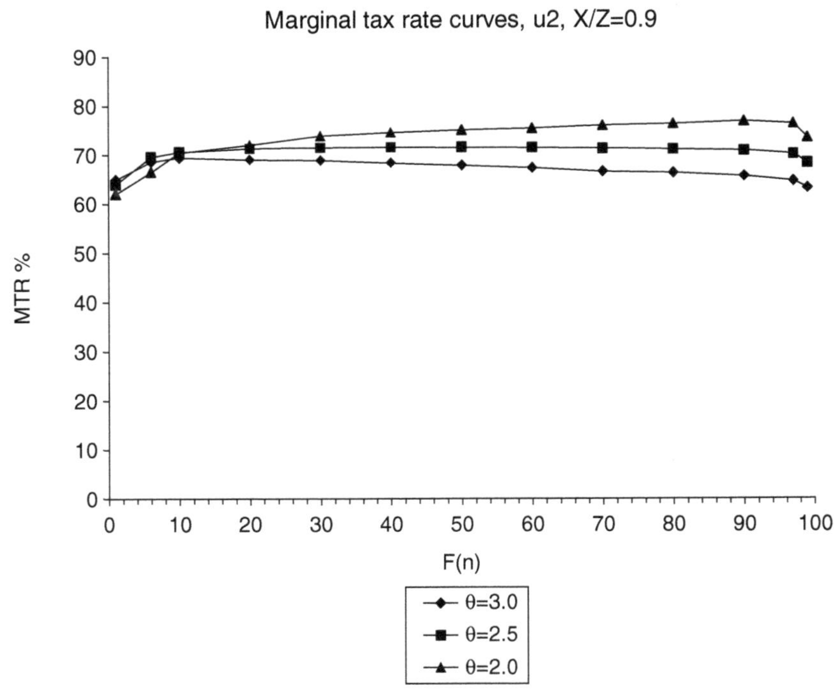

Figure 5.12 Equal opportunity: 1 − F preferences

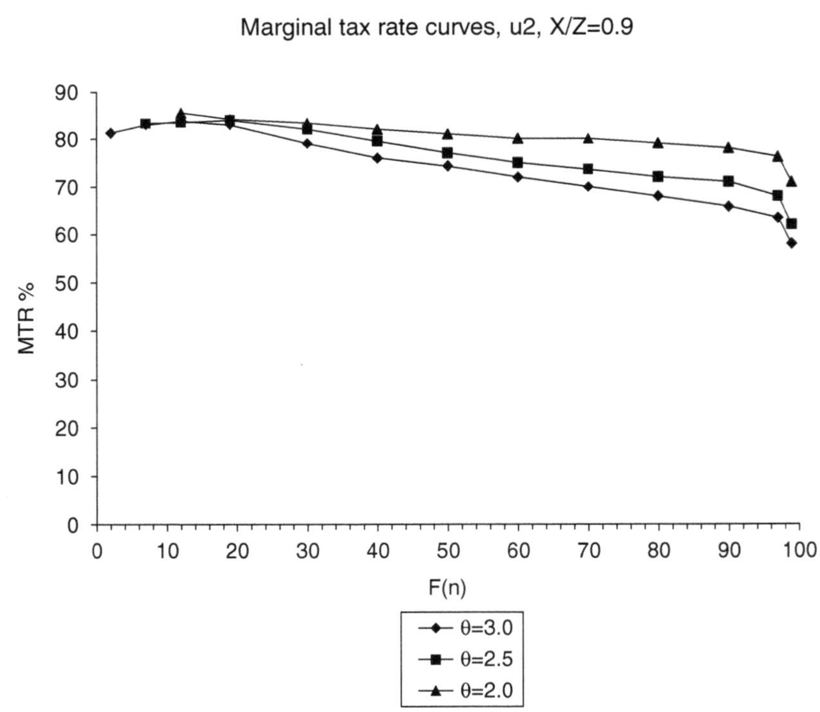

Figure 5.13 Poverty radicalism

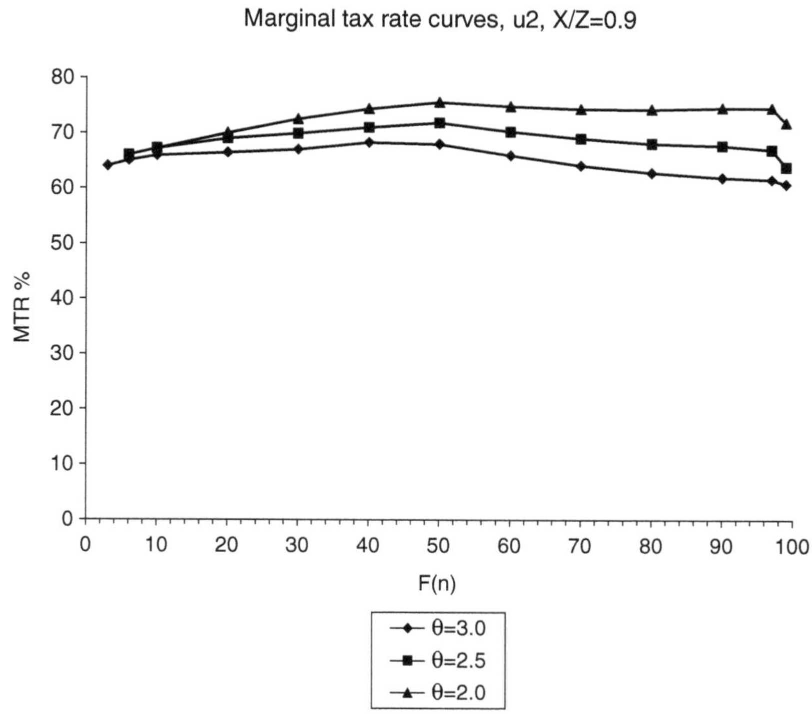

Figure 5.14 Charitable conservatism

are related to the concavity of the utility of consumption, as people are willing to work more when after-tax income is lower. In the charitable conservative case this means that weights $W'U_x$ are decreasing both below and above the poverty line and the weights jump to a lower value at n_{pov}. This suggests that this effect, through $W'U_x$, with relatively low k, the utility function (5) (case u2), and n-distribution (lognormal or Champernowne), leads to increasing marginal rates below the poverty line.

5.12 Bunching and the interplay between the curvature of utility over consumption and the social marginal weighting function

The optimum is typically characterized by a certain fraction of individuals, at the bottom end, choosing not to work (where we have dx/dn=dz/dn=0, there is bunching of individuals of different n). Given that high marginal tax rates are optimal near the bottom when θ is greater than 2.5, the finding that the percentage of those choosing not to work at all is rather high might be unsurprising. It turns out to be the case that things are not that straightforward. Namely, in the case u2 we have the highest marginal tax rates near the bottom, but the percentage of those choosing not to work is smaller than in other cases calculated. One interesting aspect in numerical results is that the amount of bunching is quite sensitive to the choice of θ and the curvature of utility over consumption. When θ is greater than 2.5, in the case of u2, there is very little bunching. It turns out to be practically zero. In the case of u2 and (θ=2, k=2, X/Z=0.9) the amount of bunching is 3 per cent, i.e. $F(n_o)=0.03$.[28] But in the case of u12 and (θ=2, k=2, X/Z=0.9), the amount of bunching is 16 per cent. Hence it is not only the inherent inequality that is crucial in determining the amount of bunching, but also the interplay between the curvature of utility over consumption and the social marginal weighting function. It is increasing with β (see more on this in Tuomala 1984). As seen in Figure 5.10b (maximin) and Figure 5.13 (poverty radicalism), when θ=2, the amount of bunching is around 18 per cent and 13 per cent, respectively. Hence the combination of high inequality aversion and high inherent inequality is crucial in determining the amount of bunching.

5.13 Guaranteed income and redistribution

How sensitive is the level of the guaranteed income or lump-sum transfer component of the tax system to the different specification of the model? And what is the relationship between the lump-sum transfer and the progressivity of the tax schedule? Table 5.5 displays the ratio of the guaranteed income to the average gross income with social welfare functions (utilitarian and Rawlsian), utility function u2, and different revenue requirement, R (=1–X/Z). This ratio is clearly higher in the Rawlsian case than in the utilitarian one. It may be slightly surprising that the ratio is not, in the Rawlsian case, sensitive to the choice of revenue requirement. From Figures 5.5a and b we see, in the case u2, that the marginal tax rates at the lower part of income distribution are much higher than in other cases considered. From Tables 5.6 and 5.7 we in turn see that the guaranteed income x_o is also much higher and rather substantial compared with other cases. Tables 5.5–5.8 display the ratio of the guaranteed income to the average gross and net income with different welfare weights and θ when utility is either u2 or u12 and revenue requirement, X/Z = 0.9. This ratio is clearly higher in the case of $\beta = 1$ and Gini weights $2(1-F)$ (k = 2) than in the case of the pure utilitarian $\beta = 0$. The ratio is

Table 5.5 The ratio of the guaranteed income to the average gross income: u2 and $\theta = 3.3$

X/Z	Rawlsian	utilitarian β=0
1.0	0.76	0.53
0.9	0.68	0.46
0.8	0.59	0.39

28 But when θ=1,5 (u2, X/Z=0.9 and linear utilitarian) the amount of bunching is 6%, i.e. $F(n_o)=0.06$.

Table 5.6 The ratio of the guaranteed income to the average gross income: u2 and $X/Z = 0.9$

Θ	Rawlsian	utilitarian $\beta = 0$	Gini weights
2.5	0.68	0.51	0.60
2.0	0.70	0.56	0.68

Table 5.7 The ratio of the guaranteed income to the average net income: u2 and $X/Z = 0.9$

Θ	$\beta = 0$	$\beta = 1$	Gini weights
3.3	0.52	0.66	0.62
2.5	0.61	0.69	0.67
2.0	0.62	0.70	0.71

Table 5.8 The ratio of the guaranteed income to the average net income: u12 and $X/Z = 0.9$

Θ	$\beta = 0$	$\beta = 1$	Gini weights
3.3	0.06	0.25	0.33
2.5	0.15	0.35	0.42
2.0	0.25	0.44	0.51

increasing with pre-tax inequality (Tables 5.6–5.8). Tables 5.8, 5.9, and 5.10 show the extent of redistribution (in terms of our measure) in the case of u2, u12, and different distributional objectives.

It is of some interest to compare our results with other studies. In a linear income tax, in Stern's (1976) central case with a tax rate slightly higher than 50 per cent, a lump-sum transfer is around one-third of average income. In the optimal two-bracket scheme, Slemrod, Yitzhaki, Mayshar, and Lundholm (1994) have a similar lump-sum transfer and a slightly higher marginal tax rate at the low bracket (around 60 per cent) than at the top bracket. Numerical simulations for the non-linear case in Saez (2001) show that the guaranteed benefit may be as high as 40 per cent of average earnings even for moderate redistributive tastes and that the phasing-out rate is very high, typically around 70–80 per cent. The desirability of such a schedule is to some extent based on constant labour supply elasticities used in Saez's (2001) simulations—namely, that kind of schedule targets benefits at the most needy individuals in the economy and concentrates labour supply disincentives to individuals with low earnings ability. These reductions in labour supply incentives at the bottom are not very costly because their labour supply elasticities

Table 5.9 The extent of redistribution (RD):[29] u2, X/Z=0.9

Θ	$\beta=0$	$\beta=1$	Gini weights
3.3	52.6	67.0	61.6
2.5	71.8	86.1	80.3

Table 5.10 The extent of redistribution (RD):[30] u12, X/Z=0.9

Θ	$\beta=0$	$\beta=1$	Gini weights
3.3	31.1	49.5	28.1
2.5	52.3	55.0	44.4

are the same as those higher up in the distribution, and because the beneficiaries would not have had very high earnings even in the absence of the programme. Diamond (1968, p. 296) also offers the conjecture that the low-ability group might best be given a higher grant and higher marginal tax rates, the latter because distortion is not that great.

In sum: a typical conclusion from numerical simulations (Mirrlees 1971; Tuomala 1984; Saez 2001) has been that the Mirrlees model suggests a relatively generous lump-sum grant for those with no earnings and very high phasing-out rates up to the median income (see the thin curve in Figure 6.1a in Chapter 6). This conclusion can be argued against. There are good grounds to feel that these simulations are based on overly restrictive and unrealistic specifications of the utility function and the skill distribution. For example, Mirrlees (1971) assumes log–log utility implying too-high labour supply elasticities, Tuomala (1984) uses lognormal skill distribution which has a too thin upper tail, and Saez (2001) assumes constant labour supply elasticity (a one-parameter constant elasticity utility) at all income levels. Above we showed that when we take a more flexible specification for the utility function—quadratic utility function—empirically better grounded skill distribution, and relatively mild redistribution preferences, we obtain the following low-income support programme: relatively generous lump-sum grant (basic income) and increasing marginal tax rates[31] (see the thick curve in Figure 6.1a in Chapter 6). Interestingly, we also obtain this pattern with CES function when the pre-tax inequality is sufficiently high but not unrealistically so. What is also important is that increasing top income inequality (smaller θ in the Champernowne distribution) leads to more progressive taxation (in the sense of increasing average tax rates in income).

[29] We measure the extent of redistribution, denoted by RD, as the proportional reduction between the decile ratio for market income, z, and the decile ratio for disposable income, x.

[30] In the case of Gini weights RD is based on P(90/50).

[31] Colombino (2009) provides an interesting discussion from the empirical point of view on the lessons of optimal income tax simulations for designing low-income support programmes. See also De Vincenti and Paladini (2009).

APPENDIX 5.1 LABOUR SUPPLY ELASTICITIES

Static model: setup

An individual's preference ordering is represented by a utility function over consumption x and hours worked y. The individual earns wage w per hour (net of taxes) and has b in non-labour income. The function $u = u(x,y)$ is strictly increasing in x, strictly decreasing in y, defined for $x \geq 0$, i.e. the consumption is unbounded, while $0 \leq y \leq 1$ with $u_x > 0$ and $u_y < 0$. Also, $u(x,y)$ is assumed to be strictly concave. Individual solves max; $u(x,y)$ subject to $x = wy + b$.

The first-order condition for the choice of work hours, $wu_c + u_y = 0$, defines uncompensated (Marshallian) labour supply function $y(w,b)$.

The possibilities open to the worker include working anywhere between 0 and some maximum hours at a fixed hourly wage rate. These possibilities are shown by the budget constraint AB in Figure A5.1, where OB is a non-labour income. The choice made by the worker is a function of the parameters describing their economic opportunities, here w and b. As w and b change, so too will y. A convenient way of representing these changes is in terms of elasticities.

Define the elasticities: uncompensated elasticity of labour supply: $E^u = \frac{\partial y}{\partial w}\frac{w}{y}$. The elasticity of labour supply with respect to the net wage is the percentage change in y (hours of work) when net wage w increases by 1 per cent. For example, where the elasticity is equal to 0.5, this implies that a 10 per cent rise in wages produces a 5 per cent rise in hours of work.

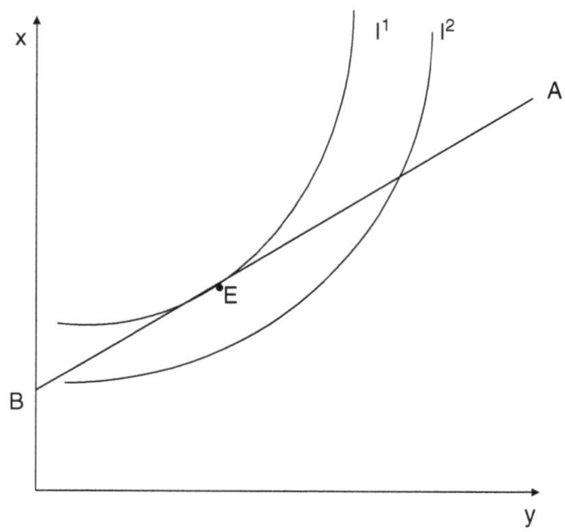

Figure A5.1 Labour supply

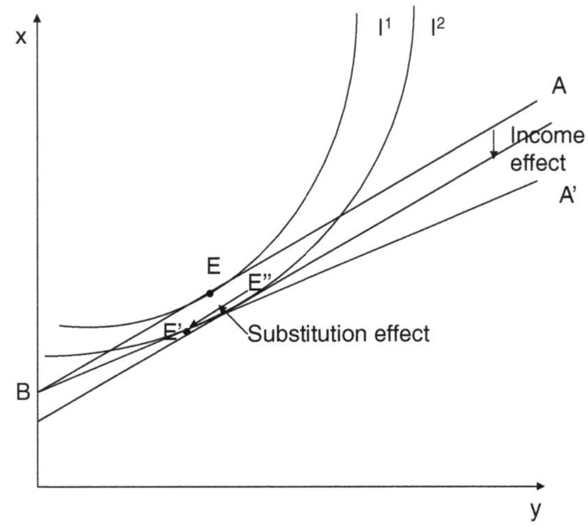

Figure A5.2 Substitution and income effects

Income effect parameter: $\xi = w\frac{\partial y}{\partial w}$. € increase in earnings if person receives €1 extra in non-labour income. Compensated (Hicksian) labour supply function $y^c(w,u)$, which minimizes expenditure $wy-x$ st to constraint $u(x,y)\geq u$. Compensated elasticity of labour supply: $E^c = \frac{\partial y^c}{\partial w}\frac{w}{y}>0$.

It has long been known that taxing earnings may have a discouraging effect on labour supply, although the effect is on the whole uncertain because the fact that a tax impoverishes people may induce them to work more to retain their consumption level. It is a standard balancing act in consumer–worker theory between a substitution effect (the tax makes leisure less expensive in forgone consumption, therefore they work less) and an income effect (the tax makes one poorer, and people may want to share this scarcity between lower consumption and lower leisure, therefore they work more).

Next we examine the effect of a tax on labour income in this textbook model. The change in net wage due to the increase of a tax on labour income reduces the worker's disposable income to $w(1-t)y+b$. Now y may have changed as a result of the tax. In Figure A5.2 we see that the budget line still starts from B but the slope is now $w(1-t)$. The new budget line is BA'. The labour supply choice shifts to point E' on the indifference curve 2. This shift can be decomposed into two effects: (1) The substitution effect, shift from E" to E', is moving along the indifference curve. (2) The income effect means a shift from E to E". The worker is now worse off, being on a lower indifference curve. The substitution effect is negative. The income effect in turn is typically expected to be positive so that the worker is less well-off and therefore less able to afford leisure. Hence the overall effect is ambiguous. It depends on the relative strength of these two effects. It means that the tax may cause people to work less or more. In other words, the elasticity of labour supply may be negative rather than positive.

Formally, the Slutsky equation: $\frac{\partial y^c}{\partial w} = \frac{\partial y}{\partial w} - y\frac{\partial y}{\partial b}$. This implies $E^c = E^u - \xi$

Table A5.1 and A5.2 show elasticities for male and women.

Table A5.1 Elasticity estimates for males: static models

Authors of study	Year	Uncompensated elasticity	Compensated elasticity
Ashenfelter–Heckman	1973	−0.16	0.11
Boskin	1973	−0.07	0.10
Eight British studies[a]	1976–83	−0.16	0.13
Eight NIT studies[a]	1977–84	0.03	0.13
Burtless–Hausman	1978	0.00	0.07
Wales–Woodland	1979	0.14	0.84
Hausman	1981	0.00	0.74
Blomquist	1983	0.08	0.11
Blomquist–Hansson–Busewitz	1990	0.12	0.13
MaCurdy–Green–Paarsch	1990	0.00	0.07
Triest	1990	0.05	0.05
Van Soest–Woittiez–Kapteyn	1990	0.19	0.28
Kuismanen	1998	0.06	0.08
Ecklof–Sacklen	2000	0.05	0.27
Blomquist–Ecklof–Newey	2001	0.08	

Notes: Where ranges are reported, mid-point is used to take means.
a = Average of the studies surveyed by Pencavel (1986).
b = Effect of surprise permanent wage increase.
Source: Keane (2011) and Meghir and Phillips (2010).

Table A5.2 Elasticity estimates for women: static models

Authors of study	Year	Uncompensated elasticity	Compensated elasticity
Cogan	1981	0.89[a]	
Heckman–Macurdy	1982	2.35	
Blundell–Walker	1986	−0.20	0.01
Blundell–Duncan–Meghir	1998	0.17	
Ilmakunnas	1997	0.10	0.29
Kimmel–Kniesner	1998	3.05[b]	
Kuismanen	1998	0.23	0.23
Moffitt	1984	1.25	

Notes:
a = Elasticity conditional on positive work hours.
b = Sum of elasticities on extensive and intensive margins.
Source: Keane (2011) and Meghir and Phillips (2010).

APPENDIX 5.2 NUMERICAL SOLUTION PROCEDURE

Now we consider a case with $u=U(x)+V(1-y)$. Two differential equations (see appendix 4.5)

$$\frac{dv}{dn}=-\frac{v}{n}\left(2+\frac{nf'}{f}\right)+\frac{1}{n^2}\left(\frac{W'}{\lambda}-\frac{1}{U_x}\right) \tag{1}$$

and

$$\frac{du}{dn}=-\frac{yV_y}{n} \tag{2}$$

in u and v provide the solution to the optimal income tax problem, together with the condition

$$n^2fv=\int_0^n((W'/\lambda)-(1/U_x))f(n)dn \tag{3}$$

and at $n=n_o$[32];

$$n_o{}^2f(n_o)v_o=\int_0^{n_0}((W'/\lambda)-(1/U_x))f(n)dn \tag{4}$$

and the transversality condition $\mu(h)=0$ and (4) requires that

$$\lambda n^2fv\rightarrow 0(n\rightarrow\infty) \tag{5}$$

The condition (4) guarantees an accurate value for n_o .

We can write the optimal marginal tax rate

$$\left(n+\frac{V_y}{U_x}\right)n^2f(n)=\xi_y\int_n^\infty\left(\frac{1}{U_x}-\frac{W'}{\lambda}\right)f(n')dn' \tag{6}$$

where $-\xi_y=(V_y+yV_{yy})$ and λ is the multiplier on the revenue constraint, at n_o

$$\lambda n_o f(n_o)\left(1+\frac{V_y^0(x_0,0)}{n_0u_x^0(x_0,0)}\right)=\frac{\mu(n_o)V_y^0(x_0,0)}{n_o} \tag{7}$$

$$\left(1+\frac{V_y^0(x_0,0)}{n_0u_x^0}\right)=g_y(u_0,0)\frac{F(n_0)}{n_0^2f(n_0)}\left[\frac{W'}{\lambda}-\frac{1}{u_x(x_0,0)}\right] \tag{8}$$

where $\xi_y=-(V_y(n_0)+y(n_0)V_{yy}(n_0))$

[32] n_o, largest n for which $y(n)=0$, may be in some cases rather large. In the interval $[0, n_o]$, $y=0$ and $x=x_0$ and then $u=U(x_o)-V(0)$ (*). (*) and (13) in Chapter 4 are needed for starting values in numerical solutions of (1) and (2) conditional on a trial value for n_o.

And further

$$\left(1+\frac{V_y^0(x_0,0)}{n_0 u_x^0(x_0,0)}\right)=-\frac{V_y^0(x_0,0)}{n_0 u_x^0(x_0,0)}\frac{F(n_0)}{n_0 f(n_0)}\left[\frac{W' u_x(x_0,0)}{\lambda}-1\right] \tag{9}$$

Equations (1) and (2) form a pair of non-linear differential equations, which can be solved only by numerical integration methods. In this study, a forward Euler and a fourth-order Runge–Kutta method are used. In equations (1) and (2) the unknowns are u, v, and λ. Instead of solving λ, a value is assumed for it. A rough estimate can be obtained by calculating $\int_0^\infty (1/U_x)f(n)dn/\int_0^\infty W'f(n)dn$ for some plausible y and x. The condition, $\mu(\infty)$=0, makes the numerical solution difficult. A trial-and-error method is used to obtain a value n_0 which enables fulfilment of the condition $y(n_0)$=0. The value of x at n_0 is solved from equation (9) by using Newton's iteration method. When λ is given and $x(n_0)$ is solved, the integration of (1) and (2) can begin. The general step is:

$$v^{i+1} = v^i + \phi_v dn \tag{10}$$

$$u^{i+1} = u^i + \phi_u dn \tag{11}$$

where ϕ is an integration operator and dn is the step length. In the case of the Euler method,

$$\phi_v = -\frac{v}{n}\left(2+\frac{nf'}{f}\right)+\frac{1}{n^2}\left(\frac{W'}{\lambda}-\frac{1}{U_x}\right)\Big|_i$$

$$\phi_u = -\frac{yV_y}{n}\Big|_i$$

i.e. the derivatives evaluated at the beginning of the step.

When u^{i+1} and v^{i+1} are obtained, the new values for y and x are calculated from (6) and from the utility function by using Newton's iteration method. In numerical applications, the following functions were used: $u = \log x + \log(1-y)$ and $u = -\frac{1}{x}-\frac{1}{(1-y)}$. f(n) is the Champernowne distribution with the probability density function and the cumulative distribution function $f(n)=\theta\left(\frac{m^\theta n^{\theta-1}}{(m^\theta+n^\theta)^2}\right)$ $F(n)=1-\frac{m^\theta}{(m^\theta+n^\theta)}$, where θ is a shape parameter and m is a scale parameter. A constant absolute utility–inequality aversion form was used for the social welfare function of the government, $W(u)=-\frac{1}{\beta}e^{-\beta u}$, where β measures the degree of inequality aversion in the social welfare function of the government (in the case of β = 0, we define W = u). If we write $W^{-\beta}=\int e^{-\beta u}f(n)dn$ then the limit as $\beta\to\infty$ is given by W=$\min_n[e^u]$.

Solutions of x and y as functions of u and v where u and v are known from (10) and (11):

$$-\frac{1}{x}-\frac{1}{1-y}-u=0$$

$$1+\frac{V_y}{nU_x}/\xi_y - v = 0$$

or generally,

$$g(x, y; u) = 0$$

$$h(x, y; v) = 0$$

Again, using Newton's method,

$$\begin{pmatrix} x^{n+1} \\ y^{n+1} \end{pmatrix} = \begin{pmatrix} x^{n} \\ y^{n} \end{pmatrix} - \begin{pmatrix} g_x(\underline{x}^n) & g_y(\underline{x}^n) \\ h_x(\underline{x}^n) & h_y(\underline{x}^n) \end{pmatrix} \begin{pmatrix} g(\underline{x}^n) \\ h(\underline{x}^n) \end{pmatrix} \text{ where } \underline{x}^n = \begin{pmatrix} x^{n} \\ y^{n} \end{pmatrix}$$

where $g_x \approx \frac{g(x+ds,y)-g(x,y)}{ds}$ by numerical integration.

The range of n was from n_0 to 1.5, at which point the integrated value of f(n) was more than 0.9999. The step length dn was 0.02 in most computations and the forward and forward Euler methods were used for the integrations. Some cases were calculated by using the Runge–Kutta method and a smaller step length to assess the accuracy of the computations. Extra care was taken to obtain an accurate value for n_0 and to satisfy $y(n_0)$=0.

In sum: the formulae (1) and (2) form a pair of non-linear differential equations in u and v. These two differential equations provide the solution to the optimal income tax problem together with the revenue requirement and $\mu(\infty)$=0. This differential equation system can be solved only by numerical integration methods. In this study, a fourth-order Runge–Kutta method is used. In equations (1) and (2) the unknowns are u, v, and λ. Instead of solving for λ, a value is assumed for it. The condition, $\mu(\infty)$=0, makes the numerical solution difficult. A trial-and-error method is used to obtain a value n_0, which enables us to satisfy the condition $y(n_0)$=0. Extra care was taken to obtain an accurate value for n_0 and to satisfy $\mu(\infty)$=0. The value for x at n_0 is solved from equation (8) by using the Newton method. When λ is given and $x(n_0)$ is solved, the integration of (1) and (2) can be started. When u^{i+1} and v^{i+1} (i refers to an iteration cycle) are obtained, the new values for y and x are calculated from equation (6) and from the utility function by using the Newton method. The range of n was from n_0 to 1.5, at which point the integrated value of f(n) was more than 0.9999. In our calculations this transversality condition takes the form $\mu(\infty)\rightarrow 0$, when $n\rightarrow\infty$ because we use the density function with infinite range.

APPENDIX 5.3 FORTRAN PROGRAM WITH SOME COMMENTS

```
>C ###### OTO #######
C select function u:
C NUSEL=1 u=ln(x)+ln(1−y)
C NUSEL=2 u=-1/x-1/(1−y)
```

```
C select formulation for g:
C NGSEL=1 EXP(BY)
C NGSEL=2 B=0 (beta=0)
C maxmin case: NFORM=0
  IMPLICIT REAL*8 (A-H,O-Z)
  COMMON /DPAR/NDIS,SIG,RK,TTH,XMY,ALF
  COMMON /CONTR/IFXY
  DIMENSION TUL(10)
  DIMENSION TULO(500,9),NT(500)
C data:
C NUSEL (1 or 2), NGSEL (1 or 2), NFORM 0=maxmin, BET=beta
C INCR (output incr, at every INCR step)
C ITKMAX max number of iterations
C DN increment of n
C XIO, guess for initial value of X (XI to be determined by iteration)
C ERMAX maximum allowed error in iterations
C DS increment of X in numerical differentiation, small for accuracy
C RNOI RNOF ND, guess of initial value for N, N-final, increment of N-initial
C (RNO is guessed, RN is usually stepped with negative DN
C to obtain final terminal condition: TEST=0 and FK=1, by trial)
C NTUL, number of output points
C TUL, output point values of N
C RLAI RLAF DRLA, lambda initial, lambda final, increment of lambda
C (usually lambda is constant, RLAI=RLAF and DRLA=0,
C lambda can also be stepped (incremented) in trying to find a solution)
C SIG, RK parameters for lognormal distribution
C TTH, XMY parameters for Champernowne distribution
C ALF parameter for exponential distribution
C read data
  READ(5,*)NUSEL,NGSEL,NFORM,INCR,ITKMAX,NTUL,NDIS
  READ(5,*)BET,RNMAX,DN,XIO,ERMAX,DS
  READ(5,*)RNOI,RNOF,DNO
  READ(5,*)(TUL(I),I=1,NTUL)
  READ(5,*)RLAI,RLAF,DRLA
  IF(NDIS.EQ.1)READ(5,*)SIG,RK,ZKA,ZMYA
  IF(NDIS.EQ.2)READ(5,*)TTH,XMY
  IF(NDIS.EQ.3)READ(5,*)ALF
  WRITE(6,100)
100 FORMAT(' NUSEL NGSEL NFORM INCR,ITKMAX,NTUL,NDIS
  .'/' BET RNMAX DN XIO ERMAX DS
  .'/' RNOI RNOF DNO
  .'/' (TUL(I),I=1,NTUL )
  .'/' RLAI RLAF DRLA')
  WRITE(6,120)NUSEL,NGSEL,NFORM,INCR,ITKMAX,NTUL,NDIS
  WRITE(6,121)BET,RNMAX,DN,XIO,ERMAX,DS
```

```
  WRITE(6,121)RNOI,RNOF,DNO
  WRITE(6,121)(TUL(I),I=1,NTUL)
  WRITE(6,122)RLAI,RLAF,DRLA
  WRITE(6,123)
123 FORMAT('distribution parameters')
  IF(NDIS.EQ.1)WRITE(6,121)SIG,RK,ZKA,ZMYA
  IF(NDIS.EQ.2)WRITE(6,121)TTH,XMY
  IF(NDIS.EQ.3)WRITE(6,121)ALF
120 FORMAT(1X,16I5)
121 FORMAT(8F12.6)
122 FORMAT(1X,8E13.5)
  FMLT=1.
  IF(NFORM.EQ.0)FMLT=0.
C
C step lambda from RLAI to RLAF with increment DRLA (in interval
C of DILA), DRLA can be negative also,
C lambda affects the ratio XF/ZF,
C for greater accuracy refined search with smaller DRLA
C
C intervals for searching parameters lambda and rno:
C DINO and DILA
C
  DINO=RNOF-RNOI
  DILA=RLAF-RLAI
  LLM=0
2000 CONTINUE
  LLM=LLM+1
  RLA=RLAI+(LLM-1)*DRLA
  WRITE(6,2030)RLA
2030 FORMAT(' RLA=',E14.6)
  LKM=0
1000 CONTINUE
C
C step N0 from RNOI to RNOF with increment DNO
C to obtain finally TEST=0 at FK=1,
C (as close to 1 as required),
C program is run interactively with monitoring results,
C for greater accuracy refined search from known values with smaller DRLA
C etc.
C
  LKM=LKM+1
  RNO=RNOI+(LKM-1)*DNO
  WRITE(6,80)RNO
80 FORMAT(' RNO=',E14.8)
  ITU=1
```

```
C
C output points at FK1, FK2, ... (FK=integral f(n)dn)
C first output point, TULOS=FK1
C
  TULOS=TUL(ITU)
C
C initialize variables
C
  N=0
  Y=0.
  Z=0.
  ZF=0.
  ZZF=0.
  ZFDZ=0.
  ZZFDZ=0.
  ZMY=0.
  ZSIG=0.
  XI=XIO
C
C initial value for X is XI
C and initial value for RN (i.e. N) is RNO
C
C calculate some values at RN=RNO
C the same results (with marginally less computation effort) if INIT is called here?
C
  CALL INIT(XI,RNO,DN,NUSEL,NGSEL,BET,F,FD,FK,XF,UF,UXF,EF,RNF,
  .RNNF,U,UX,UY,PSY,GD)
  APU=FK/F/RNO/RNO
C
C calculate initial value fox X (XI) by iteration
C DS is increment of XI (small for accuracy)
C DH/DX calculated by numerical differentiation
C
  ITK=0
48 CONTINUE
C CALL INIT(XI,RNO,DN,NUSEL,NGSEL,BET,F,FD,FK,XF,UF,UXF,EF,RNF,
C .RNNF,U,UX,UY,PSY,GD)
C APU=FK/F/RNO/RNO
  ITK=ITK+1
  CALL HS(XI,NUSEL,NGSEL,NFORM,FK,H1,APU,RLA,BET,RNO)
C
C store XI temporarily
C
  XII=XI
  XI=XI+DS
```

```
   CALL HS(XI,NUSEL,NGSEL,NFORM,FK,H2,APU,RLA,BET,RNO)
   XI=XII
   HX=(H2-H1)/DS
   DX=-H1/HX
   XI=XI+DX
   ER=ABS(DX/XI)
   IF(ER.GT.ERMAX.AND.ITK.LT.ITKMAX) GOTO 48
   IF(ER.GT.ERMAX.AND.ITK.EQ.ITKMAX)WRITE(6,141)
141 FORMAT(' XI iteration failed in ITKMAX cycles => try next N0')
C
C or STOP (not active)
C141 FORMAT(' XI iteration failed in ITKMAX cycles => STOP')
C IF(ER.GT.ERMAX.AND.ITK.EQ.ITKMAX)STOP
C
C
C ER>ERMAX and ITK=ITKMAX, i.e. not converged, try next N0 value
C (GOTO 900)
C
   IF(ER.GT.ERMAX.AND.ITK.EQ.ITKMAX) GOTO 900
C
C calculation of initial value for X successful, output some results
C
   WRITE(6,140)ITK,RNO,XI,H1
140 FORMAT(' ITK RNO XI H1',I4,E18.7,2E14.4)
C
C set initial values for X and N for integration from N0
C
   X=XI
   RN=RNO
C
C calculate (again) some values at N=NO
C
   CALL INIT(X,RN,DN,NUSEL,NGSEL,BET,F,FD,FK,XF,UF,UXF,EF,RNF,
   .RNNF,U,UX,UY,PSY,GD)
   FO=F
   FKO=FK
   VO=(1.+UY/UX/RN)/PSY
   V=VO
C
C test if V negative at NO
C (if so goto next trial NO)
C
   IF(V.LT.0.)WRITE(6,400)V,U,UX,GD
400 FORMAT(' VO<0, UO UXO GDO',/4E14.6)
   IF(V.LT.0.)GOTO 900
```

```
  ITO=0
  RN=RN-DN
C
C integration from RN=RNO starts here
C
40 CONTINUE
C
C call subroutine DIS to calculate distribution values
C F(N) and its derivate FD(N)
C
  CALL DIS(RN,F,FD)
C
C step (integrate) with constant DN
C (N is step number)
C
  N=N+1
  RN=RN+DN
  IF(RN.GT.RNMAX)WRITE(6,960)
960 FORMAT(' STOP, RN > RNMAX => increase RNMAX')
  IF(RN.GT.RNMAX)STOP
  FDN=F*DN
  FK=FK+FDN
  XF=XF+X*FDN
  UXF=UXF+FDN/UX
  ZF=ZF+Z*FDN
C
C ZKA given as data (value known after running the program)
C (does not affect the solution)
C
  ZZF=ZZF+(Z-ZKA)*(Z-ZKA)*FDN
  GD=1.
  IF(NGSEL.EQ.1)GD=EXP(-BET*U)
  EF=EF+GD*FDN
  RNF=RNF+RN*FDN
  RNNF=RNNF+RN*RN*FDN
  FU=-Y*UY/RN
  FV=-V/RN*(2.+RN*FD/F)+(FMLT*GD/RLA-1./UX)/RN/RN
  U=U+FU*DN
  V=V+FV*DN
C WRITE(6,410)V,U,UX,GD
C410 FORMAT(' V U UX GD',/4E14.6)
  UF=UF+U*FDN
C
C if iteration in XY fails, then IFXY=1
C
```

```
      IFXY=0
C
C solve for X and Y by Newton's iteration method in XY
C
      YO=Y
      CALL XY(X,Y,NUSEL,NGSEL,RN,U,V,DS,ERMAX,ITKMAX)
      IF(IFXY.EQ.1)WRITE(6,950)
950 FORMAT(' iteration in XY failed, IFXY=1 => GOTO 900')
      IF(IFXY.EQ.1)GOTO 900
      INDXY=0
C
C also required that X(N) > 0 and Y(N) < 1
C (if not try next RNO)
C
      IF(X.LT.1.E-7.OR.Y.GT..999999)INDXY=1
      IF(INDXY.EQ.1)WRITE(6,62)RN,X,Y
62 FORMAT(' **** INDXY=1, N X Y',3E14.4)
C IF(INDXY.EQ.1) STOP
      IF(INDXY.EQ.1) GOTO 900
      ZO=Z
      Z=RN*Y
      DZ=Z-ZO
      IF(N.EQ.1)goto 889
      ZFDZ=ZFDZ+Z*F*DZ
889 CONTINUE
C
C ZKA and ZMYA given as data (initially zero)
C (known after running the program)
C
      IF(N.EQ.1)goto 908
      ZZFDZ=ZZFDZ+(Z-ZKA)*(Z-ZKA)*F*DZ
      DLOGZ=DLOG(Z)
      ZMY=ZMY+DLOGZ*F*DZ
      ZSIG=ZSIG+(DLOGZ-ZMYA)*(DLOGZ-ZMYA)*F*DZ
908 CONTINUE
C ##############################################
C required DZ(N)=Z(N)-Z(N-DN) > 0
C if not try next RNO
C
      IF(DZ.GE.0.) GOTO 60
      WRITE(6,980)RN,Y,YO,DZ,FK
980 FORMAT(' N Y YO DZ<0 FK',5E14.6)
      GOTO 900
60 CONTINUE
C
```

```
C ATR, average TR
C
   ATR=(Z-X)/(Z+.0000001)
   IF(DABS(ATR).GT.1.D0)ATR=DSIGN(1.D0,ATR)
C
C TEST for terminating condition: TEST=0 (from above) and FK=1
C
   TEST=V*RN*RN*F
   GOTO(21,22),NUSEL
21 UX=1./X
   UXX=-1./X/X
   UY=1./(Y-1.)
   UYY=-1./(Y-1.)/(Y-1.)
   GOTO 299
22 UX=1./X/X
   UXX=-2./X/X/X
   UY=-1./(1.-Y)/(1.-Y)
   UYY=-2./(1.-Y)/(1.-Y)/(1.-Y)
   GOTO 299
299 CONTINUE
   THE=(1.+UY/UX/RN)
C
C output after certain FK-values and
C after INCR number of steps
C
   INDT=0
   IF((N/INCR)*INCR.EQ.N)INDT=1
   IF(FK.GE.TULOS)INDT=1
   IF(FK.GE.TULOS)ITU=ITU+1
C
C next output point
C
   TULOS=TUL(ITU)
   IF(TEST.LT.0.0)INDT=1
   IF(INDT.NE.1)GOTO 910
   ITO=ITO+1
   NT(ITO)=N
   TULO(ITO,1)=RN
   TULO(ITO,2)=X
   TULO(ITO,3)=Y
   TULO(ITO,4)=Z
   TULO(ITO,5)=FK
   TULO(ITO,6)=ATR
   TULO(ITO,7)=TEST
   TULO(ITO,8)=THE
```

```
  TULO(ITO,9)=UF
910 CONTINUE
  IF(TEST.LT.0.)GOTO 930
  IF(RN.LT.RNMAX)GOTO 40
930 CONTINUE
  WRITE(6,500)N,TEST,THE,RN,FK
500 FORMAT(' *****N TEST THE RN FK'/,I6,4E16.7)
  XZ=XF/(ZF+1.E-8)
C
C requirement: TEST goes to zero at approximately FK=1 (here at FK>0.995)
C
  IF(FK.LT..995)GOTO 1100
  WRITE(6,70)NUSEL,NGSEL,NFORM,VO,RNO,FO,FKO,APU
70 FORMAT(' NUSEL NGSEL NFORM VO RNO FO FKO APU',/3I2,5E13.4)
  WRITE(6,180)
  DO 920 NN=1,ITO
920 WRITE(6,200)NT(NN),(TULO(NN,J),J=1,8),TULO(NN,9)
200 FORMAT(I5,8F7.4,F8.4)
  WRITE(6,940)XF,ZF,XZ
940 FORMAT(' XF/ZF=',E14.5,' /',E14.5,'=',E14.5)
  WRITE(6,943)ZF,ZZF,ZFDZ,ZZFDZ
943 FORMAT(' ZF ZZF ZFDZ ZZFDZ'/,4E14.5)
  WRITE(6,636)N,ZMY,ZSIG
636 FORMAT(' N ZMY ZSIG',I5,2E13.4)
105 FORMAT(1X,2I4,6F10.4)
110 FORMAT(' INCR ITKMAX RNMAX DN XI RLA ERMAX DS')
180 FORMAT(' N RN X Y Z FK'
  1,T43,'ATR TEST MTR U ')
C180 FORMAT(' N RN X Y Z FK'
C 1,T43,'ATR TEST EU RI ')
  GOTO 1100
900 CONTINUE
  WRITE(6,130)RN,FK,X,Y
130 FORMAT(' failed, RN FK X Y',6E12.4)
1100 CONTINUE
  IF(DINO.GT.0.AND.RNO.LT.RNOF)GOTO 1000
  IF(DINO.LT.0.AND.RNO.GT.RNOF)GOTO 1000
  IF(DILA.GT.0.AND.RLA.LT.RLAF) GOTO 2000
  IF(DILA.LT.0.AND.RLA.GT.RLAF) GOTO 2000
  STOP
  END
  SUBROUTINE
INIT(X,RN,DN,NUSEL,NGSEL,BET,F,FD,FK,XF,UF,UXF,EF,RNF,
  .RNNF,U,UX,UY,PSY,GD)
C
C integrate numerically (here with 3-point Gaussian rule)
```

```
C some initial values from 0 to NO
C
   IMPLICIT REAL*8 (A-H,O-Z)
   DIMENSION GP(3),WEI(3)
      NGP=3
   GP(1)=-.774596669241483
   GP(2)=0.
   GP(3)=-GP(1)
   WEI(1)=.5555555555555555
   WEI(2)=.8888888888888888
   WEI(3)=.5555555555555555
   M=0
   FK=0.
   XF=0.
   UF=0.
   UXF=0.
   RNF=0.
   RNNF=0.
   EF=0.
C
C number of intervals DN from 0 to NO
C
   NA=RN/DN
C
C test if number of intervals sufficient for integration
C from 0 to N0,
C (here taken arbitrarily 10)
C
   DNA=RN/NA
   IF(NA.LT.11)GOTO 50
   GOTO(41,42),NUSEL
41 U=DLOG(X)
   UX=1./X
   UY=-1.
   PSY=1.
   GOTO 499
42 U=-1./X-1.
   UX=1./X/X
   UY=-1.
   PSY=1.
499 CONTINUE
   GD=1.
   IF(NGSEL.EQ.1)GD=EXP(-BET*U)
   DO 30 M=1,NA
   RNA1=(M-1)*DNA
```

```
      RNA2=RNA1+DNA
      DO 35 IP=1,NGP
      PSI=GP(IP)
      P1=.5*(1.-PSI)
      P2=.5*(1.+PSI)
      RNA=P1*RNA1+P2*RNA2
      CALL DIS(RNA,F,FD)
      DLE=.5*DNA*WEI(IP)
      FDN=F*DLE
      RNF=RNF+RNA*FDN
      RNNF=RNNF+RNA*RNA*FDN
      FK=FK+FDN
      XF=XF+X*FDN
      UXF=UXF+FDN/UX
      EF=EF+GD*FDN
35 CONTINUE
30 CONTINUE
      CALL DIS(RN,F,FD)
      RETURN
50 CONTINUE
      WRITE(6,60)NA,RN,DN,DNA
60 FORMAT(' number of intervals too small in INIT',/,
      .' smaller DN needed NA RN DN DNA',/
      .I3,3E12.4)
      STOP
      END
      SUBROUTINE HS(X,NUSEL,NGSEL,NFORM,FK,H,APU,RLA,BET,RNO)
C
C calculate function H
C
      IMPLICIT REAL*8 (A-H,O-Z)
      GOTO(11,12),NUSEL
11 CONTINUE
      IF(X.LE.0)GOTO 20
      U=DLOG(X)
      UX=1./X
      UY=-1.
      PSY=1.
      GOTO 199
12 U=-1./X-1.
      UX=1./X/X
      UY=-1.
      PSY=1.
199 CONTINUE
      GD=1.
```

```
      IF(NGSEL.EQ.1)GD=EXP(-BET*U)
      GDR=GD/RLA
      IF(NFORM.EQ.0)GDR=1./RLA/FK
      H=APU*(GDR-1./UX)-(1.+UY/RNO/UX)/PSY
      RETURN
20    CONTINUE
      WRITE(6,40)
40    FORMAT(' X le 0, STOP')
      STOP
      END
      SUBROUTINE XY(X,Y,NUSEL,NGSEL,RN,U,V,DS,ERMAX,ITKMAX)
C
C calculate X and Y by Newton's iteration method
C DS is increment of X
C ITK is iteration cycle counter
C
      IMPLICIT REAL*8 (A-H,O-Z)
      COMMON /CONTR/IFXY
      IFXY=0
      ITK=0
10    ITK=ITK+1
      CALL GH(X,Y,NUSEL,NGSEL,RN,G1,H1,U,V)
C
C present value of X saved temporarily
C
      XV=X
      X=X+DS
      CALL GH(X,Y,NUSEL,NGSEL,RN,G2,H2,U,V)
      X=XV
      XJ11=(G2-G1)/DS
      XJ21=(H2-H1)/DS
      YV=Y
      Y=Y+DS
      CALL GH(X,Y,NUSEL,NGSEL,RN,G2,H2,U,V)
C
C present value of Y saved temporarily
C
      Y=YV
      XJ12=(G2-G1)/DS
      XJ22=(H2-H1)/DS
      DET=XJ11*XJ22-XJ12*XJ21
      DUM=XJ11
      XJ11=XJ22/DET
      XJ22=DUM/DET
      XJ12=-XJ12/DET
```

```
   XJ21=-XJ21/DET
   DX=-XJ11*G1-XJ12*H1
   DY=-XJ21*G1-XJ22*H1
   X=X+DX
   Y=Y+DY
   ER=ABS(DX/X)+ABS(DY/Y)
   IF(ER.GT.ERMAX.AND.ITK.LT.ITKMAX) GOTO 10
   IF(ER.GT.ERMAX.AND.ITK.EQ.ITKMAX)WRITE(6,20)
C20 FORMAT(' ER gt ERMAX and ITK eq ITKMAX in XY => STOP')
20 FORMAT(' ER gt ERMAX and ITK eq ITKMAX in XY => IFXY=1')
C IF(ER.GT.ERMAX.AND.ITK.EQ.ITKMAX)STOP
   IF(ER.GT.ERMAX.AND.ITK.EQ.ITKMAX)IFXY=1
   RETURN
   END
   SUBROUTINE GH(X,Y,NUSEL,NGSEL,RN,G,H,U,V)
C
C calculate G and H needed in solving X and Y
C
   IMPLICIT REAL*8 (A-H,O-Z)
   GOTO(11,12),NUSEL
11 G=DLOG(X)+DLOG(1.-Y)-U
   UX=1./X
   UY=1./(Y-1.)
   UYY=-UY*UY
   GOTO 199
12 G=-1./X-1./(1.-Y)-U
   UX=1./X/X
   UY=-1./(1.-Y)/(1.-Y)
   UYY=2.*UY/(1.-Y)
199 CONTINUE
   PSY=-UY-Y*UYY
   H=(1.+UY/UX/RN)/PSY-V
   RETURN
   END
   SUBROUTINE DIS(RN,F,FD)
   IMPLICIT REAL*8 (A-H,O-Z)
   COMMON /DPAR/NDIS,SIG,RK,TTH,XMY,ALF,AA
C
C Lognormal distribution
C
   GOTO(10,20,30),NDIS
C ONE=1.D0
C TWO=2.D0
C PI=TWO*ASIN(ONE)
10 CONTINUE
```

```
   PI=3.14159265
   SIGP=SIG*SQRT(2.*PI)
   APU3=DLOG(RN)-RK
   APU=-APU3*APU3/SIG/SIG/2.
   F=EXP(APU)/(RN*SIGP)
   APU2=(-1./RN-APU3/SIG/SIG/RN)
   FD=F*APU2
   RETURN
C
C Champernowne distribution
C
20 CONTINUE
   APU=XMY**TTH+RN**TTH
   F=TTH*XMY**TTH*RN**(TTH-1.)/APU**2.
   FD=TTH*XMY**TTH*(TTH-1.)*RN**(TTH-2.)/APU**2.
   j -2.*TTH**2.*XMY**TTH*RN**(2.*TTH-2.)/APU**3.
C write(6,200)rn,f,fd
C200 format(' n f fd',3e12.4)
   RETURN
C
C Exponential distribution
C
30 CONTINUE
   F=EXP(-RN/ALF)/ALF
   FD=-F/ALF
c write(6,200)rn,f,fd
c200 format(' n f fd',3e12.4)
   RETURN
   END
```

Further comments:

The value of n0 or RNO in the program is found by stepping from RNOI to RNOF using a constant increment for DNO. The value of RNO is accepted when the test value TEST goes to zero at a point where the probability integral FK is close enough to unity (in the program version this value was set to 0.995 but more stringent criteria could be set); it could also be made a data item. The results are that output for every value of RNO after the above criteria is fulfilled. If DNO is small, only small changes in results are expected.

This program is executed interactively, so that the user can monitor how the solution develops. It is found that in most cases a proper value of RNO can be searched from an initial value of RNO downwards, i.e. putting in negative DNO. RNO can obtain quite different values in different cases. A more refined search algorithm could be programmed. The value of lambda affects the X/Z ratio, but also the value of RNO has an effect on this ratio. If one aims at a certain exact value of X/Z, this can be obtained by trial and error with several runs. In the final run, by giving the same value for RNOI and

RNOF, the amount of output is restricted (or by giving, for example, RNOI then RNOF larger than that and DNO negative), and this is the case for lambda RLA as well. Altering other data parameters may require quite different RNO. For some values, due to non-linearity, a solution may not be obtained at all. Trial and error can be tried. In all computations we select an n-distribution which, through the model, produces an earnings distribution that matches empirical earnings distributions.

6 Optimal income tax/transfer programme in the extensive margin model

Many existing transfer programmes with very high phasing-out rates have often been held responsible for the low work-participation rates among welfare recipients. This has led politicians to advocate programmes that would make work sufficiently attractive to reduce the need for income support. In the early 1990s, the Earned Income Tax Credit (EITC) programme in the United States was substantially increased, and is now the largest cash transfer programme for the poor. The United Kingdom has introduced and expanded a similar programme (Working Family Tax Credit). Many other European countries have also implemented such programmes on a more modest scale, or are contemplating introducing such programmes (see Gradus and Julsing 2001). The EITC schedule, shown in Figure 6.1b, is fundamentally different from a traditional means-tested programme (Figure 6.1a). The EITC does not provide any income support for individuals with no earnings, but all earnings below a given threshold are partially matched by the government, creating a strong incentive to enter the labour force and work. As a result, the slope of the budget constraint in the phasing-in range (depicted in Figure 6.1b) is higher than 1: an extra euro of earnings translates into more than one euro in after-transfer income.

Since Mirrlees (1971), the theory of optimal taxation has largely been developed in the intensive model setup, where labour supply is continuous. The Mirrlees model considers labour supply behaviour on its intensive margin, with changes in continuous variables such as working hours. In such models, tax rates are always positive, so an EITC would not be optimal. However, much of labour supply is the decision to work or not to work, such as the labour force participation of parents with small children, retirement decisions, and responses to disability. Diamond (1980), Saez (2002), and Laroque (2005) among others have studied the extensive margin—that is, participation decision—and show that negative taxes may be optimal in a model where the only decision is to work or not to work.

Liebman (2001) analyses the incentive and income distribution effects of changing the many parameters of the EITC for single taxpayers. He finds that a schedule close to the current US one is optimal for plausible relative weights put on efficiency and equity concerns. Saez (2002) integrates labour force participation into an optimal tax model and shows that with sufficiently high participation elasticities, transfer schemes such as

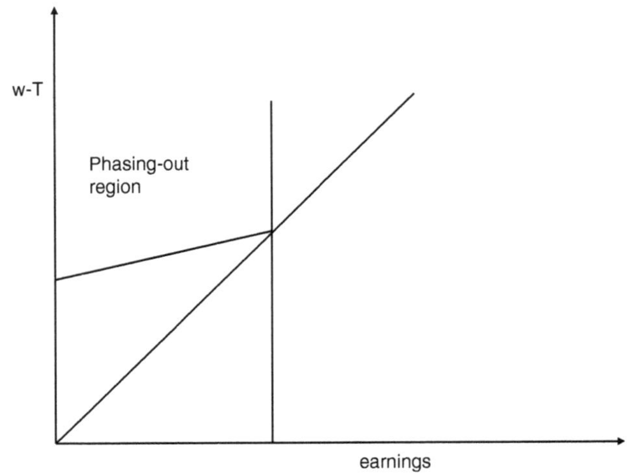

Figure 6.1a Negative income tax

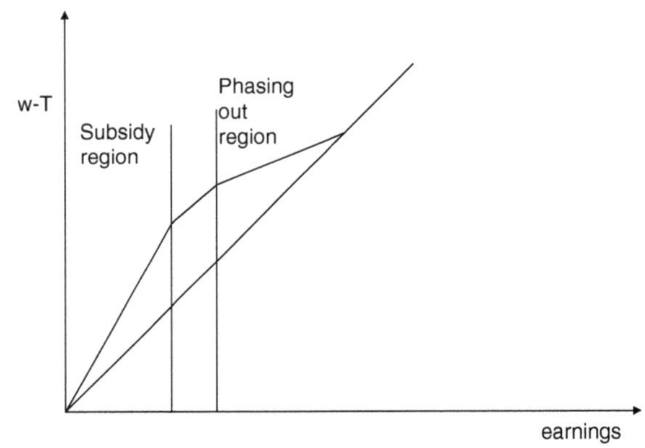

Figure 6.1b Earned Income Tax Credit

the EITC can be optimal. These analyses by Saez and Liebman suggest that there is a significant theoretical justification for a policy such as the current US EITC. There are, however, studies of alternative policies that assume that policy-makers can collect information on hours (and wages), which suggest that such policies are better targeted and have fewer distortions than an EITC (see Macurdy and McIntyre 2004, for example).

Empirical studies have shown that the extensive-margin response (choosing whether or not to enter the labour force) is much more elastic than the intensive-margin response (choosing how many hours to work once one has decided to enter the labour force). The main reason why this is the case is the fixed costs of working: the search costs of finding a job; transportation costs; child-care expenses; and so on. Moreover, Meghir and Phillips (2010) clearly show the heterogeneity of responses: for the highly educated participation elasticity is zero, but the estimate for men with low educational qualifications is 0.23 for single men and 0.43 for men in couples. The fixed cost of working may differ substantially between countries. In the Nordic countries, which have very developed child-care systems, the elasticity of participation among parents with young children may differ from that in the US or the southern part of Europe. For instance, subsidizing goods that are complements to labour supply, such as day care and care of the elderly, may be attractive, since they support labour force participation.[1]

Let us consider the discrete version of Saez's (2002) model. There are I + 1 possible earnings levels $w_0 = 0 < w_1 < \ldots < w_I$. Each individual has a potential earning level w_i and can choose either to work and earn w_i or be out of the labour force and earn $w_0 = 0$. The government sets the tax schedule depending on earnings $T_i = T(w_i)$. This is an integrated tax and transfer program: T can be positive or negative. Consumption in work state i: $c_i = w_i - T_i$. Individual choice to work depends on the difference between $c_i = w_i - T_i$ (work) and $c_0 = w_0 - T_0$ (not work). In other words, type i takes a job with fixed hours, pays a tax T_i and consumes $c_i = w_i - T_i$.

The proportion of individuals of type i who decide to work is a function h_i that is increasing in $c_i - c_0$. With no income effects and quasi-linear utility function, the optimal tax formula becomes:

$$\frac{T_i - T_0}{c_i - c_0} = \frac{(1 - \phi_i)}{\eta_i} \tag{1}$$

where ϕ s are welfare weights; the social marginal utility of income. This formula is a simple inverse elasticity tax rule.[2] $E\phi_i = 1$ (average $\phi = 1$) and η is participation elasticity:

$$\eta = \frac{c_i - c_0}{h_i} \frac{\partial h_i}{\partial (c_i - c_0)} \tag{2}$$

ϕ_i is decreasing wages (w) and η is positive.

There are three effects on a small reform, $dc_i = -dT_i > 0$:

1. Mechanical change in revenue $dM = h_i dT_i$.
2. Behavioural effect: $dh_i = -\eta_i h_i dT_i \,/\, (c_i - c_0)$, hence the tax loss: $dB = -(T_i - T_0)dh = -e_i h_i dT_i (T_i - T_0) \,/\, (c_i - c_0)$.
3. Welfare effect: each individual in job i loses dT_i and the welfare loss is $dW = \phi_i h_i dT_i$ at the optimum $dM + dB + dW = 0$. This implies the formula (1).

The striking implication of (1) is that if $\phi_1 > 1$, then T_1 must be lower than T_0. Hence the low-income earners should receive an earnings subsidy.[3]

[1] Bastani et al (2013) estimate participation elasticities using unique tax variation created by the Swedish housing allowance reform in 1997. Their preliminary central estimate of the participation elasticity is 0.06.

[2] This formula is essentially the same as the formula (4) in Mirrlees (1982). Mirrlees (1982) considers the model of optimal taxation in the presence of migration. In that model, individuals can either choose to work in their (home) country or to leave the country and work and be taxed abroad.

[3] Christiansen (2012) elaborates further on this result and shows the conditions required for the result to be valid. He argues that the result depends crucially on the labour supply responses of people in income brackets above that of the working poor. Then, distinguishing between more and less poor working people,

But in the maximin (Rawlsian) case ϕ_1 is zero; then the negative marginal tax rates (subsidies) disappear. In particular, the welfare weight attached to the working poor should be lower than that of the non-employed. This is not surprising: a government with maximin objective would never want to use participation subsidies, since these subsidies imply a redistribution from the non-working to the working population.[4]

Rewriting (38) as follows, $T_i = \frac{(c_i - c_0)(1-\phi_i)}{\eta_i} + T_0$, we can consider how taxes change as one goes up the earnings scale. If the right-hand side of this formula increases in income, T_i will rise with income and marginal rate is positive. Meghir and Phillips (2010) provide some support that η_i declines with income. So T_i will rise with income when c_i and $1 - \phi_i$ also rise with income and η_i is not increasing in income (see Jacquet et al 2009).

Saez (2002) also analyses optimal income transfers for low incomes in the case of no income effects when labour supply responses are modelled along the intensive margin (intensity of work on the job) and along the extensive margin (participation in the labour force). When behavioural responses are concentrated along the intensive margin, the optimal transfer programme is a classical negative income tax programme with a substantial guaranteed income support and a large phasing-out tax rate. However, when behavioural responses are concentrated along the extensive margin, the optimal transfer programme is similar to EITC, with negative marginal tax rates at low income levels and a small guaranteed income. It is often neglected both in empirical and theoretical studies that in most welfare schemes, individuals are not free to choose to live on social benefits.

6.1 **Intensive and extensive margin**

In the Mirrlees model, individuals can only adjust their labour supply on the intensive margin. They can decide to work more or less, but they cannot decide to enter or exit the labour market entirely. In contrast, Diamond (1980) derives the optimal tax schedule where individuals can only adjust their labour supply along the extensive margin. Saez (2002) and Jacquet et al (2009) combine the Mirrlees model with the Diamond model to analyse the optimal non-linear income tax and the optimal participation tax. Allowing both intensive and extensive margins, it turns out that optimal taxes (transfers) are characterized by budget constraint and

$$\frac{T_i - T_{i-1}}{c_i - c_{i-1}} = \frac{1}{\varepsilon_i h_i} \sum_{j=1}^{I} h_j \left(1 - \phi_j - \eta_j \frac{T_j - T_0}{c_j - c_0}\right) \text{ for } i \geq 1 \tag{3}$$

where

he shows that if a single working type faces a negative tax it is the poorer one. He also extends the analysis by endogenizing wages and shows that key conditions will be of the same form as with exogenous wages.

[4] Jacquet et al (2009) and Zoutman et al (2012a) demonstrate for the US and the Netherlands that participation is subsidized only on a net basis using utilitarian social objectives.

$$\varepsilon = \frac{c_i - c_{i-1}}{h_i} \frac{\partial h_i}{\partial(c_i - c_{i-1})}$$

It may be illuminating to note that $\frac{T_i - T_{i-1}}{c_i - c_{i-1}}$ is the same thing as $\frac{T_i'}{1-T_i'}$ in the standard formulation of optimal tax rules, where $T_i' = \frac{T_i - T_{i-1}}{Z_i - Z_{i-1}}$ is the effective 'marginal' tax rate (EMTR) faced by group i defined at the income group level. Formula (3) is highly comparable to the standard marginal tax formula in the Mirrlees model. The marginal tax is inversely related to the size of the group and the intensive-margin elasticity ε_i. A noticeable difference is the presence of the extensive-margin elasticity η_i.

Whether marginal tax rates are positive or negative depends on the relative magnitudes of two different elasticities, ε and η . To see this we can take the extreme case where the participation elasticity η is zero. Now optimal taxes satisfy

$$\frac{T_i - T_{i-1}}{c_i - c_{i-1}} = \frac{1}{\varepsilon_i h_i} \sum_{j=1}^{I} h_j(1 - \phi_j) \text{ for } i \geq 1. \tag{4}$$

This is simply a discrete version of Mirrlees. In that case, negative marginal tax rates resulting from in-work support, such as the US EITC, are never optimal, since they discourage productive workers at the intensive margin.

When both elasticities are positive, the sign of marginal rates depends on the relative magnitude of these two elasticities. So it means that it is not necessary so that marginal tax rates at the bottom should be zero.

Numerical simulations in Saez (2002) show that a subsidy for low-skilled workers is optimal when labour supply responses are concentrated along the extensive margin. The intuition is as follows: introducing a subsidy for low-skilled workers is good for redistributive purposes and also induces some individuals to enter the labour force, and thus allows the government to save on welfare outgoings. In contrast, in a model with intensive-margin responses, a subsidy for low-skilled workers would induce some higher-skill workers to work less in order to take advantage of the subsidy, and would thus increase the cost of the programme. That is why such subsidies are not optimal in the Mirrlees (1971) model. Therefore, a government contemplating an increase of incentives for low-skilled workers must precisely weigh the positive effect on work participation and the negative intensive labour-supply effect for higher-skilled workers. Saez (2002) presents simulations of this optimal transfer model using empirical estimates of the intensive and extensive elasticities of labour supply. Since the extensive elasticity appears to be much larger than the intensive elasticity, the simulations show that the optimal programme should have lower guaranteed benefits (perhaps around 20 per cent of the average earnings in the economy) but that the phasing-out rate should be close to zero on the first \$6,000 of earnings, so as to make work pay and not deter labour force participation. The benefits should then be phased out at substantial rates for earnings between \$6,000 and \$15,000. A high phasing-out rate in that earnings range creates only moderate reduction in labour supply because effort on the job (intensive margin) is not very sensitive to incentives. The transfer programmes we have described here are individually based and not family-based. During the 1990s, US income transfer and tax policies shifted towards trying to encourage work among low-income families. Optimal tax theory, however, suggests that work subsidies are usually an inefficient way to raise the incomes of poor families unless the work effort of recipients has external benefits and/or taxpayers/voters prefer redistributing income to the working poor rather than the idle poor. Saez (2002) discusses the conditions under which work subsidies may be economically efficient and assesses empirical evidence that suggests welfare reform and expansions of the EITC have increased work effort among low-income families, but is inconclusive about whether the policy shift has enabled them to advance beyond entry-level jobs or benefited their children.

Jacquet et al (2009) also derive the optimal tax schedule under both intensive and extensive labour-supply responses. The extensive margin is introduced using the so-called random participation model. When individuals participate they incur an idiosyncratic utility cost or benefit on top of the changes in income and leisure. The disutility is individual-specific and reflects the individuals' outside options such as household production or income from the black labour market.

Jacquet et al (2009) extend Saez (2002) by providing analytical and numerical results about the sign of optimal marginal tax rates in a model with both intensive and extensive margins. They analytically derive a fairly mild sufficient condition under which optimal marginal tax rates are positive almost everywhere. In their model, individuals are heterogeneously endowed with two unobserved characteristics: their skill level and disutility of participation. Using US data they find that, for the least skilled workers, participation taxes are typically negative under a utilitarian case, while they are always positive under maximin. Under utilitarian objectives, with a strictly positive lower bound for the earnings distribution, their simulations show a negative participation tax rate at this minimum (as for the EITC) and positive (as for the NIT) marginal tax rates.

It is again important to note that decisions about participation and occupational choices are driven by heterogeneous working preferences. We face the question of how to treat heterogeneous preferences for social welfare purposes.

The extensive margin and its reaction to monetary incentives has a role at the beginning and the end of working life. Therefore it is perhaps surprising that there is not that much work on the interaction between non-linear income taxes and pension systems. Diamond (2009, p. 6) comments on this situation as follows:

> Apart from some simulation studies, theoretical studies of optimal tax design typically contain neither a mandatory pension system nor the behavioural dimensions that lie behind justifications commonly offered for mandatory pensions. Conversely, optimizing models of pension design typically do not include annual taxation of labour and capital incomes. Recognizing the presence of two sets of policy institutions raises the issue of whether normative analysis should be done separately or as a single overarching optimization.

6.2 Involuntary unemployment and optimal redistribution

There are various kinds of labour market models in which unemployment is affected by taxation.[5] Empirical evidence in turn suggests the importance of these effects as shown in the literature (e.g. Manning 1993; Røed and Strøm 2002; Sørensen 1997). The effect of the marginal tax rate on pre-tax wages obtained in these models is also consistent with the empirical findings on the elasticity of taxable income with respect to the marginal tax rate surveyed by Saez et al (2012). According to them, the most plausible estimates for the elasticity of earnings to one minus the marginal tax rate range from 0.1 to 0.4 in the US. Whether this elasticity is due to a labour-supply response (as in a Mirrleesian model), to a non-competitive wage setting response, or to tax avoidance, to our knowledge, remains an open empirical issue.

It is possible to identify different categories of involuntary unemployment. Here we focus on involuntary unemployment due to labour market failure. There is already some literature in which optimal redistribution analysis has been extended to the extensive-margin models with frictional/search unemployment—by Boone and Bovenberg (2002), Boadway, Cuff, and Marceau (2003), Hungerbuhler et al (2006), and Lehmann, Parmentier, and Van der Linden (2011), among others—and to efficiency-wage unemployment—by Boadway, Cuff, and Marceau (2003) and Holzner, Meier, and Werding (2010) among others. The frictional/search unemployment models have been deployed in two different contexts: (1) optimal income redistribution when involuntary unemployment is treated as permanent; (2) the form of insurance when frictional unemployment is temporary.

Engström (2009) extends the Stiglitz–Stern (1982) two-skill model of optimal taxation by introducing search unemployment, but with exogenous hourly wages. As we have seen above, there have been many contributions to the theory of optimal taxation based on the so-called self-selection approach with two types of individuals. Engström (2009) studies the rationale for unemployment benefits as a complement to optimal non-linear income taxation. Given that unemployment is mostly a low-skilled phenomenon, the paper shows that the mimickers do not benefit from unemployment benefits intended for the low-skilled individuals to the same extent as the true low-skilled workers do. If the mimickers do not face spells of unemployment, they will not benefit from this transfer at all, which makes the unemployment benefit an attractive tool for redistribution. The results also hold in the case with search unemployment.

In the Mirrlees setting, hourly wages equal marginal products of labour and are independent of taxation. Therefore labour supply is the source of inefficiencies.

[5] For example; the monopoly union model (Hersoug 1984), the right-to manage union model (Lockwood and Manning 1993), the matching model (Manning 1993) and the efficiency wage model (Pisauro 1991).

Hungerbuhler et al (2006) in turn consider an alternative source of inefficiency: taxes alter the outcomes of the wage bargain and hence affect labour demand. Hungerbuhler et al (2006) focus on two issues: (1) what is the effect of redistributive policy on unemployment; (2) what are the implications of unemployment for the extent of redistribution in the tax-transfer system. In the search model (Mortensen and Pissarides 1999) it is assumed that there is heterogeneity in the labour market such that it is not easy for the firm to find a worker for its vacant job with whom it can produce output, and vice versa. Therefore this process is costly for both parties. Frictions are implicitly modelled by a matching function that gives the number of successful matches M as a function of the number of workers searching, o, and the number of vacancies υ. Following empirical studies (see Blanchard and Diamond 1989 or Petrongolo and Pissarides 2001) with the simplest model, the number of vacancies filled is based on a constant-returns-to-scale matching function of the Cobb–Douglas form, $M(o_n, v_n) = o^{\gamma}v^{1-\gamma}$. The number of type-n matches is a function of the number of type-a vacancies v_n and of the number of type-n searching workers o_n, according to the M function. The probability of a vacancy being filled is given by $\pi(\kappa) = M(o, v)/v$, $\pi'(\kappa) < 0$, where $\kappa = \frac{o}{v}$ is the ratio of the number of vacancies to the number of unemployed competing for them. In other words, the ratio measures the labour market tightness. The probability of a worker obtaining a job, assumed to be the same for all workers, is $\pi(\kappa) = M(o,v)/v = \kappa\pi(\kappa)$, which is increasing in κ. Once a match is found, the wage rate w is determined by Nash bargaining over the surplus. If ρ is the bargaining power of workers, assumed to be given, w maximizes the Nash product $(w_n - t(w_n) - b)^{\rho} + (t(w_n) - b)^{1-\rho}$, where t(w) is the tax function on earnings as in the extensive-margin model, b is the transfer to the unemployed, and n is the skill level of the worker.

Posting and searching vacancies produces potential benefits for the job-seekers and the posting firm, but causes potentially offsetting externalities. When a firm creates a vacancy, this increases the probability of workers finding a job, but decreases the probability that other firms find a match; when a worker chooses to search, that increases the probability that firms will find a match, but decreases the probability of other job-seekers finding a job. These externalities are offsetting and search is efficient if $\rho = \gamma$. This is shown by Hosios (1990). The share of the worker's surplus from bargaining then equals the worker's relative productivity at generating matches, and similarly for firms, so workers' search effort and firms' choice in vacancies will be efficient. In this case, the equilibrium bargaining wage maximizes the expected surplus of workers, $\kappa\pi(\kappa)(n - t(w_n) - b)$.

Hungerbuhler et al (2006) assume that working hours are fixed and workers choose whether to participate in the labour market in a job corresponding to their skill level, denoted n. Workers have a common value of leisure, which implies there is a cutoff skill level n* such that workers participate if and only if $n \geq n^*$. Those workers who participate but fail to be matched are classified as unemployed, while those who do not participate are considered as inactive. Matching frictions create search externalities and generate rents. Wage rates are then the outcome of bilateral worker–firm bargaining and wage bargaining at each skill level is assumed to be $\rho = \gamma$. The government observes negotiated wages w, and imposes a non-linear income tax t(w) and a transfer to the unemployed b. However, worker skill n is private information to the worker and employer. As in standard extensive-margin models, the average tax applying to each skill level affects participation, which in this model is the marginal skill level n^*. For employed workers, the tax affects labour market outcomes in conflicting ways. Namely, a higher marginal tax rate reduces the incentive for workers to bargain, leading to a lower w, while a higher tax level reduces a worker's surplus and yields an increase in the wage payment and a decrease in employment. Unlike in the pure extensive-margin model (Diamond 1980; Saez 2002), the participation tax applying to the marginal participant is positive. Employment varies inversely with w. In the social optimum, average tax rates rise with the wage rate and marginal taxes are all positive, including at the top. The average tax rate is increasing and the marginal tax rate is positive everywhere, including those at the top of the distribution. Yet, like in the Mirrlees model, interesting results are produced numerically. For comparisons, Hungerbuhler et al (2006) calibrate the Mirrlees model to generate the same distribution of earnings and the same elasticity of gross earnings with respect to the marginal tax rate as their model. Marginal tax rates and unemployment benefits tend to be substantially higher than those obtained in the Mirrlees intensive-margin model. The comparison between the numerical results of their model and the Mirrlees setting may give a misleading picture of the differences in these two cases. Namely, Hungerbuhler et al (2006) assume quasi-linear preferences in consumption in their simulation; as mentioned earlier, quasi-linearity eliminates declining marginal utility of consumption, which is typically motivation for redistribution.

The Hungerbuhler et al (2006) approach embodied some strong assumptions; Lehmann, Parmentier, and Van der Linden (2011) relax some of the stronger ones.[6] First of all, they allow for heterogeneity in the value of leisure at all skill levels. The consequence of this is that it creates voluntary unemployment at all skill levels alongside involuntary unemployment. The participation decision at each skill level then creates an additional margin of choice that constrains redistributive taxation, and makes possible a comparison with the pure extensive-margin model of Diamond (1980) and Saez (2002). In the maximin case they show that marginal tax rates are positive throughout and higher than in the competitive labour market setting. As in the Diamond–Saez maximin case, participation tax rates are positive at the bottom. Furthermore, assuming that the participation elasticity falls with skills, average tax rates are rising. When the social welfare function exhibits finite aversion to inequality, simulations show that the marginal tax rate and participation rate can be negative at the bottom, as in the Diamond–Saez case, while the marginal tax rate at the top continues to be positive.

Boadway, Cuff, and Marceau (2003) relax the assumption on the inability to distinguish the voluntarily from the involuntarily unemployed. They study optimal policies in

[6] Jacquet, Lehmann, and Van der Linden (2011) modify the pure extensive margin case by assuming the government can observe wage bargains by skill level, so mimicking is not possible.

an extensive-margin model with high and low-skilled workers and both voluntary and involuntary unemployment, where the latter could be due to either matching frictions or efficiency wages. When equilibrium is based on matching process, either an employment tax or an employment subsidy should be used, depending on the relative magnitude of positive and negative externalities of matching. However, when unemployment is induced by efficiency wages, the optimal level of unemployment can be obtained through the personal tax-transfer system rather than by subsidizing firms. The involuntarily unemployed are better off than those working. The efficiency wage model is, however, of somewhat limited relevance in economies characterized by strict firing regulations and high job security.

It is usually assumed that all unemployed workers obtain the same benefit b regardless of their type, or whether they have chosen to search. In practice, benefits to the unemployed differ between the voluntarily and involuntarily unemployed. Workers are monitored to verify if they are genuinely involuntarily unemployed and are active job-seekers. The monitoring system is an essential element of transfer programmes for the unemployed. Boadway and Cuff (1999) study monitoring in the context of both temporary involuntary unemployment and long-run unemployment, where involuntary unemployment is generated by a simple matching technology. Unlike in Hungerbuhler et al (2006), wages are set competitively by firms in the matching framework rather than being determined by bilateral bargaining. In their model, as you might expect, the more accurate the monitoring, the greater can be the transfer given to the involuntary and long-run unemployed without attracting those who prefer to remain voluntarily unemployed. On the more general level, their analysis emphasizes the importance of monitoring in the optimal redistribution literature.

It is obvious that search models are more appropriate for explaining temporary rather than permanent unemployment. In temporary cases, unemployment insurance becomes a relevant policy instrument. There is a large literature on the optimal design of unemployment insurance.[7] Earlier models of unemployment considered sources other than matching frictions, such as efficiency wage or turnover cost models, temporary layoffs and implicit contracts (Baily 1974; Azariadis 1975; Feldstein 1978) and displaced workers (LaLonde 2007).

Recent models analyse important trade-offs in designing efficient unemployment insurance systems in search environments (Chetty 2008). It is an insurance-incentive trade-off in the presence of moral hazard. Unemployment insurance helps workers smooth consumption when they are unemployed. Unemployment insurance is necessarily incomplete, even though the problem can be mitigated by monitoring the unemployed. Optimal unemployment insurance—including eligibility requirements, wage replacement rates, and duration—trades off these liquidity and moral hazard effects. This view of unemployment insurance has been extended in various ways. Chetty and Saez (2010)

[7] See for a survey of search-based theories of optimal unemployment insurance Coles (2008).

allow for the fact that some private unemployment insurance exists in practice, if only implicitly—an example being negotiated severance pay. Publicly provided unemployment insurance crowds out private insurance, so reduces the optimal amount of unemployment insurance, that is, the earnings replacement rate. Spinnewijn (2010) supposes that the unemployed may mistakenly both overestimate the chances of finding an employment match and underestimate the return to search. These effects tend to make the optimal level of unemployment benefits higher.

The search-and-matching model has become the standard theory of equilibrium unemployment, but recent literature highlights its shortcomings in explaining periods of high unemployment (Shimer and Werning 2005). An objection to the relevance of the job-search theory has been the experience that a very high fraction of unemployed workers are re-hired by their previous employers (Feldstein 1978). However, of greater interest in a European context is that one may question the significance of the job-search model when one observes that there are typically numerous applicants for each vacant job, especially during times of recession. Moreover, a person who is eligible for unemployment benefits is not free to search for as long as he or she wants for a new job. If offered a job, he or she may have to accept it or lose unemployment benefit (Atkinson and Micklewright 1991). The modelling should also allow for institutional diversity, such as the degree to which there is centralized bargaining. With many trade unions, each trade union is likely to take the total unemployment as given. In the polar case of a single union, it will fully internalize the effect on unemployment, and it is harder to get unambiguous tax effects (Calmfors 1982).

In recessions with high unemployment people want to work, but they cannot find jobs. This suggests that employment is constrained by demand effects rather than supply effects, as in the standard optimal tax analysis. As a result, in recessions, unemployment is likely to be less sensitive to supply-side changes in search efforts and job search is likely to generate a negative externality on other job-seekers in queueing the same job. Landais, Michaillat, and Saez (2010) take into account this effect in a search model where job rationing arises in recessions and show that unemployment insurance should be more generous during recessions. In severe recession, redistribution becomes close to lump-sum.

6.3 Social norms and redistribution

There is some literature on redistribution that takes a view that the social objective function reflects social norms. One way to interpret this is that the social welfare function is endogenized (see Saez and Stantcheva 2013). The notion of social norms was particularly prominent in the Nordic welfare state debate literature in the 1990s. Lindbeck (1995) argues that initially the welfare state did not affect labour market behaviour, but over time people became more willing to live off unemployment benefits and gradually negative effects began to emerge. Lindbeck (1995) does not, however, provide any empirical evidence about the formation of social norms and their impact on people's behaviour in the labour market. Boadway and Martineau (2013) model optimal redistributive taxation when a social norm affects work participation.[8] They examine the role of societal consensus for the pursuit of redistribution, when this consensus is induced by social norms that affect work-participation decisions. Their main findings are that in the presence of a social norm affecting participants, the optimal extent of redistribution—measured by the participation tax as chosen by a social planner, in the sense of Diamond and Saez—is reduced, compared with the case when it is not. One reason for this is the feedback effects of a decrease in participation, which lower the incitements to sustain societal co-operation, thus increasing the budgetary costs of redistribution. This result is less stark when the social norm is included as a cost of stigma for non-participants.

[8] Such norms concerning the intensity of labour supply were also applied to the context of optimal income taxation by Aronsson and Sjögren (2010).

7 Relativity and optimal non-linear labour income taxation

There is growing empirical evidence questioning the assumption that an individual's preferences are independent of the consumption of others.[1] The major alternative to this assumption is that an individual's well-being depends on his or her relative consumption—how it compares to the consumption of others. This 'relativity' idea is not new, of course. More than a hundred years ago, Thorsten Veblen[2] maintained that consumption is motivated by a desire for social standing as well as for enjoyment of goods and services per se. Pareto and Pigou also doubted that an individual's utility depends only on his or her income (consumption). Pareto's (1917) concept of utility was totally different from the standard textbook definition. It was not restricted to the satisfaction that an individual could get from his or her own consumption, but also included all available sources of satisfaction, including those aroused by the consumption and relative income levels of others. Pigou (1962, p. 91) in turn wrote that 'the satisfaction which a man derives from the possession of a given income depends, not only on the absolute amount of income, but also on the relation substituting between it and the incomes of other people'. Pigou then concludes that the so-called proportional sacrifice principle indicates continued progression at the upper end of the income scale.[3]

Relative consumption (or income) concern or status-seeking creates negative externalities because a gain in one's status is a loss to someone else. If these externalities are important as empirical research seems to suggest, taxing consumption externalities might be welfare-enhancing in just the same way as any other Pigouvian tax. However, this simple intuition does not tell us anything about the detailed effects of relative income concern on the optimal tax schedule. Do status considerations lead to a more progressive tax system or a less progressive tax system? Is income tax an effective tool for reducing

[1] Clark, Frijters, and Shields (2008) provide a good survey.

[2] Later on Duesenberry (1949), Galbraith (1958), Hirsch (1976), Frank (1985, 1997), Bowles and Park (2005), and Hopkins (2008), among others, wrote about the importance of relative position as a dominant spending motivation.

[3] More recent empirical research findings show that relative consumption concerns have important effects on consumption but little, if any, on leisure: for example, Alpizar et al (2005), Solnick and Hemenway (2005), and Carlsson et al (2007) all seem to indicate that leisure is typically less positional than many private goods.

inequalities and attenuating possible externalities arising from relative income concerns? How do inequality and relativity together determine the shape of the optimal tax schedule?

There are relatively few papers asking these questions in the optimal income tax framework—those that are include Boskin and Sheshinski (1978), Oswald (1983), Tuomala (1990), Blomquist (1993), Ireland (2001), Corneo (2002), and Aronsson and Johansson-Stenman (2011). The reference point for Kanbur and Tuomala (2013) is the paper by Oswald (1983), which also examines the impact of relativity on optimal non-linear income taxation and which specifies the relativity in terms of an individual's consumption compared to population average.[4] The key proposition of Oswald's (1983) paper is that '... optimal marginal tax rates are higher in a predominantly jealous world' (p. 89). This theoretical result is confirmed with numerical calculations by Tuomala (1990).

The Oswald (1983) result is of the '*ceteris paribus*' variety—in other words, endogenous variables such as the marginal social value of public funds, which would normally change when the relativity parameter changed, are held constant. Kanbur and Tuomala (2013) show, using numerical calculations, that the result still holds when full account is taken of all endogenous variations. Second, the Oswald (1983) result, and the results of the other papers in the literature, are about the level of marginal tax rates, and say nothing about how the shape of the marginal tax rate schedule changes with relativity. Kanbur and Tuomala (2013) show that higher relativity increases the progressivity of taxation in the sense that marginal tax rates now rise faster with income. Third, they address a question not touched by the literature—how does the impact of relativity on optimal tax structure depend on the degree of inequality in society? Using analytical results for specific cases and numerical calculations for more general specifications, they show that the impact of relativity on the level and steepness of the marginal tax rate schedule is dampened by greater levels of inequality. Although they provide some intuition for this result, further analysis is needed to fully understand its structure.

This chapter is set out as follows. Section 7.1 presents the optimal income tax model with relative consumption concern. Section 7.2 considers implications of relative concern in the optimal non-linear income tax model with utilitarian and Rawlsian social objective functions and with special assumptions on preferences and distributions. Section 7.3 presents numerical simulations in the utilitarian case. Section 7.4 elaborates on the interplay between relativity and inequality in determining optimal tax rates. Section 7.5 concludes.

[4] Boskin-Sheshinski (1978) and Blomquist (1993) stay within a linear income tax framework. Aronsson and Johansson-Stenman (2011) use a two-type model. Ireland (2001) uses a Mirrlees (1971) optimal non-linear income taxation framework, but his specification of relative concern is very different from Oswald (1983) and the other papers in the literature. In his paper individuals signal status with consumption (e.g. large houses, cars, boats, etc.), and there is a signalling equilibrium. It is not, therefore, easy to provide direct comparison of his results with our results or those of Oswald (1983) and the other papers.

7.1 Optimal non-linear taxation and relative consumption concern

Do people make comparisons between or among individuals of similar incomes? Or is the lifestyle of the upper middle-class and the rich a more salient point of reference for people throughout the income distribution? A comparison consumption level, x_r, can be constructed as follows. Let x denote consumption, and let

$$x_r = \int \omega(n)x(n)f(n)dn \tag{1}$$

where a distribution of wages (productivities), denoted by n, on the interval $(0,\infty)$ is represented by the density function f(n). There are a number of alternative interpretations of the variable x_r. The simplest one is obtained if each of the ω weights is equal to one. In this case the average consumption is the comparison consumption level. We can choose the weights ω so that x_r is the consumption of the richest individual (this corresponds to Veblen's idea), of the median individual, or of something in between the richest and the median. It is difficult to say without empirical evidence which is the most plausible interpretation. Moreover, as Layard (1980) suggests, people may have different x_r values. In this paper, we restrict attention to the case where ω=1 for all n so that x_r is the average consumption of people in the economy.

There is a continuum of individuals, each having the same preference ordering, which is represented by an additive utility function

$$u = U(x) + \psi(x_r) + V(1 - y) \tag{2}$$

where x is a composite consumption good, x_r is a comparison consumption level, and hours worked are y, with $U_x > 0$, $\psi_{x_r} <(>) 0$ and $V_y < 0$ (subscripts indicating partial derivatives) and where V(.) is convex. As is typical in optimal tax literature, we have to make simplifying assumptions like this separability assumption in order to be able to make progress in our understanding of optimal tax schedules. Workers differ only in the pre-tax wage n they can earn. Gross income is $z = ny$ and consumption, x, is after-tax income.

Suppose that the aim of policy can be expressed as maximizing the following social welfare criterion:

$$W = \int_0^\infty W(u(n))f(n)dn \tag{3}$$

where W(.) is an increasing and concave function of utility.

We should note before moving on that there are many difficult problems in formulating the social welfare function. For example, we must decide whether the government ought to accept relative income concerns in social welfare. This is closely related to the awkward question of whether we should include antisocial preferences such as envy, malice, and so on in the social welfare function, or not. If so, it would be important to consider the case where the government is 'non-welfarist' (paternalistic). But it could be argued that to the extent that relative concerns or Veblen effects are real, they should be respected when evaluating social welfare.[5] In this chapter we follow the latter, 'welfarist', route.

The government cannot observe individuals' productivities and thus is restricted to setting taxes and transfers as a function only of earnings, $T(z(n))$. The government maximizes W subject to the revenue constraint $\int_0^\infty T(z(n))f(n)dn = R$ and the incentive compatibility constraints, $\frac{du}{dn} = \frac{-yV_y}{n}$.

Since $T=ny-x$, we can think of government as choosing schedules $x(n)$, $y(n)$, and x_r. In fact it is easier to think of it choosing a pair of functions, $u(n)$, $y(n)$, and x_r, which maximize welfare index (3) subject to the revenue requirement, the incentive compatibility condition, and the comparison condition (1). We focus on the case where $\omega=1$ for all n so that x_r is the average consumption of people in the economy.

We can now write the formula for marginal rates as follows (see appendix 7.1 for detail of the derivation):

$$\frac{t}{1-t} = \frac{\gamma}{\lambda} + \underbrace{\left[\frac{1+E^u}{E^c}\right]}_{A_n} \underbrace{\left[\frac{[1-F(n)]}{nf(n)}\right]}_{B_n} \underbrace{\left[\frac{(1+\gamma/\lambda)U_x \int_n^\infty [1-\frac{W'U_x^{(p)}}{\lambda(1+\gamma/\lambda)}]\frac{1}{U_x^{(p)}}f(p)dp}{(1-F(n))}\right]}_{C_n} \tag{4}$$

where E^u is the uncompensated supply of labour and E^c in turn is the compensated elasticity. The first term on the right-hand side of (4) is analogous to a Pigouvian tax correcting for an externality. It could also be called a first-best motive for taxation, as it corrects the individual activity to correspond to social preferences. From (4), there are in

[5] Examples of the first include Kanbur, Keen, and Tuomala (1994a,b) and Pirttilä and Tuomala (2004), while O'Donoghue and Rabin (2001), Bernheim and Rangel (2005), and McCaffery and Slemrod (2006) are examples of the latter. See Seade (1980) for seminal work. However, it is not clear whether utility interdependence should be allowed to enter the social welfare function: is envy a trait one wants to honour? For example, Harsanyi (1982) does not accept antisocial preferences such as envy, malice, etc. in a utilitarian social welfare function. See also Aronson and Johansson-Stenman (2011). They show that if relativity concerns are based on mean value comparisons and all consumers are equally positional, the first-best allocations under paternalist and welfarist governments are implemented through exactly the same marginal income tax formulas. In the second-best situation there are remaining differences.

addition to the externality term three elements on the right-hand side that determine optimum tax rates: elasticity and income effects (A&C), the shape of the skill distribution (B&C), and social marginal weights (C). The B-term reflects the ratio of the numbers of people at higher levels (1−F) relative to the total income of those affected by the marginal tax rate at this income level (nf). The C-term reflects the average redistributional gain of having the marginal tax rate at this income level. In other words, the C-term in (4) is a measure of the social cost of taking one euro away from everyone above that skill level. The C-term tends to favour rising marginal rates. This is especially so when income is low or moderate. On the basis of (4) we can also notice that if the utility of individuals depends negatively on the comparison consumption, the marginal tax rate of the highest income is positive. Finally, (4) tells us that a higher γ, i.e. a higher relativity concern, will tend to increase marginal tax rates.

This discussion provides some analytical insight into a presumption in the literature that relativity concerns will raise marginal tax rates. But it should be clear from (4) that the determination of the optimal tax schedule is a complex matter. Further insight can be gained by simplifying assumptions and numerical calculations. We turn first to the case of quasi-linear preferences.

7.2 **Quasi-linear preferences: the utilitarian case**

The terms in (4) simplify if we assume quasi-linear preferences with $U_x = 1$. But even this is still too complex, with a number of different influences in play, to allow useful interpretation. This expression simplifies further if the n-distribution is a Pareto distribution $f(n) = \frac{1}{n^{1+a}}$ for a>0, i.e a Pareto tail with the coefficient a, and the utility function is $u = x - \upsilon x_r - y^{1+\frac{1}{\varepsilon}/(1+\frac{1}{\varepsilon})}$, i.e. quasi-linear in consumption, υ is the relativity parameter, and there is constant labour supply elasticity ($E^C = E^u = \varepsilon$). A Pareto distribution implies that the term B is constant and equal to a^{-1}. If W' goes to zero as n rises, then in the C-term the integral term converges to 1 from below. Then for sufficiently large n, t/(1−t) is increasing and converges to $\frac{\gamma}{\lambda}(1 + \frac{1+\varepsilon^{-1}}{a}) + \frac{1+\varepsilon^{-1}}{a}$.

Thus the marginal tax rate t increases with n and converges to a positive limit. Hence the result shown by Diamond (1998) without relative consumption concern also holds here. Note that the positive limit increases with the scope of relativity γ and a^{-1} (i.e. with increasing inequality). To get a better understanding quantitatively, we calculate an example: assume an elasticity of 0.3; the social marginal welfare weight at the top decile is 0.5 where $\frac{(1-F(n))}{nf(n)}$=0.5 [6]; and ν = ½. The optimal marginal tax rate at this income level is 75 per cent; without any relative consumption concern it would be 50 per cent. Clearly, the impact of relativity on the marginal tax rate is quantitatively significant.

[6] This is based on the 2005 US empirical income distribution (see Diamond and Saez 2011).

There may also be some interest in noting that when $W' = 1$, i.e. when there is complete distributional indifference (given the quasi-linearity in preferences), then all taxation must be Pigouvian. From (4), it is also easy to see that without relativity concern ($\upsilon = 0$), the optimal income tax is simply the Mirrleesian tax.

7.3 Quasi-linear preferences: the Rawlsian case

Assuming the Rawlsian social objective of maximizing the utility of the worst-off person in society[7] (the factor C_n in (4) is constant), then the pattern of marginal tax rates is given by:

$$\frac{t}{1-t} = \frac{\gamma}{\lambda} + \underbrace{\left[1 + \frac{1}{E^c}\right]}_{A_n}\underbrace{\left[\frac{1-F(n)}{nf(n)}\right]}_{B_n}\underbrace{\left(1 + \frac{\gamma}{\lambda}\right)}_{C_n} \tag{5}$$

When the upper part of the n-distribution is the unbounded Pareto distribution and the utility function is quasi-linear in consumption, we have:

$$\frac{t}{1-t} = \phi + \left[1 + \frac{1}{\varepsilon}\right]\frac{1}{a}[1 + \phi] \tag{6}$$

where $\phi = \frac{\upsilon}{1-\upsilon}$.

(6) implies that the optimal marginal tax rate is increasing in the inequality parameter a^{-1}, and also increasing in the relativity parameter ν.[8]

Table 7.1 illustrates and presents the marginal tax rates for different parameter values, when a=2 and 3, ν =0 and 1/2, and ϵ=1/3, ½, and 1. It shows how the top marginal tax rate decreases when the elasticity of labour supply ϵ increases, the Pareto parameter a increases and the degree of relative consumption concern declines. If the whole distribution of wages is an unbounded Pareto distribution, then optimal marginal tax rates are constant and positive.[9]

From (6) we see that the effect of an increase in the relativity parameter on progressivity (in the sense of steepness of t) depends on the sign of $\frac{d}{dn}\frac{(1-F(n))}{nf(n)}$. In particular, when

[7] Note that while maximizing the utility of the worst-off person in society is commonly interpreted as 'Rawlsian' in the literature, it is not the original version of Rawlsian thought but a kind of welfarist version of Rawls. 'To interpret the difference principle as the principle of maximin utility (the principle to maximize the well-being of the least advantaged person) is a serious misunderstanding from a philosophical standpoint' (Rawls, 1982, p. 175, footnote 13).

[8] This result can be also derived with quasi-linear in-leisure preferences.

[9] This implies that the optimal tax function is linear; $T(z) = k + \kappa z$. The average tax rate is $\frac{T(z)}{z} = \frac{k}{z} + t$ (*) where $t = \frac{b}{1+b}$ is between zero and one and where $b = \phi + \left[1 + \frac{1}{\varepsilon}\right]\frac{1}{a}[1 + \phi]$. Equation (*) implies that average tax rates are increasing if and only if k is negative. If preferences are quasi-linear in consumption and the distribution of n is an unbounded Pareto distribution, a maximin criterion implies increasing average tax rates in income.

Table 7.1 Rawlsian marginal tax rates (%) when people care about relative consumption (Source: Kanbur and Tuomala 2013)

	ϵ =1/3	ϵ =1/3	ϵ=1/2	ϵ=1/2	ϵ=1	ϵ=1
Relative concern	a=2	a=3	a=2	a=3	a=2	a=3
ν=0	66.6	57	60	50	50	40
ν =1/2	83.3	78.6	80	75	75	70

Table 7.2 Rawlsian marginal tax rates (%) with Champernowne distribution

	ϵ=1/3	ϵ=1/3	ϵ=1/3	ϵ=1/3	ϵ=1	ϵ=1	ϵ=1	ϵ=1
	ν=0	ν=1/2	ν=0	ν=1/2	ν=0	ν=1/2	ν=0	ν=1/2
F(n)	θ=2	θ=2	θ=3	θ=3	θ=2	θ=2	θ=3	θ=3
0.10	94.7	97.2	93.3	96.4	89.2	94.6	86.7	93.4
0.50	81.2	90.0	74.1	86.3	66.6	83.3	56.9	78.4
0.90	70.4	84.3	61.4	79.8	52.3	76.2	42.3	71.2
0.99	67.0	82.6	58.2	78.1	48.4	74.2	39.5	69.5
0.999	58.7	78.4	52.2	75.1	39.9	69.2	33.5	66.8

Table 7.3 Rawlsian marginal tax rates (%) with lognormal distribution

	ϵ=1/3	ϵ=1/3	ϵ=1/3	ϵ=1/3	ϵ=1	ϵ=1	ϵ=1	ϵ=1
	ν=0	ν=1/2	ν=0	ν=1/2	ν=0	ν=1/2	ν=0	ν=1/2
F(n)	σ=0.7	σ=0.7	σ=0.39	σ=0.39	σ=0.7	σ=0.7	σ=0.39	σ=0.39
0.10	93.4	96.7	89.4	94.7	87.8	93.9	80.8	90.4
0.50	77.7	88.9	65.9	82.9	63.6	81.8	49.1	74.6
0.90	61.5	80.7	46.9	73.5	44.4	72.2	30.7	65.9
0.99	51.7	75.8	36.9	68.5	34.9	67.4	22.6	61.3
0.999	47.5	73.8	31.7	65.9	31.1	65.6	18.8	59.4

it is negative (positive), the income tax schedule becomes more (less) progressive as a result of an increase in relativity.

Table 7.2 displays optimal marginal tax rates for different percentile points of the distribution two alternatives to the Pareto distribution: (i) Champernowne (1952) distribution and (ii) lognormal distribution (with parameters m and σ; see Aitchison and Brown, 1957).[10]

Note that in Tables 7.2 and 7.3 (as well as in Table 7.1), these are marginal rates for all taxes that vary with income, and should be compared with the schedules for total of taxes on income and expenditures in real economies. From Tables 7.2 and 7.3 we can see that

[10] $Ln(n; m, \sigma^2)$ with support $[0,\infty)$. The first parameter m is log of the median and the second parameter is the variance of log wage. The latter is itself an inequality measure.

the marginal tax rates decrease with labour supply elasticities as expected. We also see that marginal tax rates throughout are lower for the lognormal case than for the Champernowne distribution. The results in Tables 7.2 and 7.3 again confirm that zero is a poor approximation even for the top 0.1 per cent. Finally, and most importantly from our point of view, as the degree of relative consumption concern increases, (i) marginal tax rates increase throughout; (ii) they increase more at higher levels of income; and (iii) the result is that the fall-off of marginal tax rates is less steep, and in this sense the tax structure is more progressive.

7.4 The utilitarian case with income effects

When the elasticity of labour supply is not constant, the problem becomes more complicated. Then it is not possible without simulations to say anything about the shape of the tax schedule. The special cases considered in the previous section yield insights, but within the framework of the assumptions made. How robust are these insights? What happens when we move away from quasi-linearity?

This section presents optimal tax schedules with alternative assumptions. In Kanbur and Tuomala (2013), simulations are performed for the utilitarian case. The distribution f(n) is either the lognormal density (m,σ) (mean, standard deviation) or the Champernowne distribution (m,θ).

The utility function takes the following form:[11]

$$U = \log x + \phi \log \frac{x}{x_r} + \log (1 - y) \tag{7}$$

where x_r is the comparison consumption level and ϕ is a degree of relative income concern.[12] Of course, the form in (7) restricts the range of the elasticity of labour supply. It is important to note that (7) not only affects directly individual utility levels but also has behavioural effects, namely, relativity concerns (ϕ) can change an individual's marginal rate of substitution between consumption and labour supply. This can be seen from individuals' utility maximization condition; $x/(1+\phi)(1-y) = 1-t$.

The empirical research on relativity (status) also employs the log-linear specification as in (7) (see Clark et al 2008, eqs (2) and (4)). One of the key findings of this research is that the estimated coefficients on income (consumption) and income comparison are statistically almost equal and opposite (see e.g. Clark and Oswald 1996, Blanchflower and Oswald 2004, Luttmer 2005). This finding is robust to a variety of controls and is highly statistically significant. Thus, relative consumption matters approximately as much as own consumption; one euro of increased consumption increases utility by about the

[11] Boskin and Sheshinsky (1978) employ the same functional form.

[12] Note that ϕ=1 corresponds to a degree of relativity concern ν = 0.5 in section 3.

Table 7.4 Utilitarian optimal taxation with relativity: lognormal skills distribution

β=0	σ=0.5	R=0.0	ϕ=0				
F(n)	y	z	x	ATR%	MTR%	E^c	E^u
0.10	0.32	0.06	0.09	−50	30	1.06	0.56
0.50	0.41	0.15	0.15	−4	29	0.72	0.22
0.90	0.46	0.32	0.28	13	26	0.59	0.09
0.99	0.48	0.57	0.47	18	23	0.54	0.04
P(90/10)		5.33	3.11				
RD%			41.7				

$F(n_o)=0.0003$, $x(n_0)=0.05$, $x(n_0)/x(\text{median})=0.33$

Table 7.5 Utilitarian optimal taxation with relativity: lognormal skills distribution

β=0	σ=0.5	R=0.0	ϕ=1				
F(n)	y	z	x	ATR%	MTR%	E^u	E^c
0.10	0.22	0.04	0.13	−202	58	2.03	2.36
0.50	0.41	0.15	0.17	−14	60	0.67	0.95
0.90	0.53	0.37	0.26	30	61	0.26	0.59
0.99	0.59	0.68	0.38	44	60	0.13	0.46
P(90/10)		9.25	2.0				
RD%			78.4				

$F(n_o)=0.015$, $x(n_0)=0.11$, $x(n_0)/x(\text{median})=0.65$

Table 7.6 Utilitarian optimal taxation with relativity: lognormal skills distribution

β=0	σ=0.7	R=0.0	ϕ=1				
F(n)	y	z	x	ATR%	MTR%	E^u	E^c
0.12	0.01	0.001	0.13	–	61		
0.50	0.34	0.14	0.17	−38	65	0.96	1.29
0.90	0.51	0.48	0.28	39	68	0.31	0.64
0.99	0.60	1.06	0.48	55	67	0.11	0.44
P(90/50)		3.4	1.64				
RD%			51.8				

$F(n_o)=0.12$, $x(n_0)=0.125$, $x(n_0)/x(\text{median})=0.7$

same amount as a euro reduction in average consumption in the society. Hence relative income is close to a zero-sum game.

The optimal tax schedules are calculated numerically. The results of the simulations are summarized in Tables 7.4–7.10. In these Tables, R (or X/Z) is revenue requirement (R=0 means pure redistributive system), ATR is average tax rate, and MTR is marginal tax rate. The Tables give labour supply, y, gross income, z, net income, x and optimal

Table 7.7 Utilitarian optimal taxation with relativity: lognormal skills distribution

β=0	σ=0.5	R=0.0	ϕ=3				
F(n)	y	z	x	ATR%	MTR%	E^u	E^c
0.10	0.11	0.02	0.15	−643	78		
0.50	0.41	0.15	0.18	−20	79	0.95	1.15
0.90	0.58	0.40	0.23	42	80	0.38	0.58
0.99	0.66	0.76	0.30	60	81	0.21	0.41
P(90/50)		2.66	1.66				
RD%			37.6				

$F(n_o)=0.07$, $x(n_0)=0.14$, $x(n_0)/x(\text{median})=0.78$

Table 7.8 Utilitarian optimal taxation with relativity: lognormal skills distribution

β=0	σ=0.7	R=0.0	ϕ=3				
F(n)	y	z	x	ATR%	MTR%	E^u	E^c
0.22	0.01	0.001	0.16	–	81		
0.50	0.30	0.11	0.18	−64	82	1.66	1.86
0.90	0.56	0.50	0.25	51	84	0.42	0.63
0.99	0.67	1.21	0.36	71	85	0.19	0.39
P(90/50)		4.54	1.56				
RD%			66.0				

$F(n_o)=0.22$, $x(n_0)=0.16$, $x(n_0)/x(\text{median})=0.89$

average (ATR) and marginal tax rates (MTR) at various percentiles of the ability distribution. The Tables also provide the decile ratios (P90/P10) and ((P90/P50)) for net income and gross income and the ratio between the guaranteed income $x(n_0)$[13] and median income. Since marginal tax rates may be a poor indication of the redistribution powers of an optimal tax structure we measure the extent of redistribution, denoted by RD, as the proportional reduction between the decile ratio for market income, z, and the decile ratio for disposable income, x. Tables 7.4–7.10 give comparisons as ϕ and σ (θ) vary. Figures 7.1–7.5 show marginal tax rates for different parameters.

Several patterns emerge from the simulations presented here, focusing specifically on the impact of relativity on progressivity. As the parameter ϕ increases, (i) marginal tax rates increase at all levels of income; (ii) the drop-off in marginal tax rates for higher income levels is mitigated; and (iii) our redistribution measure, RD, increases. The argument for greater progressivity as a function of relativity comes through in the cases examined here—it is not just a property of the Rawlsian objective function, nor restricted to the Pareto or the Champernowne distributions.

[13] There is a critical n_0 such that $y(n) = 0$ for $n \leq n_0$ and $y(n)>0$ for $n>n_0$.

Table 7.9 Utilitarian optimal taxation with relativity: Champernowne skills distribution

β=0	θ=3	R=0.0	ϕ=3				
F(n)	y	z	x	ATR%	MTR%	E^u	E^c
0.12	0.01	0.002	0.16	–	79		
0.50	0.37	0.14	0.18	−33	80	1.06	1.36
0.90	0.55	0.42	0.24	44	83	0.45	0.65
0.99	0.65	1.06	0.34	68	85	0.23	0.43
P(90/50)		2.8	1.33				
RD%			52.5				

$F(n_o)=0.117$, $x(n_o)=0.155$, $x(n_o)/x(\text{median})=0.86$

Table 7.10 Utilitarian optimal taxation with relativity: Champernowne skills distribution

β=0	θ=2	R=0.0	ϕ=3				
F(n)	y	z	x	ATR%	MTR%	E^u	E^c
0.38	0.01	0.001	0.18	–	84		
0.50	0.15	0.06	0.19	−228	85	1.32	1.52
0.90	0.51	0.56	0.25	55	88	0.57	0.77
0.99	0.69	1.06	0.44	69	90	0.16	0.36
P(90/50)		9.33	1.32				
RD%			85				

$F(n_o)=0.38$, $x(n_o)=0.178$, $x(n_o)/x(\text{median})=0.93$

To further examine how sensitive the shape of the tax schedule and working hours are to the choice of the parameter ϕ in the utility function and inherent inequality, we computed solutions for ϕ=1.0 and 3.0 in the case of the utility function (7) and σ=0.5 and 0.7 in the lognormal distribution (shown in Figures 7.1–7.6) and θ=2 and 3 in the Champernowne distribution (see Tables 7.9 and 7.10). We find that when ϕ and inherent inequality increase the marginal tax rates are higher and increasing with income, up to around F(n)=0.99.[14]

7.5 **Relativity and inequality**

From the results in Sections 7.2 and 7.3, we know that progressivity increases with greater relativity concern. Greater relativity concern increases marginal tax rates throughout, and they increase more at the higher levels of income. We also know, from these sections and from Kanbur and Tuomala (1994), that progressivity increases

[14] These results reinforce the findings of Kanbur and Tuomala (1994) that when higher values of inherent inequality are used, optimal marginal tax rates increase with income over the majority of the population.

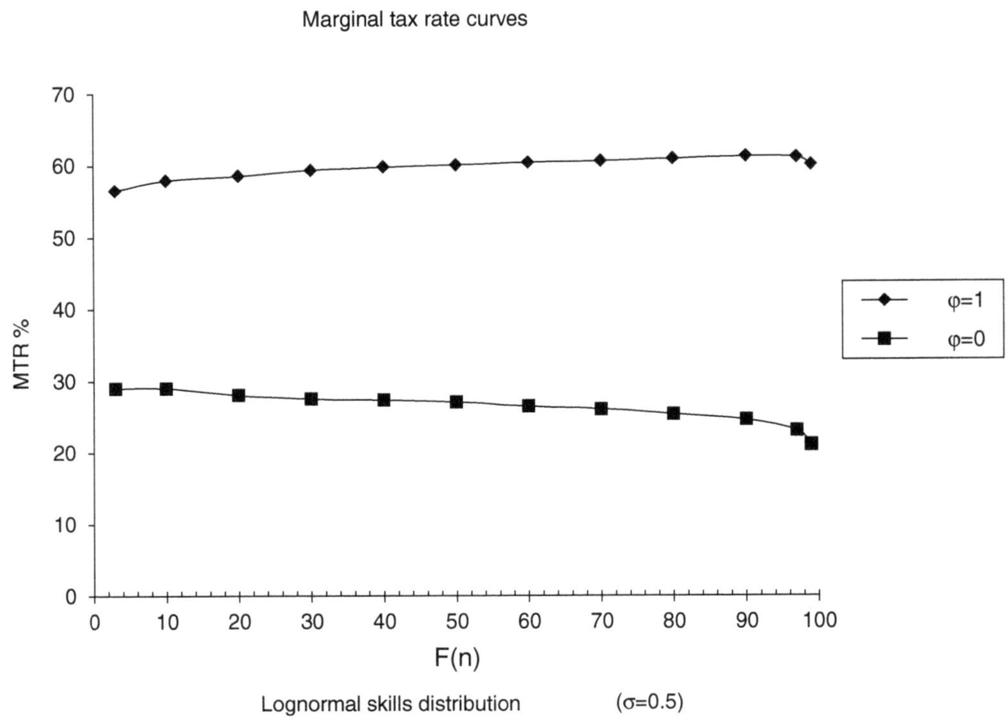

Figure 7.1 Lognormal skills distribution (σ = 0.5)

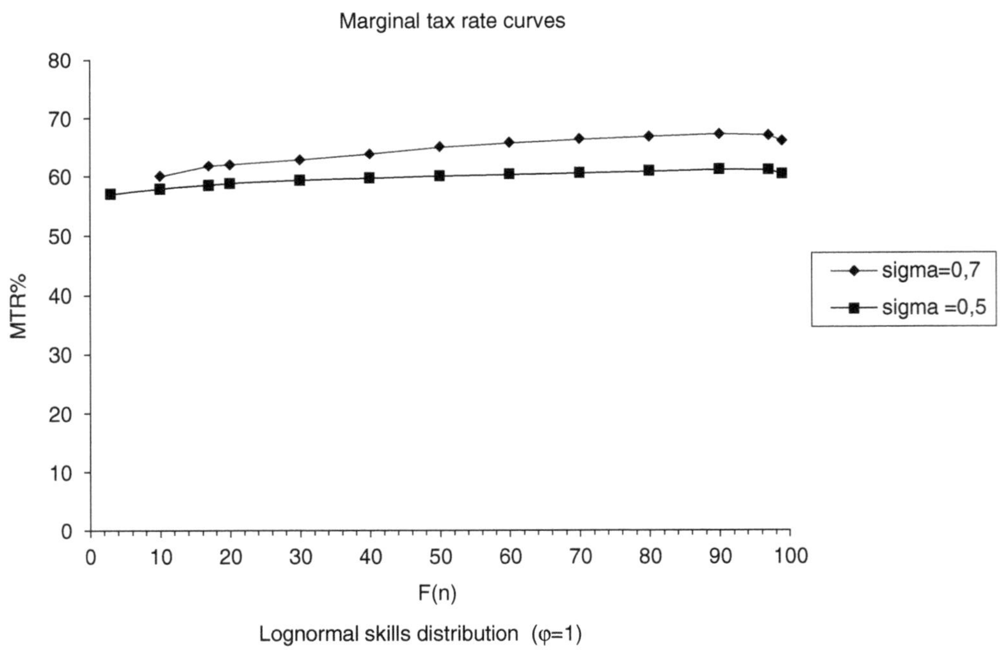

Figure 7.2 Lognormal skills distribution (ϕ =1)

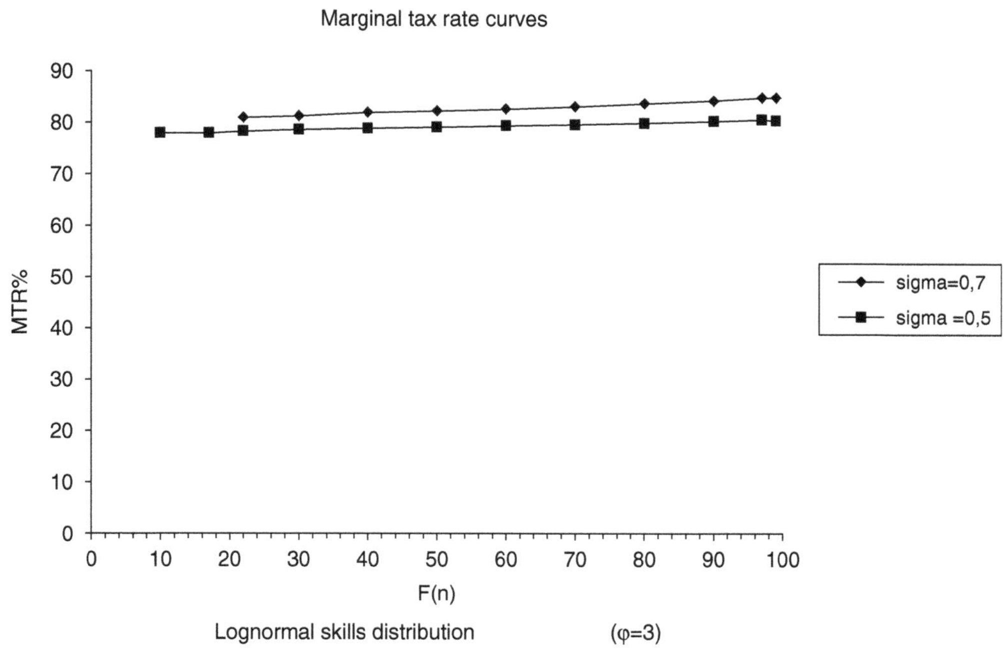

Figure 7.3 Lognormal skills distribution (ϕ =3)

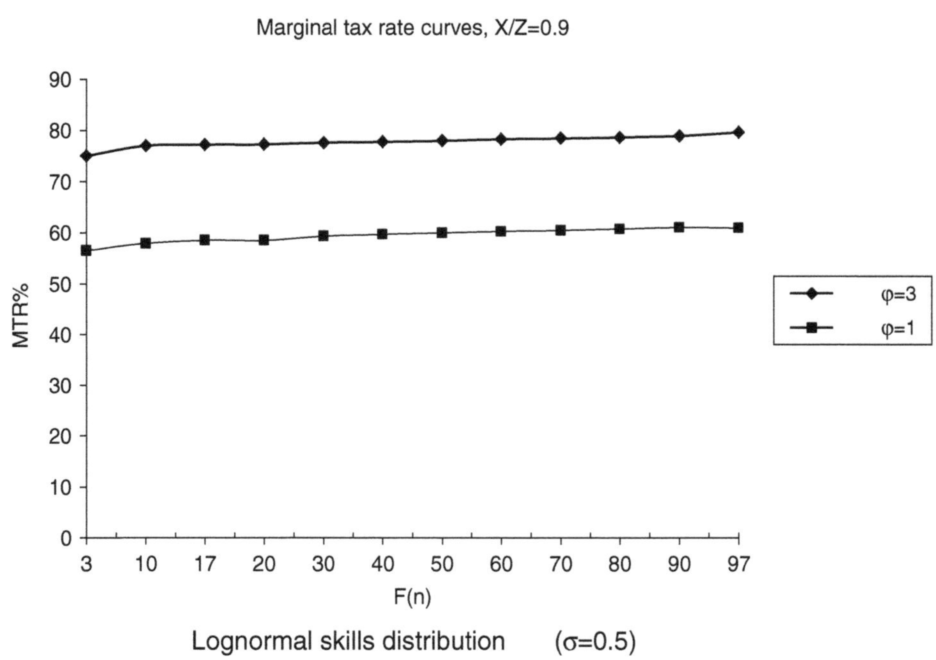

Figure 7.4 Lognormal skills distribution (σ =0.5)

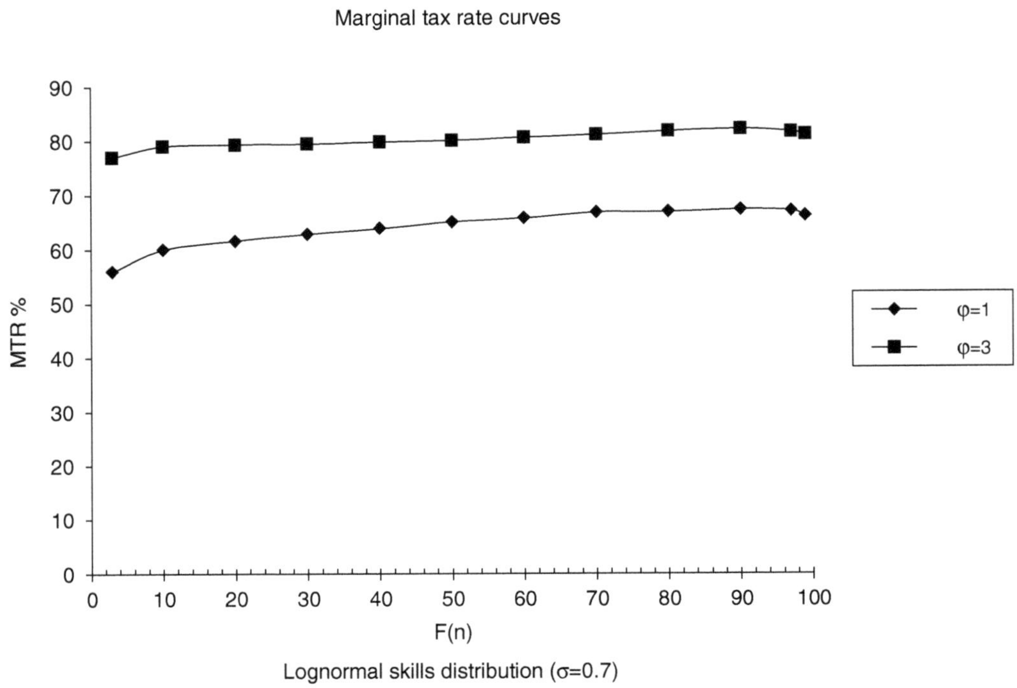

Figure 7.5 Lognormal skills distribution (σ =0.7)

with inequality. In this section we look at the interaction of inequality and relativity in determining the optimal tax schedule. How does the effect of relativity on progressivity change with inequality? And how does the effect of inequality on progressivity change with relativity?

We have some theoretical guidance on these questions from the special case of the Rawlsian objective function with an unbounded Pareto distribution. The marginal tax rates for this case are given in equation (9). From this it is seen that the marginal tax rate depends on the inequality parameter a^{-1} and the relativity parameter ϕ. The impact of one on the optimal marginal tax rate thus depends on the level of the other. Differentiating (6) first with respect to a^{-1} and then with respect to ϕ shows that the second order cross-partial derivative of t is negative. This leads us to the following result: with quasi-linear preferences, a Rawlsian objective function, and a Pareto distribution, the higher inequality is, the lower is the effect of relativity in raising marginal tax rates. Similarly, the higher relativity is, the lower is the effect of inequality in raising marginal tax rates.

Numerical illustrations of this proposition can be seen in Table 7.1. For example, with labour supply elasticity of unity, (i) with $a^{-1} = 1/2$ when the relativity parameter increases from 0 to ½, the optimal marginal tax rate increases from 50 per cent to 75 per cent; but (ii) with $a^{-1} = 1/3$, for the same increase in the relativity parameter, the optimal marginal tax rate rises from 40 per cent to 70 per cent. The results of Proposition 3[15] are

[15] In Kanbur-Tuomala (2013).

for a special case. Do they hold for more general preferences, for the more general utilitarian social welfare function, and for more general distributions? In what follows we generalize by assuming preferences in (7), the classical utilitarian social welfare function used in Section 4, and lognormal and Champernowne distributions. Moreover, Proposition 3 is only for the level of the marginal tax rate. It does not speak to the progression of marginal tax rates when they are not constant.

To see how the impact of greater relativity affects progressivity at successively higher levels of pre-tax inequality, we have computed solutions for different parameter values of relative consumption concern ϕ given pre-tax inequality, and then repeated the exercise at a higher level of inequality. From Figures 7.3 and 7.4 we see that the greater relativity raises marginal tax rates and increases progressivity, but this impact is dampened by increasing inequality. Similarly, we can ask how the impact of greater inequality affects progressivity with greater strength of relativity. From Figures 7.5 and 7.6 we see that greater inequality increases progressivity, but this impact on progressivity is in turn declining with an increase of relativity. Thus it seems that, in these numerical simulations at least, relativity and inequality do not compound each other's incremental effect on progressivity. The numerical simulations provide support for the narrower theoretical result in Proposition 1 see Kanbur-Tuomala (2013).

Given the inherent complexities of optimal non-linear income taxation, it is not straightforward to develop an intuition for this result. But we can take the first steps towards understanding, as follows. Consider the effects of an increase in the marginal tax rate at some income level, $z^* = ny$ (say, in a small interval from z^* to $z^*+\Delta$), leaving all other marginal tax rates unaltered. There are four effects of such a change: (i), individuals at that income level face a higher marginal rate, which will distort their labour supply, the term A in equation (4); (ii), all individuals above income level z^* will pay more tax, but these individuals face no new marginal distortion. That is, the higher marginal rate at z^* is infra-marginal for them, the term B; (iii), since those thus giving up income are an above-average slice of the population (it is the part of the population with income above z^*), there tends to be a redistributive gain; (iv), on top of those effects there is a Pigouvian term $\frac{\gamma}{\lambda}$. Now an increase in pre-tax inequality implies that more of the extra revenue gained due to effect (i) comes from taxpayers far above average and whose losses under effect (iii) are therefore valued well below average. This means that the benefit of effect (ii) increases in relation to the loss of effect (iii), making higher marginal tax rates more attractive. The benefit of effect (ii) in relation to the loss of effect (iii) further increases when we take into account externality effect through $\lambda(1 + \frac{\gamma}{\lambda})$, i.e. an augmented shadow price of public funds. Hence, in addition to a direct Pigouvian effect, the marginal tax rate further increases.

This still leaves open the question of the progression of optimal marginal tax rates. As should be clear from (4), this is an even more intricate issue than the level of marginal tax rates. The numerical calculations suggest that, for the cases examined, the cross-effect of inequality and relativity on the progression of marginal tax rates is negative. However, a satisfactory theoretical explanation for this must await further research.

How does relativity affect the structure of optimal non-linear income taxation? Kanbur and Tuomala (2013) provide three sets of answers to this general question. First, it supports the conclusion in the literature that relativity leads to higher marginal tax rates. In doing so it both generalizes some of the conditions under which this result is obtained in the literature and fleshes out the detailed structure for optimal marginal tax rates for specific functional forms of distribution, utility function, and social welfare function. Second, it may also be the case that this is a more suitable framework within which to examine the optimal top tax rate. Third, the paper goes beyond the literature and examines the impact of relativity on the progression of optimal marginal tax rates. By and large, we find support for greater progressivity, defined as the steepness of the rise of the marginal tax rate schedule, as relativity concern increases. Fourth, it examines the interplay of relativity and inequality in determining the optimal structure of taxes. Their special analytical cases and more general numerical calculations support the conclusion that higher inequality dampens the positive impact of greater relativity on the level and progression of marginal tax rates.

APPENDIX 7.1 DERIVATION OF RESULTS

Introducing Lagrange multipliers λ, α(n) and γ for the constraints (5), (6), and (1) and integrating by parts, the Lagrangean becomes

$$L=\int_0^\infty [(W(u)+\lambda(ny-x)f(n)+\gamma(\mu-xf))-\mu' u-\mu\Psi]dn+\mu(\infty)u(\infty)-\mu(0)u(0) \quad (1)$$

Differentiating with respect to u, y, and x_r gives the first-order conditions[16]

$$L_u = [W' - h_u(\lambda+\gamma)]f(n) - \mu'(n) = 0 \quad (2)$$

$$L_y = \lambda(n-h_y)f(n) - \gamma h_y f(n) - \mu(n)(V_y + yV_{yy})/n = 0 \quad (3)$$

$$L_{x_r} = \int -\lambda h_{x_r} f(n)dn + \gamma - \int \gamma h_{x_r} f(n)dn = 0 \quad (4)$$

(3) implies

$$\frac{\gamma}{\lambda} = \frac{\int h_{x_r} f(n)dn}{1-\int h_{x_r} f(n)dn} \quad (5)$$

where $\frac{\gamma}{\lambda}$ is the shadow price of the average consumption constraint expressed in public funds.

[16] Inverting the utility function we have $x = h(u, y, x_r)$ and calculating the derivatives $h_y = -V_y/U_x, h_u = 1/U_x, h_{x_r} = -\psi_{x_r}/U_x$

(2) satisfies the transversality conditions

$$\frac{\partial L}{\partial u(0)} = \mu(0) = 0; \frac{\partial L}{\partial u(\infty)} = \mu(\infty) = 0$$

and

$$\mu(n) > 0, \text{for } n \in (0, \infty).$$

Integrating equation (2),[17]

$$\mu(n) = \int_n^\infty \left[\frac{(\lambda + \gamma)}{u_x} - W' \right] f(p)dp \tag{6}$$

From the first-order conditions of government's maximization, we obtain the following condition for optimal marginal tax rate $t(z) = T'(z)$; [Note: $\frac{t}{1-t} = \frac{1}{1-t} - 1 = \frac{U_x n}{V_Y} - 1$]

$$\frac{t}{1-t} = \frac{\gamma}{\lambda} + (\zeta) \frac{U_x}{\lambda n f(n)} \int_n^\infty \left[\frac{(\lambda + \gamma)}{U_x} - G' \right] f(p)dp \tag{7}$$

where $\zeta = 1 + \frac{yV_{yy}}{V_y}$.

It is worth noting that the so-called end-point results no longer hold. From (13) and the transversality conditions $\mu(o) = \mu(\infty) = 0$, the marginal tax rates are positive at both ends when $\psi_{x_r} < 0$ (see Oswald 1983). This is also true with other comparators. As shown in Tuomala (1990), the separability assumption used in Oswald (1983) can be weakened so that μ affects individuals' choices. Unfortunately we are not able to say more on the shape of the tax schedule with a weaker separability condition.

For more general distributions, the marginal tax rate will not be constant. To gain further understanding on the relationship between the degree of progressivity represented by the steepness of t, and relativity, we solve for marginal tax in (16). It is given by

$$t = 1 - \frac{1}{(1+\phi)\left[1 + (1+\varepsilon^{-1}) \frac{(1-F(n))}{nf(n)}\right]}. \tag{8}$$

A measure of the degree of progressivity of t is given by:

$$\frac{dt(n)}{dF(n)} = \frac{1}{f(n)} \frac{dt}{dn} = \frac{1}{f(n)} \frac{\frac{d}{dn} \frac{(1-F(n))}{nf(n)} (1+\varepsilon^{-1})}{(1+\phi)\left[1 + (1+\varepsilon^{-1}) \frac{(1-F(n))}{nf(n)}\right]^2}. \tag{9}$$

[17] Integrating equation (8) note $\int_n^\infty \frac{d\mu}{dn} dn = \mu(\infty) - \mu(n)$.

With this formula we calculate the effect of an increase in ϕ on progressivity as follows:

$$\frac{d^2 t(n)}{d\phi dF(n)} = -\frac{1}{f(n)} \frac{\frac{d}{dn}\frac{(1-F(n))}{nf(n)}(1+\varepsilon^{-1})}{(1+\phi)^2\left[1+(1+\varepsilon^{-1})\frac{(1-F(n))}{nf(n)}\right]^2}. \tag{10}$$

From (10) we see that the effect of an increase in the relativity parameter on progressivity (in the sense of steepness of t) depends on the sign of $\frac{d}{dn}\frac{(1-F(n))}{nf(n)}$. In particular, when it is negative (positive) the income tax schedule becomes more (less) progressive as a result of an increase in relativity.

8 Optimal income taxation and tagging

In the analysis so far, individuals have been assumed to differ only in their unobserved ability. It is widely recognized that there are potentially severe incentive and other costs of administering income-related transfers. One way of overcoming these costs is to differentiate the population by easily observable indicators that are correlated with the unobservable characteristic of interest. An individual's labour market status or demographic attributes, for instance, may convey information on underlying productivity.[1] Transfers can then be made contingent upon such characteristics. Akerlof (1978)[2] was among the first to recognize that the use of contingent information to implement several tax/transfer schedules, one for each group, was bound to be superior to being restricted to a single schedule for the whole population. However, he did not say much about the quantitative gain from such differentiation, nor about the shapes of the schedules for the different groups.

The two decades following Akerlof's (1978) seminal publication saw the application and extension of the idea in a number of different directions and settings. Kanbur (1987) and Besley and Kanbur (1988) applied the idea to the targeting of anti-poverty transfers in developing countries. Kanbur and Keen (1989) provide some characterizations of linear group-specific tax/transfer schedules with incentive effects. The design of distinct non-linear income tax/transfer schemes for sub-groups of the population linked by intergroup transfers was provided by Immonen, Kanbur, Keen, and Tuomala (1998) (hereafter IKKT), with a focus on two key issues: what are the shapes of optimal tax/transfer schedules when categorical information can be used to apply different schedules to different groups, and how substantial are the potential welfare gains from applying distinct schedules to distinct groups? The interplay between income relation and categorical benefits is also examined by Stern (1982). A number of other papers have considered optimal taxes with tagging: for example, Bennett (1987) explores lump-sum transfers between different types of individuals, and Parsons (1996) studies the optimal benefit structure of an earnings insurance programme when 'eligibility requirements' are used as a tag to (imperfectly) identify those who are out of work.

1 Mirrlees (1971, p. 175) noticed: 'One might obtain information about a man's income-earning potential from his apparent I.Q., the number of his degrees, his address, age or colour . . .'

2 In fact the two-tier social dividend system in the Meade report (1978) pp. 271–6 is a very similar idea.

The continuing power of the tagging idea is shown by a burgeoning literature post-2000, which has become more specific and considers tagging across different types of groupings. Viard (2001a, b) studies tagging in an optimal linear income tax framework allowing the demogrants to differ across groups but not the income tax rates; Alesina et al (2007) advocate tagging based on gender; Blumkin, Margalioth, and Sadka (2007) examine the redistributive role of affirmative action policy, asking whether in an egalitarian society, supplementing the tax-transfer system with an affirmative action policy would enhance social welfare; Mankiw and Weinzierl (2010) study a model with many skill types who can be tagged on the basis of height; Jacquet and Van der Linden consider stigma in the tagging model; Cremer et al (2010) study the properties of tagging in an optimal income tax framework assuming quasi-linear preferences and a Rawlsian social welfare function; and Boadway and Pestieau (2006) have studied the issue of tagging with optimal income taxation in a two-group-two-skill-level setting.[3]

Following Kremer (2001), age-based taxation, in particular, has received especially close attention in the last decade. Banks and Diamond (2010) argued that tagging based on age may be socially acceptable because everyone can reach a given age at some time during their life. The Mirrlees Review (2011) found this argument to be persuasive in advocating some age-related tax reforms to influence labour market participation decisions by older workers and parents with school-age young children. Blomquist and Micheletto (2008) consider age-dependent non-linear taxation in a dynamic Mirrleesian setting with heterogeneous agents and private savings using an overlapping generations (OLG) model where individuals face a stochastic wage process. Bastani, Blomquist, and Micheletto (2013) examine the quantitative implications of implementing an optimal age-dependent non-linear labour income tax. Weinzierl (2011) provides a quantitative assessment of the welfare gains from age-dependent non-linear income taxes.[4]

The tagging literature has thus grown, and is still growing, in leaps and bounds. However, its central assumption is still that the groupings available to the government are given and fixed. The government cannot rearrange these groupings—it cannot increase or decrease the number of groups, nor can it choose one type of grouping over another. Thus the assumption on the one hand is that the groupings are available to the government without cost, yet on the other hand that it is too costly for the government to deviate from the groupings specified by the analyst. However, if the implementation of tagging is itself costly, and if the costs are a function of the number

[3] Further, Kanbur and Tuomala (2006) analyse optimal aid allocation when the donor is faced with two potential recipient countries with their own specific characteristics. Each recipient government chooses its policies in light of its technology, preferences, and aid allocation. The donor has the task of choosing the aid allocation from a fixed pool of aid resources, to optimize the donor's welfare function. Among their findings is that a key indicator for aid effectiveness is the degree of inequality in a country—more unequal countries should get less aid. Bastani (2013) explores the optimal tax implications in a model with both singles and couples and inequality across as well as within households.

[4] Yet other recent analyses of age-dependent taxes include Erosa and Gervais (2002), and Lozachmeur (2006).

and type of grouping available, the question arises: how many and which types of groups should the government choose to tag? This is the question addressed by Kanbur and Tuomala (2014).

Although it can be shown that tagging is welfare-improving we can find very little tagging in the actual income tax system. There are many reasons why tagging may be unappealing in practice. First, tagging could induce stigma. Errors in tagging cast a shadow on all persons tagged (Moffitt 1983; Jacquet and Van der Linden 2006). Akerlof (1978, p. 17) writes that 'the disadvantages of tagging... are the perverse incentives to people to be identified as needy (to be tagged), the inequity of such a system, and its cost of administration.' Another concern of Akerlof is that tagging could violate horizontal equity: 'equals ought to be treated equally'. This is a prominent concern. For example, Boadway and Pestieau (2006, p. 2) write: 'Of course, such a system may be resisted because, if the tagging characteristic has no direct utility consequences, a differentiated tax system violates the principle of horizontal equity'. Similar statements are made by, e.g., Atkinson and Stiglitz (1980). As stated by Musgrave (1959, p. 160) the principle of horizontal equity provides an unsatisfying explanation for the limits to tagging: 'If there is no specified reason for discriminating among unequals, how can there be a reason for avoiding discrimination among equals?' On the other hand, a welfarist approach to social welfare would overrule objections based on horizontal equity concerns (Kaplow 2008a).

Mankiw and Weinzierl (2010, p. 15) offer two critiques of utilitarianism, coming from the areas of libertarianism and horizontal equity. They are 'sceptical of the redistribution of income or wealth because they believe that individuals are entitled to the returns on their justly-acquired endowments'. More recently, Weinzierl (2012) provided an explanation for limited use of tagging in actual income tax system. He argues that 'this puzzle is a symptom of a more fundamental problem. Conventional theory neglects the diverse normative criteria with which, as extensive evidence has shown, most people evaluate policy. In particular if the classic principle of Equal Sacrifice augments the standard Utilitarian criterion, optimal tagging is limited.'

Weinzierl's (2012) approach has its own weaknesses—namely, it is not obvious how to guarantee commensurability between two very different ethical frameworks. Utilitarianism is based on the end-state principle; libertarianism ('equal sacrifice') not.

It should be intuitively obvious, and it is clear from the literature, that there are gains to be made in moving from no grouping to some grouping, unless of course the groups chosen are identical to each other. But how do these gains depend on the nature of the groups? How do they depend on the differences between groups? And how do they depend on the number of groups? Answers to these questions are the building blocks for a deeper analysis of the design of tagging, where the groupings can also be chosen by the government. Kanbur and Tuomala (2013) take the first steps in such an analysis. Starting with a simple framework and ending with numerical simulations based on data from Finland, they show how groupings should be formed for tagging and provide a quantitative assessment of how group differences affect the gains from tagging, and the welfare gains from increasing the number of groups being tagged.

The plan of this chapter is as follows. First, following Kanbur and Tuomala (2014), we set out a starting framework, with two groups, simple transfers, and no behavioural responses. It derives results for special cases in order to sharpen intuition on the determinants of the gains from grouping. The results are illustrated with Finnish data on income distribution by age. Section 3 stays with the two-group case but moves to a more general framework of optimal non-linear income taxation with labour supply responses. The optimal tax/transfer problem with tagging proves to be too complex for an unambiguous analytical answer concerning the intra-group patterns of optimal marginal tax rates without simplifying assumptions. Assuming quasi-linear preferences with constant elasticity of labour supply, we can analytically understand the pattern of marginal rates in different groups and redistribution between two groups. To pursue this further we turn to numerical simulations. The numerical results in IKKT (1999) are based on utilitarian social objectives. Here we extend their analysis in several ways. We consider non-utilitarian social welfare functions, other utility functions and the pre-tax inequality in the tagged groups based on the Finnish income distribution data. We also quantify the welfare gains from having the ability to implement separate tax/transfer schedules by solving the optimal income taxation problem when different groups can face different non-linear tax/transfers. Section 4 then takes up the case with more than two groups and, again using Finnish data for application, provides a quantitative assessment of the gains from increasing the number of groups to be tagged schedules. Section 5 concludes with a agenda for future research.

8.1 A simple framework

Kanbur and Tuomala (2013) develop a simple framework for assessing the gains from different types of groupings. There are no behavioural responses and attention is restricted to very simple tax and transfer regimes. The government's objective is to maximize a utilitarian social welfare function. Only two groups are allowed. The question, of course, is—which two groups? Because of its simplicity, the analytical framework allows us to derive closed-form solutions, which in turn help to develop intuitions on what sorts of group differences are relevant for tagging. Section 8.2 presents a more general model which relaxes many of these assumptions.

Two groups are mutually exclusive and exhaustive groups, indexed 1 and 2. Let income be denoted z and let the density function of income in the groups be $f_1(z)$ and $f_2(z)$ with means $\bar{z}_1$ and $\bar{z}_2$ respectively. Let the population shares of the groups be N_1 and N_2, with $N_1 + N_2 = 1$. The overall density is then:

$$f(z) = N_1 f_1(z) + N_2 f_2(z) \tag{1}$$

The government's objective function is given by:

$$W = \int u(z)f(z)dz = N_1 \int u(z)f_1(z)dz + N_2 \int u(z)f_2(z)dz \tag{2}$$

where u(z) is an individual level valuation function with u'>0 and u"<0 in the usual way.

Consider now the simplest case of a group-specific tax-transfer regime. A lump-sum tax a_1 is imposed on each member of group 1 and the proceeds are used to finance a lump-sum payment of a_2 to each member of group 2. The self-financing constraint implies that:

$$a_2 = \frac{N_1}{N_2} a_1 \tag{3}$$

Social welfare after the transfer is:

$$W = N_1 \int u(z - a_1)f_1(z)dz + N_2 \int u(z + \frac{N_1}{N_2} a_1)f_2(z)dz \tag{4}$$

and the impact of increasing a_1 on welfare is:

$$\frac{dW}{da_1} = N_1 \left\{ -\int u'(z - a_1)f_1(z)dz + \int u'(z + \frac{N_1}{N_2} a_1)f_2(z)dz \right\} \tag{5}$$

The optimal value of a_1 can be found by setting $\frac{dW}{da_1}$ equal to zero. This solves for a_1 implicitly and we can then find the maximized value of W. Although simple, the structure of the model still does not yield a closed-form solution. We can, however, focus attention on small taxes and transfers. Evaluation $\frac{dW}{da_1}$ at $a_1 = 0$ gives us:

$$\left.\frac{dW}{da_1}\right|_{a_1=0} = N_1 \left\{ \int u'(z)f_2(z)dz - \int u'(z)f_1(z)dz \right\} \tag{6}$$

This depends solely on α and on the properties of u', $f_1(z)$ and $f_2(z)$, and can be used to sharpen our intuitions on what types of differences between $f_1(z)$ and $f_2(z)$ will maximize the welfare gain from the introduction of a tagged tax-transfer regime.

The two terms in curly brackets in (6) can be interpreted as the 'distributional characteristic' of each group (Feldstein 1972). The term in curly brackets as a whole is thus a measure of how different the two groups are along this metric. Equation (6) tells us that there are two features which determine groupings which will give the biggest impact on welfare with tagging—how different the groups are in terms of their population shares, and how different the groups are in terms of their distributional characteristic. Now, it might seem from the first feature that is it best to choose one very small and one very large group in terms of population share. But notice that in the limit, as one group comes closer and closer to becoming the whole population, the difference in the curly brackets will disappear. There thus appear to be subtle trade-offs in group choice, which will depend on also the exact form of the valuation function $u(.)$. We now develop a number of special cases to investigate this further.

8.1.1 SPECIFIC FUNCTIONAL FORMS

If f_1 and f_2 are not in the relation of a mean preserving spread, then more specification of functional forms of either f_1 and f_2, or of u(.), or of both, will be needed to get clear results. Let

$$u(z) = -\left(\frac{z^p - z}{z^p}\right)^{\gamma}; z \leq z^p \tag{7}$$

$$0; z > z^p$$

for $\gamma \geq 0$. Then W will be recognized to be nothing other than the negative of the famous FGT family of poverty indices (Foster, Greer, and Thorbecke 1984):

$$P_{\gamma} = \int_0^{z^p} \left(\frac{z^p - z}{z^p}\right)^{\gamma} f(z)dz \tag{8}$$

Here z^p is the poverty line and γ is interpreted as the degree of poverty aversion. When $\gamma = 0$, P_{γ} is simply the head count ratio of poverty. When $\gamma = 1$ and $\gamma = 2$, the depth of poverty is also emphasized to different degrees.

Noting:

$$u'(z) = \frac{\gamma}{z^p}\left(\frac{z^p - z}{z^p}\right)^{\gamma - 1}; \quad z \leq z^p \tag{9}$$

$$0; z > z^p$$

expression (6) now becomes:

$$\left.\frac{dW}{da_1}\right|_{a_1=0} = \frac{N_1\gamma}{z^p}\{P_{2,\gamma-1} - P_{1,\gamma-1}\} \tag{10}$$

where the subscript 1 and 2 on P indicates group-specific poverty, and the subscript $\gamma - 1$ indicates a poverty aversion of $\gamma - 1$.

Expressions such as (10) are to be found in the literature on anti-poverty targeting (Kanbur 1987, Besley-Kanbur 1988). For our purposes, what it shows is that if its objective is to minimize poverty P_{γ}, then for given population shares the government should choose groups with the biggest difference in $P_{\gamma-1}$. Thus if the objective is to minimize the poverty gap measure P_1, the transfer should be across groups with the biggest difference in P_0—in other words, the biggest differences in the head count ratio.

If the utility function is with constant absolute inequality aversion,

$$u(z) = -\frac{1}{\beta}e^{-\beta z}, \tag{11}$$

where β is the inequality aversion parameter, then substituting this in Equation 6 still does not give a closed-form solution. While this can be calculated for empirical distributions, as it will be in sub-section 8.1.2, further specification is needed for an analytical closed form. With this in mind, let the densities be exponential:

$$f_i(z) = h_i e^{-h_i z}, \ i = 1, 2 \tag{12}$$

Then

$$\left.\frac{dW}{da_1}\right|_{a_1=0} = N_1 \left\{ \frac{h_1}{\beta + h_1} - \frac{h_2}{\beta + h_2} \right\} \tag{13}$$

Thus the impact is greatest when the two densities are most different from each other, as measured by the difference between their exponential parameters h_1 and h_2.

8.1.2 APPLICATION TO FINNISH DATA ON AGE STRUCTURE OF INCOME DISTRIBUTION

Estimates on age structure of income distribution from 1990 to 2007 have been calculated from the Income Distribution Statistics (IDS) data based on a representative national sample. The IDS is a sample survey of around 9,000–11,000 households drawn from private households in Finland. The IDS contains information on incomes, taxes, and benefits together with various socio-economic characteristics of the Finnish households. Most of the information contained in the IDS has been collected from various administrative registers. Auxiliary information is collected through interviews. Figure 8.1a shows pre-tax mean incomes in different age groups in Finland in 1990, 2000, and 2007. They display an inverse U-shaped pattern, except in 2007. Figure 8.1b in

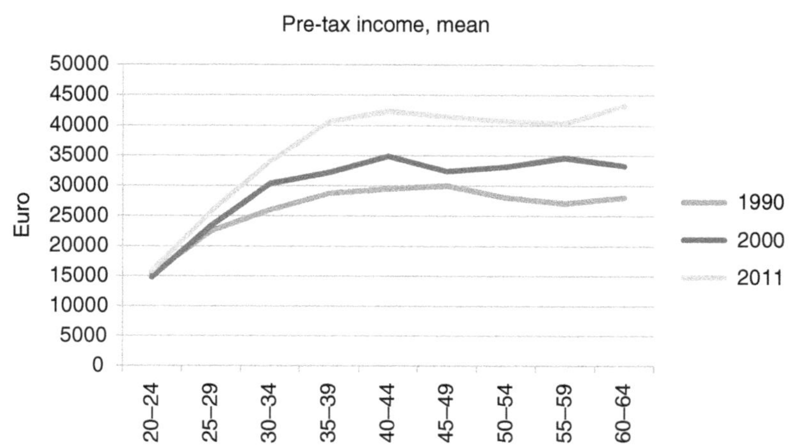

Figure 8.1a Pre-tax income (mean) in age groups (excl. pensioners, unemployed, and students, etc.) in Finland 1990, 2000, 2007

Source: Riihelä et al 2013.

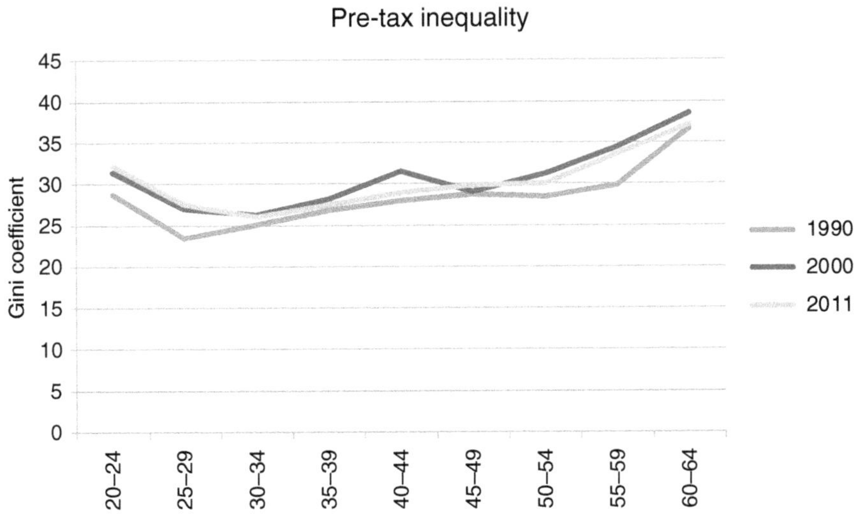

Figure 8.1b Gini coefficient for pre-tax income in age groups (excl. pensioners, unemployed, and students, etc.) in Finland 1990, 2000, 2007

Source: Riihelä et al 2013.

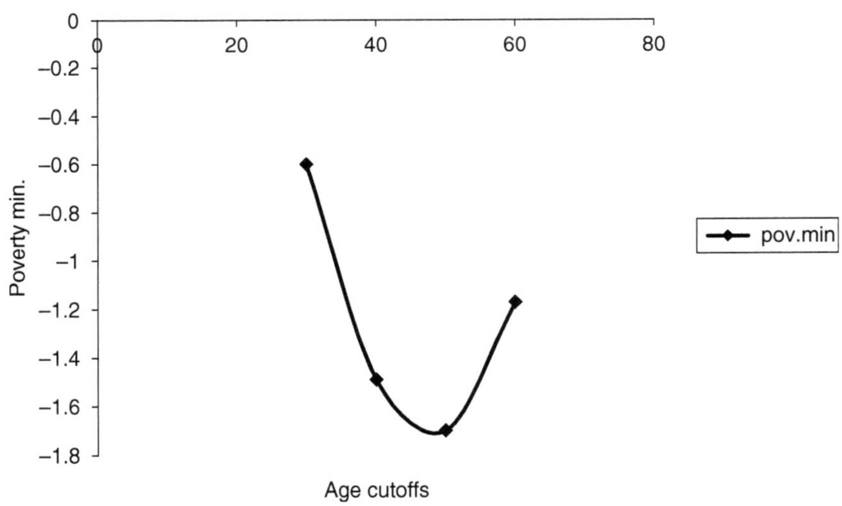

Figure 8.2 The government's objective is to minimize poverty gap

turn displays Gini coefficients in the same age groups and years. The Gini coefficients are higher in younger and older groups than in middle-age groups.

Figures 8.2 and 8.3 display welfare gains as in (6) for different specifications from grouping through different age cut-offs: age 20, age 30, age 40, age 50, and age 60. In Figure 8.2, based on poverty gaps in Finland in different age groups in 2001, we see that if the government's objective is to minimize poverty gaps, then the biggest impact in the sense of poverty alleviation is achieved with age cut-off 30. Figure 8.3 shows welfare gains as in (6), where $u'(z) = \frac{1}{z}(\beta = 0)$ and $u'(z) = e^{-z}(\beta = 1)$ and the distribution of $f_1(z)$

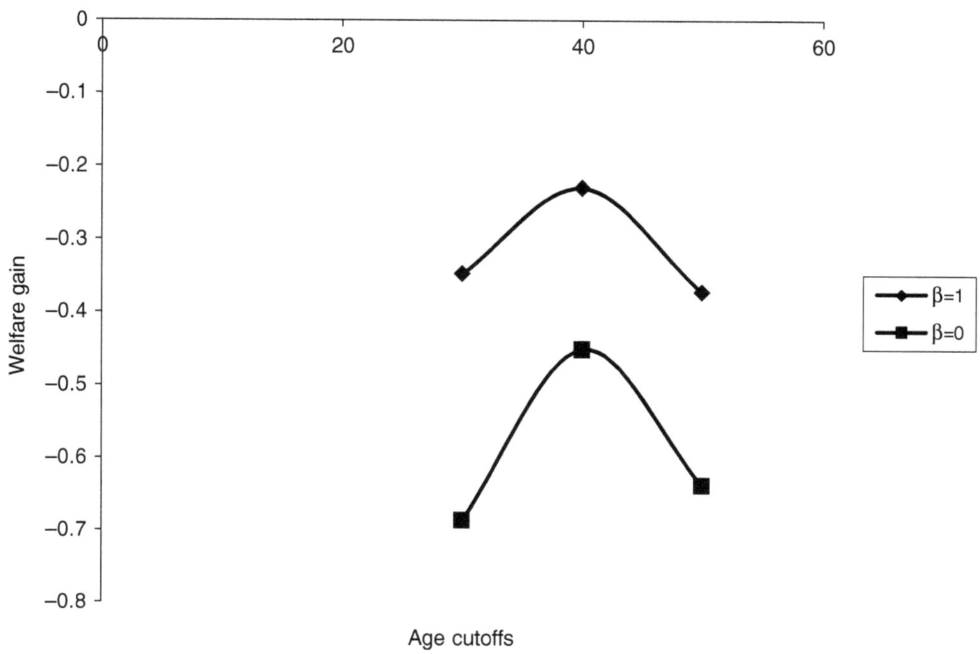

Figure 8.3 Equation (6) with exponential utility function (11) with β=0 and β=1

and $f_2(z)$ are the Champernowne distribution with parameters θ and m.[5] Figure 4 also shows that the biggest impact from tagging is achieved when age cut-off is at age 40.

8.2 Tagging and optimal non-linear income taxation

The simple analytical framework of the last section, and the special functional forms used there, are useful for developing and sharpening intuition. However, they are clearly special in: (i) the form of the tax-transfer regime; (ii) the government's objective function; (iii) the distributional forms used; and, perhaps most important, (iv) the assumption of no behavioural responses. In this section we turn to a more general formulation where these restrictions are relaxed. We do this by setting the problem of choosing groups in the Mirrlees (1971) framework of optimal non-linear income taxation.

Before going to the formal analysis, let us start with informal discussion of Dilnot, Kay, and Morris (1984; henceforth DKM), who argue diagrammatically for a particular pattern of Figure 8.4c. Suppose, as we henceforth shall, that group 1 is the poorer of the two in the sense of having a less favourable distribution of abilities; for brevity, we shall simply call group 2 'rich' and group 1 'poor'. Representing members of group 1 by o and

[5] We calculate (8) with this specification both analytically and numerically. It turns out to be so that when dz=0.0001 in numerical integration, the results are in both methods the same.

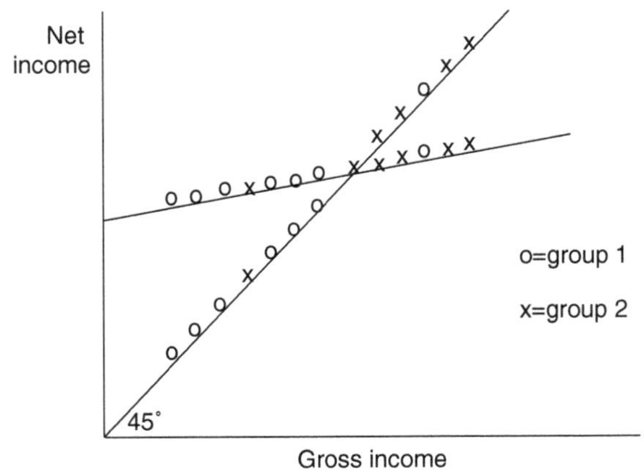

Figure 8.4a (Basic income system)

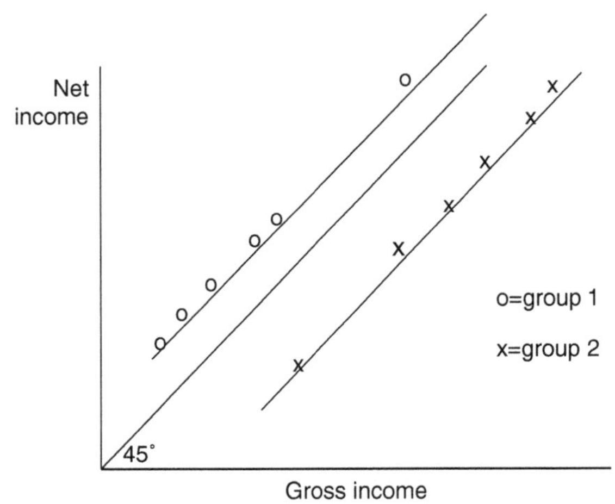

Figure 8.4b (Pure social insurance)

members of group 2 by x, the no-tax outcome is then as in Figure 8.4a, with members of group 1 clustered at relatively low levels of income. Figure 8.4b shows the effect of a purely categorical benefit: a poll subsidy to members of group 1 financed by a poll tax on members of group 2. This clearly brings about a considerable equalization of average post-tax incomes in the two groups. But clearly, too, the scheme is very generous to the outlying 'rich' member of the poor group 1 and, at the same time, very harsh on the outlying poor member of the rich group 1. This then points to a gain from introducing non-linearities in the group-specific schedules of the kind shown in Figure 8.4c, increasing the tax paid by the rich outlier in the poor group and using the proceeds to reduce that paid by the poor outlier in the rich group. Such a reform has the merit of increasing intergroup transfers to the poorest of the poor but the disadvantage of raising the marginal tax rates on these outliers; but since there are, by definition, few outliers, the

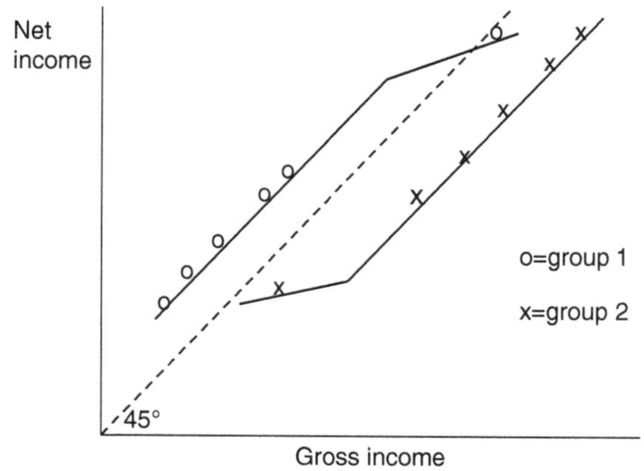

Figure 8.4c (Tagging and taxing)

first-order distributional gain will (up to some point) outweigh the additional deadweight loss. The implication of this line of argument is that the optimal combination of categorical and income information has the feature that the marginal tax rate decreases with income in the rich group but increases with income in the poor group. The argument is intuitively appealing. On closer inspection, however, there is a puzzle. Recall from the discussion above that the optimal group-specific schedules are the solution to a standard one-dimensional Mirrlees problem (in which the revenue to be raised reflects the optimal intergroup transfer determined in the second step of the two-dimensional problem). And, while there are no general analytical results on the pattern of marginal tax rates required to solve the Mirrlees problem, the solutions that have emerged in many simulations typically have the feature that optimal marginal tax rates decrease with income. This would lead one to expect simulations using standard functional forms and parameter values to generate decreasing marginal tax rates within both groups. But the DKM argument points, on the contrary, to increasing marginal rates within the poor group.

Suppose, as before, that the population (the size of which is normalized to unity) can be divided into two mutually exclusive and exhaustive groups, labelled 1 and 2. Individuals are unable to alter or disguise the group to which they belong, which is observed as costless by the government. Members of each group i (=1, 2) have preferences $u_i = U(x) + V(1 - y)$ defined over consumption x and labour supply y, but differ in their hourly gross wage (alternatively, their skill or ability), n. with $U_x > 0$ and $V_y < 0$ (subscripts indicating partial derivatives). Individuals differ only in the pre-tax wage n they can earn. Gross income is z = ny. The groups differ in the form of their preferences and/or the distribution of their abilities, the latter being described for each group by a continuous density function f_i (with corresponding distribution $F_i(n)$) on support $[0, \infty]$. The within-group structure of the model is thus exactly as in Mirrlees (1971).

Suppose that the aim of policy to design tax/benefit schedule $T^i(z)$ for two different groups i=1, 2 can be expressed as maximizing the following social welfare criterion:

$$W = \int_0^\infty \sum N_i(W(u_i(n))f_i(n)dn \tag{14}$$

where N denotes the proportion of the population in each group i and W is an increasing and concave function of utility. The government cannot observe individuals' productivities and thus is restricted to setting taxes and transfers as a function only of earnings, $T_i(z)$. The government maximizes W subject to the revenue constraint:

$$\int_0^\infty \sum N_i(z_i(n) - x_i(n))f_i(n)dn = R \tag{15}$$

and the second constraint making use of workers' utility maximization condition—in each group, a person with wage n chooses y to maximize u_i subject to $x = ny - T_i(ny)$. We obtain the incentive compatibility constraint constraints,

$$\frac{du_i}{dn(i)} = \frac{-y_i V_{y(i)}}{n(i)} \text{ for i} = 1, 2.(\text{IC}) \tag{16}$$

It is helpful to think of this problem as consisting of two steps. First we derive group-specific optimal tax schedules, given a group-specific revenue requirement R_i. This means solving the standard optimal income problem for each group (see Chapter 4).

The government's problem is to design possibly non-linear tax/benefit schedules $T_i(z)$ for the groups. Its objective, we assume, is to maximize a social welfare function of the general form. Comparing the separate schedule model with the single non-linear form of the Mirrlees model, it is important to note the following result. First, let us assume two groups. It is almost trivially true that if $u_1 = u_2$ and $f_1 = f_2$, the optimal policy yields $T = T_1 = T_2$.[6] Thus we only have an interesting situation when either preferences or distributions or both are different in different groups.

So solving the Mirrlees problem for all conceivable R_i then gives the maximized contribution of group i to collective welfare as a function $W^i(R^i)$ of the revenue constraint imposed on it, with associated shadow price of revenue $\lambda^i = -W^{i\prime}(R^i) > 0$.[7]

In the second step, the government chooses the optimal allocation of the aggregate R over two groups selecting R^1 so that is to maximize, $W^1(R^1) + W^2(R - R^1)$. In other

[6] Let $\{T_1(z) = T_2(z)\}$ be optimal tax schedule implied by the solution of the tagging problem. Then there is no such $T(z)$ so that (i) $T(z) = T_1(z) = T_2(z)$. (ii) $\max W[n; T(z)] > \max W[n : T_i, i = 1, 2]$ and (iii) the condition (2) and the incentive compatible condition (IC) hold. Proof: If $\max W[n; T(z)] > \max W[n : T_i, i = 1, 2]$ and (2) and (IC) hold, then $T(z) = T_1(z) = T_2(z)$ should be the solution of the tagging problem. This is a contradiction.

[7] Derivatives are indicated by subscripts for functions of several variables and a prime for functions of just one.

words it chooses optimal intergroup transfer and requires $\lambda_1 = \lambda_2 = \lambda$, where λ is the marginal social cost of funds.

Hence we can conclude that if characteristic i is immutable, the redistribution across characteristics will be complete until the average social welfare weights are equated across characteristics. In the case where characteristics can be manipulated but they are correlated with skill, then taxes will depend on both income, z, and characteristics, i.

The difference between this formula and the marginal tax formula in the Mirrlees model is that the tax/transfer function $t_i(z)$ here is allowed to depend on i and f and F to depend on i. The optimizations for each value of i are linked by common shadow price on revenue λ.

Using formulas for E^u and E^c, where E^u is the uncompensated supply of labour and E^c in turn is the compensated elasticity, we obtain the following condition for optimal group-specific marginal tax rate:

$$\frac{t_i}{1-t_i} = \underbrace{\left[\frac{1+E_i{}^u}{E_i{}^c}\right]}_{A_n}\underbrace{\left[\frac{1-F_i(n)}{n_i f_i(n)}\right]}_{B_n}\underbrace{\left[\frac{U_x^i \int_{\underline{n}}^{\infty}(1-W'U^i{}_x/\lambda)(1/U_x^i)f_i(p)dp}{1-F_i(n)}\right]}_{C_n} \tag{17}$$

where the group-specific marginal tax rate is $t_i = \left(1+\frac{V_y}{nU_x}\right)$.

8.2.1 MAXIMIN AND NO-INCOME EFFECTS

We turn now to stronger assumptions, on the government's objective function and the individual's utility function, to provide further insights. If we assume the Rawlsian social objective of maximizing the utility of the worst-off person $u(\underline{n})$. in society, the factor C_n in (17) is constant. As in Cremer et al (2010), making some simplifications, we can analytically understand the pattern of marginal rates in different groups and redistribution between these groups. The terms in (17) simplify if we assume quasi-linear preferences with constant elasticity of labour supply,[8]

$$u = x - y^{1+r} \,.\, U_x = 1(E^c = \varepsilon) \tag{18}$$

Suppose further there are two groups 1 and 2 with the same size. Group 1 is taken to be poorer, having a lower average wage. The density function and the distribution function for the whole working population are $f(n) = [f_1(n) + f_2(n)]/2$ and $F(n) = [F_1(n) + F_2(n)]/2$, respectively.

The marginal tax rate formula is in the maximin case

[8] The individual first order condition $[n(1-t)]^r$ implies that everybody with n>0 works. Hence there is no bunching.

$$\frac{t_i}{1-t_i} = \underbrace{[1+\varepsilon]}_{A_n} \underbrace{\left[\frac{1-F_i(n)}{n_i f_i(n)}\right]}_{B_n} \tag{19}$$

Now t depends only on $\frac{1-F(n)}{nf(n)}$, i.e. on the properties of the distribution.

We can solve the optimal income z(n) for both groups and the whole working population (see appendix 8.2).

The marginal tax rate for the whole working population is a weighted average of the marginal tax rates of groups 1 and 2.

$$\frac{t}{1-t} = \frac{f_1(n)}{f_1(n)+f_2(n)} \frac{t_1}{1-t_1} + \frac{f_2(n)}{f_1(n)+f_2(n)} \frac{t_2}{1-t_2} \tag{20}$$

Now we can summarize the following results:

Proposition 1: If we assume quasi-linear preferences and constant labour supply elasticity in both groups with equal size, then with the maximin or the Sen social welfare functions[9] *(Gini weights) the pattern of marginal rates is* $t_1 < t < t_2$ *for all* n, *if* f_2 *dominates* f_1 *in the sense of the inverse hazard rate (divided by* n,)[10] *i.e.* $\left[\frac{1-F_1(n)}{nf_1}\right] \leq \left[\frac{1-F_2(n)}{nf_2}\right]$[11].

Proposition 2: With the same assumptions as in Proposition 1, tagging implies redistribution from group 2 to group 1 when the government has either the maximin or the Sen social welfare functions (Gini weights).

It is important to note that with the assumption of quasi-linearity, the external revenue requirement has no effect on marginal tax rates. They depend only on the distribution and the elasticity of labour supply in this group, not on the corresponding characteristics in the other group. The distribution has a key role in the marginal tax formula in this specification. We should know the relationship between $\Phi_1(n)$ and $\Phi_2(n)$in order to be able to say who are gainers and who are losers from tagging. We adopt in simulations later on, the Champernowne distribution. For the Champernowne distribution,

$$\Phi = \frac{1-F(n)}{nf(n)} = \frac{m^\theta + n^\theta}{\theta n^\theta} \tag{21}$$

and

$$\frac{d}{dn}\frac{m^\theta + n^\theta}{\theta n^\theta} = \frac{-m^\theta}{n^{\theta+1}} < 0. \tag{22}$$

[9] In the Sen social welfare function, $G' = 2(1-F)$, in turn we have

$$\frac{t_i}{1-t_i} = \underbrace{[1+\varepsilon]}_{A_n} \underbrace{\left[\frac{1-F_i(n)}{n_i f_i(n)}\right]}_{B_n} \underbrace{F_i(n)}_{C_n}$$

[10] This holds e.g. in the case of the Champernowne distribution.

[11] With a constant elasticity of labour supply, the second order condition $\left(\frac{dz(n)}{dn} \geq 0\right)$ holds here if and only if $\Phi(n)$ is nondecreasing.

Figures 8.5, 8.6, 8.7, and 8.8 illustrate the two possible cases when the inverse hazard rates of Champernowne distribution do not intersect and when they do. Unlike with lognormal n-distribution as analysed by Cremer et al (2009), when $m_1 < m_2$ and $\theta_1 = \theta_2$, the distribution ratios $\Phi_1(n)$ and $\Phi_2(n)$ do not cross with the Champernowne distribution (as in Figure 8.5). Then in the two-group case, all individuals of the poorer (on average) group 1 are the gainers from tagging. Again, as in the previous section with no behavioural effects, this says that the government should use groupings with the largest difference in mean.

If in turn $m_1 = m_2$ and $\theta_1 < \theta_2$, then $\Phi_1(n)$ and $\Phi_2(n)$ cross (as in Figure 8.6). Suppose $\theta_1 = 2$ and $\theta_2 = 4$, $\Phi_1 = \Phi_2$ yields a quadratic equation. The positive root is n*=0.2367[12]. Hence every individual in group 2 n is higher than n* (n* is the point where $\Phi_1 = \Phi_2$) benefits from tagging. Now $F(n^* = 0.2367) = 0.22$. In the (on average) richer group there are 2, 78 per cent who benefit from tagging[13]. This sounds rather surprising.

Figures 8.7 and 8.8 display graphical solutions to the case where both mean ratios m_1/m, m_2/m and θ_1 and θ_2 and the population shares of the groups are estimated from

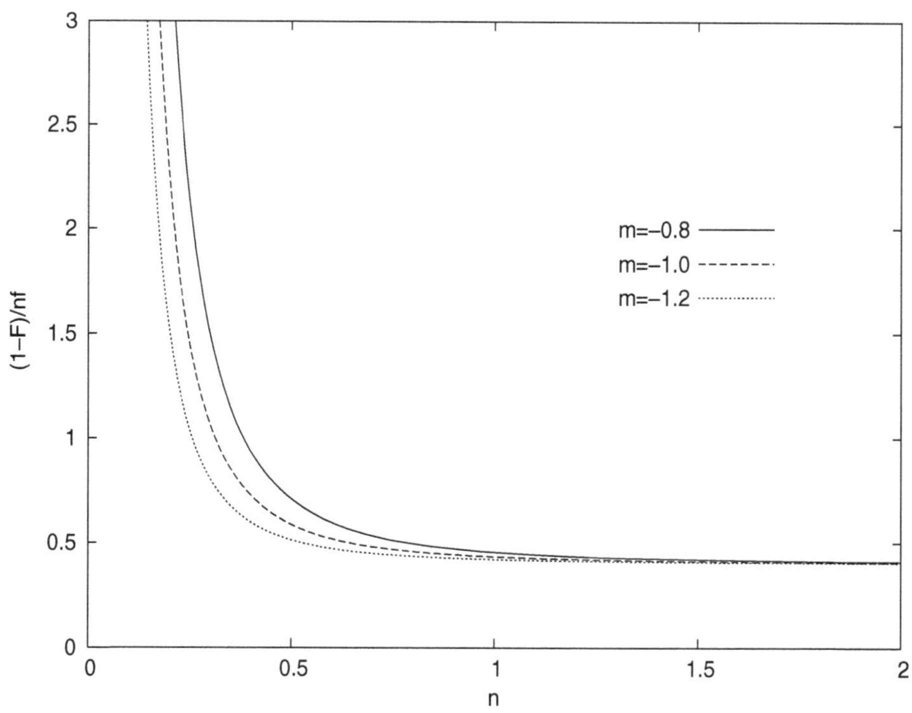

Figure 8.5 (1−F)/nf Champernowne distribution m=e^{-i}. i=−0.8,−1, −1.2, $\theta = 3$

[12] $\Phi_1 = \Phi_2$ implies $n^4 + 2m^2n^2 - m^2 = 0$. The solution of this equation is $n^2 = \pm(\sqrt{2} - 1)m^2$ (m=0.368). Hence $n^2 = 0.056$.

[13] Cremer et al (2010a) do not provide any corresponding estimate in their case with lognormal n-distribution.

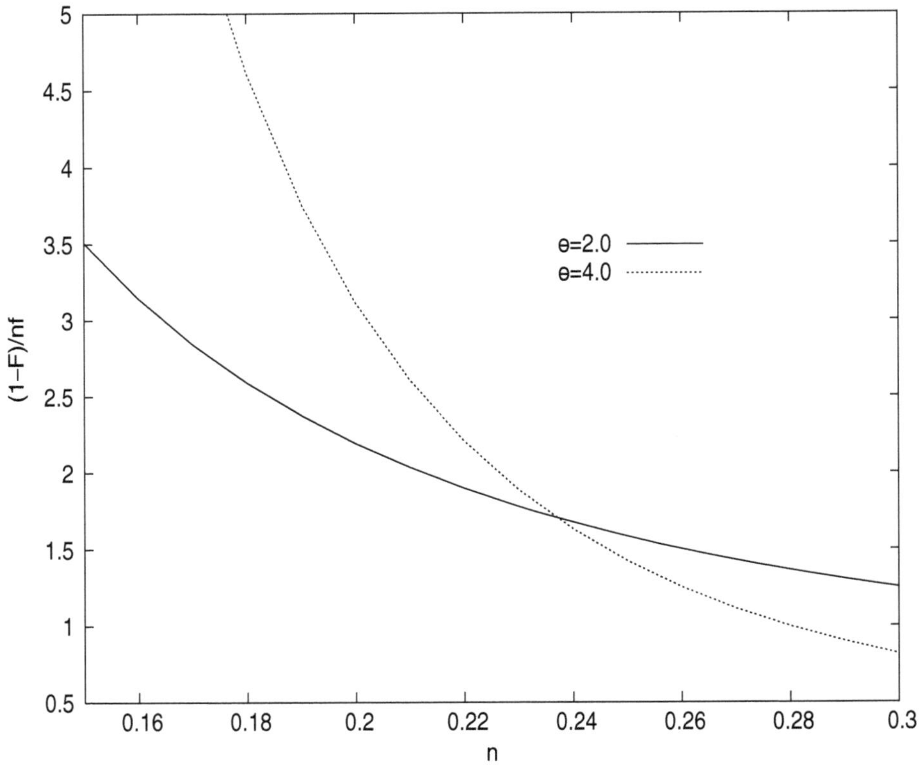

Figure 8.6 (1−F)/nf Champernowne distribution, $m = e^{-1}$

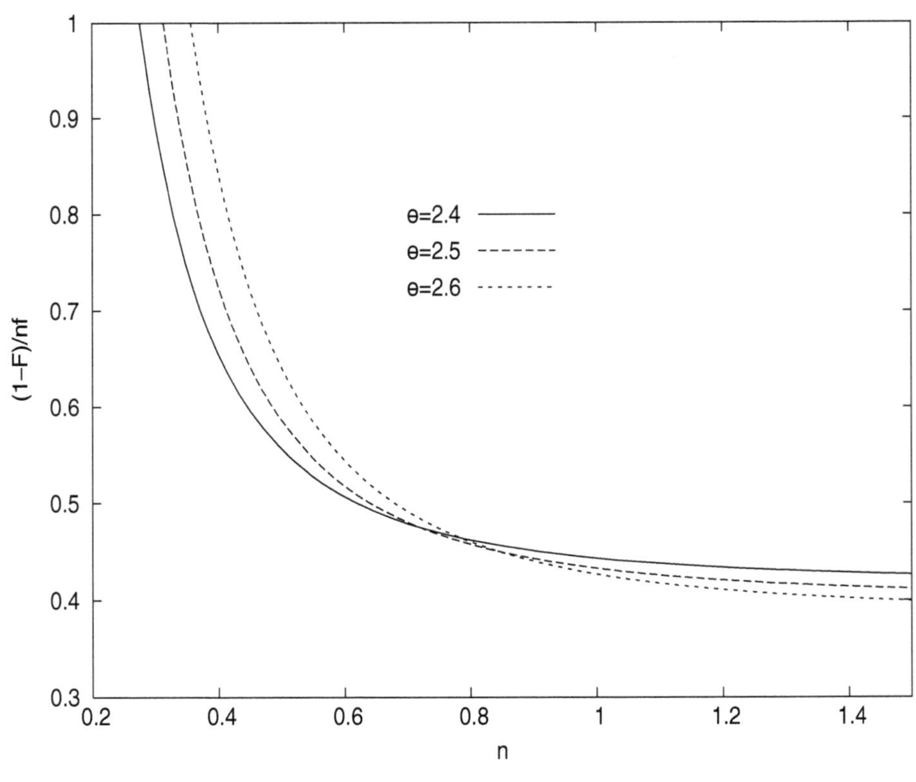

Figure 8.7 group 1 [$\theta_1 = 2.3$, $m_1/m = 0.55$, $\alpha_1 = 0{,}21$], group 2 [$\theta_2 = 2.6$ $m_2/m = 1.05$ $\alpha_2 = 0{,}79$]

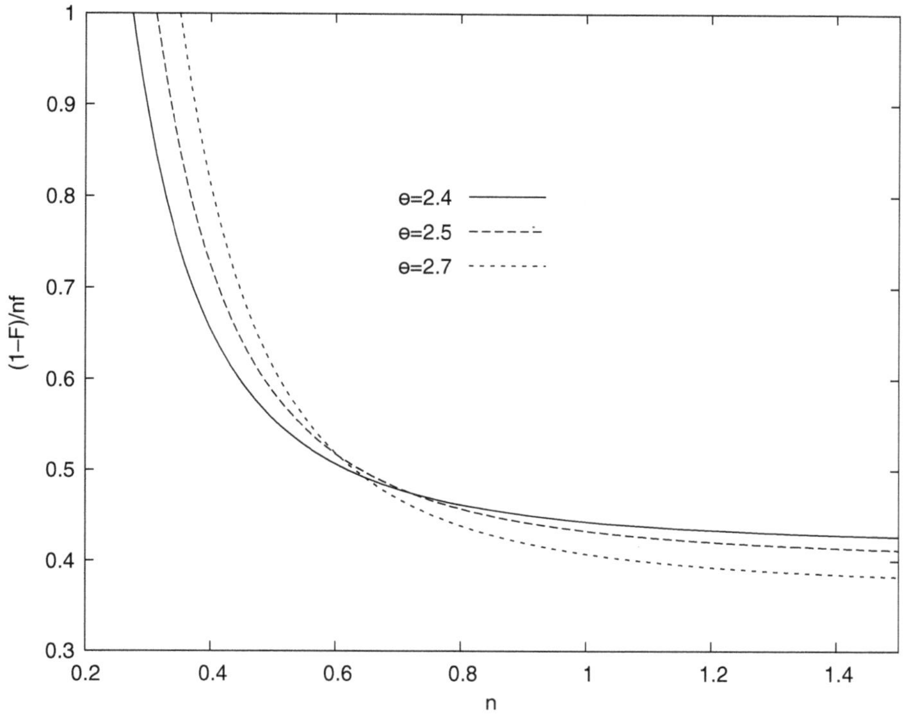

Figure 8.8 group 1 [θ_1=2.3, m_1/m = 0.55, α_1 = 0,21], group 2 [θ_2 = 2.6 m_2/m = 1.05 α_2 = 0,79]

the Finnish data. From the graphical solutions in Figure 8.7 and 8.8, we see that the number of those who benefit in group 2 from tagging is much smaller: somewhere between 15 and 20 per cent.

8.2.2 INCOME EFFECTS: AN APPLICATION TO THE FINNISH DATA

It is important to note that the special case considered in the previous section yields insights, but within the framework of the assumptions made. When preferences are not quasi-linear and the elasticity of labour supply is not constant, the problem becomes more complicated. Then it is not possible to say anything about the shape of tax schedule and gainers and losers from tagging without simulations. How robust are these insights? What happens when we move away from quasi-linearity and the dominance requirement in the n-distribution? This section presents optimal tax schedules with alternative assumptions. Let us now apply this framework to the specific case of the data on the age structure of income distribution in Finland, as described in the previous section. We begin by specifying social objectives further.

Social objectives: Social welfare is taken to be the function of utilities cardinalized as a constant absolute utility–inequality aversion form: $W(u) = -\frac{1}{\beta}e^{-\beta u}$ where β measures the degree of inequality aversion in the social welfare function of the government (in the case of $\beta = 0$, we define $W = u$). If we write $W^{-\beta} = \int e^{-\beta u} f(n)dn$ then the limit as $\beta \rightarrow \infty$ is given by $W = min_n[e^u]$. This is of course the Rawlsian maximin. The curvature in the utility of consumption modifies social marginal weights $W'U_x$ and makes the government preferences (implicit) more redistributive. An alternative social weighting function is that where the social marginal valuation declines according to the ranking in the n-distribution. In other words, we have the rank-order social welfare function. The essential feature of rank-order social welfare functions is that they put more weight on the utility of the worst-off. Rank-order weights represent society's aversion to inequality. An example of the rank-order social welfare criterion is the Gini or Sen social welfare function. For example, the social marginal valuation implicit in the Gini coefficient depends on the income rank order and is bounded above by 2 and below by 0. Initially the social marginal valuation falls slowly with income, but then the decline accelerates. The ethical justification behind this rank-order social welfare function is at least equally convincing as the justification behind the traditional 'constant elasticity' class of welfare functions. When $W' = 2(1 - F)$, we have in effect the weighting underlying the Gini coefficient, as shown by Sen (1974), who provided an axiomatic justification for such a social welfare function.

Preferences are in each groups of the form $u = -\frac{1}{x} - \frac{1}{(1-y)}$, implying an elasticity of substitution between consumption and leisure in each group of 0.5.

The distribution of the pre-tax wage within each group is assumed to be the Champernowne distribution with parameters m_i and θ_i. We also assume that the tagged groups differ only in the distribution of ability.[14] Based on Finnish income distribution data (cross-section) we estimated by using maximum likelihood methods, several two- and three-parameter distributions with corresponding measures of goodness of fit (several of them plus the log-likelihood value for the estimated model). Among two-parameter distributions, Champernowne is the best fit for pre-tax income distribution in Finland (2002–2010). The θ parameter varies from 2.78 to 2.34. Over the period from the latter part of the 1990s to 2010, the θ-parameter was almost constant at around 2.5. Hence θ =2 reflects a low range estimate (high inequality) and θ =3 in turn a high range estimate (low inequality). The Gini coefficients estimated by this distribution (Gini=$1/\theta$) are quite close to those calculated from the data. Interestingly, the location parameter m in our notations (median) in the Champernowne distribution is quite close to that calculated from the data.

First we divide the Finnish working population into two groups on the basis of age, with different age cut-offs, as discussed earlier, so that group 1 refers to all workers between the age of 20 and 29. The proportion of the working people in this group is 0.21. All workers between the ages of 30 and 64 belong to group 2. The proportion of working

[14] It might be of some interest to look at the case in which members of the poorer group also have a lower disutility of effort, and so work more hours at any given wage (in the absence of tax). In other words, in this case the poor are also the hardest-working.

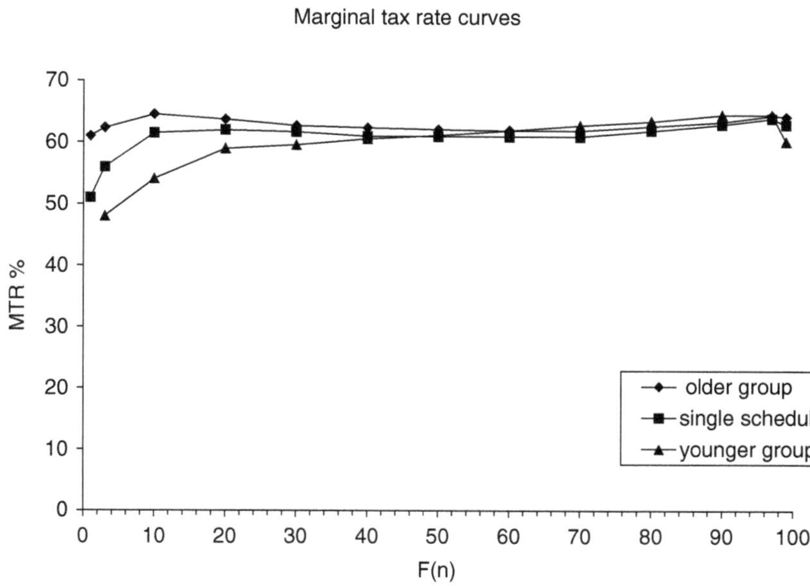

Figure 8.9 Single schedule and two separate schedules: utilitarian
Group 1 [θ_1=2.3, m_1=0.202, N_1=0.21], group 2 [θ_2=2.6, m_2=0.407, N_2=0.79]

people in turn in this group is 0.78. Next we increase the number of groups from two to three. Now group 1 is the same as in the two-group case, group 2 refers to those between 30 and 54 (0.55), and those people between 55 and 64 belong to group 3 (0.24). For all groupings we calculate tax schedules for the three social welfare functions introduced in this section—utilitarian, Rawlsian and rank-order weights. The marginal tax rates of different cases are shown in Figures 8.9–14. Figure 8.9 displays marginal tax rates in the two-group case with utilitarian objective when the values for m and θ in different groups are $\theta_1 = 2.3$, $m_1 / m_2 = 0.55$ and $\theta_2 = 2.6$, $m_2 / m = 1.05$. For the case of single schedule, $\theta = 2.5$. The marginal rates of the on average poorer group 1 increase throughout with income both in Figures 8.9 and 8.10. The marginal rates of the richer group (on average) are mainly declining in income, but they are no longer declining throughout in income. The marginal tax rates of the single tax schedule increase in income. The marginal rates of groups 1 and 3 increase in income, but the pattern of group 2 is more complicated. It first increases up to the 10th percentile, then declines slightly, until it begins again to rise. Figures 8.11–8.14 display the marginal tax schedules in maximin and rank-order (Gini weights) cases. As expected, in the maximin case, the marginal tax rates decline with income. In the rank-order case the pattern of marginal tax rates is very similar to that of the utilitarian case, except the levels of rates are much higher throughout.

Unlike the marginal income tax rates, average tax rates increase in income in all cases (except in the maximin case at the very top), indicating the progressivity of the three schedules (see appendix 8.2). They are substantially affected by tagging. At the upper part of the income distribution the average tax rates of the whole working population

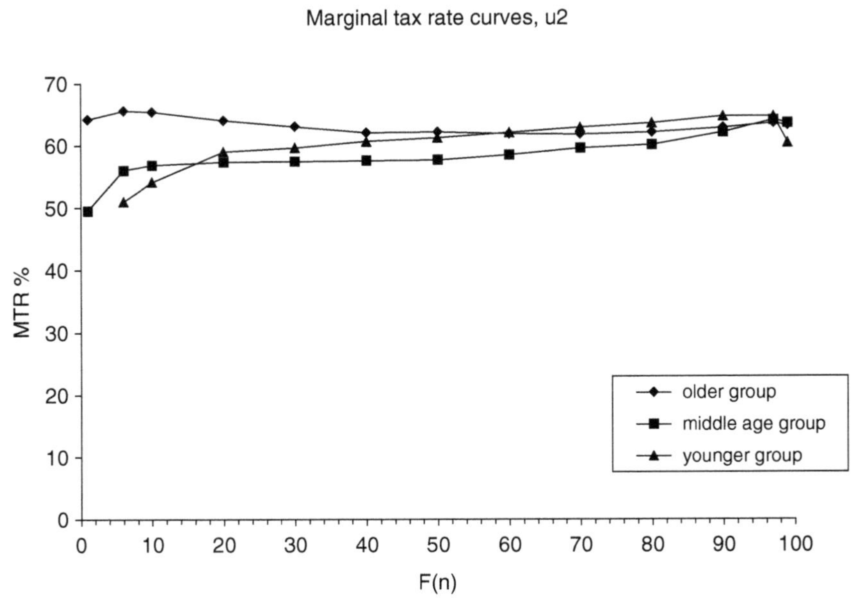

Figure 8.10 Three separate schedules: utilitarian

Three groups: group 1 [$\theta_1 = 2.3$, $m_1 = 0.202$, $N_1 = 0.21$], group 2 [$\theta_2 = 2.4$, $m_2 = 0.317$, $N_2 = 0.20$], group 3 [$\theta_3 = 2.7$, $m_3 = 0.427$, $N_3 = 0.59$]

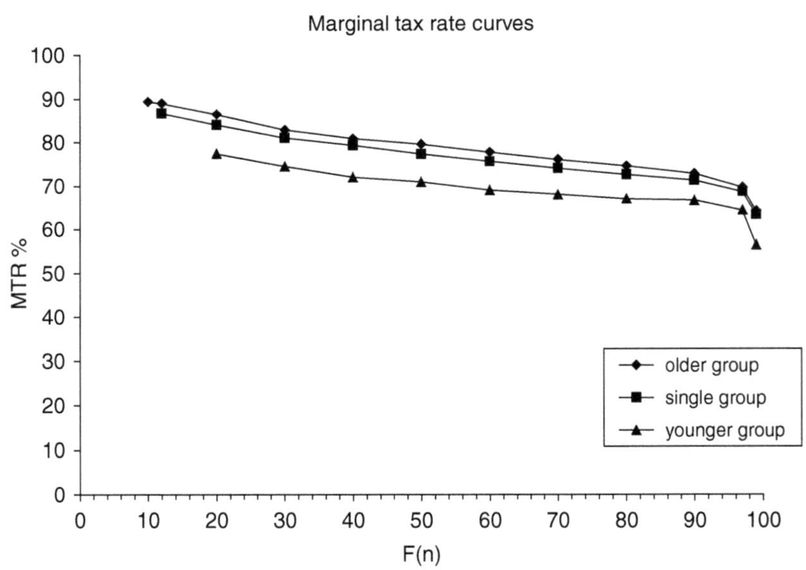

Figure 8.11 Single schedule and two separate schedules: maximin

Group 1 [$\theta_1 = 2.3$, $m_1 = 0.202$, $N_1 = 0.21$], group 2 [$\theta_2 = 2.6$, $m_2 = 0.407$, $N_2 = 0.79$]

and the richer group 2 are very close to each other. The lower average tax rates faced by individuals in group 1 means that they are the gainers in the tagging procedure.

IKKT (1998) argue that the key to understanding the shapes of schedules lies in the revenue requirement. In the simulations of the one-dimensional Mirrlees problem, the

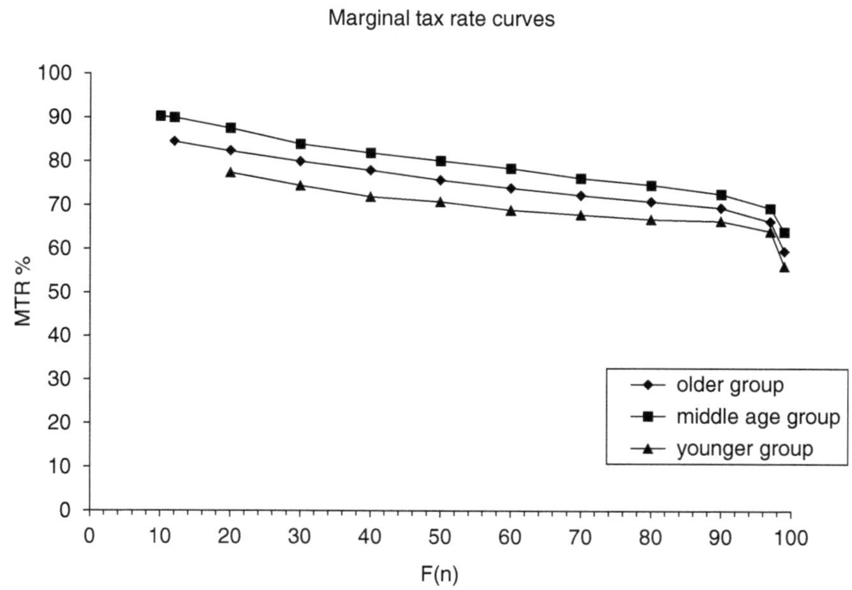

Figure 8.12 Three separate schedules: maximin

Three groups: group 1 [$\theta_1 = 2.3$, $m_1 = 0.202$, $N_1 = 0.21$], group 2 [$\theta_2 = 2.4$, $m_2 = 0.317$, $N_2=0.20$], group 3 [$\theta_3=2.7$, $m_3 = 0.427$, $N_3=0.59$]

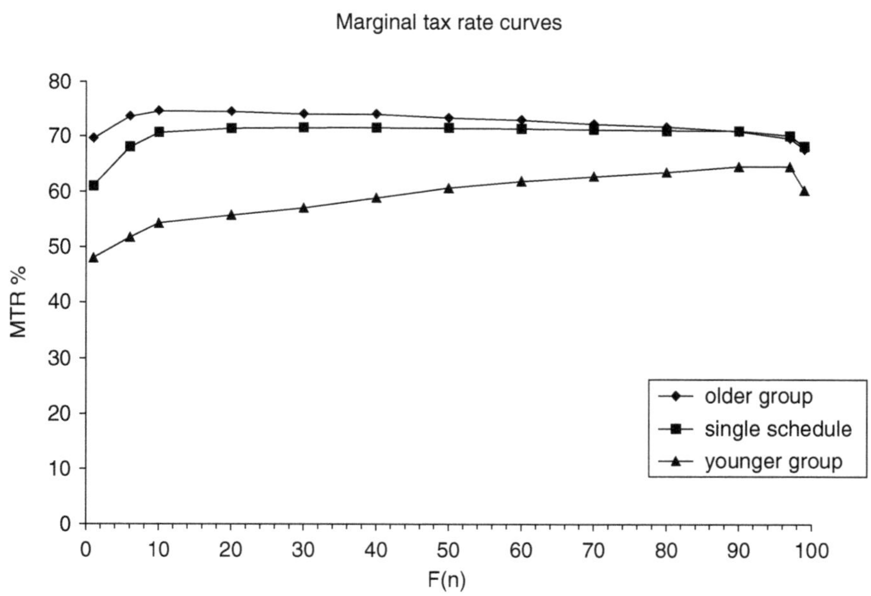

Figure 8.13 Single schedule and two separate schedule: rank order social preferences

Group 1 [$\theta 1 = 2.3$, $m1 = 0.202$, $N1 = 0.21$]

revenue requirement is usually set at levels taken to correspond broadly to observed levels of national expenditure on public goods: between, say, 10 per cent and 30 per cent of aggregate gross income. The optimal group-specific revenue requirements, however, reflect optimal intergroup redistribution and so can be of an entirely different order of

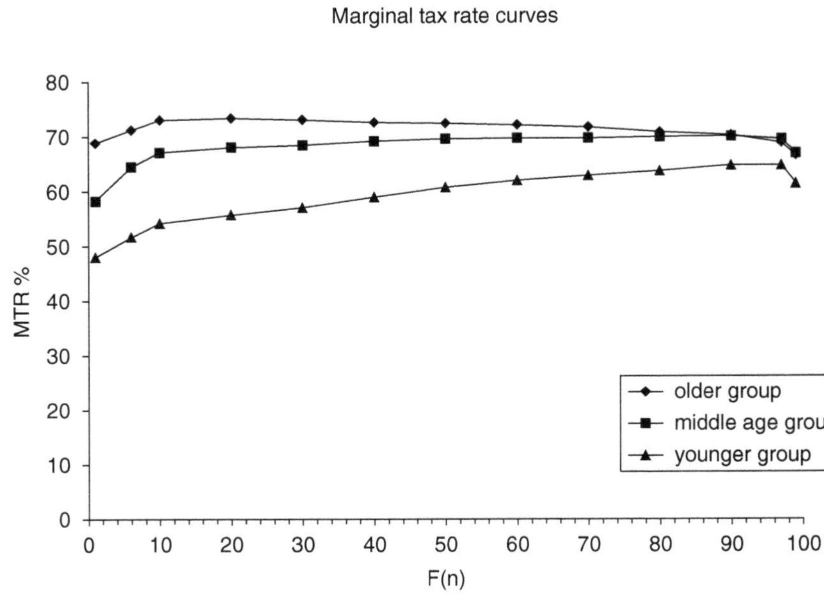

Figure 8.14 Three separate schedules: rank-order preferences

Three groups: group 1[$\theta_1 = 2.3$, $m_1 = 0.202$, $N_1 = 0.21$], group 2 [$\theta_2 = 2.4$, $m_2=0.317$, $N_2 = 0.20$], group 3 [$\theta_3 = 2.7$, $m_3 = 0.427$, $N_3 = 0.59$]

magnitude and indeed sign: much higher for richer groups; much lower, and quite possibly negative, for poorer.

The differences in the shape of the skill (wage) distributions may be an equally or even more important source of the different patterns in rates. In the two-group case for the poorer group 1, a distribution with a lower mean will tend to have a lower B term in expression (17) at the low end of the income distribution because *1-F* in the numerator is lower and f in the denominator is larger, favouring lower marginal rates. The C-term in turn will continue to favour somewhat higher marginal rates. If the guaranteed income is more generous, as we expect it to be in this group, and initial marginal rates are low, then the welfare cost of higher payments by those with greater income will be less than otherwise. For the richer group, the results at the low end of the income distribution reverse. The *1-F* component will be larger than in the single schedule case, and *f* will be much smaller; these factors favour high marginal rates in this income range. Some offset will be provided by the C-term.

Utility changes from moving a single schedule to separate schedules vary quite a lot at different parts of the distribution. The last column in Tables A8.2.2–A8.2.18 in appendix 8.2 tells who are gainers (+)/losers (−). In the two-group case, losers in group 1 are those in the top decile. In group 2, gainers are those at the very top. If the differences in means between groups are big enough then all individuals of group 2 are losers in the utilitarian case (see Table A8.3.5 in appendix) but not in maximin and rank-order cases. It may sound rather surprising that even the most well-off people in the richer (on average) group are better off from tagging. But we have to remember that tagging is done to make redistribution more efficient from higher to lower-skilled individuals. In the three-group case, no one in group 2—the middle-age group—gains in the utilitarian case. In maximin and rank-order cases the picture is otherwise the same, but there are fewer losers in group 1 at the top decile and gainers at the top in this middle-age group.

The optimum is typically characterized by a certain fraction of individuals, at the bottom end, choosing not to work (where we have $\frac{dz}{dn} = \frac{dx}{dn} = 0$), there is bunching of individuals of different n. The combination of high inequality aversion and high inherent inequality is crucial in determining the amount of bunching. In the utilitarian case, the amount of bunching turns out to be very little. As seen in the Tables in appendix 8.2, in the maximin case the amount of bunching varies between 10 per cent (F_0=0.10) and 20 per cent (F_0=0.20). This is in strong contrast to what we observed in the case with quasi-linearity and the constant elasticity of labour supply. The different amount of bunching in maximin cases explains why the marginal tax schedules are quite similar but the extent of redistribution between and within groups differs.

8.2.3 CHOICE OF GROUPS AND OPTIMAL NON-LINEAR INCOME TAXATION

Next we focus on the gains from having two tagged groups rather than being forced to apply a single schedule to the population as a whole. This takes us to the second step. Given the solution to the first step, the government chooses the optimal allocation of aggregate R over groups; in other words, it selects R^i to maximize overall social welfare, having first maximized each W_i for given R.

We divide the Finnish working population into two groups on the basis of age, with different age cut-offs, as discussed above. For each cut-off, we calculate the welfare gain from grouping for each of the three social welfare functions introduced in this section—utilitarian, Rawlsian, and rank-order weights. The welfare gain reported in Table 8.1 is the proportional increase in equivalent consumption in moving from the optimal single schedule to the optimal group-specific—two groups—schedules. Table 8.1 immediately gives us the answer to the question of which grouping is best for tagging; it is the one which uses the age cut-off of 40 years.

Table 8.1 shows the results when two groups are formed by the following cut-offs: (i) age 20 (i.e. single group), (ii) age 30, (iii) age 40, and (iv) age 50. The gains are modest, but far from negligible. The rise in aggregate equivalent consumption x^0 using categorical information varies between 1.8 and 2.8 per cent, as shown in Table 8.1. In the utilitarian case, welfare gain from tagging is clearly larger than other cases.

Table 8.1 Welfare effects of different age cut-offs (Estimates of θ and m are based on year 2005)

	Utilitarian		Rank-order		Maximin	
	x^0	change %	x^0	change %	x^0	change %
Single schedule	0.163		0.163		0.178	
two groups*	0.166	1.84	0.165	1.23	0.183	2.81
two groups**	0.164	0.61	0.164	0.61	0.178	
two groups***	0.164	0.61	0.164	0.61	0.178	

x^0: Consumption equivalent: x^0 is that consumption which, if equally distributed with zero work hours, would give the same social welfare integral as the allocation $((x, y_i))$ arising from a given tax schedule.
Single: θ=2.5
Two groups *: group 1 [θ_1=2.3, m_1/m=0.55, N_1=0,21], group 2 [θ_2=2.6 m_2/m=1.05 N_2=0,79],
Two groups **: group 1 [θ_1=2.4, m_1/m=0.86, N_1=0,41], group 2 [θ_2=2.6 m_2/m=1.10 N_2=0,59],
Two groups ***: group 1 [θ_1=2.5, m_1/m=0.90, N_1=0,64], group 2 [θ_2=2.7 m_2/m=1.16 N_2=0,36]

8.2.4 INCREASING THE NUMBER OF GROUPS

The discussion so far has maintained the number of groups at two. But each of these groups could be further sub-divided, until there are as many tax schedules as individuals. Of course if increasing the number of instruments in this way was costless, it would make sense to do so, because welfare cannot decrease with more instruments available. However, what if instruments are costly—what if the costs of distinguishing between and monitoring across groups increases in the number of groups? Then it would be optimal to limit the number of groups to well before each individual is a group by themselves. But how many groups is optimal? The answer depends on the costs of managing each additional group and, crucially, the marginal welfare gain from increasing the number of groups. This section begins the analysis of quantifying the gains from additional groups, in the specific context of our Finnish data set.

We proceed as follows. We already know the optimal welfare levels when there is no tagging, and when there are two groups with an age cut-off at 30. We will now calculate the welfare level with three groups (under 30, between 30 and 40, and over 40) and four groups (under 30, between 30 and 40, over 50). In each case we calculate the welfare when the government uses all the information available to tag groups and implements separate non-linear income tax schedules on each group to maximize overall social welfare. These welfare levels are given in Table 8.2. Table 8.2 shows welfare levels for one group, two groups, three groups, and four groups for three welfare functions—utilitarian, Rawlsian, and rank-order.

The biggest impact from tagging is achieved with three groups in utilitarian and maximin cases, but moving from two to three schedules does not just increase welfare gain much; it should be clear from Table 8.2 that there are strong diminishing returns to

Table 8.2 Welfare levels of increasing the number of groups (Estimates of θ and m are based on year 2005)

	Utilitarian		Rank-order		Maximin	
	x^0	change %	x^0	change %	x^0	change %
Single schedule	0.163		0.163		0.178	
2 groups*	0.166	1.84	0.166	1.84	0.183	2.81
3 groups**	0.1675	2.76	0.166	1.84	0.185	3.93
4 groups***	0.1678	2.94	0.167	2.45	0.185	3.93

x^0: Consumption equivalent: x^0 is that consumption which, if equally distributed with zero work hours, would give the same social welfare integral as the allocation ((x, y,)} arising from a given tax schedule.
Two groups: group 1 [θ_1=2.3, m_1=0.202, N_1=0.21], group 2 [θ_2=2.6 m_2=0.407. N_2=0.79],
Three groups: group 1[θ_1=2.3, m_1=0.202, N_1=0.21], group 2 [θ_2=2.4, m_2=0.317, N_2=0.20],
group 3 [θ_3=2.7, m_3= 0.427, N_3=0.59],
Four groups: group 1[θ_1=2.3, m_1=0.202, N_1=0.21], group 2 [θ_2=2.4, m_2=0.317, N_2=0.20],
group 3 [θ_3=2.6 m_3=0.407, N_3=0.23], [θ_4=2.5, m_4=0.387, N_4=0.36]

increasing the number of groups. For example, in the utilitarian case, welfare increases by 1.84 per cent with the introduction of two groups compared to the single-group case, but only a further 0.92 per cent of the base welfare is added when the groupings are increased to three, and going from three groups to four groups only gives an additional 0.18 per cent. Thus the gains from increasing the number of groupings fall off quite rapidly.

The large literature on 'tagging' shows that group-specific tax and transfer schedules improve welfare over the case where the government is restricted to a single schedule over the whole population. The central assumption of this literature, however, is that the groupings available to the government are given and fixed. But how many and which types of groups should the government choose to tag? This is the question addressed in this chapter. Starting with a simple framework and ending with numerical simulations based on data from Finland, Kanbur and Tuomala (2014) show how groupings should be formed for tagging, and provide a quantitative assessment of how group differences affect the gains from tagging. They also provide a quantitative assessment of the welfare gains from increasing the number of tagged groups.

Earlier we mentioned that the differences in the shape of the skill (wage) distributions may be an equally or even more important source of the different patterns in rates. Another reason for carrying out tagging analysis lies in which people's preferences about working vary with different age. In this kind of situation it may be desirable to have income tax schedules varying with age and, in particular, having very different low-income marginal tax rates at different ages. In fact, it is not only the preferences of people that change with age; the distribution of skills within the age group also changes considerably.

APPENDIX 8.1 DERIVATION OF DIFFERENT TAX/TRANSFER SCHEDULES

The optimality conditions for this problem are obtained by treating, in each group, u as a state variable and y as a control variable; x is determined from the utility function. Now there must exist a dual function $\mu(n)$ such that

$$\frac{d\mu_i(n)}{dn_i} = \left[W' - \frac{\lambda}{U_x}\right] f_i(n) \qquad \mathrm{i} = 1, \ldots, N \tag{1}$$

and differentiating with respect to $\mathrm{y_i}$ i=1,2

$$\lambda t_i f_i(n) = -\mu_i(n)(V_y + yV_{yy})/n^2 \quad \mathrm{i} = 1, \ldots, N \tag{2}$$

where the group-specific marginal tax rate is $t_i = (1 + \frac{V_y}{nU_x})$.

In addition we have transversality condition on $\mu_i(n)$

$$\mu_i(0) = 0, \quad \lim_{n\to\infty}\mu_i(n) = 0 \tag{3}$$

Using formulas[15] for E^u and E^c, where E^u is the uncompensated supply of labour and E^c in turn is the compensated elasticity, we obtain the following condition for optimal group-specific marginal tax rate:[16]

$$\frac{t_i}{1-t_i} = \underbrace{\left[\frac{1+E_i^u}{E_i^c}\right]}_{A_n} \underbrace{\left[\frac{1-F_i(n)}{n_i f_i(n)}\right]}_{B_n} \underbrace{\left[\frac{U_x^i \int_n^\infty (1 - W'U^i{}_x/\lambda)(1/U_x^i) f_i(p)dp}{1-F_i(n)}\right]}_{C_n}$$

The incentive compatibility condition $\frac{du_i}{dn_i} = \frac{-y_i V_y}{n_i}$ can be written—following Mirrlees (1971), eq. (15)—in integrated form:

$$u_i(n) = u_i(0) + \int_{\underline{n}}^{n} \frac{V_i'(z(n')/n')}{n'^2} z_i(n')dn', \quad i = 1, \ldots, N \tag{4}$$

Substituting (4) into the revenue constraint (19) in the text for $u(n)$ where $x(n) = u(n) + V(y(n))$ yields

15 Differentiating the FOC of the individual maximization, $U_x n(1-\tau) + V_y = 0$, with respect to net wage, labour supply, and virtual income, b, we have after some manipulation elasticity formulas: $E_i^u = \frac{(V_y/y)-(V_y/U_x)^2 U_{xx}}{V_{yy}+(V_y/U_x)^2 U_{xx}}$, (income effect parameter) $\xi_i = \frac{-(V_y/U_x)^2 U_{xx}}{V_{yy}+(V_y/U_x)^2 U_{xx}}$, and from the Slutsky equation $E_i^c = E_i^u - \xi_i$, then $E_i^c = \frac{(V_y/y)}{V_{yy}+(V_y/U_x)^2 U_{xx}} = i = 1.2$.

16 From the first-order condition of the individual we obtain $nt = -(V_y/U_x)t/(1-t)$. We also multiply and divide by $(1 - F(n))$ to get formula (8).

$$\int_{\underline{n}}^{\bar{n}}\left[z_i - V_i\left(\frac{z(n)}{n}\right)\right]f_i(n)dn - u_i(\underline{n}) - \int_0^{\infty}\frac{V_i'(z(n)/n)}{n^2}z_i(n)(1-F_i(n))dn = R_i,\ i=1,\ldots,N \tag{5}$$

Here we have applied Fubini's theorem for the double integral. The government now chooses $u(n)$ and $z(n)$ to maximize $u(\underline{n})$. Differentiating with respect to z(n) and using the first-order condition of individual's maximization $\frac{V'(y)}{n} = 1 - t$ (t marginal tax rate), then the pattern of marginal tax rates is given by:

$$\frac{t_i}{1-t_i} = \underbrace{\left[1 + \frac{1}{e(n)}\right]}_{A_n}\underbrace{\left[\frac{1-F_i(n)}{n_i f_i(n)}\right]}_{B_n} \tag{6}$$

The first-order condition also gives $\lambda = 1$.

Moreover, the quasi-linearity in consumption implies that $\frac{dx(n)}{dR} = -1$. This can be seen as follows. From the utility function we have

$$x(n) = u(n) + V(y(n)) \tag{7}$$

and substituting this into the government revenue requirement we have

$$\int_0^{\infty}(z_i(n) - u_i(n) - V_i(y(n))x_i(n))f_i(n)dn = R$$

Using the first-order condition of the government problem and Fubini's theorem we obtain

$$u_i(\underline{n}) = -R + \int_{\underline{n}}^{\bar{n}}\left[z_i - V_i\left(\frac{z(n)}{n}\right)\right]f_i(n)dn - \int_0^{\infty}\frac{V_i'(z(n)/n)}{n^2}z_i(n)(1-F_i(n))dn,\ i=1,\ldots,N$$

Substituting this into (A7) and using (A4) yields

$$x(n) = -R + M(n) \tag{8}$$

where

$$M(n) = \int_{\underline{n}}^{\bar{n}}[z_i - V_i(\frac{z(n)}{n})]f_i(n)dn - \int_0^{\infty}\frac{V_i'(z(n)/n)}{n^2}z_i(n)(1-F_i(n))dn + V_i(\frac{z(n)}{n}),\ i=1,\ldots,N$$

Hence M(n) depends only on the n-distribution and the specification of $V(z/n)$.

Solving the optimal income z(n) for both groups and the whole working population takes the following form $z(n) = \left[1 + \frac{1}{e}\right]^{1+r} n^{1+r}[(1+e)\Phi(n) + 1]^{-r}$

The expression for $u^*(n)$, $x^*(n)$, $u^*{}_i(n)$ and $x_i^*(n)$

$$u^{\star}(n) = u^{\star}(0) + \left[1 + \frac{1}{e}\right]^{1+r} \int_0^n n^{1+r}[1 + (1+e)\Phi(n')]^{-1-r} dn' \tag{9}$$

$$x^{\star}(n) = u^{\star}(n) + \left[1 + \frac{1}{e}\right]^{1+r} n^{1+r}[1 + (1+e)\Phi(n')]^{-1-r} \tag{10}$$

$$u_i^{\star}(n) = u^{\star}(\underline{n}) + \left[1 + \frac{1}{e}\right]^{1+r} \int_0^n n^{1+r}[1 + (1+e)\Phi_i(n')]^{-1-r} dn', \ i = 1, \ldots, N \tag{11}$$

$$x_i^{\star}(n) = u_i^{\star}(n) + \left[1 + \frac{1}{e}\right]^{1+r} n^{1+r}[1 + (1+e)\Phi_i(n')]^{-1-r}, i = 1, \ldots, N \tag{12}$$

Let $\Phi = \frac{1-F(n)}{nf(n)}$. For the whole working population, $\Phi(n)$ is a weighted average of $\Phi_1(n)$ and $\Phi_2(n)$. From (19) in the text we can see that $z(n)$ lies between $z_1(n)$ and $z_2(n)$ at the optimum.

Using the closed-form solution (19) in the text and (4) and (8) we can solve $u^{\star}(n)$, $x^{\star}(n)$, $u^{\star}{}_i(n)$ and $x_i^{\star}(n)$.

APPENDIX 8.2 NUMERICAL SIMULATIONS

Table A8.2.1 Utilitarian no tagging

β= 0	θ=2.5							
F(n)	y	Z	x	ATR%	MTR%	E^u	ξ	u
0.10	0.41	0.06	0.14	−133	62	0.38	−0.19	−8.675
0.50	0.50	0.18	0.19	3	61	0.08	−0.28	−7.247
0.90	0.50	0.44	0.29	35	63	−0.04	−0.36	−5.455
0.97	0.47	0.73	0.39	45	64	−0.1	−0.43	−4.439
0.99	0.45	1.05	0.50	52	64	−0.16	−0.48	−3.813
n_0=0.03	x_0=0.12	F_0=0.0						

Table A8.2.2 Utilitarian tagging

β= 0	θ=2.3	$\frac{m_1}{m} = 0.55$						
F(n)	y	z	x	ATR%	MTR%	E^u	ξ	u
0.10	0.03	0.001	0.16	−261	50	10.1	−0.14	−7.180 +
0.50	0.32	0.07	0.19	−171	61	0.59	−0.22	−6.764 +
0.90	0.43	0.22	0.25	−11	65	0.17	−0.30	−5.804 −
0.97	0.45	0.38	0.30	21	65	−0.04	−0.35	−5.117 −
0.99	0.46	0.62	0.39	37	61	−0.09	−0.42	−4.413 −
n_0=0.04	x_0=0.16	F_0=0.04						

Table A8.2.3 Utilitarian tagging

β= 0	θ=2.4	$\frac{m_3}{m} = 0.86$						
F(n)	y	z	x	ATR%	MTR%	E^u	ξ	u
0.10	0.37	0.05	0.15	−180	57	0.51	−0.19	−8.297 +
0.50	0.47	0.15	0.19	−29	58	0.14	−0.27	−7.085 +
0.90	0.48	0.38	0.28	25	62	−0.004	−0.35	−5.438 +
0.97	0.46	0.61	0.37	39	64	−0.06	−0.41	−4.580 −
0.99	0.44	0.94	0.48	48	64	−0.13	−0.47	−3.853 −
n_0=0.03	x_0=0.10	F_0=0.001						

Table A8.2.4 Utilitarian tagging

β= 0	θ=2.6	$\frac{m_2}{m} = 1.05$						
F(n)	y	z	x	ATR%	MTR%	E^u	ξ	u
0.10	0.44	0.08	0.14	−80	64	0.3	−0.2	−9.239 −
0.50	0.52	0.21	0.19	10	62	0.05	−0.28	−7.363 −
0.90	0.51	0.48	0.29	40	63	−0.06	−0.37	−5.479 −
0.97	0.48	0.74	0.38	48	65	−0.12	−0.43	−4.528 +
0.99	0.45	1.08	0.50	53	64	−0.17	−0.48	−3.621 +
n_0=0.03	x_0=0.11	F_0=0.00						

Table A8.2.5 Utilitarian tagging

β= 0	θ=2.7	$\frac{m_2}{m} = 1.22$						
F(n)	y	z	x	ATR%	MTR%	E^u	ξ	U
0.10	0.47	0.09	0.14	−45	67	0.3	−0.2	−9.218 −
0.50	0.54	0.24	0.19	22	63	0.05	−0.28	−7.482 −
0.90	0.52	0.53	0.29	44	64	−0.06	−0.37	−5.497 −
0.97	0.49	0.83	0.40	52	64	−0.12	−0.43	−4.439 ()
0.99	0.46	1.13	0.51	54	64	−0.17	−0.48	−3.813 ()
n_0=0.03	x_0=0.11	F_0=0.00						

Table A8.2.6 Utilitarian tagging

β= 0	θ=2.5	$\frac{m_3}{m} = 0.82$						
F(n)	y	z	x	ATR%	MTR%	E^u	ξ	U
0.10	0.37	0.05	0.15	−180	54	0.50	−0.19	8.155 +
0.50	0.47	0.16	0.20	−38	55	0.14	−0.27	−7.001 +
0.90	0.48	0.39	0.28	18	59	0.00	−0.35	−5.443 +
0.97	0.46	0.65	0.37	35	61	−0.06	−0.41	−4.555 −
0.99	0.45	0.93	0.47	43	61	−0.13	−0.46	−3.919 −
n_0=0.03	x_0=0.10	F_0=0.0						

Table A8.2.7 Maximin no tagging

	θ=2.5							
F(n)	y	z	x	ATR%	MTR%	E^u	ξ	U
0.11	0.005	0.001	0.14	−139	88		−0.12	−8.297
0.50	0.42	0.15	0.18	−6	79	0.33	−0.22	−7.859
0.90	0.52	0.45	0.23	47	72	−0.01	−0.33	−6.258
0.97	0.51	0.74	0.32	57	70	−0.11	−0.40	−5.171
0.99	0.51	1.08	0.43	60	63	−0.21	−0.47	−4.335
n_0=0.16	x_0=0.137	F_0=0.11						

Table A8.2.8 Maximin tagging

	θ=2.3	$\frac{m_1}{m} = 0.55$						
F(n)	y	z	x	ATR%	MTR%	E^u	ξ	U
0.20	0.02	0.0001	0.16		77	–	–	– 7.336 +
0.50	0.29	0.06	0.17	−121	71	0.8	−0.19	−7.203 +
0.90	0.45	0.23	0.23	1	67	0.14	−0.29	−6.214 +
0.97	0.48	0.40	0.28	28	64	0.003	−0.35	−5.426 –
0.99	0.50	0.62	0.37	41	56	−0.13	−0.42	−4.678 –
n_0=0.12	x_0=0.16	F_0=0.20						

Table A8.2.9 Maximin tagging u2

	θ=2.4	$\frac{m_3}{m} = 0.86$						
F(n)	y	z	x	ATR%	MTR%	E^u	ξ	U
0.13	0.005	0.001	0.14		86	–	−0.13	−8.032 +
0.50	0.38	0.12	0.16	−36	77	0.43	−0.21	−7.689 +
0.90	0.50	0.40	0.24	40	72	0.03	−0.32	−6.243 +
0.97	0.50	0.68	0.32	53	69	−0.08	−0.30	−5.141 +
0.99	0.50	0.97	0.42	57	64	−0.19	−0.45	−4.400 –
n_0=0.12	x_0=0.14	F_0=0.13						

Table A8.2.10 Maximin tagging

β= 0	θ=2.6	$\frac{m_2}{m} = 1.05$						
F(n)	y	z	x	ATR%	MTR%	E^u	ξ	U
0.10	0.02	0.002	0.13		89	–	−0.12	−8.489 –
0.50	0.44	0.18	0.16	10	79	−0.27	−0.23	−7.976 –
0.90	0.53	0.50	0.24	52	73	−0.04	−0.34	−6.283 –
0.97	0.52	0.80	0.33	59	70	−0.13	−0.41	−5.145 +
0.99	0.51	1.13	0.44	61	64	−0.22	−0.47	−4.329 +
n_0=0.18	x_0=0.13	F_0=0.10						

Table A8.2.11 Maximin tagging

	θ=2.7	$\frac{m_2}{m}=1.22$						
F(n)	y	z	x	ATR%	MTR%	E^u	ξ	U
0.10	0.05	0.01	0.13	−100	90	7.5	−0.12	−8.690 –
0.50	0.46	0.21	0.16	24	80	0.22	−0.23	−8.099 –
0.90	0.54	0.54	0.24	54	73	−0.06	−0.34	−6.303 –
0.97	0.53	0.86	0.33	55	69	−0.15	−0.41	−5.123 +
0.99	0.51	1.19	0.44	64	64	−0.23	−0.43	−4.312 +
n_0=0.19	x_0=0.13	F_0=0.08						

Table A8.2.12 Maximin tagging u2

	θ=2.5	$\frac{m_3}{m}=0.82$						
F(n)	y	z	x	ATR%	MTR%	E^u	ξ	U
0.13	0.005	0.01	0.14		85	–	−0.13	−7.929 +
0.50	0.38	0.11	0.17	−46	76	0.43	−0.21	−7.602 +
0.90	0.50	0.36	0.24	34	70	0.03	−0.32	−6.236 +
0.97	0.51	0.60	0.31	48	67	−0.08	−0.30	−5.230 –
0.99	0.51	0.86	0.41	53	60	−0.19	−0.45	−4.447 –
n_0=0.12	x_0=0.14	F_0=0.13						

Table A8.2.13 Rank order no tagging

	θ=2.5							
F(n)	y	z	x	ATR%	MTR%	E^u	ξ	U
0.10	0.31	0.05	0.15	−200	71	0.7	−0.17	−8.264
0.50	0.45	0.17	0.18	−10	71	0.23	−0.25	−7.358
0.90	0.49	0.44	0.26	41	71	0.001	−0.34	−5.838
0.97	0.49	0.72	0.34	52	70	−0.08	−0.4	−4.862
0.99	0.47	1.07	0.45	58	68	−0.15	−0.45	−4.110
n_0=0.04	x_0=0.13	F_0=0.003						

Table A8.2.14 Rank-order tagging

	θ=2.3	$\frac{m_1}{m}=0.55$						
F(n)	y	z	x	ATR%	MTR%	E^u	ξ	U
0.10	0.12	0.01	0.12		54		−0.14	−7.180 +
0.50	0.32	0.07	0.19		61	0.6	−0.22	−6.764 +
0.90	0.43	0.22	0.25	−11	65	0.17	−0.30	−5.804 +
0.97	0.45	0.42	0.32	25	64	−0.02	−0.37	−4.983 –
0.99	0.46	0.62	0.39	37	60	−0.09	−0.42	−4.413 –
n_0=0.05	x_0=0.16	F_0=0.04						

Table A8.2.15 Rank-order tagging

	θ=2.4	$\frac{m_3}{m}=0.86$						
F(n)	y	z	x	ATR%	MTR%	E^u	ξ	U
0.10	0.26	0.03	0.15	–	67	1.0	−0.17	−7.948 +
0.50	0.41	0.13	0.18	−39	70	0.3	−0.24	−7.198 +
0.90	0.48	0.38	0.26	32	70	0.04	−0.33	−5.816 +
0.97	0.48	0.63	0.33	47	69	−0.05	−0.39	−4.910 −
0.99	0.47	0.98	0.44	55	67	−0.15	−0.45	−4.141 −
n_0=0.05	x_0=0.14	F_0=0.01						

Table A8.2.16 Rank-order tagging

	θ=2.5	$\frac{m_2}{m}=1.05$						
F(n)	y	z	x	ATR%	MTR%	E^u	ξ	U
0.10	0.35	0.06	0.13	−100	73	0.6	−0.18	−8.481 −
0.50	0.47	0.19	0.18	6	72	0.22	−0.24	−7.648 −
0.90	0.50	0.48	0.26	45	71	−0.02	−0.35	−5.847 −
0.97	0.49	0.77	0.35	55	70	−0.10	−0.41	−4.842 +
0.99	0.48	1.12	0.46	59	67	−0.18	−0.47	−4.084 +
n_0=0.04	x_0=0.125	F_0=0.002						

Table A8.2.17 Rank-order tagging

	θ=2.7	$\frac{m_2}{m}=1.22$						
F(n)	y	z	x	ATR%	MTR%	E^u	ξ	U
0.10	0.38	0.08	0.14	−86	75	0.50	−0.18	−8.721 −
0.50	0.49	0.22	0.18	20	73	0.13	−0.26	−7.578 −
0.90	0.51	0.52	0.26	50	71	−0.05	−0.35	−5.869 −
0.97	0.50	0.82	0.35	57	70	−0.12	−0.41	−4.847 +
0.99	0.48	1.18	0.46	61	68	−0.18	−0.47	−4.083 +
n_0=0.04	x_0=0.12	F_0=0.002						

Table A8.2.18 Rank-order tagging

	θ=2.5	$\frac{m_3}{m}=0.82$						
F(n)	y	z	x	ATR%	MTR%	E^u	ξ	U
0.10	0.26	0.03	0.15	–	65	1.0	−0.17	−7.837 +
0.50	0.41	0.12	0.18	−49	67	0.3	−0.24	−7.121 +
0.90	0.47	0.34	0.26	26	68	0.05	−0.33	−5.819 +
0.97	0.47	0.592	0.34	43	68	−0.05	−0.39	−4.887 −
0.99	0.47	0.86	0.43	51	65	−0.13	−0.44	−4.228 −
n_0=0.05	x_0=0.14	F_0=0.03						

9 Optimal income taxes/transfers and non-welfarist social objectives

Optimal tax theory has often been criticized for taking insufficient account of developments in other disciplines, notably philosophy and psychology. In particular, public economics has remained too rooted in utilitarianism. The welfarist approach ranks social outcomes solely according to how they affect individual utilities. Utility also plays a dual role in the welfarist literature on the optimal taxation. It is the same utility function employed by individuals in their decision that enters the social welfare function. Both of these are open to question. The modelling of individual decision-making has been particularly questioned in the recent literature on behavioural public economics. As Peter Diamond put it, 'In standard modelling, we assume consistent behaviour across economic environments, captured in preferences that are defined only in terms of commodities acquired (absent externalities). One of the key messages of behavioural economics is that context (also referred to as situation) matters in ways that are not recognized in standard modelling' (Diamond, 2008, p. 1).

As noted in the introduction, however, there is a striking and fundamental dissonance between the welfarist approach and the tone of much policy debate. It is the consequences of reform for the incomes of the poor—the money in their pockets, not something akin to money metric measures of their welfare—that are commonly discussed and analysed. This chapter therefore examines the implications of an alternative approach to the design of non-linear income tax schemes. Governments may also take a non-welfaristic approach attaching weight to objectives that do not reflect individual preferences (see e.g. Sen 1985). Kanbur et al (1994a,b) adopt this kind of approach. First, they take the objective of policy to be the minimization of a poverty index rather than the maximization of a social welfare function. This approach is not without its critics (see, for instance, Stern 1987), but in a technical sense at least it is relatively straightforward. Loosely speaking, a poverty index defined on utility—attaching zero weight to all households above some threshold—is merely a special form of social welfare function. The second point of departure is more fundamental. The motivation for this departure begins with the observation that the poverty indexes on which much policy discussion focuses are, in practice, almost invariably defined in terms not of utility but of income. In the presence of incentive effects, these criteria are very different things (and can move in different directions). Indexes that focus on income attach no significance to the effort put into earning income, or, put another way, attach no weight to the leisure of the poor. And indeed it is clear that much policy debate is cast in precisely these terms: the focus is on the income of the poor, not on how hard they work to get it. First, to the extent that—rightly or wrongly—policy is often evaluated, at least in part, by the use of such indexes, it is helpful to know what kind of policy would be implied by the explicit pursuit of such a minimand. To make the point more formally, we take a constant elasticity labour supply function with elasticity ε; $y = n^{\varepsilon}$ where n is the wage rate. Now the indirect utility function can be written as $v = ny/(1+\varepsilon) + b$, where b is lump sum income (benefits and unearned income). In the welfarist case, the level of indirect utility enters a welfarist measure of poverty so that labour income is discounted by the factor $(1+\varepsilon)$. This factor in turn takes into account the cost of working. The individual situation in much of the policy debate is evaluated in terms of ny+b.

The government might also be concerned with particular aspects of a given low-income support programme. For example, it might care about the cost of the programme, programme take-up and the social stigma associated with the programme, and how the programme will affect assistance recipients receive from private sources. Governments may also take a paternalistic approach in the sense of giving weight to the well-being of persons, but judging that well-being not according to the preferences revealed by individuals themselves but according to preferences chosen by the government. These preferences may be justified from an altruistic perspective as reflecting the weights that the non-poor put on the consumption patterns of the poor. For example, Moffitt (2006) suggests that society might care about work per se, independent of well-being as perceived by the individual. Tuomala (1990) notices that, even if the individual's income were independent of the amount he or she chose to work (the linear earnings function has this fairly realistic property), he or she would choose a certain amount. It turns out that in the linear income tax model, an increase in the subsistence quantity of labour increases the optimal maximin income tax rate. In other words, the subsistence quantity of labour mitigates the disincentive effects of income taxation. Mirrlees (2002) in turn studies the optimal non-linear income tax schedule under the assumption that the marginal utility of labour is positive for a sufficiently small amount of labour. He shows in a wide class of cases that the marginal tax rate is 100 per cent for those on a low income. (Figure 9.1 illustrates this possibility but does not prove it.) This requires that the subsidies should be large enough to generate full employment by inducing sufficiently large demand for all types of work.

Paternalism may also emerge in an otherwise welfaristic framework if one adopts recent findings in the behavioural economics literature. That literature has stressed various ways in which individual behaviour does not conform with the rational, well-informed, far-sighted, self-interested view of standard economic theory. This has major implications for positive economic analysis, as the apparatus of behavioural economics has made progress in explaining a number of empirical phenomena that are not

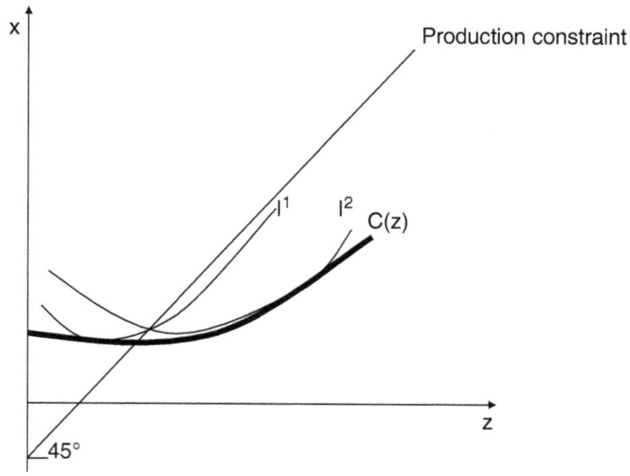

Figure 9.1 The marginal tax rate on a low income

consistent with standard rational choice models.[1] It also has implications for normative analysis. For example, limited self-control may lead to over-consumption of alcohol and drugs and underinvestment in human capital. In situations like these, individuals might benefit if an outsider induced them to behave as if they had perfect self-control. This outsider could be the government, and the inducements might be through tax and subsidy policies. A new kind of market imperfection, mistakes in individual behaviour, brings us, then, to the realm of public economics—specifically, behavioural public economics.

Behavioural public economics is a rapidly expanding field whose central focus is on public policy when individual preferences differ from social ones.[2] O'Donoghue and Rabin (2003) consider optimal paternalistic taxes that the government imposes to correct individual behaviour regarding consumption of harmful goods. Sheshinski (2003) proposes a general model with faulty individual decision-making, where restricting individuals' choices leads to welfare improvements. Kanbur et al (2008) examine taxation under income uncertainty when individuals behave according to the tenets of prospect theory,[3] but the government uses expected utility theory to evaluate the outcomes of this behaviour. The situation in the normative part of this research agenda is, therefore, one where market behaviour is generated by one set of preferences, but society evaluates it with respect to another set of preferences. In many respects, the situation described above is fairly common in welfare and normative public economics. Perhaps the most well-known example is the analysis of so-called merit goods (Sandmo 1983, Besley 1988, Schroyen 2005). The consumption of these goods, in the viewpoint of the government, is

[1] For surveys of the literature, see Camerer and Lowenstein (2004) and Bernheim and Rangel (2008).

[2] A general discussion is to be found in Camerer et al (2003).

[3] Kahneman and Tversky's (1979) prospect theory is a much-used alternative to the expected utility theorem, with empirical support.

meritorious and should be encouraged or imposed, ignoring individual choice.[4] We discuss these questions in Chapters 11 and 12.

9.1 Additively separable individualistic social evaluation function

Kanbur, Pirttilä, and Tuomala (2006) (KPT hereafter) provide a general non-welfarist formulation of the income tax problem, which unifies special cases that have been studied in non-welfarist tax literature. The way in which the individual optimization is modelled in KPT (2007) is the same as the approach in welfarist tax literature.[5] As in Mirrlees (1971), there is a continuum of individuals, each having the same preference ordering, which is represented by an additive utility function $u = U(x) + V(1 - y)$ over-consumption x and hours worked y, with $U_x > 0$ and $V_y < 0$. Individuals are otherwise identical, but they differ in their income-earning ability, or the wage rate, n. Workers differ only in the pre-tax wage n they can earn. There is a distribution of n on the interval $\underline{n}, \bar{n}$ represented by the density function $f(n)$. Gross income is given by $z = ny$.

It is usual in optimal tax theory to assume an additively separable individualistic welfare function. One can of course allow for any increasing transformation of individual utilities here, so as to capture a greater or lesser concern with inequality on the part of the government. Suppose, therefore, that the aim of policy can be expressed as maximizing the following social evaluation criterion (allowing for non-individualistic preferences):

$$S = \int P(x, y, n) f(n) dn, \tag{1}$$

where $P = P(.,n)$, following Seade (1980), is 'the social utility' derived from an n-individual's consumption and labour (leisure), which may in particular coincide with, or be related in some special form to, $u(.,n)$. S is restricted to be additively separable in individual utilities, but the formulation still allows, e.g., the social welfare to depend in any linear form on utilities or on specific goods such as income.[6]

[4] Perhaps at some level one could also argue that redistribution—where the government can evaluate individual welfare in a different way than the individuals themselves—and correction of externalities are additional examples in which the social welfare function differs from the individual utility.

[5] Note it is assumed that individuals are perfectly rational when assessing the self-selection constraint. That individuals can make mistakes with respect to incentive compatibility constraints as well is clearly a somewhat different topic from the one we consider. This is examined further in Sheshinski (2002).

[6] The individualistic form of the welfare function has been criticized, most notably by Sen (1985), as unable to meet in many instances common-sense notions of equality, which would generally relate to distribution of consumption, i.e. directly to quantities not necessarily through utilities (non-welfarism).

From the first-order conditions of government's maximization, we obtain the following condition for optimal marginal tax rate $t(z) = T'(z)$; (see appendix 9.1 for the derivation)

$$\frac{t}{1-t} = \frac{P_x(\varpi - \varpi^p)}{\lambda} + \underbrace{\left[\frac{1+e^u}{e^c}\right]}_{A_n} \underbrace{\left[\frac{[1-F(n)]}{nf(n)}\right]}_{B_n} \underbrace{\left[\frac{U_x \int_n^\infty \left[\frac{1}{U_x^{(p)}}(1 - P_x U_x/\lambda)\right] f(p)dp}{(1-F(n))}\right]}_{C_n} \tag{2}$$

where $\varpi^p = -\frac{P_y}{nP_x}$ denotes the social (paternalist) marginal rate of substitution. The ABC terms on the right are familiar from the welfarist literature, whereas the first term is novel. It captures the social value of divergence between private and social preferences, and is therefore called the paternalistic motive for taxation. It could also be called a first-best motive for taxation, as it corrects the individual activity to correspond to social preferences. It is analogous to a Pigouvian tax correcting for an externality.[7] The conventional terms, the ABC terms at the right of (2) elasticity and income effects (A&C), the shape of the skill distribution (B&C), and social marginal weights (C), represent in turn the second-best motive for marginal distortion, arising from the asymmetric information. It should be clear from (2) that the variation of the optimal marginal tax rate with the level of income is a complex matter. Applying (2), it appears that there are four elements on the right-hand side of (6) that determine optimum tax rates.

At the end points of income distribution, the ABC is zero, and the marginal tax is completely determined by paternalistic motives. Suppose, for instance, that the social planner regards very high incomes as unwanted per se. In this case, $\varpi^P > \varpi$. Therefore, the marginal tax rate at the top is positive, despite the fact that this policy is not Pareto-efficient. The marginal tax rate is used as a device to correct 'undesirable' social outcomes. The sign of the marginal rate will depend on the interaction between these terms. We might think of a government that has redistributive goals but more 'Calvinistic' or 'puritanical' views on working than taxpayers, so that it would like to see people work harder and earn more. In this case, $\varpi^p < \varpi$. As is known from Mirrlees (1971), the second term implies a non-negative marginal tax rate. The first term in turn implies a marginal subsidy as an incentive to promote labour supply. At the top the marginal tax rate is negative. Hence the property of welfarist optimal income tax—the non-negativity of marginal rate—no longer holds.

[7] The marginal tax formula takes the same formal structure in the case when individuals care about their relative position (see Kanbur and Tuomala 2013).

9.2 Special cases; poverty reduction

In the absence of incentive effects (and with sufficient resources available for poverty relief), the design of income-based targeting is a trivial exercise. After the poverty line is established, those individuals who are initially below it are given exactly that transfer needed to bring them just above it. Such a scheme involves no leakages. If there are no labour supply or other effects in transferring or raising these resources, and if the informational and administrative requirements can be met without cost, this method provides perfect targeting. But once incentive effects are admitted, difficulties arise. Because perfect targeting implies an effective marginal tax rate of 100 per cent on those below the poverty line, the poor have no incentive to earn income. Their rational labour supply decisions would then be likely to greatly increase the revenue costs of alleviating their poverty. Incentive effects thus rule out marginal rates of 100 per cent on the poor. The questions of precisely how high or low those rates should be, and of how they should vary with income, then become considerably more complex.

Much of the attention of non-welfarist approaches has focused on a particular form of non-welfarism, namely poverty reduction. Policy discussion on poverty alleviation and the targeting of social policy often concentrates almost exclusively on income. Little weight is typically given to issues such as the disutility the poor experience when working. Indeed, sometimes work requirements are seen in a positive light, as is often the case with workfare. This is in marked contrast with conventional, utility-based objectives in optimal income taxation literature. Therefore it is worthwhile examining the implications of poverty-reduction objectives on optimal income tax rules.[8] It must also be remembered that the dividing line between welfarism and non-welfarism is not very clear. Conventional tax analysis utilizes social welfare functions with inequality aversion, which already implies a deviation of assessing individual welfare with the same function which the individual uses himself. In some sense, the social objective functions form a continuum in the welfarism–non-welfarism scale.

9.2.1 LINEAR INCOME TAX

Kanbur et al (1994a) examine the properties of the Mirrlees-type optimal income tax model when the government objective is alleviation of income poverty.[9] Instead of social welfare maximization, the government aims to minimize an income-based poverty index of the general additively separable form. First, following Kanbur, Pirttilä, Tuomala, and Ylinen (2015) (hereafter KPTY), we analyse linear income tax. Particularly in a

[8] The literature makes clear that it does not necessarily advocate these objectives; rather, the aim is to explore their implications.

[9] Besley and Kanbur (1988) analyse commodity tax/subsidy rules (when no income taxation is available) for poverty alleviation. Kanbur, Keen, and Tuomala (1994b) and Bradbury (2004) offer surveys. Ravallion (2013) provides an excellent overview on anti-poverty policy.

developing country context, linear taxation can be justified as an easily implementable instrument. We have the same instruments, t, b, and R, that are used not for welfare maximization, as in Chapter 3, but instead for poverty minimization. Note first that the revenue-maximizing tax rate is in fact equivalent to the tax rate obtained from a maximin objective function, since when the government only cares about the poverty (consumption) of the poorest individual, its only goal is to maximize redistribution to this individual, i.e. maximize tax revenue. The social evaluation function $P(x,y,n)$ reduces to $D(x,x^*)$ ($P_y = 0$ and $P_x = D_x$). In the discrete case the objective function is now:

$$S = \sum D(x^i, x^*) \tag{3}$$

where x^* is the poverty line. D is non-negative for $x < x^*$ and zero otherwise. It satisfies the following properties:

$$D_x < 0,\ D_{xx} > 0\, \forall\, x \in (0, x^*). \tag{4}$$

This specification captures a number of widely used poverty measures, such as the headcount ratio and the Gini-based measure of Sen (1976). Note that while it has a similarity with a Rawlsian social welfare function (focusing on the poor), the poverty index depends only on income. In the Rawlsian difference principle, an individual's well-being is judged according to an index of primary goods.[10]

The optimal tax rate becomes (see appendix 9.1 for a derivation):

$$\frac{t}{1-t} = \frac{1}{e}\left[1 - \frac{\hat{D}}{\bar{z}}\right] \tag{5}$$

where $\hat{D} = \dfrac{\sum D_c(1 + (1-t)z^i{}_{1-t}/z^i)z^i}{\sum D_c(1 + (1-t)z^i{}_b)} = \dfrac{\sum D_c(1+e)z^i}{\sum D_c(1 + (1-t)z^i{}_b)}$ (e=elasticity).

Here $\hat{D}$ describes the relative efficiency of taxes and transfers in reducing deprivation: the higher $\hat{D}$ is, the lower the tax rate should be. Both the numerator and denominator of $\hat{D}$ depend on D_c, so the difference in the relative efficiency of the two depends on z^i_{1-t} and z^i_b. The more people react to taxes (relative to transfers) by earning less, the higher $\hat{D}$ is and the lower the tax rate should be. In Chapter 3, the formula (3), $z(\beta)$ has a similar impact: the higher the welfare-weighted income $z(\beta)$, the lower the tax rate should be. The difference is in using deprivation reduction as the guiding measure for taxation instead of welfare measures. In addition, the same efficiency result comes from the term $\frac{1}{e}$.

Thus the $\hat{D}$ in the optimal tax formula (5) entails a further efficiency consideration, lowering optimal tax rates to induce the poor to work more. Kanbur, Keen, and Tuomala

[10] Economists have, however, narrowed Rawls's theory into one that allocates according to 'maximin utility'.

(1994a) find a similar result in their non-linear poverty-minimizing tax model. Here, in linear income tax, however, we are restricted to lowering the tax for everyone instead of only the poorest individuals.

To summarize, the non-welfarist tax rules differ from the welfarist ones, depending on the definition of non-welfarism in question (the P_x and P_y terms). However, when we take poverty minimization as the specific case of non-welfarism, the tax rules are quite similar to welfarist ones. The basic difference is that equity is not considered in welfare terms but in terms of poverty-reduction effectiveness. A more notable difference arises from efficiency considerations. With linear taxation, taking into account labour supply responses means that everybody's tax rate is affected, instead of just the target group's. If we want to induce the poor to work more to reduce their poverty, we need to lower everyone's tax rate. The welfarist linear tax rule does not take this into account. It is not however possible to state that under poverty-minimization tax rates are optimally lower than under welfare maximization, since we cannot directly compare the welfare and deprivation terms. However, there is an additional efficiency consideration involved under poverty minimization. Non-linear tax rules of course make it possible to target lower tax rates on the poorer individuals, but in a developing country context with lower administrative capacity this is not necessarily possible, and such considerations affect everyone's tax rate.

9.2.2 NON-LINEAR TAX

Next we turn to non-linear tax in a continuum case and write the government's income-based poverty index in the following additively separable form:

$$S = \int D[x(n), x^*] \, f(n)dn \tag{6}$$

In a second step, take the following form:

$$\frac{t}{1-t} = \frac{D_x}{\lambda} s + \underbrace{\left[\frac{1+e^u}{e^c}\right]}_{A_n} \underbrace{\left[\frac{[1-F(n)]}{nf(n)}\right]}_{B_n} \underbrace{\left[\frac{U_x \int_n^\infty \left[\frac{1}{U_x^{(p)}}(1 - D_x U_x/\lambda)\right] f(p)dp}{(1-F(n))}\right]}_{C_n} \tag{7}$$

In (7) we have defined the variable $s = -V_y/nU_x > 0$ to denote the marginal rate of substitution between x and y. Preferences are taken to satisfy the further restriction that $s_n < 0$. This is assumption B of Mirrlees (1971) and the agent monotonicity assumption of Seade (1982). It implies that indifference curves in consumption–gross income space become flatter the higher an individual's wage rate is, which in turn ensures that both consumption and gross earnings increase with the wage rate.

Do the three central welfarist results continue to apply? Result 3 in Appendix 4.1 clearly does. Using $\mu(\underline{n}) = 0$ in (7) and noting that $D(x(\underline{n}), x^{\star}) = 0$ (so long as the highest earner is not poor), it follows that $t(z(\bar{n})) = 0$: the marginal rate at the top of a bounded distribution should again be zero. This is as one would expect, for in the context of poverty alleviation, the only reason to care about the highest earner—indeed, about any of the non-poor—is as a source of revenue, and it is well known that in these circumstances one would want a zero marginal rate at the top: if it were strictly positive, additional revenue could be extracted by slightly lowering it and thereby inducing the highest earner to earn additional taxed income.

Results 1 and 2, in contrast, are overturned. Taking limits in (7) thereby assuming that it is optimal for all to work, and using $\mu(\underline{n}) = 0$, one finds $t(z(\underline{n}))=\frac{D_x(x(\underline{n}),x^{\star})}{\lambda}s<0$ by the condition $D_x < 0$ (and assuming too that poverty is not entirely eliminated). Hence if some amount of work is always desirable,[11] the ABC at the right of (6) vanishes. However, in the poverty alleviation case, the first term at the right remains, and the marginal tax rate for the lowest earner is negative. In these circumstances the marginal rate at the bottom of the gross income distribution should be strictly negative: if it is optimal to have everybody work, poverty alleviation calls for a marginal subsidy on the earnings of the very poorest. Indeed, the conclusion to be drawn here is of a rather more general kind than the welfarist lower endpoint result in Chapter 4. Whereas the latter applies, only at the lower extreme of the distribution, a set of measure zero, (7) implies—given continuity—that there exists an interval over which a negative marginal rate is appropriate.

Over some intervals at the bottom of the wage distribution, the marginal tax rate derived in the poverty alleviation case is therefore lower than in the conventional welfarist case. This policy, via inducing the poor to work and earn more, contributes to poverty reduction. The finding is potentially important in policy terms, motivating the use of wage subsidies such as the EITC (earned income tax credit).[12] Note that the policy outlined above would not necessarily raise welfare, because of the foregone leisure. Its desirability arises from the fact that the social planner does not evaluate its policy based on individual utility, but uses a different, non-welfarist notion.

Bradbury (2004) points out that policy discussion often goes beyond this, giving a negative weight to leisure. One reason for this is paternalism. Compulsion to work may be seen as in individuals' best interests, for instance because of learning-by-doing reasons that the individuals fail to see. Another reason relates to notions of obligation and reciprocity. The recipients of the welfare benefits have 'no rights without responsibilities'. They may have a responsibility to work to be entitled to social welfare programmes, irrespective of the desirability of the work to themselves.

[11] This is the so-called no-bunching case.

[12] Note this is a quite different argument favouring EITC than those based on Saez (2002).

The formula (7) implies that if it is optimal for the lowest-ability earner to work, the marginal tax rate at the lower end of the distribution should be strictly negative; that is, a marginal earnings subsidy should be paid to the very poorest. The reason why this is optimal from the non-welfarist perspective even though it cannot possibly be optimal from a welfarist one can be seen in Figure 9.2, taken from KKT(1994).

Suppose that the initial position is one in which the marginal tax rate on the very poorest individual is indeed strictly negative. This initial equilibrium is shown as point a in Figure 9.2, an indifference curve of an n-individual being tangential to the segment AA of the budget constraint implied by the tax system in force. The assumption of a negative marginal rate implies that the slope of AA exceeds that of CC, which is the 45-degree line through a. Consider now a tax reform that increases the marginal rate at a while retaining a itself as a feasible point; diagramatically the budget constraint rotates clockwise about a to arrive at BB. The effects of this rotation of the poorest worker's budget constraint through the initial consumption-leisure bundle are that the individual's welfare rises (because if the initial consumption-leisure bundle remains feasible, any change in the individual's behaviour must signify an increase in welfare); the individual's net income falls (because the only incentive effect is a substitution toward leisure induced by the higher marginal tax rate); and the government's revenue increases (because the subsidy is paid at a lower rate on a narrower base). From the welfarist perspective, the combination of the utility gain to the individual and the revenue gain to the government makes this reform ambiguously desirable. From the non-welfarist perspective, however, opposing effects are at work. The revenue gain is desirable, but the net income loss to the poorest worker is not. Minimization of an income-based poverty index will require striking a balance between the two effects, which will make a

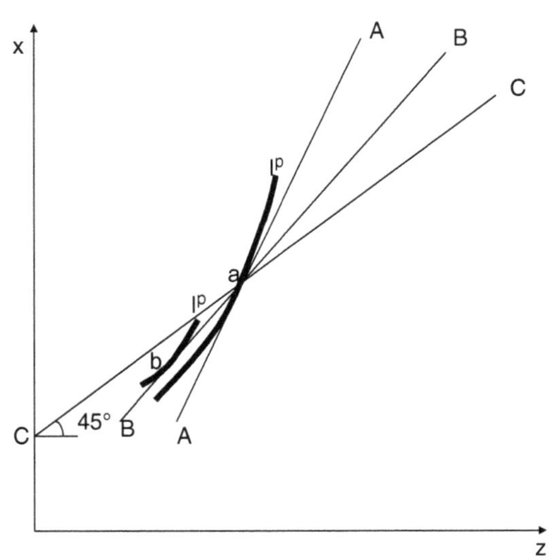

Figure 9.2 Negative marginal tax rate

marginal subsidy on the very poorest optimal. The possibility of an optimally negative marginal tax rate is confined, however, to the poorest of the poor. For those who find themselves exactly on the poverty line, the optimal marginal rate can be shown to be strictly positive. These qualitative implications of the non-welfarist approach thus point to a pattern of marginal tax rates below the poverty line that is both complex and potentially very different from that suggested by the welfarist tradition.

But how far do low or even negative marginal tax rates on the very poorest individuals extend into the range of incomes? And how is the poverty-minimizing rate structure affected by the precise location of the poverty line x* and by the form of the deprivation function? The revenue requirement R will be taken to be 10 per cent of gross income, again a conventional figure (intended as a very rough approximation to the levels of expenditure on public goods commonly observed). Typically, poverty indices consist in computing some average measure of deprivation by setting individual needs as defined above at the agreed-upon poverty line x^*. For this purpose, KKT (1994) take a poverty index of the form developed by Foster, Greer, and Thorbecke (1984). They have proposed defining a poverty index, $P_\beta = \int_0^{n^*} \left[\frac{x(n)-x^*}{x^*}\right]^\beta f(n)dn$, as the average of these poverty gaps raised to some power β across individuals. The parameter β reflects the degree of aversion to the depth of poverty. For example, when $\beta = 0$, the poverty index does not take into account the size of existing poverty gaps—it is simply the proportion of units below the poverty line. When $\beta = 1$, by contrast, it is just the proportion of units below the poverty line multiplied by the average poverty gap. As the parameter a increases beyond unity, the index P_β becomes more sensitive to the poverty gap of the poorest among the poor. This has been widely used in the analytical literature on targeting (as for instance in Besley 1990 and Kanbur and Keen 1989). In KKT (1994), $\beta = 2$. One immediate implication of this specification should be noted. With Cobb–Douglas preferences (so that the marginal rate of substitution between consumption and work is strictly positive at zero hours) and a lognormal wage distribution (so that the lower bound of n is zero), there are some who will work only if the marginal tax rate at the bottom of the distribution is infinitely negative. In both the welfarist context and that of income-poverty minimization, it would be optimal to have some of the population idle. As noted above, in the welfarist case, the optimal marginal rate at the bottom of the income distribution is then strictly positive. However, for the case in which the objective is to minimize income poverty and some households are idle at the optimum, we have been unable to derive any general result on the sign of the optimal marginal rate at the lower endpoint. The simulations provide some indication of the extent to which the argument for non-positive marginal rates at the lower end (when the poorest work) continues to exert some force when instead the wage distribution is not bounded away from zero.

Several features stand out from numerical simulations in KKT (1994). First, the marginal rate on the lowest gross income—which, as just noted, we are unable to sign in principle—emerges as very strongly positive: not only is it not negative, it is not even low. Second, marginal tax rates decline monotonically from the poorest to the richest individual, implying that the dictates of effective targeting can run exactly counter to the popular notion that equity concerns require the marginal tax rate to increase with income. Such declining marginal tax rates run counter to the conclusion sometimes drawn from the welfarist literature that the administrative advantages of linear taxation can be bought at relatively little loss in terms of policy effectiveness. As seen in Chapter 5, this pattern of marginal tax rates seems to be quite specific. The third feature is that increases in the poverty line reduce optimal marginal rates at and below the poverty line. The intuition for this seems to be that the case for low marginal rates intended to encourage those at or near the poverty line to move out of poverty becomes stronger as the poverty line moves into denser parts of the distribution. Fourth, comparing the maximin case with the others, increases in the extent of aversion to inequality among the poor tend to increase the marginal rates that they optimally face. Other simulations suggest that moderate variation in the revenue requirement affects the general level of marginal tax rates (which tend to increase with the revenue required), but not the qualitative pattern of their variation with income. This is perhaps as would be expected because the greater the concern with alleviating poverty, the more attractive schemes that approach minimum income guarantees are likely to be: the emphasis is then on raising the consumption of the very poorest, and financing the transfer this requires calls for relatively high marginal tax rates in the lower part of the distribution in order to impose sufficiently high average tax rates further up the distribution. But perhaps the most important feature of the results is the finding of marginal tax rates on the poor that are invariably rather high (bearing in mind the fairly minimal revenue requirement). In most cases marginal rates on the bulk of the poor exceed 60 per cent, and in all cases they exceed 50 per cent. The case for low marginal tax rates to encourage the poor to help themselves thus is less discernible in the simulations than expected. Even with the relatively elastic labour supply responses implicit in Cobb–Douglas preferences (the elasticity of substitution between consumption and leisure being unity), a stronger mark is left by the case for high marginal rates associated with the unattainable ideal of perfect targeting described at the start of this section. Simulations for the case in which the elasticity of substitution is 0.5 (reported in Kanbur, Keen, and Tuomala 1994a) confirm this impression. The optimal marginal tax rates that emerge from these simulations are not necessarily higher in the non-welfarist case than in the welfarist one. Indeed, it is not clear that a coherent comparison between the two approaches can be made, because the latter, but not the former, depends on the cardinal representation of preferences.

9.3 Poverty rate minimization

The obvious objection to the poverty rate or headcount poverty measure is that it does not indicate the severity of poverty; namely, people may be far below or close to the poverty line. Atkinson (1998, p. 49) defends the use of this measure: 'If a minimum income is a basic right, the head count measures the number of deprived of that right. It is indeed an either/or condition.'

Suppose the government cares only about the number of people living in poverty, that is, the poverty rate. In that case, the government puts more value in lifting people above the poverty line than helping those substantially below the poverty line. We simplify further by assuming $u = x - \frac{y^{1+\frac{1}{\varepsilon}}}{1+\frac{1}{\varepsilon}}$.

Now if the government minimizes poverty rate ($\beta = 0$ in FGT-index), the optimal tax formula becomes:

$$\frac{t}{1-t} = \underbrace{\left[1+\frac{1}{\varepsilon}\right]}_{A_n} \underbrace{\left[\frac{1-F(n)}{nf(n)}\right]}_{B_n} \qquad n>n^* \tag{8}$$

$$\frac{t}{1-t} = \underbrace{\left[1+\frac{1}{\varepsilon}\right]}_{A_n} \underbrace{\left[\frac{-F(n)}{nf(n)}\right]}_{B_n} \qquad n \leq n^* \tag{9}$$

Hence the marginal tax rate above n^* is the same as in the revenue maxining or maximin case. The marginal tax rates are negative below the poverty line. The optimal tax schedule resembles an EITC schedule with negative marginal tax rates at the bottom.

APPENDIX 9.1 LINEAR AND NON-LINEAR INCOME TAXES

Linear income tax

Equation (8) in appendix 3.1 now becomes

$$\frac{\sum D_c(z^i + az^i{}_a)}{\sum D_c(1 + az^i{}_b)} = \frac{\sum z^i/N - (1-a)\sum z^i{}_a/N}{1-(1-a)\sum z^i{}_b/N}$$

$$\hat{D} = \frac{\sum D_c(1+(1-t)z^i{}_{1-t}/z^i)z^i}{\sum D_c(1+(1-t)z^i{}_b)} = \frac{\sum D_c(1+e)z^i}{\sum D_c(1+(1-t)z^i{}_b)}$$

Using the same steps as in the appendix to Chapter 3, the optimal tax rate becomes (5) in the text.

Non-linear tax

Suppose that the aim of policy can be expressed as maximizing the following social welfare criterion:

$$S = \int_0^\infty P(x(n), y(n))f(n)dn. \tag{1}$$

Introducing Lagrange multipliers λ, μ(n) for the revenue and incentive-compatibility constraints (as in the Mirrlees model) and integrating by parts, the Lagrangean becomes

$$L = \int_0^\infty (P(x,y) + \lambda(ny - x))f(n) - \mu' u - \mu u_n)dn + \mu(\infty)u(\infty) - \mu(0)u(0) \tag{2}$$

Differentiating with respect to u and y gives the first-order conditions

$$L_u = \left[(P_x - \lambda)\frac{1}{U_x}\right]f(n) - \mu'(n) = 0 \tag{3}$$

$$L_y = \left[P_x h_y + P_y + \lambda(n + \frac{V_y}{U_x})\right]f(n) + \mu(n)(V_y + yV_{yy})/n = 0 \tag{4}$$

(3) satisfies the transversality conditions

$$\frac{\partial L}{\partial u(0)} = \mu(\underline{n}) = 0; \frac{\partial L}{\partial u(\bar{n})} = \mu(\infty) = 0 \tag{5}$$

and

$$\mu(n)>0 \text{ for } n \in (0, \infty), \tag{6}$$

Integrating (7)

$$\int_0^n \left[(P_x - \lambda)\frac{1}{U_x}\right] f(p)dp = \int_0^n \frac{d\mu}{dn}dn = \mu(n) - \mu(0) \tag{7a}$$

or

$$\int_n^\infty \left[(P_x - \lambda)\frac{1}{U_x}\right] f(p)dp = \int_n^\infty \frac{d\mu}{dn}dn = \mu(\infty) - \mu(n) \tag{7b}$$

10 Heterogeneous work preferences and optimal redistribution

Although the models of the one-dimensional population have been useful for computations and examinations of the optimal income tax/transfer problem, they are not in all respects accurate pictures of reality. To analyse redistribution policies more fully, it would be useful to consider situations in which individuals are characterized by more than just one parameter. In the simple model with identical preferences, all workers earning the same level of income also have the same wage rates (marginal productivities). When preferences vary in unspecified ways across individuals, this will no longer be the case. Some people will be earning a given income because they are more productive, others because they are more hard-working. The assumption that differences in earnings are completely to be explained by differences in preferences (working or leisure preferences) is obviously an unrealistic one, just as the alternative explanation in terms of ability differences is also a simplification of reality. A more realistic model should take account of both. There are still other ways to relax the homogeneity assumption. One way is to differentiate the population through easily observable indicators that are correlated with the unobservable characteristic of interest. An individual's labour market status or demographic attributes, for instance, may convey information on underlying ability. When these characteristics are observable and convey some information on ability, we face the issue of tagging (considered in Chapter 8). When they are not observable, we face the analytical difficulty of dealing with a multidimensional principal agent problem. The government can only condition taxation on endogenous earnings and not on the exogenous characteristics whose heterogeneity in the population are at the origin of the redistribution problem.

To see this difficulty, let us return to the two-type case with homogenous preferences. There the more able or skilled individuals need less extra consumption to accept earning an additional euro, and if the social objective is redistributive, we know that the constraint is that the more skilled may want to mimic the less skilled. In order to prevent that, the less skilled must be induced to work less than would be efficient at their wage rate. This makes mimicking behaviour less attractive to the better-skilled. Therefore we have to put up the distortive taxation. In the case of heterogeneous preferences, the analysis of incentive compatible allocations becomes complex. It means that incentive constraints may then operate in all directions of skills. The pattern of the set of binding incentive compatible constraint is then hard to know a priori. Only with some simplifications can theoretical solutions can be found in this context. One way to avoid this difficulty is to assume that there is a perfect correlation between skills and preferences.[1,2] We return to these issues in the context of capital income taxation in Chapter 14.

How might these factors included in the optimal income tax model affect our views as to the optimal level of income taxation and transfer payments? Should this, as many seem to believe, be an argument for a more regressive tax/transfer system? In fact, considerations of that kind can be seen to lie behind income tax reforms implemented in several countries during the past decades. It is clear that the theory of optimal non-linear income taxation becomes more complicated since we allow for individuals to differ in more than one dimension. Papers in this area are few. Mirrlees (1976a, 1986) sets out the framework of a multidimensional optimal tax problem and derives first-order conditions for the optimal tax schedule. It is well known that formal results about the optimal (one-dimensional) income tax are limited. Hence it is not surprising that Mirrlees (1976a, 1986) has no general results concerning the shape of the optimal tax schedule in the multidimensional case. In the context of non-linear pricing, Armstrong (1996) and Wilson (1993) have analysed the problem of multidimensional types. Armstrong (1996) shows a class of cases that allow explicit solutions. Wilson (1993) also computes numerical solutions. These contributions are to some extent important in the context of optimal income taxation. As is typically the case with non-linear pricing literature, Armstrong (1996)[3] excludes income effects. The motivation for ignoring income effects when constructing non-linear tariffs for services and goods offered to household customers is that their income elasticities are small and/or their residual incomes are large in relation to their expenditures on non-linearly priced goods and services. This assumption cannot be easily justified in the context of an optimal income taxation model. In particular, in conjunction with the welfarist objective, it eliminates the equity considerations that motivate the income tax problem in the first place. Therefore we face a more complex problem in the context of the optimal income tax/transfers problem.

Tarkiainen and Tuomala (1999) (TT hereafter) build on a model in which individuals are assumed to differ in abilities, n, and work preferences, ω. They also do not rule out income effects. When individuals have different tastes for work, their welfare is no longer

[1] In Ebert (1988) the problem is considered with some strict restrictions on the utility function which allow transforming the two-dimensional problem into the one-dimensional one. There are also methods to avoid the technical problems with multidimensional income-earning ability—see Lockwood and Weinzierl (2012) and Rothschild and Scheuer (2013).

[2] Sandmo (1993) (section 6) discusses the difficulty of signing a marginal tax rate in a linear income tax model when individuals differ both in tastes and productivities. A number of other papers have considered optimal taxes with heterogeneous preferences in a two-skills setting. See, for example, Blomquist and Christiansen 2004; Boadway et al 2002; Cremer et al 2001; Cuff 2000; Kaplow 2008; Diamond and Spinnevijn 2009; and Tenhunen and Tuomala 2010.

[3] Laffont, Maskin, and Rochet (1987); McAfee and MacMillan (1988); Rochet (1985); Rochet and Choné (1998); Wilson (1993).

necessarily an increasing function of the productivity level. If everyone has the same wage (skill), TT (1999) show numerically that in the utilitarian case the marginal tax rates turn out to be non-decreasing over the majority of the population. Thus there is redistributive taxation in this case. Some people would, however, say that if individuals have the same opportunities then, while their choices may differ, there is no ethical basis for redistributive taxation.

As we discussed in Chapter 2, when individuals have heterogeneous preferences, comparing welfare across population becomes conceptually problematic. It may be the case that an individual with a high disutility for work will work less than those with a lower disutility for work at the same wage. In this case individuals with a high disutility for work will be lower income earners. Are they also individuals with lower welfare? Should the government redistribute towards these individuals? Unfortunately, it seems to us that we do not have good answers for this. One possible case to think about here is to view a high disutility for work as some form of disability that limits possibilities of participation in the labour market.

Heterogeneity of preferences can be given different interpretations. Although economists typically think of preferences in terms of psychological characteristics of the individual in question, those characteristics may also have non-psychological dimensions. Sandmo (1993) noted that there is a parallel here to Sen's discussion of capabilities (see Sen 1982). Namely there is an important general problem of interpersonal variations in converting incomes into the actual ability of an individual to do this or be that. This could be rephrased to refer to work preferences in this kind of model. It is not obvious that one would want to redistribute income from those who prefer to work a lot to those who prefer to work little. Many of those politically on the right seem to believe in that way.

As is often the case with the one-dimensional optimal income tax model, we have to rely on numerical simulations. In a two-dimensional model this is even more the case. Moreover, now, the computation is much more demanding. TT (1999) used a uniform distribution of parameters (taste for work and productivity). TT (2007) in turn used a more realistic bivariate lognormal distribution, but in order to implement this more complicated distribution numerically, new computational techniques had to be developed and employed. Rather than solve the first-order conditions associated with the problem as in TT (1998), they directly compute the best tax function which can be written in terms of a second order B-spline function.

The government chooses T(.) by solving the following optimization problem:

$$\max_T \left\{ G(T, z(T)) = \int\int_{t,\omega} u(z/n, z - T(z)) f(n, \omega) dn d\omega \right\} \tag{1}$$

$$s.t. \qquad \int\int_{t,\, s} [T(z)] f(n, \omega) dn d\omega = R \tag{2}$$

where *z(T)* is a solution of the following individual's optimization problem

$$z(T) = \arg\max_z u(z/n, z - T(z)) \text{ for all } (n, \omega) \in \Omega. \quad (3)$$

There are several features of numerical results that can be seen in Figures 10.1 and 10.2. First, in the two-dimensional cases, the marginal tax rates are not monotone functions of gross income. Second, in terms of levels of marginal tax rate, there is a substantial difference between the one and two-dimensional cases. Optimal marginal tax rates are higher for almost all income levels in the two-dimensional case compared to those obtained from the one-dimensional model. In fact, there are two possibilities in the case of the one-dimensional population. Namely, if people have identical preferences but differ in abilities, we are back in the Mirrlees model. The opposite case to the Mirrlees model is the one in which diversity of preferences is the sole source of inequality. Numerical simulation was carried out for the log–log utility function:

$$u = \ln x + \omega \ln (1 - z/n) \quad (4)$$

These results shown in Figures 10.1 and 10.2 may be obvious to some, and surprising to others. At least, they are surprising to those who believe that by taking into account work preferences in the population we have an argument for a less redistributive tax/benefit system. Given our specifications, numerical results suggest that this is not necessarily so. Note also that a higher correlation between n and ω lowers marginal tax rates uniformly—or, put another way, marginal tax rates are higher when there is positive (negative) correlation between work (leisure) preferences and productivity. From Figures 10.1 and 10.2 we can also see that the marginal tax rates are increasing around average z (0.28 negative correlation, 0.26 positive correlation). What might be an intuitive explanation of these results? We know from the numerical results in Chapter 5 that a greater inherent inequality leads to higher marginal tax rates at each income level in the one-dimensional income tax model. We might reasonably expect a greater

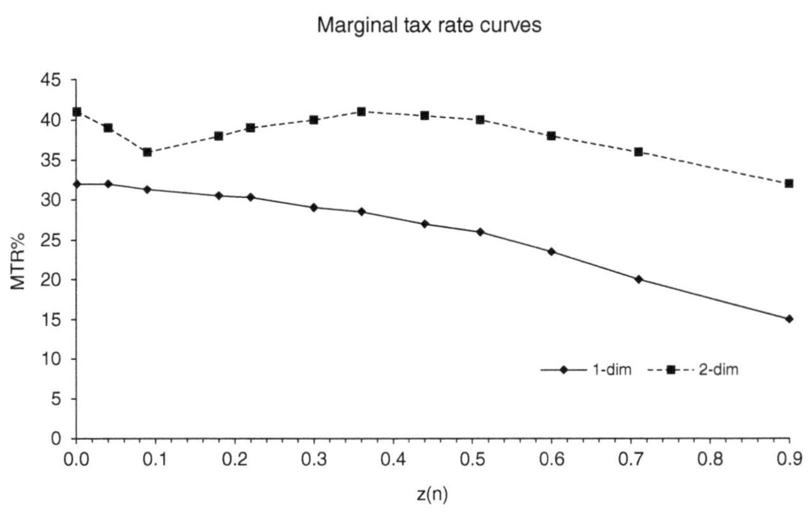

Figure 10.1 Marginal tax rates

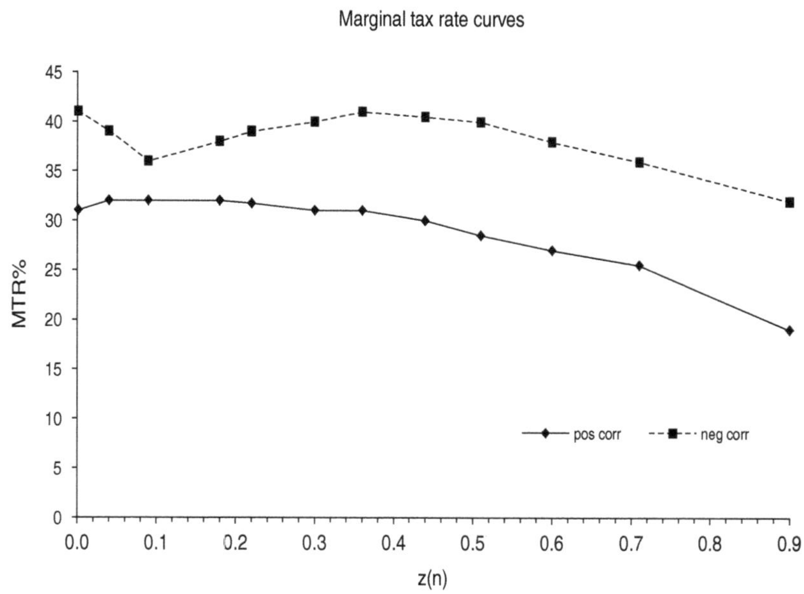

Figure 10.2 Marginal tax rates

dispersion of income in the two-dimensional world—at least, it seems to us that this is so when there is a positive correlation between work preferences and productivity. The maximization of the concave social welfare together with a greater dispersion of income will imply higher marginal tax rates. The levels of z and x are considerably higher with heterogeneous work preferences than with identical preferences. In other words, the economy with heterogeneous work preferences seems to be richer than that of identical work preferences. How can we explain this? It may be useful to consider how things are in a no-tax economy in which diversity of work preferences is the sole source of inequality. Thus people face equal opportunities in the labour market. To simplify further, this economy consists of two types of individuals who differ in their work preferences, ω_1 and ω_2, where $\omega_2 > \omega_1$. Given the utility function (4) in a no-tax economy, the demand for leisure is $(1-y) = \omega/(1+\omega)$. If we now increase dispersion of ω in this economy, average leisure decreases—or, put another way, the average labour supply increases and consequently the average gross income increases so that the economy becomes richer. One has to be careful in making comparisons between the one and two-dimensional problems. It is simply that we have different populations in different cases. Therefore we should not take literally our comparisons in Figure 10.1. They just show the solutions in the two-dimensional and the case when $\omega = 1$.

The guaranteed income, x at z=0, is higher in the two-dimensional case compared to that obtained from the one-dimensional model. Moreover, one interesting aspect of the numerical results is that there was quite little bunching. In the circumstances under which bunching occurs, each individual faces the same pre-tax income and consumption. This means that $\partial z(n;\omega)/\partial n = \partial z(n;\omega)/\partial\omega = 0$ in a subdomain of Ω. In two-dimensional problems one might expect more bunching, simply because some taxpayers with different work preferences will end up supplying the same amount of labour. In the case of Figure 10.1 ($\rho = -0.3$) the amount of bunching was about 3 per cent. In the one-dimensional case the amount of bunching turns out to be, practically speaking, zero.

The numerical results obtained direct us to influences that a richer picture of population would have on the optimal income tax schedule. On the basis of our numerical results, we conclude that the tax system is more redistributive compared to that obtained from the one-dimensional case. This may be surprising to those who believe that taking into account different work preferences is an argument for having less redistribution and hence lower levels of income taxation and social security payments. It is not easy in the two-dimensional problem to see through the mechanisms at work to determine the extent of redistribution. For example, what is the role of preferences as in (6)? Numerical results in TT (2007) seem to suggest that the correlation between n and s has a central role in determining the extent of redistribution.

TT (2007) has relied on a particular cardinalization of working preferences. One may feel uneasy about the analysis' dependence on cardinalization, but this unease concerns only the utilitarian approach as such. Indeed, within the utilitarian approach, some reliance on a specific cardinalization is unavoidable; however, it would be desirable to have a clear view of the ordinal properties of individual utility specifications and which properties depend on the cardinalization. As suggested by Sandmo (1993), these results may be interpreted in two different ways. One may fully accept the utilitarian approach even in the case of different working preferences, and read our results as such. On the other hand, one may interpret the results as an exploration of the serious limitations of the utilitarian approach.

If one supposes that persons are responsible for their own preferences, while they are not responsible for their productivity, the principles of compensation and responsibility suggest that they should be compensated for differences in their productivity, but should be neither penalized nor rewarded for differences in their preferences (Fleurbaey and Maniquet 2005). Fleurbaey and Maniquet (1998) provide an earlier analysis of optimal taxation which builds on an ordinal approach to social preferences. Boadway et al (2002) provide a general analysis of this situation and demonstrate how the tax structure depends on weights given on different types of households in the social welfare function. A plausible case is, for example, where the weight given to the utility of a hard-working low-skilled worker is higher than that of a lazy high-skilled agent. In a framework with two-dimensional heterogeneity, Schokkaert et al (2004) find the social planner may have a different idea than the individuals themselves about the 'correct' or 'reasonable' preferences for leisure. The social planner may, for instance, want to restrict the hours worked to protect the workers from exhaustion or to impose limits to work (and consumption) for ecological reasons. The latter motivation can also be related to quality-of-life vs. material welfare considerations. Applying these principles in practice is not easy, although some attempts have been made (Roemer 1998 and Roemer el al

2003).[4] In a world with full information and lump-sum taxes, it is impossible to satisfy both principles simultaneously. In their recent study, Jacquet and Van de Gaer (2011) make the interesting finding that the equality-of-opportunity approach tends to favour the negative income tax against the EITC. This is an important result because it shows that the choice between the EITC and the NIT is not only related to the nature of labour supply margins (extensive or intensive), but very much dependent on social objectives.

For those who prefer to think of the justification for redistribution as being based on inequality of opportunity, differences in preferences may provide a suitable basis for distinguishing economic rewards but differences in abilities in turn do not. This point of view raises questions on the nature of the parameters. Namely, it may be argued that both attributes (working preferences and productivity) are circumstances of birth; or, as Sandmo (1993) pointed out, there is a very fine dividing line between differences in preferences that are due on the one hand to physiological characteristics and on the other hand to psychological attitudes to work. Therefore, it is far from clear how unsuitable the welfarist (such as utilitarian) criterion is in this context. Or: how appealing are equality-of-opportunity principles inherently?

APPENDIX 10.1 A TWO-DIMENSIONAL OPTIMAL INCOME TAX PROBLEM

The economy consists of many different types of individuals who are distinguished both by earnings abilities, denoted by n, and work (or leisure) preferences, denoted by ω. Thus each individual is characterized by a vector $[n, \omega]'$ of type parameters that varies among individuals. Both characteristics, n and ω, are assumed to be private information that is not available to the government. The distribution of these type parameters in the population is given by a density function f such that $f(n, \omega) \geq 0$ on a rectangular domain $\Omega = [n_0, n_1] \times [\omega_0, \omega_1]$. There are two commodities in this economy, namely a consumption good x and labour supply y. The economy is competitive so that pre-tax pay in each job is the worker's marginal product in that job. Hence his gross income z is given by $z = ny$. The government knows that when it provides a non-linear income tax schedule $T: R^+ \rightarrow R$, where T(z) is the tax paid on gross income z, each individual maximizes his or her utility function of the following additive form:

$$u = U(x) + \omega V(y) \tag{1}$$

subject to

$$x + T(z) = z; z = ny \tag{2}$$

[4] The paper also departs from the traditional welfarist literature by considering 'responsibility-sensitive' egalitarianism, due to Roemer (1998), where individuals should only be compensated for differences in their innate skill levels, while they should be responsible for their preferences for leisure. Introducing these concerns leads typically to smaller tax rates than in the welfarist case.

in choosing his or her labour supply. We assume that u $\in C^2$, $U_x > 0$ and $V_y < 0$ for all x, y$\geq$ 0, y < 1. The higher the value of ω, the stronger is the preference for leisure or the weaker is the preference for work (or the greater is the disutility of work). The additivity assumption in (1) has very strong implications. Namely, the marginal utility of consumption is independent of work preferences.

The labour supply behaviour can be modelled by first-order partial differential equations. These are so called incentive-compatibility conditions. Next we formally introduced these conditions. For that we define the maximum value function v: $\Omega \rightarrow$R by

$$v(n,\omega) = \max\ _{x,y}\{U(x) + \omega V(y); x + T(z) = z; z = ny\} \tag{3}$$

For each (n,s) we denote the optimum of (1)-(2) by (x(n, ω), y(n, ω)), and then we have

$$v(n,\omega) = U(x(n,\omega)) + \omega V(y(n,\omega)) \tag{4}$$

We assume that x and y are differentiable with respect to n and s. When the government chooses a tax schedule T, the individuals react to this schedule and modify their labour supply behaviour. These reactions are presented by the following conditions (5) and (6). Then, by differentiating (4) with respect to n and s and making use of necessary first-order conditions of the individual's problem, (1)-(2) we obtain 'envelope' (or incentive compatibility) conditions

$$v_n = -\omega V_y/n \tag{5}$$

$$v_\omega = V \tag{6}$$

for all (n,s) $\in \Omega$.

Conditions (5) and (6) are only necessary for the individuals' choices to be optimal. Sufficient conditions for a global maximum are considered in Mirrlees (1976a). We only assume that conditions (5) and (6) are also sufficient for a global maximum so that we can substitute the individuals' utility maximization conditions by the weaker conditions (5) and (6).

We may eliminate x by inverting (4) so that x(n, ω) = ξ(v(n, ω),y(n, ω),n, ω) for all (n, ω) $\in \Omega$. Given the tax schedule T, the government can calculate the gross income z(n,s) and the consumption (net income) x(n, ω) for an individual with characteristics (n, ω). Now, by choosing y as a control and v as a state function, the problem of the utilitarian government in choosing the optimal income tax schedule can be described as follows:

$$\max_{x,v} W = \iint\limits_{\Omega} v(n,\omega) f(n,\omega) dn d\omega \tag{7}$$

subject to the envelope conditions

$$v_n = -\omega V_y/n \text{ for all } (n, \omega) \in \Omega \tag{8}$$

$$v_\omega = V \text{ for all } (n, s) \in \Omega \tag{9}$$

and the revenue constraint

$$\iint_\Omega [ny(n,\omega) - \xi(n,\omega)]f(n,\omega)dnd\omega = R \tag{10}$$

We can construct a Lagrangean[5] by defining multipliers λ for (10) and $\gamma(n, \omega)$ for (8) and $\alpha(n, \omega)$ for (9)

$$L(v,y,\lambda,\gamma) = \iint_\Omega \{[v(n,\omega)f(n,\omega) + \lambda(ny(n,\omega) - \xi(n,\omega))]\, f(n,\omega)$$
$$+\gamma(n,\omega)(v_n + \omega V_y/n) + \alpha(n,\omega)(v_\omega - V)\}dnd\omega \tag{11}$$

Using Green's formula, taking into account that $\gamma(n_0, \omega) = \gamma(n_1, \omega) = 0$, $\omega \in [\omega_0, \omega_1]$, and $\alpha(n, \omega_0) = \alpha(n, \omega_1) = 0$, $n \in [n_0, n_1]$ (transversality conditions), where n_0, ω_0, n_1, ω_1 are lower and upper bounds for n and ω, and setting the derivatives of L with respect to y and v equal to zero, we obtain:

$$T'(z) = (1 + \frac{sV_y}{nU_x}) = -\frac{\gamma(n,\omega)\omega[V_{yy}y/n + (V_y/n)]}{\lambda nf(n,\omega)} + \frac{\alpha(n,\omega)V_y}{\lambda nf(n,\omega)} \tag{12}$$

$$(1 - \frac{\lambda}{U_x})f(n,\omega) = \gamma_n + \alpha_\omega \tag{13}$$

where we have used the facts that $\xi_v g_x = 1$, $\xi_y = \xi_v \omega V_y = -\omega V_y/U_x$. Equation (12) is the marginal tax-rate formula. To say something about the properties of the tax schedule, we should be able to deduce from (12) and (13) the sign of multipliers. It is still a necessary condition for an optimum that the marginal tax rate faced by the highest income earner should be zero. This can be deduced from (12) and the transversality conditions. Thus, the optimal income tax schedule must have a zero marginal tax rate at the top, even when the preference structures underlying the work-behaviour of different consumers differ in any number of ways. The top-income person will now not necessarily be the one with the highest wage rate. This result is interesting in the sense that this property is not purely the result of an assumption that taxpayers differ only by a scalar parameter (the additivity assumption in (1) is not crucial for the result here). Unfortunately these endpoint results offer us little concrete guidance for tax policy purposes.

[5] Following Wilson (1993), this formulation can be called a relaxed version of the problem in which some of the possibly relevant constraints are omitted. Namely, we know in a one-dimensional model that relatively weak conditions suffice to ensure that the solution of the relaxed problem is the solution of the complete problem.

In sum, we can conclude that, analytically, we have no results concerning the shape of the optimal tax schedule. Therefore computer simulation is the only way to gain further insights. In fact, the most interesting results obtainable in the optimal income tax theory are numerical calculations for specific examples. It can be said that the very basic nature of income tax problems requires quantitative results. It is also good to remember that in modern physics and applied mechanics, the many partial equations encountered are almost invariably solved numerically.

If we solve y and v from (12) and (13) as a function of λ, α, γ, α_s, γ_t, n and ω, substitution in the state equations yields a system of partial differential equations for α and γ. This system seems to be rather complicated even to be solved numerically.[6] Therefore we will adopt a direct method to solve this problem numerically. Wilson (1993, 1995) describes various computational methods and solves some examples of non-linear pricing without income effects. The complexity of the multidimensional non-linear income tax problem addressed here suggests that an entirely different formulation and computational method might be useful in practice (see Tarkiainen and Tuomala 2007).

[6] In principle, the problem could be solved indirectly using necessary conditions, which must hold for a solution of the problem. However, in practice this turned out to be very difficult even in very simple cases.

11 Income uncertainty and optimal redistribution

So far we have assumed that the inequality of earnings arises from differences in abilities (and tastes) which are unalterable and are perfectly known to people when they decide what training to undergo, what jobs to do, and how many hours, weeks, and years to work. All the evidence tells us that this is not always the case. Much of inequality of earnings seems to reflect random factors that were unpredictable when many of the relevant decisions were taken. It is highly uncertain what kind of job opportunities a first-class degree will open up, how the demand for engineers will vary in the long run, etc.

An important limitation of the standard model is that there is no income uncertainty. Once skill type is revealed, individual controls income perfectly. In practice, there is considerable uncertainty in incomes. There are many relationships in economics where the agents are no better informed than the principal. This is known in insurance as moral hazard. If the agent's behaviour is unobservable, it is usually not possible to deduce the individual's action from performance when the connection between action and performance is uncertain. In many relationships this better describes the situation than the adverse selection (hidden information) model does. Therefore it is also interesting to examine the optimal income tax problem in the model as though it were a moral hazard (hidden action) model. In the pure moral hazard model, everyone is identical at the point when labour supply decisions are taken. In an optimal tax system with moral hazard, income is partly due to individual effort and partly due to luck, but the planner can only observe realized income, not effort. Mirrlees (1974) was the first to examine the design of optimal redistributive income tax under income uncertainty. This moral hazard model, later used by, among others, Varian (1980a, b); Tuomala (1984); Low and Maldoom (2004); Pirttilä and Tuomala (2007); and Boadway and Sato (2011)[1], is an alternative to the more well-known adverse selection model of Mirrlees (1971), where income dispersion arises from differences in innate skill levels. The optimal redistribution scheme is a balance between providing the workers with adequate incentives to acquire skills and sufficient insurance. Low and Maldoom (2004) show how the degree of progressivity reflects a trade-off between an insurance effect, which favours progressivity in the sense

[1] Mirrlees (1990) and Hsu and Yang (2013) analyse linear income tax with uncertainty. Both papers show that adding uncertainty always increases the marginal tax rate of the linear income tax.

of increasing marginal tax rates, and an incentive effect, which works against such progressivity.

The important question is how opinion as to the relative contributions of skill and luck to observed inequality should affect the optimum income tax system. We could describe individuals by their mean productivity M and postulate that effort y(M) maximizes $Eu(c(MSy),y)$ where S is a random variable representing the element of luck in labour supply, c is the consumption allowed by the tax system to someone who earns MSy, and u is utility function. The distribution of S is independent of M, the sum of utilities is a social objective, and total production is the sum of individual earnings (before tax). We seek the function c that maximizes $\int Eu(c(MSy),y)f(M)dM$ st.$\int E[c(MSy) - MSy]f(M)dM = R$ where y=y(M) is the function of M defined by the maximization of $Eu(c(MSy),y)$.

We should want to compare cases in which the differentiation of MS is the same but the relative variances of the components M and S are different. The case with S as a constant is studied in Mirrlees (1971). The case with M as a constant is studied in Mirrlees (1974) and Tuomala (1984).

There has been relatively little attention devoted to studying optimal income taxation when both ability differences and earnings uncertainty are present. Eaton and Rosen (1980b) considered the choice of a linear progressive income tax in a model with two ability-types and uncertain earnings. Given the difficulty of obtaining analytical results in even this simple setting, they solved some numerical examples. Depending on the parameters chosen, such as the degree of risk aversion, adding uncertainty to the standard optimal redistribution problem with two ability-types could either increase or decrease the optimal linear tax rate. Tuomala (1979, 1990) considers non-linear taxation when individuals do not fully know their productivity skills in making labour supply decisions. Again, given the complexity of the problem, numerical solutions are needed.

It seems to us that the right kind of model in which to examine the question of implications of luck and ability is one in which some labour decisions are made early, under imperfect information, while others are made at the last moment, under full information. Along these lines, Tuomala (1986) considers a model in which individuals first decide how much educational training to have without accurately knowing their own abilities. Educational training reveals their abilities to themselves, and on the basis of known abilities they make their labour supply decisions.

There is another, more recent, body of literature on the effect of uncertainty on optimal redistribution policy. In the so-called new dynamic public finance literature, the emphasis is on uncertainty in an intertemporal setting (Golosov et al 2007; Kocherlakota 2010). Ability is heterogeneous, but evolves in a stochastic manner period-by-period. In each period, individuals choose their labour supply and their saving knowing their current skills, but having only expectations of their future skills. Much of the emphasis in this literature is on the implications for the taxation of capital income, with the typical finding that capital income should face positive taxation. We shall return to this topic in the context of capital income taxation in Chapter 14. A lower level of saving makes it more difficult for taxpayers who turn out to be high-skilled to mimic those with lower skills. In a related context, Cremer and Gahvari (1995) show that with wage uncertainty, a case can be made for giving preferential commodity tax treatment to consumer durables. They assume that individuals or households allocate their disposable income to many goods. Some goods can be purchased after wages are known, while others—durables—must be chosen before wage uncertainty is resolved. Subsidizing the purchase of consumer durables makes it more difficult for the high-skilled to mimic the low-skilled.

Income tax is only one element, albeit an important one, in the design of optimal government redistributive policy. Indeed, recent optimal tax literature has devoted a lot of attention to the use of other instruments, such as commodity taxation, minimum wages, and public provision of public or private goods. Introducing distortions to the choice in these tools can be useful if the additional distortions help alleviate existing distortions arising from asymmetric information. We come back to these questions in Chapters 12 and 13 both with and without income uncertainty. Income uncertainty, and the need to deal with it by offering social insurance, is also an important part of the concerns of real-world tax policy.

As does much of the moral hazard literature, this chapter utilizes the so-called first-order approach for solving the optimization problem. In this approach, the incentive compatibility constraint is captured by a local maximization constraint of the individuals in a way shown below. Mirrlees (1975, 1999) was the first to point out that this procedure may not necessarily be valid and, consequently, may fail to provide a global optimum.

11.1 **The moral hazard optimal income tax model**

Consider an economy, as in Mirrlees (1974), where the worker–consumer does not know what income, z, he or she will receive for each possible level of effort, y. In other words, income is determined both by effort and by some random element. We denote the distribution for z, given that effort y is undertaken by the worker, as $F(z,y)$, and its density as $f(z,y)$. It is assumed that $f(z,y)$ and $F(z,y)$ are continuous and continuously differentiable for all $z \in [z_0,z_1]$ and y. Moreover, we assume that the support of this distribution is independent of y. The worker–consumer chooses effort y to maximize expected utility:

$$\int u(x)f(z,y)dz - y, \tag{1}$$

where $x = z - T(z)$ is the after-tax income/consumption. As in much of the literature, we concentrate on an additively separable specification of the utility function. The consumer is risk-averse, hence $u' > 0$, $u'' < 0$. The first-order condition for the maximization of (1) is

$$\int u(x)f_y dz - 1 = 0. \tag{2}$$

The government is utilitarian and maximizes (1) subject to the individual optimization constraint (2) and the budget constraint which, for a large identical population with independent and identically distributed states of nature, can be written in the form:

$$\int [z - x]f(z, y)dz = 0. \tag{3}$$

Taking multipliers α and λ for the constraints (2) and (3) respectively, from the first-order condition we obtain the marginal tax rate ($MTR = T'(z)$)

$$MTR = 1 - x' = 1 - \frac{\alpha u'\zeta'}{\lambda\delta} \tag{4}$$

where $\zeta = f_y/f$ is the likelihood ratio or the elasticity of output probability with respect to effort and $\delta = -(u'')/(u')$ is the coefficient of absolute risk aversion. This approach, where incentive compatibility is modelled using equation (2), is the so-called first-order approach (FOA).[2] In the non-linear income tax model, the most interesting question is without doubt how marginal tax rates behave as a function of income. When the incentive compatibility constraint is slack, $\alpha = 0$, the optimal marginal tax rate is 100 per cent. This is the case of full insurance, which risk-averse individuals value. However, when incentives to undertake effort matter, the optimal marginal tax rate is a compromise between risk aversion and providing incentives. If the consumers become more risk-averse (δ increases), the marginal tax rate increases, *ceteris paribus*. On the other hand, if effort is more tightly connected with income (ζ' goes up), workers' effort can be more reliably tracked, and the optimal marginal tax rate is reduced. Key steps for demonstrating this include showing that the after-tax income is increasing in income ($x'(z) > 0$) and that the government's maximization problem is concave.[3] As shown in Tuomala (1984), the sign of $x''(z)$ is not unambiguous. Hence we cannot comment on the progressivity in the sense of an increasing marginal tax rate with income. Note, however, that in this setting it is not possible to prove the zero marginal tax rate at the top. In fact, it is more likely that the marginal tax rate of top incomes is rather high. While the probability of being the most productive in the society is so small, the incentive losses from the severe taxing of the ex post most productive taxpayer is in turn very small. By and large, the tax schedule in this simple model is so complicated that it is difficult to say much about the shape of the optimal tax schedule without numerical

[2] Mirrlees (1975, 1999) was the first to point out that FOA is not necessarily a valid procedure in a potentially large number of cases, because it might lead to a local instead of a global optimum. Mirrlees (1976b), Rogerson (1985), Jewitt (1988), and Alvi (1997) have explored conditions for the validity of the FOA.

[3] In numerical simulations, one can also find solutions that are valid but do not satisfy CDFC (See e.g. Low and Maldoom 2004).

solutions for some specific examples. Before turning to numerical examples it is of some interest to note that in the case where the utility function takes the Cobb–Douglas form and the income distribution is gamma distribution, the tax schedule becomes linear (see Tuomala 1984). Thus marginal tax rate is constant, but of course, when the intercept of the consumption schedule is positive, the average tax rates are increasing in income, z. Another interesting question is the existence of optimal policy in this setting—namely, Mirrlees (1974) noted that under quite reasonable assumptions (income is distributed lognormally and utility is unbounded), there is strictly speaking no optimal policy. In the lognormal case, f_y/f tends to $-\infty$ when z tends to 0. But now according to equation (4) this is inconsistent with any positive value of α. Such a case is possible only when α=0 holds. This situation does not give an optimal policy. In this case, from the government's point of view, it is more advantageous to induce taxpayers to approach the efficient level of effort by threatening them with a sufficiently large penalty if they fail to meet some minimum income level. In other words, any feasible consumption schedule that is positive for all z yields expected utility which is strictly less than the first-best solution. Hence the government can achieve this outcome as though the incentive constraint could be ignored. It should be emphasized, however, that this result is true only under certain conditions. In particular, unbounded utility is essential. Another questionable assumption in this model is that people can calculate events of a small probability. Does this result have any practical relevance? It is clear an outcome of this kind is unacceptable. Does this then imply that we need an additional constraint or a different social welfare function? This is also closely related to the question of whether one should formulate the welfare function using the ex post or ex ante utilities of individuals. One of the main arguments against ex ante utilities is the potential difference between subjective and objective probabilities. In fact, we have assumed that the two are equal. Thus discussions about this issue do not arise in this model here. For such discussions, see e.g. Mirrlees (1974); Broome (1978); Atkinson and Stiglitz (1980).

11.2 **Numerical simulations**

In the tradition of the non-linear taxation literature, Pirttilä and Tuomala (2007) provide further insight of the form of $c(z)$ through numerical simulations. They consider the case where the worker has the following non-separable utility function $u(c,y) = \frac{c^{1-\gamma}}{1-\gamma}(a + by^{-\beta}) - y$, where $a > 0$, $b > 0$, $\beta > 0$.[4] Suppose further that $\gamma > 1$ (i.e. the consumer's risk aversion corresponds to empirically valid measures). The utility function reduces to a standard separable case, used among others by Low and Maldoom (2004), when $a + by^{-\beta} = 1$. The consumption function c(z) takes the form $c(z) = ((1+\alpha h)(a+by^{-\beta}) - \alpha\beta by^{-\beta-1})/\lambda)^{1/\gamma}$. Then c(z) is concave in its positive section, meaning that the marginal tax rate

[4] The cross-derivative $u_{cy} = -\beta by^{-\beta-1}c^{-\gamma}<0$, as required by the assumptions of the FOA.

has a convex shape. The calculations were carried out, for simplicity, with the exponential distribution,[5] $f(z,y) = (1/y)e^{-(z/y)}$.

Table 11.1 displays the average (ATR) and marginal (MTR) tax rates across the income distribution. Table 11.1 shows that marginal and average tax rates are higher for all income levels in a non-separable case than in a separable case. Furthermore, individuals put in more effort in a non-separable case than in a separable case.

Table 11.2 compares effort, y, and inequality measure, P(90/50) (percentile ratio), under autarky (= no social insurance) and social insurance (socins) for the distribution of consumption, c, and gross income, z. Note the gross income (pre-tax) distribution is here endogenous. The consumption (post-tax) P(90/50) under social insurance (2.20, 2.04) is lower than the ratio under autarky (3.32, 3.33). To sum up, both informal examination of the tax rule and the simulation results suggest that the marginal tax rates, solved with a non-separable utility function, tend to rise in comparison to those based on standard, separable, utility.

11.3 **Prospect theory and moral hazard**

Above, as in most principal-agent analysis, expected utility theory is used as a description of agents' behaviour under uncertainty. In his Nobel Lecture, Mirrlees (1997, p. 1324) calls for closer scrutiny of this approach:

Table 11.1 Tax rates

γ =1.2	Separable utility	Revenue requirement=0	Non-separable utility	a=0.5, b=0.1, β=0.5
F(z,y)	ATR%	MTR%	ATR%	MTR%
0.10	−25	30	−31	40
0.50	−8	39	−10	47
0.90	29	48	33	54
0.99	40	53	45	58
		y=0.30	y=0.37	

Source: Pirttilä and Tuomala, 2007.

Table 11.2 Effort and inequality

	Effort y		P(90/50)		
	Autarky	Socins	Autarky	Socins(c)	Socins (z)
Separable	0.50	0.30	3.32	2.20	3.35
Non-separable	0.48	0.37	3.33	2.04	3.34

Source: Pirttilä and Tuomala, 2007.

[5] This satisfies the MLRC property since $\partial(f_y/f)/\partial z = \frac{1}{y^2} > 0$.

Problems of this kind are usually analysed with the assumption that people try to maximise their expected utility. There are good reasons for thinking that may be a mistake. At least the consequences of alternative theories of decisions under uncertainty for these situations should be explored.

One such alternative theory of decision-making under uncertainty is prospect theory, developed by Kahneman and Tversky (1979) and modified by Tversky and Kahneman (1992), which has garnered significant empirical support (see Kahneman's Nobel lecture, 2003, and Camerer and Lowenstein 2003). In prospect theory, an individual's utility depends on how the outcome deviates from some reference point, rather than directly on the absolute value of the outcome. Individuals are loss-averse; in other words, a loss leads to a larger change in welfare than a gain of a similar size. Finally, individuals may misperceive probabilities underlying the decision problem. In his review of alternative theories for expected utility theory, Starmer (2000, p. 376) concludes that because of many appealing features of rank-dependent or sign-dependent models of decision-making under uncertainty, such as prospect theory, 'there seems good reason to push forward the task of examining what implications such models have in general economic contexts'. In the original Mirrlees (1974) formulation of the income tax model, workers and the government maximize workers' expected utility over income and effort. Kanbur, Pirttilä, and Tuomala (2008) (KPT hereafter) introduce elements of prospect theory into individual behaviour, in keeping with the emerging empirical consensus, to examine how optimal taxation results change with the introduction of prospect theory preferences. They first assume that the government respects the individual preferences, i.e. it is a 'welfarist' government. However, there are elements in prospect theory that may or may not be desirable from the social welfare point of view. For instance, the social planner may dislike the consumers' tendency to be risk-seeking for losses. Therefore, they also consider the case where the government is 'non-welfarist' (paternalistic) and its objective function may differ from that used by the individuals.

We consider first the welfarist case where individual behaviour is described by prospect theory, and this is also accepted as a basis for social welfare. In prospect theory, the utility function is replaced by a value function. The key assumptions about the value function are that it 'is (i) defined on deviations from the reference point; (ii) generally concave for gains and convex for losses; (iii) steeper for losses than for gains' (Kahneman and Tversky 1979, p. 281). The two latter properties capture the idea that individuals are loss-averse.

For simplicity, let us concentrate on the case where prospect theory is only related to the utility of income. Individuals now maximize the expectation of the value function v(c)

$$\int v(d)f(z,y)dz - y, \tag{5}$$

where $d = x - \bar{x}$ denotes the change in realized income from a reference income, depicted by $\bar{x}$. The reference income is assumed to be exogenous. Note that the utility function is still assumed to be additively separable between effort and income.

If there was a reference point for effort level, too, within this quasi-linear model, along the lines of $\int v(d)f(z,y)dz - (y - \bar{y})$, the reference level would not change (1'). However, with a general, non-separable, formulation, $\int v(d, y - \bar{y})f(z,y)dz$, the validity of the FOA is a complicated matter even without reference levels, as shown by Alvi (1997). A possibility for loss aversion on either side of the reference level for y—the individuals could lose both from working less or more than the reference level—would add to the complexity.

The individual's first-order condition can be rewritten as

$$\int v(x)f_y dz - 1 = 0. \tag{6}$$

The marginal tax rate is

$$MTR = 1 - x' = 1 - \frac{\alpha v'\zeta'}{\lambda \delta_e} \tag{7}$$

where $\delta_v = -v''/v'$ is the coefficient of the individual attitude towards risk (see appendix 11 for the derivation).

To provide incentives for exerting effort, x should be increasing in z.[6]

An example: it is difficult to characterize the tax schedule in more detail within the general model. KPT (2008) therefore consider the following example, where the utility function and the distribution function are assumed to take certain functional forms. Note this also explicitly allows for the kink in the utility function. Suppose first that the utility function is

$$v(x) = \frac{(x - \bar{x})^{1-\beta}}{1 - \beta}, \quad if \quad (x - \bar{x}) \geq 0 \tag{8a}$$

$$v(x) = -h\frac{(\bar{x} - x)^{1-\beta}}{1 - \beta}, \quad if \quad (x - \bar{x}) < 0, h \geq 1. \tag{8b}$$

The form in (8a) is of CRRA form and similar to what has been used in simulations of the moral hazard model, such as those in Tuomala (1984). The function in (8b) is otherwise similar, but it includes h, which is a loss-aversion parameter. The function also satisfies the conditions that $v'' < 0$ above the reference point and $v'' > 0$ below the reference point.

[6] In order to be sure that the first-order approach is valid in this case with prospect theory preferences we need to see how consumption is related to effort.

Consider first the area above the reference point. Substituting (8a) in the first-order condition yields:

$$x = \left(\frac{1}{\lambda} + \frac{\mu}{\lambda}\zeta\right)^{(1/\beta)} + \bar{x}. \tag{9}$$

Suppose now that the distribution function is a gamma distribution, $f(z,y) = \{b/\Gamma(r)\}(bz)^{r-1} y^{-r} e^{-(bz/y)}$. Then it can be shown that the likelihood ratio has the following form, $\zeta = f_y/f = bz/y^2 + (1+r)/y$. The likelihood ratio is also linear in z. Assuming $A + Bz > 0$, consumption is determined by

$$x(z) = (A + Bz)^{(1/\beta)} + \bar{x}, \tag{10}$$

where $A = (1/\lambda - \alpha s/\lambda y)$, $B = \alpha b/\lambda y^2$, and $s = r - 1$. In the example below, r=2.75 and b=3. If g is linear in z (as in gamma and exponential distributions), the tax schedule will have a declining marginal tax rate if $\beta < 1$ and increasing marginal tax rate if $\beta > 1$. These results are the same as in the standard model. In calculations we have $\beta = 1.2$.

We now turn to the implications of (8b). Combining it with the first-order condition implies

$$x(z) = \bar{x} - h(A + Bz)^{(1/\beta)}. \tag{11}$$

This equation implies that x is decreasing in $z \in (z_0, z^*)$, where z_0 is the smallest z and x $=\bar{x}$ at z = z*. In this example the consumption level offered at the lower end is just equal to the reference consumption. Therefore, using these functional forms, the optimal contract offers full insurance below the reference point, as illustrated in Figure 11.1. Needless to say, this is not a general result, but it does suggest that it can be optimal to lengthen the flat part of the consumption schedule downwards from reference consumption.

In Figure 11.1 we see that the shape of the optimal income tax schedule becomes more progressive when $\bar{x}$ increases. Our calculations showed that the flat segment covers about 4 per cent of the population with $\bar{x}$=0.1 (30 per cent of mean consumption) and 3 per cent with $\bar{x}$=0.23 (50 per cent of mean income). The mean x and z also increase with $\bar{x}$.

As is well known, in the expected utility version, one can approximate the first best outcome with an extreme punishment for the worst possible outcome and full insurance for all other outcomes. Usually the possibility for this 'capital punishment' is assumed away, but its existence is still an undesirable outcome of the basic moral hazard model, as Mirrlees (1997) has pointed out. It is interesting that our example provides an escape route from this problem by providing full insurance for low values of gross income. In this sense, prospect theory helps the motivation to work with the otherwise standard version of moral hazard.

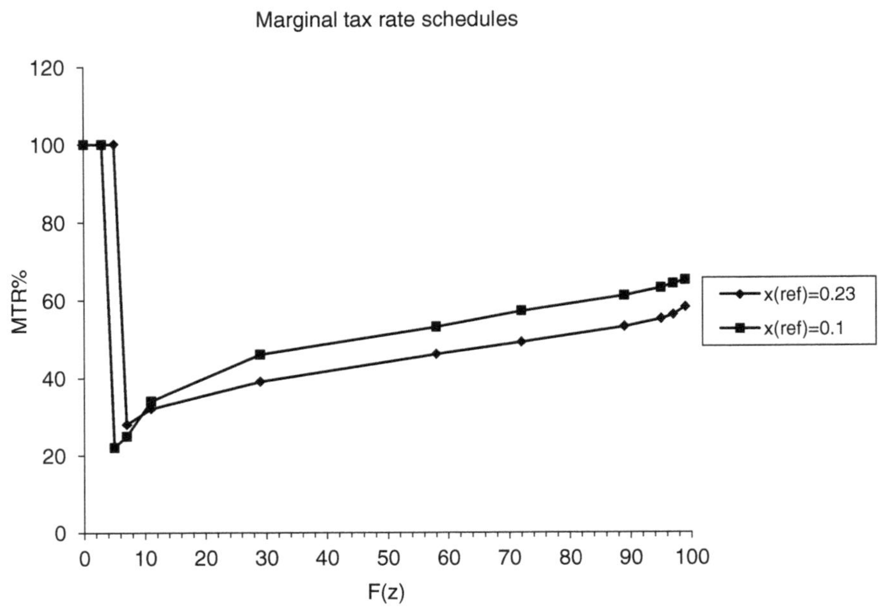

Figure 11.1 Marginal tax rates with two different reference consumption levels

11.4 **Prospect theory non-welfarism**

It is not necessarily clear that the social planner ought to accept all facets of prospect theory when forming its social objectives. There is, for example, some evidence according to which people underestimate their ability to cope with negative life-events, for instance income losses (see the discussion in Frey and Stutzer 2004). Loewenstein et al (2002) provide theoretical reasoning for this behaviour based on projection bias. The projection bias can therefore imply that the utility function governing individuals' long-term welfare is different from that of their short-term welfare.[7] But to the extent that loss aversion is real, it should, of course, be respected when evaluating social welfare.

Perhaps a stronger case for paternalism could be built on the idea that the government is not willing to accept risk-loving over the domain of losses. The society may want to restrict gambles on stakes involved in income taxation. We therefore also consider the case where the government's and the individual's objective functions differ. The individual still maximizes the same value function (v) as in the previous section, but the government's objective function is globally concave, as in the expected utility model, and denoted by u. Because of the concavity, it does not also involve any approximated kink near the reference point.

[7] Some forms of prospect theory also include biases in evaluating probabilities. These biases provide further reasons for paternalism, akin to Sandmo (1983).

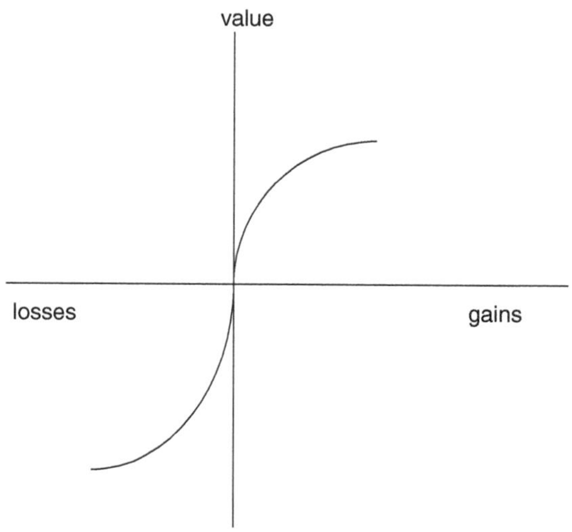

Figure 11.2 An example of a value function

The introduction of non-welfarism brings with it the interesting point that if the government's willingness to override loss-seeking behaviour is sufficiently strong, one can avoid randomization over the domain of losses. Because of the potential complexities of carrying out randomization in the real world, this may be a desirable outcome from paternalism. But at the reference point, the tax schedule still offers full insurance (marginal tax rate equal to 100 per cent).[8] Even though the government is non-welfarist, and its objective function does not directly include loss aversion, it must take individuals' preferences into account through the incentive compatibility constraint (see appendix 11.1 for technical details).

APPENDIX 11.1 THE MORAL HAZARD MODEL: THE STANDARD MODEL

Taking multipliers α and λ for the constraints (2) and (3) in the text respectively, the Lagrangean and the first-order condition with respect to x (pointwise optimization) are as follows:

$$L = \int \{[u(x) + \lambda(z - x)]f(z, y) + \alpha u(x) f_y\} dz - \alpha - y \tag{1}$$

$$1 + \alpha\zeta = \frac{\lambda}{u'}, \tag{2}$$

[8] It is of some interest to note that consumption is (weakly) monotonically increasing in gross income. Namely, when the FOA is valid below the reference point, consumption is increasing in gross income for small gross incomes, it is constant at the reference point over some interval of gross incomes, and finally above that interval consumption is increasing in gross income.

where $\zeta = f_y/f$ is the likelihood ratio. This approach, where incentive compatibility is modelled using equation (2), is the so-called FOA. Mirrlees (1975, 1999) was the first to point out that FOA is not necessarily a valid procedure in a potentially large number of cases, because it might lead to a local instead of a global optimum. Mirrlees (1976b), Rogerson (1985), Jewitt (1988), and Alvi (1997) have explored conditions for the validity of the FOA. When the utility function is separable as in our set-up, sufficient conditions are:

1. Monotone likelihood ratio condition, MLRC: $\partial\zeta/\partial z > 0$. Income is increasing stochastically in effort, that is, higher output is more likely for higher effort than lower effort.
2. Convexity of the distribution function condition, CDFC: $F_{yy}(z,y) > 0$. This is like a diminishing returns condition, applied to the production of information of worker's action.

Key steps for demonstrating this include showing that the after-tax income is increasing in income ($x'(z) > 0$) and that the government's maximization problem is concave. Appendix 1 in KPT (2008) provides details of the proof. In numerical simulations, one can also find solutions that are valid but do not satisfy CDFC (see e.g. Low and Maldoom 2004).

We can now turn to the properties of the solution. Differentiation of (5) again with respect to z, substitution and reorganisation yield the shape of $x'(z)$:

$$x' = -\frac{\alpha(u')^2\zeta'}{\lambda u''}. \tag{3}$$

Denote the coefficient of absolute risk aversion as $\delta = -(u'')/(u')$. Hence we get eq. (4) in the text.

This equation shows that without the need to consider incentives, i.e. when the incentive compatibility constraint is slack, $\alpha = 0$, the optimal marginal tax rate is 100 per cent. This is the case of full insurance, which risk-averse individuals value. However, when incentives to undertake effort matter, the optimal marginal tax rate is a compromise between risk aversion and providing incentives. If the consumers become more risk-averse (δ increases), the marginal tax rate increases, *ceteris paribus*. On the other hand, if effort is more tightly connected with income (ζ' goes up), workers' effort can be more reliably tracked, and the optimal marginal tax rate is reduced.

KPT (2008) show in appendix 1 that the following assumptions are sufficient conditions for the validity of the first-order approach for the problem at hand.

1. Monotone likelihood ratio condition, MLRC: $\partial\zeta/\partial z > 0$. Income is increasing stochastically in effort, that is, higher output is more likely for higher effort than lower effort. The MLRC also implies the stochastic dominance condition (SDC), $F_y(z,y) \leq 0$.
2. Convex distribution function condition, CDFC: $F_{yy}(z,y) > 0$. This is like a diminishing returns condition, applied to the production of information of worker's action.

3. Normality of leisure, $\frac{\partial(-\frac{u_y}{u_c})}{\partial c}$ >0. This is implied by $u_{yc} \leq 0$ and $u_{cc} < 0$. Note $x = c(z)$
4. Increasing effort increases absolute risk aversion (IEIARA), $\frac{\partial \kappa}{\partial y} \geq 0$, where $\kappa(c(z), y) = \frac{-u_{cc}}{u_c}$ is the coefficient of absolute risk aversion.

APPENDIX 11.2 PROSPECT THEORY AND MORAL HAZARD

In prospect theory, the utility function is replaced by a value function. The key assumptions about the value function are that it 'is (i) defined on deviations from the reference point; (ii) generally concave for gains and convex for losses; (iii) steeper for losses than for gains' (Kahneman and Tversky 1979, p. 280). The two latter properties capture the idea that individuals are loss-averse. Hence, the value function takes the S-shaped value as in Figure 1.

The reference income is assumed to be exogenous.[9] Note that the utility function is still assumed to be additively separable between effort and income.

To capture the shape of the value function, we make the following assumptions about the properties of the utility function:

$(i)\ v' > 0$
$(ii)\ v'(-d) \geq v'(d)$
$(iii)\ v'' > 0\ for\ d < 0,\ v'' < 0\ for\ d > 0$

Assumption (ii) captures the principle of loss aversion: 'losses loom larger than corresponding gains' (Tversky and Kahneman 1992, p. 303). Assumption (iii) refers to 'diminishing sensitivity for losses and gains', i.e. a diminishing marginal utility for losses and diminishing marginal disutility for losses.

The specification in (ii) allows for non-differentiability in $v(d)$ at d=0. In fact, much of the standard representation of prospect theory is in terms of a 'kink' at zero. However, in this chapter we assume that the function $v(d)$ is everywhere differentiable. This is because the purpose of this paper is to study to what extent one can utilize first-order conditions for analysing tax optima, and in particular the extent to which the standard first-order approach can be modified. This implies that we are by definition in a world of differentiable functions, thus excluding kinks. However, even without kinks the key features of prospect theory as stated in (i), (ii), and (iii) can be captured with differentiable functions and, furthermore, one can with suitable functional forms and parameter values approach arbitrarily closely the description of individuals' choices even if they were generated by a function with a kink. Nevertheless, we return to the case where the kink exists via an example at the end of this section.

[9] Some of the implications of endogenizing the reference point were explored in an earlier version of this chapter (see Kanbur et al 2004).

We are now in a position to rewrite the government's optimization problem. The individual's first-order condition can be rewritten as

$$\int v(x)f_y dz - 1 = 0.^{10} \tag{1}$$

The Lagrangean and the first-order condition with respect to x (pointwise optimization) are now as follows:

$$L = \int \left\{ [v(d) + \lambda(z - x)] f(z, y) + \alpha v(d) f_y \right\} dz - \alpha - y, \tag{2}$$

$$1 + \alpha\zeta = \frac{\lambda}{v'}. \tag{3}$$

We first examine whether the first-order approach is valid in this case with prospect theory preferences. For this, we need to see how consumption is related to effort. Differentiate (3) again with respect to z and reorganize to obtain the shape of $x'(z)$:

$$x' = -\frac{\alpha (v')^2 \zeta'}{\lambda v''}. \tag{4}$$

The marginal tax rate is then written as (7) in the text.

To provide incentives for exerting effort, x should be increasing in z. Depending on whether realized income is above or below the reference income, $\bar{x}$, three cases emerge.

1) For income above the reference income, $d > 0$, consumption x is indeed increasing in income z, since the value function has similar properties to the standard case of Section 2. In other words, $u = v$. The first-order approach is valid (following the arguments of equations (A1)–(A4) in KPT (2008)), and the marginal tax rate is given by (7).
2) If $d = 0$, the right-hand side of (A1) is not defined.
3) If the income is below the reference income, $c < 0$, the right-hand side of (4), i.e. $x'(z)$, is non-negative only if $\alpha < 0$, since $v''>0$. Using a similar procedure as in appendix 1 in KPT (2008), one can determine the sign of α from

$$\begin{aligned} \frac{\alpha}{\lambda}\int v f_y dz &= cov(v, \frac{1}{v'}) \\ \frac{\alpha}{\lambda} &= cov(v, \frac{1}{v'}), \end{aligned} \tag{5}$$

where the second line follows from (1). Equation (5) is a counterpart of the earlier equation (A3). Now v and v' covary in the same directions for $d < 0$, we necessarily have

[10] Similarly to the standard model, the second-order condition of individual optimization will be satisfied when the first-order approach as a whole is valid.

$\alpha \leq 0$. However, the only case where the covariance is zero is when x is constant irrespective of income. But then the worker has no incentives to provide positive effort. Therefore, to induce effort, $\alpha < 0$.

However, if $\alpha < 0$, a relaxation in the incentive constraint reduces the social welfare determined by (2). For a meaningful government optimization problem this cannot hold. Therefore, one must conclude that the FOA is not valid for income below the reference level. Proposition 1 summarizes the earlier discussion.

Proposition 1. In a moral hazard tax problem, when the individuals' decision-making is based on prospect theory, the FOA is valid if income is above the reference point. When income is below the reference point, the FOA is not valid.

The optimal solution is therefore non-continuous. For consumption above the reference level, the marginal tax rate is given by (7). For income below the reference point, a randomized schedule is optimal. To see this, recall that the convexity of the value function implies that the consumer is in fact risk-loving if income is below the reference point. It is therefore conceivable why conditions needed for an insurance scheme are then not valid. The point that randomization may be desirable in a moral hazard context is not new. Holmström (1979) and Arnott and Stiglitz (1988) have shown, however, that randomization is never optimal for a standard, concave, moral hazard problem as in Section 2. Rather, it can become optimal in more complicated situations (Arnott and Stiglitz 1988).[11] The optimality of randomization depends on the magnitude of diminishing sensitivity for losses. It may be the case that for stakes on the scale involved in income taxation, diminishing sensitivity for losses may not hold. In this case, the tax rate could remain continuous.

The next step is to characterize the tax schedule in more detail. Usually loss aversion is introduced by a kink at the reference consumption. This is not necessarily a major issue. We can always approximate arbitrarily well any kinked value function.[12] If −v'' is very large in the neighbourhood of the reference consumption, we can approximate a kinked function by a differentiable one. In an approximation, e' would fall continuously in an interval $[\bar{x}, \bar{x} + \varepsilon]$ and v'' would approach $-\infty$. From (4) we see that when v'' is very large, x' is close to zero. Let denote $x(z^{\star}) = \bar{x}$ and $x(\hat{z}) = \bar{x} + \varepsilon$. Since e'(x) is constant over the short interval, it implies $v'(\bar{x})\zeta(z^{\star}) \approx v'(\bar{x} + \varepsilon)\zeta(\hat{z})$. This shows that consumption x(z) is constant at $\bar{x}$ over the interval $[z^{\star}, \hat{z}]$. The net income is insensitive to gross income over this interval. In other words, the marginal tax rate is 100 per cent in that range. Beyond $\hat{z}$, consumption is monotonically increasing in z. Combining this discussion and the point about randomization, one can deduce the following.[13]

[11] Of course, the question remains how randomization can be implemented in real-world tax policy. One of the ideas presented in this context is lax control of tax evasion. Another example is related to poverty traps due to the interaction of social benefits and taxation. Then for low incomes, a minor change in before-tax income can generate a large variation in after-tax income.

[12] We are very grateful to a referee for this point.

[13] It is possible that x(z) cannot cross the reference level. We rule out this possibility here.

Proposition 2. In a moral hazard tax problem, when the individuals' decision-making is based on prospect theory and MLRC holds, the following features characterize optimal tax schedule:

(i) 100 per cent marginal tax rate at the reference point over the interval of gross income $[z^*, \hat{z}]$.
(ii) Optimal consumption is increasing above the reference point (as in the standard model without loss aversion).
(iii) It is not optimal to have consumption between a minimum consumption and the reference consumption.

The intuition for this result is that around the reference point, the individual is extremely risk-averse, and therefore it is locally optimal to provide full insurance. In the area below the reference point the individual prefers a gamble. Hence we have a randomized tax schedule between a minimum consumption and the reference consumption below the reference point. Above the reference point, the determinants of the tax schedule are similar to the standard model with expected utility.

Prospect theory non-welfarism

The Lagrangean and the first-order conditions can now be written as

$$L = \int \left\{ [u(x) + \lambda(z - x)] f(z, y) + \alpha v(x) f_y \right\} dz - \alpha - y, \tag{6}$$

$$u' f + \alpha v' f_y - \lambda f = 0. \tag{7}$$

To determine how consumption is related to income, differentiate (7) with respect to z to get

$$x' = \frac{\alpha v' \zeta'}{u' \delta_u + \delta_v (\lambda - u')}, \tag{8}$$

where $\delta_u = -u''/u'$ is the social coefficient of absolute risk aversion and $\delta_v = -v''/v'$ is the coefficient of the individual attitude towards risk. For $c > 0$, the individual is risk-averse, and δ_v is defined to be positive. However, for $c < 0$, because of diminishing marginal disutility for losses the individual is in fact risk-loving, and $\delta_v < 0$. The term $\lambda - u'$ is positive because of (7). The marginal tax rate is

$$MTR = 1 - x' = 1 - \frac{\alpha v' \zeta'}{u' \delta_u + \delta_v (\lambda - u')}. \tag{9}$$

Let us now examine the conditions for the validity of the first-order approach. Appendix 2 demonstrates that the same conditions, namely MLRC and the CDFC, still constitute part of the sufficient conditions. In addition, consumption x should be increasing in income z. For $c > 0$, this is always the case because then $\delta_e \geq 0$, and the denominator in (4) and the term at the right of (8) are positive.

If $c < 0$, the denominator in (8) may be either positive or negative, depending on the strength of diminishing marginal disutility for losses. Then the FOA remains valid if the individuals' risk-loving is sufficiently smaller than the social coefficient of risk aversion, i.e. $v'\delta_v > -\delta_e(\lambda - v')$. However, if the individual is sufficiently risk-loving, $v'\delta_v < -\delta_e(\lambda - v')$, the denominator and the right-hand side of (8) are negative, i.e. consumption would be decreasing in income (effort). The following proposition summarizes:

Proposition 3. In a non-welfarist moral hazard tax problem, when the individuals' decision-making is based on prospect theory, the FOA is valid if income is above the reference point. The FOA is also valid below the reference point if the government's risk aversion sufficiently outweighs individuals' diminishing sensitivity for losses.

Notice that around the reference consumption level, the individual is very risk-averse, and therefore $\delta_v = -v''/v'$ is very large. This means that at the reference level, $v'\delta_v < -\delta_v(\lambda - u')$ always holds. Even if the FOA would hold in the area below the reference point, it can never be a global solution.

APPENDIX 11.3 NUMERICAL SOLUTION: THE STANDARD MODEL

From the Lagrangean

$$L = \int\{[u(c) + \lambda(z - c)]f(z, y) + \mu u(c)f_y\}dz - \mu - y$$

we get

$$\frac{\partial L}{\partial c(z)} = u_c f + \mu u_c f_y - \lambda f = 0$$

eli $1 + \mu\zeta = \frac{\lambda}{u_c}$,

where $\zeta = f_y / f$.

and

$$\frac{\partial L}{\partial y} = \lambda\int(z - c)f_y dz + \mu\int u f_{yy} dz = 0$$

If $u = \frac{c^{1-p}}{1-p} - y$, so $(p \geq 1)$

$$c(z) = ((1 + \mu\zeta)/\lambda)^{1/p}.$$

Suppose f is the gamma distribution, $\zeta = f_y/f = \frac{bz}{y^2} + \frac{1-r}{y}, f(z, y) = \frac{b}{\Gamma(r)}(bz/y)^{r-1}e^{-(bz/y)}$

Now $c(z) = (A + Bz)^{1/p}$, $p \geq 1$,

where $A = (\frac{1}{\lambda} - \frac{\mu s}{\lambda y}), B = \frac{\mu b}{\lambda y^2}$, where s=r−1

A solution method: **x**= $(y,\mu,\lambda)^T$ can be solved by Newton's iteration method from the equation system

$$\frac{\partial L}{\partial y} = \lambda \int (z-c) f_y dz + \mu \int u f_{yy} dz = 0 \qquad GL(\text{inprogram})$$

$$\frac{\partial L}{\partial \mu} = \int u(c) f_y dz - 1 = 0 \qquad \text{GY(inprogram)}$$

$$\frac{\partial L}{\partial \lambda} = \int [z - c(z)] f(z,y) = 0 \qquad \text{ZCA.(inprogram)}$$

$$R = (L_y, L_\mu, L_\lambda)^T = 0$$

and then substitute to c(z):

Non-separable utility $u = u(c,y)$ with $u_{cy} \neq 0$. From the Lagrangean

$$L = \int \{[u(c,y) + \lambda(z-c)] f(z,y) + \mu(u_y f + u f_y)\} dz$$

we get

$$u_c f + \mu u_c f_y + \mu u_{yc} f - \lambda f = 0$$

or

$$u_c = \frac{\lambda}{1+\mu\zeta} - \frac{\mu u_{yc}}{1+\mu\zeta}.$$

$$\frac{\partial L}{\partial y} = \lambda \int (z-c) f_y dz + \mu \int (u_{yy} f + 2u_y f_y + u f_{yy}) dz = 0$$

Now the equation system is the following:

$$\mu = -\lambda \int (z-c) f_y dz \Big/ \int (u_{yy} f + 2u_y f_y + u f_{yy}) dz (= \text{YLP/ALP}) \qquad \text{GL}$$

$$\frac{\partial L}{\partial \mu} = \int (u_y f + u f_y) dz = 0 \qquad \text{GY}$$

$$\frac{\partial L}{\partial \lambda} = \int [z - c(z)] f(z,y) = 0 \qquad \text{ZCA}$$

$$\text{If } u(c,y) = \frac{c^{1-p}}{1-p}y,$$

$$u_y = \frac{c^{1-p}}{1-p}, u_c = c^{-p}y, u_{cc} = -pc^{-p-1}y, u_{cy} = c^{-p}, u_{yy} = 0,$$

$c(z) = (((1+\mu\zeta)y+\mu)/\lambda)^{1/p}$. As above we solve **x**= $(y,\mu,\lambda))^{T}$ from the system and substitute to c(z). We obtain

$$c(z) = (A + Bz)^{1/p}, p \geq 1,$$

where $A = (\frac{1}{\lambda}(1 - \frac{\mu s}{y^2} + \mu), B = \frac{\mu b}{\lambda y^3}$, where s=r−1. If r=1 f is exponential distribution $f = y^{-1}e^{-z/y}$. Now $c(z) = (((1 + \mu(\frac{z}{y^2} - \frac{1}{y}))y + \mu)/\lambda)^{1/p}$ or $c(z) = \left(\frac{y^2}{\lambda} + \frac{\mu z}{\lambda y}\right)^{1/\gamma}$.

If in turn $u(c,y) = \frac{c^{1-p}}{1-p}y^{-1}$,

$$u_y = -\frac{c^{1-p}}{1-p}y^{-2}, u_c = c^{-p}y^{-1}, u_{cc} = -pc^{-p-1}y^{-1}, u_{cy} = -c^{-p}y^{-2}, u_{yy} = 2\frac{c^{1-p}}{1-p}y^{-3},$$

Now $c(z) = ((\frac{(1+\mu\zeta)}{y} - \frac{\mu}{y^2})/\lambda)^{1/p}$.

FORTRAN program with some comments

```
C OPZB 17.12.2004
C NAG instead of imsl
  IMPLICIT REAL*8 (A-H,O-Z)
  COMMON /MATR/XJ(3,3),DX(3)
  COMMON
/PAR/NUSEL,LTUL,NINTPZ,JAK,ZMAX,A,D,P,Q,S,CMIN,A1,A2,A3
C IMSL
C DIMENSION WKAREA(200)
C NAG
  DIMENSION AA(41,41),RHS(41),WKS1(41),WKS2(41)
  DIMENSION X(3),YJ(3,3)
C#### NJF=0 CONSTANT JACOBIAN MATRIX
C#### NJF=1 RLA EQUATION NOT INCLUDED
C#### NJF=2 RMY = 0
C#### U-FUNCTIONS
C#### NUSEL=1: U=LOG(C)+ 2: U=-1/C+
C#### DISTRIDUTION 1: EXP 2: GAMMA
C IMSL
C IDGT=0
  MN=3
  WRITE(6,50)
50 FORMAT(' NUSEL NJF ITKMAX ERMAX CMIN RELM'/
  1,' LTUL JAK NINTPZ NINCR A D P Q S'/
```

```
   2,' DY DRMY DRLA'/
   3,' ZMAX'/
   4,' YA MYA RLAA'/
   5,' A1 A2 A3')
   READ(5,*)NUSEL,NJF,ITKMAX,ERMAX,CMIN,RELM
   READ(5,*)LTUL,JAK,NINTPZ,NINCR,A,D,P,Q,S
   READ(5,*)DY,DRMY,DRLA
   READ(5,*)ZMAX
   READ(5,*)YA,RMYA,RLAA
   READ(5,*)A1,A2,A3
   WRITE(6,51)NUSEL,NJF,ITKMAX,ERMAX,CMIN,RELM
   J,LTUL,JAK,NINTPZ,NINCR,A,D,P,Q,S
   J,DY,DRMY,DRLA
   J,ZMAX
   J,YA,RMYA,RLAA
   J,A1,A2,A3
51 FORMAT(3I3,3E12.4,/,4I3,5E12.4,/,3E12.4,/,E12.4
   J,/,3E12.4,/,3E12.4)
   UFMAX=-1.E33
   DZ=ZMAX/NINTPZ
   IF(NJF.EQ.2) RMYA=0.
   X(1)=YA
   X(2)=RMYA
   X(3)=RLAA
   JF=1
   ITK=0
910 CONTINUE
   ITK=ITK+1
   IF(NJF.EQ.0.AND.ITK.GT.1) JF=0
   IF(NJF.NE.1) CALL ZCA(X,ZCA1,ZF,CF,UF,FK)
   CALL FUNCT(X,GL1,GY1)
   DX(1)=-GY1
   DX(2)=-GL1
   Y=X(1)
   X(1)=Y+DY
   CALL FUNCT(X,GL2,GY2)
   CALL ZCA(X,ZCA2,ZF,CF,UF,FK)
   X(1)=Y
   XJ(1,1)=(GY2-GY1)/DY
   XJ(2,1)=(GL2-GL1)/DY
   XJ(3,1)=(ZCA2-ZCA1)/DY
   RMY=X(2)
   X(2)=RMY+DRMY
   CALL FUNCT(X,GL2,GY2)
   CALL ZCA(X,ZCA2,ZF,CF,UF,FK)
```

```
      X(2)=RMY
      XJ(1,2)=(GY2-GY1)/DRMY
      XJ(2,2)=(GL2-GL1)/DRMY
      XJ(3,2)=(ZCA2-ZCA1)/DRMY
      IF(NJF.NE.2)GOTO 559
      XJ(2,2)=XJ(2,2)*1.E20
      DX(2)=0.
  559 CONTINUE
      IF(NJF.EQ.1) GOTO 112
      RLA=X(3)
      X(3)=RLA+DRLA
      CALL FUNCT(X,GL2,GY2)
      CALL ZCA(X,ZCA2,ZF,CF,UF,FK)
      X(3)=RLA
      XJ(1,3)=(GY2-GY1)/DRLA
      XJ(2,3)=(GL2-GL1)/DRLA
      XJ(3,3)=(ZCA2-ZCA1)/DRLA
      DX(3)=-ZCA1
  112 CONTINUE
      DO 911 I=1,3
      IF(LTUL.EQ.22) WRITE(6,912)(XJ(I,J),J=1,3),DX(I)
  911 CONTINUE
  912 FORMAT(' XJ',3E12.4,E15.4)
      WRITE(6,861)
  861 FORMAT(' RESIDUAL')
      WRITE(6,860)(DX(I),I=1,3)
  860 FORMAT(2E12.4)
      NEQ=3
      IF(NJF.NE.1) GOTO 510
      DX(3)=0.0
      NEQ=2
  510 CONTINUE
      DO 500 I=1,3
C NAG (following is not needed if IMSL)
      RHS(I)=DX(I)
      DO 500 J=1,3
  500 YJ(I,J)=XJ(I,J)
C CALL LEQT1F(YJ,1,NEQ,MN,DX,IDGT,WKAREA,IER)
C IF(IER.LT.34)GOTO 20
C WRITE(6,14)IER
C14 FORMAT(' IER=',I5)
C STOP
C NAG
      IFAIL=0
      CALL F04ATF(YJ,MN,RHS,NEQ,DX,AA,MN,WKS1,WKS2,IFAIL)
```

```
  WRITE(6,732)(DX(I),I=1,3)
732 FORMAT(' DX',3E12.4)
  IF(IFAIL.EQ.0)GOTO 20
  WRITE(6,14)IFAIL
14 FORMAT(' IFAIL=',I5)
  STOP
20 CONTINUE
  IF(NJF.EQ.2)X(2)=1.E-7
  DO 950 N=1,3
  REL=DABS(DX(N)/X(N))
  IF(REL.GT.RELM)DX(N)=RELM*DX(N)/REL
950 CONTINUE
  ER=0.0
  Y=X(1)+DX(1)
  RMY=X(2)+DX(2)
  IF(Y.LT.1.E-6)Y=1.E-6
  IF(Y.GT.0.99999)Y=.99999
  IF(RMY.LT.0.01)RMY=0.01
  IF(NJF.EQ.2)RMY=1.E-7
  X(1)=Y
  X(2)=RMY
  ER=ER+DABS(DX(1)/X(1))+DABS(DX(2)/X(2))
  RLA=X(3)+DX(3)
  X(3)=RLA
  ER=ER+DABS(DX(3)/X(3))
  WRITE(6,830)ITK,ER,X(3),DX(3)
830 FORMAT(' ITK ER RLA DRLA ',I5,3E12.4,/' Y MY DY DMY')
  WRITE(6,850)X(1),X(2),DX(1),DX(2)
850 FORMAT(4E12.4)
  IF(ER.GT.ERMAX.AND.ITK.LT.ITKMAX) GOTO 910
C
C **** CALCULATE ZCA
C
  CALL ZCA(X,ZCA1,ZF,CF,UF,FK)
  WRITE(6,88)ZCA1,ZF,CF,UF,FK
88 FORMAT(' ZCA ZF CF UF FK',5E11.3)
  WRITE(6,720)
720 FORMAT(' I Z C(Z) FK D(Z-C):DZ (Z-C):C UF')
  DZ=ZMAX/NINTPZ
  FK=0.0
  UFK=0.
  DZC=0.0
  ZCZ=0.0
  C=0.0
  DO 730 I=1,NINTPZ
```

```
   Z=(I-.5)*DZ
   COLD=C
   CALL FF(Z,Y,F,FY,FYY)
   FK=FK+F*DZ
   CALL CFUNCT(X,Z,C)
   GOTO(41,42),NUSEL
41 CONTINUE
   U1=DLOG(C)
   GOTO 49
42 CONTINUE
C U1=C**(1-P)/(1-P)
C U1=Y*C**(1-P)/(1-P)
   U1=(A1+A2*Y**A3)*C**(1-P)/(1-P)
49 CONTINUE
   U2=-Q*Z*Z
   U=U1+U2-S*Y
   UFK=UFK+U*F*DZ
   IF(I.NE.(I/NINCR)*NINCR)GOTO 730
   IF(I.EQ.1) GOTO 731
   DZC=1.+(COLD-C)/DZ
   ZCZ=(Z-C)/Z
731 CONTINUE
   WRITE(6,740)I,Z,C,FK,DZC,ZCZ,UFK
730 CONTINUE
740 FORMAT(I5,6E11.3)
1000 CONTINUE
   STOP
   END
   SUBROUTINE FUNCT(X,GL,GY)
   IMPLICIT REAL*8 (A-H,O-Z)
   COMMON /MATR/XJ(3,3),DX(3)
   COMMON /PAR/NUSEL,LTUL,NINTPZ,JAK,ZMAX,A,D,P,Q,S,CMIN,A1,A2,A3
   DIMENSION X(3)
   Y=X(1)
   RMY=X(2)
   RLA=X(3)
   GL=0.0
   ALP=0.0
   YLP=0.0
   DZ=ZMAX/NINTPZ
   DO 200 I=1,NINTPZ
   Z=(I-0.5)*DZ
   CALL CFUNCT(X,Z,C)
   CALL FF(Z,Y,F,FY,FYY)
   GOTO(10,20),NUSEL
```

```
10 CONTINUE
   U1=DLOG(C)
   GOTO 100
20 CONTINUE
C U1=C**(1-P)/(1-P)
C U1Y=C**(1-P)/(1-P)
C U1=Y*U1Y
   U1=(A1+A2*Y**A3)*C**(1-P)/(1-P)
   U1Y=A2*A3*Y**(A3-1.)*C**(1-P)/(1-P)
100 CONTINUE
   U2=-Q*Z*Z
   U=U1+U2-S*Y
   YLP=YLP+(Z-C)*FY*DZ
c GL=GL+(U1+U2)*FY*DZ
c ALP=ALP+(U1+U2)*FYY*DZ
   GL=GL+((U1+U2)*FY+U1Y*F)*DZ
   ALP=ALP+((U1+U2)*FYY+2.*U1Y*FY)*DZ
200 CONTINUE
   GL=GL-S
   GY=GL+RLA*YLP+RMY*ALP
   IF(LTUL.EQ.2)WRITE(6,300)Y,RMY,RLA,U1,U2,GL,YLP,ALP
300 FORMAT(' Y MY L U12GYA',3E12.4,/,5E12.4)
   RETURN
   END
   SUBROUTINE CFUNCT(X,Z,C)
   IMPLICIT REAL*8 (A-H,O-Z)
   COMMON /MATR/XJ(3,3),DX(3)
   COMMON /PAR/NUSEL,LTUL,NINTPZ,JAK,ZMAX,A,D,P,Q,S,CMIN,A1,A2,A3
   DIMENSION X(3)
C
C CALCULATE C(Z)
C
   C=0.0
   Y=X(1)
   RMY=X(2)
   RLA=X(3)
   CALL FF(Z,Y,F,FY,FYY)
   GOTO(10,20),NUSEL
10 C=(1.+RMY*FY/F)/RLA
   GOTO 100
20 CONTINUE
C C=((1.+RMY*FY/F)/RLA)**(1/P)
C C=(((1.+RMY*FY/F)*Y+RMY)/RLA)**(1/P)
   C=(((1.+RMY*FY/F)*(A1+A2*Y**A3)
   J +RMY*A2*A3*Y**(A3-1.))/RLA)**(1/P)
```

```
100 CONTINUE
   IF(C.LT.CMIN)C=CMIN
   RETURN
   END
   SUBROUTINE ZCA(X,ZCAA,ZF,CF,UF,FK)
   IMPLICIT REAL*8 (A-H,O-Z)
   COMMON /MATR/XJ(3,3),DX(3)
   COMMON /PAR/NUSEL,LTUL,NINTPZ,JAK,ZMAX,A,D,P,Q,S,CMIN,A1,A2,A3
   DIMENSION X(3)
C
C CALCULATE ZCAA
C
   ZF=0.0
   CF=0.0
   UF=0.0
   FK=0.0
   Y=X(1)
   RMY=X(2)
   RLA=X(3)
   DZ=ZMAX/NINTPZ
   DO 10 I=1,NINTPZ
   Z=(I-.5)*DZ
   CALL CFUNCT(X,Z,C)
   CALL FF(Z,Y,F,FY,FYY)
   FDZ=F*DZ
   ZF=ZF+Z*FDZ
   CF=CF+C*FDZ
   FK=FK+FDZ
10 CONTINUE
   IF(DABS(D-1.0).GT.0.00001) A=(1.0-D)*ZF
   ZCAA=ZF-CF-A
   IF(LTUL.EQ.2)WRITE(6,85)ZF,CF,UF,FK,ZCAA,A
85 FORMAT(' ZAC',6E12.4)
   RETURN
   END
   SUBROUTINE FF(Z,Y,F,FY,FYY)
   IMPLICIT REAL*8 (A-H,O-Z)
   COMMON /PAR/NUSEL,LTUL,NINTPZ,JAK,ZMAX,AA,DD,P,Q,S,CMIN,A1,A2,A3
   GOTO (10,20,30),JAK
10 F=(EXP(-Z/Y))/Y
   FY=(-1./Y+Z/Y/Y)*F
   FYY=(1./Y/Y-2.*Z/Y/Y/Y)*F+(-1./Y+Z/Y/Y)*FY
   RETURN
20 RLAM=2.75
   RLAM=3.
```

```
   R=2.5
   GAR=1.33
C R=2.75
C GAR=1.61
   R1=R-1.
   APU=EXP(-RLAM*Z/Y)
   F=RLAM/GAR*(RLAM*Z/Y)**R1*APU/Y
   FY=F*(RLAM*Z/Y-R)/Y
   FYY=FY*(RLAM*Z/Y-R-1)/Y-RLAM*Z*F/Y/Y/Y
   RETURN
30 CONTINUE
   ALF=2.
   BET=2.
   GAM=.75
   A=ALF/(1.-GAM)
   B=BET/GAM
   AK=A*B/(B-A)
   C=-Z*A
   D=-Z*B
   EA=EXP(C/Y)
   EB=EXP(D/Y)
   F=AK*(EA-EB)/Y
   DUM=(C*EA-D*EB)*AK
   FY=-F/Y-DUM/(Y**3)
   FYY=F/Y/Y-FY/Y+3*DUM/(Y**4)+AK*(C*C*EA-D*D*EB)/(Y**5)
   RETURN
   END
```

12 Optimal mixed taxation

So far we have focused on optimal labour-income taxation. What happens when the government has access to additional instruments? One additional instrument is commodity or indirect taxation.[1] There is a long history of optimal commodity taxes without income taxes. Inspired by Pigou, Ramsey (1927) developed a theory for optimal commodity taxes in his article 'A Contribution to the Theory of Taxation'. He was concerned with how commodities should be taxed to achieve a given revenue from a representative consumer. Ramsey showed that the optimal commodity taxes would be set so that, roughly speaking, they reduce all commodity demands proportionately. Assuming quasi-linear in-leisure preferences, optimal commodity tax rates are inversely proportional to elasticities of demand, i.e. the inverse elasticity rule. Corlett and Hague (1953) generalized Ramsey's model for more general preferences. They consider a representative household that consumes two goods and leisure. The government can tax the two goods, but not leisure. The Corlett–Hague rule states that a good which is more complementary with leisure should be taxed at a higher rate.

Diamond and Mirrlees (1971) generalized Ramsey's (1927) optimal tax analysis to heterogeneous individuals that differed in their wage rates but had the same preferences. In their analysis we face a fundamental conflict between equity and efficiency: goods with the lowest price elasticity of demand should have high tax rates for the sake of efficiency, but they are also the ones with the lowest income elasticity of demand that should be taxed leniently on equity grounds. Deaton (1979) in turn extended the Corlett–Hague theorem to this setting.[2] An important result from Diamond and Mirrlees (1971) is the production efficiency theorem, which says that if the optimal commodity tax system is in place, and if pure profits are all taxed away,[3] production efficiency should apply for the economy as a whole (see appendix 12.1). This result is surprising since it is at odds with the Lancaster–Lipsey (1956) second-best theorem, which says that in the second-best situation we cannot just say anything on the nature of the optimum. The Diamond–Mirrlees result in turn says that when there is a pre-existing distortion, introducing another distortion to the economy may improve welfare. Its implications are that taxes on producer inputs are eliminated, thus promoting production efficiency. This means no taxes on, e.g., investment goods, office space, fuel, etc. The value-added tax (VAT)

[1] According to OECD Revenue Statistics (2006) indirect taxation represents on average around 30 per cent of total tax revenue in the EU19 countries.

[2] The Deaton theorem has been generalized by Hellwig (2009).

[3] See Munk (1978) on the qualification of this condition.

achieves this. The credit-and-invoice VAT used in most countries ensures that taxes on producer inputs are eliminated. The use of producer prices for project evaluation within the public sector is consistent with aggregate production efficiency (Little and Mirrlees 1974). There are, however, obvious limitations in the efficiency theorem. For example, if profits cannot be fully taxed and/or not all goods are taxed optimally, the theoretical case for production efficiency no longer applies. One important counter-argument is shown by Naito (1999) in a model with non-linear income taxation and public production. Suppose the public good is produced using two types of labour, skilled and unskilled. Then it is optimal to deviate from production efficiency in public production and use more unskilled labour, relative to market equilibrium, in public production. The reason is that this increases demand for unskilled labour, increases their wage rate, and reduces the burden to redistribute income by the distortive income tax.

Can the government design a better redistribution system combining income taxation and commodity taxation? Can it meet then the same distributional objectives but with smaller efficiency costs? In most developed countries, labour income is taxed on a non-linear scale, whereas indirect taxation is linear. This system can also be defended on the basis of information constraints: it is difficult to observe the amount of purchases by individual consumers which would be needed to implement non-linear commodity taxation on most goods. In other words, resale possibilities hinder, in most cases, the implementation of fully non-linear taxation. The mixed taxation framework has the attractive feature that it corresponds to the type of tax systems actually used. It corresponds to the mixed taxation case in optimal tax literature (see Mirrlees 1976a; Atkinson and Stiglitz 1976; Christiansen 1984; Revesz 1986, 2005; and Guesnerie 1995). The availability of tax instruments in use in the optimal mixed tax model is not just assumed but derived from the presence of asymmetric information between the government and the taxpayers.

In the mixed tax framework, the most influential result is that of Atkinson and Stiglitz (1976): when consumer preferences are separable between goods and leisure, there is no need for differentiated commodity tax rates.[4] Deaton (1979) in turn shows that if preferences are weakly separable in goods and leisure and exhibit linear Engel curves with the same slope for all individuals, then the optimal tax is a linear progressive income tax: commodity taxes are not needed. The Atkinson–Stiglitz result has considerably played down the potential role of differentiated commodity tax rates as a redistributive device. Although such preference structure is not likely to be empirically valid,[5] optimal tax theory is quite often seen to provide a limited role for commodity taxation in redistribution. Much policy advice has similarly argued that the scope of redistribution achieved by differentiated commodity tax rates is relatively minor and similar impacts

[4] There is a large literature on the A-S theorem, recently excellently summarized in Boadway (2012). See also Hellwig (2010).

[5] There is much empirical research rejecting weak separability in the utility function. See, e.g., Browning and Meghir (1991), Crawford et al (2010), Gordon and Kopczuk (2013), and Pirttilä and Suoniemi (2014).

could be more easily obtained by income-based targeting. For example, the IMF fiscal affairs department seemed to subscribe to this view (Ebrill et al 2001).[6] More recently one key policy recommendation of the Mirrlees Review (2011), influenced by optimal tax theory, is the proposal for a more broad-based VAT. Optimal tax theory is not the only background to their argument for uniform rates of VAT. The Review emphasizes administrative advantages of uniform VAT structure; moreover, it regards a uniform tax as less vulnerable to lobbying pressure. A background study by Crawford, Keen, and Smith (2010, Chapter 6) focuses mainly on the optimal taxation argument. In the optimal tax literature, individual behaviour is mainly modelled by utility maximization and social welfare is typically based on welfarism, i.e. assessed in terms of individual utilities. Based on this kind of analysis, the Mirrlees Review concludes that 'there is a strong case for broadening the VAT base and moving towards a uniform rate. This would increase consumers' welfare' (2011, p. 229). The Review also argues that it is possible to devise a tax reform package that broadens the base for VAT, removing zero rating 'to raise net revenue for the Exchequer and to redistribute more resources from better off households to less well-off households' (2011, p. 217).[7] The Review recognized, however, the limitation of this kind of analysis at a number of points. For instance, it says in a footnote on page 156: '... lower taxes can offset the effects of market power where firms are able to charge above the efficient price, but we do not pursue those here.'[8]

12.1 The discrete-type model with individuals of two skill levels

As in standard optimal income tax analysis, optimal policy is constrained by asymmetric information between the government and individuals. Individuals' income-earning abilities are private information and tax policy must be based on (observable) income instead. In designing the tax policy, the government must therefore take into account the incentive compatibility or self-selection constraints of the individual. So it can deploy a non-linear income tax $T(z)$, leaving individuals with disposable income $c(z)=z-T(z)$. The government cannot observe individual purchases of the goods, but can tax market transactions anonymously. The question of interest is whether it is optimal for the

[6] Political economy considerations may also limit the desirable number of VAT rates. With a large number of existing tax rates, interest groups may find it easier to lobby for further tax concessions.

[7] More precisely, the Mirrlees Review recommends uniform commodity taxation, but with some goods such as child care (needed for working) left untaxed. Bastani, Blomquist, and Pirttilä (2013) show that even if all goods other than the good needed for working are separable from leisure, the optimal tax on these goods should not be uniform. The key message of Bastani et al (2013) is that the optimal commodity tax system is dependent on the expenditure side of the government.

[8] See Myles (1989) on commodity taxation with imperfect competition.

government to use differential commodity tax rates alongside this. In other words, should commodity tax rates be uniform, or should they be different for different goods? The tax policy tools include non-linear income tax and commodity taxes, t_i. Thus, we analyse a similar situation to that in Mirrlees (1976a): with an income tax $T(ny)$ and commodity taxes (tax vector) $t=q-p$, an individual's budget constraint is $qx=z-T(z)$.

To make things simpler we consider the discrete-type model with individuals of two skill levels or abilities and government facing the self-selection constraint. Within these models the seminal contributions are Guesnerie and Seade (1982), Stiglitz (1982), and Stern (1982), while the presentation here draws on the framework developed in Edwards et al (1994). The appeal in using this approach is in the simplicity of analytics and, more importantly, easily interpretable results. At the heart of the non-linear income tax analysis are the incentive compatibility constraints restricting redistributive policy. Perhaps the most prominent advantage in the self-selection approach is its capability to address the incentive issue explicitly through the analysis of the self-selection constraint.

We consider an economy consisting of two types: a type-1 individual has low productivity with wage rate n^1; a type-2 individual has higher ability so that $n^2 > n^1$.[9] Individuals earn labour income $z^i = n^i y^i$, with y^i denoting the labour supply of individual i. We normalize time endowment so that leisure is given by $l^i = 1 - y^i$. Individuals have identical preferences defined on their consumption commodities, $x = (x_1, x_2)$.[10] Income is taxed on a non-linear scale, and consumers allocate the after-tax income B^h over consumption goods $x = (x_1, x_2)$.

It turns out to be useful to break the consumer's optimization into two stages, as in Mirrlees (1976a), Christiansen (1984), and Edwards et al (1994). First, the consumers allocate a fixed amount of expenditure B (i.e. their income after income taxation) optimally over the consumption goods, holding labour supply as given. We denote consumer prices by $q_i = p_i + t_i$, where p_i and t_i refer to (constant) producer price and tax rate of good i. Furthermore, in the subsequence we will very often omit the superscript h to avoid clutter. Consumer's first-stage optimization gives conditional indirect utility:

$$V(q, B, z, n) = \max_X \left\{ U(x, \frac{z}{n}) \Big| \sum_i q_i x_i = B \right\}, \tag{1}$$

For brevity, we write $V(q, B, z, n^h)$ as $V^h(q, B, z)$. We introduce the agent monotonicity condition by assuming that the level curves of V in (z,B)-space are, *ceteris paribus*, the

[9] For simplicity, we have not included N^1 of type-1 and N^2 of type-2 consumers into the economy. This extension could, however, readily be made.

[10] The number of goods is restricted to two only for ease of presentation; generalization to a many-good economy gives rise to no other difficulties.

flatter the higher the wage rate of the individual is. This means that $-\frac{V_z^h}{V_B^h}$ decreases with n. Finally, solving (1) gives conditional demand functions, with $V_i = \partial V / \partial q_i$:

$$x_i(q, B, z, n) = -\frac{V_i}{V_B}. \tag{2}$$

At the second stage of individual's optimization, hours worked (earnings) are chosen to maximize the conditional utility function, subject to the budget equation $B^h = z^h - T(z^h)$, with T denoting the non-linear income tax function. The second-stage maximization yields the following condition (where T' indicates the marginal tax rate):

$$V_B^h(1 - T') + V_z^h = 0 \Leftrightarrow T'(z^h) = \frac{V_z^h}{V_B^h} + 1. \tag{3}$$

In the government's optimization problem we will concentrate on Pareto-efficient tax structure, so that the social planner is assumed to maximize the welfare of the low-ability class subject to a given level of utility to the high-ability individual. Since the government cannot differentiate taxes by ability, its maximization problem is restricted by the self-selection constraints of different types. This means that for both types, it has to be optimal to select their own level of labour and not to mimic the choice of the other class.[11] As in Chapter 2, the more interesting case is where the binding self-selection constraint is that of the high-ability individual; consequently, the government's problem has to be solved subject to the following constraint:

$$V^2(q, B^2, z^2) \geq V^2(q, B^1, z^1). \tag{4}$$

Moreover, the government is restricted by its budget constraint: the public good provision (rG) must be financed by income taxes T and indirect taxes t_i:[12]

$$T(z^1) + \sum_i t_i x_i^1 + T(z^2) + \sum_i t_i x_i^2 = rG. \qquad i = 1, 2. \tag{5}$$

12.2 **Optimal commodity taxes**

From the first-order condition with respect to q (or equivalently with respect to tax rate t), we have the formula for the optimal commodity taxes (see appendix 12.2 for the derivation). We simplify things further so that there are two goods, x_1 and x_2. We normalize the tax on x_2 to be zero, so that the only indirect tax will be t_1 on x_1.

[11] This solution is a separating equilibrium which Pareto-dominates pooling equilibrium in a two-class society, as is demonstrated in Stiglitz (1982).

[12] In addition, consumers' budget constraints are used to rewrite the government budget equation.

$$t_1 = \mu^* \frac{(x_1^1 - \hat{x}_1^2)}{(x_{t_1}^{c1} + x_{t_1}^{c2})} \tag{6}$$

where $\mu^* = \frac{\hat{V}_B^2 \mu}{\lambda} < 0$ where the hat-term $\hat{V}^2$ refers to type 2 individual mimicking low-ability person. μ and λ Lagrange multipliers relate to (4) and (5) respectively and c refers to the Hicksian (compensated) demand. There is thus in general no simple relationship between the optimal tax on some commodity and its (compensated conditional) own-price elasticity.

What can we conclude from (6)? The sign of the optimal commodity tax is negative if the consumption of x_I is bigger for the true type 1 person than for the mimicker, i.e. $x_1^1 > \hat{x}_1^2$. The tax is positive if the mimicker consumes more of that good, i.e. $x_1^1 < \hat{x}_1^2$.

The mimicker and true type 1 have identical preferences; they only differ by the amount of labour supply (the high-skilled mimicker can earn the income of the low-skilled with fewer hours of labour supply). Therefore, the mimicker enjoys more leisure. Consider the case where the mimicker's consumption is higher. Then start from a zero commodity tax. Assume that tax t is increased by a small amount, dt. The purchasing power of type 1 decreases by $x_1^1 dt$. This loss can be compensated by decreasing income tax for type 1, T^1, by an equal amount. Equivalently, the loss for type 2 can also be compensated. But the mimicker is now worse off, because $\hat{x}_1^2 dt - x_1^1 dt$ is positive when $x_1^1 < \hat{x}_1^2$. This makes mimicking less desirable and thus mitigates self-selection constraint. When self-selection constraint is mitigated, a Pareto improvement in income taxation is possible.

(6) is an implicit formulation for the optimal commodity tax structure. Edwards, Keen, and Tuomala (1994) provide a straightforward intuition for why it would be optimal to introduce a subsidy to a good which is complementary to labour supply. Subsidizing such a good reduces the incentives of high-ability households to work less, which is the distortion stemming from income taxation. Therefore, the pre-existing distortions from the income taxation can be mitigated. Likewise, introducing a tax on a good complementary with leisure would reduce the valuation of leisure and lead to an increase in labour supply. Therefore if a commodity is a complement (substitute) to leisure, optimal commodity tax is positive (negative). This resembles the Corrlett–Haque (1953) result, which states that increasing the tax on the good most complementary with leisure will increase welfare. Imposing a higher tax on leisure complements relaxes the incentive constraints and allows the non-linear income tax to be more progressive. A worker who is mimicking the income of a lower-wage worker will obtain the same disposable income but have more leisure, so will consume more of those goods that complement leisure. Imposing higher taxes on such goods makes it more difficult to mimic, so relaxes the incentive constraint. It is important to note that goods that are more complementary with leisure are not necessarily luxury goods. This is one argument for the Mirrlees Review (2011) support for uniform goods taxation.

12.3 Effective marginal tax rates

From the first-order condition we get also the effective marginal tax rates: how the total tax payment of type i changes when income increases. Denote the total tax payment by $\tau(z^i) = T(z^i) + tx^i(q, B^i, z^i)$. Therefore, differentiating gives the effective tax rate:

$$\tau'(z^i) = T'(z^i) + t\frac{\partial x_i}{\partial B}(1 - T') + \frac{\partial x_i}{\partial z}. \tag{7}$$

Using the first-order condition, it can be shown that at the optimum (see appendix 8.2), $\tau'(z^2) = 0$ and $\tau'(z^1) > 0$.

These are the same results as in the case where income taxation only is used (see Chapter 2), but here in terms of effective tax rates. Notice that for $\tau'(z^2) = 0$, if $t > 0$, the marginal income tax rate for type 2 must be negative. The zero effective marginal tax rate of a type-2 individual means that if they have an infinitesimal increase in income, the indirect taxes paid from extra income have to be compensated in direct taxation. Hence this result is a kind of strengthening of the familiar end-point result deduced, for instance, in Chapter 2, again with same qualifications.

12.4 The Atkinson–Stiglitz theorem

As shown by Atkinson and Stiglitz (1976), if consumer preferences are weakly separable between goods and leisure, i.e. utility takes the form $U(\psi(x_1, x_2), y)$, differential commodity taxation should not be used. In other words demand does not depend on the amount of leisure, and the mimicker and true type-1 person consume the same amount, i.e. $x_1^1 = \hat{x}_1^2$. In this case, the demand for different commodities does not vary with the wage rate (or labour supply), and that term at the right of (6) is always zero. The Atkinson–Stiglitz result is often used as an argument against the use of differentiated commodity taxation as a redistributive device. Direct income transfers (as a part of an optimal income tax scheme) would be sufficient instead. It has to emphasize that this is a result regarding the structure of tax system. It does not tell us about the appropriate tax mix between labour income tax and commodity taxes. In fact, the appropriate mix between income (direct) and commodity (indirect) taxes is one of the oldest issues in tax literature. The modern optimal tax literature recognizes that the balance between direct and indirect taxes is to some degree arbitrary. In other words, there is an equivalence between consumption and labour-income (wage) taxes. This equivalence holds for any form of tax on final consumption when taxes are proportional. Hence direct and indirect taxes are similar in terms of their impact on individuals' budget constraints and hence, in the absence of fiscal illusion, on their behaviour. To say something on tax mix we have to add to the model some extra feature. For example, Boadway, Marchand, and Pestieau (1994) incorporate tax evasion into the design of an optimal mix tax system. Their paper is based on the assumption that indirect taxes may be more difficult to evade than direct taxes. Of course, this is a rather controversial assumption.[13]

The Atkinson–Stiglitz result was extended by Deaton (1979) to the case where the government can only apply linear progressive taxes. If the linear progressive tax is set optimally, preferences are weakly separable and if the demand for goods is quasi-homothetic, differential commodity taxes cannot improve social welfare. It is still possible that goods have very different income elasticities of demand (as the case of Stone–Geary preferences confirms). Both results (Atkinson–Stiglitz and Deaton) have been generalized in cases with non-optimal income tax. Laroque (2005a) and Kaplow (2006), following an approach suggested by Konishi (1995), showed the following. Start with a set of differential indirect commodity taxes and any arbitrary non-linear income tax, not necessarily optimal, and assume that preferences are weakly separable. There exists a Pareto-improving tax reform that eliminates differential commodity taxes and adjusts the income tax such that both the government revenue and incentive constraints are satisfied. So, as long as there are no restrictions on changing the non-linear income tax, there is a case for eliminating differential commodity taxes (or adopting a uniform VAT)[14,15] (see appendix 12.3 for formal proof). The Mirrlees Review used this argument for moving uniform VAT tax rates in a roughly distributive neutral way.[16]

How convincing is this argument? Boadway (2012) has some doubts:

> It relies heavily on income-specific tax adjustments being undertaken as part of the commodity tax reform. If they are not undertaken, the result would be convincing only if one subscribed to the hypothetical compensation criterion of Little (1957) or Coate (2000) where by a change is judged to be worth undertaking if the gainers could compensate the losers. Moreover, if the income tax is not fully optimized for some reason and income tax reform is ruled out, preferential tax treatment of necessities can be welfare improving... if a substantial number of low-income persons are not in the labour force, complementarity with leisure loses its policy relevancy. In these circumstances, preferential VAT treatment of necessities has more justification. (Boadway, 2012, pp. 1154–5)

12.5 Support for differential commodity taxation

The Atkinson–Stiglitz result is one of the most important single results in optimal tax analysis, but its applicability is limited. There are several considerations that support

[13] The standard expected utility model of tax evasion predicts that evasion is decreasing in the marginal tax rate. See Yitzhaki (1987).

[14] If the income tax is less progressive than optimal for some reason, redistribution can then be improved by favouring necessities in the commodity tax system (Boadway and Pestieau 2011).

[15] In fact, the Laroque–Kaplow result might support a move to uniform commodity taxes even if the income tax reform is potentially Pareto-improving satisfying in the sense of a second-best compensation test. See Coate (2000) for further discussion of second-best compensation tests.

[16] The Mirrlees review supports its VAT recommendation with their finding based on the UK data that those goods are not complementary with leisure. The only exception was child care.

differential goods taxation, though again not necessarily preferential treatment of necessities. Examples include differences in unobserved endowments of some commodities (Cremer, Pestieau, and Rochet 2001), differences in preferences (Saez 2002a; Marchand, Pestieau, and Racionero 2003; Blomquist and Christiansen 2008); differences in the need for particular goods (Boadway and Pestieau 2003), and differences in labour utilization in producing commodities (Naito 1999). Boadway and Gahvari (2006) show that a higher tax should be levied on goods whose consumption is more time-intensive as long as consumption time is a substitute for labour.

Cremer et al (2001) study optimal income design in a setting in which individuals differ in both ability and an unobserved endowment. They show how a differential commodity tax system can improve welfare if used alongside the income tax in a setting in which the Atkinson–Stiglitz (1976) theorem otherwise applies. In other words, in their model, separability is no longer enough to obtain the Atkinson–Stiglitz result. They also find that the self-selection constraints can take very surprising patterns (see more on this in Chapter 14, section 2).

Saez (2002b) shows that a small tax on a given commodity is desirable if high-income earners have a relatively higher taste for this commodity or if consumption of this commodity increases with leisure. A small linear tax on a commodity preferred by individuals with higher ability generates a smaller efficiency loss than does an increase in the optimal non-linear income tax that raises the same revenue from each individual. Saez (2002b) also investigates the conditions necessary to restore the Atkinson–Stiglitz result with heterogeneous preferences.

As previously mentioned, in the optimal tax literature, individual behaviour is mainly modelled by utility maximization, and social welfare is typically based on welfarism. The limitation of this analysis for both the explanation of individual behaviour and the formulation of social objectives is, however, recognized by several scholars. Another limitation of the optimal tax literature is the assumption of perfect competition. Based on the optimal tax model with this assumption of perfect competition, the Mirrlees Review recommends to devise a tax reform package that broadens the base for VAT, removing the zero rating, notably for food. Because food retailing in the UK (and in many other countries)[17] is highly concentrated, Atkinson (2012) criticises the review's recommendation. Namely, oligopolistic supermarkets may raise their prices higher than the tax. The design of commodity taxes such as VAT has to consider the degree of market competition. But how does the existence of imperfect competition affect the optimal design of indirect taxation? It may be the case that lower taxes can offset the effects of market power where firms are able to charge above the efficient price.

Fleurbaey (2006) studies how to combine linear commodity taxes and non-linear income tax in a model where taxpayers have unequal skills and heterogeneous

[17] Atkinson (2012, p. 775): 'food retailing in the United Kingdom is highly concentrated. The top four supermarkets in the United Kingdom have a market share of over 75 per cent. These firms are unlikely to act as perfect competitors'. The top two supermarkets in Finland have a market share around 80 per cent.

preferences about consumption goods and leisure. He proposes a particular social welfare function on the basis of fairness principles and then derives a simple criterion for evaluating the social welfare consequences of various tax schedules. Under the proposed approach, the optimal tax should have no commodity tax for some range of consumptions, and income redistribution would feature high subsidies to the working poor. It is also shown that, even when the income tax fails to be optimal, commodity taxes may not improve social welfare. Pirttilä and Tuomala (2004) in turn study mixed taxation when the government uses non-welfarist social objectives. They show that if the government aims to minimize poverty, lower tax should be levied on goods included in the bundle that defines the poverty line. We return to this later on in this chapter.

Allowing for endogenously determined wages, Naito (1999) also extended the argument to the case with multiple consumption goods. In this case, applying a differential commodity tax on the most skill-intensive good also increases $\frac{w^1}{w^2}$, so the Atkinson–Stiglitz theorem does not carry over.

Using the discrete occupational model, Saez (2004) notes that, in the absence of profits, in the case of endogenous wages the demand effects are a pure transfer from low to high-skilled workers. Through demand effects an increase in high-skill taxes leads to a reduction in the high-skilled workers' labour supply and hence an increase in their wages, plus a decrease in low-skilled wages. By readjusting the tax on high and low-skilled workers the government can offset those demand effects on the net consumption levels at no net fiscal cost. Hence the optimal tax formula does not change. Formally, the discrete occupational model used by Saez (2004) is effectively identical to a Diamond and Mirrlees (1971) optimal commodity tax model where each occupation is a specific good taxed at a specific rate. In Diamond and Mirrlees (1971), optimal commodity tax rules do not depend solely on production functions. Consequently the production efficiency result of Diamond and Mirrlees (1971) carries over to the discrete occupational choice model, implying that distortions in the production process (no taxes on input) are not desirable. Extended to many consumption goods, the theorem of Atkinson and Stiglitz (1976) also holds. Differentiated commodity taxation is not desirable to supplement optimal non-linear earnings taxation under the weak separability assumption just presented.

Saez (2004) argues that the discrete occupational model captures the long term when individuals choose their occupations, while the Stern–Stiglitz model with endogenous wages captures a short-term situation where individuals have fixed skills and only adjust hours of work. Suppose an increase in high-skill taxes leads to a reduction in high-skilled labour supply and hence an increase in high-skilled wages (and a decrease in low-skilled wages) through demand effects. Because of the absence of profits, those demand effects are a pure transfer from low to high-skilled workers. Therefore, the government can readjust the tax on high and low skills to offset those demand effects on the net consumption levels at no net fiscal cost, leaving the optimal tax formula unchanged. Those results are formally proven in Saez (2004). They stand in sharp contrast to results obtained in the Stiglitz (1982) discrete model with endogenous wages where it is shown that the optimal tax formulas are affected by endogenous wages (Stiglitz 1982).

12.6 **Fully non-linear taxation on commodities**

The idea that goods preferred by the highly able ought to be taxed has a long history in tax literature.[18] Mirrlees (1976a) shows for the fully non-linear taxation on commodities, 'the marginal tax rates should be greater on commodities the more able would tend to prefer' (Mirrlees 1976a, p. 337). As put by Mirrlees (1976a, p. 337), 'This prescription is most agreeable to common sense.' In other words, taxes on goods preferred by high-ability individuals contribute to progressivity and the redistribution of income.[19] Non-linear commodity taxation has not got much attention, one obvious reason being that non-linear taxation is impractical for most commodities. This is not the case in taxing capital income, to which we return in Chapter 14. This is also not necessarily the case with housing consumption. Governments typically have information on personal housing consumption levels. Housing is the most important item in family budgets and housing outlays are influenced by government policy in a number of ways, either in the form of tax relief or direct subsidies. It is argued that the higher the housing outlays, the lower the taxable capacity, and therefore there should be a tax deduction or a tax credit for housing outlays. On the other hand there is an argument that tax deductions are unacceptable because under progressive income taxation it means that different individuals pay different effective prices for housing and the price is lowered more for the rich than for the poor. Therefore it has been proposed that a tax credit would be preferable to tax deductions. A tax credit is simply equivalent to a proportional subsidy for housing: it involves an equal reduction in the price of housing to all individuals. However, in many countries housing costs are taken into account in basic maintenance supports. Thus, the subsidy is not necessarily equal to all, but in effect housing subsidies might be non-linear.

From the Atkinson–Stiglitz theorem we know that if there is a freely variable non-linear income tax, people differ only with respect to their earning potential, and the weak separability between labour and other commodities holds, then neither tax deductibility nor a tax credit would be desirable (see Atkinson 1977 or Atkinson and Stiglitz 1980). Thus, the desirability of tax deductions or tax credit must be based on recognition of the facts that there are long-run inequalities in access to housing, the weak separability does not apply in preferences, and there are restrictions in the use of non-linear income tax schedules. The third of these is explored by Atkinson (1977), who considers a model where the individuals have identical utility functions but they differ in their earning abilities (wage per hour). He shows in the case of linear taxation, when all goods are normal and substitutes in the Hicksian sense, the optimal rate of subsidy on housing is strictly less than the rate of income taxation. He also considers the case where the price of

[18] For example, Tuomala (1990, p. 167) writes that 'the marginal tax rates on commodities that the more able people tend to prefer should be greater', while Kaplow (2008, p. 140) argues 'it tends to be optimal to impose a heavier burden on commodities preferred by the more able and a lighter burden on those preferred by the less able'.

[19] Golosov, Troshkin, Tsyvinski, and Weinzierl (2011) revisit to the general Mirrleesian setting, characterizing optimal policy analytically and, for capital taxation, quantitatively.

housing varies across individuals, but so that housing prices and wages are independent. In housing markets with market imperfections this is not necessarily true. It is possible that more able individuals have higher earning prospects and might thus have better access to mortgages required for owner-occupied housing with lower unit costs. There is some evidence from Finland (see Tenhunen and Tuomala 2007) that the correlation between income and housing price is negative.

The potential redistributive role of housing subsidies has had relatively little attention in the literature. However, non-linear housing subsidy schemes are commonly used by many countries. Tenhunen and Tuomala (2007) examine the role of housing subsidy schemes as a redistributive mechanism when tax policies are not artificially restricted to be linear. They are optimized given the structure of information in the economy. The underlying information structure is the standard one in the optimal taxation literature. Unlike in the original Mirrlees model (1971), they address the design of housing taxes/subsidies when individuals differ both in their productivity and the unit price of housing they face. This leads to a four-type model. A bi-dimensional setting complicates the analysis notably, as is discussed in Chapter 10 (see also Boadway et al 2002). The biggest challenge in multidimensional problems is the choice of the binding self-selection constraints (see more on this in Chapter 14 in the context of capital income taxation). There are some analytical studies in a discrete case with two-dimensional heterogeneity, but they are usually simplified further to a three-type case with strong assumptions on binding self-selection constraints.[20] Cremer and Gahvari (1998) study optimal taxation of housing in the model where there are two types of housing goods (low and high quality) for which the agents have different tastes. They assume that tastes for housing and wages are positively correlated, and consider a two-type model with one particular configuration of binding self-selection constraint.

Instead of choosing the binding self-selection constraints a priori, Tenhunen and Tuomala (2007) include all of them in the optimization problem. To gain better understanding of the housing subsidies and binding constraints, they solve the problem numerically. A two-type model with perfect correlation between productivity and housing prices is considered as a special case.

In the previous analysis, assumptions were chosen so that they rule out changes in pre-tax (subsidy) housing cost. There is no good reason to think that distribution of housing prices is fixed and given. The endogenous price determination is shown to have essential effects on the optimal tax policy (Naito 1999; Micheletto 2004). Tenhunen and Tuomala (2007) also extend the analysis of the optimal tax treatment of housing to take into account the possibility that taxes (subsidies) affect housing prices.

Housing is typically analysed in the literature in such a way that there is nothing to distinguish housing services from any other commodity. Atkinson (1977) gives two interesting examples of this kind of view, from Milton Friedman and Friedrich Engels.

[20] Discrete three-type models are considered e.g. in Cuff (2000) and Blomquist and Christiansen (2004). A continuous case is considered numerically in Tarkiainen and Tuomala (1999; 2007).

> Public housing is proposed not on the ground of neighbour hood effects but as a means of helping low-income people. If this is the case, why subsidize housing in particular. (Friedman, quoted in Atkinson 1977, p. 8)

> The rent agreement is quite an ordinary commodity transaction which is... of no greater and no lesser interest to the worker than any other commodity transaction, with the exception of that which concerns the buying and selling of labour power. (Engels, quoted in Atkinson 1977, p. 8)

Housing policy in many countries suggests that the commodity is, indeed, a 'special' or merit commodity. Rosen (1985) discusses both the efficiency and equity arguments to subsidize housing. The question of the optimal tax treatment for housing is closely related to analysis of merit goods, starting with Musgrave (1959). The optimal tax treatment of merit goods has been analysed by, for example, Besley (1988), Racionero (2001), and Schroyen (2005). Also, 'specific egalitarianism', originally introduced by Tobin (1970) suggests that intervening in the distribution of certain goods essential to life, such as housing, might be beneficial. Thus paternalism may be a more plausible characterization of housing policy in many countries. It may take the form that government wants all households to receive a certain minimum level of housing services. As an example, Tenhunen and Tuomala (2009) consider a specific type of paternalism, where housing is introduced directly into the social welfare function.

Tenhunen and Tuomala (2009) provide some support for a view that a general income tax based on earning abilities alone would not be sufficient for redistributive purposes when individuals differ also in access to housing. The pattern of binding incentive compatibility constraints plays a crucial role in determining the optimal tax treatment of housing. The key lesson from their paper is that housing subsidy schemes have a redistributive role and they are non-linear. Because of the two-dimensional heterogeneity, a distortion in the housing price is an effective way to relax an otherwise binding self-selection constraint. This follows from the fact that even under separability, mimicker and mimicking individual do not consume the same amount of housing.

A justification for subsidizing or taxing housing consumption holds also without introducing any merit-good argument to the analysis; in the optimal tax model where agents differ in their abilities and access to housing it is optimal to tax and subsidize housing, even with separable preferences. An important feature of their results is that they do not depend on the specific form of social welfare function, but they hold also with all constrained Pareto-efficient allocation.

12.7 Non-welfarist social objectives: poverty minimization and commodity taxes

In contrast to much other policy discussion, where the emphasis is on income poverty (and sometimes other measures of social situations), the traditional concern in public economics is related to utility. This is reflected in the use of social welfare functions as governmental objectives. As in Chapter 5, one may wonder if the apparent difference in objectives between much policy discussion and optimal tax analysis has some important bearings on the optimality of different policies. It is therefore interesting to consider some non-welfarist objectives as well.[21]

There are of course many possible alternatives of non-welfarism, such as the pioneering work by Sen (1985). Here we have extended recent work on one perhaps crude form of non-welfarism, one that has the merits of capturing the common preoccupation with income-based measures of poverty and, moreover, of being readily tractable. Here we follow the approach taken in Kanbur, Keen, and Tuomala (1994a) and focus on a particular form of non-welfarism, namely alleviation of poverty. Poverty is defined here to capture either consumption or income poverty but can be interpreted to include other measures as well, such as the social indicators suggested by Atkinson et al (2002). Poverty alleviation provides a parsimonious form of social objective and yet can capture key elements of the tone of policy discussion.[22] It has to be stressed, however, that we do not set out to capture the richness of Sen's capabilities approach.

We discussed in Chapter 9 some earlier studies that examine optimal tax and transfer schemes under non-welfarist objectives.[23] Kanbur and Keen (1989) analyse what kind of linear income tax schedules could be used to alleviate poverty. Kanbur, Keen, and Tuomala (1994a) extend the analysis to a Mirrlees (1971) type of model to cover non-linear income taxation.[24] Besley and Kanbur (1988) analyse commodity tax/subsidy rules (when no income taxation is available) for poverty alleviation. Besley and Coate (1992, 1995) consider income-maintenance schemes, especially the role of workfare, when the objective is to minimize the costs related to these schemes. They all find that the some of the earlier results in tax analysis are no longer valid with non-welfarist objectives.

Pirttilä and Tuomala (2004) analyse optimal non-linear income taxation, linear commodity taxation, and public good provision when the government objective is to minimize poverty.[25] The tone of much policy discussion and a recent emphasis on social policy and poverty, especially in the EU, motivate exploring the implications of such a non-welfarist approach. The results from optimal tax policy under poverty alleviation may therefore help understand further why real-world tax policy often differs from recommendations from optimal tax literature. This analysis may also be seen as a

21 For example, the Mirrlees Review recognizes the nonutilitarian dimensions but it does not make these explicit.

22 One can criticize this objective for not guaranteeing Pareto efficiency in all cases. For example, people could be forced to work despite prohibitively high disutility of labour, to push them above the poverty line.

23 See Kanbur, Keen, and Tuomala (1994b) and Bradbury (2002) for surveys.

24 A related analysis by Wane (2001) considers a case where poverty is a public 'bad' that enters the individual's utility function.

25 Blomquist and Micheletto (2006) provide, in a two-type setting, a characterization of the properties of an optimal redistributive mixed tax scheme when the government evaluates individuals' well-being using a different utility function than the one maximized by individuals.

robustness analysis of optimal tax results in the mixed tax case when the objective is to alleviate poverty.

As discussed, the result found by Atkinson and Stiglitz (1976) has considerably played down the potential role of differentiated commodity tax rates as a redistributive device. Although the preference structure required for this result is not likely to be empirically valid (Browning and Meghir 1991), optimal tax theory is quite often seen to provide a limited role for commodity taxation in redistribution. Much policy advice has similarly argued that the scope of redistribution achieved by differentiated commodity tax rates is relatively minor and similar impacts could be more easily obtained by income-based targeting.

Yet most countries continue to use multiple commodity tax rates. How can one reconcile what we observe in practice and the message of the Atkinson–Stiglitz theorem? As discussed, one obvious option is non-separability of preferences between goods and leisure. In this case, the insight from optimal tax analysis (such as Christiansen 1984 and Edwards et al 1994) is that commodity tax rates should be lower for goods which are substitutes for leisure/complements with labour supply. However, it seems difficult to explain many of the lower VAT rates employed in EU countries with the help of this principle.[26] We previously listed cases that can explain some part of the observed commodity tax structures,[27] but it still seems plausible that the selection of many commodities for the lower taxed groups, such as foodstuffs, pharmaceutical products, and social housing, may well have been motivated by the simple desire to alleviate the tax burden on the poor. Pirttilä and Tuomala (2004) examine whether there is a theoretical case, based on poverty alleviation, for such favourable tax treatment. They also examine optimal effective marginal tax rates (combined influence of income tax and commodity taxes) under poverty alleviation.

The standard approach to poverty measurement compares individual or household h's income, z^h, to a poverty line x^*. Following the approach by Kanbur et al (1994b), poverty is measured by an index of

$$P = \int_0^\infty D(x^*, z) f(z) dz. \tag{8}$$

$D(x^*, z)$ denotes a deprivation index of individual earning income z and f(z) denotes the density function of z. It is assumed that D is differentiable and takes positive values if individual's income is below the poverty line z and is zero otherwise. In addition, $D_z < 0$; in other words, poverty decreases as income increases. For our purposes, this very general type of poverty index is sufficient. For instance, formulation (8) encapsulates the aggregate poverty gap (if $D(x^*, z) = \max(x^* - z, 0)$).

[26] Indeed, some commodities with lower tax rates (such as TV broadcasting and sporting events) are more likely to be complements with leisure. Subsidized or free public provision of day care can, however, be motivated by complementarity with labour supply.

[27] Boadway and Pestieau (2003) point out tax-evasion considerations.

In the simplest case, poverty is related to the lack of sufficient amount of one consumption good. We need to enlarge the set-up to cover a multiple-good case as well. One starting point is a reference-good bundle, to which actual consumption bundles are compared. In a general case, the reference-good bundle may also include an individual's labour supply. Denote this target by a vector (x', y'), where x refers to N commodity goods and y denotes labour supply. For the moment, we skip the discussion on how the reference bundle is determined. We need to decide how the gap between the reference bundle and actual consumption is measured. For simplicity, we consider a deprivation measure $D[x^*, z(q, n)]$, where

$$x^{*h} = s_x x' - s_y^h y' \tag{9}$$

and

$$z^h(q, n^h) = s_x x(q, n^h) - s_y^h y(q, n^h), \tag{10}$$

where q denotes consumer prices and $x(q, n^h)$ and $y(q, n^h)$ depict the uncompensated commodity demand and labour supply, respectively. Equation (9) determines the poverty line x^{*h} which is defined as the resources needed to attain the target vector at some shadow prices (s_x, s_y). Equation (10) determines, in turn, the resources that are actually at the disposal for h. Kanbur et al (1994b) point out that if y increases with n, and x^{*h} does not increase too rapidly with n (it would typically fall), then there exists a unique wage rate n* at which $z(q, n^*) = x^*$. Poverty can then be measured by varying n so that

$$P = \int_0^{n^*} D\left[x^*, z(q, n)\right] f(n) dn. \tag{11}$$

One also needs to determine the shadow prices (s_x, s_y) used in calculating the target vector. Technological reasons would suggest using producer prices p, so that $p_x = p = q - t$, where t denotes commodity taxes. Emphasis on the purchasing power of the poor would support the use of consumer prices. But there can be other weights attached to different commodities. One may include only some necessities with their producer prices, but goods that are not included in the target vector have zero weights. The social indicator approach by Atkinson et al (2002) may give some guidance on what sort of commodities are included in the target vector. The poverty line can then be interpreted as a broad measure consisting of basic consumption goods and goods that are deemed valuable to acquire (e.g. medicine, children's equipment, housing, etc.).

A benefit associated with measuring poverty by consumption is that it may convey better information about actual deprivation than information on income. This is why many economists working on poverty measurement prefer consumption-based poverty measures.

Giving the government the choice to include/exclude goods from the reference consumption bundle opens up the possibility for paternalism. Paternalism itself may or may not be desirable,[28] but the fact that not all goods are included in actual poverty measures defends our choice. The choice of the reference bundle nevertheless has many implications for poverty measurement. To exemplify, a person with a given income may not be poor, but another person with the same income but a consumption pattern where goods in the reference bundle are underrepresented is considered so. Pirttilä and Tuomala (2004), while considering identical preferences, abstract from these considerations.[29]

In what follows, we do not consider labour supply when measuring the target commodity groups, and concentrate on income(expenditure)–poverty measures alone. As discussed earlier, this captures the policy-makers' tone of focusing on income instead of leisure enjoyed by the poor. Then, $x^{*h} = sx^*$, and one may write the poverty index directly in terms of commodity demand as follows:

$$P = \int_0^{n^*} D[x^*, sx(q, w)]f(n)dn. \tag{12}$$

12.8 Optimal commodity taxation and non-linear income taxation

As shown in appendix 12.4, maximizing with respect to q yields the following formula:

$$t\int x_q^c f dn = -\int \pi(n)x_n(q, b, y, n)dn + \int \frac{1}{\lambda} D_m s x_q^c(q, y, v, n) f dn, \tag{13}$$

where $\pi = E_v^{-1}\alpha/\lambda > 0$ and $E_v = 1/v_E$.[30] where $D_m = \frac{\partial D}{\partial m} = \frac{\partial D}{\partial sx^c}$. The expression in (13) is an implicit formulation for the optimal commodity tax structure. The left-hand side of this formula measures, as pointed out by Mirrlees (1976a), the extent to which commodity taxation encourages/discourages consumption of different commodities. The first term on the right is similar to Mirrlees (1976a). It links the 'index of discouragement' at the left to the differences in consumption of a particular good among people with different abilities, n. $\frac{\partial x_i}{\partial n} < 0$ implies that the consumption of commodity i should be discouraged and $\frac{\partial x_i}{\partial n} > 0$ in turn implies that it should be encouraged. In other words, commodity taxes should be higher on the commodities that more able people tend to prefer.

[28] For a defence of paternalism, see Thaler and Sunstein (2003).

[29] A special case of poverty measurement is one where all goods are included in the measure with their consumer prices. Implications of such a choice will be briefly considered presently.

[30] The income tax is also assumed to be optimally chosen.

The second term on the right measures the impact of commodity taxation on poverty. Consider a case where good i is included in the deprivation measure and the tax (consumer price) of good j is increased. Then the index of discouragement at the left measures the discouragement of the consumption of j. If these goods are complements, then $x_q^c < 0$, and the consumption of good j is encouraged. Likewise, if i and j are substitutes, i.e. $x_q^c < 0$, the consumption of good j is discouraged through the tax system. Finally, since we know that the compensated own-price effect is always negative, we can infer that the consumption of goods that themselves feature in the deprivation measures should be encouraged.

These remarks can be summarized as follows: (i) when the government minimizes poverty, the consumption of goods that enter the deprivation measure (or are complementary to goods entering the deprivation measure) and that are favoured relatively strongly by low-ability households should be encouraged; (ii) consumption of goods that are substitutes for goods entering the deprivation measure or are favoured relatively strongly by high-ability households should be discouraged.

In terms of tax rates, commodity taxes should therefore be the highest for goods for which the high-ability households have a relatively strong taste and that are substitutes for goods in the poverty measure. Commodity taxes should be the lowest for goods for which the low-ability households have a relatively strong taste and that are included in the deprivation measure or are complementary to goods in the poverty measure.

The intuition for the first part of the result (i) is straightforward. If a good is included in the deprivation index, a decrease in its price leads to an increase in its consumption, and thus to a reduction in poverty. Likewise, setting a relatively low (high) tax for goods that are complements (substitutes) with goods in the deprivation measure reduces poverty indirectly. The magnitude of the tax effects also depends on the weight/shadow price(s) the goods have in the deprivation measure. For goods that are seen as essential in reducing deprivation, poverty concerns have a strong impact. Goods that have secondary importance for poverty reduction get less favourable tax treatment.[31]

On top of the income tax, it is therefore optimal to introduce a small subsidy to directly reduce the cost of consumption of goods that are deemed necessary/important for poverty alleviation. Since the starting point of income taxation alone also includes the possibility that all commodities are taxed equally, the result also suggests that a commodity tax structure with a basic VAT rate applicable to most commodities and lower rates applied to some basic commodities can be optimal when the government seeks to alleviate poverty. Many of the real-world commodity tax systems have such a feature. Allowing the government to minimize poverty may therefore explain many existing commodity tax structures, which have been hard to combine with messages of conventional tax theory.

[31] A special case where all goods enter the deprivation measure with their consumer price (q) implies that the last term at the right of (13) is the following $\int \left(\frac{1}{\lambda}\right) D_m \left(x^c + q x_q^c\right) f dn$. It is unfortunate that in this case, if $x_q^c < 0$, one cannot sign the term.

The interpretation of the second part (ii) of our summary results is the same as earlier tax analysis. The government is still constrained by asymmetric information, and it must design its tax schedules so that individuals' incentive compatibility constraints are not violated. Christiansen (1984) and Edwards et al (1994) show that goods that are negatively related to labour supply should be taxed relatively more. Holding income constant, a reduction in hours worked can be achieved by an increase in skills. Therefore, a good for which people with higher abilities have stronger taste is negatively related to labour supply.

The incentive effect vanishes if consumer preferences are separable between goods and leisure (Atkinson and Stiglitz 1976). In this case, the demand for different commodities does not vary with the wage rate (or labour supply), and the first term on the right of (13) is always zero. However, even with separable preferences, the second term on the right in (13) may still be positive or negative. This gives rise to the following observation: when the government seeks to minimize poverty, even with separable preferences between goods and leisure, non-uniform commodity taxation is still optimal.

Based on utility maximization and welfarist social welfare objectives, the Atkinson–Stiglitz result and its generalizations are often used as an argument against the use of differentiated commodity taxation as a redistributive device (most notably in the Mirrlees Review). Direct income transfers (as part of an optimal income tax scheme) would be sufficient instead. In the present context, there is no reason to suppose that influencing income is better than affecting consumption of the commodities. The poverty index depends directly on the consumption of some of the commodities, and it is in the interest of the government to promote their consumption. This also implies that income-based targeting is not necessarily superior to targeting based on consumption goods.

12.9 **Effective marginal tax rates**

From the first-order conditions we obtain the effective marginal tax rates[32]

$$1 + tx_z + (1 - tx_b)\phi = \frac{1}{f}\pi\phi_n + \frac{1}{\lambda}D_m p x_z^c, \qquad (14)$$

where τ is defined to be the marginal rate of substitution between income and expenditure on goods that are taxed on linear scale, i.e. $\phi(x, y, n) = -(\partial b/\partial z)_u = -E_z(q, z, n, v)$. As in Mirrlees (1976a), the left-hand side of (14) measures the total increase in the tax liability (including commodity taxes and the income tax), or the effective marginal tax rate, of a household when income increases.

[32] See appendix 12.1 for details.

These observations can be summarized as follows: when the government minimizes poverty, the effective marginal tax rate is zero at the top of the income distribution, but it may be positive or negative at the bottom of the income distribution. If some work is always desirable, and additional income increases the demand for goods that are needed to alleviate poverty, then the effective marginal tax rate is negative at the bottom of the income distribution.[33]

The standard result in optimal tax analysis—there should be no distortion at the top—carries over to the present case with poverty minimization. This is not surprising since the individual at the top is not the concern in poverty alleviation programmes. But the result differs from standard welfarist tax analysis, where the marginal tax rate at the bottom of the income distribution is also zero. The effective marginal tax rate at the bottom of the income distribution can in general be positive or negative. The intriguing case is the one where the goods in the poverty index are normal (additional income increases their demand). With the negative effective marginal tax rate, the government can motivate the poor individual to work more and earn more income. When no weight is given to the leisure of this individual, such a policy is clearly desirable from the poverty alleviation point of view. The result can also be seen as a justification for various policies of wage subsidization that are currently applied in some countries, either through cuts in employer's social security contributions or through systems such as the EITC.

Kanbur et al (1994a) (see Chapter 9) derived similar results for the case where the government has access to income tax only. The novelty here is to calculate the effective marginal tax rates that include both the income tax and commodity taxes. Typically, one would assume that commodity taxes are on average positive, and therefore the result would tend to reduce the marginal tax rates of the income tax only. However, in the present case the consumption of commodities that are relevant for poverty calculation should be subsidized. If no other commodity taxes are in use, the observation based on (14) would tend to increase the marginal tax rates relative to those derived in the case of no commodity taxes or subsidies.

The analysis shows that relatively low commodity tax rates (or subsidies) should be placed on goods that are included in the poverty measure. This conclusion holds even if preferences are separable between goods and leisure. In contrast to the result by Atkinson and Stiglitz (1976), non-uniform commodity taxation can therefore be optimal in a large number of situations. More generally, the consumption of goods that are complements (substitutes) for goods entering the deprivation measure should be encouraged (discouraged).

[33] Proof: Consider first the end point at the top of income distribution. Then the transversality condition in (14) implies that the first term at the right of (14) is zero. Assuming that the highest income earner is not poor, the second term is zero as well. At the bottom of income distribution, if some work is always desirable (no bunching), the first term at the right is again zero. However, in general the second term may be positive or negative. If $x_z > 0$, the second term is negative, since $D_m < 0$. QED

The simple, parsimonious, deprivation index applied here may be too crude a formulation of a real-world government objective function. One important avenue would be to explore if there are political economy arguments—such as altruistic preferences or efficiency losses from poverty—that would motivate such a choice. What is sufficient for our qualitative results to hold is, however, that, in addition to standard welfarist objectives, the government also cares about poverty. The social welfare function could therefore also be a weighted average of social welfare and poverty. Another important area for further research would be to analyse the quantitative importance of the results using simulations. However, to our knowledge, no computational results are available in the mixed tax case even under welfarist objectives.

12.10 **Optimal mixed taxation and externalities**

The mixed taxation case opens up a forum to discuss issues that are, though perhaps not totally neglected, at least rarely addressed in environmental tax analysis. These include the impact of externalities on marginal tax rates and the accurate role of commodity taxation in the presence of externalities. The Atkinson–Stiglitz result allows us to achieve all the desired redistribution through income taxation and there is no need to use indirect taxes for equity objectives. One caveat which is entered is that efficiency may require taxes to be levied, or subsidies paid, on goods and services that are socially costly or beneficial—or so-called externalities. The seminal paper in environmental tax analysis that addresses redistributional concerns is that by Sandmo (1975), which, among other things, analyses optimal commodity taxation structure in the presence of an externality in a many-person economy.

In political discussion, the idea of using environmental taxation to finance part of government's budget has had great interest. This possibility has also produced a growing body of economic research analysing this public finance aspect of environmental taxes. The models used to study the issue, such as Bovenberg and van der Ploeg (1994) and Bovenberg and de Mooij (1994), consist typically of an identical individual economy with proportional taxes and have efficiency as the sole objective of the tax system.[34]

This approach lacks, however, some features that might be relevant in environmental tax analysis. First of all, concentration on a representative consumer economy excludes the analysis of redistributional concerns' influence on environmental policy. These redistributional considerations are, however, likely to become an important determinant of environmental tax policy, since the results from some empirical studies (Smith 1992, Harrison 1994, Fullerton, Leicester, and Smith 2010) suggest that environmental taxes tend to be, at least slightly, regressive. Second, analysing solely the choice between

[34] For surveys on the double dividend theme (as it is known in the literature), see Goulder (1995) and Oates (1995).

proportional income tax and pollution tax, as in Bovenberg and de Mooij (1994), restricts the use of various tax instruments in an unnecessary way compared to the taxation systems actually in use: in most developed countries, income is taxed on a non-linear scale, whereas indirect taxation is linear. Hence, a thorough analysis of the way the use of environmental taxes as a source of public revenues influences the choice between income and other forms of taxation calls for the use of a relevant framework, which in most cases is the mixed taxation one.

Pirttilä and Tuomala (1997), Cremer and Gahvari (1998), Micheletto (2008), and Tenhunen (2008) study environmental policy within the mixed taxation framework. This setting for tax analysis contains very many relevant features of tax policy objectives encountered in reality—namely, consideration of revenue drawing, redistribution, and environmental quality. Among other things, this approach provides the opportunity to examine whether the earlier models targeted to analyse the public finance aspect of environmental taxation, while abstracting from the analysis of non-linear taxation and redistributional concerns, still derive reliable findings.

With only income taxation in use, Pirttilä and Tuomala (1997) derive a rule for the shadow price of the externality, measured in terms of public funds, that determines the magnitude of the externality-based parts in the marginal tax rates. The results reveal that while the externality's direct harmful effect raises the marginal tax rates, the indirect impact, arising from the self-selection constraint, dampens the rise in the most plausible case. This is because the exacerbation of pollution decreases the value of leisure and hence the incentive of the high-ability type to mimic the choice of the low-ability one, which in turn facilitates redistribution and alleviates the harmfulness of the externality. Although the sign of the marginal tax rates under most general conditions is indefinite, introducing separability between leisure and the externality excludes the self-selection effect and implies an unambiguous rise in marginal tax rates.

The reasoning above carries over to the mixed taxation case as well, but the shadow price of the externality is then determined also by the commodity tax revenue effects arising from changes in pollution level. The rules of the (effective) marginal tax rates are also slightly revised in this case: with harmful externality, the marginal tax rates rise (fall) if the environmentally harmful goods are normal (inferior). These conclusions concerning the marginal tax rates therefore suggest that the results derived in some earlier models, abstracting from income tax analysis and containing decreasing progressivity, might be partly misleading.

In the first-best world Pigouvian corrective taxes are equal to the marginal social damage. Suppose the utility function of consumer i is $U = U(x_c^i, x_d^i, y^i, E)$, where x_c is the consumption of a clean good, X_d is the consumption of a 'dirty' good, y is labour supply, and E is environmental quality, $E(\sum_i x_d^i)$, $E' < 0$. Hence 0 environmental damage depends negatively on the aggregate consumption of the good. Consumers are 'atomistic'. They do not take environmental harm into account in consumption decisions. Consumer optimization implies that $\frac{U_d^i}{U_c^i} = \frac{q_d}{q_c}$, where $q_i = p_i + t_i$ consumer prices. This means that the government can implement the first-best situation by setting taxes $t_c = 0$

and $t_d = \frac{-\sum_i U_E^i E'}{\lambda}$. This implies that the marginal environmental damage is equal to the Pigouvian corrective tax.

How should corrective taxes with pre-existing tax distortions be set, i.e. when taxes are also used both to collect revenue and to redistribute income? The first analysis of this question is by Sandmo (1975). He showed that the so-called additivity property holds. The corrective or environmental term is only present in the tax formula for the dirty good, i.e. $t_c = t_c^R$ and $t_d = t_d^R + t_d^P$ where R refers to the (Ramsey) tax rule without externalities and P to the corrective part of the tax rule.

The findings regarding the role of commodity taxation in the mixed case indicate, first of all, that the additivity property discovered by Sandmo also applies in the broader set-up of the present paper. The property shows that the externality-based part of commodity taxation is added to the tax rules of the environmentally harmful good only; the level of this term is determined by the shadow price of the externality, and its interpretation corresponds therefore to the discussion in the previous paragraph. A striking feature concerning the externality-internalizing taxation is that, with suitably chosen preference restrictions (that are not less general than those used in many related papers), the externality-based part of commodity taxation is exactly the same as the first-best Pigou principle. Moreover, expressing the commodity tax rule by means of aggregate compensated demand reveals that commodity taxation is determined by the self-selection considerations targeted to facilitate redistribution on the one hand, and by the externality-based objectives on the other.

Tenhunen (2007) shows that the Sandmo result of the separability of environmental taxes fails with two-dimensional heterogeneity in the pooling optimum, but not in the separating optimum. The explanation for this is that there are too few policy instruments in the pooling equilibrium: commodity taxes should take care of both redistribution and externality internalization.

Pirttilä and Tuomala (1997) and Cremer et al (1998) have shown that when preferences are separable so that $U = U(\zeta(x_c^i, x_d^i), y^i, E)$, i.e. consumer demand depends neither on the amount of leisure nor environmental quality, and the income tax is set optimally, then the first-best Pigouvian tax can be used even in a second-best setting. This means that redistributional concerns need not be taken into account when setting environmental taxes. Tax distortions do not affect the corrective part of taxation as opposed to the earlier 'double dividend' literature. Needless to say, the conditions for this result are unlikely be true in real life.

12.11 Merit goods and commodity taxation

The notion of merit goods, as initiated by Musgrave (1959), is used as another motivation for public intervention that is distinct from those cases just described. Examples for merit-good arguments are easy to find in reality. Compulsory education is perhaps the best known example of merit goods, whereas banning drug use is used to protect consumers from a harmful demerit good. In all such arguments, the principle of consumer sovereignty is ignored. The government's intervention is thought to be justified, since consumers make faulty choices. Public policy is then designed to correct consumers' choice, often against their will.

First-best commodity tax rules for merit goods, derived in the situation where there is no need to resort to distortionary taxation, are directly targeted to correct the difference between private and social valuations of these goods. In a second-best situation with distortionary linear taxation, Ramsey-type rules emerge. Consumption of commodities that are complementary to the merit goods should be encouraged, while substitutes should be discouraged (see e.g. Besley 1988).

Racionero (2001) considers linear commodity taxation in the presence of merit goods when the government has access to non-linear income taxation as well.[35] Racionero (2001) utilizes a merit-good modelling due to Besley (1988), where individuals disregard the beneficial impact of consumption of one good on health, whereas the health effect is taken into account in the government's assessment of individual welfare. Assuming that preferences are weakly separable between consumption and leisure—when no commodity taxes would be needed without merit-good considerations—there should still be a subsidy on the consumption of the merit good. The size of the subsidy is shown to be a sum of two elements. It depends, first, on the average of the marginal effects on health over individuals of different income level. Second, a covariance term emerges, which measures the dispersion of the marginal effects on health across population. If, for instance, workers with low income-earning ability are more sensitive to the subsidy (increase the consumption of the merit good relatively more when subsidized), the subsidy tends to be higher.[36]

Following Kanbur et al (2006), suppose that the individuals do not care about additional positive effects of certain goods on health, while the government does. This divergence can be expressed in the following way:

$$u^g = u(x, x_h, y) + \psi(x_h), \tag{15}$$

where u^g reflects government's preferences and u refers to individuals' preferences. $\psi(x_h)$ denotes the health function ($\psi' > 0$ and $\psi'' < 0$). Schroyen (2005) has provided an alternative formulation, where the idea is that the marginal rate of substitution between the (de)merit good and a numeraire good is higher (lower) for the government than for the individual. The general structure of the tax rule below would remain similar if the merit good was modelled along the lines of Schroyen (see Pirttilä and Tenhunen 2008 for details).

[35] Racionero (2000) examines the case where individuals also differ in their preferences over the merit good, but government only utilizes income taxation.

[36] Similar modelling has been used by Racionero (2001) and, more generally, by Besley (1988).

Using partially indirect utility functions, we write the government's welfare function as follows:

$$W = \int (v(q, y, b, n) + \psi(x_h))f(n)dn, \tag{16}$$

where $b = \sum q_i x_i + q_h x_h$. Now with weakly separable preferences we can derive, using the same procedure as in appendix 8.2, the implicit commodity tax formula for a merit good:

$$t^m \int (x^h)^c_q f dn = -\int \frac{1}{\lambda} \psi'(x^h)(x^h)^c_q f dn, \tag{17}$$

where $(x^h)^c$ is compensated demand. The left-hand side of (17) measures the extent to which commodity taxation encourages/discourages consumption of merit good. The term on the right-hand side measures the impact of health effect of merit good. Since $(x^h)^c_q < 0$, the term is positive, suggesting that the consumption of merit goods should be encouraged. In terms of tax rates, commodity tax on merit goods should be low or negative (a subsidy).

12.12 **Sin taxes**

One reason why people can end up making choices against their own good is excessive discounting of future. This may result in e.g. over-consumption of goods that offer initial satisfaction but belated suffering. O'Donoghue and Rabin (2003) consider how a paternalistic government could respond to such a situation by designing appropriate, corrective, 'sin' taxes.[37]

We can capture some of the arguments developed by O'Donoghue and Rabin (2003) in the mixed tax framework. Consider a case where consumers have self-control problems, i.e. they end up consuming more of a harmful good than they ex ante would consider the right amount. Utility is $u = u^*(x, a, z, n)$, where a is a 'sin' good (x is untaxed). All consumers have some degree of self-control problem so that there is an over-consumption of a. By contrast, optimal behaviour maximizes $u = u^{**}(x, a, z, n)$, so that $a^* > a^{**}$. Otherwise the model is the same as the one used above. Typically self-control models involve a dynamic element (e.g. the harm from eating unhealthy food occurs in the future), but the static formulation of the self-selection constraint is still possible, since the choice between healthy and harmful consumption occurs at present. Now we have, using the same procedure as in appendix 8.2,

[37] Similar modelling has been used by Racionero (2001) and, more generally, by Besley (1988). See also Haavio and Kotakorpi (2011).

$$t_a \int a_q^c f dn = -\int \pi(n) a_n dn - \int \frac{1}{\lambda} P_a a_q^c f dn. \tag{18}$$

With weakly separable preferences (the first term on the right-hand side is zero), we have $t_a > 0$, i.e. the consumption of the sin good should be taxed. If the first term of the right is non-zero, the optimal commodity taxes are a combination of traditional welfarist concerns and the need to influence the consumption of the harmful good.

An alternative formulation of sin goods might be one where the degree of irrationality is assumed to vary across individuals. As optimal taxation exercises where agents differ in two respects (as ability and tastes) are difficult, we concentrate on a simpler case where individuals do not differ in terms of their income-earning ability. Utility may now be defined by $u(x, a, \phi)$, where ϕ is an index of irrationality, with density f. The government objective function takes the non-welfarist form $NW = \int_{\underline{\phi}}^{\overline{\phi}} \hat{u}(x, a) f(\phi) d\phi$. In other words, $\hat{u}$ is the social utility derived from a ϕ individual's consumption. Now we can reinterpret our model in Chapter 9.

The optimal marginal tax rate formula can be written as follows:

$$T' = \frac{\hat{u}_x (s - \hat{s})}{\lambda} - \frac{\mu(\phi) u_x s_\beta}{\lambda f}, \tag{19}$$

where s is again the (individual) marginal rate of substitution between a and x and $\hat{s} = -\frac{\hat{u}_a}{\phi \hat{u}_x}$ denotes the social marginal rate of substitution. The second term on the right is again familiar from the welfarist literature, whereas the first term is novel. It captures the social value of divergence between private and social time preferences. Suppose that for the most irrational individual we have $\hat{s} > s$, so that society would like to see him to consume less of the sin good than he would choose to do at any given prices. At the optimum, the relative price of x faced by this individual is lowered to discourage his consumption of a.

12.13 **Optimal commodity taxes and income uncertainty**

Next we extend the mixed taxation framework in the case with income uncertainty. The model is otherwise the same as in Chapter 7. Once income z is realized, a worker-consumer pays income taxes according to schedule $T = z - c(z)$ and uses the rest of his or her income to choose the bundle of commodities x by maximizing utility.[38] The worker

[38] Note that while consumption takes place after the resolution of uncertainty, the consumer can still take commodity demand and prices into account when choosing his or her level of effort. In order to preserve the analysis analogous to conventional tax models under adverse selection, we abstract from explicit inter-temporal modelling.

is risk-averse with a partially indirect utility function $V(q, c(z), G, y)$, where $V_c > 0 V_{cc} < 0$, $V_y < 0$ and $V_{yy} < 0$. The consumer chooses a bundle x conditional on his choice of $y \in (y_L, y_H)$ (effort belongs to an interval from low to high) and expenditure on commodities, c. q denotes consumer prices and g the public good.

The worker-consumer chooses effort y to maximize private expected utility

$$\int V(q, c(z), G, y) f(z, y) dz, \tag{20}$$

The necessary condition of (20) is

$$\int (V_y + V f_y / f) f dz = 0, \tag{21}$$

where $f_y/f = \zeta$. It measures the impact of unobservable effort on the log-likelihood of income.

The government maximizes expected utility with respect to c(z), y, and q subject to the incentive compatibility condition (21) that individuals choose their effort optimally. This approach, where the incentive compatibility condition is captured by (21), is called the first-order approach (see Chapter 11 for more on this). To reiterate, in the optimal tax problem the government maximizes:

$$\int V(q, c(z), G, y) f(z, y) dz \tag{22}$$

subject to

$$\int (V_y + V\zeta) f dz = 0 \tag{23}$$

and a revenue constraint which, for large identical population with independent and identically distributed states of nature, can be written in the form

$$\int (z - px(q, c(z), g, y) - rg) f(z, y) dz = 0 \tag{24}$$

where p denotes producer prices of commodities and r is the production price of the public good.

From the first-order condition we get for each row of the matrix/vector equation

$$\int \sum_k x^c_{ik} t_k f dz = \mu \int V_c \frac{\partial x_i}{\partial y} f dz \tag{25}$$

Equation (25) is analogous to equation (86) in Mirrlees (1976a). The left-hand side of (25) is a measure of the extent to which commodity taxes encourage consumption of the different commodities. $\frac{\partial x_i}{\partial y} < 0$ implies that the consumption of commodity i should be discouraged and $\frac{\partial x_i}{\partial y} > 0$ in turn implies that it should be encouraged.

The redistributive income tax system involves distortions because of the reduced effort. The government wants to enhance effort, and one way to do so is to encourage consumption of goods whose valuation increases with effort. In other words, it is optimal to use differentiated commodity taxation (i.e. introduce an additional distortion), if the additional distortion reduces the overall distortions of the tax system.

Note that there is an interesting analogy to the commodity tax rule derived in the standard optimal taxation framework, where the government cannot observe the income-earning ability of individuals. In other words, income-earning ability is hidden information. In the standard model of Mirrlees (1976a), the consumption of goods for which, at a given income level, highly skilled people have a relatively strong taste should be discouraged. This policy reduces the value of leisure, encourages labour supply, and may reduce the overall distortions of the tax system. In the present framework, effort is unobservable to the government, i.e. it is hidden action. Therefore, the government seeks to encourage effort by its commodity tax policy. The analogy is therefore related to how the tax policy aims to reduce the efficiency losses stemming from asymmetric information: in standard optimal tax setting from hidden information (ability), and in the present, income-uncertainty framework, hidden action (effort).

Finally, from (25) we see that if preferences are separable between consumption and effort, i.e. the indirect utility takes the form $V[v(q, c(z)), G, y]$, there is no need to use differentiated commodity taxation. Income taxation alone or income taxation with uniform commodity taxation would be sufficient to achieve redistributive aims with minimal efficiency losses. The separability result of Atkinson and Stiglitz (1976), derived under varying income-earning ability, is therefore valid also in the case with income uncertainty.

The conditions for when the first-order approach is a valid solution procedure are rather stringent. However, it seems that for the Atkinson–Stiglitz separability result, these conditions are not needed. To see this, denote $v(q, c(z)) = w(z)$. Using Roy's identity we have $x = \xi(q, w(z))$. Now the worker/consumer minimizes the expenditure on goods with respect to prices, $\int pxf(z,y)dz = \int p\xi(q, w(z))f(z,y)dz$, subject to the condition that the consumer attains the maximum expected utility, $\int V[v(q, c(z)), G, y]f(z,y)dz = V^*$. For these preferences, the consumer gains nothing from commodity taxes. Costs are minimized if the consumer pays the producer prices only, i.e. there are no commodity taxes (q=p). Therefore, the Atkinson–Stiglitz separability result appears to be valid in the income-uncertainty case even without the assumptions required for the first-order approach.[39] Practical commodity tax policy rules remain therefore the same irrespective of whether income differences arise from uncertainty or differences in skills.

[39] It appears that even if we adopted the timing structure used by Cremer and Gahvari (2001)—that consumers commit to a consumption of some goods prior to the resolution of uncertainty—the Atkinson–Stiglitz result would still remain valid for the goods consumed after the resolution of uncertainty, if there is weak separability between these goods and effort. The taxation rule of the precommited consumption good would presumably have a complicated structure, a topic analysed by Cremer and Gahvari (2001).

12.14 Fully non-linear taxation and income uncertainty

In the analysis of fully non-linear taxation, one can proceed with standard direct utility functions of the form

$$\int u(x, y) f(z, y) dz, \tag{26}$$

where x is a vector of many goods. The necessary condition of (26) is

$$\int (u_y + u f_y / f) f dz = 0, \tag{27}$$

The government can directly control x for a given income. The first-order condition gives

$$\frac{u_{x_i}}{u_{x_j}} = \frac{p_i - \mu u_{yx_i}}{p_j - \mu u_{yx_j}}, \tag{28}$$

where $\mu = \alpha/\lambda$ (see appendix 8.4). Note first that with separable preferences, $u_{yx_i} = 0$. This means that there ought to be no distortion between goods; in other words, the marginal rate of substitution between i and j on the left should be equal to the marginal rate of transformation on the right. Therefore, a counterpart of the Atkinson–Stiglitz result holds under non-linear commodity taxation as well.

If i is more complementary[40] with effort than j is—or if i is a complement and j is a substitute with effort—the right-hand side of (5) goes down ($u_{yx_i} > 0$ and $u_{yx_i} > u_{yx_j}$). This means that the relative price of i decreases at the margin. Therefore its consumption is encouraged by the tax system, i.e. its marginal tax rate is negative. Likewise, the consumption of goods which are substitutes with effort is discouraged by a positive marginal tax rate.

This result is again connected with one derived by Mirrlees (1976a) for the fully non-linear case without income uncertainty. In his analysis, 'the marginal tax rates should be greater on commodities the more able would tend to prefer' (Mirrlees 1976a, p. 337). The marginal tax rates in Mirrlees (1976a) are related to the skill level (hidden information), whereas here they are related to the effort level (hidden action).

APPENDIX 12.1 PRODUCTION EFFICIENCY

The government maximizes social welfare function $W(u^1.,,,.u^H) = W(v(q, b^h), ...)$ $s.t \sum_h x^h(q, b^h) = z + g$ where x^h is h's individual net demands, $q = (q_1, ..., q_k)$ is a consumer price vector, $b = (b^1, ..., b^H)$ is a distribution of income, but h is not

[40] Complementarity here must be interpreted as increasing the value (or decreasing the discomfort) of effort, since $u_y < 0$.

individually observable. The private production $z = (z_1, \ldots, z_k)$ is chosen when prices are $p = (p_1, \ldots, p_k)$. The public production is $g = (g_1, \ldots, g_k)$ with shadow prices $s = (s_1, \ldots, s_k)$. In the pure commodity tax problem, b=0. In the more general problem, b^h = [profit share of individual h + b (lump sum transfer)]. Constant returns in the private sector imply zero profit in equilibrium and therefore all profit shares are zero. In this case, many alternative tax systems yield the same equilibrium. Suppose q, p, etc. are associated with an equilibrium (all market clear - $\sum_h x^h(q, b^h) = z + g$, private production $z = (z_1, \ldots, z_k)$ is chosen when prices are $p = (p_1, \ldots, p_k)$). Now let $p' = \lambda p, q' = \mu q, s' = \upsilon s, b' = \mu b$ for positive numbers λ, μ, υ. Then behaviour does not change, but the implied tax rates are now $t' = \mu q - \upsilon s, r' = \upsilon s - \lambda p$ where $r = s - p$ producer tax rate. These do not need be proportional to t and r. Some goods previously taxed may not be subsidized, and vice versa. Therefore one cannot answer such a question as: ought commodity i be taxed? There is no unique answer. We can choose some commodity as untaxed numeraire. This fixes the tax system for given relative prices, but changing the numeraire changes results.

Diamond and Mirrlees theorem: Assuming $p = (p_1, \ldots, p_k)$ and $s = (s_1, \ldots, s_k)$ under constant returns q^*, b^* maximize social welfare function $W(v(q, b^h), \ldots) s.t \sum_h x^h(q, b) \in X$, then $\sum_h x^h(q, b)$ is in the frontier of X.X is the aggregate production set, Z+G, where $Z = \sum Z^j$ is the private production set and G is in turn the public production set. $\sum_h x^h(q, b)$ in the frontier of X means that it is efficient; in other words, it is not possible to produce more of everything. This also implies that, if $\sum_h x^h(q, b^h) = z^* + g^*$, and z^* maximizes $p.z$ with z in Z, then p also gives shadow prices for the public sector; $s = p$.

Proof: Suppose $\sum_h x^h(q, b)$ lies in the interior of X. Then a small increase in b is possible while keeping $\sum_h x^h(q, b)$ in X. But increasing b increases every $v^h(q, b)$, and hence increases W. Therefore, q^*, b^* is not optimal. This contradicts the assumption, and proves the theorem.

If there are private profits (decreasing returns in the private sector) but the government taxes them at 100 per cent, the efficiency theorem still holds, because consumer demands and welfare are still independent of producer prices.

APPENDIX 12.2 OPTIMAL MIXED TAXATION

The government maximizes the welfare of the low-ability individual, given its budget constraint, the fixed utility to the high-ability class, and the self-selection constraint of the higher binding.

The Lagrangean of the government's problem is:[41]

[41] Alternatively, we could restrict the analysis to the same kind of externality modelling as in section (2); in this case, the FOC for commodity tax would not depend on E.

$$L = V^1(q, B^1, z^1) + \delta[V^2(q, B^2, z^2) - \bar{V}^2]$$
$$+ \mu[V^2(q, B^2, z^2) - V^2(q, B^1, z^1)] \tag{1}$$
$$+ \lambda\left[\sum_h \left(z^h - \sum_i p_i x_i^h(q, B^h, z^h)\right) - rG\right].$$

The first-order conditions with respect to z^h:s, B^h:s, the price q_j, and E are:

$$V_z^1 - \mu\hat{V}_z^2 + \lambda\left(1 - \sum_i p_i \frac{\partial x_i^1}{\partial z}\right) = 0, \tag{2}$$

$$V_B^1 - \mu\hat{V}_z^2 - \lambda\sum_i p_i \frac{\partial x_i^1}{\partial B} = 0 \tag{3}$$

$$(\delta + \mu)V_Y^2 + \lambda\left(1 - \sum_i p_i \frac{\partial x_i^2}{\partial z}\right) = 0 \tag{4}$$

$$(\delta + \mu)V_B^2 - \lambda\sum_i p_i \frac{\partial x_i^2}{\partial B} = 0 \tag{5}$$

$$-V_B^1 x_j^1 - (\delta + \mu)V_B^2 x_j^2 + \mu\hat{V}_B^2 \hat{x}_j^2 - \lambda\sum_h \sum_i p_i \frac{\partial x_i^h}{\partial q_j} = 0 \tag{6}$$

where the hat still refers to person 2 mimicking a type-1 individual.

In a Pareto-efficient mixed taxation scheme, the aggregate compensated change in the demand of commodity j is given by

$$\Delta x_j = \mu^*(x_j^1 - \hat{x}_j^2) \tag{7}$$

where

$$\mu^* = \frac{\hat{V}_B^2 \mu}{\lambda(x_q^{c1} + x_q^{c2})} < 0$$

Proof: In order to show this, we need to manipulate the first-order condition given in equation (6) in the following way:

$$\sum_h \sum_i t_i \frac{\partial x_i^{ch}}{\partial q_j} = \sum_h \sum_i t_i \frac{\partial x_j^h}{\partial q_i} \equiv \Delta x_j$$
$$= -\sum_h \sum_i p_i \frac{\partial x_i^h}{\partial B} x_j^h + \frac{1}{\lambda}\left[V_B^1 x_j^1 + (\delta + \mu)V_B^2 x_j^2 - \mu\hat{V}_B^2 \hat{x}_j^2\right], \tag{8}$$

where use has been made of the Slutsky relation

$$\frac{\partial x_i^{ch}}{\partial q_j} = \frac{\partial x_i^h}{\partial q_j} + \frac{\partial x_i^h}{\partial B} x_j^h \text{ and } \frac{\partial x_i^{ch}}{\partial q_j} = \frac{\partial x_j^{ch}}{\partial q_i} \text{(symmetry property)} \tag{9}$$

Then, substitution for V_B^1 from first-order condition (3), and for $(\delta + \mu)V_B^2$ from (5) in equation (7) gives the result in equation (6) in the text.

We may now proceed to calculate the effective marginal tax rates for both ability types. When the tax system consists of both direct and indirect tax components, the total taxes (denoted by τ) paid by individual h are (where $B = z - T(z)$):

$$\tau(z) = T(z) + \sum_i t_i x_i(q, z - T(z), z, n) \tag{10}$$

Differentiating this with respect to z gives the marginal effective tax rate

$$\tau(z) = T'(z) + \sum_i t_i \left(\frac{\partial x_i}{\partial B}(1 - T') + \frac{\partial x_i}{\partial z} \right) \tag{11}$$

Substituting (4) into (44) gives:

$$\tau'(z) = 1 + \sum_i t_i \frac{\partial x_i}{\partial z} + \left(\frac{V_z}{V_B} \right) \left(1 - \sum_i \frac{\partial x_i}{\partial B} \right) \tag{12}$$

This can be further modified if we utilize the following conditions, which can be derived from the adding-up conditions:[42]

$$\sum_i p_i \frac{\partial x_i}{\partial B} = 1 - \sum_i t_i \frac{\partial x_i}{\partial B} \tag{13}$$

$$\sum_i p_i \frac{\partial x_i}{\partial z} = - \sum_i t_i \frac{\partial x_i}{\partial z} \tag{14}$$

With the help of these equations we can write the formula for a marginal effective tax rate as:

$$\tau'(z) = 1 - \sum_i p_i \frac{\partial x_i}{\partial z} + \left(\frac{V_z}{V_B} \right) \sum_i p_i \frac{\partial x_i}{\partial B} \tag{15}$$

For this definition we can deduce the following proposition:

The effective marginal tax rates in a Pareto-efficient mixed taxation scheme:

(a) the marginal effective tax rate faced by the high-ability type is zero; (b) the marginal effective tax rate faced by the low-ability type is positive.

[42] $\sum_i q_i \frac{\partial x_i}{\partial B} = 1$ and $\sum_i q_i \frac{\partial x_i}{\partial z} = 0$.

Proof: The marginal effective tax rate faced by the high-ability household can be derived by dividing (4) by (5),

$$\frac{V_z^2}{V_B^2} = \frac{-1 + \sum_i p_i \frac{\partial x_i^2}{\partial z}}{\sum_i p_i \frac{\partial x_i^2}{\partial B}} \tag{16}$$

which can be rewritten after some rearrangements as

$$\frac{V_z^2}{V_B^2} \sum_i p_i \frac{\partial x_i^2}{\partial B} = -\left(1 - \sum_i p_i \frac{\partial x_i^2}{\partial z}\right). \tag{17}$$

Combining (15) and (17), the marginal tax rate faced by the high-ability type is given by $\tau'(z^2) = 0$.

Turn now to the tax rule for the low-ability type. Dividing (2) by (3) yields

$$\frac{V_z^1}{V_B^1} = \frac{\frac{\mu}{\lambda} \hat{V}_Y^2 - \left(1 - \sum_i p_i \frac{\partial x_i^1}{\partial z}\right)}{\frac{\mu}{\lambda} \hat{V}_B^2 + \sum_i p_i \frac{\partial x_i^1}{\partial B}} \tag{18}$$

Rearranging gives

$$\frac{V_z^1}{V_B^1} \sum_i p_i \frac{\partial x_i^1}{\partial B} = -\left(1 - \sum_i p_i \frac{\partial x_i^1}{\partial z}\right) + \frac{\mu \hat{V}_B^2}{\lambda} \left(\frac{\hat{V}_Y^2}{\hat{V}_B^2} - \frac{V_Y^1}{V_B^1}\right) \tag{19}$$

which can be substituted into equation (15) to give the marginal effective tax rate faced by the low-ability type

$$\tau'(z^1) = \mu^* \left(\frac{\hat{V}_z^2}{\hat{V}_B^2} - \frac{V_z^1}{V_B^1}\right) \tag{20}$$

The first term on the right-hand side is positive by the agent monotonicity condition (see appendix 2.1).

APPENDIX 12.3 KAPLOW'S RESULT

Kaplow's proof:

Individual's weakly separable—between labour and all other commodities—utility function can be expressed as $U = u(\psi(x_1, ..., x_k), y)$, where the subutility function ψ is homogenous across individuals. In other words the ratio of the marginal utilities of consumption for any two commodities i and j, at given levels of consumption of those commodities and of all other commodities, is independent of the level of labour supply.

The idea of the proof is that a tax system $(t_1, \ldots, t_k, T(ny))$ that includes both a non-linear income tax and a vector of commodity taxes can be replaced by a pure income tax $(t_1^*, \ldots, t_n^*, T^o(ny))$ that keeps all individual utilities constant and raises at least as much tax revenue.

We will examine an income tax schedule T°(ny) that has the property that, if all individuals continue to choose the same level of labour supply y(n) as under the initial tax system, then their utility will be unchanged. In other words, it is possible to construct such an income tax schedule for each income level due to the continuity of utility in income.

Let $\zeta(p_1 + t_1, \ldots, p_k + t_n, ny - T(ny)) \equiv \max_x \{\psi(x_1, \ldots, x_k) s.t. \sum_i (p_i + t_i)x_i(ny) = ny - T(ny)(1)\}$ be the indirect subutility function for all n individuals. Next we construct a Pareto-improving tax reform starting from an initial, differentiated commodity tax regime $(t_1, \ldots, t_n, T(ny))$. For simplicity, we then choose from among the multitude of equivalent undifferentiated tax systems the one for which $t_i^* = 0$, for all i. Moving to this commodity tax vector will tend to change individuals' utility because they no longer pay commodity taxes (or receive subsidies) and because, with a new relative price vector, they will change their consumption vector.

Define intermediate tax function T°(ny) such that

$$\zeta(t_1, \ldots, t_k, ny - T(ny)) = \zeta(t_1^*, \ldots, t_1^*, ny - T^0(ny))$$

Then such a T°(ny) (and is unique) as $\zeta(ny - T^o(ny), p)$ is strictly increasing in $ny - T^o(ny)$. This implies that $u(\zeta(t_1, \ldots, t_k, ny - T(ny))) = u(\zeta(t_1^*, \ldots, t_1^*, ny - T^0(ny))$ for all ny.

Hence, both the utility and the labour supply choice are unchanged for each individual. The next question is how revenue compares between the initial tax system and the new one. The idea will be to show that no individual under the new tax system $(t_1^*, \ldots, t_k^*, T^o(ny))$ can still afford the consumption vector purchased under the initial tax system $(t_1, \ldots, t_k, T(ny))$, and that the only way this can be true is if each individual pays more tax (commodity taxes and the income tax taken together) under the new system than under the initial one.

From the budget constraint and since $t_i^* = 0$, for all ny, we obtain

$$\sum_i p_i x_i > ny - T^o(ny) \tag{2}$$

or, using the budget constraint (1) for the initial system to substitute for $\sum p_i x_i(ny)$ on the left side of expression (2), we obtain

$$ny - T(ny) - \sum t_i x_i > ny - T^o(ny) \text{ or}$$
$$T^o(ny) > T(ny) + \sum t_i x_i \text{ for all ny.}$$

Hence the total revenue is higher under the new tax system $(t_1^*, \ldots, t_k^*, T^o(ny))$ than the initial tax system $(t_1, \ldots, t_k, T(ny))$.

APPENDIX 12.4 POVERTY MINIMIZATION AND COMMODITY TAXATION

Because of the need to deal with both non-linear and linear price structures, it is helpful to apply dual techniques to solve the optimization problem. We utilize partial expenditure and indirect utility functions, first discussed by Mirrlees (1976a), which are calculated for given income. Let the expenditure function for individual be $E(q, z, n, v) = \min[qx : \; u(x, z, n) = v]$ and the partially indirect utility function $v(q, b, z, w) = \max[u(x, z, n) : \; qx = b]$, where expenditure on linearly taxed goods is b = E.

Household optimization will be used to generate the incentive compatibility constraint for the government optimization. In the case where one good only is subject to non-linear taxation, for each n, x(n),z(n), maximize u subject to $qx=z-T(z)$. We want to express this in terms that can more easily be manipulated.

The individual's optimization implies that for any n, n',

$$E(q, z(n), u(x(n), z(n), n), n) \leq E(q, z(n), u(x(n), z(n), z'), n'). \tag{1}$$

since the right-hand side is by definition greater than or equal to $qx(n)$, which is in turn equal to the left-hand side. Thus $n' = n$ minimizes the right-hand side, and the derivative with respect to w' vanishes at w:

$$E_v u_n + E_n = 0 \tag{2}$$

On the other hand, using the envelope theorem, we know that $u_n = v'(n)$, since individuals are all maximizing utility subject to the same budget constraint. Therefore (2) implies that

$$v'(n) + E_n/E_v = 0. \tag{3}$$

The resource constraint for this economy is

$$\int (wz - px^c) f dw = A, \tag{4}$$

where $x^c = x^c(q, z, v, n)$ (= E_q) and w is a shadow price for z. (We assume w=1.) The Lagrangean of the government optimization problem can then be written as:

$$\begin{aligned} L &= \int \Big\{ (-D[x^*, sx^c(q, z, v, n)] + \lambda(z - px^c))f + \alpha v' + \alpha E_n/E_v \Big\} dn \\ &= \int \Big\{ (-D[x^*, sx^c(q, z, v, n)] + \lambda(z - px^c))f - \alpha' v + \alpha E_n/E_v \Big\} dn \\ &\quad - \alpha(0)v(0) + \alpha(\infty)v(\infty), \end{aligned} \tag{5}$$

where the latter formulation follows from integrating $\alpha v'$ by parts. Maximizing with respect to q yields the following first-order condition:

$$-\int D_m s x_q^c f dn - \int \{\lambda p x_q^c f + \alpha \partial(E_n/E_v)/\partial q\} dn = 0, \tag{6}$$

where $D_m = \frac{\partial D}{\partial m} = \frac{\partial D}{\partial s x^c}$.

Combining Slutsky symmetry and the fact that $q x_q^c = 0$, we have:

$$p x_q^c = (q - t) x_q^c = -t x_q^c = -(q - p) x_q^c. \tag{7}$$

Using the properties of the expenditure function,

$$\begin{aligned}\partial(E_n/E_v)/\partial q &= (E_{nq}E_v - E_{vq}E_n)/E_v^2 = \left(x_n^c - (E_n/E_v)x_v^c\right)/E_v \\ &= E_v^{-1}(x_n^c + x_v^c u_n) = E_v^{-1} x_n(q, E, n)\end{aligned} \tag{8}$$

Substituting (7) and (8) for (6) then gives the expression in equation (9), i.e. (13) in the text.

$$t\int x_q^c f dn = -\int \pi(n) x_n(q, b, y, n) dn + \int \frac{1}{\lambda} D_m s x_q^c(q, z, v, n) f dn, \tag{9}$$

where $\pi = E_v^{-1}\alpha/\lambda > 0$ and $E_v = 1/v_E$.[43]

To obtain the necessary conditions for the effective marginal tax rates, (5) is differentiated with respect to v and z:

$$-D_m x_v^c f - \lambda p x_v^c f + \alpha\{\partial(E_n/E_v)/\partial v\} - \alpha' = 0, \tag{10}$$

$$\alpha(0) = \alpha(\infty) = 0, \tag{11}$$

$$-D_m s x_z^c f + \lambda(1 - p x_z^c) f + \alpha\{\partial(E_n/E_v)/\partial z\} = 0. \tag{12}$$

Bearing in mind the definition of ϕ, the following properties hold:

$$\partial(E_n/E_v)/\partial z = E_v^{-1}\{E_{nz} - (E_n/E_v)E_{nz}\} = E_v^{-1}(E_{zn} + E_{zn}u_n) = -E_v^{-1}\phi_n(x, z, n) \tag{13}$$

and

$$p x_z^c = q x_z^c - (q - p) x_z^c = E_y - t(x_z + x_b E_z) = -(1 - t x_b)\phi - t x_z. \tag{14}$$

Combining these with (12) enables one to write equation (14) in the text.

APPENDIX 12.5 OPTIMAL COMMODITY TAXES AND INCOME UNCERTAINTY

The Lagrangean function of the optimization problem is:

$$L = \int \left\{ V + \alpha(V_y + V\zeta) + \lambda(z - px - rG) \right\} f(z, y) dz \tag{1}$$

[43] The income tax is also assumed to be optimally chosen.

The first-order conditions with respect to c(z) (point-wise maximization) and q are:

$$\frac{\partial L}{\partial c(z)} = V_c(1+\alpha\zeta) + \alpha V_{yc} - \lambda p x_c = 0 \text{ for all z} \tag{2}$$

$$\frac{\partial L}{\partial q} = \int \{V_q(1+\alpha\zeta) + \alpha V_{yq} - \lambda p x_q\} f dz = 0 \tag{3}$$

The solution does not depend on optimality of y and therefore the first-order condition for it is not shown. Note that (2) can be rewritten as $V_c = \frac{\lambda p x_c}{1+\alpha\zeta} - \frac{\alpha V_{yc}}{1+\alpha\zeta}$. Without commodity taxation and separable preferences it would reduce to the standard first-order condition in this class of models, i.e. $V_c = \frac{\lambda}{1+\alpha\zeta}$.

Finally, we rule out the possibility of obtaining the first-best solution by imposing an extremely large penalty on the worst outcome and allowing for almost perfect insurance for other outcomes (Mirrlees 1974). This solution would invalidate the interior solution on which we concentrate. Extreme penalties would also be undesirable in practical applications.

We will first concentrate on characteristics of optimal commodity taxation. From Roy's identity, $V_q = -xV_c$. Therefore, we can write in (3) the cross-derivatives

$$V_{yq} = V_{qy} = -xV_{cy} - x_y V_c \tag{4}$$

Manipulating the first-order condition, we obtain

$$\int -p x_q^c f dz = \mu \int V_c x_y f dz \tag{5}$$

where $\mu = \alpha/\lambda$.

Slutzky symmetry implies $p x_q^c = (q-t)x_q^c = -t x_q^c = -x_q^c t$.

Reorganizing the term $p x_g^c$, one arrives at equation (25) in the main text.

Using (4) and the Slutsky equation, we have:

$$\int \{-x(V_c(1+\zeta) + \alpha V_{cy} - \lambda p x_c) - \alpha x_y V_c - \lambda p x_q^c\} f dz = 0.$$

In addition to those assumptions 1–4 in Chapter 11, appendix 11.1, we now need the following assumption 5. Engel curves are either convex or linear (Engel curve condition ECC). An increase in income must not increase consumption in a diminishing way, i.e. $x_{cc} \geq 0$. This assumption is not needed if commodity taxes are zero.

Assumptions 1–2 are sufficient when utility is separable between consumption and effort. The unseparable case—which we want to focus on, since then commodity taxes may play a role—requires conditions 3 and 4, as shown by Alvi (1997). Assumption 5 is needed because of the inclusion of multiple commodities.

There is no doubt that these conditions are rather stringent and they may not necessarily hold. However, some of them are less restrictive than they first seem. For a large number of non-separable utility functions, condition (4) is valid because $\frac{\partial \kappa}{\partial y} = 0$. An earlier example often used in this strand of literature is a constant relative risk aversion utility function, $\frac{c^{1-\gamma}}{1-\gamma} - y$. Its non-separable counterpart, $\frac{c^{1-\gamma}}{1-\gamma}(a + by^{-\beta})$, for example, satisfies condition (4).

Assumption (5) is, in turn, valid for the so-called Gorman form of utility functions used extensively in traditional empirical analysis of consumption behaviour (see e.g. Deaton and Muellbauer 1980). There, the consumers' cost function is of the form $c(v, q, y) = a(q, y) + vb(q, y)$. Inverting it gives indirect utility: $v(q, c, y) = \frac{c - a(q,y)}{b(q,y)}$.

The (compensated) demand for good k is then $x_k^c = a_k(q, y) + \frac{b_k(q,y)}{b(q,y)}[c - a(q, y)]$, which is indeed linear in c, but it still allows consumer demand to be dependent on effort, y. Finally, it is important to remember that the conditions 1–5 above are sufficient, not necessary. There may therefore be other cases when FOA is a valid solution procedure.

APPENDIX 12.6 OPTIMAL NON-LINEAR TAXES AND INCOME UNCERTAINTY

The Lagrangean and the first-order condition for x_i are therefore

$$L = \int \{u(x, y) + \alpha(u_y + u\zeta) + \lambda(z - px - rG)\} f(z, y) dz \tag{1}$$

$$u_{x_i}(1 + \alpha\zeta) + \alpha u_{yx_i} - \lambda p_i = 0 \tag{2}$$

Dividing the optimality rule for x_i with one for another good, x_j, gives formula (3) in the text.

$$\frac{u_{x_i}}{u_{x_j}} = \frac{p_i - \mu u_{yx_i}}{p_j - \mu u_{yx_j}},$$

where $\mu = \alpha/\lambda$.

13 Public provision and optimal taxation

As in the case of commodity taxation, publicly provided private goods and pure public goods, when these goods are financed by non-linear income taxation, can be seen as additional instruments for public redistribution policy. Much of the activities of the modern welfare state are related to provision of private goods (pensions, education, health care, childcare, care of the elderly, etc.). In practice, a large share of public expenditure is indeed allocated to the provision of those goods. In some advanced countries the share of GDP would be as much as 15–20 per cent (see Figure 13.2 on some European countries), whereas the share of pure public goods (general administration, defence, etc.) is quite small (see Figure 13.1).

13.1 Provision of public goods

In the case of pure public goods, exclusion of consumers is neither possible nor desirable. In the first-best world, optimality for public goods requires that the sum of each individual's marginal valuation on the extra unit is equal to the marginal cost; $\Sigma MRS = MC$. How should this Samuelson provision rule be adjusted when the provision is funded by distortionary taxation and the government has redistributive aims? In particular, since collecting public funds imposes distortions, should the public good be underprovided relative to the Samuelson rule? As noted by Gahvari (2006), we can distinguish two different strands of research literature. One of them studies the question of the optimal provision of public goods in the presence of a general income tax (see, e.g., Mirrlees 1976a, Christiansen 1981, and Boadway and Keen 1993). The second generalizes the concept of the marginal cost of public funds (MCPF) to take account of the government's redistributive concerns (see, e.g., Dahlby 1998, 2008; Sandmo 1998; Slemrod and Yitzhaki 2001; and Christiansen 1999, 2007).

Long ago, Pigou (1947, pp. 33–4) claimed that the existence of distortionary taxes was a reason for not 'carrying public expenditures as far' as would be done if we could apply the rule of equating marginal cost to marginal benefit of individuals. Pigou's claim has often been employed also in political debate on the size of the public sector.[1] Actual

[1] These tools can also be used in debate about austerity programmes (see Atkinson 2014).

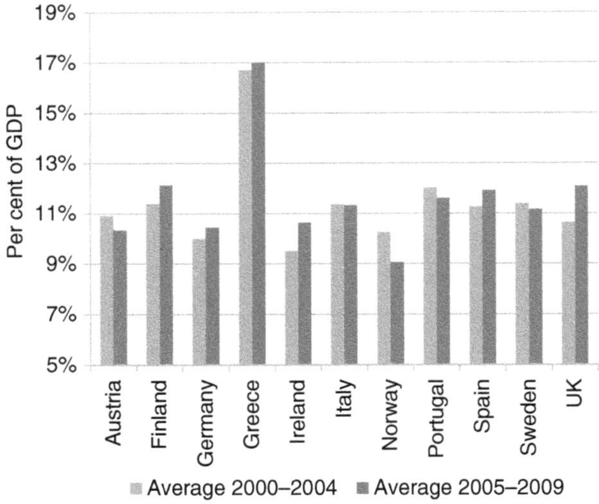

Figure 13.1 Public goods in kind
Source: OECD COFOG.

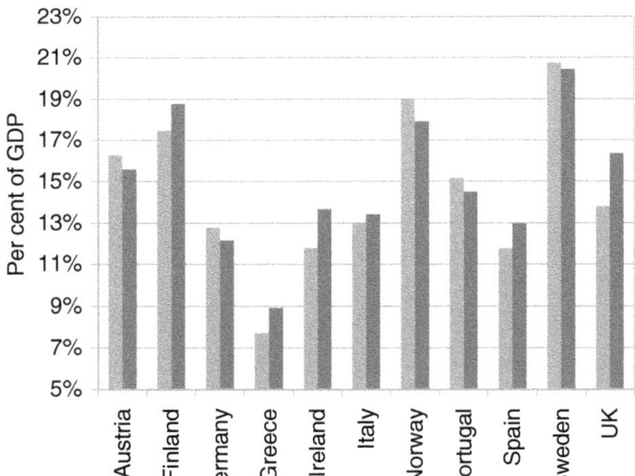

Figure 13.2 Publicly provided private goods
Source: OECD COFOG.

economies should thus attain a lower level of public expenditure than in the situation where lump-sum taxes are assumed to be available. The validity of Pigou's reasoning, however, is usually justified in the Ramsey economy, where linear taxes and a representative consumer are assumed. This issue was analysed by Atkinson and Stern (1974) in the Ramsey tax model, following Dasgupta and Stiglitz (1971),[2] who had noticed that Pigou's argument is not necessarily correct in an optimal tax framework. Atkinson and Stern (1974) provide an example which is consistent with Pigou's claim. Later on this example was generalized by Wilson (1991) and Gaube (2000b). These papers study a Ramsey economy, where individuals are identical and there is no lump-sum tax. It is obvious that this issue needs to be considered in an economy with heterogeneous individuals. The comparison between the first- and second-best levels of public good with an identical individual is clearly uninteresting, since there is no plausible reason to rule out a poll tax. Wildasin (1984), King (1986), Wilson (1991), and Mirrlees (1994) consider an economy with heterogeneous individuals and point out that the government's informational constraints allow for the introduction of a lump-sum tax in addition to linear consumption taxes. Although in real-world economies we do not find anything exactly corresponding to a lump-sum tax or subsidy, Mirrlees (1994, p. 223) explains that 'personal tax allowances are not dissimilar in effect for those not on the lowest incomes, and welfare payments apply to many on the lowest incomes'.

These papers show that in this setting, the second-best optimal level of provision can be greater that the first-best level. This is explained by the observation that the lump-sum tax accommodates the public sector with a non-distortionary source of marginal finance and may hence lead to a higher level of public provision in second-best than in first-best. More specifically, Mirrlees (1994) introduces a perturbation by a small amount of inequality in n (skill/wage) and compares the resulting change in the first-best and second-best levels of public good, Furthermore, he assumes that utility is separable between private goods and public good, $v(q,b,n)+ \psi(G)$ (q=commodity prices and b=lump-sum income). Mirrlees (1994) shows that the second-best level of the public good is higher than the first-best one if $\frac{v_{bbn}}{v_{bn}} > \frac{v_{bbb}}{2v_{bb}}$. This condition can be expressed in the following form, $\frac{2v_b}{v_{bn}} A_n + A + \frac{A_b}{A} < 0$, where $A = -\frac{v_{bb}}{v_b}$ is the coefficient of absolute inequality aversion. The first two terms are positive ($v_{bn} < 0$ and $v_{bb} < 0$) and the third negative. Thus the optimal level of public provision is greater in the second-best situation if $-\frac{A_n}{A}$ is relatively large. This is so if, for example, A is small. Mirrlees (1994, p. 231) concludes: 'It is disappointing, but not surprising, that one should not be able to find a really simple, easily checked criterion for lower public expenditure in a second-best economy. The main lesson of the analysis is that we cannot easily tell which way the balance goes.'

Mirrlees (1976a) and Christiansen (1981) have extended the Mirrlees (1971) model of optimal non-linear income taxation with a continuum of households to include the use of the revenues for the provision of public goods. Here we follow a two-type simplification according to Boadway and Keen (1993) and Edwards et al (1994). They analyse the conditions for optimal supply of public goods in a two-type model with non-linear taxes using the self-selection approach to optimal taxation. They derive a modified Samuelson

[2] See also Diamond and Mirrlees (1971).

rule that has a simple and appealing interpretation in terms of the self-selection constraint at the heart of the problem. They give a remarkably simple criterion for determining which way to deviate from the Samuelson rule when that decentralization result cannot be invoked: when all households have the same preferences, under- (over-) provision is optimal if and only if the public good is in a natural sense complementary with (substitutable for) leisure.[3]

Consumer utility is $V(x^i, z^i, G)$, where G is the public good. The government sets non-linear income taxes and public provision optimally given the binding self-selection constraint that the skilled person should not be better off mimicking the unskilled type than choosing 'his own' consumption bundle $V^2(x^2, z^2, G) = \hat{V}^2(x^1, z^1, G)$ and government budget constraint $z^1 + z^2 - x^1 - x^2 = rG$, where r is the producer price of the public good. The producer price of private consumption is normalized to 1. From the first-order conditions of this optimization we obtain the following modified Samuelson rule (see appendix 13.1 for the derivation of the rule):

$$\sum_i MRS^i = r + \mu^*(\hat{MRS}^2 - MRS^1) \tag{1}$$

where $\mu^* = \frac{\mu \hat{V}_X^2}{\lambda} > 0$.

Following Boadway and Keen (1993), we will refer to the situation in which $\sum_i MRS^i > r$ at the second-best optimum as involving 'under-provision' of the public good relative to the Samuelson rule, and to $\sum_i MRS^i < r$ as involving 'over-provision'. As emphasized by Boadway and Keen, the direction of this inequality does not indicate relative levels of provision.

Rule (1) can be interpreted intuitively by applying the same logic as in the context of the mixed taxation in Chapter 12. Consider the case in which the low-skill type values the public good more than the mimicker, i.e. $\hat{MRS}^2 < MRS^1$. Now, equation (1) shows that at the optimum, $\sum_i MRS^i < r$ so, the public good should be 'over-provided' relative to the Samuelson rule. Therefore it should be possible to show that a Pareto improvement is possible starting at an optimal income tax equilibrium with the first-best Samuelson rule satisfied. To see this we start at $\sum_i MRS^i = r$, and then increase G incrementally, and adjust the income tax structure such that each type's tax liability rises by their marginal willingness to pay, MRS_{GX}. There will be no change in the welfare of either type 1 or type 2, and the government budget will not have changed. However, since the tax liability of the mimicking person will rise by MRS^1, which is greater than their valuation $\hat{MRS}^2$, the mimicker will be worse off. Since the mimicker and true type 1 have the same preferences, but the mimicker has more leisure, the public good should be over-provided if it is complementary with labour supply. In this case, over-provision of the public good renders mimicking less attractive, relaxes the self-selection constraint, and improves

[3] Gahvari (2006) generalizes Boadway and Keen (1993) to a model with many types of individuals, many private goods, and without making any assumptions regarding which self-selection constraints are or are not binding.

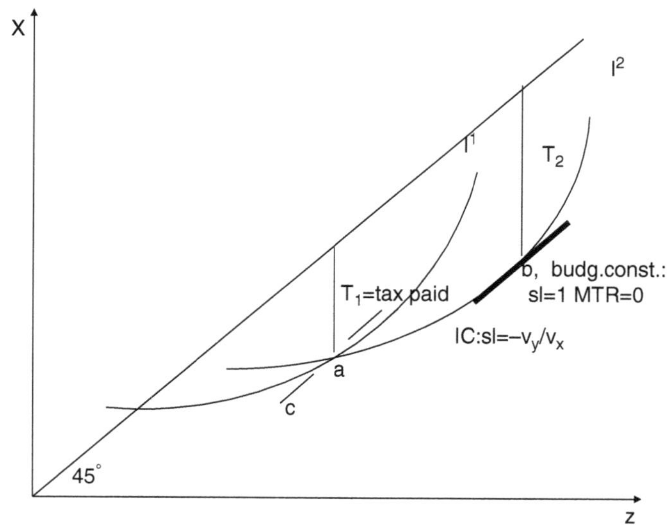

Figure 13.3 Provision of public good

welfare. This is captured by the last term of equation (1). With the welfare of both types unchanged at their intended bundles, but mimicking less attractive (i.e. the self-selection constraint relaxed), a change in the optimal income tax structure can then be undertaken which will make both types better off. Thus the intuition for diverting from the first-best Samuelson rule is exactly the same as the intuition for setting non-uniform commodity taxes. Figure 13.3 taken from Boadway and Keen (1993) illustrates.

Let us start at point c in Figure 13.3, which is along the locus of constant T^1 (tax paid by type 1s). The marginal tax rate on type 1s can be lowered with the same total tax revenue being collected. Type 1s are made better off, without inducing type 2s to mimic. Over-provision of the public good will thus be a useful adjunct to income taxation as part of redistributive policy because of its effect on the self-selection constraint. The argument is symmetric for the opposite case in which the mimicker has a higher marginal evaluation of G than the low-ability type. In this case, the exercise involves reducing G starting from the Samuelson rule, and simultaneously reducing tax liabilities by the respective MRSs. Again, a Pareto improvement is possible in which both types can be made better off. Equivalently, social welfare can be improved in the sense that more redistribution can take place.

Formula (1) also implies that MCPF is less than 1 if $\hat{MRS}^2 < MRS^1$, and vice versa. In other words, if labour is more complementary with G than with private consumption, then MCPF < 1.

The Samuelson rule in the second-best optimum: The central result and the analogue of the Atkinson-Stiglitz theorem in this area is that of Christiansen (1981),[4] who shows

[4] Tuomala (1990) also provides a decentralization result involving separability of the utility function. However, his result is cast in a slightly different form than the usual Samuelson condition because he chooses

that if all households have the same preferences (over private goods, labour, and a public good), then public goods provision can be decentralized if labour is weakly separable from goods (public and private) in the utility function. This is the case if $\hat{MRS}^2 = MRS^1$. Then the first-best Samuelson rule remains valid in the second-best world as well. It is valid only if the valuation of the public good is independent of labour supply, i.e. preferences are separable $V(\zeta(x_i,G),z_i)$.

Kaplow (2004) has extended this result to circumstances under which neither the tax system nor the provision of public goods are optimal. Kaplow (2008)[5] has argued that the Samuelson rule should be satisfied even if the income tax is not set optimally as long as preferences are separable as above. He employs the same intuition as in the context of commodity taxes in Chapter 12. There is a problem, as in Chapter 12, with taking this position, as pointed out by Christiansen (2007, p. 38).[6] He writes:

> Suppose that the (increase in the) public good is provided on the grounds of the Pareto principle in a situation where the tax policy fails to be socially optimal. Then assume that the non-optimality of the tax policy is being redressed. In general, we cannot know that the public good provision is then optimal. It might have been the case that the provision was driven by a high willingness to pay for the public good among people whose income and willingness to pay are being substantially reduced by the tax reform. Maybe one would rather have shrunk the public good provision as part of the total reform package. Hence, one might regret the more generous provision. It can be noted that this is a problem that is not due to second-best constraints, but arises already when applying the Samuelson rule in the first-best regime.

The provision rule (1) and the Christiansen (1981) result refer to the rule, not the level, of public provision, since the rule is evaluated at a different optimum.[7] Gaube (2005) studies the validity of Pigou's claim within the two-type version of non-linear income taxation employed by Boadway and Keen (1993), where lump-sum taxes are ruled out. Boadway and Keen (1993) explore whether the social marginal benefit, $\sum MRS_{Gx}$ or $\sum MRS_{Gz}$, of the public good exceeds its marginal production cost r in second-best. This investigation corresponds to the common belief that the relationship indicates under-provision of the public good in second-best (i.e. G(2.best) < G(1.best)) while $\sum MRS_{Gx} < r$ or $\sum MRS_{Gz} < r$ indicates over-provision (i.e. G(2.best) > G(1.best)). However, Boadway and Keen point out that these notions of over- and under-provision depend on the choice of the private reference commodity: x or z. Gaube (2005) expands the results of Boadway and Keen, providing sufficient conditions for both under- and over-provision of the public good in the income tax optimum. In particular, he shows that the separability assumption of Christiansen (1981) implies under-provision of the public good in second-best. Although over-provision is also possible, Gaube's results make it clear that such an outcome is not very likely to happen as long as the public good is strictly normal.

to use an effective labour supply, z=ny, as a numeraire. It implies a different kind of separability condition. As is clear from Boadway and Keen (1993) and Gaube (2005), the choice of numeraire makes a difference.

[5] See also Gauthier and Laroque (2009). [6] See also Gahvari (2006).

[7] See also King (1986), Mirrlees, (1994), Arnott (1994).

13.1.1 PUBLIC GOOD PROVISION AND LINEAR INCOME TAX UNDER POVERTY MINIMIZATION

How should we modify the provision rule if we consider social objectives other than welfarist ones? For example, we could consider not just willingness to pay for public goods but also their contribution to alleviating poverty. Public goods may also reduce poverty, either directly or indirectly through the impact on consumer choice. One may think of, loosely speaking, e.g. programmes against social exclusion or basic education spending. Now we use the deprivation index as before in Chapter 9, defined over consumption of the public good G and other private consumption c. Kanbur et al (2015) derive from the first-order conditions (see appendix 13.1.2) the following expression.

$$D^{*}\left(1 - t\sum\frac{\partial z^{i}}{\partial b}\right) = r - t\sum\frac{\partial z^{i}}{\partial G} \tag{2}$$

where $D^{*} = \frac{\sum D_G + \sum D_c a \frac{\partial z^i}{\partial G}}{\sum D_c (1 + a \frac{\partial z^i}{\partial b})}$ captures the efficiency of the public good in reducing deprivation relative to the income transfer (because $D_G, D_C <, D^{*} > 0$).

The result is analogous to 11' in Chapter 3: the left-hand side captures the relative efficiency of public good provision and the right-hand side shows the relative cost. The tax-revenue impacts are important to determining the optimal level of public good provision and income transfers. We can further rewrite this to achieve comparability with equation (11'):

$$r = D^{*} - t\left(D^{*}\sum\frac{\partial z^{i}}{\partial b} - \sum\frac{\partial z^{i}}{\partial G}\right) \tag{3}$$

This shows how the price of the public good relates to the relative deprivation efficiency of public good provision. Using the same example as in the context of (11'), if, for example, labour supply is independent of the level of public good provision if $\frac{\partial z^i}{\partial G} = 0$, and $\frac{\partial z^i}{\partial b} < 0$ (or if $\frac{\partial z^i}{\partial G} > 0$, and $\frac{\partial z^i}{\partial b} = 0$), the price r of the public good would be higher than its relative efficiency in eliminating deprivation.

13.1.2 PUBLIC GOOD AFFECTS PRODUCTIVITY

Suppose now that the public good can have a productivity-increasing impact. An example could be publicly provided basic education that affects individuals' productivity via the wage rate. We therefore suppose that the direct impact of the public good on deprivation cancels out (i.e. $D_G = 0$), whereas the wage rate becomes an increasing function of G, i.e. $w'(G) > 0$ (denoting z = w(G)y). This means that the expression in (2) is written as:

$$\frac{\sum D_c a(w\frac{\partial y}{\partial G} + w'y)}{\sum D_c(1 + aw\frac{\partial y}{\partial b})} = \frac{r - (1-a)\sum w\frac{\partial y}{\partial G}}{1 - (1-a)\sum w\frac{\partial y}{\partial b}} \tag{4}$$

This means that even if labour supply would not react to changes in public good provision, public good provision would still be potentially desirable through its impact on the wage rate. In this way, public good provision can be interpreted as increasing the capability of individuals to earn a living wage, which serves as a poverty-reducing tool, and which can in some cases be a more effective way to reduce poverty than direct cash transfers. The optimality depends on the relative strength of $w'(G) > 0$ versus the direct impact of the transfers.

13.1.3 THE OPTIMAL PROVISION OF PUBLIC GOODS IN THE CONTINUUM CASE

The deprivation index we consider in (12) in Chapter 12 is therefore reformulated as:

$$P = \int_0^{n^*} D\left[x^*, sx^c(q, y, G, v, n), G\right] f(n)dn. \tag{5}$$

In a second-best world with asymmetric information, the government must worry about the effects of public good provision on individuals' incentives—in other words, the costs of raising revenue for the public good using distortionary taxation. Pirttilä and Tuomala (2004) derive the optimality condition for public good provision under non-linear income taxation and linear commodity taxation when the government aims to minimize poverty.

To analyse this, suppose x, z, and E are also functions of G, and the production constraint now includes the public good—in other words, a term λrg is subtracted from the Lagrangean in (5) in appendix 12.4. Let us now define the marginal willingness to pay for the public good by the expression a. The Lagrangean is then maximized with respect to G. From this condition (see appendix) we have the following rule for the supply of public good:

When the government minimizes poverty, the optimal provision of a public good is determined by (see appendix 13.1.3):

$$r = -\frac{1}{\lambda}\int D_G f dn - \frac{1}{\lambda}\int D_m sx_G^c f dn + \int (1 - tx_b)\sigma f dn + \int tx_G f dn + \int \pi\sigma_n dn. \tag{6}$$

Despite its complicated appearance, the interpretation of the rule above is relatively straightforward, given the existing knowledge from the welfarist case. The left-hand side of (6) is the marginal rate of transformation, r. It is to be equated to a number of terms at the right, capturing the benefits of public good provision. The last three of these are familiar from the welfarist case. The third term at the right refers to the individual marginal willingness to pay for the public good, reduced by a proportion equal to the derivative of commodity taxes with respect to income spent on them. The fourth term at the right is the direct tax-revenue effect of G, while in the fifth term σ_n measures how the personal marginal willingness to pay or preference for the public good varies with n. This term takes into account distributional considerations and corrects the direct estimates (the first four terms on the right-hand side of (6)) for the social value of public good.

The first term on the right measures the direct marginal benefit of G in terms of poverty reduction, weighted by the inverse of the Lagrange multiplier of government budget constraint (λ). The second term is the effect of public good provision on poverty through the demand for commodities that are important for avoiding deprivation. If public good provision increases the demand for these goods, the second term on the right is positive, which increases the benefits of public good provision. Other things equal, this effect tends to increase public good provision.

We can deduce $\pi\ (n)$ from the optimal marginal tax condition (see equation (14) in Chapter 12) and substitute it into (6). In the case of zero commodity taxes we have:

$$r = -\frac{1}{\lambda}\int D_G f dn - \frac{1}{\lambda}\int D_m s x_G^c f dn + \int \left(\sigma + \tau\frac{\sigma_n}{\phi_n}\right) f(n) dn \tag{7a}$$

or alternatively

$$r = -\frac{1}{\lambda}\int D_G f dn - \frac{1}{\lambda}\int D_m s x_G^c f dn + \int \left(\sigma(1 + \frac{\sigma_n/\sigma}{\tau_n/\tau}\right) f(n) dn. \tag{7b}$$

The single crossing condition implies that $\phi_n < 0$. Hence the sign of the latter term in (7a) depends on the sign of the denominator, i.e. $\sigma_n = (E_{nG} + E_{vG}v)$. This term is negative if the more able have a stronger preference for the public good and positive if the less able have this. The latter term in (7b) implies, as suggested by Mirrlees (1976a, p. 353), that 'the social value of the public good is enhanced when its value for some individual responds more sensitively to n than do his marginal tax rates'. It is interesting to note that in Mirrlees (1976a),[8] conditions (122) and (123) are a set of welfare-independent conditions necessary for Pareto efficiency. In our case with poverty minimization, this is no longer so.

As mentioned above, welfarist literature has established some decentralization results about public good provision (see Christiansen 1981 and Tuomala 1990). In the decentralized case, the decisions related to public good supply need not depend on

[8] Kreiner and Verdelin (2012) derive the same conditions as (122) in Mirrlees (1976a).

distributional concerns. Roughly speaking, when preferences between private and public goods and leisure are separable, the first-best Samuelson rule is valid even in the case where funds for the public good need to be raised with non-linear income taxation. Or, put another way, this is the case if σ and τ are equally sensitive to n.[9] In the present context, if preferences are separable between consumption (of private and public goods) and leisure, then the last term on the right of (6) is zero. Even if one supposes that there are no commodity taxes (when the fourth term at the right vanishes), the rule given in (6) still differs from the welfarist Samuelson rule, as $x_G^c \neq 0$, and because the direct impact of public good provision (the first term on the right) stays in the rule.

13.1.4 PUBLIC GOOD PROVISION AND INCOME UNCERTAINTY

Let the expenditure function be E(q,v,G,y). Then we can define the marginal willingness to pay for the public good, σ, by the expression $\sigma = -\frac{\partial E}{\partial G} = E_G$. Using analogous arguments to those in the case of commodity taxation, we show in appendix 13.1.2 that the rule for public good provision can be written in the following form:

$$r = \int \sigma f dz - \int \sigma t x_c f dz + \int t x_G f dz + \mu \int \frac{\partial \sigma}{\partial y} f dz \tag{8}$$

Equation (8) is analogous to equation (117) in Mirrlees (1976a). The marginal rate of transformation at the left should be equated with the sum of the marginal rate of substitution (the first term on the right), producing the Samuelson rule for public good provision, and a number of additional terms. The second and third terms on the right capture the impact of public good provision on commodity tax revenues. The key addition is the last term on the right: if the marginal rate of substitution increases with effort, the overall valuation of the public good (the right-hand side) increases as well. Other things being equal, the public good should therefore be over-provided if it increases the value of effort.[10]

There is again a clear relation to the standard optimal income taxation framework. In Mirrlees (1976a), the public good provision rule is dependent on how the marginal willingness to pay varies with income-earning ability. In the present framework, the public good rule is related to how the marginal willingness to pay varies with unobserved effort.

[9] Tuomala (1990) shows that in the case of optimal non-linear income tax the Samuelson rule is still valid if the utility function takes the form u=(x,ψ(x,z,G),n). That is, the overall utility from x, z, and G can be expressed as a function of the subutility of x, z, and G and the level of x and n.

[10] Note, however, that overprovision/underprovision rules can depend on the choice of the numeraire. For discussion of this, see Boadway and Keen (1993). Similarly, the rules may not necessarily correspond to similar differences in the level of public good provision, as the rule is evaluated in another optimum (Gaube 2005).

Finally, it is natural to ask in this set-up when (8) reduces to the first-best Samuelson rule even under asymmetric information. Clearly it is sufficient, for the Samuelson rule to be valid with optimal mixed taxation, that preferences take the form $V[v(q,c(z),G),y]$. In other words, if indirect utility takes this form, then we have both the Atkinson and Stiglitz (1976) result and the Christiansen (1981) result in the income-uncertainty framework. Namely, from the result of Atkinson and Stiglitz (1976), such preferences imply that all commodity taxes are zero at the optimum, so that at full optimum the second and third terms of (8) vanish. Similar to the validity of the Atkinson and Stiglitz result, one does not require the sufficient conditions needed for the first-order approach to prove the validity of the first-best Samuelson rule in the second-best framework. Minimization of $\int(px-rG)f(z,y)dz$ subject to $\int V[v(q,c(z,),G),y]\, f(z,y)dx=V^{*}$ suggests that costs are minimized if the public good is provided at the producer price, i.e. r.

13.2 **Public provision of private goods**

As we noted earlier, the provision of private goods forms a much larger share of government budget than the provision of pure public goods. This can be considered as somewhat odd, since it is generally supposed that the consumer knows best what amount of private goods to purchase. As a stark contrast to this, the conventional wisdom of many introductory economics textbooks has been that we should rely on the market to provide private goods.

Why are these intrinsically private goods publicly provided? Does normative public economics provide a case for public provision of private goods? Is there any other explanation why private goods are publicly provided?

Most private goods are never publicly provided. Can we find a common factor for publicly provided private goods? Christiansen (2001) identifies three factors. First, most publicly provided goods or in-kind transfers are not tradable. In other words, these goods cannot be resold or given away to others. Second, they impact more directly than other goods on human resources and capabilities (in the language of Amartya Sen). Most private goods that are publicly provided are provided mainly for children and elderly and disabled people. They typically affect people's ability to function in society and the labour market in particular. Third, they are typically the outcome of labour-intensive production. There is also a striking similarity across countries. Do these common features explain why it is these goods that are being provided by the public sector? Almost by definition, public provision implies that a good is made available free of charge or at a nominal price. There must be some kind of quantity rationing or administratively determined allocation, for example uniform provision, means-testing, income testing, vouchers, etc.

We can find several welfare-theoretic arguments that may conceivably support a role for public provision of private goods. For example, externalities, scale economies, transaction costs, and merit good arguments provide some reasons for public provision. There are also non-welfarist reasons for public provision or subsidizing, say, health care, education, and housing. As we said above, the publicly provided goods typically affect people's capability to function in society and the labour market. For many years, Amartya Sen has been arguing for consideration of alternative evaluative bases, notably individual capabilities, defined broadly as the freedom that individuals have to function in different dimensions. Rawls (1971) assessed opportunity in terms of primary goods such as income, wealth, and so on. Sen argues that opportunity is best seen directly in terms of the extent of freedom that a person actually has—that is, by one's capability to achieve alternative beings and doings—most of which depend critically on one's health and education.

For these reasons, in this context the capability approach might be more plausible than maximizing social welfare as the proper objective for the government. It is clear that provision of public goods and publicly provided goods has an important role in guaranteeing many aspects of capabilities. Hence the government should be concerned with the distribution of capabilities. Well-being assessed in terms of capabilities may lead to different conclusions. How should we modify the rules of public provision if we take into account not only willingness to pay but also the contribution to capabilities? In fact, we already saw in the case of poverty minimization, in formula (4) in section 13.1, what happens when public provision has a productivity-increasing impact. We may interpret G in formula (4) as a basic education.

13.2.1 TRANSACTION COSTS

There is evidence from a private health insurance market that 15 per cent of insurance premiums are devoted to administrative costs. The proportion of administration in health care expenditures is much higher in the US than in Canada and Europe. A simple argument for public provision is the potential saving of transaction costs, as with public provision there is not necessarily any monitoring of usage, or there are simple administrative procedures for uniform treatment of everybody.

13.2.2 MERIT GOODS: BEHAVIOURAL ECONOMICS OR SOFT PATERNALISTIC ARGUMENTS

Recent findings in behavioural economics have demonstrated that individual decision-making suffers from various biases. There are a number of reasons why individuals are particularly prone to make mistakes, for instance, in decisions related to health: the information required for rational decision-making may be too demanding, or individuals may undervalue, say, the returns on health investment accruing later in the future.

In many situations it can therefore be desirable to induce behaviour that is closer to what individuals wish they were doing.

13.2.3 SECOND-BEST EFFICIENCY ARGUMENTS

A number of studies have demonstrated that, with limited information and limited policy tools, publicly provided (non-tradable) benefits can actually be desirable in a second-best setting (see a recent summary by Currie and Gahvari 2008). This literature has argued that in-kind transfers can be an efficient complement to the tax-transfer system as a way to design a better redistribution system. It is based on the notion that in a second-best world, quantity controls can be welfare-improving. In other words, is it worthwhile for the government to use in-kind transfer (public provision) alongside cash transfers for redistribution? This is related to the general result from Guesnerie and Roberts (1984) that in a second-best situation, quantity restrictions may be optimal.

Introducing additional distortionary policies, which would not be used in a first-best world without asymmetric information, can be useful in a second-best situation if they help mitigate the distortions stemming from distortionary income taxation.[11] In other words, public provision of private goods may work to alleviate the underlying self-selection constraint and enhance economic efficiency. One way to do this would be to tax finance goods that the potential mimicker does not value very much. The argument of this literature can most clearly be seen in a setting in which the main constraint to redistribution is informational, and the government can freely use non-linear income taxation. Public provision can relax the incentive constraint that precludes higher-skilled individuals from mimicking lower-skilled ones. Thus, if a good that is substitutable for leisure (i.e. complementary with labour) is also non-tradable, a transfer of that good that forces low-wage individuals to consume more than they would freely choose will make it more difficult for higher-wage individuals to mimic them. Such mimicking can be done by supplying less labour, in which case the forced consumption of the good in question will be less valuable to the mimicker than to the low-wage individual. Then the mimicker will be made worse off as the benefits from the goods do not offset the additional tax burden. The goods that are suitable for public provision are those that are less valued when the consumer enjoys more leisure. The reason, as pointed out in Chapter 2, is that what distinguishes a mimicker from the low-skilled person he will potentially mimic is that, being more productive, he or she will earn the same income in less time, and thus enjoy more leisure. Suppose public childcare is provided for the benefit of people working long hours. If high-skilled persons were to mimic by working short hours, they would no longer benefit very much from the childcare but still face the tax liability, and mimicking would become less appealing. Day care, care of the elderly, and provision

[11] We have already analysed above such policies' over- or under-provision of public goods (Boadway and Keen 1993) or differentiated commodity taxation (Edwards, Keen, and Tuomala 1994).

of basic education can all be seen as complements to labour supply. Therefore their public provision may help reduce distortions from income taxation.

The intuition of this argument was first noted by Nichols and Zeckhauser (1982), but was subsequently formally developed by Blackorby and Donaldson (1988); Blomquist and Christiansen (1995), (1998a), and (1998b); Boadway and Marchand (1995); and Cremer and Gahvari (1997). Note that this is similar to the argument for using differential commodity taxes: lower tax rates should also apply to goods that are more substitutable for leisure. What if both public provision and price subsidies are available? Blomquist and Christiansen (1998b) and Boadway, Marchand, and Sato (1998) have shown that, even when optimal commodity taxation is allowed for, the use of public provision can still be welfare-improving. They show that public provision tends to dominate price subsidies, since price subsidies distort the consumption bundles of all true-type persons, whereas this is not necessarily the case for public provision.

Blomquist, Christiansen, and Micheletto (2010) examine implications of public provision for tax distortions: suppose public provision is strictly tied to working hours (e.g. day care) and paid by the income tax. Then part of the tax is a direct payment, like a service fee or market price. Hence this implies that not all of the marginal tax rate is distortionary. Therefore, to analyse how tax distortions differ between countries, one must also look at how the taxes are employed.

Public provision can take two broad forms. Two major schemes that have been identified are often labelled 'topping up' and 'opting out'. Topping up implies that the consumers can supplement any publicly provided amount by purchasing any additional amount they want in private markets. Opting out means that the alternative to accepting the public provision is to forego it and instead buy the whole amount in the private market: for instance, children are sent to private schools rather than state schools.

Although such second-best arguments for public provision have attracted the most attention in the optimal tax literature, they have received very little attention in the public debate, which focuses primarily on the other justifications we discussed above. But we can combine second-best and behavioural economies arguments. While price subsidies and public provision can both be used as corrective devices, public provision can be especially important in situations with individual mistakes. With public provision, the government can make sure that the individuals consume at least a certain minimal amount of goods deemed meritorious. So we can analyse optimal tax policy with redistributive objectives and the public provision of a good that is undervalued by individuals relative to government's view. In other words, the government is paternalistic, i.e. tries to correct these mistakes by basing its own decision on what it thinks is truly best for the individuals. We account for two potential constraints to optimality: asymmetric information of agents' productivity and mistakes in individual decision-making. Intuitively, individuals' undervaluation which is to be rectified should imply desirability of public provision.

Pirttilä and Tenhunen (2008) analyse the optimal tax policy and public provision of private goods when the government is paternalistic and has a redistributive objective.

When individuals only differ with respect to their income-earning abilities, the publicly provided goods should be over-provided, relative to the decentralized optimum, if society's marginal valuation of them exceeds the individual valuation and if these goods are complements to labour supply. However, when the individuals also differ in terms of their valuation of the publicly provided good, this simple conclusion does not hold. Optimal marginal income tax rates are shown to differ from the standard rules if publicly provided goods and labour supply are related.

All these above studies model the production side in a simple way with exogenous wage rates for different types of households in a static setting. Pirttilä and Tuomala (2002) extend the literature above in two main ways. First, they allow for a richer description of the production technology that enables the before-tax wage rate to depend on the labour supply of different households and, in various ways, the level of publicly provided private goods. Many of the publicly provided goods (e.g. education) can have a sizeable influence on the productivity of different households. It is also the case that in practice, government involvement in public provision is indeed often motivated by attempts to reduce wage inequality. Allowing for endogenously determined wages is also interesting because it gives rise to new forms of distorting taxation and production inefficiency, along the lines of the important contribution by Naito (1999).

Next, we analyse a simple static set-up, but with the endogenous wage structure. Now, in contrast to results in earlier literature, there can be reasons for public provision of private goods, even if we assume weakly separable preferences between goods and leisure. The reason is that public provision can affect productivities of different kinds of labour, thus affecting wage dispersion and the possibilities for redistribution. The following section considers an example whereby the public provision itself influences productivity—i.e. education that raises income-earning abilities—and discusses the characteristics of optimal public provision in those circumstances.

13.2.4 PUBLIC PROVISION WITH PRODUCTIVITY AND RELATIVE WAGE EFFECTS

There are two types of households in the economy: households of type 1 are less skilled and earn income n^1, while the more skilled household, type 2, earns a wage n^2 ($> n^1$). The number of households of each type is 1. Households supply labour, denoted by y, and consume two types of goods: a normal private good, c, and a quasi-private[12] good, d. The overall level of the latter good for the household is a sum of the public provision of the good, depicted by g, and the private, topping-up part, d. We apply the terminology introduced by Boadway and Marchand (1995) and call the situation where an increase in

[12] The term 'quasi-private' only refers to the idea that this good is both provided by the government and purchased by the household itself.

g leads to a reduction in the private purchases, z, one where the household's private purchases of the quasi-private good are crowded out. The government supplies the same amount of g to all households. In addition, we assume that g cannot be resold.

It is useful to break the household optimization into two parts. In the first, the households make the optimal consumption decision for a given after-tax income (x) and public provision. Denote household utility function by $u(c^i,y^i,d^i+g)$, where the subscript $i \subseteq (1,2)$ refers to household type and is dropped below. Then, using the household budget constraint, the household maximization of $u(x-d,y,d+g)$ with respect to z yields the following Kuhn–Tucker conditions:

$$-u_c + u_d \leq 0; \quad d(-u_c + u_d) = 0, \tag{1}$$

where subscripts refer to partial derivatives.[13] Conditions in (1) give the conditional indirect utility function $v(x, y, g)=u[x-d(x, y, g), y, d(x, y, g)+g]$ and conditional demand for d, $d(x, l, g)$.[14]

In the second step of consumer optimization, the household maximizes $v(x,y,g)$ with respect to its labour supply, subject to a given tax schedule, T(ny), and the budget constraint $x=ny-T(ny)$, where $z=ny$ denotes the household's gross income. The optimization enables the marginal income tax to be expressed in terms of the utility function:

$$T'(ny) = MTR(ny) = \frac{1}{n}\frac{v_y}{v_c} + 1. \tag{2}$$

The production side of the economy is modelled using an aggregate, constant returns to scale, production function $F(y^1,y^1,e)$, where e denotes the aggregate level of the quasi-private good in the economy, i.e. the sum of private and public parts for the two consumers. Note that the same technology is used to produce both goods. They thus have similar producer prices as well. For simplicity, the prices for both goods are normalized to unity. This specification captures two important features of the model. First, the wage rates are endogenous in a similar way to those in Stern (1982) or Stiglitz (1982). In the following, $\Omega = \frac{n^1}{n^2}$ depicts the relative wage of the low-skilled type. Assuming a competitive labour market, Ω is a function of y^1/y^2 and e, $\frac{n^1}{n^2} = \frac{F_1(y^1, y^2, e)}{F_2(y^1, y^2, e)}$. It captures the idea that the relative wage rate of type 1, determined at the market, is a decreasing function of y^1/y^2. Hence, if the government uses its policy instruments so that the relative labour supply of the type 2 household rises, it carries a redistributive benefit through an increase in the relative wage of the low-skilled household.[15] The second key feature of our framework is that the overall level of the publicly provided good is allowed to affect not only consumers directly, but also the production side of the economy by

[13] The derivative Uz refers to the derivative with respect to the third argument in the utility function.

[14] Using the envelope theorem, the following properties hold:

$$v_x = u_c, v_y = u_y, v_g = u_d.$$

[15] See Stiglitz (1982) or Stern (1982) for details.

influencing the productivity and the wage rates in the economy. Thus e has a positive externality feature.

Following the standard idea of Pareto-optimal taxation, the government maximizes the utility of the less-skilled households subject to the constraint that the skilled household must stay at a given utility level. The government redistributes income by taxing income on a non-linear scale. It may also use a uniform public provision of g as a policy variable. The government can observe the labour income ny, but it observes neither the income-earning abilities (the wage rates) of the households nor their consumption allocation decisions (between c and z). Therefore, the government must select the tax schedule subject to the self-selection constraint that the skilled household has an incentive to work $n^2y^2/n^2 = y^{2_1}$, report income n^2y^2, and consume x^2 (after-tax income), instead of wishing to pretend to be the unskilled household, i.e. mimic, working $n^1y^1/n^2 = \Omega y^1$, reporting income n^1y^1 and consuming x^1. The government chooses the tax schedule (or labour-after-tax income) bundles optimal to the two different household types subject to the constraint that the skilled household be at a given utility level, the self-selection constraint of the skilled household, and the resource constraint of the economy. Given this income tax schedule, we may use the envelope theorem to detect the change in the social welfare from an increase in the level of the publicly provided good as follows (see appendix 13.2 for the derivation):

$$\frac{dL}{dg} = (v_g^1 - v_x^1) + (\delta + \mu)(v_g^2 - v_x^2) + \mu(\hat{v}_x^2 - \hat{v}_g^2) - \mu\hat{v}_l^2 \frac{d\Omega}{dg} y_1 + \rho F_e \frac{de}{dg}. \qquad (3)$$

The first three terms in (3) restate the Boadway and Marchand (1995) result (their proposition 1) that public provision of private good is welfare-improving if the mimicker becomes crowded out (i.e. his private purchases, d, fall to zero), while households of type 1 and type 2 that report their types are honestly not yet crowded out.[16] The intuition is that pushing g above the point where the private purchases of the mimicker fall to zero makes the mimicker worse off, but if households of type 1 and 2 are not crowded out, it increases social welfare by relaxing the self-selection constraint (that a type 2 household honestly reporting its income must be better off than a mimicker). Boadway and Marchand also note that in the case where the publicly provided good enters the households' utility functions, if preferences are weakly separable between goods and leisure, the mimicker and a true type-1 representative become crowded out at the same point, because of which there is no benefit from having a positive provision of the publicly provided good.

With separable preferences, the three first terms of (3) are zero. Hence the following result emerges:

[16] This may be seen by using the properties in (2) in appendix 13.2.1 and combining (3) with the households' first-order conditions in (1).

If preferences are weakly separable between goods and leisure, public provision of private good is welfare-improving if it (a) increases productivity and (b) reduces the wage differentials of the households.

The results can be seen from the last two effects in (3). The direct productivity effect (last term in (30)) is usually positive (if it is negative, then it offsets part of the potential benefits for households, i.e. the original Boadway–Marchand part). What is more interesting, however, is the link between the publicly provided private good and the wage structure of the economy (the term $-\mu \hat{v}_l^2 \frac{d\Omega}{dg} y^1$). If its provision leads to a relative increase in the wage rate for type 1 households, then indirect redistribution through public provision will Pareto-improve welfare by mitigating the incentive problem of the non-linear income tax system. Intuitively this would be a case where the publicly provided good augments the productivity of type 1 labour supply more than that of type 2 labour supply. This effect is similar to the impact of labour supply on the wage rates, as originally analysed by Stiglitz (1982) and Stern (1982). The result is also important in that it bears resemblance to the interesting findings by Naito (1999) that if wage rates are endogenous, redistribution devices that otherwise would not be applied—in Naito's case, public inputs and commodity taxation; in our case, public provision of private goods—become welfare-improving.

13.2.5 PUBLICLY PROVIDED EDUCATION

Education is often considered a great equalizer in a society, capable of lifting less advantaged children and improving their chances of success as adults. One widely accepted social objective is to provide access to education for everyone, regardless of his or her social background. To what extent do individuals differ in access to education, especially for higher education? How does it depend on their social background, i.e. their parents' income and wealth? A growing body of research in developed countries suggests that the achievement gap between rich and poor children is widening. As in the context of housing above, we can find some support for a view that a general income tax based on earning abilities alone would not be sufficient for redistributive purposes when individuals differ also in access to education.

The issue of human capital investment raises the question of whether education should be used as a policy tool to reduce inequality in skills. That is, should redistribution policy focus on reducing ex post income inequality as in the standard model, or should it be complemented by ex ante policies to reduce the source of earnings inequality? There is a body of literature on optimal provision of publicly provided goods such as education and health, beginning with Arrow's (1971) paper. Arrow (1971) examines the normative characteristics of redistribution using targeted government expenditures. Arrow suggests that education is characterized by a correlation of ability with securing of benefits from expenditures at the margin and in total. This yields output regressivity. However, health expenditures are the opposite. Arrow assumes implicitly that ability or health status is observable, so that the optimal expenditure policy can be implemented. Given this assumption, tax policy would dominate expenditure policy. In that sense Arrow does not establish the normative basis for using expenditures for redistributive purposes; instead, he assumes it. The interaction of optimal income taxation and educational choices has been examined, among others, by Ulph (1977), Hare and Ulph (1979), and Tuomala (1986). Following Arrow, the first two papers assume that ability to benefit from education is observed by the education authorities. Assuming that low-skilled persons are also less productive in education, it is inefficient to redistribute using education to reduce inequality in skills. Education policies favouring the low-skilled at the expense of the high-skilled reduce the amount of income available for ex post redistribution (Hare and Ulph 1979). This information on educational abilities is not available to the tax officials, however. Earnings inequality arising from human capital investment cannot practically be disaggregated from that arising from endowed differences in ability. De Fraja (2002) considers optimal education policy when households are allowed to differ with respect to their income and the intellectual ability of their children. Income is observed by the government. In this model the optimal education policy is input-regressive, in sense of Arrow (1971). How surprising is this result in this framework? It is mainly driven by the incentive compatibility condition and the fixed budget of the Ministry for Education. Krause (2006) analyses the case in which more equal wage rates tighten the incentive constraints that restrict redistribution and increase the efficiency cost of redistribution (see also Stephens 2009). As a result, low-ability persons might be better off if education were targeted at those of higher ability.

The most recent literature on public provision departs from earlier contributions by assuming that public provision cannot be related to an individual's ability. Tuomala (1986) in turn focuses on the question of how educational choices affect the progressivity of the optimal income tax when labour productivity is no longer innate, but depends also on the amount of education received. Optimal income tax progressivity can be affected by incentive effects on human capital investment. If earnings are taxed progressively, investment in human capital is discouraged, and this reduces optimal progressivity. There are, however, offsetting forces. Bovenberg and Jacobs (2005) argue that this can be mitigated by subsidizing human capital investment. As in Tuomala (1986), Brett and Weymark (2003) consider an optimal non-linear income tax problem when individuals can enhance their skills through education. Individuals vary both in skills and in their education productivity. The authors show that marginal tax rates at the bottom of the skill distribution might be negative to encourage education, and they might also be increased at the top. They do not focus on the overall effect on progressivity. Blumkin and Sadka (2005) examine the desirability of taxing (subsidizing) education as a supplement to an optimal labour income tax in a model where individuals differ in both innate ability and scholastic aptitude.

Next we focus on public provision of education. Similar to the previous section, the individual may supplement publicly provided education from the private markets. The individual optimization now changes somewhat from the case presented above. The individual utility now depends only on private consumption, c, and labour, y. Education itself does not enter the utility function; it affects the individual's wage through its influence on productivity.

The marginal tax rate condition is similar to the one given in (2). The production function now depends not only on the labour supply of the individuals, but also on the level of their education. To simplify the production function somewhat, we assume that it takes a specific, two-factor form with education-weighted effective labour supplies of both household types. The production function may then be written as $F(e^1y^1,e^2y^2)$. This also means that $\Omega = \frac{\omega^1}{\omega^2}$ depends on g.

Since the government optimization remains the same as in the previous section, the optimality conditions with respect to the tax rates are also the same. Given the optimal tax schedule, the change in the social welfare with respect to public provision of education is:

$$\begin{aligned}\frac{dL}{dg} &= (v_g^1 - v_x^1) + (\delta + \mu)(v_g^2 - v_x^2) + \mu(\hat{v}_x^2 - \hat{v}_g^2) \\ &\quad + \rho\left(F_1y^1\frac{de^1}{dg} + F_2y^2\frac{de^2}{dg}\right) - \mu\hat{v}_l^2\frac{d\Omega}{dg}\mu_1.\end{aligned} \tag{4}$$

Boadway and Marchand (1995) show that with exogenous wages, public provision of education is welfare-improving if the mimicker becomes crowded out before the true-type households. This effect can be seen from the first three terms in expression (4). Here, when the production function is more general, there are also additional impacts. We can summarize the effects as follows:

Public provision of education tends to be welfare-improving if it (a) renders the mimicker to be crowded out first, (b) increases productivity, and (c) reduces the wage differentials of the households.

As discussed above, part (a) has already been shown by Boadway and Marchand (1995). Part (b) is due to the fourth term in (4) and measures the value of additional production arising from an increase in publicly provided education. Unlike in the case of exogenous wages, the productivity effect is unambiguously non-negative, and positive, if private education purchases are not crowded out. Part (c) is due to the last term in expression (4), with a similar interpretation as before: if publicly provided education reduces wage differentials, its provision becomes welfare-improving, other things being equal.

Boadway and Marchand (1995) also show that if the mimicker becomes crowded out at the same point as the true-type, there is nothing to be gained from the public provision of education. More precisely, this is the case if the elasticity of the wage rate toward education is similar for the mimicker and the true type 1. A similar result holds in our framework as well: if type 1 and type 2 individuals also become crowded out, the fourth term in (4) vanishes. In addition, with an equal elasticity of the wage rate toward education, additional education raises the wage rates of both types in a similar manner, and therefore no impacts arise from the fifth term in (4).

13.3 Public sector employment

Public sector employment has grown in most OECD countries since the early post-war period, but the cross-country differences are quite marked. In Germany[17] and the UK, public sector employment accounted for 15 and 14 per cent of the labour force in the mid-1990s, whereas in the Nordic countries, the proportions were much bigger: in Sweden, for example, the public sector employed 32 per cent of the labour force. In countries with a high level of public employment, the extent of public provision of goods such as education, health care, and social services is also much larger than in other OECD countries. There also seems to be less inequality in countries where public production is widespread (Lundholm and Wijkander 2002). Several explanations have been suggested for public sector employment. One popular explanation in the political economy literature is that governments have used public sector employment as a tool for generating and redistributing rents. In other explanations, government employment has been seen as way of ensuring income security. In other words, it can be used as a form of social insurance.

When discussing public sector employment, it is also natural to examine the use of public capital in connection to public production. As shown in several empirical studies (see e.g. Aschauer 1990), the accumulated stock of public capital is an important factor in enhancing the productivity capacity of the economy. Thus, decisions on public investment taken by the government today have long-lasting effects on the well-being of both present and future generations. Therefore the choice of discount rate that ought to be used in evaluating public projects is one of the most important decisions taken by the government (more on this in Chapter 14, section 14.6). It is not only important for accepting or rejecting a specific project but, in particular, for the allocation of resources between the public and the private sectors of the economy.

Pirttilä and Tuomala (2004) analyse the potential role of public sector employment and public investment as redistributional devices along with a non-linear income tax. The government cannot observe productivity and must design its redistributive policy subject to the self-selection constraint that the skilled households do not want to mimic the choice of the unskilled households. A key assumption of their approach is, following Naito (1999) and Pirttilä and Tuomala (2002), that the relative wage rates of different types of workers depend on their relative supplies and complementarity with capital. Another key assumption is that there are two production sectors in the economy (private and public) which both use low-skilled and skilled labour, but the factor intensities and

[17] The public employment figures in Germany are not comparable with the Nordic countries. In Germany there are a lot of quasi-private (NGO) agencies in the health care sector.

complementarity with capital may differ. Using a two-type and two-sector optimal non-linear income tax model with endogenous wages, they show that, to produce a given amount of consumption, the government should employ more unskilled workers and less-skilled workers than is necessary to minimize costs at the prevailing gross wage rate. This policy reduces the relative supply of low-skilled labour in the private job market and contributes to higher market wages for the low-skilled. In these circumstances, the pressure to redistribute income using distortionary income taxes is reduced. The production function in the public sector is given by $F^g(y_1^g, y_2^g, n_g)$, where y_i^g denotes the labour input of skill i used in the public sector.

These observations may provide one explanation for the large proportions of the public sector and the combination of public production and public provision in some countries, particularly the Nordic countries. It also implies that a larger public sector may not necessarily hamper efficiency as much as is sometimes thought. The government can mitigate the harmful effects of higher tax rates with suitably organized public production/provision schemes. The Nordic countries seem to provide, again, a case in point: countries such as Sweden have not suffered in terms of income level despite their exceptionally large public sectors. In more general terms, the results in this chapter are compatible with the empirical evidence related to the size of the public sector and economic growth. While the overall picture the evidence provides is mixed, many studies, such as Krusell et al (2000), Kneller, Bleaney, and Gemmell (1999), and Padovano and Galli (2002), find that there is no robust relationship between the size of the public sector per se (and hence average tax rates) and growth.

Earlier literature in optimal taxation has paid relatively little attention to the redistribution motive in public sector employment. On public employment, a notable exception is a paper by Wilson (1982), who studies optimal employment policy in a linear income tax model with two types of labour. In the model where workers choose the type of labour they supply, Wilson shows that the government should hire less unskilled labour and more skilled labour than is necessary to minimize costs at the prevailing gross wage rates. But this result is reversed when labour quantity is the choice variable. A number of papers have extended the analysis to a setting with non-linear taxation. Naito (1999) shows that production inefficiency in public production is desirable if it leads to an increase in the relative wage of less-skilled workers. Gaube (2000a) demonstrates how production efficiency is violated not only in special cases, but in all potential regimes of second-best, two-sector, optimal taxation models. Lundholm and Wijkander (2002) explicitly focus on public employment decisions and conduct numerical simulations.

An interesting trade-off arises. Namely, the private sector may be more productive in manufacturing some of the goods, but by having these goods produced by the public sector, the government can enhance the wage rate of low-skilled workers in the labour market more. This observation may explain one mechanism leading to a relatively large scope of public employment and public sector in general in modern welfare states. It also implies that through suitably arranged public production and expenditure policies, the government can offset some of the harmful effects of higher tax rates. A larger government may not necessarily therefore harm efficiency as much as is sometimes thought. This property is compatible with much empirical evidence failing to find a robust negative link between the size of the government and the size of the public sector.

13.4 The potential role of minimum wages

The minimum wage is a widely used but among the most controversial policy tools. Several introductory economics textbooks using the usual first-best reasoning demonstrate that the minimum wage legislation is well intended but misguided. However, it is shown by Guesnerie and Roberts (1984, 1987) that the use of first-best results is inappropriate in a second-best world. The minimum wage is a potentially useful tool for redistribution because it increases low-skilled workers' wages at the expense of higher-skilled workers or capital. The other side of the coin is that it may also lead to involuntary unemployment, thereby worsening the welfare of workers who lose their jobs. A large empirical literature has studied how the minimum wage affects the wages and employment of low-skilled workers. There is also the normative literature on the minimum wage.

This normative literature has examined whether the minimum wage is desirable for redistributive reasons in situations where the government can also use an optimal income/transfers system for redistribution. The key idea in early studies by Guesnerie and Roberts (1984, 1987) and Allen (1987) is that the beneficial effect of a minimum wage occurs if it relaxes the incentive constraint and hence expands the redistributive power of the government. In the context of the two-skill Stern–Stiglitz (1982) model with endogenous wages, Guesnerie and Roberts (1987) show that a minimum wage can sometimes usefully supplement an optimal linear tax, but is not beneficial in the case of an optimal non-linear tax even in the most favourable case where unemployment is efficiently shared. This result is obtained because a minimum wage does not in any way prevent high-skilled workers from mimicking low-skilled workers.

Marceau and Boadway (1994) in turn show that a minimum wage is welfare-improving in the case of optimal non-linear income tax. They assume that the minimum wage induces firms to reduce the number of workers employed. In the absence of a minimum wage, a binding participation constraint determines labour supply. A minimum wage that applies only to low-wage workers is welfare-improving, and accompanying the minimum wage with unemployment insurance will improve social welfare further. More specifically, the authors show that redistributive policy could be improved by allowing the government to use a minimum wage and unemployment insurance as additional tools. The beneficial effect of a minimum wage occurs even though it tightens the incentive constraint (since the higher wage makes mimicking more attractive). This is so because the minimum wage, assuming it can be enforced, targets low-wage workers and makes them better off. Boadway and Cuff (2001) show that a minimum wage policy combined with forcing non-working welfare recipients to look for jobs and accept job offers indirectly reveals skills at the bottom of the distribution. Using a continuous-wage Mirrlees optimal income tax setting with bunching at the bottom (voluntary unemployment), the minimum wage causes unemployment for all those with abilities below the minimum wage. Combining a minimum wage with a policy rule that requires low-income workers to accept jobs that are offered to them relaxes the incentive constraint applying at the minimum wage level and improves social welfare. It might even increase employment.

This approach is not without its critics. Critique focuses on informational assumptions of these models; namely, they assume that the government can enforce the minimum wage despite the fact that optimal income tax (intensive-margin) models assume that wage rates are private information. Though this problem may be addressed by assuming the minimum wage law is enforced by audit-and-penalty mechanisms, that is costly and diminishes the effectiveness of the programme.

Guesnerie and Roberts (1984) and Allen (1987) assumed that minimum wages reduce employment along the intensive margin (hours worked) rather than the extensive margin (job loss). Lee and Saez (2010) avoid the informational issue by adopting the extensive-margin approach of Diamond (1980) and Saez (2002).[18] In the Lee–Saez model, the government observes all wage rates.[19] Workers choose whether to participate, and those with the least taste for leisure do so. There are two different skill levels for workers, w^1(low skill) and w^2. There are hi number of workers at ability level w^i. The production function is $f(h^1, h^2)$ and different types of labour are imperfect substitutes. So wages are endogenous due to imperfect substitutability of skills in the production. The workers face different kinds of cost of effort, θ^i. The government can observe the wage rates of different ability types, but not the individuals' cost of effort. Individual utility is assumed to be $u^t = c^t - \theta^t$, where c is consumption. They show, in a model with a discrete number of jobs and endogenously determined wage rates for different types of occupations, that introducing minimum wages can be useful even in the presence of an optimal non-linear income tax under welfarist social objectives. A key assumption[20] for the result in Lee and Saez (2012) is that of efficient rationing. It implies that those who lose their job first when the minimum wage is increased above the equilibrium wage of low-skilled workers are those with the smallest surplus from work. This means that the social planner is indifferent regarding whether they work or not (implying little efficiency

[18] Blumkin and Danziger (2014) extend the Lee–Saez analysis to an environment with deserving and undeserving poor and where labour supply decisions are concentrated along the intensive margin.

[19] This is a stronger requirement than that in Boadway–Cuff and Guesnerie–Roberts, in which wages are observable at the firm level.

[20] Further assumptions employed are that the elasticity of supply of low-skilled workers is positive and the elasticity o—f demand for them is finite.

losses from the minimum wage) and what is left is the desirable redistributive effect in terms of higher wages for those earning the minimum wage. Of course, the requirement that the rationing of available jobs is efficient is a strong one. Also here we face the problem of how to treat different preferences for social welfare purposes. If we adopt poverty minimization as a social objective, we can avoid this problem.

Pirttilä and Tuomala (2002) consider a model with two sectors in which some low-income workers may end up unemployed due to the minimum wage. Now suppose that the government imposes a minimum wage w^m ($F^c_{y_1} < w^m$). The government has a new control variable w^m in addition to the old ones (non-linear income taxation, public employment, and production) and a new constraint $w^1 \geq w^m$. So the minimum wage does not restrict the labour supply of low-income workers directly, but it raises the wage. The public sector hires more low-skilled workers, reducing the number of unemployed due to the minimum wage in the private sector. By employing more low-income workers at the minimum wage than the private sector would, the public sector does not minimize costs, but the government can offset this efficiency loss by distributional gains.

Finally, some studies have explored the issue of jointly optimal minimum wages and optimal taxes and transfers in imperfect labour markets. Blumkin and Sadka (2005) consider a signalling model where employers do not observe productivities perfectly and show that a minimum wage can be desirable to supplement the optimal tax system. Cahuc and Laroque (2007) show that in a monopsonistic labour market model, with participation labour supply responses only, the minimum wage should not be used when the government can use optimal non-linear income taxation. Hungerbuhler and Lehmann (2007) analyse a search model and show that a minimum wage can improve welfare even with optimal income taxes if the bargaining power of workers is sufficiently low. If the government can directly increase the bargaining power of workers, the desirability of the minimum wage vanishes.

There are still considerations not analysed in this literature. A typical doubt regarding the minimum wage is that employers have no interest in recruiting workers whose productivity is less than the wage cost. But productivity is not fixed. It may increase with the wage paid. Hence, for example, taking into account the idea of learning by doing might strengthen the case for a minimum wage even in the case of a competitive labour market.

13.5 **Tax evasion and optimal redistribution**

Although labour supply would be rather insensitive to taxes for most people, declarations of earnings may be sensitive to taxes. Hence a problem relates more to the design of a good tax-monitoring administration than a real incentive problem. The standard approach simply assumes that taxpayers willingly report their true incomes. This may sound slightly odd given the importance of asymmetric information in optimal redistribution analyses. There is nonetheless evidence that under-reporting of income represents an informational constraint for at least some taxpayers.

The pioneering work on modelling tax evasion within the optimal tax theory is by Allingham and Sandmo (1972). In their model individuals are deterred from evasion by a fixed probability of auditing and a proportional penalty to be applied over and above the payment of the true liability. In addition, taxpayers are risk-averse and taxable income is exogenous.[21] Yitzhaki (1987) extended the original model by assuming the probability of auditing to be an increasing function of evaded income, but with risk-neutral agents. The standard expected utility model of tax evasion predicts that evasion is decreasing in the marginal tax rate. This is sometimes called the Yitzhaki puzzle.[22] Sandmo (1981) was the first to combine tax evasion and optimal income taxation approaches in the linear income tax model.[23] Using the two-type model (high- and low-wage individuals), Cremer and Gahvari (1995) and Schroyen (1997) analyse evasion within a non-linear optimal income tax framework. The two-type setting greatly simplifies the problem, but it also implicitly generates some of the most relevant results of the papers, such as the optimality of the zero marginal tax rate for high-skilled workers. As discussed in Chapters 4 and 5, Mirrlees (1971) only considers, realistically, an unbounded wage (skill) distribution, and therefore he did not get the zero tax rate result.

There are quite straightforward ways to revise the standard optimal income tax formulas to take account of the possibility of evasion or avoidance.[24] The optimal marginal tax rate depends inversely on the elasticity of labour supply. However, earnings' responses can reflect either changes in labour supply or changes in reported income. As Feldstein (1999) has argued, if evasion is costly to the taxpayer, the welfare cost of taxation depends on the elasticity of earnings with respect to the tax rate, whether changes in earnings come from labour supply effort or from efforts in evading or avoiding taxes. As Chetty (2009) puts it, the elasticity of earnings is a 'sufficient statistic' to measure the deadweight loss of taxation.

As we saw earlier, some empirical estimates suggest that the elasticity of taxable income is much higher at high income levels than elsewhere in the income distribution (e.g. Gruber and Saez 2002). That clearly tends to favour lower marginal tax rates at the top, and therefore less income tax progressivity. Of course, this depends on all changes in earnings representing welfare costs: some earnings responses are due to tax avoidance or evasion activities or simply costless transfers of income to other tax brackets, or result in penalty payments to the government (Chetty 2009).

[21] Several authors relaxed the risk-neutrality assumption and introduced expenditure on concealment (see Cowell 1990; Kaplow 1990; Cremer and Gahvari 1995, among others).

[22] There is some literature replacing the expected utility approach by Prospect Theory. However, this literature disagrees on whether Prospect Theory overturns the puzzle (see Piolatto and Rablen 2013).

[23] For a comprehensive review of tax evasion literature see Cowell (1990), Sandmo (2005), Sandmo (2012), and Slemrod and Yitzhaki (2002).

[24] Of course, tax evasion is conceptually different from avoidance, since it always implies an illegal action.

Piketty et al (2014) build a model where the top incomes respond to marginal tax rates through three channels: labour supply elasticity, avoidance elasticity, and bargaining elasticity. They argue that the third channel is the main source of response. Labour supply elasticity is typically small and is the real factor limiting the top tax rate. Finally, tax avoidance elasticity reflects a poorly designed tax system, and can be confined to be close to zero mostly by costless tax design reforms. Hence a reasonable response would be to tighten up the tax administration rather than compromising tax progressivity.

In the spirit of Piketty et al (2014), Balle et al (2015) study optimal non-linear labour income taxation when taxpayers are allowed to evade taxes. Their main finding is that the optimal marginal tax schedule is the same as in the Mirrlees problem and the government should enforce no evasion by imposing a sufficiently large penalty under a constant auditing probability.

APPENDIX 13.1.1 PROVISION OF PUBLIC GOOD

The government optimization problem is

$$\begin{aligned} L = V^1(x^1, z^1, G) + V^2(x^2, z^2, G) \\ \text{Max } \mu[V^2(x^2, z^2, G) - V^2(x^1, z^1, G)] \\ +\lambda(z^1 + z^2 - x^1 - x^2 - pG) \end{aligned}$$

The first-order condition with respect to G:

$$V_G^1 + V_G^2 + \mu V_G^2 - \mu \hat{V}_G^2 - \lambda p = 0 \quad (1)$$

Notice that the first-order conditions x and z are the same as in the two-type case earlier.

Reorganize equation (1)

$$\frac{V_G^1}{V_x^1} V_x^1 + (1+\mu)\frac{V_G^2}{V_x^2} V_x^2 - \mu \hat{V}_G^2 = \lambda p \quad (2)$$

where $\frac{V_G^1}{V_x^1} = MRS_{G,x}$. To see this we differentiate consumer utility function keeping utility constant to get

$$V_x dx + V_G dG = 0, \text{ i.e. } \left.\frac{dx}{dG}\right|_{dV=0} = -\frac{V_G}{V_x}$$

Since we want a positive number, we set $MRS^i = \frac{V_G^i}{V_X^i}$ and return to (2) and substitution from the first-order conditions with respect to x and z yields

$$MRS^1 + MRS^2 + MRS^1 \mu \hat{V}_X^2/\lambda - \mu \hat{V}_G^2/\lambda = p$$

APPENDIX 13.1.2 POVERTY MINIMIZATION AND PUBLIC GOOD

Linear income tax

Dividing the government's first-order condition for G with that of b, we have the following relationship:

$$\frac{\sum D_G + \sum D_c a \frac{\partial z^i}{\partial G}}{\sum D_c (1 + a \frac{\partial z^i}{\partial b})} = \frac{r - (1-a)\sum \frac{\partial z^i}{\partial G}}{1 - (1-a)\sum \frac{\partial z^i}{\partial b}}$$

where $D^* = \frac{\sum D_G + \sum D_c a \frac{\partial z^i}{\partial G}}{\sum D_c (1 + a \frac{\partial z^i}{\partial b})}$ captures the efficiency of the public good in reducing deprivation relative to the income transfer (because $D_G, D_c < 0, D^* > 0$).

$$D^* \left(1 - t \sum n \frac{\partial y}{\partial b}\right) = r - t \sum n \frac{\partial y}{\partial G}$$

Non-linear income tax

Suppose x, y and E are also functions of g, and the production constraint now includes the public good; in other words, a term λrg is subtracted from the Lagrangean in (5) in appendix 12.4 in Chapter 12. The Lagrangean is then maximized with respect to g, which yields the following first-order condition:

$$-\int (D_G + D_m s x_G^c) f dn - \int \lambda p x_G^c f dn - \lambda r + \int \alpha \{\partial (E_n / E_v) / \partial G\} dn = 0. \qquad (1)$$

With the definition, $\sigma = \frac{v_G}{v_b} = -E_G$, we have

$$\partial (E_n / E_v) / \partial G = (E_{nG} E_v - E_{vG} E_n) / E_v^2 = E_v^{-1} (E_{nG} + E_{vG} v') = E_v^{-1} \sigma_n. \qquad (2)$$

By usual manipulation in tax theory (as in Mirrlees 1976a) we have

$$p x_G^c = (q - t) x_G^c = E_G - t(x_G + x_b E_G) = (1 - t x_b) E_G - t x_G. \qquad (3)$$

Using (2) and (3) the first-order condition for the public good we have (3) in the text.

APPENDIX 13.1.3 PUBLIC GOOD PROVISION AND INCOME UNCERTAINTY

The first-order condition with respect to G is

$$\frac{\partial L}{\partial G} = \int \{V_G (1 + \alpha h) + \alpha V_{yG} - \lambda p x_G - \lambda r\} f dz = 0 \qquad (1)$$

Let the expenditure function be E(q,v,G,y). Then we can define the marginal willingness to pay for the public good, σ, by the expression $\sigma = -\frac{\partial E}{\partial G} = E_G$.

First note that

$$-E_G = -E_V V_G \tag{2}$$

Then, since $E_v V_c = 1$,

$$\sigma = -E_G = V_G / V_c \tag{3}$$

In (2) and (3) we have used the fact that there is a duality between the prices of private commodities and the quantity of public good and the willingness to pay for the public good. In (3) we have used the analogues of the derivative property of the expenditure function and Roy's identity for the public good. Now we can write the cross derivatives

$$V_{yG} = V_{Gy} = -E_G V_{cy} - E_{Gy} V_c \tag{4}$$

where $E_{gy} = \dfrac{\partial E_g}{\partial y}$.

Using (3) and the Slutsky equation for the public good $x_G = x_G^c + x_c E_G$ we have

$$\int \left\{ -E_G(V_c(1+h) + \alpha V_{cy} - \lambda p x_c) - \alpha E_{Gy} V_c - \lambda p x_G^c - \lambda r \right\} f dz = 0 \tag{5}$$

Again using (3) in (4) and noting that

$$p.x_G^c = (q-t)x_G^c = E_g - t.(x_G + x_c E_G) = -t.x_g + (1 - t.x_c)E_G \tag{6}$$

we have

$$\int \left\{ \alpha V_c \frac{\partial \sigma}{\partial y} - \lambda p x_G^c - \lambda r \right\} f dz = 0 \tag{7}$$

Reorganising the term px_G^c one arrives at equation (4) in the main text.

One possibility is that the public good affects the distribution of $f(y,z)$, as in Anderberg and Andersson (2003). This might mean e.g. that the public good enhances income-earning abilities so that the distribution with $G > 0$ stochastically dominates one with $g = 0$. Denoting $V + \alpha(V_y + Vh) + \lambda(z - px - rG) = W$, the Lagrangean can be written as $\int Wf(z, y, g)$. Then the first-order condition with respect to g is the following:

$$\frac{\partial L}{\partial G} = \int \{ V_G(1 + \alpha h) + \alpha V_{yG} + \alpha V h_G - \lambda p x_G - \lambda r \} f dz + \int W f_G = 0. \tag{8}$$

For brevity, let us concentrate on the case where $V_{yG} = x_G = 0$. The provision rule can be rewritten as

$$r = \int \sigma f dz + \alpha \int V h_G f dz + \int W f_G dz, \tag{9}$$

where the deviation from the first-best Samuelson rule is dependent on how the public good affects the distribution of f directly (the last term at the right of (9)) and how it influences the incentive compatibility constraint through the impact on the likelihood ratio, h_G. One possibility is that the public good enhances overall productivity. This tends to lead to over-provision of the public good relative to the first-best rule. At the same time, the public good might blur the relationship of effort on income, reducing the likelihood ratio and leading to under-provision of the public good through the middle term at the right of (9).

APPENDIX 13.2.1 PUBLIC PROVISION AND EXOGENEOUS WAGES (BOADWAY AND MARCHAND 1995; BLOMQUIST-CHRISTIANSEN 1995)

Now the instruments available for the government are non-linear income taxation and public provision of private goods. When 'topping up' is allowed, the government sets a minimum consumption for the publicly provided good, but the consumer may buy more of it on the market:

2 types, $n^2 > n^1$. gross income $z = ny$, and individual budget constraint: $x^i = z^i - T(z^i)$

There is a private good, c^i and a quasi-private good, $d^i = e^i + g$, where g is the publicly provided amount and e refers to the private purchases of the good. Hence $c^i = d^i = x^i$

Consumer optimization:

Max $V(c^i, z^i, d^i)$ = Max $V(x^i - e^i, z^i, e^i + g)$. The idea is to write an indirect utility function where the arguments are observable (x, y, g); $v[x^i - e^i(x^i, z^i, g), z^i, e^i(x^i, z^i g)+g]$.

Consumer's private optimization implies (at interior solution)

$$MRS = \frac{v_g}{v_x} = MRT = 1$$

The situation where the publicly provided amount is so large that the private part e = 0 is referred to as 'crowding out' the government optimization:

$$\begin{aligned} L = v^1(x^1, z^1, g) + v^2(x^2, z^2, g) \\ \text{Max}\, \mu\left[v^2(x^2, z^2, g) - v^2(x^1, z^1, g)\right]. \\ +\lambda(z^1 + z^2 - c^1 - c^2 - 2g) \end{aligned} \quad (1)$$

The first-order conditions with respect to z and x are the same as earlier. Therefore, the MTR results are the same as earlier. What is the change of social welfare if public provision is increased? This is given by

$$\frac{dL}{dg} = v_g^1 + v_g^2 + \mu v_g^2 - \mu \hat{v}_g^2 - 2\lambda \quad (2)$$

As in the Boadway–Keen model, this can be written as:

$$\frac{dL}{dg} = \frac{v_g^1}{v_x^1} + \frac{v_g^2}{v_x^2} - 2 + \frac{\mu v_g^2}{\lambda}\left(\frac{v_g^1}{v_x^1} - \frac{\hat{v}_g^2}{\hat{v}_x^2}\right) \quad (3)$$

Suppose we start from the initial situation with no public provision. This implies that the consumers are not at a corner solution.

$$\text{Therefore} \quad \frac{v_g^1}{v_x^1} + \frac{v_g^2}{v_x^2} - 2 = 0. \tag{4}$$

The sign of $\frac{dL}{dg}$ is determined by the term in the brackets.

Again, if the true type 1 person values the good relatively more than the mimicker, the term in the brackets is positive. This holds as long as neither of the true type (1 or 2) is crowded out.

Let us denote the crowding out level as $\tilde{g}^i$.

When $\frac{dL}{dg} > 0$ and g is complementary with labour supply and $\tilde{g} < \min\{g^1 . g^2\}$

When g is complementary with labour supply, the mimicker is crowded out before a true type 1 person. Since the mimicker also works less than the true type 2 person, the mimicker is crowded out first. Therefore there exists a positive level of public provision which enhances social welfare.

The intuition is again to make mimicking less attractive and to boost labour supply that will otherwise be distorted downwards because of the presence of redistribution.

Public provision education and endogeneous wages

Let us denote the wage rate for household i as $\omega^i = \omega(y^1, y^2, e^i)$, where $e^i = d^i + g$. The utility function is now $u(c, y) = u\left(x - d, \frac{z}{\omega}\right)$. The first-order conditions with respect to z are now:

$$-u_c - u_y z \frac{\omega_e}{(\omega)^2} \leq 0; \quad d\left(-u_c - u_y z \frac{\omega_e}{(\omega)^2}\right) = 0, \tag{1}$$

where $\omega_e = \frac{\partial \omega}{\partial e}$. Now, the following properties hold for the conditional indirect utility function $v(x, y, g)$:

$$v_x = u_c, \; v_y = u_y, \; v_g = -u_y z \frac{\omega_e}{(\omega)^2}. \tag{2}$$

The Lagrangean of the government optimization problem can therefore be written as

$$\begin{aligned} \underset{x_1, y_1, x_2, y_2}{Max} \; L = {} & v(x^1, y^1, g) + \delta[v(x^2, y^2, g) - \bar{v}^2] \\ & + \mu[v(x^2, y^2, g) - v(x^1, \Omega y^1, g)] \\ & + \rho[F(y^1, y^2, e) - x^1 - x^2 - 2g]. \end{aligned}$$

where the hat terms refer to the so-called mimickers, i.e. type 2 households when mimicking the choice of type 1. Stern (1982) and Stiglitz (1982) show that in this framework, the marginal tax rate for the skilled household is negative and the marginal tax rate for the less-skilled household is positive.[25] Given this income tax schedule, we may use the envelope theorem to detect the change in the social welfare from an increase in the level of the publicly provided good as follows:

$$\frac{dL}{dg} = v_g^1 + (\delta + \lambda)v_g^2 - \lambda\hat{v}_g^2 - \lambda\hat{v}_y^2\frac{d\Omega}{dg}y_1 + \rho F_e\frac{de}{dg} - 2\rho. \tag{3}$$

Rewriting (3) by substituting for ρ from the first-order condition with respect x_1 and x_2 yields

$$\frac{dL}{dg} = (v_g^1 - v_x^1) + (\delta + \mu)(v_g^2 - v_x^2) + \mu(\hat{v}_x^2 - \hat{v}_g^2) - \mu\hat{v}_l^2\frac{d\Omega}{dg}y_1 + \rho F_e\frac{de}{dg}. \tag{4}$$

Since the government optimization remains the same as in the previous section, the optimality conditions with respect to the tax rates are also the same. Given the optimal tax schedule, the change in the social welfare with respect to public provision of education is

$$\frac{dL}{dg} = v_g^1 + (\delta + \mu)v_g^2 - \mu\hat{v}_g^2 + \rho\left(F_1y^1\frac{de^1}{dg} + F_2y^2\frac{de^2}{dg}\right) - \mu\hat{v}_y^2\frac{d\Omega}{dg}y_1 - 2\rho. \tag{5}$$

Rewriting (5) by substituting for ρ from the first-order condition with respect x_1 and x_2 yields (4) in the text.

[25] This result can be obtained by combining (7) and (8), as well as (6) and (5).

14 Optimal capital income taxation

14.1 Introduction

Starting around 1980, many developed countries abolished annual or inherited wealth taxes. At the same time, almost all developed countries have seen a sharp decline in tax progressivity. Moreover, a growing fraction of capital income was gradually left out of the income tax base. Consequently, in the tax system, only a labour income tax is any more progressive. In the Nordic dual income tax system, this has been done explicitly. Dual income tax systems in turn have suffered from income shifting from progressively taxed labour income to capital income, which is taxed at a lower, flat rate.[1]

We have also seen a rising share of capital in many advanced countries since the 1980s (see Piketty and Zucman 2014). This, in turn, directly increases inequality, because ownership of capital is much more unequally distributed than labour income. Therefore, equity considerations suggest capital income should be taxed more than labour income. If capital accumulation is sensitive to the net-of-tax return, these considerations in turn suggest going in a different direction. Moreover, capital is more mobile internationally than labour. Given these considerations, how should capital income be taxed? Roughly classifying, we can distinguish four alternatives to taxing capital income: not at all; linearly (Nordic dual income tax); relating the marginal tax rates of capital and labour incomes; and taxing all income with the same schedule.

There is much tax research implying that there is no need to impose any tax on capital or capital income. The often-cited results by Judd (1985) and Chamley (1986) finding that no capital taxation is optimal arises asymptotically in models with infinitely lived individuals. The significance of these findings is limited for a number of reasons. The Ramsey setting assumes both identical individuals and unavailability of an income tax. There is no redistribution problem and thus no need in principle to rely on distortionary taxation. Many have questioned the model's assumptions, especially that of an infinitely lived agent (e.g. Banks and Diamond 2009). Piketty and Saez (2012, p. 1) describe these results as follows:

[1] As pointed out to me by Vidar Christiansen, in Norway there is a progressive element in the capital income tax, since shareholders pay a tax on what is defined as above-normal return on shares. Other capital income is taxed linearly. The Finnish dual income system is no longer purely linear.

Taken seriously, those results imply that all inheritance taxes, property taxes, corporate profits taxes, and individual taxes on capital income should be eliminated and that the resulting tax revenue loss should be recouped with higher labor income or consumption or lump-sum taxes. Strikingly, even individuals with no capital or inheritance would benefit from such a change. E.g. we should be explaining to propertyless individuals that it is in their interest to set property taxes to zero and replace them by poll taxes.

Perhaps the most important doubts regarding the Chamley–Judd results come from Straub and Werning (2014). They show that, in both models, taxation may be positive even in the long run. They also argue that even when optimal taxes are zero in the long run, this may only be true after centuries of high taxation.

There have been views on capital income taxation that deviate from the Chamley–Judd prescription. For example, Johansen writes in his book *Public Economics* (1965, p. 197):

In some countries income derived from wealth has been regarded as a surer and more permanent form of income than earned income, and it has therefore been considered that a definite amount of an income of this kind provided a higher tax ability than a corresponding amount of other income, within a particular period.

Mirrlees (2000, p. 8) in turn writes:

some of [the] variations in the return on capital are the result of the application of the skill and effort: but most is surely the result of risky outcomes. To that extent, there might be advantage in a high tax on the returns, offset by a subsidy on the capital; for that would provide people with insurance against investment risks. When one then takes account of the redistributive element of taxation, there is case for taxing wealth . . . I suggest there is a case for a rather progressive tax on income from capital after all, with perhaps some small offset related to capital value.

Diamond and Saez (2011, p. 181) in turn argue: 'The difficulties in telling apart labour and capital income are perhaps the strongest reason why governments would be reluctant to completely exempt capital income and tax only labour income'.

These zero tax rate results are a striking contrast with the fact that all advanced countries impose still substantial, although declining, capital taxes. For example, as of 2008, the European Union raised 8.9 per cent of GDP in capital taxes and 22.7 per cent as a percentage of total taxation.[2] Hence, there is a good reason why Piketty and Saez (2012, p. 1) argue 'the large gap between optimal capital tax theory and practice [is] one of the most important failures of modern public economics'.

Another result in the literature in support of zero capital income taxation is the Atkinson–Stiglitz (1976) theorem interpreted in the intertemporal context. If (i) all consumers have preferences that are separable between consumption and labour, and (ii) the same sub-utility function of consumption, $u^i(c, x, z) = U^i(\psi(c, x), z)$, where c is the first period consumption, x the second period consumption, and z earnings, then the

[2] Taxation trends in the European Union, for GDP weighted EU-27 averages.

government should use only labour income tax and should not use tax on savings. Condition (i) says that the intertemporal marginal rate of substitution of consumption does not depend on labour supply and (ii) requires all consumers to be the same in their interest in smoothing consumption across their life cycle. In other words, there should be zero differential taxation of first- and second-period consumption (no 'wedge' between the intertemporal marginal rate of substitution and the intertemporal marginal rate of transformation between consumer goods in different periods) if two conditions are satisfied. To put it differently: if inequality entirely comes from labour income inequality, then it is useless to tax capital; one should rely entirely on the redistributive taxation of labour income. Under separable preferences, there is no point taxing capital income; it is more efficient to redistribute income by using solely a labour income tax. Atkinson and Stiglitz (1980, pp. 442–51) were themselves very well aware of the implausibly strong assumptions (most notably the absence of inheritance and the separability of preferences) behind their zero capital tax result.

As in Banks-Diamond (2010, p. 559), the Atkinson–Stiglitz theorem can be seen in the two different roles: 'one is to show that limited government action is optimal in an interesting setting, and the second is to provide, through the assumptions that play a key role in the theorem, a route towards understanding the circumstances calling for more government action (in this case distorting taxation of saving and therefore implicitly taxing (or subsidizing) consumption in the second period relative to consumption in the first period)'. This interpretation by Banks and Diamond (2010) is important because this result has been misused as straightforward support for zero capital income taxation. There is also an important difference between these two zero tax results. The Chamley–Judd results focus on given initial wealth, whereas there is no inherited wealth in the Atkinson and Stiglitz result. The wealth is saved from labour earnings. Hence new money turns into old money.

14.1.1 A TWO-PERIOD AND TWO-TYPE MODEL

Tax rate schedules typically do not take into account the taxpayer's pattern of earnings over time. Instead, they are based on a snapshot—the taxpayer's current annual income. In fact, Mirrlees (1971, p. 175) suggests that one of the limitations of his analysis is that it does not address intertemporal problems, even if 'in an optimum system, one would no doubt wish to relate tax payments to the whole life pattern of income . . . '. Vickrey's (1939) is the famous early contribution to the normative theory of lifetime income taxation. He proposed a cumulative averaging system for personal income taxation. Basing his argument on horizontal equity, Vickrey argued that if the tax schedule were convex, then individuals with fluctuating incomes would pay more taxes on average than individuals with steadier incomes. Diamond (2003) analyses the lifetime redistribution of income across individuals within a cohort. Thereby he avoids the dynamic complications that arise from intergenerational redistribution. More specifically, he considers a two-period variant of the Mirrlees (1971) income tax problem, where all individuals work in the first period and then retire.

The Mirrlees model as an annual tax system requires that the government can commit to ignoring the information that has been revealed by individuals' choices. Therefore, reinterpreting the Mirrlees model as a model of lifetime redistribution, we have to assume that the government can commit to a lifetime tax. The lifetime version of the Mirrlees model can be interpreted either such that the government controls first- and second-period consumption and labour supply directly, subject to the self-selection constraints. Alternatively, if we assume that there are no private savings, we have a model of labour income taxation in the first period and public provision of pension in the second period. This means that we consider the many-good non-linear tax model.

To introduce return to capital and the possible taxation thereof, it is useful to consider a two-period and two-type model (low skill, L and high skill, H), with labour supply in the first period and consumption in both the first and second periods. Savings from the first-period earnings are used to finance second-period consumption and so generate capital income that is taxable in the second period. With only a single period of work, the model is about the taxation of savings for retirement. The government wishes to design a lifetime tax system that may redistribute income between individuals in the same cohort. There is asymmetric information in the sense that the tax authority is informed about neither individual skill levels, labour supply, nor discount rates. The two types of individuals, labelled L and H, are endowed with productivities (skill levels) that are reflected by their respective wage rates n^L and $n^H > n^L$. Individual i (=L, H) gets labour income z = ny in the first period where n = wage rate, y = labour supply, and chooses how much to consume c (first-period consumption) and x (second-period consumption). The lifetime utility of an individual of type i is additive in the following way:

$$U^i = u(c^i) + \delta v(x^i) + \psi(1 - y^i), \tag{1}$$

where c and x denote, respectively, consumption when young and when retired; y is labour supply when young; and δ is a discount factor (here we assume $\delta^L = \delta^H = \delta$). U is increasing in each argument and $u', v', \psi' > 0$ and $u'', v'', \psi'' < 0$ and strictly concave. We also assume that all goods are normal.

Individuals are free to divide their first-period (when young) income between consumption, c, and savings, s. Each unit of savings yields a consumer an additional $1+\phi$ units of consumption in the second period after tax income, x. As further simplifications, we assume that there is a fixed rate of return to savings, which may be justified by assuming that we consider a small open economy facing a world capital market. Consumption in each period is given by $c^i = n^i y^i - T(n^i y^i) - s^i$ and $x^i = (1 + \phi)s^i$, i = 1. Now let us assume that the government controls c^i, x^i, and y^i directly, subject to the self-selection constraints. The optimization problem is maximization of a following utilitarian social welfare function:

$$\sum N^i(u(c^i) + \delta v(x^i) + \psi(1 - y^i)) \tag{2}$$

subject to the revenue constraint:

$$\sum N^i(n^i y^i - c^i - rx^i) = R \tag{3}$$

where $r = \frac{1}{1+\phi}$, and self-selection constraint:

$$u(c^H) + \delta v(x^H) + \psi(1 - y^H) \geq \hat{u}(c^L) + \delta\hat{v}(x^L) + \hat{\psi}\left(1 - \frac{n^L}{n^H}y^L\right). \tag{4}$$

The self-selection constraint requires that a high-skilled individual weakly prefers the bundle (c^H, x^H, z^H) to the two time periods intended for him or her to the bundle (c^L, x^L, z^L) designated for a low-skilled individual.[3] We consider the more interesting case, where only the incentive compatibility or self-selection constraint of the high-skilled type binds. This amounts to the region where redistribution takes place from high-skilled to low-skilled.

The first-order conditions (presented in appendix 14.2.1 setting $\delta^L = \delta^H = \delta$) can be written in a form:

$$\left(\frac{u_c}{v_x}\right)^L = \left(\frac{u_c}{v_x}\right)^H = \frac{\delta}{r}, \tag{5}$$

which says individual i's (i =L, H) marginal rate of substitution between consumption in period one and consumption in period two should be equal to the intertemporal marginal rate of transformation. Hence, there is no intertemporal distortion.

A much-discussed problem with taxing capital income concerns the inability of the government to commit to future tax policies. Can the government commit to a tax policy for two periods? Most analyses simply assume this away by allowing governments to commit to policies, even in cases where lifetime optimal taxation is studied. In fact, Roberts (1984, proposition 4), in an optimal dynamic taxation model without government commitment, raises doubts about the government's ability to use information from early periods of life to accomplish redistribution in later periods of life with lower welfare cost. The well-known problem with relaxing the commitment assumption is that it may no longer be social welfare-maximizing for the government to design a non-linear income tax system in which individuals are willing to reveal their skill types. Instead, it may be optimal to pool the individuals so that skill-type information is not revealed. Roberts (1984) concludes that if the time horizon is infinite and there is no discounting, separation never occurs. This means that if high-skilled individuals live forever, they will forever face personalized lump-sum taxation if they reveal their type. Moreover, since they do not discount the future, they cannot be compensated in the present for the everlasting personalized lump-sum taxation they would face after revealing their type. Hence, separation is not possible. Berliant and Ledyard (2005) in turn examine a

[3] The terms with a hat refer to mimicking behaviour. Note that regardless of different notation, the functional form is the same with or without a hat.

two-period model with discounting. In their model, the separation occurs when the discount rate is high. The intuition is that if high-skilled individuals are not too concerned about their future welfare, there exists a relatively low level of compensation that they can be given in the first period for revealing their type and when facing personalized lump-sum taxation in the second period. The assumptions on discounting made by Roberts (1984) and by Berliant and Ledyard (2005) are extreme, and not necessarily empirically plausible.

The so-called new dynamic public finance literature instead assumes that wages change stochastically in each period, so what is learned about an individual's type in one period is not relevant for the next. Alternatively, it might be assumed that government decision-making is sufficiently time-consuming that re-optimizing in the face of recent information would not be feasible. The commitment assumption might be criticized as being inconsistent with the information-based approach of the Mirrlees model. The government cannot observe each individual's skill type, which is the reason it must use distortionary taxation. Ruling out lump-sum taxation in a dynamic Mirrlees model using a commitment assumption might be considered somewhat artificial. The commitment assumption might be criticized as being inconsistent with one of the motivations behind the new dynamic public finance literature—to remove the need for ad hoc constraints on the tax instruments available to the government, which must be imposed in standard macro-style dynamic models (see Golosov et al (2007, 2010) for further discussion[4]).

If government policy can be changed after private agents have accumulated asset wealth, there will be an incentive for even benevolent governments to impose excessive taxes on capital income (Kydland and Prescott 1977; Fischer 1980). Given this, one expects capital income taxes to be higher than optimal, leading to a case against imposing capital income taxes in the first place.[5] Farhi et al (2011) provide a political economy theory without government commitment that addresses both the level and the progressivity of capital taxation. They point out that rising inequality is a destabilizing political force, which may encourage future governments to expropriate capital through heavy taxation. That threat could discourage saving and investment now. Hence, a progressive tax on capital in the present may lead to more investment by preventing an increase in inequality and by convincing firms that their wealth is (mostly) safe over the long term. Gaube (2007) in turn interprets the practice of taxing current income in each period as a partial commitment device. Gaube (2007) assumes that the government can commit to a

[4] Examples of this literature include Kocherlakota (2005), Albanesi and Sleet (2006), and Werning (2007), among others. Surveys of the new dynamic public finance literature are provided by Golosov et al (2006) and Golosov et al (2011). For a textbook treatment of the new dynamic public finance, see Kocherlakota (2010).

[5] For example, Farhi and Werning (2008) and Acemoglu et al (2008, 2010) relax the commitment assumption. The latter two papers, in particular, are concerned with the revelation and use of skill-type information, but where politicians may use this information partly for their own benefit, rather than only to maximize social welfare. Their analyses are therefore mostly positive in nature.

tax policy at least for two periods. This assumption can be justified by the fact that the income tax schedule is usually not redesigned each fiscal year. In the end, however, full commitment may not be realistic. Roberts (1984) and Gaube (2007) do not, however, consider taxes on savings as possible tax instruments. Gaube (2007) examined the difference between general and period tax functions. He showed that the one-period result of a zero marginal tax rate at a finite top of the earnings distribution does not apply to the two-period model with separate taxation in each period when there are income effects on labour supply, since additional earnings in one period would lower earnings, and so tax revenues in the other period.[6]

In what follows we focus on the case where the government can commit. Extending the analysis to the case where labour is supplied in both periods, the above results carry forward. If individuals have the intertemporal and intratemporal separable utility function $U^i = u(c^i) + \psi(1 - y^i) + \delta^i[v(x^i) + \psi(1 - y'^i)]$, there should be no capital income tax, while if the utility discount factor is correlated with wage rates, the capital income tax rate should be positive, as shown later on in the case with labour supply only in the first period. This can be seen as a simple extension of the above analysis. Now the government chooses consumption and income in both periods. The lifetime self-selection or incentive constraint becomes:

$$\begin{aligned} u(c^H) + \psi(1 - y^H) + \delta[v(x^H) + \psi(1 - y'^H)] \geq \hat{u}(c^L) + \hat{\psi}\left(1 - \frac{n^L}{n^H}y^L\right) \\ +\delta\left[\hat{v}(x^L) + \hat{\psi}\left(1 - \frac{n^L}{n^H}y'^L\right)\right] \end{aligned} \tag{6}$$

where y' is the second-period labour supply. From the first-order condition, we can see that also in this case there is no intertemporal distortion on consumption for either skill type.

With variable earnings in both periods, the pattern of tax rates on earnings over time becomes relevant. Marginal tax rates for the high-wage persons will be zero in both periods, as expected. For low-wage persons, optimal marginal tax rates will be positive and will rise over time if the rate of growth of wage rates is less for low-wage types than for high-wage types, and vice versa (Diamond 2007).

The Atkinson–Stiglitz result has been subject to considerable scrutiny in the literature, and special attention has been devoted to circumstances in which it is violated. One reason for departure is nonseparability in preferences. From the Corlett and Hague (1953) analysis with linear tax, we know that commodities that are complements to leisure should be taxed more heavily so as to increase work incentives. However, a similar argument will hold when we consider consumption today and consumption tomorrow. It may be efficient to discriminate against or in favour of saving if, given the

[6] See also Berliant and Ledyard (2005).

level of income, the way in which people want to divide their expenditure between consumption today and consumption tomorrow depends upon how many hours they work. By acting as a tax on future consumption, taxing savings may increase the incentive to work if consumption tomorrow is related to leisure today. With non-separability between consumption and labour, a key issue for the sign of taxing capital income—taxing versus subsidizing—is the pattern of the cross-elasticities between labour supply and consumption levels in the two periods. However, not much is known about these cross-elasticities and thus there is not a strong reason from this argument to reject the zero tax policy implication.

Boadway et al (2000) and Cremer et al (2003) show that where skill and inherited wealth are not observable, a capital income tax might become desirable even with separable preferences. A major focus of these two papers is to study capital income taxation as an instrument to indirectly tax inherited wealth, particularly when it is not perfectly correlated with skills. In the real world inheritances strongly influence income levels, particularly among the very rich. Solow (2013) (http://www.newrepublic.com/article/115956/alan-greenspans-map-and-territory-reviewed-robert-solow) puts this as follows:

> The actual outcome, including the relative incomes of participants, depends on 'initial endowments,' the resources that participants bring when they enter the market. Some were born to well-off parents in relatively rich parts of the country and grew up well-fed, well-educated, well-cared-for, and well-placed, endowed with property. Others were born to poor parents in relatively poor or benighted parts of the country, and grew up on bad diets, in bad schools, in bad situations, and without social advantages or property. Others grew up somewhere in between. These differences in starting points will be reflected in their marginal products and thus in their market-determined incomes. There is nothing just about it.

Hence, taxes on labour income are inadequate to the task of limiting inequality because they punish those who owe high incomes to greater ability and effort, rather than to inheritance.

The logic of Mirrlees' (1976a) result for taxing goods preferred by those with higher skill can also be used as an argument for capital income taxation. In fact, Saez (2002) argues, in the context of present and future consumption, that individuals with higher earnings save relatively more, which suggests that high-skilled individuals are more likely to have higher discount factors. Like Saez (2002), Diamond (2003) assumes that the correlation between skills and time preferences is perfect so that problems of multi-dimensional screening do not arise. Banks and Diamond (2010), in the chapter on direct taxation in the Mirrlees Review, conclude: 'With the plausible assumption that those with higher earnings abilities discount the future less (and thus save more out of any given income), then taxation of saving helps with the equity-efficiency trade-off by being a source of indirect evidence.'

On average, those with higher earning capacity are more likely to save and will achieve a higher return on any savings they have. This provides a strong case for taxing savings because saving is an indicator of having high earnings capacity. Tenhunen and Tuomala (2010) extend Diamond's (2003) analysis of non-linear taxation of savings into the three-type and four-type models (two wage rates and two discount factors) where time preferences and productivity abilities are imperfectly correlated. An individual may be high or low-skilled, and they may have a high or low discount factor. They mainly focus on numerical solutions to the multi-dimensional screening problem. They also examine the possibility that the government's discount factor may differ from that of individuals, which creates a paternalistic motive for taxation. Diamond and Spinnewijn (2009) build a model with jobs rather than choice of hours by workers facing a given wage rate. They avoid problems of the multi-dimensional screening assuming that jobs have fixed earnings and are specific to skill type in equilibrium. In a four-type model they show that, starting with the optimal earnings tax, the introduction of a small tax on savings of high earners raises social welfare, as does introduction of a small subsidy on savings of low earners. Both introductions ease the binding incentive compatibility constraint. The result makes no use of the correlation across types, although it does assume that at the optimum all higher-skilled workers hold the higher output job. With a restriction on preferences, they also show that the optimal linear earnings-varying savings tax has the same character. The intuition behind this is that those valuing the future more (relative to the disutility of work) are more willing to work than those valuing the future less. The incentive constraint binds for high wage/low savers but not for high wage/high savers. This generates scope for taxing savings. Both Tenhunen and Tuomala (2010) and Diamond and Spinnewijn (2011) assume full commitment.

The so-called new dynamic public finance has extended the Mirrlees optimal income tax approach to a dynamic setting (see e.g. Golosov, Tsyvinski, and Werning 2007; Kocherlakota 2010). This is far from an easy task. Uncertainty is a key feature of the analysis. If future earnings are uncertain, it is desirable to tax savings to maximize social welfare. This is the key message of this literature. Intuitively, this means that if an individual plans to work less because of high taxes later on in life, the individual saves more. Therefore, discouraging saving makes it harder for individuals to respond to taxes. Without doubt, these models require a high level of rationality from individuals.

The models examined by Golosov, Troshkin, and Tsyvinski (2011) (or Golosov et al (2010)) avoid the complexities associated with multi-dimensional screening by assuming that preferences for savings are a function of skills. They derive and illustrate optimal labour wedges in connecting their generalized formulas to the static Mirrlees expressions. They show that the size of the optimal implicit capital income tax wedge is quantitatively fairly modest on average (figure 2, p. 25). Farhi and Werning (2012) characterize the evolution of the labour implicit tax rates (wedge) over time analytically and numerically in such an environment.

A typical assumption in the theoretical literature is that the tax authority can easily distinguish the respective types of income. In practice, it is difficult to distinguish between capital and labour income (e.g. small businesses, self-employed, professional traders). Differential tax treatment can induce shifting. Examples follow:

1. US C-corporations vs S-corporations: shift from corporate income and realized capital gains toward individual business income (Gordon and Slemrod 2000).
2. Carried interest in the US: hedge fund and private equity fund managers receive fraction of profits of assets they manage for clients. Those profits are labour income but are taxed as realized capital gains.
3. The Finnish Dual income tax system has taxed capital income separately at preferred rates since 1993. Pirttilä and Selin (2011) show that it induced shifting from labour to capital income, especially among the self-employed.

Christiansen and Tuomala (2008) examine a model with costly (but legal) conversion of labour income into capital income. Despite preferences that would result in a zero tax on capital income in the absence of the ability to shift income, they find a positive tax on capital income. With finite shifting elasticity, differential marginal tax rates for labour and capital income taxation induce an additional shifting distortion. The higher the shifting elasticity, the closer the tax rates on labour and capital income should be (Christiansen and Tuomala 2008). Gordon and Slemrod (1998) raise the issue of shifting between corporate and personal tax bases. Even with an infinite horizon, the Chamley–Judd result of asymptotically zero capital income taxation does not hold in a model with an inability to distinguish between entrepreneurial labour income and capital income (Correia 1996; Reis 2007). In the extreme case, government cannot distinguish at all between labour and capital income. It means government observes only total income (labour income plus capital income). Then the only option is to have identical marginal tax rates at individual level. In practice, this seems to be a very important consideration when designing income tax systems, especially for top incomes. It is a strong reason for having marginal tax rates on labour and capital income identical at the top.

An early contribution to redistributive tax policy in the presence of asymmetric information in dynamic settings is that of Ordover and Phelps (1979). They consider optimal non-linear taxation of income and savings in an overlapping generation's model. In their model, individuals live for two periods, but work only when young. Ordover and Phelps (1979) show that it is optimal to tax the savings of most individuals (but not the savings of the most skilled) whenever the marginal rate of substitution between consumption when young and consumption when old depends on labour supply. On the other hand, savings should remain untaxed at the margin whenever preferences are separable across time. Using a similar generational structure and informational assumptions, Pirttilä and Tuomala (2001) (see also Brett 1997) argue that distorting savings decisions can be optimal even when preferences are separable across time when future relative wages are sensitive to current savings via their effect on capital accumulation.[7]

[7] Naito (1999) has shown that the Atkinson–Stiglitz result does not hold with non-linear technology.

In other words, they have shown that capital income taxation may be desirable even when preferences are separable across time where future relative wages are sensitive to current savings via their effect on capital income. In the context of an OLG model where the concern is inter-generational redistribution, Blackorby and Brett (2000) show that capital income taxes can implement parts of the Pareto frontier that would otherwise be unattainable.

The Atkinson–Stiglitz theorem also implies that a consumption or expenditure tax[8] is superior to an income tax. The intuition is that one can achieve any degree of redistribution by adjusting the rate schedule, so the only remaining question concerns efficiency, as in the original commodity tax problem. That is, we can ask whether an individual of a given earnings level should be taxed relatively more or less depending on whether more income is allocated to first-period or second-period consumption. In this basic case, neutrality (no differentiation in tax rates) is optimal because it avoids an additional distortion (of the intertemporal pattern of consumption), whereas differentiation would not help to offset the pre-existing distortion (of labour supply). There are reasonably convincing arguments from behavioural economics that a subset of the population systematically under-saves, and taxing capital income would provide further discouragement. This is one reason for the Mirrlees Review's opting for a form of progressive expenditure tax regime that sheltered all capital income with the exception of super-normal returns. The Meade report and Kay and King (1986) present an argument for expenditure tax that the individual's annual income is difficult to measure. It is, however, so that consumption and income are equally difficult to measure for top wealth holders. There are, however, arguments working against expenditure tax. There is evidence from advanced economies on the growing gap in life expectancy between low and high-income people. If gains in expected life spans are increasingly concentrated among the well-to-do, we should not ask the less affluent to bear the main burden of an aging society. This is clearly an argument against expenditure tax. This is also an argument against increasing VAT on food.

In sum, from a point of view of equity, it seems fair to not discriminate against savers if labour earnings are the only source of inequality and are taxed non-linearly. In reality, capital income inequality is due to many different reasons: differences in savings behaviour; difference in rates of returns (often lucky returns); shifting of labour income into capital income; inheritances, etc. At the same time, there are other arguments working against capital income taxation. Capital income taxes are costly to administer and give rise to costly tax planning, relocation, and evasion. Some forms of asset income are difficult to tax, such as the imputed return on human capital and consumer durables, so inter-asset distortions are inevitable.

[8] See on expenditure tax e.g. Kaldor 1955; Meade 1978; Kay and King 1978; King 1980.

14.2 On informational rationales for taxing capital income

14.2.1 HETEROGENEOUS TIME PREFERENCES

It is quite plausible to assume that in reality, for all sorts of reasons, both ability and time preferences are not observable. Multidimensional heterogeneity in individuals' characteristics is a realistic assumption but it complicates the analysis notably as seen in Chapter 10 (see also an excellent discussion on this in Boadway 2012). In the case with heterogeneous time preferences, incentive constraints may then operate in all directions of skills. The structure of the set of self-selection constraints or incentive-compatible constraints is then difficult to deal with, and no theoretical solution has yet been found to the multi-dimensional optimization problem in this context. There are some analytical studies in a discrete case with two-dimensional heterogeneity,[9] but they are simplified further to a three-type case (Cuff 2000; Blomquist and Christiansen 2004). Cremer, Lozachmeur, and Pestieau (2004) also consider social security and retirement decision in a static model with agents differing in two dimensions: productivity and health status. Cremer et al (2009) also examine a non-linear social security scheme when the government has a paternalistic view and wants to help to overcome individuals' myopia problems. They all find some support for public intervention in terms of a pension policy or a non-linear taxation of savings.

However, as discussed earlier, the problem of heterogeneous preferences is not just about incentives. It is also a hard normative question, because the social objective must then involve interpersonal comparisons of individuals with heterogeneous preferences. In the welfarist tradition there is no principle on which such comparisons can be grounded. This tradition always assumes that the relevant utility functions are provided by some external authority. Economists who want to say something about the optimal tax therefore can only consider the various possible results that can come for the various possible weights attached to different utility functions.

The standard argument against taxing the return to saving relies on the assumption that taxing saving creates inefficiencies and cannot help with redistribution. The recent research in behavioural economics has demonstrated that individual decision-making often suffers from various biases. Some people save more for the future than others because they are more patient. Some save more because they have a greater understanding of the options available and the consequences of saving, or not saving. In particular, those with low earnings capacity do not save enough. They can be impatient and have difficulty making appropriate calculations and decisions. In these situations, when there

[9] An exception is Tarkiainen and Tuomala (1999; 2007), who present numerical calculations in the two-dimensional optimal tax problem for a continuum of agents.

is a possible conflict between an individual's long-term preference and his short-term behaviour, the government may want to intervene. If the observed level of saving is a good proxy for earnings capacity, then taxing savings might be a useful way of redistributing. We might then want to subsidize or otherwise encourage them to save. At the margin, by taxing savings the government could raise revenue and redistribute from those with higher earning capacity while reducing tax rates on labour supply.

Economists such as Wicksell, Pigou, Ramsey, and Allais[10] have argued that the social planner should be more patient than the individual. For example, Ramsey (1928) claimed that it was 'ethically indefensible' not to take into account discounting of the future utilities. Any such argument can be called paternalistic. The notion that individuals may not make the best choices for themselves raises difficult issues. Individuals may be fully rational and just happen to have a high preference for the present, which causes them to save little, because too little weight is given to future contingencies. Should the government be welfarist and maximize individual welfare, as the individual sees it? Alternatively, as suggested in recent behavioural public economics literature, should it be paternalistic, or non-welfarist, and discount the future at a different rate than individuals? In fact, individuals may want the government to intervene, to induce behaviour that is closer to what individuals wish they were doing. For example, in models with quasi-hyperbolic preferences it is typically desirable to impose a particular savings plan on individuals.

Tenhunen and Tuomala (2010) characterize the optimal lifetime redistribution policy within a cohort. They consider the optimal tax treatment of savings when individuals differ both in abilities and time preferences in both welfarist and paternalistic cases.[11] The case with two-dimensional heterogeneity is considered both in analytical form and, to gain a better understanding, also in the light of numerical examples. Next we consider a two-period and two and four-type version of the Mirrlees model with different correlations between skill and discount factor, with both welfarist and paternalistic governments.[12]

[10] 'In actual societies it seems to be common that social choices deviate from consumer preferences in the assessment of the relative importance of future needs with respect to present needs ... Public saving and legal arrangements such as compulsory pension schemes allow this objective to be realised. ... It was in order to generalise optimum theory to such a collective attitude that M. Allais put forward the concept of 'rendement social généralisé'. His idea is to define and investigate a notion of optimum in which individual preferences are retained for the choice between consumption relating to the same date, but not necessarily between those relating to different dates.' (Malinvaud 1972, p. 244)

[11] In a longer working paper version (Tenhunen and Tuomala 2007) a case of Rawlsian government is also considered.

[12] Sandmo (1993) considers a case where people differ in preferences, but are endowed with the same resources. Tarkiainen and Tuomala (1999, 2007) also consider a continuum of taxpayers simultaneously distributed by skill and preferences for leisure and income.

A benchmark model: two types with a positive correlation between skill and discount factor

Each individual has a skill level reflecting his wage rate, denoted by n, and a discount factor, denoted by δ. We denote low-skilled types by the superscript L and high-skilled types by the superscript H. The assumption of positive correlation implies that $\delta^L \leq \delta^H$. The proportion of individuals of type i in the population is $N^i > 0$, with $\sum N^i = 1$.

Do we have empirical evidence that high-type people are more patient? The assumptions on preferences that are made in this model imply that high-skilled people have higher earnings and that people who discount the future less heavily have higher savings rates. Given this, the statement 'high-type people are more patient' follows from the empirical correlation between savings rates and earnings. In Figure 14.1, based on Consumer Surveys in Finland over the period 1976–2012, we see that savings rates are increasing in income.

Saez (2002) also argues that individuals with higher earnings save relatively more, which suggests that high-skilled individuals are more likely to have higher discount factors. In this case, discount factor is positively correlated with productivity level. For this reason, we take as a starting point separable utility with different time preference.[13] The lifetime utility of an individual of type i is additive in the following way:

$$U^i = u(c^i) + \delta^i v(x^i) + \psi(1 - y^i), \tag{1}$$

where we make the same assumptions as previously.

The government wishes to design a lifetime tax system that may redistribute income between individuals in the same cohort. There is asymmetric information in the sense that the tax authority is informed about neither individual skill levels, nor labour supply,

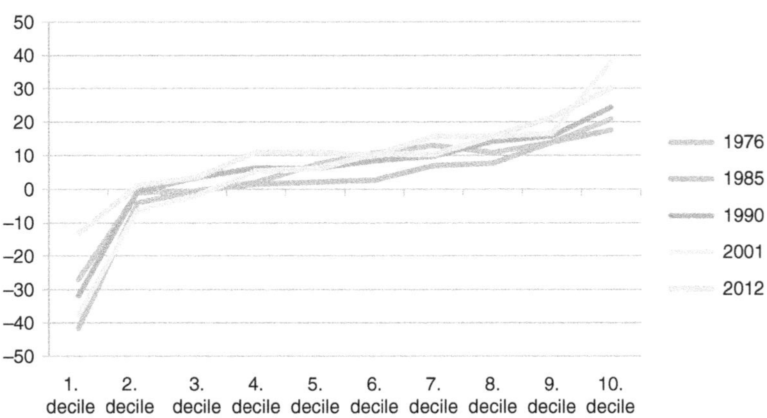

Figure 14.1 Savings rates in Finland in different deciles

Source: Riihelä, Sullström, and Tuomala (2015).

[13] Alternatively, the same outcome could be reached by assuming homothetic preferences and linear Engel curves.

nor discount rates. It can only observe before-tax income, ny. In this setting, where taxes both on earnings and savings income are available, we examine whether or not savings ought to be taxed. The separability assumption makes it possible to isolate the significance of variations in time preferences.

The welfarist government: The government respects the individual sovereignty principle and evaluates individuals' well-being using their own discount rates. Assume that the government controls c^i, x^i, and y^i directly. Alternatively, if we assume that there are no private savings, we have a model of labour income taxation in the first period and public provision of pension in the second period.

In the welfarist case, government's problem is to maximize the following social welfare function:

$$\sum N^i(u(c^i) + \delta^i v(x^i) + \psi(1 - y^i)) \tag{2}$$

subject to the revenue constraint:

$$\sum N^i(n^i y^i - c^i - rx^i) = R \tag{3}$$

where $r = \frac{1}{1+\phi}$, and the self-selection constraint[14]

$$u(c^H) + \delta^H v(x^H) + \psi(1 - y^H) \geq u(c^L) + \delta^H v(x^L) + \psi\left(1 - \frac{n^L}{n^H}y^L\right). \tag{4}$$

The first-order conditions[15] can be expressed in the form:

$$\left(\frac{u_c}{v_x}\right)^i = \frac{\delta^i}{r}[1 - d^i], \tag{5}$$

where the left-hand side is individual i's marginal rate of substitution between consumption in the first and in the second period, and d^i is the distortion. A positive (negative) d^i implies that type i should have an implicit tax (subsidy) on savings. It is useful to define a relative difference in discount factors as $\Delta^{ij} \equiv \frac{\delta^i - \delta^j}{\delta^j}$, for any pair of discount factors. The first-order conditions (see appendix) imply that

$$\begin{aligned} d^L &= (\phi^1 - 1)\Delta^{HL} \\ d^H &= 0 \end{aligned} \tag{6}$$

where $\phi^1 = \frac{N^L}{N^L - \mu^{HL}}$. The returns to savings of type i should not be taxed when d^i is zero.

[14] The direction of the binding self-selection constraint is assumed to be, following the tradition in the one-dimensional two-type model, from high-skilled individual toward low-skilled individual. This pattern is also confirmed by the numerical simulations.

[15] In the numerical solution we also consider the marginal labour income tax rates. As has become conventional in the literature, we may interpret the marginal rate of substitution between gross and net income as one minus the marginal income tax, $\frac{\psi'(ny/n)}{nu_c} = 1 - T'(ny)$, which would be equivalent to the characterization of the labour supply of an agent facing an income tax function $T(ny)$. The marginal labour income tax rates satisfy the usual properties: $T'(n^L y^L) > 0$ and $T'(n^H y^H) = 0$.

With d^H=0, the optimal implicit marginal tax rate for the high-skill type is zero. When we assume, empirically plausibly, $\delta^H > \delta^L$, we have d^L>0 implying implicit taxation of savings for the low-skill type. This is the same result as in Diamond (2003).

As a result of the two-dimensional heterogeneity, a tax on capital income is an effective way to relax an otherwise binding self-selection constraint. This is because even under separability the mimicker and the individual mimicked do not save the same amount. A high-skilled individual choosing to mimic someone with less skill values savings more than a low-skilled individual, since discount of the future is less for the potential mimicker. Thus, taxing savings relaxes the self-selection constraint. Alternatively, put another way: distortions generate second-order efficiency costs but first-order redistributional benefits. The implication is that there should be a tax on the savings of low-wage persons. Intuitively, lower saving by low-skilled (wage) persons reduces their second-period consumption, making it more difficult for high-skilled (wage) persons to mimic them. Hence, the tax rate on capital income should be positive if the discount rate increases with the wage rate.

Differences in governments' and individuals' discount rates

Assume now that the government does not respect the individual sovereignty principle and evaluates individuals' well-being using a discount rate different from those of individuals. Now the paternalistic government with a discount factor δ^g maximizes social objective given by:

$$\sum N^i(u(c^i) + \delta^g v(x^i) + \psi(1 - y^i)) \tag{7}$$

The form giving the implicit marginal taxes for savings is now $\left(\frac{u_c}{v_x}\right)^i = \frac{\delta^g}{r}[1 - \alpha^i]$, where α^i gives the distortion. There is a correspondence between α^i and d^i, given by $\alpha^i = d^i + \Delta^{ig}(d^i - 1)$, for all types i. It can be observed that as long as $d^i < 1$, $\alpha^i > d^i$. In other words, a positive (negative) α^i implies that the savings decision of type i is under-subsidized (over-subsidized) relative to the first-best.

From the first-order conditions of government's problem (appendix 14.2.1), we get the following expressions:

$$\begin{aligned} \alpha^L &= (\phi^1 - 1)\Delta^{Hg} \\ \alpha^H &= (\phi^2 - 1)\Delta^{Hg} \end{aligned} \tag{8}$$

where $\phi^1 = \frac{N^L}{N^L - \mu^{HL}}$ and $\phi^2 = \frac{N^H}{N^H + \mu^{HL}}$.

From (8) we see that α^L is negative and α^H is positive, when type H individual's discount factor is smaller than that of the social planner. Relaxing the self-selection constraint in this paternalistic case means an upward distortion for the savings of type L and a downward distortion for the savings of type H. Contrary to the welfarist case, the savings of the low-skill type are now subsidized. In other words, compared to the savings required to the first-best optimum, it is socially beneficial to have the high-skill type save less and the low-skill type save more.

In the first-best situation with perfect information and a paternalistic government, the distortion is $-\Delta^{gi}$. This marginal subsidy on savings corrects the effect of the difference in the discount rates between individuals and government. In the second-best case without paternalistic objectives, the results in (8) suggested a marginal tax on the low-skill type and no distortion for the high-skill type. However, in the case where these two phenomena (paternalistic objectives and imperfect information on both productivity and time preferences) appear at the same time, the low-skill type is subsidized and the high-skill type is taxed. One possible explanation for this somewhat surprising result is that in addition to the separate effects[16] of the two sources of distortions, they are also likely to interact. This interaction can be expected to affect the incentive structure of the economy. In this framework it is not possible to isolate the effects due to self-selection constraint and to discount factors (paternalism) in distortions. It is only possible to say that $\alpha^H > -\Delta^{gH}$, i.e. in the second-best optimum the tax overcompensates the first-best subsidy, and for the low-skilled type in the second-best optimum there is an additional subsidy compared to first-best situation, i.e. $\alpha^L < -\Delta^{gL}$.

Comparing the solution of the second-best problem given in equation (8) to the laissez-faire we have a positive tax on savings for the high-skilled type and a negative one for the low-skilled type. This implies that non-linear taxes and subsidies of savings are a useful complement to non-linear taxation of labour income for a government interested in redistribution.

In sum: as long as $\delta^H < \delta^g$, the savings of the high-skill type should be implicitly taxed at the margin (under-subsidized relative to the first-best situation), while the savings of the low-skill type should be implicitly subsidized (over-subsidized relative to the first-best situation) when individuals differ both in their productivities and time preferences.

A four-type model, numerical considerations

To investigate further the properties of the optimal lifetime redistribution, Tenhunen and Tuomala (2010) analyse a four-type case with numerical tools. Thus, instead of deriving analytical results that are not very tractable in a general case, we consider the four-type model only numerically. In a four-type model, the types are indexed, as in Table 14.1. Without any assumptions on the interdependence of these two characteristics, we end up having a four-type economy, with types denoted according to Table 14.1. The proportion of individuals of type i in the population is $N^i > 0$, with $\sum N^i = 1$.

[16] The separate effects would have suggested that high-skill type should only face the subsidy resulting from the paternalistic objectives, while the distortion of the low-skilled type would consist of a subsidy due to paternalistic objectives and a tax resulting from the aim to avoid mimicking behaviour.

The social planner maximizes a sum of utilities, (3), and the paternalist planner maximizes (7) subject to the revenue constraint (3) and the self-selection constraints given by

$$u(c^i) + \delta^i v(x^i) + \psi(1 - y^i) \geq u(c^j) + \delta^i v(x^j) + \psi\left(1 - \frac{n^j y^j}{n^i}\right), \ \forall i, j \text{ and } i \neq j \qquad (9)$$

There appear twelve self-selection constraints in the optimization problem. The parameterization is as presented in Table 14.2. First, a uniform distribution of types is assumed, i.e. $N^i = 0.25$, implying that there is no correlation between skill level and time preference. The utility function takes the following separable forms of $U^i = -\frac{1}{c^i} - \delta^i \frac{1}{x^i} - \frac{1}{1-y^i}$ (CES). The results of the numerical solution are given in Tables 14.3 and 14.4.

No a priori assumptions of the binding self-selection constraints are made in numerical simulations. We do not choose the direction of redistribution a priori, i.e. the pattern of the binding self-selection constraints is not restricted a priori. Tables 14.3 and 14.4 present the numerical results for CES function in the welfarist and paternalist cases: private utilities in the optimum; the values of the marginal rates of labour income T'; the marginal tax rates of savings, given by distortion d^i in the welfarist case and α^i in the

Table 14.1 Individual types

		Wage	
		Low	high
Discount factor	Low	type 1	type 3
	High	type 2	type 4

Table 14.2 Parameterization in the two-type economy

Fraction of individuals in each group	$N^i = 0.25$ for i = 1,2,3,4
Discount factors	$\delta^L = 0.6$, $\delta^H = 0.8$, $\delta^g = 1$, r = 0.95
Productivities (wages)	$n^L = 2$, $n^H = 3$

Table 14.3 Utility levels at the optimum, marginal tax rates, and replacement rates in the welfarist case. The binding self-selection constraints are (3.1), (3.2), and (4.3)

	U	T'	d	y	x/ny	means
type 1	−4.73	7.80	0	0.51	50.88	$\bar{c}$= 0.72
type 2	−5.10	13.17	−11.38	0.52	56.40	$\bar{x}$= 0.62
type 3	−4.22	0	5.14	0.52	41.29	
type 4	−4.52	0	0	0.54	45.06	

Table 14.4 Utility levels at the optimum, marginal tax rates and replacement rates in the paternalistic case. The binding self-selection constraints are (3.1), (3.2), and (4.3)

	U	T′	α	y	x/ny	means
type 1	−4.84	12.81	−17.63	0.54	59.58	$\bar{c}$= 0.68
type 2	−5.15	12.81	−17.63	0.54	59.58	$\bar{x}$= 0.71
type 3	−4.23	0	14.13	0.54	46.54	
type 4	−4.50	0	4.49	0.55	47.99	

paternalistic case; and the replacement rates in terms of second-period consumption relative to the first-period gross income (x/ny).

In both the welfarist and the paternalistic case, type 2 consumers are worst off in terms of utilities while type 3 consumers have the highest utility. The pattern of binding self-selection constraints is the same in both cases. It can be noted that constraint (4,3) binds even though type 3 consumers have higher utility. In our case this results from the fact that the consumption levels available for a true type 3 are different (present consumption relatively larger and future consumption relatively lower) from those that would be chosen by type 4, given the possibility to allocate income freely between present and future period consumption. Technically speaking, those individuals that are mimicked in the optimum should be taxed. In the two-type case, we had a positive marginal tax on both labour income and savings for the mimicked type. With two-dimensional heterogeneity, the pattern of binding self-selection constraints can be less straightforward. Similarly, the constraint (4,3) binds to the three-type case here even though type 3 has higher utility than type 4. The direction of other binding constraints (3,1) and (3,2) is something we could expect on the basis of the one-dimensional case with differences only in productivity. We note that the most socially desirable redistribution is from type 3 to type 2 (from the best-off to the worst-off). This binding constraint in turn limits the opportunities to redistribute between other pairs of types. For instance, it would be socially desirable to redistribute from type 4 to type 1, but this is constrained by the fact that type 3 has to be provided with some information 'rent' ((4,3) binds). Therefore, if we tax type 4 too heavily, he or she may begin to mimic type 3.

In the optimum of the welfarist case there are positive marginal labour income tax rates on both low-skilled types. The savings decisions of types 1 and 4 are not distorted. Type 2 consumers, who are the worst-off types in terms of utilities, have a positive marginal income tax and a marginal subsidy on savings, whereas type 3, the best-off type in terms of utilities, faces a marginal tax on savings. There is bunching of types 1 and 2 in the paternalistic cases, i.e. they always choose a common bundle of labour supply and consumption. This means that the second-order incentive compatibility conditions are not satisfied. This finding gives further validation for the three-type case considered earlier: in the paternalistic case only three different types of consumers can be distinguished.[17] With the pattern of binding self-selection constraints, we could conclude that type 3 mimicking the common choice of types 1 and 2 is prevented by setting a positive marginal income tax on types 1 and 2. This is compensated (at least partly) by a subsidy on savings. The marginal tax on savings for types 3 and 4 is driven by the paternalistic preferences of the social planner.

Tenhunen and Tuomala (2010) also checked how sensitive the results are for parameter values of discount factors, group sizes, and productivity (wage) differences. Marginal tax rates for income from savings for types with lower discount factor are larger. Increasing wage inequality marginal tax rates for both labour income tax and tax on savings increase, which is in accordance with findings in the atemporal continuous Mirrlees model (see Kanbur and Tuomala 1994; see also Chapter 5).

Correlation between skill level and time preference

A uniform distribution of all types implies that the correlation between skill level and time preference is zero. However, this may not be the case; the two characteristics may be imperfectly correlated. At the same time, changing the assumption of the correlation allows us to consider the robustness of our results with respect to the distribution of types. Figures 14.2 and 14.3 present the marginal tax rates on savings in the welfarist and paternalist cases with the CES utility function.

From the figures we can see that the results for the marginal tax on savings are fairly robust except for type 3. As the correlation between skill level and time preference

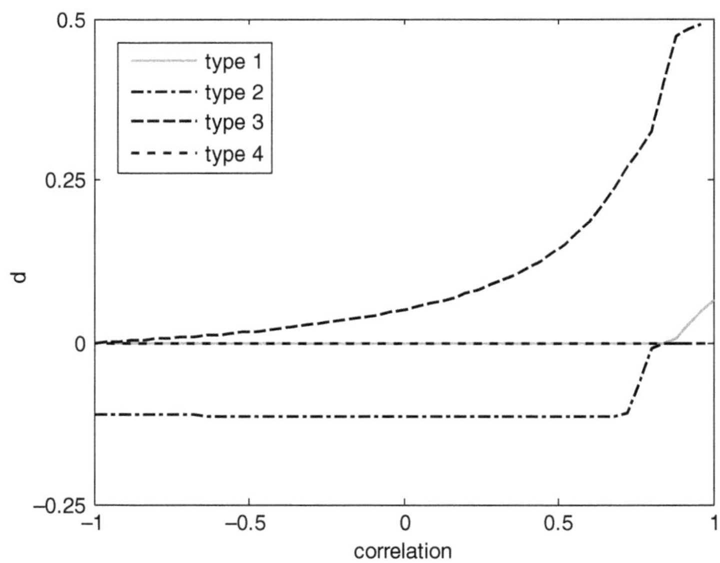

Figure 14.2 Marginal tax on savings in the welfarist case

[17] Blomquist and Christiansen (2004) and Cuff (2000) also apply a three-type version of a Mirrlees (1971) optimal income tax model with heterogeneity in preferences between leisure and consumption.

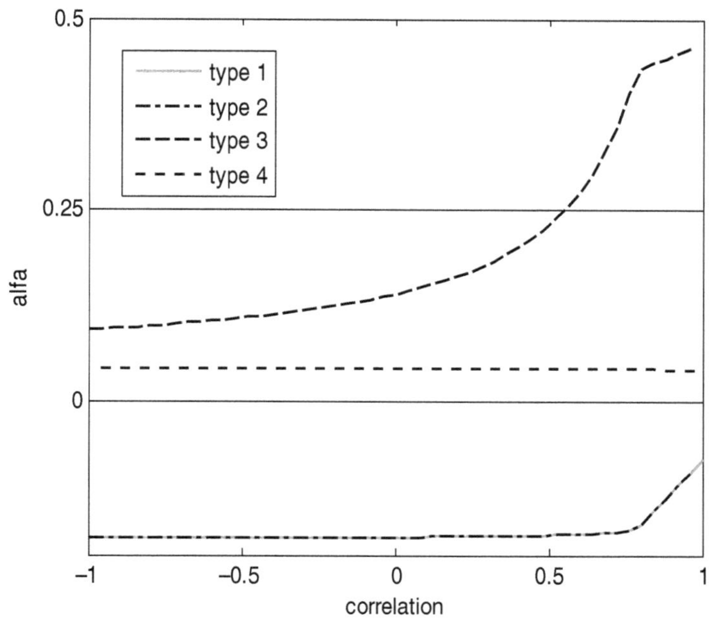

Figure 14.3 Marginal tax on savings in the paternalistic case

increases, or as the fraction of types 2 and 3 decreases, the distortion on type 3's savings decision increases significantly with both types of government preferences. In the welfarist case, type 4 remains undistorted regardless of the structure of the economy. Type 1 is also undistorted except at very high levels of correlation, where his savings become taxed. In the paternalistic case, types 1 and 2 remain pooled, and the tax on savings for type 4 is almost fixed at all levels of correlation. Note that the two-type case above which is equivalent to a correlation of one corresponds to the right boundaries of Figures 14.2 and 14.3.

Myopic behaviour

Next we analyse the model in which all individuals do not save voluntarily and, in their labour supply decisions, they ignore the implications of their earnings when young for retirement income—i.e. they are myopic. Myopic behaviour may be quite common for a substantial proportion of individuals who hardly save and rely almost entirely on public pension benefits. Does this model generate less dispersed retirement consumption than the models with rational behaviour? Diamond (2003, chapter 4) and Diamond and Mirrlees (2000) consider a benchmark situation where individuals do not save at all.[18] In their model workers are otherwise identical, but their skills differ, and the government's

[18] See also Cremer and Roeder (2013).

objective is to design an optimal redistributive policy for the working-age and for the retired. If the social welfare function exhibits inequality aversion, the optimal retirement consumption is shown to be higher for those whose lifetime income has been smaller.

It is worth stressing that myopic behaviour is distinct from the behaviour associated with heavy discounting of the future. If individuals have low discount factors, they will save little for their retirement consumption, but this reflects optimizing behaviour. By contrast, if individuals are myopic and are subjected to forced saving, their welfare will increase. Although the behavioural foundations of myopia differ essentially from those of time-consistent utility maximization, the analysis developed above can be used with minor modifications. We simply interpret the discount factor δ as either 0 for perfectly myopic types and 1 for completely rational individuals.

Myopic labour supply implies that the retirement consumption does not enter the incentive compatibility constraint of a myopic mimicker. The social welfare function depends on ex post utilities given by $u(c^i) + \delta^g v(x^i) + \psi(1 - y^i)$.

By assuming that all types are myopic, we get a two-type version of the continuum model analysed in Diamond (2003). A more interesting case is to extend Diamond's analysis into a more realistic case in which some people save and some do not, i.e. assume that myopia and ability are imperfectly correlated. To maintain the tractability, we simplify the four-type model by assuming that there are actually only three types: low-skilled types with a low discount factor δ^L, indexed as type 1; high-skilled types with a low discount factor, type 3; and high-skilled types with a high discount factor, type 4.[19] We assume that $\delta^L = 0$, but unlike in Diamond (2003), we allow social planner and type 4 individuals to have different discount factors.

Myopic types perceive only the apparent utility $u(c^i) + \psi(1 - y^i)$. Thus there is now no first-best case, where the government could induce myopic types to save voluntarily through a subsidy on savings.[20] As a result, the interpretation based on private distortion d cannot be used here. However, in the optimum, from the government point of view, there is a distortion a also for myopic types. Myopic types take only the apparent utility into account, also when mimicking. But rational type 4 perceives the changes in second-period consumption that would occur if he mimicked myopic types, so the part reflecting the utility from the second period remains in the self-selection constraints binding type 4 but vanishes from those binding types 1 and 3.

The social planner maximizes (7) subject to the revenue constraint (3) and the self-selection constraints (see appendix 14.2.1). Numerical simulation suggests that whereas none of the upwards self-selection constraints are binding, all of the downward constraints are. For type 1 the marginal taxation of saving is negative; for type 4 it is positive; and the sign of the distortion is indeterminate for type 3 (see appendix 14.2.1).

[19] There are also other possible structures for a three-type economy. A discussion on the issue is presented in appendix 14.2.2.

[20] The first-best distortion $-\frac{\delta^g - \delta^i}{\delta^i}$ approaches $-\infty$ when δ^i goes to zero.

Table 14.5 The numerical solution in the paternalistic case with myopia. The binding self-selection constraints are (3.1), (4.1), and (4.3)

	U	T′	α	x/ny	means
type 1	−3.96	14.61	−40.07	62.86	$\bar{c}$= 0.72
type 3	−3.35	0	33.85	42.90	$\bar{x}$= 0.71
type 4	−4.52	0	4.37	47.48	

The numerical solution (Table 14.5) with otherwise the same parameters as in the earlier case, except for δ^L=0, also follows the same lines as the paternalistic case presented earlier. The optimal savings tax rate for type 1 is negative, i.e. there is an implicit subsidy for savings as suggested by the analytical part. For types 3 and 4 we have a tax.

In a three-type model when there are myopic individuals in the economy, the paternalist government policy increases the savings of the low-skilled type and decreases the savings of the high-skilled types compared to the paternalist government policy without myopic individuals. When we interpret the model as a public pension system and no private savings, the previous result indicates that the pension system is more generous to low-skilled types and less generous to high-skilled types in the economy with myopia.

Marginal labour income tax rates satisfy the usual properties: zero marginal rates for both skilled types 3 and 4, $T'(n^3y^3) = 0$ and $T'(n^4y^4) = 0$. The government with paternalist views and with myopic individuals yields higher marginal labour income and savings tax rates than in the case without myopia. Also in the latter case, marginal savings tax and subsidy rates are smaller. It may be surprising that when there are myopic individuals in the economy, paternalist government policy increases saving and makes saving larger than a paternalist government policy without myopic individuals. In all cases considered, type 3—high-skilled and low discount factor—attains the highest utility level. This may be interpreted so that there is in all cases a kind of bias towards the present. In paternalistic cases our simulations show that in the optimum, type 1 and type 2 are always pooled. This result can be used as a justification for a three-type model.[21] Numerical results in the four-type case also help us to choose a particular pattern of self-selection constraints.

In sum: in this section we have examined the optimal redistribution policy when society consists of individuals who do not differ only in productivity, but also in time preference. Tenhunen and Tuomala (2010) extend Diamond's (2003) analysis of the non-linear taxation of savings to the three and four-type models and consider the problem both analytically and numerically. In this section it is shown that when there are both paternalistic objectives and imperfect information on individuals' productivities and time preferences, the results are not just the sum of distortion suggested by these

[21] Blomquist and Christiansen (2004) and Cuff (2000) apply a three-type version of a Mirrlees (1971) optimal income tax model with heterogeneity in preferences between leisure and consumption.

phenomena alone. A possible explanation is that these sources of distortion, paternalism, and two-dimensional unobservable heterogeneity interact. Tuomala and Tenhunen (2010) results provide a rationale for distortions (upward and downward) in the savings behaviour in a simple two-period model where high-skilled and low-skilled individuals have different non-observable time preferences beyond their earning capacity.

This model can also be interpreted as analysis of a pension programme. When insufficient saving is caused by a low discount factor,[22] our analytical and numerical results support the view that there is a case for a non-linear public pension programme (second-best redistribution) in a world where individuals differ in skills and discount factor.

APPENDIX 14.2.1

Two types

Multipliers λ and μ are attached respectively to the budget constraint and the self-selection constraint. The Lagrange function of the optimization problem is:

$$L = \sum_i N^i\left[u(c^i) + \delta^i v(x^i) + \psi(1-y^i)\right] + \lambda\left[\sum N^i(n^i y^i - c^i - rx^i) - R\right]$$
$$+\mu^{HL}\left[u(c^H) + \delta^H v(x^H) + \psi(1-y^H) - u(c^L) - \delta^H v(x^L) - \psi\left(1 - \frac{n^L y^L}{n^H}\right)\right]$$

The first-order conditions with respect to c^i, x^i and y^i, i=L,H from the Lagrange function given in equation (5) are:

$$N^L u_c^L - \lambda N^L - \mu^{HL} u_c^L = 0 \tag{1}$$

$$N^L \delta^L v_x^L - \lambda r N^L - \mu^{HL}\delta^H v_x^L = 0 \tag{2}$$

$$-N^L \psi'^L + \lambda N^L n^L + \mu^{HL}\frac{n^L}{n^H}\psi'^L = 0 \tag{3}$$

$$N^H u_c^H - \lambda N^H + \mu^{HL} u_c^H = 0 \tag{4}$$

$$N^H \delta^H v_x^H - \lambda r N^H + \mu^{HL}\delta^H v_x^H = 0 \tag{5}$$

[22] We also analysed the model in which not all individuals save voluntarily and ignore the implications for the retirement income of their earnings when young in their labour supply decisions, i.e. they are myopic. The analytical results follow the earlier case (proposition 3). For type 1 the marginal taxation of saving is negative, for type 4 it is positive, and for type 3 the sign of the distortion is indeterminate (see Tenhunen and Tuomala 2007).

$$-N^H \psi'^H + \lambda N^H n^H - \mu^{HL} \psi'^H = 0 \tag{6}$$

In the paternalistic case the first-order condition with respect to c^i, and $1y^i$, i=L,H, remains unchanged, while (A2) and (A5) are replaced by

$$N^L \delta^g v_x^L - \lambda r N^L - \mu^{HL} \delta^H v_x^L = 0 \tag{7}$$

$$N^H \delta^g v_x^H - \lambda r N^H + \mu^{HL} \delta^H v_x^H = 0 \tag{8}$$

Four types

Welfarist case:

The first-order conditions with respect to c, x, and y for type *i*, *i*=1,...,4 are:

$$N^i u_c - \lambda N^i + \sum_j \mu^{ij} u_c - \sum_j \mu^{ji} u_c = 0 \tag{1}$$

$$N^i \delta^i v_x - \lambda N^i r + \sum_j \mu^{ij} \delta^i v_x - \sum_j \mu^{ji} \delta^j v_x = 0 \tag{2}$$

$$-N^i \psi_y + \lambda N^i n^i - \sum_j \left(\mu^{ij} - \frac{n^i}{n^j} \mu^{ji} \right) \psi_y = 0 \tag{3}$$

where λ and μ^{ij} are the Lagrange multipliers for the production constraint and self-selection constraint preventing type *i* from mimicking type *j* and u_c, v_x and ψ_y are partial derivatives of sub-utility functions with respect to variable denoted by subscripts.

Paternalist case

The first-order condition with respect to y is the same as in the welfarist case. The conditions with respect to c and x for i=1,...,4 are:

$$N^i u_c - \lambda N^i + \sum_j \mu^{ij} u_c - \sum_j \mu^{ji} u_c \tag{4}$$

$$N^i \delta^g v_x - \lambda N^i r + \sum_j \mu^{ij} \delta^i v_x - \sum_j \mu^{ji} \delta^j v_x \tag{5}$$

14.2.2 HABIT FORMATION AND OPTIMAL CAPITAL INCOME TAXATION

Above and in the previous studies taxing the return to saving, it is usually assumed that saving is non-positional. In an early work, Duesenberry (1949) in turn argued that saving is positional and presented evidence to the effect. He proposed the idea of habit formation—that the utility from consumption can be affected by the level of past consumption.[23] The optimal tax design should also take into account the fact that individuals with different preferences for savings (or myopic individuals) may be subject to habit-formation or standard-of-living effects under which present consumption influences the utility of future consumption. In recent years, models which allow for various kinds of habit formation have been used to analyse a wide variety of phenomena both in macro and microeconomics.

There is evidence that people tend to make errors in predicting changes in their future tastes.[24] All models considering under-saving due to high discounting or myopia can be seen as special cases of the more general phenomenon of projection bias. Projection bias implies that people, while understanding the direction of changes in tastes, systematically make mistakes in predicting the magnitude of the changes. When projection bias is combined with habit formation, there exist two mechanisms that affect the savings behaviour. First, projection bias leads to underestimation of the effect the current consumption has on future utility, and hence encourages excessive consumption when young. The second effect arises in a dynamic setting. As one gets used to higher consumption levels, the new standard of living induces even higher consumption, and also less saving, than what was earlier planned. Thus, both effects tend to leave savings below the optimal level (see Loewenstein, O'Donoghue, and Rabin 2003).

In this section, following Tuomala and Tenhunen (2014), we study optimal lifetime redistribution when individuals in a life-cycle cohort have habit-forming preferences over period consumption. We assume that individuals are heterogeneous in a binary fashion (i.e. high and low) with respect to their respective rate of labour productivity and time preference. The government faces information asymmetry in that it is only able to observe and verify the gross income and saving of individuals but not the labour supply, labour productivity, and discount rates of individuals. We derive general mathematical expressions that characterize optimal marginal tax/subsidy rates for the case of habit formation with two-dimensional individual heterogeneity. The first-order conditions suggest that habit formation affects results qualitatively. The pattern of marginal labour income taxes depends on habit formation. To gain a better understanding, we examine numerically the properties of an optimal lifetime redistribution policy with habit formation. The effect of changes in the degree of habit formation is explored in the numerical simulations, as well as the implications of different degrees of correlation between skill and projection bias.

A four-type model with habit formation

Otherwise, the model is the same as in the previous section, except the utility of the retirement-period consumption depends on past levels of consumption through a habit-

[23] The idea was formalized by Pollak (1970) and Ryder and Heal (1973).

[24] Loewenstein, O'Donoghue, and Rabin (2003) present a survey of some empirical evidence on the presence of projection bias. People tend to underappreciate the adaptation to the change in the standard of living, i.e. changes in their long-term preferences.

formation or standard-of-living channel. In other words, preferences are not additive over time. Parameter ρ describes the degree of habit formation: the closer to zero ρ is, the smaller the effect of the habit is to the retirement period utility.[25] Individuals' utility is given by

$$U^i = u(c^i) + \delta^i v(\rho c^i, x^i) + \psi(1 - y^i). \tag{1}$$

The sub-utility functions u and ψ are increasing and strictly concave. In addition, v is increasing and strictly concave with respect to x, whereas with respect to c it is decreasing and strictly convex. The first-period consumption reduces second-period utility. We also assume that all goods, both consumption goods and leisure, are normal.

Government optimization problem

Without any assumptions of the mimicking behaviour, there are twelve possible self-selection constraints given by:

$$u(c^i) + \delta^i v(\rho c^i, x^i) + \psi(1 - y^i) \geq u(c^j) + \delta^i v(\rho c^j, x^j) + \psi\left(1 - \frac{n^j y^j}{n^i}\right) \tag{2}$$

for $i,j = 1, \ldots 4$ and $i \neq j$.

Should the government be welfarist and maximize individual welfare, as the individual sees it? Or, as suggested in recent behavioural public economics literature, should it be paternalistic, or non-welfarist, and discount the future at a different rate than individuals? In fact, individuals may want the government to intervene, to induce behaviour that is closer to what individuals wish they were doing.

In the welfarist case the government maximizes the sum of individuals' utilities:

$$\sum N^i [u(c^i) + \delta^i v(\rho c^i, x^i) + \psi(1 - y^i)] \tag{3}$$

whereas the non-welfarist or paternalistic government evaluates the future with a higher discount factor δ^g than the individuals, i.e. $\delta^g > \delta^i$ for all $i=1,\ldots,4$.[26]

The optimization in both cases is subject to the self-selection constraints given in (2) and the production constraint:

$$\sum N^i (n^i y^i - c^i - r x^i) - R \geq 0 \tag{4}$$

where $r = \frac{1}{1+\theta}$ is the discount factor for production.

[25] Non-separability of utilities alone would already imply habit formation, but we have chosen to use parameter ρ to make the effect of habit formation clearer.

[26] Another case, where some of the individuals over-save, i.e. use too high a discount factor to maximize their lifetime utility, can also easily be analysed with the same framework. Similarly, the case where government uses the same discount factor as those suffering less from projection bias can be obtained as a special case of the analysis presented here. In this chapter, however, we concentrate on the case where all individuals suffer from projection bias and under-save as a result of it.

Welfarist case

From the first-order conditions (1) and (3) in appendix 14.2.2 we can solve the marginal tax of labour income in terms of the marginal rate of substitution between leisure and working period consumption, $T^{i'} = 1 - \frac{\psi_y}{n^i(u_c + \delta^i \rho v_c)}$. This can also be interpreted as the implicit tax (or subsidy) on prolonged activity.

The marginal tax of labour income for type i is given by

$$T^{i'} = 1 - AB.^{27} \tag{5}$$

At this level of generality it is difficult to obtain clear-cut results. Any results depend on the pattern of binding self-selection constraints. We cannot predict this on the basis of the first-order conditions alone. The marginal rates of type *i* depend both on the pattern of those constraints deterring others from mimicking type *i* and also on those self-selection constraints preventing type *i* from mimicking others.

Based on our numerical simulations, we assume the following pattern of downward-binding self-selection constraints, $\mu^{31}>0$, $\mu^{32}>0$ and $\mu^{32}>0$ while $\mu^{ij}=0$ and $\mu^{ji}=0$, for all other self-selection constraints. Given these binding constraints, we have the following signs for marginal rates: $T^{1'}>0$ $T^{2'}>0$ $T^{3'}<0$ $T^{4'} = 0$. The so-called 'no distortion at the top' result holds here too. There is a type nobody wants to mimic at equilibrium. It means that no self-selection constraint is binding toward this type (in our case type 4). Then $\mu^{ji} = 0$ for all $j \neq 4$. Intuitively, because at equilibrium nobody wants to mimic type *I*, there is no advantage in distorting such a person's choices from the first best. If we further assume that the government has to some extent redistributive concerns, at least one μ^{ji} is non-zero. In fact, if the optimal tax policy is truly second-best, then at least one of the self-selection constraints must bind at the optimum. Hence the non-linear policy scheme is a useful mechanism if the government has sufficient redistributive aims.

It is worth noting a special case in which people do not differ in discount factors. From (5) we see that in this case, habit formation has no impact on the standard results that the high-skill type should face a zero marginal tax rate and the low-skill type should face a positive marginal tax rate. This is because the consumers rationally consider the effects on their second-period utility when deciding their first-period consumption levels. Hence, there is no need for the government to implement marginal tax-rate distortions to correct the negative internality that an individual's first-period consumption imposes on their second-period utility.

Habit formation appears explicitly in the marginal tax rate formula (in the term A). This term implies that the marginal labour income tax of type *i* is increased when type *i* is mimicked by those with a more severe projection bias, and decreased if mimicked by those suffering less from projection bias. The two sources of distortion, imperfect information on both skill level and level of projection bias, interact. The effect of

[27] $A = \frac{\lambda N^i}{\lambda N^i + \rho \sum_j \mu^{ji}(\delta^j - \delta^i)v_c}$ and $B = \frac{N^i + \sum_j (\mu^{ij} - \mu^{ji})}{N^i + \sum_j \left(\mu^{ij} - \frac{n^i}{n^j}\mu^{ji}\right)}$

mimicking also comes from the coefficients μ^{ji} in the part B in (5), so the effect is not separable.

It is also worth noting that the idea that marginal labour income tax rates must be non-negative does not necessarily hold here.[28] The term A becomes greater than one when $\rho \sum_j \mu^{ji}(\delta^j - \delta^i)v_c < 0$, i.e. when the sum of the discount factors of the mimickers are greater than those of the mimicked (for the pairs for which the incentive constraint is binding), and the term B, when $n^i > n^j$ the mimicker has lower wage rate than the mimicked (for the pairs for which the incentive constraints are binding).

The intuition behind this result is that in the Mirrlees model only those individuals with a lower wage rate were in danger of being mimicked, but in the two-dimensional case the pattern of the binding constraint can also be the other way around. The additional disutility obtained from mimicking a type with higher wage rate by having to work more than the mimicked type can be more than compensated by the additional utility of the higher retirement consumption if the difference in the levels of projection biases is high enough. In terms of support for prolonged activity, this result means that it might be desirable to encourage longer working careers of some types with a wage subsidy. However, without making any assumptions on the direction of binding incentive constraints, it is not clear whether this outcome ever occurs. We will return to this question in the numerical part of the paper.

Next we consider marginal tax rates on savings. The marginal rate of substitution between consumption in the working period and retirement period is given by $\sigma^i = \frac{u_c + \delta^i \rho v_c}{\delta^i v_x}$.

From the first order conditions (5) and (6), we can write[29]

$$\sigma^i = \frac{1}{r}\left[1 - \frac{u_c}{\lambda N^i}\sum_j \mu^{ji}\Delta^{ji}\right] = \frac{1}{r}(1 - d^i) \tag{6}$$

where $\Delta^{ji} = \frac{\delta^j - \delta^i}{\delta^i}$ is the relative difference in the level of projection bias and where d^i captures the implicit marginal tax on savings. A positive d reflects marginal tax on savings, and a negative d implies a marginal subsidy.

Equation (6) implies that we have to consider only downward incentive constraints. When type i is mimicked by a type with a less severe projection bias, the distortion (marginal tax rate) for type i tends to increase. And similarly, when type i is mimicked by a type with a more severe projection bias, the distortion (marginal subsidy rate) decreases. The overall effect might be positive, negative, or zero, depending on the binding self-selection constraints. Given the binding constraint, we have $d^1 = d^4 = 0$, $d^2 < 0$, $d^3 > 0$. It is also true here that far-sighted high-ability individuals (type 4) face no distortion on their savings (a zero marginal tax rate). Perhaps slightly surprisingly, the

[28] Our result contradicts the traditional Mirrlees result. In multidimensional optimal tax problems, however, negative marginal labour income taxes are sometimes found (see e.g. Boadway et al 2002, Judd and Su 2006, Cremer et al 2001).

[29] See appendix 14.2.2 for a derivation.

savings decision of the low-skilled type 1 is also undistorted. This is due to the fact that the individuals who should be deterred from mimicking the low-skilled are the high-skilled with the same time preference as the low-skilled. Thus, no gain could be achieved by taxing the savings decision of type 1.

It is also worth noticing that there is nothing that explicitly reveals the effect induced by habit formation on the right-hand side of (6). Parameter ρ, which is equal for all types, cancels out in the derivation. This does not imply that the implicit tax rates are not affected by habit formation; the magnitude of marginal rates will, however, depend on habit formation.

Paternalistic case

Now the government using its own discount factor in the social welfare function maximizes $\sum N^i[u(c^i) + \delta^g v(\rho c^i, x^i) + \psi(1 - y^i)]$, subject to self-selection constraints (2) and the production constraint (4).

The marginal labour income tax in the paternalistic case can be solved from the first order conditions (3) and (4) (see appendix 14.2.2): $T^{gi'} = 1 - \frac{\psi_y}{n^i(u_c+\delta^g \rho v_c)}$.

In this case $T^{gi'} = 1 - A'B'$.[30]

There are now two sources for distortions that affect the design of optimal policy: paternalistic view of correcting projection bias, and imperfect information on both productivities and projection bias. These features interact so that the effects cannot be separated from each other, i.e. labour income taxation is used at the same time to take care of all distortions in the economy. As in the welfarist case the possibility of negative marginal labour tax rates cannot rule out here. In the paternalistic case in turn the 'no distortion at the top' result does not hold any longer.[31,32]

$$T^{g1'}>0, \ T^{g3'}>(<)0, \ T^{g4'}<0$$

The labour supply of type 4 is encouraged by a marginal subsidy. The bunch of types 1 and 2 faces a positive marginal tax on labour income. Type 3, however, may be taxed or subsidized: $T^{g3'}$ can be positive as well as negative.

There are two possible ways to consider the distortion in savings: government's and individual's points of view.[33] Government's view represents the actual distortion required to implement the second-best optimum, whereas what determines the behavioural effects is the distortion perceived by the individual. The marginal rate of substitution between first and second-period consumption from the government's point of

[30] $A' = \frac{\lambda N^i}{\lambda N^i - \rho \sum_j \mu^{ij}(\delta^i - \delta^g) v_c + \rho \sum_j \mu^{ji}(\delta^j - \delta^g) v_c}$ and $B' = \frac{N^i + \sum_j (\mu^{ij} - \mu^{ji})}{N^i + \sum_j \left(\mu^{ij} - \frac{n^i}{n^j}\mu^{ji}\right)}$

[31] The result is not uncommon for a model with paternalistic objectives and multidimensional self-selection constraints. A similar result is found e.g. in Cremer et al (2009).

[32] Due to the bunching, the marginal tax rates on labour income are equal for types 1 and 2.

[33] See for example Cremer et al (2009) for a similar approach.

view can be obtained from the first order conditions[34]: $\left(\frac{u_c+\delta^g\rho v_c}{\delta^g v_x}\right)^i =: \sigma^{gi}$. Using (4) and (5) we obtain:

$$\sigma^{gi} = \frac{1}{r}\left[1 - \frac{u_c}{\lambda N^i}\left(\sum_j \mu^{ji}\Delta^{jg} - \sum_j \mu^{ij}\Delta^{ig}\right)\right] = \frac{1}{r}(1-\alpha^i), \tag{7}$$

where the relative projection biases $\Delta^{jg} = \frac{\delta^j - \delta^g}{\delta^g}$ and $\Delta^{ig} = \frac{\delta^i - \delta^g}{\delta^g}$ are both negative due to assumptions made on individuals' and governments' time discount factors. α^i captures the implicit marginal tax on savings.[35]

As in previous cases, here also the signs of α^i s remain ambiguous in analytical consideration. Compared to the welfarist case, it can be noted that now type i's marginal tax rate on savings depends on both those self-selection constraints restricting others mimicking type i (as in welfarist case), but also on those self-selection constraints stopping type i mimicking others.

The marginal tax rates on savings given by Equation (7) can now in turn be written as:

$$\alpha^1 < 0 \quad \alpha^3 \geq (<) 0 \quad \alpha^4 > 0 \qquad .$$

This means that savings of the low-skilled individuals (type 1 and type 2) are subsidized. It turns out that α^3 can be positive as well negative, while type 4 faces a positive marginal tax on savings.

As habit formation and projection bias are both likely to induce too-high first-period consumption, encouraging people to work might become even more desirable than in the welfarist case. That way pension savings would also increase, as not all additional labour income is spent on first period consumption.

Numerical solution

To investigate further the properties of the optimal policy, we now turn to numerical examples.[36] The utility function is again the following a CES utility function:

[34] See appendix 14.2.2.

[35] The marginal implicit tax rate for savings chosen by the government, α, takes care of the negative internality, whereas an individual making labour supply and savings choices sees that as a pure distortion. From the perspective of the individual, the distortion is still given by d. From a similar term as in the welfarist case, (12), we get the distortions from the individuals' perspectives.

$$\sigma^i = \frac{1}{r}\left[1 - \frac{u_c}{\lambda N^i}\left(\sum_j \mu^{ji}\Delta^{ji} - N^i\Delta^{gi}\right)\right] \quad (*)$$

where $\Delta^{ji} = \frac{\delta^j - \delta^i}{\delta^i}$ and $\Delta^{gi} = \frac{\delta^g - \delta^i}{\delta^i}$.

Compared to the welfarist case, there now appears an additional term $N^i\Delta^{gi}$ in (*) that results from the difference in the discount factors between the government and individuals. This can be called a Pigovian term. When all μs are zero we are in the first-best situation.

[36] To reach reliable quantitative results a general equilibrium approach would be more suitable. However, introducing endogenous wages and interest rate would require a more sophisticated simulation model, and it is left for future challenge.

$$U^i = -\frac{1}{c^i} - \delta^i \frac{1}{x^i - \rho\, c^i} - \frac{1}{1 - y^i}. \tag{8}$$

The degree of habit formation, ρ, is assumed to be positive and less than one. The pattern of the binding self-selection constraints is not restricted a priori, and there are 12 self-selection constraints in the optimization problem.

The parameterization is the same as in Table 14.2 and the degree of habit formation, $\rho=0.3$, in the central case. First in the central variant specification the correlation between skill and time discounting is zero and there is a uniform distribution of types in the economy, i.e. the size of the groups of each type is identical, 0.25. The value for ρ is chosen to be 0.3, indicating that the utility of second-period consumption is mostly made up of retirement-period consumption, and the relative consumption has a rather moderate effect.

The pattern of binding self-selection constraints is presented in Table 14.6. A reduced-form consideration of the optimum, taking into account only the downward binding self-selection constraints, seems to be a reasonable simplification: none of the Lagrange coefficients for the upward binding self-selection constraints is non-zero in the welfarist case.[37] In a welfarist case there are three binding constraints: one that prevents the patient high-skilled type (type 4) from mimicking the short-sighted high-skilled type (type 3), and two restricting type 3 from mimicking either of the low-skilled types. However, in the paternalistic case the same self-selection constraints bind, but in addition to that, constraints preventing type 1 from mimicking type 2 and vice versa are binding, although the Lagrange multipliers are zero. Hence types 1 and 2 are actually pooled in the optimum. A similar pattern of binding self-selection constraints was also found with other parameter values for habit formation and number of types in the economy.[38]

Table 14.6 Binding self-selection constraints: welfarist and paternalistic case

	n^L	n^H		n^L	n^H
δ^L	type 1	type 3	δ^L	type 1	type 3
δ^H	type 2	type 4	δ	type 2	type 4

[37] By downwards and upwards binding self-selection constraints we refer here to our numbering. As the numbering is chosen here more or less randomly, it is important not to make assumptions of the reduced-form optimization before checking the actual pattern of binding constraints.

[38] The only exception was the extreme case where types 1 and 3 suffered from full myopia. In the case with myopia, the same three constraints (arrows in Table 14.6) are still binding, but the constraints between

The results of the numerical solution of the central variant are presented in Tables 14.7 and 14.8. The marginal distortions for savings show that in the optimum, the tax programme is non-linear: some types are subsidized at the margin while others are taxed. In the welfarist case, savings of types 1 and 4 remain undistorted. In other words, for type 4, the so-called 'no distortion at the top' result holds. However, type 2, the patient low-skilled type, is subsidized at the margin. Type 3, the impatient high-skilled type, is marginally taxed.

The treatment of savings observed by the individuals in the paternalistic case shows, rather as expected, that all types receive a marginal subsidy for savings (negative d^i:s), as the government with a higher discount factor wants to induce individuals to save more for their retirement. The actual distortion for savings, i.e. the ones that also individuals afterward perceive as true, however, shows a pattern of both subsidizing and taxing savings income (α^i:s). In the paternalistic case low-skilled types' pension savings are subsidized at the margin, while high-skilled types' pension savings face marginal tax.

There are some negative marginal labour income tax rates, even in the welfarist case. The short-sighted high-skill type (type 3) gets a wage subsidy, while both the low-skilled are marginally taxed, or undistorted as in the welfarist case.

Labour supply can also consider the retirement age of type i individuals. People work y years and then retire. In our example, labour supply varies between 52 to 56 per cent of

Table 14.7 Numerical results, welfarist case

type	U	d	α	T′	y	x/ny	x/c	means
1	−5.12	0	–	0.08	0.52	63.19	120.09	$\bar{c}$= 0.61
2	−5.50	−0.14	–	0.15	0.54	67.38	139.55	$\bar{x}$= 0.78
3	−4.56	0.07	–	−0.02	0.54	51.31	117.76	
4	−4.88	0	–	0	0.56	54.06	134.02	

Table 14.8 Numerical results, paternalistic case

type	U	d	α	Tg′	y	x/ny	x/c	means
1	−5.23	−1.22	−0.22	0.16	0.55	69.55	155.73	$\bar{c}$= 0.58
2	−5.55	−0.59	−0.22	0.16	0.55	69.55	155.73	$\bar{x}$= 0.86
3	−4.58	−0.56	0.18	−0.05	0.56	55.43	137.99	
4	−4.85	−0.25	0.06	−0.01	0.56	56.56	143.72	

types 1 and 2 are now genuinely binding, and in addition the constraint stopping the patient high-skilled from mimicking the impatient high-skilled binds.

the total time endowment. The labour supply of high-skilled types with lower projection bias is the highest, while the differences between the types remain rather moderate.

The effect of the degree of habit formation

The magnitude of the distortion (subsidy or tax) on savings increases with the degree of habit formation (Figure 14.4). In the welfarist case pension savings of types 1 and 4 remain undistorted. It can be noted that the marginal subsidy on savings perceived by type 1 is required to be more than 100 per cent in order to induce the second-best outcome, regardless of very low levels of habit formation.

The increase in the marginal tax or subsidy rates alongside rising habit formation results from the fact that with a higher level of habit formation, projection bias causes bigger welfare losses to (partly) myopic individuals. To maximize overall welfare, bigger distortions are required to induce the optimal outcome. More surprisingly, a similar pattern, although to a much smaller extent, appears also in the welfarist case, where time discounting is interpreted as a pure time preference and is respected by government.

Correlation between skill level and time discounting

In the central variant specification, the correlation between skill and time, discounting is zero. Assuming a perfect correlation between productivity and the level of projection bias, we are back in a two-type economy. However, the two characteristics may also be imperfectly correlated. Changing the assumption of the correlation allows us to consider the robustness of our results with respect to the distribution of types.

In our case, perfect positive correlation between skill level and projection bias means that the economy consists of types 1 (low-skilled with high projection bias) and 4 (high-skilled with low projection bias) only, whereas perfect negative correlation means that there are only types 2 (low-skilled with low projection bias) and 3 (high-skilled with high projection bias) in the economy. To maintain the tractability of the numerical problem, we have fixed the fractions so that half of each discount rate group has a low and the other half a high wage, i.e. $N^1+N^3=N^2+N^4=\frac{1}{2}$, and that the fraction of individuals with high projection bias is the same in both wage groups, i.e. $N^1=N^3$ and $N^2=N^3$.

Overall, the results in Tenhunen and Tuomala (2013) regarding optimal tax policy seem to be rather robust with respect to the structure of the economy. Most changes happen at the level of strong negative correlation between skill level and discount factor, as in the previous section without habit formation.

In sum: Tuomala and Tenhunen (2013) studied the optimal lifetime tax policy in a two-period model where individuals differ in both productivity and time discounting and where their utility of the retirement period consumption is not independent of the earlier standard of living. They considered both welfarist government maximizing

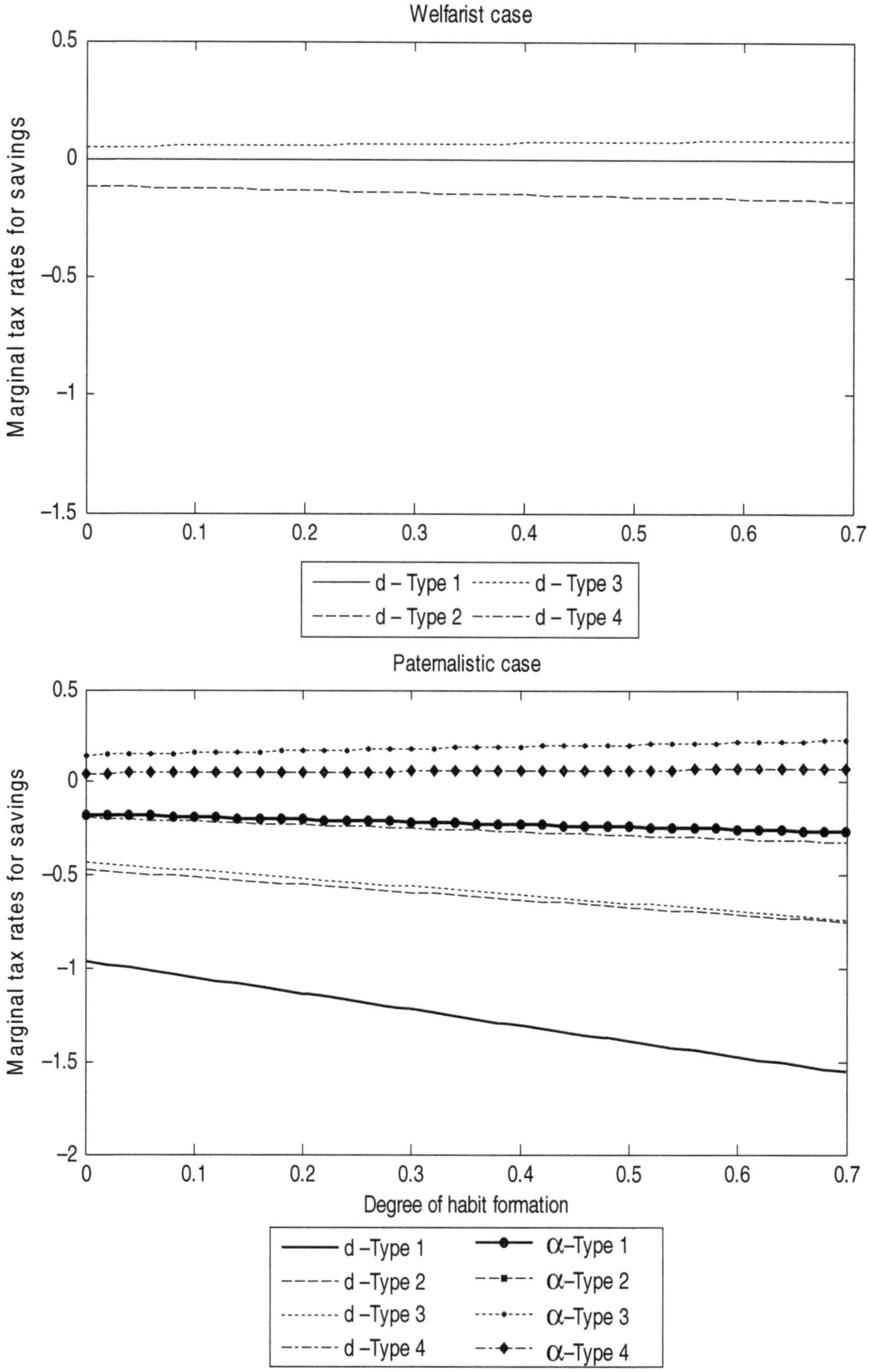

Figure 14.4 Marginal tax rates for savings and the degree of habit formation

the sum of individual utilities and the case where the government aims at correcting the short-sightedness of individuals by using a higher discount factor for retirement period utility. With imperfect information and two-dimensional heterogeneity of the individuals, the optimal tax and pension policy depends crucially on the pattern of binding self-selection constraints. Hence the tax policy can be based on both gross income and saving of each type. The two sources of imperfect information interact. As both tax devices are used at the same time to deter mimicking, the effects of each source of heterogeneity cannot be separated. Indeed, with habit-forming utilities and individuals suffering projection bias, both labour supply and consumption decisions are sub-optimal without government intervening with tax policy. To get an idea of the tax and the effect of the degree of habit formation on it, we solved the problem numerically. The numerical analysis shows that in the optimum the tax program is non-linear: some types are subsidized at the margin while others are taxed. Taxation or subsidization of savings provides indirect evidence about who has higher or lower earnings potential and thus contributes to more efficient redistribution through the tax system. Negative marginal labour income taxes are also possible in the optimum. The marginal distortions for labour income and pension savings increase when habit formation increases. Labour income subsidies (marginally) increase as habit formation increases for high wage earners under a non-welfarist social welfare function. The pattern looks the same with marginal tax rates on savings: the magnitude of distortion (subsidy or tax) in savings increases with the degree of habit formation. Our numerical results also show that the length of working career increases with the degree of habit formation. Overall, the results regarding optimal tax policy seem to be rather robust with respect to the correlation between skill level and discount rates. Most changes happen at the level of strong negative correlations between skill level and discount rate.

APPENDIX 14.2.2

The first-order conditions of maximizing (3) subject to (2) and (4) with respect to c, x, and y for type i, i=1,. . .,4 are:

$$N^i(u_c + \delta^i \rho v_c) - \lambda N^i + \sum_j \mu^{ij}(u_c + \delta^i \rho v_c) - \sum_j \mu^{ji}(u_c + \delta^j \rho v_c) = 0; \tag{1}$$

$$N^i \delta^i v_x - \lambda N^i r + \sum_j \mu^{ij} \delta^i v_x - \sum_j \mu^{ji} \delta^j v_x = 0; \tag{2}$$

$$-N^i \psi_y + \lambda N^i n^i - \sum_j \left(\mu^{ij} - \frac{n^i}{n^j} \mu^{ji} \right) \psi_y = 0; \tag{3}$$

where λ and μ^{ij} are the Lagrange multipliers for the production constraint and self-selection constraint preventing type i from mimicking type j and u_c, v_x and ψ_y are partial derivatives of sub-utility functions with respect to variable denoted by subscripts.

The first-order condition with respect to y is the same as in the welfarist case, given in (7). The conditions with respect to c and x for i=1,...,4 are:

$$N^i(u_c + \delta^g \rho v_c) - \lambda N^i + \sum_j \mu^{ij}(u_c + \delta^i \rho v_c) - \sum_j \mu^{ji}(u_c + \delta^j \rho v_c); \tag{4}$$

$$N^i \delta^g v_x - \lambda N^i r + \sum_j \mu^{ij} \delta^i v_x - \sum_j \mu^{ji} \delta^j v_x. \tag{5}$$

Derivations of implicit taxes on savings

Derivation for equation 6 in the text

Step 1: To rewrite the marginal rate of substitution $\frac{u_c+\delta^i \rho v_c}{\delta^i v_x}$ with the help of the first-order conditions we first solve the numerator from equation (1). By adding and subtracting a term $\sum_j \mu^{ji} \delta^i \rho v_c$ the first-order condition with respect to c given in equation (1) can be written as:

$$\begin{aligned} &N^i(u_c + \delta^i \rho v_c) - \lambda N^i + \sum_j \mu^{ij}(u_c + \delta^i \rho v_c) \\ &-\sum_j \mu^{ji}(u_c + \delta^i \rho v_c) - \sum_j \mu^{ji}(\delta^j - \delta^i)\rho v_c = 0 \end{aligned} \tag{A1}$$

From this we can solve:

$$u_c + \delta^i \rho v_c = \frac{\lambda N^i + \sum_j \mu^{ji}(\delta^j - \delta^i)\rho v_c}{N^i + \sum_j \mu^{ij} - \sum_j \mu^{ji}} \tag{A2}$$

Next we solve similarly the denominator of the marginal rate of substation. By adding and subtracting term $\sum_j \mu^{ji} \delta^i v_x$ to the first-order condition with respect to x given in equation (2), it can be written as

$$N^i \delta^i v_x - \lambda N^i r + \sum_j \mu^{ij} \delta^i v_x - \sum_j \mu^{ji} \delta^i v_x - \sum_j \mu^{ji}(\delta^j - \delta^i) v_x = 0 \tag{A3}$$

From this we can solve

$$\delta^i v_x = \frac{\lambda N^i r + \sum_j \mu^{ji}(\delta^j - \delta^i) v_x}{N^i + \sum_j \mu^{ij} - \sum_j \mu^{ji}}. \tag{A4}$$

By combining (A1) and (A2) and making use of definition of the proportional difference in discount rates, $\Delta^{ji} = \frac{\delta^j - \delta^i}{\delta^i}$, we can write:

$$\frac{u_c + \delta^i \rho v_c}{\delta^i v_x} = \frac{\lambda N^i + \delta^i \sum_j \mu^{ji} \Delta^{ji} \rho v_c}{\lambda N^i r + \delta^i \sum_j \mu^{ji} \Delta^{ji} v_x}. \tag{A5}$$

Step 2: Manipulating equation to useful form.

The next trick is to multiply the both sides of equation (A5) by term $\frac{\lambda N^i r + \delta^i \sum_j \mu^{ji} \Delta^{ji} v_x}{\delta^i \sum_j \mu^{ji} \Delta^{ji} v_x}$. This gives us:

$$\frac{\lambda N^i r}{\delta^i \sum_j \mu^{ji} \Delta^{ji} v_x} \frac{u_c + \delta^i \rho v_c}{\delta^i v_x} + \frac{u_c + \delta^i \rho v_c}{\delta^i v_x} = \frac{\lambda N^i}{\delta^i \sum_j \mu^{ji} \Delta^{ji} v_x} + \frac{\delta^i \rho v_c}{\delta^i v_x}. \tag{A6}$$

Rearranging terms gives us:

$$\frac{\lambda N^i r}{\delta^i \sum_j \mu^{ji} \Delta^{ji} v_x} \left[\frac{u_c + \delta^i \rho v_c}{\delta^i v_x} - \frac{1}{r} \right] - = -\frac{u_c}{\delta^i v_x}. \tag{A7}$$

From this form we can solve for the marginal rate of substitution, $\frac{u_c + \delta^i \rho v_c}{\delta^i v_x}$, in a form given in Equation (6).

Derivation of Equation (7) in the text

The paternalistic case follows a similar procedure to the welfarist case, so details of the derivations are omitted. The terms to be added and subtracted to first-order conditions are now $\sum_j \mu^{ij} \delta^g \rho v_c - \sum_j \mu^{ji} \delta^g \rho v_c$ and $\sum_j \mu^{ij} \delta^g v_x - \sum_j \mu^{ji} \delta^g v_x$. The term that is used to multiply equation in step 2 is given by $\frac{\lambda N^i r - \delta^g \sum_j \mu^{ij} \Delta^{ig} v_x + \delta^g \sum_j \mu^{ji} \Delta^{jg} v_x}{-\delta^g \sum_j \mu^{ij} \Delta^{ig} v_x + \delta^g \sum_j \mu^{ji} \Delta^{jg} v_x}$.

Derivation of Equation (*) in footnote 35

Derivation proceeds similarly to earlier cases. The terms to be added and subtracted to the first order conditions are $N^i \delta^i \rho v_c - \sum_j \mu^{ji} \delta^i \rho v_c$ and $N^i \delta^i v_x - \sum_j \mu^{ji} \delta^i v_x$. In step two, the multiplier to be used is $\frac{\lambda N^i r - \delta^i (N^i \Delta^{gi} - \sum_j \mu^{ji} \Delta^{ji}) v_x}{-\delta^i (N^i \Delta^{gi} - \sum_j \mu^{ji} \Delta^{ji}) v_x}$.

Marginal tax rates (welfarist case)

$$T^{1'} = 1 - \frac{N^i - \mu^{31}}{N^i - \frac{n^1}{n^3} \mu^{31}} > 0$$

$$T^{2'} = 1 - \frac{\lambda N^2}{\lambda N^2 + \rho \mu^{32} (\delta^3 - \delta^2) v_c} \frac{N^i - \mu^{32}}{N^i - \frac{n^1}{n^3} \mu^{32}} > 0$$

$$T^{3'} = 1 - \frac{\lambda N^3}{\lambda N^3 + \rho \mu^{43} (\delta^4 - \delta^3) v_c} < 0$$

$$T^{4'} = 0$$

$$d^1 = d^4 = 0,\ d^2 = \frac{u_c}{\lambda N^2}\mu^{32}(\frac{\delta^3 - \delta^2}{\delta^2})<0,$$

$$d^3 = \frac{u_c}{\lambda N^3}\mu^{43}(\frac{\delta^4 - \delta^3}{\delta^3})>0$$

Marginal tax rates (paternalist case)

$$T^{g1'} = 1 - \frac{(N^1 - \mu^{31})}{[N^1 - \frac{n^1}{n^2}\mu^{31}]}\frac{\lambda N^1}{[\lambda N^1 + \rho v_c \mu^{31}(\delta^1 - \delta^g)]}>0$$

$$T^{g3'} = 1 - \frac{\lambda N^3}{\lambda N^3 - \rho\mu^{31}(\delta^3 - \delta^g)v_c + \rho\mu^{43}(\delta^4 - \delta^g)v_c}>(<)0$$

$$T^{g4'} = 1 - \frac{\lambda N^4}{\lambda N^4 - \rho\mu^{43}(\delta^4 - \delta^g)v_c}<0$$

$$\alpha^1 = \frac{u_c}{\lambda N^1}\mu^{31}(\frac{\delta^3 - \delta^g}{\delta^g})<0$$

$$\alpha^3 = -\frac{u_c}{\lambda N^3}[\mu^{43}(\frac{\delta^4 - \delta^g}{\delta^g}) - \mu^{32}(\frac{\delta^3 - \delta^g}{\delta^g})] \geq (<)0$$

$$\alpha^4 = -\frac{u_c}{\lambda N^4}\mu^{43}(\frac{\delta^4 - \delta^g}{\delta^g})>0$$

Numerical simulations

Procedure

Numerical simulation was carried out with the Matlab programme. The function used (*fmincon*) solves the optimum of a multivariable function with equality and inequality constraints that may be linear or non-linear. It also determines which of the constraints are binding. The same procedure is applied to all cases considered in this chapter.

Note that as the optimization function also allowed slack constraints, we were not restricted to a priori assumptions on the binding self-selection constraints. Thus, we included all possible constraints in the optimization procedure and simply determined the binding constraints with the help of numerical solutions.

Multidimensional screening problems are numerically challenging to solve, as discussed in Judd and Su (2006). We also encountered some difficulties with the solvability of the problem, as the matrix including the constraints with opposite self-selection constraints is very close to being singular. These difficulties were met during the sensitivity analysis; with some combinations of parameters, the problem was not solvable, or gave irrational values.

Parameterization

The distribution of the economy was chosen to be uniform merely for the simplicity and comparability for the following cases. The discount factors, δ^L and δ^H, are set at 0.6 and

0.8, while δ^g is set equal to 1. These values are in line with e.g. Cremer et al's (2006) similar numerical calculations. The wage rates reflecting the productivities were chosen to be 2 and 3 respectively. The magnitude of the wage rates was determined by the solvability of the problem; with these wage rates, the labour supply decision, restricted to lie between 0 and 1, was at reasonable levels.

Numerical table A14.2.2

	WELFARIST	PATERNALISTIC
Λ	2.0469	2.2483
μ^{12}	0	0
μ^{13}	0	0
μ^{14}	0	0
μ^{21}	0	0
μ^{23}	0	0
μ^{24}	0	0
μ^{31}	0.0502	0.0741
μ^{32}	0.0759	0.0741
μ^{34}	0	0
μ^{41}	0	0
μ^{42}	0	0
μ^{43}	0.0498	0.0704

	WELFARIST		PATERNALISTIC	
	C	X	C	X
type 1	0.55	0.66	0.49	0.77
type 2	0.51	0.72	0.49	0.77
type 3	0.70	0.83	0.67	0.93
type 4	0.68	0.91	0.67	0.96

Sensitivity analysis

We have considered the sensitivity of the analysis with the help of varying i) the degree of habit formation, which allows us to compare the cases with and without habit effect, and ii) the correlation between the characteristics of the individuals, skill level, and discount factor. With some combinations of the parameters there is a failure to find the optimum, but it is due to technical problems in the optimization algorithm.

The first part, sensitivity with respect to degree of habit formation, is presented in the main text. The results considering sensitivity with respect to correlation between the two unobservable features follow here.

14.2.3 HETEROGENEOUS PREFERENCES, EQUALITY OF OPPORTUNITIES, AND OPTIMAL CAPITAL INCOME TAXATION

The assumption that differences in lifetime earnings are completely to be explained by time preferences is obviously an unrealistic one, just as the alternative explanation in terms of ability differences is also a simplification of reality. A more realistic model should take both into account. There are well-known technical difficulties related to incentive constraints to study multidimensional optimal tax problems including both of the elements. Another problem is how to incorporate heterogeneous preferences into social welfare function in analysing optimal tax policy. Social welfare functions can be quite straightforwardly parameterized when individuals have the same preferences represented by a utility function. In fact, there are two possibilities in the case of one-dimensional population. Namely if people have identical preferences but they differ in abilities, we are back in the Mirrlees model. The opposite case of the Mirrlees model is that in which diversity of preferences is the sole source of inequality.

In the case of diversity in preferences some people would, however, say that if individuals have the same opportunities while their choices may differ, there is no ethical basis for redistributive taxation. According to this view individuals should be compensated for circumstances affecting their wellbeing over which they have no control, such as their family background or disability at birth. On the other hand, individuals should be held responsible for circumstances which they can control, such as how many hours or weeks they work. Hence, no redistribution should take place based on such choices. The former is referred to as the principle of compensation and the latter the principle of responsibility (see Fleurbaey 1994; Roemer 1998). By the principle of compensation, it is fair to redistribute from high-ability to low-ability individuals. By the principle of responsibility, it is unfair to redistribute from goods-lovers to leisure-lovers. In the one-dimensional population, those principles are easy to apply. For example, if individuals differ only according to their earnings ability (wage rate) and not in their preferences, then the principle of compensation reduces to a maximin criterion whereby the tax and transfer system should provide as much compensation as possible to the worst-off people. If individuals differ solely in preferences, the principle of responsibility calls for no redistribution at all because everybody has the same opportunities. It would be unfair to redistribute based on tastes. The standard welfarist approach can obtain this result only in the case where social marginal utilities of net income are the same across individuals (absent transfers).

When individuals differ in preferences, the problem of choosing different utility functions for representing those preferences is more complex. If individuals have different preferences, it is not clear how to weight their utilities in a social welfare function. For example, with differences in time preferences, simply adding the utility functions for different types will give arbitrarily heavier weight to those with higher discount factors. One way to deal with this is to assume a paternalistic government, which uses not the subjective discount factors in the welfare maximization but instead a desired discount rate. It can be argued that the fundamental distinction is not so much between earning abilities and preferences but between those factors that are beyond an individual's control and those that are purely a matter of individual choice. Redistribution policies should aim to eliminate disparities in those matters that are beyond individual control, but should be neutral about those matters within their control. How to apply these two principles? There is a fundamental conflict between them. Namely, even in the world of perfect information with lump sum redistribution tools, the government cannot generally satisfy these two principles at the same time.

There are some recent contributions that incorporate heterogeneous time preferences into optimal tax analysis while remaining agnostic about the appropriate cardinalization (see Cremer et al 2009; Tenhunen and Tuomala 2010). In this setting the principle of responsibility says that these differences should not be a base for redistribution, as an individual has control over his timing of consumption. In the spirit of Roemer (1998) and Van de Gaer (1993),[39] Ravaska et al (2015) apply a compromise between the principle of compensation and the principle of responsibility. For individuals with same discount rates but different wage rates, the maximin criterion is applied, and then the least well-off from each preference group are simply added together. In other words, a zero aversion of inequality can be applied along the dimension of responsibility (in this case time preference) whereas a high aversion to inequality is acceptable along the dimension of circumstances (in this case skill).

A benchmark model: two types with a positive correlation between skill and discount factor

Ravaska et al (2015) employ the same model as previously shown, except the social objectives differ. In the case with positive correlation between skills and discount factors, Romer and Van de Gaer's approaches are equivalent with the maximin social welfare function: now the government maximises the welfare of the worst-off group:

$$[u(c^L) + \delta^L v(x^L) + \psi(1 - y^L)] \tag{1}$$

subject to the revenue constraint (3) and the self-selection constraint[40] (4).

Again assuming, empirically plausibly, $\delta^H > \delta^L$, we have $d^L>0$, implying implicit taxation of savings for the low-skill type. This is the same result as in the utilitarian case in section 14.2.1 and in Diamond (2003).

[39] Bossert (1995) and Fleurbaey (1994) have studied the idea of compensating inequalities due to circumstances only, while leaving other inequalities untouched.

[40] The direction of the binding self-selection constraint is assumed to be, following the tradition in the one-dimensional two-type model, from high-skilled individual towards low-skilled individual. This pattern is also confirmed by the numerical simulations.

Equality of opportunity and four types

In order to study the equality of opportunity, a compromise has to be made between the principles of compensation and responsibility, by first computing the minimum within each responsibility group (discount rates here) and then applying the utilitarian criterion. This means that for individuals with the same discount rates but different wage rates, the maximin criterion is applied and thus we have a social ordering over each discount group. Then these minimum numbers are added together.[41] Thus we have:

$$N^1[u(c^1) + \delta^L v(x^1) + \psi(1 - y^1)] + N^2[u(c^2) + \delta^H v(x^2) + \psi(1 - y^2)] \qquad (2)$$

The government now maximizes (2) subject to self-selection constraints (without any assumptions of the mimicking behaviour, there are twelve possible self-selection constraints) given by $u(c^i) + \delta^i v(x^i) + \psi(1 - y^i) \geq u(c^j) + \delta^i v(x^j) + \psi\left(1 - \frac{n^j y^j}{n^i}\right)$ for i, j = 1,...,4 and i ≠ j. and the production constraint $\sum N^i(n^i y^i - c^i - rx^i) - R \geq 0$.

Numerical simulations

Ravaska et al (2015) use the CES utility function in numerical simulations, with parameterization as in Table 14.2. There are no a priori assumptions made on the binding self-selection constraints in the numerical simulations. The formulas derived from the first-order conditions do not reveal the signs of the distortions, so again we turn to the numerical results. In the first specifications the discount factor remains the same as earlier, $\delta^L = 0.6$, $\delta^H = 0.8$, but the size of the low-productivity group is set to 0.4 and the high-productivity group to 0.6. These in turn are divided equally to the two preference groups. Table 14.6 presents these results. The binding self-selection constraints in this optimization are (3,1), (3,2), (4,2), and (4,3).

Interestingly, the results show that the labour supply of impatient and patient low-productivity workers is nearly the same. This occurs because in the equality of

Table 14.9 Utility levels at the optimum, marginal tax rates, replacement rates in the equality of opportunity. The binding self-selection constraints are (3.1), (3.2), (4.2), and (4.3)

	U	T′	d	y	x/ny	means
type 1	−4.6	47	0	0.36	64	$\bar{c}$= 0.67
type 2	−4.9	57	−0.65	0.37	79	$\bar{x}$= 0.66
type 3	−4.3	0	18	0.53	38	
type 4	−4.7	0	0	0.55	43	

[41] Or we can first calculate the average utility in each skill group and then apply the maximin criterion to such average figures.

opportunity case, the saving decision of the patient worker is heavily subsidized, and this leads to the situation that type 2's replacement rate is also high. From Table 14.3 we see that marginal tax rates on labour are significantly higher compared to the utilitarian case. Interpreting the results without private savings, it can be noticed that the pension system is progressive, i.e. the replacement rates are smaller for high-productivity workers than in the utilitarian case (see Table 14.3). Compared to the utilitarian case (see Figure 14.3), the labour supply or the length of career or retirement age of the low productivity type is smaller. There are also significant differences in replacement rates compared to the utilitarian case.

Concluding remarks

Although the present section in several respects extends the literature on optimal lifetime redistributive policy, there are still many important aspects left. As in most two-period models of optimum taxation, the present one also assumes that each individual lives for two periods, but is work-active, earns income, and pays taxes on labour income only in the first period. This is a useful simplification for many purposes, but it means that the model fails to capture the problems arising when an individual is due to pay labour and capital taxes in the same period. For example, labour supply of the elderly is one of the most debated issues in many countries in the context of pension design. Furthermore, if government and individuals have different views on the desirable level of leisure for old people, we may have an additional case for paternalism. To include these concerns we should consider a model in which the individual also works and pays labour taxes in the second period when he or she receives the return on capital accumulated in the first period. These questions and possible extensions to the OLG economy are analysed later on in this book. If dynamic decision-making at the beginning of each period was allowed, this would give opportunity to consider retirement decisions in more detail. Given that in aging societies, the demand for labour is becoming an important issue, a consideration of tax policy in a world where individuals have habit-forming utilities but suffer from projection bias would be valuable information. Furthermore, we have assumed that individuals do not differ in the degree of habit formation. This may crucially affect individuals' choices of retirement age, and the optimality of tax and pension policies. These questions are left for future research.

14.3 Uncertain future earnings and capital income tax

None of us can be certain about how much we will be able to earn in the future. In the Atkinson–Stiglitz model, a worker knows their full lifetime income before making any consumption decisions. When consumption decisions are taken before earnings uncertainties are resolved, the Atkinson–Stiglitz result does not hold. It means that in a two-period model, second-period consumption should be taxed at the margin relative to first-period consumption. We may save not just to smooth our consumption over predictable life events—having children or retiring—but also to protect ourselves in case something goes wrong—being made redundant or getting sick, for example. Those of us lucky enough to maintain a high earnings capacity may find ourselves with more wealth than we had planned. Alternatively, to put it another way, most of us save to hedge against a bad outcome and if the outcome turns out good, we will have 'over-saved'. This might lead to reduced labour supply and some form of tax on savings may increase efficiency. At the margin, taxing savings will weaken the desire to work less and will therefore reduce the distortionary effects of redistributive taxation. The underlying logic of this result is that welfare is enhanced by providing insurance about future earnings opportunities through the tax system. When leisure is a normal good, those who save more, *ceteris paribus*, will tend to work less later on. Thus, discouraging savings enhances the ability to provide insurance against future poor labour market possibilities.

Diamond and Mirrlees (1978, 2000) have already made this point in a special case. They apply this approach to the adjustment of retirement benefits as a function of the age at retirement in a setting where the alternatives are a particular job or no work at all and there is uncertainty about the ability to hold the job. Implicitly taxing both work and savings allows for more redistribution to those who should retire early by discouraging savings made in order to take advantage of an early retirement pension. The implicit tax comes from a benefit level that rises at less than an actuarially fair rate with continued work. The insight is that when less future work with lower future consumption results in a higher marginal utility of consumption (and so a greater incentive to save), making savings less available eases the incentive compatibility constraint. Golosov and Tsyvinski (2006) revisit this case. They consider the problem of implementation of optimal disability insurance when disability status is unobservable and show what instruments can implement the optimum. Asset testing allows control of joint deviations in which an individual, in anticipation of falsely claiming disability, increases his savings compared to those implied by the optimal allocation. Golosov and Tsyvinski (2006) provide numerical results that suggest the welfare gains from asset testing might be large. In fact, asset testing is a feature of many real-world benefit schemes.

The case for taxing savings is also made by the new dynamic public finance literature (see Golosov, Tsyvinski, and Werning 2006 and Kocherlakota 2010 for recent comprehensive surveys) using the mechanism design approach of social welfare optimization with the government controlling individual consumption and labour, subject to incentive compatibility constraints and aggregate resources. With additive preferences, a robust finding of this literature is the 'Inverse Euler Equation'—that the reciprocal (inverse) of the marginal utility of consumption is equal to the expectation of the reciprocal (inverse) of the future marginal utility of consumption—$\frac{1}{u'(c)} = E\frac{1}{u'(x)}$ where c is the first-period consumption and x the second-period consumption (Jensen inequality).

In a certainty model, the Inverse Euler Equation and the familiar Euler Equation are the same. However, with uncertainty, the marginal utility of present consumption is less than the expected marginal utility of future consumption when the Inverse Euler Equation holds. To see this, first note that Jensen inequality $E\frac{1}{u'(x)} > \frac{1}{E\frac{1}{u'(x)}}$. This implies $\frac{1}{E\frac{1}{u'(x)}} < Eu'(x)$, since the inverse function is convex. Using this with the inverse Euler equation gives $u'(c) = \frac{1}{E\frac{1}{u'(x)}} < Eu'(x)$. Thus in the absence of restrictions, an individual would want to save more than with the socially optimal plan. To implement such an allocation one needs to have a 'wedge' reflecting implicit marginal taxation of future consumption relative to earlier consumption, and so an implicit marginal tax on savings or capital income.

The inverse Euler condition comes from optimally balancing the incentives for today's work coming from additional compensation today and from anticipated changes in future resources because of today's additional earnings, since the inverse of marginal utility is the resource cost of increasing utility. Making it less attractive for someone with higher future earnings skills to mimic someone with lower earnings skills improves the equity efficiency trade-offs. The mechanism design approach generates the allocation that is optimal, which is then supplemented by analysis of ways to implement such an optimum, sometimes using familiar tax tools.

Following Diamond (2007), we consider uncertain future earnings in a two-period model with work only in the second period and consumption in both periods. The key assumption is that a consumption decision is made before the individual's second-period wage is known. With earnings occurring only in the second period, first-period consumption is chosen before the uncertainty about future earnings is resolved. In this model, second-period consumption should be taxed at the margin relative to first-period consumption. This result holds whether there is general taxation of earnings and savings or only a linear tax on savings with a non-linear tax on earnings. Indeed, in this case we get an inverse Euler equation.

With the same notation as above, consider a one-type model with uncertainty about second-period skill, but not first-period skill. There are not insurance markets to mitigate uncertainty. Let π_i now stand for the probability of having skill i in the second period. We continue to assume that the only binding incentive compatibility constraint is that type H does not want to imitate type L, which now refers only to the second period.

In the welfarist case, the government's problem is to maximize the following social welfare function:

$$u(c) + \psi(1 - y_1) + \delta[\sum \pi^i(u(x^i) + \psi(1 - {y_2}^i))] \tag{1}$$

subject to t $G + c - z_1 + \sum \pi^i r(x^i - {z_2}^i) \leq 0$ (2)

where $r = \frac{1}{1+\theta}$, and the self-selection constraint[42]

[42] The direction of the binding self-selection constraint is assumed to be, following the tradition in the one-dimensional two-type model, from high-skilled individual towards low-skilled individual. This pattern is also confirmed by the numerical simulations.

$$u(x^H) + \psi(1 - y_2{}^H) \geq u(x^L) + \psi\left(1 - \frac{n^L}{n^H} y_2{}^L\right) \tag{3}$$

This problem has the FOCs for consumption levels:

$$u'(c) = \lambda \tag{4}$$

$$(\pi^H + \mu)\delta u'^H(x^H) = \lambda r \pi^H \tag{5}$$

$$(\pi^L - \mu)\delta u'(x^L) = \lambda r \pi^L. \tag{6}$$

Adding and taking a ratio to the first equation, we obtain:

$$\frac{u'(c)}{(\pi^H + \mu)u'(x^H) + (\pi^L - \mu)u'(x^L)} = \delta r^{-1}. \tag{7}$$

Comparing this with the case without distortion, the taxpayer would gain from taxing savings if

$$\frac{u'(c)}{\pi^H u'(x^H) + \pi^L u'(x^L)} < \delta r^{-1}. \tag{8}$$

Thus, we have implicit marginal taxation of savings, provided $u'(x^H) < u'(x^L)$, as follows from the need to have $x^H > x^L$, to induce type H not to mimic type L.[43] If a high-skilled person works less (to mimic a lower-skilled person), this person would also like to reduce the first-period consumption and hence save more, so tax on savings is a good way to discourage mimicking. The intuition for this intertemporal wedge is that implicit savings affect the incentives to work.

The mimicker prefers to implicitly save more than the agent who is planning to tell the truth. An intertemporal wedge worsens the return to such behaviour. Intuitively, when preferences are separable between consumption and leisure, leisure is a normal good. Normality of leisure means that workers with a large amount of accumulated wealth in period 2 are harder to motivate in that period. Hence, on the margin, good tax systems deter wealth accumulation from period 1 to period 2 to provide people with better incentives to work in the latter period.

Thus in a setting where everyone is the same in the first period, a plausible condition is sufficient for a positive intertemporal consumption wedge. The insight, paralleling the argument through the inverse Euler condition, is that with this condition, less future work and lower future consumption will result in a higher marginal utility of consumption and a greater incentive to save (unless the condition is not satisfied and the impact of

[43] The underlying argument does not need the additive structure of preferences, provided that preferences are such that keeping x^H enough larger than x^H to just induce the higher labour supply implies a lower marginal utility of consumption at the higher consumption level.

hours worked on the marginal utility of consumption overcomes the higher level of consumption). Easing the incentive compatibility constraint then comes from making the return to saving smaller.

With uncertain (future) wage rates, the government would like to provide insurance by lowering after-tax earnings in the event of high wages in order to raise after-tax earnings in the event of low wages. With asymmetric information, the government is inferring wage rates from earnings and is limited by the ability of someone with a high wage rate to choose low earnings nevertheless. The incentive compatibility constraint is that those with high wage rates must find it in their interest to work harder and earn a higher amount. However, a worker intending to earn a low amount despite a high wage rate has a higher valuation of savings than if the worker were planning to earn a high amount (assuming normality of consumption). Thus, taxing savings eases the incentive compatibility constraint by making it less attractive to work less in the future. One example is that retirement tends to come at an earlier age for those with more accumulated savings (earnings opportunities held constant). Thus, discouraging savings encourages later retirement and permits pensions that are more generous for those who need to retire early and so have lower accumulated lifetime earnings.

This result has appeared in the pension literature as part of the design of a pension system to recognize that some workers lose good earnings opportunities while others do not. To provide lifetime earnings insurance, the encouragement of delayed retirement should be less than actuarial, implying an implicit tax on continued work. In the setting of providing insurance in this way, discouraging savings is part of providing insurance more efficiently. This result appears in models of pension design that have no income taxes, so it is not clear how it would carry over, if at all, in models that also have standard annual taxation of earnings, not just lifetime taxes.

Cremer and Gahvari (1995) consider a model where wage rates are uncertain and some goods must be purchased before the wage rate is revealed, while other goods and labour supply must be chosen after the wage rate is revealed. Their setting is similar to that used in Chapter 11 when we studied income taxation under uncertainty. Individuals are identical ex ante but face uncertain wage. There is no differential tax on goods purchased ex post. Instead, there is lower tax on goods purchased ex ante: under-demanded for self-insurance. This provides justification for preferential treatment of housing and other consumer durables. The intuition is that it is more difficult for those with higher skill ex post to mimic those with lower skill, since the ex post consumption requirement is higher (leisure is a normal good). It appears that even if we adopted the timing structure used by Cremer and Gahvari (2001)—that some goods (durables and housing) are purchased before the resolution of uncertainty—the Atkinson–Stiglitz result fails. The Atkinson–Stiglitz result would still remain valid for the goods consumed after the resolution of uncertainty, if there is weak separability between these goods and effort.

The wage uncertainty may itself be partly the result of uncertain returns to human capital investment. Anderberg (2009) shows that if human capital accumulation increases wage risk (i.e. increases the wage obtained with good shocks relative to bad shocks), it should be taxed, and vice versa. The tax causes the utility cost to an individual with a good productivity shock pretending to have had a bad productivity shock to be higher, thus relaxing the incentive constraint.

14.4 Hard to distinguish capital income from entrepreneurial earnings and capital income tax

One of the key issues in the optimal tax literature is how to differentiate taxes on labour income and capital income, respectively. A typical assumption in the theoretical literature is that the tax authority can easily distinguish the respective types of income. In practice, however, this is far from easy, as has been realized and discussed at length in connection with the dual income tax in the Nordic countries. Norway witnessed extensive circumvention of the income-splitting model introduced by the 1992 tax reform. Any gap between the labour income tax rate and the capital income tax rate may induce tax avoidance. Rather than having a substantial part of their income taxed as labour income, many entrepreneurs found ways to have it taxed much more leniently at the rate applied to capital income.[44] This problem was a major motivation for appointing a tax reform committee (the Skauge committee) that delivered its report in 2003 and led to the introduction of a new shareholder income tax with a marginal tax rate close to that of the labour income tax in order to remove the motivation for artificially channelling the income earned through a corporation into dividends or capital gains. Opportunities for income-shifting also exist for a large number of top executives (e.g. via stock options and capital gains). There is extensive empirical evidence that income-shifting is a significant issue, and accounts for a large fraction of observed behavioural responses to tax changes.

Jäntti et al (2010) argue that the 1993 tax reform in Finland had an impact on the level and composition of top incomes.[45] Figure 14.5 documents a surge in capital incomes (mainly dividends) of top 1 per cent starts just after the 1993 reform. Figure 14.6 also shows that top tax rates on upper income earners have declined significantly after the 1993 reform. There is not much change in the composition of incomes among the next 4 per cent. The gap between the tax rates on labour and capital income was huge after the

[44] In particular, many active owners of corporations have escaped the split model. One way to do this was to invite more passive owners into the company to bring the ownership share of active owners below 66 per cent. Between 1992 and 2000 the percentage of corporations subject to income-splitting fell from 55 to 32. By avoiding mandatory income-splitting the owners were free to work for a very low official salary, while reaping large dividends.

[45] The proportion of capital income in 2007 was 53 per cent of income in the top one per cent group (Figure 14.6). It was 11 per cent in 1990.

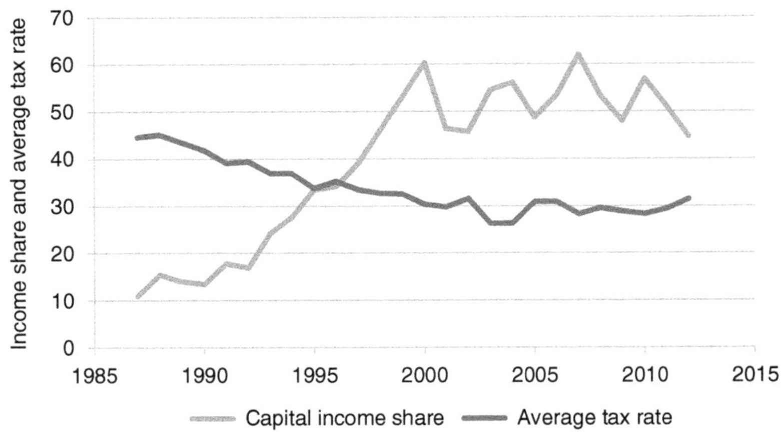

Figure 14.5 Capital income share and average tax rate for top 1 per cent in Finland 1987–2012

Source: Riihelä, Sullström, and Tuomala (2013).

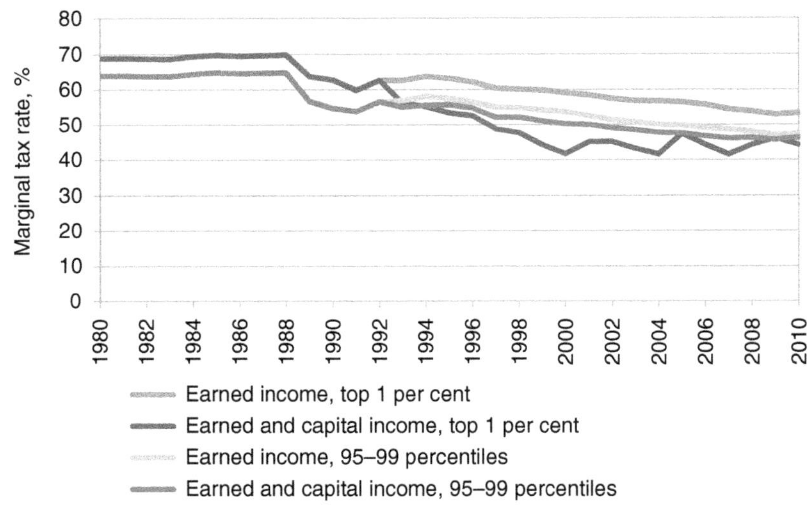

Figure 14.6 Marginal tax rates and income shares for top 1 per cent and 95–99 percentiles

Source: Riihelä, Sullström, and Tuomala (2013).

1993 reform.[46] The dual income tax dropped the marginal tax rates on capital income the higher was the person's total income before the reform. Those entrepreneurs who saw the largest reduction in the marginal tax rates on capital income also experienced the largest increase in capital income. At the same time, the share of labour income decreased for these taxpayers. The increase in the share of capital income out of total income was much more modest for high-income employees.

[46] 'The (Finnish) system seems to offer generous opportunities for tax-avoidance by transforming labor income into capital income. For example, retained corporate profits will increase the amount that is taxed as capital income, and capital gains on shares are only subject to capital income tax.' (Lindhe et al 2002, p.6)

The Finnish reform of 1993 sharply reduced the marginal tax rates on capital income for some corporate owners, but did not simultaneously change the taxation of labour income. Corporate owners who can afford to save can reduce their intertemporal tax bill by taking less labour income out of the firm, which increases the net worth of the company. The increased net worth, in turn, increases the share of dividends that can be paid tax-free in the future. People who are not owners of closely held corporations do not have an access to this route. Pirttilä and Selin (2011) examine whether the responses to the Finnish dual income tax reform of 1993 were different among entrepreneurs and employees. The idea is that entrepreneurs have more leeway for income shifting than employees. They first make the tax base as constant as possible so that legislation changes governing the tax base would not distort our inference. They then estimate, using the approach in the elasticity of taxable income literature (for this, see e.g. Gruber and Saez 2002 and Aarbu and Thoresen 2001) how taxable capital and labour income reacted to changes in the marginal tax rates on labour and capital income. They found significant shifts of labour income to capital income among the self-employed after the 1993 Finnish tax reform to a dual income tax with a lower rate on capital income.

The most dramatic changes in marginal income tax rates in Finland have taken place in the top percentile of the income distribution. It is interesting to note that the share received by the top 1 per cent of income recipients started to increase after 1993. In contrast to that for the next 4 per cent, the marginal tax rates of labour income and total income after 1993 differ only slightly from each other (see Figure 14.6). This implies that income-shifting possibilities are quite modest for this group.

A relevant question to ask is whether this increase in top incomes could have occurred had the income tax system remained the same as before 1993. It is plausible to think that the drastic reduction of top income tax rates which started in 1993 opened up the possibility of the dramatic increase in top incomes that started around the mid-1990s and accelerated in the end of the 1990s.

Landais et al (2010) found a clear regressivity in the top centiles in France. The important reason is that capital income is largely exempt from progressive taxation. There are also doubts that the U-shaped tax curve can be found in many other developed countries.

Christiansen and Tuomala (2008) (henceforth referred to as Ch-T) analyse a model wherein labour income can be camouflaged as capital income, but only at a cost, so that if tax relief can be achieved by converting capital income into taxable labour income this will be done to the extent that the marginal tax saving exceeds the marginal cost of transforming the former type of income to the latter. The issue of fiscal manipulation in the form of income-shifting has also received much attention in the context of the US tax reforms of 1986. Gordon and Slemrod (2000) have argued that a large part of the response observable in the tax return was due to income-shifting between the corporate sector and the individual sector.

While a capital income tax is sometimes assumed to be the only available instrument for certain types of redistribution (e.g. between those who inherit and those who don't, as in Boadway et al 2000), in principle any redistribution might in Ch-T's (2008) model be achieved by means of a non-linear tax on earnings. The question is whether imposing a tax on capital income may still be desirable. Income-shifting is sometimes related to the choice between being an entrepreneur or a wage earner, as in Gordon and MacKie-Mason (1995), where the role of the corporate income tax is to prevent a distortion of this choice under income-shifting. Ch-T (2008) do not model this choice explicitly, but one may conceive of income reported as capital income being earned as business income. A more important aspect of our model is that, with differential taxation of labour and capital, income-shifting allows the remuneration of marginal labour supply to be taxed at the capital tax rate. As in Gordon and MacKie-Mason, the reporting does not involve any tax evasion but is conditional on making use of perfectly legal ways to organize one's economic activities. Fuest and Huber (2001) discussed optimal taxes of labour and capital in a model with income-shifting, but in other respects their model is different from Ch-T, as we shall detail below after presenting the main structure of our model.

Ch-T (2007) employ the simplest possible model, capturing the essentials of the problem by making a number of assumptions that allow them to use a two-type, asymmetric information model of non-linear income taxation bearing strong resemblance to the models of Stern (1982) and Stiglitz (1982). The two types of persons, labelled L and H, are endowed with productivities (skill levels) that are reflected by their respective wage rates n^L and $n^H > n^L$. The two-type model has been used to analyse labour and capital taxation in overlapping generation models. It is typically assumed that each generation lives for two periods, but is work-active, earns income and pays taxes on labour income only in the first period. This is a useful simplification, implying that one can focus on the labour income tax of an agent in a single period, but it means that the model fails to capture the problems that arise when an agent is due to pay labour and capital taxes in the same period. To include the latter concern we shall consider a model in which the agent works and pays labour taxes in the second period when he receives the return to capital accumulated in the first period. As further simplifications we assume that wage rates are constant over time and that there is a fixed rate of return to savings, which may be justified by assuming that we consider a small open economy facing a world capital market. To establish a benchmark close to previous models we shall start out by considering the case in which labour income and capital income can indeed be perfectly distinguished.

The rest of the section is organized as follows. First we establish the basic structure of our model by setting up a simple benchmark model in which we address taxation of savings in a two-type model where individuals live two periods. In order to fully retain the simplicity of the conventional model, we make the assumption that the young pay no taxes. Then we provide the formulas for linear taxation of savings without and with income-shifting.

14.4.1 A BENCHMARK MODEL

The classic optimal income tax model, Mirrlees (1971), treats differences in observed income as being due to unobserved differences in ability. We will in general assume that individuals differ not only in ability but also in initial endowments, denoted by e. In the Ch-T model the initial endowment may be interpreted as representing various factors affecting capital income. Beyond representing a tangible asset, say, in terms of inherited wealth or exogenous labour income, it may, liberally interpreted, represent entrepreneurial skill, family background, social and business networks, and other circumstances that are conducive to earning capital income. It is also quite plausible to assume that in reality both ability and endowment are unobservable. This may be more plausible for intangible assets, but in practice there are a number of non-transparent ways in which even tangible assets can be transferred from one generation to the next.[47] First-best taxation is not feasible in this economy, because we cannot distinguish ex ante between the two types. Thus, only anonymous tax systems are feasible.

There are in total four types of individuals. To avoid difficulties with multidimensional optimal tax problems, variation is restricted to two types by assuming that there are only two fixed n, e bundles (n^H, e^H and n^L, e^L),[48] where we either assume that $e^H > e^L$ or $e^H = e^L$. This framework allows us to consider as special cases either variation in initial resource endowments or in skill, but also the case where one type is more richly endowed with both initial resources and skill. The latter case may be justified as an approximation to reality, as there is evidence of a strong positive correlation between the two characteristics.[49] Multidimensional variation would pose serious problems of tractability that are likely to require numerical computations.

Each agent supplies y units of labour in the second period. The labour market is perfectly competitive so that an individual's effective labour supply equals his or her gross income, $z=ny$. To simplify the exposition and notation without loss of generality, we consider the case with an equal number of individuals of each type. The government wishes to design a tax system that may redistribute income between individuals. There is asymmetric information in the sense that the tax authority is informed neither about individual skill levels and labour supply nor endowments. To introduce return to capital and the possible taxation thereof, it is useful to consider a two-period model wherein an individual starts out with the endowment e. The economy lasts two periods. Individuals are free to divide their first period (when young) endowment between consumption, denoted by c and savings, s. Each unit of savings yields a consumer $1+r$ additional units of consumption in the second period. Denote after-tax income by B. Consumption in each period is given by

[47] This is a key point in Cremer et al (2003).

[48] This is a less restrictive way to avoid multidimensional variation than the pure endowment variation adopted in Fuest and Huber (2001).

[49] See Pekkarinen et al (1985).

$$c^i = e^i - s^i, \qquad i = L, H \tag{1}$$

$$x^i = B_2^i + (1+r)s^i \qquad i = L, H. \tag{2}$$

Labour is supplied (elastically) only in the second period and all taxes are imposed in that same period. (Exogenous labour income may be permitted in the first period.) The analysis may be generalized to (elastic) labour supply in both periods but only by adding considerable analytical complexity. The individuals have identical and additively separable preferences over first and second period consumption and labour supply, represented by the utility function

$$U^i = u(c^i) + v\psi(x^i) - \psi(y^i), \qquad i = L, H \tag{3}$$

Unless otherwise stated, the functions u and ψ are increasing, strictly concave, and twice differentiable. The function v is increasing, strictly convex, and twice continuously differentiable. It is also assumed that all goods are normal. In this setting, where taxes on both earnings and savings income are available, the question is whether or not the return to savings ought to be taxed.

14.4.2 NON-LINEAR LABOUR INCOME TAX AND LINEAR TAXATION OF SAVINGS

The tax system is similar to the Nordic dual income taxation where capital income is taxed at a fixed rate (proportional tax) and a non-linear tax is levied on labour income. That means that each type of tax is conditioned only on one type of income. This tax system is similar to that of Boadway et al (2000) but is different from the taxes examined by Fuest and Huber (2001), who postulate a non-linear tax function with both capital income and labour income as arguments. While both regimes are of interest, we wish to examine what is basically the Nordic type of tax system, which is based on a mixture of principles and practical considerations that motivated this particular dual design.[50]

It is well known from the tax theory with one-dimensional population that an important role for linear taxes may be to alleviate the self-selection constraint imposed under asymmetric information. This may be a role also where individuals differ both in skills and initial endowments. Adopting standard procedures, we can characterize Pareto-efficient second-best taxes. This is done by maximizing the utility of type L

[50] One relevant concern has been the desire to have equal tax rates on corporate profits and (other) capital income (interest, dividends, etc.) and, with a constant corporate tax rate, there will be a fixed tax rate on capital income in general.

$$U^L = u(e^L - s^L) + v(B^L + (1 + \bar{r})s^L) - \psi(y^L) \tag{4}$$

for a fixed utility assigned to type H, $U^H = \bar{U}^H$, and subject to the pre-set revenue constraint

$$\sum(z^i - B^i + trs^i) = R \qquad i = L, H \tag{5}$$

and the self-selection constraint

$$\bar{U}^H \geq u(e^H - \hat{s}) + v\left(B^L + (1 + \bar{r})\hat{s}\right) - \psi\left(\frac{n^L}{n^H} y^L\right) \tag{6}$$

where t is the tax rate for capital income, $r(1 - t) = \bar{r}$, R denotes the required tax revenue, and $\bar{U}^H$ is the pre-assigned utility level of type H, and where 'hat' is used to indicate type H as a mimicker who would choose the bundle intended for type L. The maximization amounts to choosing bundles of gross and net incomes, z^H, B^H and z^L, B^L, while it is implicit that each type chooses the corresponding utility-maximizing level of savings conditional on the values of e, B, and $\bar{r}$.

The self-selection constraint requires that an individual weakly prefers the bundle over the two time periods intended for him or her to the bundle designated for the other individual. We consider the more interesting case, where only the incentive compatibility or self-selection constraint of the high-skilled type binds. This amounts to the region where redistribution takes place from high-skilled to low-skilled. The natural limit of redistribution is that, if taken too far, such redistribution might induce the high-skilled type to pretend to be the low-skilled type. Such mimicking implies that the high-skilled would choose a labour supply $n^L y^L / n^H$ to make his income equal to that of the low-skilled, and he would choose savings $\hat{s}$ to maximize intertemporal utility given the second-period income he would earn as a mimicker. Imposing (6) precludes mimicking. Multipliers α, μ, and λ are assigned to the constraints (4), (5), and (6).

From the first order conditions (see appendix) we obtain:

$$t = \frac{\frac{\lambda}{\mu} \hat{v}_B (\hat{s} - s^L)}{-\left(\frac{\partial s^{cL}}{\partial t} + \frac{\partial s^{cH}}{\partial t}\right)} \tag{7}$$

where $e^L = e^H$, the mimicker and the genuine low-skilled type have the same initial endowment and the same second period income (being a property of mimicking), and they will have the same level of savings. A larger initial endowment will induce larger first-period savings. Christiansen and Tuomala (2007) state the following results:

(i) If $e^L = e^H$ and if preferences of individuals are additively separable, $\hat{s} = s^L$, and there is no taxation of capital income at the optimum.

(ii) If $e^H > e^L$, the mimickers have a higher savings level, and there is a case for taxing capital income at the optimum.

We shall leave further interpretation to the next section.

14.4.3 INCOME SHIFTING

Above, labour income was treated as observable. In reality, the government cannot directly observe an individual's true labour income and capital income, but individuals have to report their labour income and capital income for tax purposes. Now the government faces an information problem not only because information on skill and wealth is private, but even the true labour income is unknown, since individuals have the possibility to shift labour income to capital income. Let z be the amount of income reported as labour income in the second period whilst Δ is the labour income which is converted to capital income. Hence, the actual labour income is z+Δ, and the labour supply is $y = \frac{z+\Delta}{w}$. Income-shifting involves costs, which could be modelled in different ways. As the crucial role for these costs is to determine an optimum extent of income-shifting, while their exact nature is less important, we choose the simplest possible way by assuming that shifting an amount of income Δ inflicts a loss of net income $k(\Delta)$ on the taxpayer,[51] where $k'(\Delta)>0$ and $k''(\Delta)>0$. As above, each type of agent will choose savings and income-shifting to maximize his utility.

In practice, income-shifting from labour to capital is an important issue as the marginal tax on labour income exceeds the tax rate on capital income in countries with a dual income tax, but in general whether an agent wants to shift income from labour to capital depends on relative marginal tax rates. However, we shall simply rule out the possibility of reversing the income-shifting by shifting income from capital to labour (i.e. setting $\Delta<0$) as it is an issue of minor practical interest. Thus we simply impose the restriction that $\Delta>0$. As we shall see and discuss further below, there may be theoretical cases where this constraint will be binding.

To characterize Pareto-efficient second-best taxes we now maximize the utility of type L

$$u(e^L - s^L) + v(B^L + (1+\bar{r})s^L + (1-t)\Delta^L - k(\Delta^L)) \; - \psi(\frac{z^L + \Delta^L}{w^L}) \tag{8}$$

for a fixed utility $\bar{U}^H$ assigned to type H and subject to the revenue constraint

$$\sum\left(z^i - B^i + t(rs^i + \Delta^i)\right) = R \qquad i = 1, 2 \tag{9}$$

and the self-selection constraint

$$\bar{U}^H \geq u(e^H - \hat{s}) + v\left(B^L + (1 + r(1-t))\hat{s} + (1-t)\hat{\Delta} - k(\hat{\Delta})\right) - \psi\left(\frac{z^L + \hat{\Delta}}{n^H}\right). \tag{10}$$

[51] Alternatively, one might have assumed that the cost would reduce taxable income and hence the tax liability, or that it would imply use of own labour.

The following multipliers are assigned to the constraints: α to the pre-assigned utility of type H, μ to the revenue constraint, and λ to the self-selection constraint.

From the first-order condition (see appendix) solving for t, we obtain the formula for the optimal capital tax.

$$t = \frac{\frac{\lambda}{\mu}\hat{v}_B(r\hat{s} - rs^L + \hat{\Delta} - \Delta^L)}{-\left[r\frac{\partial s^{cL}}{\partial t} + r\frac{\partial s^{cH}}{\partial t}\right] - \left[\frac{\partial \Delta^{cL}}{\partial t} + \frac{\partial \Delta^{cH}}{\partial t}\right]}. \quad (11)$$

The formula for the optimal capital income tax shows that three effects should be taken into account. Where the mimicker would report a larger capital income ($rs+\Delta$) than the genuinely low-skilled type, the mimicker is hit harder when the return to capital (rs) and the concealed labour income (Δ) are taxed more strongly, and the self-selection constraint is alleviated. This effect is captured by the numerator. On the other hand, the tax causes a distortion of the inter-temporal consumption trade-off, represented by the former term in the denominator. Finally, as it is possible to increase labour supply and have it taxed as capital income due to income-shifting, the capital tax also distorts the labour supply. This effect is captured by the latter term in the denominator. The alleviation of the self-selection constraint should be traded off against the distortions.[52] In sum:

The optimal tax is characterized by (11). If $e^L = e^H$, and there is income shifting, taxing capital income is part of the optimal tax policy.

In the absence of income-shifting there would be no tax on capital income. This would correspond to the two-period model with labour supplied only in period 1 and preferences where consumption in the two periods is weakly separable from labour (leisure), as discussed in the introduction to this chapter. Considering the expression for the tax rate t in (11) above, we note that with income, shifting the numerator is positive and the denominator is negative, and due to the minus sign, t is positive. Hence, there is a case for taxing capital due to income-shifting.

Above we have focussed on the capital income tax. To characterize the optimal labour income tax and overall tax policy we shall highlight a number of marginal tax rates which are also crucial for the existence of income-shifting but were brushed aside above. First, we note that there is a need to distinguish two tax rates on labour income, namely the marginal tax rate on reported labour income and the marginal tax rate on labour income reported as capital income. The latter is the more transparent one. As capital income is taxed at a fixed rate equal to t, this is simply the marginal tax rate on labour income disguised as capital income.

It is important to note that the crucial condition for using a capital income tax to relax the self-selection constraint is that the mimicker would like to shift income to a larger extent than the genuinely low-skilled. It is immaterial whether the high-skilled agent also

[52] Christiansen and Tuomala (2008) analyse in further detail the contents of each term in the formula for t.

shifts income. It is not even crucial that the low-skilled type shifts income, as our result would also go through with $\hat{\Delta} > \Delta^L = 0$. However, raising t to a level where income-shifting both by the mimicker and by the true low-skilled type is quenched would not be efficient, as it would then fail to relax the self-selection constraint.

14.4.4 CONCLUDING REMARKS

Ch-T (2008) addressed non-linear taxation of labour income and linear taxation of capital income in a two-period model with agents who differ in their earnings capacity. As is well known, a capital income tax may be redundant in such a setting, given certain separability assumptions on preferences. Beyond imposing those separability assumptions, we assume that the agents may organize their economic activity in perfectly legal but costly ways that allow (part of) their labour earnings to be taxed as capital income, which is a favourable option granted that the capital tax rate is lower. Even if an agent makes use of this opportunity, the government can always tax him harder by increasing the income tax on labour. A tax on capital income is strictly required neither for raising revenue nor redistributing income. We show that there may still be a role for a capital income tax, as taxation takes place under the usual asymmetric information constraint causing tax distortions, and under income, shifting the capital income tax may alleviate the effects of the information constraint.

We show our result in a simple two-period model with taxation only in a single period and where high-skilled and low-skilled individuals may have different non-observable resource endowments beyond their different earnings capacity. An important implication is that such endowments may impact on tax policy even without introducing a new distributional dimension (as between those who inherit or not in Boadway et al (2000)).

An important finding is that with pure wage rate variation, there is no case for a capital income tax unless there is income-shifting. With variation in initial endowments, there is a case for capital taxation even without income shifting in the Ch-T model with savings, but income-shifting will rather weaken this case, as the larger savers will have less incentive to earn additional labour income to be reported as capital income.

The asymmetric information argument for a capital income tax must be traded off against its distortionary effect not only on savings, as in the conventional model of capital taxation, but also on labour as, due to income shifting, the capital tax now also becomes a marginal tax on labour. The interaction between tax shifting and labour supply is a key element. Inducing a larger reported labour income weakens the incentive to earn labour income to be reported as capital income, as do a low marginal tax on labour income and a large tax rate on capital income. The Ch-T model highlights a central and complex interaction between taxes on income from labour and capital, respectively. The crucial marginal tax rate is the *effective* marginal tax rate capturing both the marginal tax on labour income tax and the marginal tax due to its income effect on savings and hence on capital income. The latter effect will to a large extent influence the discrepancy between the tax rate on (reported) labour income and the tax rate on (reported) capital income at the optimum, and thereby govern the inducement to shift income.

APPENDIX 14.1 INCOME SHIFTING AND CAPITAL INCOME TAXATION

The Lagrange function of the optimization problem is:

$$\begin{aligned}\Lambda = & u(e^L - s^L) + v(B^L + (1+\bar{r})s^L) - \psi(y^L) \\ & + \alpha(u^H(e^H - s^H) + v(B^H + (1+\bar{r})s^H) - \psi(y^H) - \bar{U}^H) \\ & + \mu[\sum(n^i y^i - B^i + trs^i - R] \\ & + \lambda\left[\bar{U}^H - u(e^H - \hat{s}) - v(B^L + (1+\bar{r})\hat{s}) + \psi\left(\frac{n^L y^L}{n^H}\right)\right]\end{aligned}$$

Let subscripts denote partial derivatives. The first-order conditions for interior solution with respect to B^i,$i = L, H$, are

$$\frac{\partial \Lambda}{\partial B^L} = v_B^L - \lambda \hat{v}_B - \mu + \mu trs_B^L = 0 \tag{1}$$

$$\frac{\partial \Lambda}{\partial B^H} = \alpha v_B^H - \mu + \mu trs_B^H = 0 \tag{2}$$

A 'hat' is assigned to a function where the suppressed arguments are those of the mimicker.

Using Roy's theorem and the Slutsky decomposition, the first-order condition with respect to t can be written as follows:

$$\begin{aligned}\frac{\partial \Lambda}{\partial t} = & - rs^L v_B^L - \alpha rs^H v_B^H + \lambda r \hat{v}_B \hat{s} + \mu(rs^L + rs^H) + \mu trs_B^L(-rs^L) + \mu trs_B^H(-rs^H) \\ & + \mu tr\frac{\partial s^{cL}}{\partial t} + \mu tr\frac{\partial s^{cH}}{\partial t} = 0\end{aligned} \tag{3}$$

where superscript c indicates compensated effects. Multiplying (1) by $-rs^L$ and (2) by $-rs^H$ and substituting in (3), we have

$$\lambda \hat{v}_B(\hat{s} - s^L) + \mu t(\frac{\partial s^{cL}}{\partial t} + \frac{\partial s^{cH}}{\partial t}) = 0$$

Consider the behaviour of an arbitrary agent supposed to maximize

$$U = u(e - s) + v(B + (1+\bar{r})s + (1-t)\Delta - k(\Delta)) - \psi(\frac{z+\Delta}{n}))$$

with regard to s and Δ, which yields the first-order conditions

$$U_s = -u'(e-s) + v'\Big(B + (1+\bar{r})s + (1-t)\Delta - k(\Delta)\Big)(1+\bar{r}) = 0$$

$$U_\Delta = v'\Big(B + (1+\bar{r})s + (1-t)\Delta - k(\Delta^L)\Big)(1-t-k') - \psi'\left(\frac{z+\Delta}{n}\right)\frac{1}{n} \leq 0$$

implicitly defining s and Δ as functions of z, B, and t. At this point we have found it handy to let a prime denote derivatives. The inequality applies where income shifting reversal would be desirable and $\Delta > 0$ is binding.

The corresponding Lagrangian is

$$\begin{aligned}
\Lambda &= u(e^L - s^L) + v\Big(B^L + (1+\bar{r})s^L + (1-t)\Delta^L - k(\Delta^L)\Big) - \psi\left(\frac{z^L + \Delta^L}{n^L}\right) \\
&+ \alpha\left[u(e^H - s^H) + v\Big(B^H + (1+\bar{r})s^H + (1-t)\Delta^H - k(\Delta^H)\Big) - \psi\left(\frac{z^H + \Delta^H}{n^H}\right) - \bar{U}^H\right] \\
&- \lambda\left[u(e^H - \hat{s}) + v\Big(B^L + (1+\bar{r})\hat{s} + (1-t)\hat{\Delta} - k(\hat{\Delta})\Big) - \psi\left(\frac{z^L + \hat{\Delta}}{n^H}\right) - \bar{U}^H\right] \\
&+ \mu[z^L - B^L + z^H - B^H + trs^L + trs^H + t\Delta^L + t\Delta^H - R]
\end{aligned} \tag{4}$$

The associated first-order conditions for an interior solution with respect to z^i and B^i, i=L,H are:

$$\frac{\partial\Lambda}{\partial z^L} = -\psi'\left(\frac{z^L+\Delta^L}{n^L}\right)\frac{1}{n^L} + \lambda\psi'\left(\frac{z^L+\hat{\Delta}}{n^H}\right)\frac{1}{n^H} + \mu + \mu trs_z^L + \mu t\Delta_z^L = 0 \tag{5}$$

$$\frac{\partial\Lambda}{\partial z^H} = -\alpha\psi'\left(\frac{z^H+\Delta^H}{n^H}\right)\frac{1}{n^H} + \mu + \mu trs_z^H + \mu t\Delta_z^H = 0 \tag{6}$$

$$\frac{\partial\Lambda}{\partial B^L} = v_B^L - \lambda\hat{v}_B - \mu + \mu t(rs_B^L + \Delta_B^L) = 0 \tag{7}$$

$$\frac{\partial\Lambda}{\partial B^H} = \alpha v_B^H - \mu + \mu t(rs_B^H + \Delta_B^H) = 0 \tag{8}$$

Using Roy's theorem and the Slutsky decomposition, the first-order condition with respect to t can be written as follows:

$$\begin{aligned}
\frac{\partial\Lambda}{\partial t} &= (-rs^L - \Delta^L)v_B^L + (-rs^H - \Delta^H)\alpha v_B^H + \lambda\hat{v}_B(r\hat{s} + \hat{\Delta}) + \mu(rs^L + \Delta^L + rs^H + \Delta^H) \\
&+ \mu trs_B^L(-rs^L - \Delta^L) + \mu trs_B^H(-rs^H - \Delta^H) + \mu t\Delta_B^H(-rs^L - \Delta^L) + \mu t\Delta_B^H(-rs^H - \Delta^H) \\
&+ \mu trs_t^{cL} + \mu trs_t^{cH} + \mu t\Delta_t^{cL} + \mu t\Delta_t^{cH} = 0.
\end{aligned} \tag{9}$$

As above, superscript c indicates compensated effects. Multiplying (7) by $(-rs^L - \Delta^L)$ and (8) by $(-rs^H - \Delta^H)$ and substituting in (9), we have:

$$\lambda \hat{v}_B(r\hat{s} - rs^L + \hat{\Delta} - \Delta^L) + \mu t(r\frac{\partial s^{cL}}{\partial t} + r\frac{\partial s^{cH}}{\partial t} + \frac{\partial \Delta^{cL}}{\partial t} + \frac{\partial \Delta^{cH}}{\partial t}) = 0 \qquad (10)$$

14.5 **Inherited wealth and capital income tax**

If savings were only made for life-cycle smoothing purposes, and everyone has the same preferences, then wealth differences for any given cohort will reflect earnings differences. However, this is not the only way in which people receive capital. For example, some people inherit it.[53] Hence, capital income inequality is due to differences in wealth due to past saving behaviour, inheritances received, and rates of return that have varied dramatically over time and across assets.

Piketty and Zucman (2013) have estimated wealth for eight advanced economies: the United States, Canada, Britain, France, Italy, Germany, Japan, and Australia. Their estimates reveal some striking trends. Wealth-to-income ratios in these nations climbed from a range of 200 to 300 per cent in 1970 to a range of 400 to 600 per cent in 2010.

Atkinson (2012, pp. 11–12) describes the role of inheritance and wealth taxes in this development as follows:

> After a long period when inheritance was declining, it is now increasing again in significance in many advanced countries. In France, this has been shown in a recent study by Piketty (2011).... Indeed, wealth taxes have been going out of favour for some time, having been abolished in Austria, Denmark, Finland, Germany, Sweden and Spain. Although, we should note that France has swum against the tide with its Solidarity Tax on Wealth.

Taxing inheritance gives rise to difficult conceptual issues.[54] Hence perhaps it is not surprising that the economic literature on inheritance taxation has been rather inconclusive. If the bequest is voluntary, then it is plausible from a strictly welfaristic perspective, as in Kaplow (2008), that both the donor and the recipient utilities should be included in social welfare. There are both efficiency and equity implications here. However, when generations are linked by altruism then there will be an externality involved in the transfer, i.e. donors take account of their own altruistic utility from the transfer, but not the additional utility to the recipients. From an efficiency point of view, a Pigovian subsidy should be made to internalize this externality. Farhi and Werning (2010) allow for the social planner to value welfare of children generation separately from dynastic welfare and show that the corresponding externality due to insufficient giving should be addressed by policy that subsidizes bequests (albeit in a 'progressive'

[53] In Boadway, Marchand, and Pestieau (2003) when wealth transfers are unobserved taxing capital income is indirect consumption tax.

[54] Boadway, Chamberlain, and Emmerson (2010) give an excellent survey on inheritance taxation.

manner). When bequests are unintended, because they arise from precautionary savings held as self-insurance against uncertainty about longevity, taxing them will not be distorting. Cremer and Pestieau (2006) suggest that the optimal taxation of accidental bequests could be at 100 per cent from an efficiency perspective. Of course, it is not easy in practice to identify which bequests are unintended. The Mirrlees Review based its argument for inheritance taxation on equality of opportunity in the sense that redistribution should aim to equalize persons' opportunities in the market economy, but should not penalize them for the way they exercise those opportunities (cf Roemer 1998). Inheritances received over the life-cycle create better opportunities for the recipients and so should be taxed.

In the real world it is very likely that inheritance affects, in particular, income levels of the very rich. Hence, taxes on labour income are not alone able to limit inequality. Piketty and Saez (2014) employ linear taxation and make many extensions of a steady state setup and generally find a role for inheritance taxation. They emphasize three main rationales for capital taxation. First, the tax authority cannot easily distinguish capital and labour income. Second, notions of income and consumption flows are difficult to define and measure for top wealth holders. Finally, there are strong meritocratic reasons why we should tax inherited wealth more than earned income or self-made wealth. This implies that the ideal tax system should combine a progressive inheritance tax, in addition to progressive income and wealth taxes. Piketty and Saez (2012) show that optimal inheritance tax formulas can be expressed in terms of estimable 'sufficient statistics', including behavioural elasticities, distributional parameters, and social preferences for redistribution (see Kopczuk 2013 for a recent survey).

One of the most famous ethical cases for inheritance tax was put by John Stuart Mill, as quoted in the Mirrlees Review (2011):

> I see nothing objectionable in fixing a limit to what anyone may acquire by mere favour of others, without any exercise of his faculties, and in requiring that if he desires any further accession of fortune, he shall work for it.
>
> The Meade Committee followed the Millian tradition: inherited wealth is widely considered—and we share the view—to be a proper subject for heavier taxation on grounds of both fairness and economic incentives. The citizen who by his own effort and enterprise has built up a fortune is considered to deserve better tax treatment than the citizen who, merely as a result of the fortune of birth, owns an equal property; and to tax the former more lightly than the latter will put a smaller obstacle in the way of effort and enterprise (Meade 1978, p. 318).

Rising inequality is often (too often) discussed in terms of differences in labour income. The standard optimal income tax analysis is also based on differences in earning capacity. In other words, there is simply one dimension along which people differ. The wage distribution is certainly important, but people differ also in wealth they have. One highly significant phenomenon in recent years in many developed countries has been the ending of the downward trend in wealth concentration, and inheritance and wealth transferred earlier in life through gifts *inter vivos* has returned as a source of inequality. As a reaction to this, the Mirrlees Review recommends a comprehensive lifetime wealth receipts tax. Atkinson (1972) proposed the application of the tax on a cumulative basis to all capital receipts over the lifetime, given the importance of transfers made earlier in life and their impact on inequality of opportunity (Atkinson 1972).

When we take into account inherited wealth, we are again in a two characteristic model. When there is greater inequality in inherited wealth, does this lead us to tax inheritance more heavily and earned income less heavily? However, the multidimensionality also introduces a new element, which is the extent to which we can operate separate progressive taxes on earned income and on inherited wealth—or do they have to be jointly taxed?

First, we start with a simple model where each individual supplies y units of labour in the second period. The labour market is perfectly competitive so that an individual's effective labour supply equals his or her gross income, $z = ny$. To simplify the exposition and notation without loss of generality, we consider the case with an equal number of individuals of each type. The government wishes to design a tax system that may redistribute income between individuals. There is asymmetric information in the sense that the tax authority is informed about neither individual skill levels and labour supply nor endowments. To introduce return to capital and the possible taxation thereof, it is useful to consider a two-period model wherein an individual starts out with the endowment e. The economy lasts two periods. Individuals are free to divide their first-period (when young) endowment between consumption, denoted by c and savings, s. Each unit of savings yields a consumer $1+r$ additional units of consumption in the second period. Denote after-tax income by B. Consumption in each period is given by

$$c^i = e^i - s^i, \qquad i = L, H \tag{1}$$

$$x^i = B_2^i + (1+r)s^i \qquad i = L, H. \tag{2}$$

Labour is supplied (elastically) only in the second period and all taxes are imposed in that same period. (Exogenous labour income may be permitted in the first period.) The analysis may be generalized to (elastic) labour supply in both periods but only by adding considerable analytical complexity. The individuals have identical and additively separable preferences over first and second period consumption and labour supply, represented by the utility function

$$U^i = u(c^i) + v(x^i) - \psi(y^i), \qquad i = L, H. \tag{3}$$

Unless otherwise stated, the functions u and ψ are increasing, strictly concave, and twice differentiable. The function v is increasing, strictly convex, and twice continuously differentiable. We also assume that all goods are normal.

In this setting, where taxes on both earnings and savings income are available, we examine whether or not the return to savings ought to be taxed. For full non-linear taxation (earnings and capital income) we have to assume that the tax authority has the ability to observe savings. Here no restrictions are placed on tax instruments. This means that we consider the many-good non-linear tax model. The tax schemes required to implement the allocation of this economy are necessarily more complicated than linear schemes we have considered so far. The self-selection constraint requires that an individual weakly prefers the bundle, over the two time periods, intended for him or her over the bundle designated for the other individual. We consider the more interesting case, where only the incentive compatibility or self-selection constraint of the high-skilled type binds. This amounts to the region where redistribution takes place from high-skilled to low-skilled. The natural limit of redistribution is that, if taken too far, such redistribution might induce the high-skilled type to pretend to be the low-skilled type. Such mimicking implies that the high-skilled would choose a labour supply $n^L y^L / n^H$ to make his income equal to that of the low-skilled, and he would choose savings $\hat{s}$ to maximize intertemporal utility given the second-period income he would earn as a mimicker. Now we maximize the utility of type L

$$U^L = u(e^L - s^L) + v(B^L + (1+r)s^L) - \psi(y^L) \tag{4}$$

for a fixed utility assigned to type H, and subject to the revenue constraint

$$\sum (n^i y^i - B^i) = R \qquad \mathrm{i} = \mathrm{L, H} \tag{5}$$

and self-selection constraint

$$\bar{U}^H \geq \hat{u}(e^H - \hat{s}) + \hat{v}\left(B^L + (1+r)\hat{s}\right) - \hat{\psi}\left(\frac{n^L}{n^H} y^L\right) \tag{6}$$

Imposing (6) precludes mimicking. The multipliers α, μ, and λ are assigned to the constraints.

From the Lagrange function the first order condition with respect s^H gives

$$-\alpha u'(c^H) + \alpha(1+r)v'(x^H) = 0 \tag{7}$$

This implies that there is no implicit marginal taxation of savings for type H (e^H, n^H)

$$\frac{u'(c^H)}{v'(x^H)} = 1 + r \tag{8}$$

where the left hand side is the marginal rate of substitution between after-tax income in period two and after-tax income in period two of type H. (17) implies that savings decisions of type H are not distorted at the margin.

The first order condition with respect s^L in turn gives

$$-u'(c^L) + (1+r)v'(x^L) - \lambda u'(c^L) + \lambda(1+r)v'(x^L(e^H)) = 0 \tag{9}$$

From the condition for type L we have

$$\frac{(1-\lambda)u'(c^H)}{(1-\lambda\frac{v'(x^L(e^H))}{v'(x^L)})v'(x^L)} = 1+r \tag{10}$$

If and only if $v'(x^L(e^H)) = v'(x^L)$, i.e. $e^L = e^H$, there is no taxation of savings for type L at the margin. In empirically plausible cases where individuals with higher initial wealth e have higher savings rates, then we have implicit taxation of savings for type L at the margin.

Hence, taxation of savings depends, among other things, on the degree of correlation between the e and n. One case is where they are independent, but that is hardly true. One extreme case is the classical class model where workers have labour income and no capital and capitalists have capital but no labour income; the correlation is minus 1. At the other extreme is the case where the amount inherited is determined by the parent's earnings and earning power is perfectly correlated across generations. For example in the United States, the correlation is 0.5—the highest of the OECD countries (see OECD 2010).

It is clear that inherited wealth and earnings are correlated but less than perfectly. In that case, in order to tax them appropriately we may need to take account of both dimensions at the same time. To gain a better understanding we need numerical simulation. Again, we are in the situation in which taxing capital income depends not only on the separability in the utility function (as in the Atkinson-Stiglitz Theorem) but also on the degree of linkage between the marginal distributions.

14.5.1 TWO-PERIOD AND TWO-TYPE MODEL WITH THE LABOUR SUPPLY IN BOTH PERIODS

When we allow the labour supply in both periods and assume the intertemporal and intratemporal separable utility function $U^i = u(c^i) + \psi(1-y^i) + \delta^i[v(x^i) + \psi(1-y'^i)]$, then the income tax system becomes more complicated with taxes in both periods. When the government can impose optimal labour income taxes in both periods, no capital income taxation is needed. This can be seen in a simple extension of the above analysis. Now the government chooses consumption and income in both periods. The lifetime self-selection or incentive constraint becomes

$$\begin{aligned} u(c^H) + \psi(1-y^H) + \delta[v(x^H) + \psi(1-y'^H)] \geq \hat{u}(c^L) + \hat{\psi}\left(1-\frac{n^L}{n^H}y^L\right) \\ + \delta\left[\hat{v}(x^L) + \hat{\psi}\left(1-\frac{n^L}{n^H}y'^L\right)\right] \end{aligned} \tag{11}$$

where y' is the second period labour supply. From the first-order condition we can see that also in this case there is no intertemporal distortion on consumption for either skill type.

Assume that $e^H > e^L$

$$u(B_1^H + e^H - s^H) + \psi(1 - y^H) + \delta[v\left(B_2^H + (1+r)s^H\right) + \psi(1 - y'^H)] \geq$$
$$\hat{u}(B_1^L + e^H - s^L) + \hat{\psi}\left(1 - \frac{n^L}{n^H}y^L\right) + \delta[\hat{v}(x^L) + \hat{\psi}\left(1 - \frac{n^L}{n^H}y'^L\right)]. \tag{12}$$

From the Lagrange function, the first-order condition with respect to s^H gives

$$-u'(c^H) + (1+r)v'(x^H) - \mu u'(c^H) + (1+r)\mu v'(x^H) = 0. \tag{13}$$

This implies that there is no implicit marginal taxation of savings for type H (e^H, n^H), as can be seen from (13)

$$\frac{u'(c^H)}{v'(x^H)} = 1 + r. \tag{14}$$

The first-order condition with respect to s^L in turn gives

$$-u'(c^L) + (1+r)v'(x^L) - \mu\hat{u}'(c^L[e^H]) + \mu(1+r)\hat{v}'({c_2}^L(e^H)) = 0 \tag{15}$$

$$\frac{u'(c^L)}{v'(x^L)} = \mu\frac{\hat{u}'}{\hat{v}'} + (1+r). \tag{16}$$

In an empirically plausible case, individuals with higher initial wealth e have a higher savings rate, then we have implicit taxation of savings for type L at the margin.

14.6 Capital income taxation and endogenous pre-tax wages in the OLG model

Next we analyse the intertemporal dimension of direct taxation in the overlapping generations model. There are several earlier papers that have analysed taxation in the OLG model. An early contribution is by Ordover and Phelps (1979).[55] Stiglitz (1987) extended the analysis to include general equilibrium considerations arising from endogenously determined pre-tax wage rates. Brett (1997), using the self-selection interpretation of optimal taxation, described capital income taxation rules if preferences are not separable. In a OLG model, Boadway, Marchand, and Pestieau (1998) treat labour and capital income taxation separately, in the spirit of the so-called dual income tax system. In their model, bequests have a key role. Finally, by means of a somewhat different methodology of dynamic programming, Atkinson and Sandmo (1980) examine

[55] There is some earlier work done by the same authors; see the references cited in Ordover and Phelps (1979).

optimal savings income taxation under the case where there is no heterogeneity within generations.[56]

Here the presentation draws from the framework used in Pirttilä and Tuomala (2001). They allow for a rich description of the production technology that enables the before-tax wage rate to depend on e.g. the labour supply of different individuals. This is a quite plausible and important assumption in an essentially long-term, dynamic framework. Pirttilä and Tuomala (2001) combine two well-known economic models: the Mirrlees (1971) model of optimal taxation and the overlapping generations model as represented in Diamond (1965). The reason for this is that this combination, encompassing heterogeneity both within and between generations, provides an appropriate means to study savings taxation and public provision (both pure public goods and publicly provided private goods) in a dynamic model with distortionary taxation.

In a general equilibrium setting in which wages are not given, capital taxes or subsidies may be optimal if they favourably influence the distribution of pre-tax income through the effects of changes in the capital stock on wage rates. In this instance and more broadly, when the government cannot directly control the capital stock through debt or other policies, taxation or subsidization of capital serves as a substitute instrument. Allowing for endogenously determined wages is also important because it gives rise to new forms of distorting taxation and production inefficiency, along the lines of Naito (1999).

14.6.1 THE FRAMEWORK

In the model, individuals are assumed to differ in two respects: by their birth date and their income-earning ability. Applying the self-selection approach to tax analysis, there are assumed to be two types of households in each generation. The government tax policy is, hence, restricted by the self-selection constraint of high-income households. The wage rates of the individuals are endogenously determined on the labour market and depend on the labour supply decisions, the capital stock, and the level of the public good. Thus, we examine a very general class of public goods, which, in addition to their impact on consumer utility, also affect the production possibilities of the economy. In an overlapping generations economy individuals live across two periods, supplying labour in the first and consuming a composite good in both periods. For simplicity, there is no population growth. Each generation consists of two households that have different productivity in the labour market. As usual in the optimal taxation literature, type 2 households' wage rate, w_2, is higher than the wage rate of type 1 individuals, w_1. The following notations are used: c_i^t denotes the consumption of a individual of type i born at

[56] Using the same approach, Park (1991) relaxes the homogeneity assumption but does not derive many concrete results. For an excellent overview of various OLG tax models, see Renström (1998).

time t when young, x_i^t the consumption of the same individual when old, y_i^t individual i's labour supply, and G^t the level of the public good at period t. The utility function, which is assumed to be identical between the individuals, may then be written as $U_i = U(c_i^t, x_i^t, y_i^t, G^t, G^{t+1})$.[57] Individual optimization, given a government's labour income tax schedule $T(w_i^t y_i^t)$, enables the marginal income tax rate to be written as:

$$MTR(w_i^t y_i^t) = \frac{1}{w_i^t}\frac{U_{i,y}^t}{U_{i,c}^t} + 1, \tag{1}$$

where $U_{i,l}^t$, for instance, depicts the partial derivative of the utility of individual i at period t with respect to its labour supply.

The production side of the economy utilizes four factors: capital denoted by k^t, the two kinds of labour, and the public good. Hence, the production function can be written as $F = F(k^t, y_1^t, y_2^t, G^t)$. The production function is assumed to exhibit constant returns to scale with respect to labour and capital under perfect competition. Factor prices are then determined by the marginal productivities as follows: $F_k^t = r^t$, $F_{l_1}^t = w_1^t$ and $F_{l_2}^t = w_2^t$. As mentioned above, the public good contributes positively to the output, i.e. F_G^t is positive. Because G appears both in the utility and the production functions, it is a good such as roads used both by consumers and for commercial traffic, or environmental quality enjoyed by consumers but at the same time beneficial for production. Note that how the production function is specified here involves endogenous determination of the wage rates of the two household types. The relative wage between the two types may therefore be written as a function $\omega^t = \frac{w_1^t}{w_2^t} = \omega(k^t, y_1^t, y_2^t, G^t)$.

The government's problem is to maximize intertemporal social welfare that includes welfare comparison both within and between generations. Applying the interpretation by Brett (1997) of the social welfare function, we assume that the government is utilitarian within the generation, but the utilities of different cohorts are taken into account via a general social welfare function G. Alternatively, we could choose a formulation with a general social welfare function within generations as well. Because the assumption of within-generation utilitarianism is not crucial for the results but may be expositionally briefer, we apply it here. In both regimes, the government chooses optimal tax rates for both income and savings taxation, subject to a resource constraint for each period.

The public good is a stock variable that evolves from one period to another according to the relationship:

$$G^t = \beta G^{t-1} + g^t, \tag{2}$$

[57] Note that households enjoy utility from the public good both when young and when old. For brevity, we omit G^{t+1} from the notation below.

where β is a depreciation parameter that takes values from zero to one, and g^t is the decision-based increase of the public good at period t. Supposing that the producer price of the incremental public good in terms of the numeraire, private consumption, is p, the resource constraint of the economy for each period may be written as

$$k^{t+1} = F(k^t, y_1^t, y_2^t, G^t) + k^t - c_t - x_{t-1} - pg^t, \tag{3}$$

where c_t depicts the aggregate consumption by the two young individuals born at time t, and x_{t-1} the aggregate consumption of the old at the same period.

The informational assumptions we apply are similar to the standard Mirrlees-type income tax problem. The government can observe the income of the two individual types but not their type, i.e. their wage rate. This implies that the tax schedule must be planned to fulfil the self-selection constraints of the individuals. Concentrating on the 'normal' case where the redistribution occurs from the high-ability type to the low ones, the self-selection constraint that may bind is

$$U(c_2^t, x_2^t, y_2^t, G^t) \geq U(c_1^t, x_1^t, \omega^t(k^t, y_1^t, y_2^t, G^t)y_1^t, G^t), \tag{4}$$

where $\omega^t(k^t, y_1^t, y_2^t, G^t)y_1^t$ gives the required labour supply of a high-ability type when mimicking the choice of the low-ability type to earn the income level of the true low-ability type. Note that as the individuals retire in the second period of their life, at that period their types are public information because of their decision at the first period. Hence, no self-selection constraints for the old need to be considered.

An important assumption to note is that the government possesses perfect control over the capital stock. As shown by e.g. Atkinson and Sandmo (1980), this implies that only one of the resource constraint and government budget constraint needs to be taken into account. Because of this, together with the observation that the resource constraint may be derived from combining the government's and the individuals' budget constraints in the Mirrleesian fashion, the multiplier associated with the resource constraint, ρ^t, may be interpreted as the shadow price of government's revenue.[58] Although the main purpose is to focus on capital income taxation and public provision, the characteristics of an optimal income tax schedule under endogenous wages derived in a static framework by Stern (1982) and Stiglitz (1982) (see also Chapter 2) also apply in the dynamic case of the present chapter. Unlike in the standard model, the marginal tax rate faced by the high-ability individuals is negative instead of zero. The intuition, as noted by Stern (1982), is clear: on top of the income tax, it is optimal for the government to rely on the redistributive capacity of the economy by pushing the labour supply of the high-ability type further, and hence to achieve an increase in the relative wage of the low-ability type.

[58] The calculations revealing how the resource constraint can be split into individual and government budget constraints are available from the authors upon request.

We now turn to the properties of the optimal non-linear taxation of capital income (savings), which may be deduced by comparing the marginal rate of substitution between the present and the future consumption imposed on the individuals.

From the first order conditions of the government's problem (details in appendix 14.6), Pirttilä and Tuomala (2001) obtain the following result:

Propostion 1: Within each generation, the optimal marginal capital income tax rate (MTR for savings) is positive (negative) for the high-ability individual, if an increase in capital reduces (raises) the relative wage rate of the low-ability type, ω^t. The MTR for savings of the low-ability individual is positive (negative), if an increase in capital reduces (raises) the relative wage rate and the mimickers value future consumption more (less) than the true low-ability types. Otherwise the MTR for savings of the low-ability type individuals is ambiguous.[59]

Its intuition is straightforward: if an increase in savings and, hence, in the capital stock, leads to a decrease in the relative wage of the low-income individuals, it becomes optimal for the government to distort the savings level downwards because of redistributional impacts that arise. The self-selection concerns expressed in the marginal tax rule for the low-ability type were, however, discussed earlier in Brett (1997). As he points out, if mimickers have a lower valuation of future consumption, taxing savings is a device to relax the self-selection constraint and obtain a Pareto improvement through easier redistribution. This part also makes it clear why, with weakly separable preferences between goods and leisure, capital income taxation cannot be used to deter mimicking.[60] The reason is that in that case, a true type 1 and a mimicker have the same valuation for savings, and the self-selection term (see (14) in appendix 14.6) vanishes.

Note that even if preferences are separable between goods and leisure, the endogenous wage term in the tax rules provides justification for distorting capital income taxation:

Corollary 1: If consumer preferences are weakly separable between goods and leisure, it is optimal to impose a tax (subsidy) on capital income, if an increase in the savings—i.e. investment—by generation t leads to an decrease (increase) of the relative wage of the low-income individuals (ω^{t+1}) of the next generation, t+1.

In the standard taxation model in an OLG economy (in the model examined by Ordover and Phelps (1979), for instance), there is no reason to rely on taxation between the generations. This is because the income-earning abilities of the generations are independent of each other, and there is no device to transfer income from one generation to another. The possibility that changes in capital stock may influence income-earning abilities and wage differences in the future provides a rationale to resort to distorting taxation of savings of the present generation in favour of future cohorts. This result can also be interpreted as a reservation to the old issue of the optimality of the so-called expenditure tax.

[59] Stiglitz (1987) provides similar results but does not discuss their implications on marginal tax rules.

[60] The result that there should be no capital income taxation if preferences are weakly separable between goods and leisure has been shown originally by Ordover and Phelps (1979).

Furthermore, this result has implications to production efficiency. The presence of the endogenous wage term (the last term) in expression (2) in appendix 14.6 implies production inefficiency at the optimum of this model. In other words, the across-time ratio of marginal social values of commodities is not equal to the marginal rate of transformation of commodities across time, i.e. $1 + r^t \neq \frac{\rho^{t-1}}{\rho^t}$. Thus, this kind of production inefficiency justifies capital income taxation in this model. This is in contrast with the famous efficiency theorem by Diamond and Mirrlees (1971). The discussion here bears an obvious similarity with the important work by Naito (1999) who shows that, in the presence of endogenous wages, the introduction of distortions in the public sector can Pareto-improve welfare.

14.6.2 THE OPTIMAL PROVISION OF A PUBLIC GOOD IN AN OLG FRAMEWORK

There are several examples of public goods that have dynamic characteristics that could, and should, be formulated as durable goods: environmental quality (e.g. climate change), the basic infrastructure of the society, as well as the material and immaterial heritage of a nation. Thus actions taken by the government today affect the position and the well-being of future generations. The aim here is a joint examination of optimal taxation of savings and the provision of public good in a genuinely dynamic framework.[61] Pirttilä and Tuomala's (2001) paper is related to those of Batina (1990) and Myles (1997). Batina considers ways to affect production efficiency by modifying a (static) public good provision rule in a representative consumer economy with linear taxes, when government debt policy is restricted. Myles, in turn, derives a dynamic formulation of the Samuelson principle using a representative consumer model with no distortionary taxation and no OLG setting.[62] The public good is modelled as a stock that preserves from period to another and provides a potentially intriguing link between the taxation of different individuals. Indeed, it is shown how our dynamic formulation of the Samuelson rule in a second-best world addresses efficiency and distributional considerations both within and between generations. Finally, worth noting is the fact that the modified Samuelson rule developed by Pirttilä and Tuomala (2001) is derived in a setting where the tax policy instruments (the possibility for non-linear income and savings taxation) are practically relevant.

[61] Using the same approach, Park (1991) relaxes the homogeneity assumption but does not derive many concrete results. For an excellent overview of various OLG tax models, see Renström (1998).

[62] John and Pecchenino (1994) examine optimal environmental policy in an OLG economy with the first-best world assumptions, where the environment is modelled as a stock variable.

The dynamic public good provision rule can be expressed as follows:

Proposition 2: In the presence of the optimal income and savings taxation scheme, the dynamic formulation of the Samuelson rule for a public good is given by

$$p = \sum_{\tau=t}^{\infty} \frac{\rho^{\tau}}{\rho^{t}} \beta^{\tau-t} SMB_{G}^{\tau}.$$

The notion of SMB_G^t measures the social marginal benefit of an increase in the level of the public good at time t; its interpretation is discussed shortly below. Let us begin the interpretation of this proposition by noting that the dynamic formulation of the Samuelson rule is written in a similar way to the static one (see Chapter 13): the left-hand side depicts the marginal rate of transformation between producing an incremental unit of public good in terms of private consumption. The right-hand side, in turn, measures the sum over time of the marginal social benefits of an incremental public good. The key aspect to note is that the expression on the right now measures not only the sum of the marginal rate of substitution within one generation, but a sum of all these intratemporal utilities together.[63]

The marginal social benefit of the public good, as given in equation (19) in appendix 14.6, takes into account all the influences of an increase in the public good stock at one period. The first term in this expression captures the sum of the marginal rate of substitution for the public good of the two types of households that are working at that period. This term is hence equal to the corresponding term in the standard Samuelson rule of the static case. Within the overlapping generations model, however, the presence of the public good affects two cohorts at the same time. Thus the optimality condition also takes into account the sum of the marginal rate of substitution for the public good of the households that are old at the examined period. This influence is encapsulated in the second term in (19) in appendix 14.6. The third and fourth terms in the public good provision rule address the impact of the public good on the self-selection constraint. Recall and as discussed in Chapter 13 that in the second-best circumstances where the government cannot observe individuals' abilities, its redistributive efforts are limited by the self-selection constraint of the more skilled (higher wages) individuals. For instance, as demonstrated by Boadway and Keen (1993), if the individual valuation of the public good decreases with leisure, the government may ease the self-selection constraint and assist redistribution by distorting the public good provision upwards. This follows from the observation that in that case, the true type 1 individuals have a higher valuation of the public good than the mimickers, and revenue-neutral increases in the public good provision hence deter mimicking. These self-selection impacts are taken into account in the present model as well, but for both generations living in the period considered.

[63] This discussion could be related to the literature on cost-benefit analysis of public projects. An important early contribution in this field within the OLG models is Pestieau (1974).

The remaining terms in (19) in appendix 14.6 refer to the presence of the public good in the production function. The first of these, F_G^t, simply measures the direct influence of the public good on the production possibilities. If this impact is positive, it increases the marginal social benefit of public good provision. The second arises from the fact that the public good may also affect the relative wage in the economy. If, for instance, the public good increases the relative wage of type-1 workers, this impact raises the social benefit of public good provision. To conclude, the divergence of the *MSB* at a given point of time from the fully efficient Samuelsonian principles stems from the imperfect redistributive capacity of the government. In these circumstances, under- or over-provision of the public good may be used for intergenerational redistributive purposes through the self-selection impact and the influence on the relative wage.

Let us move on to interpretation of the dynamics of the proposition 2. Basically, the rule measures the sum of the marginal benefits over time. The parameter $\beta^{\tau-t}$ in the rule captures the physical depreciation of the stock of the public good that, if evaluated at time *t*, starts at period *t+1*. The intuition emerging from the term $\frac{\rho^{\tau}}{\rho^{t}}$ is important and interesting. As noted earlier, the multiplier ρ is associated with the shadow price of the public funds. Now suppose that this shadow price is for some reason higher at period *t+1* than at period *t*. This means that the weight for the MSB_G^{t+1} is higher than that of MSB_G^t, which implies that the public good increase at period *t* should be relatively high. The intuitive explanation stems from the observation that as the public funds become more expensive at next period, it is useful to increase the stock already at period *t*, and take advantage of the preservation of the public good as a stock to the next period.

In second-best tax models with redistributive objectives, the interpretation of the shadow price of public funds, ρ, depends on the social value of redistribution and on the efficiency losses of taxation.[64] Therefore, under the most general second-best circumstances, the actual realized value of ρ remains unknown. Consider next a special case where the tax system may operate in the first-best world within each generation (that is, the terms referring to self-selection vanish). Then it may be deduced from equation (6) in appendix 14.6 that the ratio of the shadow prices at different periods is determined by $\frac{\rho^{t+1}}{\rho^{t}} = \frac{\partial W}{\partial U^{t+1}} / \frac{\partial W}{\partial U^{t}}$. This expression highlights the intergenerational redistribution aspect present at the dynamic public good provision rule. It states that if the social marginal

[64] This issue comes close to the notion of marginal cost of public funds (MCPF). In its usual form, as a division of shadow price of public funds by the shadow price of private income, it does not show up in non-linear tax models that follow the self-selection interpretation, such as Boadway and Keen (1993). Christiansen (1999) incorporates the notion into such a regime and shows that public funds are distortionary (MCPF>1) if the self-selection constraint is tightened, i.e. the tax increase of the high-ability type is large enough. The present set-up is more general than that of Christiansen in that it also encompasses capital income taxation. Examining the level of MCPF in our framework would certainly be interesting, but worthy of a separate analysis.

value of an extra income for generation $t+1$ is higher than that of generation t, the sum of the marginal rate of substitution of generation $t+1$ has a higher weight on the public good provision rule. This implies that the public good stock may be employed as a intergenerational redistributive device: in the described case, the increase of the public stock should be high at this period, since it increases the utility of the people living in the future. Note that similar kinds of intertemporal considerations are present in a second-best case as well, though in a muted form, as the evaluation of $\frac{\rho^{t+1}}{\rho^t}$ becomes more complicated.

The modified dynamic Samuelson rule encompasses both intra- and intergenerational distributional concerns. These concerns arise from the fact that the redistributional capacity of the government is restricted. Given these circumstances, it is usual, as discussed in Chapter 13, in the public economics literature to ask if there are some special conditions under which the second-best optimality rule reduces to the simple, first-best one. Were this the case, the public good provision rule would become much more simplified. Christiansen (1981) and Boadway and Keen (1993) show that if consumer preferences are weakly separable between goods and leisure, the first-best rule for the public good provision remains valid also for the second-best case under non-linear income taxation.

In the present model with the public good affecting the production function and the level of wages as well, these separability conditions do not hold. The following corollary summarizes this:

Corollary 2. Under the optimal income and savings taxation scheme, if consumer preferences are weakly separable between goods and leisure, the dynamic analogue of the public good provision rule does not reduce to the first-best intragenerational Samuelson principle.

The notion of the first-best rule in the intragenerational sense refers to a situation where only the direct effects of the public good are taken into account in the social marginal benefit of the public good, given in expression (19) in appendix 14.6. To put it more rigorously, the social marginal value of an incremental public in the first-best situation would then be given by $SMB_G^t \equiv \sum_i MRS_{i,GC}^t + \sum_i MRS_{i,GX}^{t-1} + F_G^t$. The dynamic Samuelson rule of Proposition 2 would still depend on intergenerational concerns, captured by the discount factors—hence, the notion of the 'intragenerational Samuelson principle'. While the separability structure mentioned in Corollary 2 makes the self-selection term disappear from the social marginal valuation of the public good [expression (19)], the last term referring to the impact of public good on wages remains in the formulation. In contrast to the results cited earlier, it is not possible to separate efficiency and equity concerns in the public good provision in conditions where standard separability assumptions are valid.

Both the capital income tax and public good provision rules depend crucially on the implications of endogenous wages. In particular, the standard rules required for decentralization of equity and efficiency concerns need to be augmented by imposing separability also in the production side of the economy. In other cases, first-best rules do not remain valid in second-best circumstances.

This section has examined the problem of optimal taxation and government expenditure in a dynamic setting combining a Mirrlees type of an optimal income tax model and an overlapping generations model, such as that used by Diamond (1965). While it is not surprising, therefore, that most of the properties of these models carry over to the present set-up, combining them makes it possible to derive some properties of optimal taxation of income from capital. In particular, it is possible to characterize the shape of an optimal tax on capital income similarly to the way in which the properties of optimal labour income taxation have been highlighted before in a static framework. Allowing the wages to be endogenously determined in the model, we also provide a rationale for distorting capital income taxation: the marginal tax rate on income from capital depends on the relative valuation between present and future consumption by true low-ability individuals and mimickers, and on the impact of capital stock on the income-earning abilities of future generations. The latter impact seems to have interesting implications: it calls for violation of production efficiency and means that the separability result derived by Ordover and Phelps (1979) does not hold within this setting.

Pirttilä and Tuomala (2001) also examined the optimal provision of a public good which is treated as a stock variable. This was addressed by deriving a dynamic analogue of the Samuelson rule of public good provision in a second-best world with distortionary labour and capital income taxation. The rule was shown to capture not only efficiency considerations, but also inter- and intragenerational redistributional concerns. As in the case of capital income taxation, the standard separability rules do not remain valid in the present set-up with endogenous wages.

14.6.3 PUBLICLY PROVIDED PRIVATE GOODS IN AN OLG FRAMEWORK

Pirttilä and Tuomala (2002) consider public provision of private goods in a genuinely dynamic overlapping generations economy. They extend the analysis into a dynamic, infinite horizon, OLG framework, where the individuals live for two periods, supplying labour in the first and retiring in the second. The purpose is to demonstrate how the extension of the production side of the economy to include a stock of publicly provided private good that preserves from period to another can affect the public provision rule. In particular, the publicly provided private good may be motivated both for intragenerational and intergenerational reasons. Many of the publicly provided goods have arguably interesting dynamic and cross-generational effects, because of financing arising from a different generation (pensions) or potential externality effects between generations (education). The government may be interested in the provision of such goods precisely because they have a special characteristic to enhance individuals, capabilities. Part of the effects of the publicly provided good can thus be modelled as a stock that preserves from period to another and provides a potentially intriguing link between the taxation of different individuals. In such a case, the decision rule for the publicly provided private good involves efficiency and distributional considerations both within and between generations.[65]

The intergenerational effects of public provision are clearly essential in public provision of pensions, for example. However, important implications also arise in the context of education: public provision of education not only affects efficiency of redistribution within one cohort; it can also have lasting effects because of accumulation of knowledge in the economy. These impacts are of key interest in this section, which focuses on the role of public provision (say education) in an OLG framework.[66]

What is novel in the OLG set-up are the intertemporal productivity effects that arise from the presence of human capital in the model. The level of education, or human capital, that is obtained at a given period partially preserves to the following periods. In the subsequent periods, therefore, present investments in education affect first the wage structure and second the overall productivity of the economy. These impacts are not taken into account by the individuals themselves in their educational decisions. Therefore, besides the present period effects, there can be intergenerational reasons for public provision of education.[67]

If future productivity effects are large enough, public provision can be welfare-improving even if we consider the case where no impacts arise from the (static) crowding out mechanism. Finally, it is interesting to note that some of these impacts may of course partially offset each other: there can be trade-offs between within-period impacts and benefits to the future generations. Balancing these requires comparison of the shadow value of public funds and the importance of the self-selection constraint in different periods, because the valuation of future benefits depends, among other things, on these terms.

[65] One of the key interest areas in the recent economic research following the asymmetric information approach to optimal redistribution has been the attempt to explain the role of public provision of private goods (such as education, health care, day care and care of the elderly) as part of a redistributive set of instruments (see e.g. Blomquist and Christiansen (1995), (1998a), and (1998b), Boadway and Marchand (1995), and Boadway, Marchand, and Sato (1998)). All these studies model the production side in a simple way with exogenous wage rates for different types of households in a static setting.

[66] For an early contribution in the intertemporal context, see Hare and Ulph (1981). The crucial element in their model is imperfect capital markets.

[67] It is interesting to compare the dynamic provision rule of the publicly provided private good to the dynamic Samuelson rule of a pure public good, analysed above and in Pirttilä and Tuomala (2001). The key difference is that if a public good is durable, its effects on the utilities of future generations must be taken into account directly, whereas the publicly provided private good affects directly only the utilities of current generation. The dynamic impacts in the private good case arise from the potential production side implications.

APPENDIX 14.2 TAXATION, THE DYNAMIC FORMULATION OF THE SAMUELSON RULE, AND THE OLG MODEL

If we ignore the generation that is old at period 1,[68] we are now in a position to write the Lagrangean for the government optimization problem as follows:

$$\begin{aligned} L = {} & W[U(c_1^1, x_1^1, y_1^1, G^1) + U(c_2^1, x_2^1, y_2^1, G^1), \ldots] \\ & + \sum_{t=1}^{\infty} \lambda^t [U(c_2^t, x_2^t, y_2^t, G^t) - U(c_1^t, x_1^t, \omega^t y_1^t, G^t)] \\ & + \sum_{t=1}^{\infty} \rho^t [F(k^t, y_1^t, y_2^t, G^t) + k^t - c^t - x^{t-1} - pg^t - k^{t+1}] \\ & + \sum_{t=1}^{\infty} \mu^t [\beta G^t + g^{t+1} - G^{t+1}] \end{aligned} \tag{1}$$

For a given level of the public good, the first-order conditions at an exemplary date t revealing the optimal tax structure are the following:

$$k^t : \rho^t (F_k^t + 1) - \rho^{t-1} - \lambda^t \hat{U}_{2,y}^t \frac{\partial \omega^t}{\partial k^t} y_1^t = 0, \tag{2}$$

$$c_1^t : \frac{\partial W}{\partial U^t} U_{1,c}^t - \lambda^t \hat{U}_{2,c}^t - \rho^t = 0, \tag{3}$$

$$c_2^t : \left(\frac{\partial W}{\partial U^t} + \lambda^t\right) U_{2,c}^t - \rho^t = 0 \tag{4}$$

$$x_1^t : \frac{\partial W}{\partial U^t} U_{1,x}^t - \lambda^t \hat{U}_{2,x}^t - \rho^{t+1} = 0, \tag{5}$$

$$x_2^t : \left(\frac{\partial W}{\partial U^t} + \lambda^t\right) U_{2,x}^t - \rho^{t+1} = 0, \tag{6}$$

$$l_1^t : \frac{\partial W}{\partial U^t} U_{1,y}^t - \lambda^t \hat{U}_{2,y}^t \left(\omega^t + \frac{\partial \omega^t}{\partial y_1^t} y_1^t\right) + \rho^t F_{y_1}^t = 0, \tag{7}$$

$$l_2^t : \left(\frac{\partial W}{\partial U^t} + \lambda^t\right) U_{2,y}^t - \lambda^t \hat{U}_{2,y}^t \frac{\partial \omega^t}{\partial y_2^t} y_1^t + \rho^t F_{y_2}^t = 0, \tag{8}$$

where the hat-terms refer to the type-2 when mimicking the choice of the type-1.

[68] It is a usual feature of dynamic optimal taxation exercises that it is optimal for the government to collect the bulk of the revenue by confiscating the capital stock at the outset. We want to abstract from these complications by leaving out the generation 0. For a good overview on these issues, see Domeij and Klein (1998).

Proof of proposition 1: The marginal income tax rate for the high-ability type may be deduced by dividing (8) by (4) and combining the result with the property in (1):

$$MTR(n_2^t y_2^t) = \frac{\lambda^t \hat{U}_{2,l}^t}{\rho^t n_2^t} \frac{\partial \omega^t}{\partial y_2^t} y_1^t, \tag{9}$$

which is negative, since $\hat{U}_{2,l}^t$ is negative and the increase in the labour supply of the high-ability type increases the relative wage of the low-ability workers (i.e. $\frac{\partial \omega^t}{\partial y_2^t} > 0$). The corresponding tax rate for the low-ability type follows from dividing (7) by (3) and some rearrangements:

$$MTR(n_1^t y_1^t) = \frac{\lambda^t \hat{U}_{2,c}^t}{\rho^t n_1^t} \left(\frac{\hat{U}_{2,y}^t}{\hat{U}_{2,c}^t} \omega^t - \frac{U_{2,y}^t}{U_{2,c}^t} \right) + \frac{\lambda^t \hat{U}_{2,y}^t}{\rho^t n_1^t} \frac{\partial \omega^t}{\partial y_1^t} y_1^t. \tag{10}$$

To sign this expression, note first that the latter term, referring to the endogenous wage structure, is positive, since increasing labour supply of the low-ability type decreases their relative wage rate ($\frac{\partial \omega^t}{\partial y_2^t}$<0). The term in the brackets is positive, because of the standard single-crossing property: the indifference curve for the high-ability type at a given point in (income, consumption) -space is assumed to be flatter than that of the low-ability type. This results from the fact that the type-2 households find it easier to transform leisure to consumption because of their higher ability. It may be shown that under the single-crossing assumption, the marginal rate of substitution for the mimicker is determined by $\frac{\hat{U}_{2,y}^t}{\hat{U}_{2,c}^t} \omega^t$, and that the term in the brackets is positive. Combining the effect of the two forces in (13), the marginal income tax rate for type-1 households is positive. *QED.*

Proof of proposition 2: Individual optimization between the present and future consumption, for a given after-income-tax income, implies that the marginal savings tax rate (with s_i^t denoting the savings of household i) may be expressed by:

$$MTR(s_i^t) = -\frac{U_{i,c}^t}{U_{i,x}^t} + 1 + r^{t+1}. \tag{11}$$

Note next that leading and rearranging (2) yields $\rho^{t+1} = \left(\rho^t + \lambda^{t+1} \hat{U}_{2,y}^{t+1} \frac{\partial \omega^{t+1}}{\partial k^{t+1}} y_1^{t+1} \right) / (1 + r^{t+1})$. By means of this property and the one in (11), and dividing (4) by (6), we obtain

$$MTR(s_2^t) = \frac{\lambda^{t+1} \hat{U}_{2,y}^{t+1}}{\rho^t} \frac{\partial \omega^{t+1}}{\partial k^{t+1}} y_1^{t+1} \frac{U_{2,c}^t}{U_{2,x}^t}. \tag{12}$$

This expression reveals that if an increase in savings (and hence in the level of capital) reduces the relative wage rate of the low-ability households, it is optimal to impose a positive marginal savings (=capital income) tax on type-2 households. The MTR for savings of the low-ability type may be derived in a similar manner. Divide first (3) by (5) and use the properties above to get:

$$\frac{U_{1,c}^{t}}{U_{1,x}^{t}}\left[\frac{1+\frac{\lambda^{t+1}\hat{U}_{2,l}^{t+1}}{\rho^{t}}\frac{\partial\omega^{t}}{\partial k^{t}}y_{1}^{t+1}}{1+r^{t+1}}\right]=\frac{\lambda^{t}\hat{U}_{2,x}^{t}}{\rho^{t}}\left(\frac{\hat{U}_{2,c}^{t}}{\hat{U}_{2,x}^{t}}-\frac{U_{1,c}^{t}}{U_{1,x}^{t}}\right)+1 \tag{13}$$

This enables us to write the tax rate as follows:

$$MTR(s_{1}^{t})=\frac{\lambda^{t+1}\hat{U}_{2,l}^{t+1}}{\rho^{t}}\frac{\partial\omega^{t+1}}{\partial k^{t+1}}l_{1}^{t+1}\frac{U_{1,c}^{t}}{U_{1,x}^{t}}-\frac{\lambda^{t}\hat{U}_{2,x}^{t}}{\rho^{t}}\left(\frac{\hat{U}_{2,c}^{t}}{\hat{U}_{2,x}^{t}}-\frac{U_{1,c}^{t}}{U_{1,x}^{t}}\right)(1+r^{t+1}). \tag{14}$$

This expression encompasses two distinct influences: the first term on the right is analogous to the expression in the MTR for savings of the high-income type, and captures the effect of extra capital on the relative wage rate. If $\frac{\partial\omega^{t+1}}{\partial k^{t+1}}$ is negative, the endogenous wage term in (14) implies a positive marginal tax rate on savings, and *vice versa* for a positive $\frac{\partial\omega^{t+1}}{\partial k^{t+1}}$. The latter term in (14), arising from the self-selection considerations, becomes positive (negative) if a mimicker has a higher (lower) valuation of future consumption than a true type-1 representative. Clearly, in the case where the two impacts have different signs, the MTR for savings of type 2 remains ambiguous. *QED*.

The optimality conditions are the following:

$$\begin{aligned}G^{t}:\ &\frac{\partial W}{\partial U^{t}}(U_{1,G}^{t}+U_{2,G}^{t})+\frac{\partial W}{\partial U^{t-1}}(U_{1,G}^{t-1}+U_{2,G}^{t-1})+\lambda^{t}(U_{2,G}^{t}-\hat{U}_{2,G}^{t})\\&+\lambda^{t-1}(U_{2,G}^{t-1}-\hat{U}_{2,G}^{t-1})-\lambda^{t}\hat{U}_{2,l}^{t}\frac{\partial\omega^{t}}{\partial G^{t}}l_{1}^{t}+\rho^{t}F_{G}^{t}+\mu^{t}\beta-\mu^{t-1}=0,\end{aligned} \tag{15}$$

$$g^{t}:\ -\rho^{t}p+\mu^{t-1}=0. \tag{16}$$

Note that the level of the public good affects at the same time t both the young and the old living in that period, and it also influences the production possibilities and the relative wage in the economy. Equation (15) may be reformulated by substituting from (3), (4), (5), and (6), and by defining the marginal rate of substitution between the public good and the consumption when young and the consumption when old as $MRS_{i,GC}^{t}=\frac{U_{i,G}^{t}}{U_{i,c}^{t}}$ and $MRS_{i,GX}^{t}=\frac{U_{i,G}^{t}}{U_{i,x}^{t}}$, respectively. Conducting these operations in (15) yields:

$$\begin{aligned}&MRS_{1,GC}^{t}\left(\frac{\lambda^{t}\hat{U}_{2,c}^{t}}{\rho^{t}}+1\right)+MRS_{1,GX}^{t-1}\left(\frac{\lambda^{t-1}\hat{U}_{2,x}^{t-1}}{\rho^{t}}+1\right)+MRS_{2,GC}^{t}+MRS_{2,GX}^{t-1}\\&-\frac{\lambda^{t}\hat{U}_{2,G}^{t}}{\rho^{t}}-\frac{\lambda^{t-1}\hat{U}_{2,G}^{t-1}}{\rho^{t}}-\frac{\lambda^{t}\hat{U}_{2,l}^{t}}{\rho^{t}}\frac{\partial\omega^{t}}{\partial G^{t}}l_{1}^{t}+F_{G}^{t}+\frac{\mu^{t}}{\rho^{t}}\beta-\frac{\mu^{t-1}}{\rho^{t}}=0.\end{aligned} \tag{17}$$

Using λ_*^t as shorthand for $\frac{\lambda^t \hat{U}_{2,c}^t}{\rho^t}$ and $\lambda_\#^{t-1}$ for $\frac{\lambda^{t-1} \hat{U}_{2,x}^{t-1}}{\rho^t}$, (17) may be rewritten as:

$$SMB_G^t + \frac{\mu^t}{\rho^t}\beta = \frac{\mu^{t-1}}{\rho^t}, \tag{18}$$

where

$$\begin{aligned} SMB_G^t \equiv & \sum_i MRS_{i,GC}^t + \sum_i MRS_{i,GX}^{t-1} + \lambda_*^t (MRS_{2,GC}^t - M\hat{R}S_{1,GC}^t) \\ & + \lambda_\#^{t-1}(MRS_{2,GX}^{t-1} - M\hat{R}S_{1,GX}^{t-1}) + F_G^t - \frac{\lambda^t \hat{U}_{2,y}^t}{\rho^t}\frac{\partial \omega^t}{\partial G^t} y_1^t. \end{aligned} \tag{19}$$

According to equation (18), the shadow value of the public good at one period should be equal to the value of an incremental unit of the public good (SMB_G^t) plus the shadow value of the public good next period. To arrive at the final formulation of the dynamic public good provision rule, lead (18) first by one period, then two, and so on, and substitute these values again in (18).[69] Combining the result with (18) enables us to state proposition 2 in the text.

14.7 **Other cases for capital income tax**

There are still many other considerations related to capital income taxation. In a multi-period model with a rising age–earnings profile, individuals might be liquidity-constrained early in life if they need to finance houses, durable goods, and human capital accumulation, or to hold assets to insure against uncertainty in the length of life. In these circumstances, postponing tax liabilities until later on in life relaxes the liquidity constraint. A number of papers have shown that the optimal tax on capital income can become positive when capital market imperfections are introduced, even in models with no inheritance. Typically, the optimal capital income tax is positive because it is a way to redistribute from those with no credit constraints (the owners of capital) toward those with credit constraints (non-owners of capital). Aiyagari (1995) and Chamley (2001) make this point formally in a model with borrowing constrained infinitely lived agents facing labour income risk. They show that optimal capital income taxation is positive when consumption is positively correlated with savings. They do not compute numerical values for optimal capital tax rates. Farhi and Werning (2011) also propose a quantitative calibration of an infinite horizon model with borrowing constraints but they find small welfare gains from capital taxation. In contrast, Conesa, Kitao, and Krueger (2009) calibrate an optimal tax OLG lifecycle model with uninsurable idiosyncratic labour productivity shocks and borrowing constraints, and find capital income tax is

[69] In other words, we simply add the first-order conditions for the public good evaluated at different periods together to obtain the present value of an increase in the public good.

36 per cent and labour income tax is 23 per cent in their preferred specification. The main effect seems to be that capital income tax is a way to shift the tax burden onto older cohorts and to alleviate the liquidity constraints faced by younger cohorts. Of course, in principle, this could also be achieved by using age-dependent taxation. In fact, public pension systems do this in practice. Jacobs and Bovenberg (2010) demonstrated that capital taxes are optimally positive even in the absence of binding credit constraints, since the capital tax reduces the disincentives of the labour tax on human capital investments. Alvarez et al (1992) show, in a representative individual two-period context with a constant wage rate in the two periods, that optimal labour income tax should fall with age if the interest rate exceeds the utility discount factor. If labour income taxes must be constant over time, capital income should face a positive tax rate if the interest rate exceeds the utility discount factor, and vice versa. Cremer, Lozachmeur, and Pestieau (2010) show that if expected longevity is increasing in skills, tax on capital income is desirable.

As we see in Chapter 12, the Atkinson–Stiglitz result is often used as an argument against the use of differentiated commodity taxation as a redistributive device. Direct income transfers (as a part of an optimal income tax scheme) would be sufficient instead. When the government seeks to minimize poverty, even with separable preferences between consumption of present and future periods and leisure, taxation of saving is optimal. As noted in Pirttilä and Tuomala (2004), this result can also be linked to the taxation of savings. When different commodities are interpreted as consumption in different points in time, the Atkinson and Stiglitz (1976) result implies that savings should not be taxed. A plausible case in practice is one where the poverty index is measured based on current consumption. This measurement, which can be defended at least if poverty is transitory, would imply a relative encouragement of present over future consumption, in other words, a positive tax rate on savings. Overall, there are reasonably strong cases for capital income tax. Taken together, these results suggest that capital income tax rates should be positive (see Banks and Diamond 2010).

15 Discussion and conclusions

The optimal tax framework developed by Mirrlees (1971) has dominated the economics of taxation for the past forty years. It provides an analytical framework for thinking through the relationship between inherent inequality and the extent of redistribution. Three elements of the model are useful for this purpose. First is the concept of inherent inequality, reflecting, among other things, skilled/unskilled wage differentials, asset inequality, and social norms. If there is no intervention by the government, the inherent inequality will be fully reflected in the disposable income. However, if the government wants to intervene—as seems to be the case in developed countries—it will find the second component of the Mirrlees model, the egalitarian objectives of the government. And if the government tries to redistribute income from high-income people to low-income people, there will be incentive and disincentive effects. In other words, the redistribution policy is the product of circumstances and objectives.

In fact, some of the basic features of redistribution in OECD countries can be explained through the Mirrlees model. Tanninen and Tuomala (2005) examine the relationship between the inherent inequality and the extent of redistribution by utilizing the Luxembourg Income Study (LIS) database. This database provides both market (pre-tax) and disposable income distributions for a number of OECD countries over the past two or three decades. They find that redistribution in these countries is positively associated with inherent inequality up to the mid-1990s. If the inherent inequality increases (decreases) for any given incentive effects and the degree of espoused egalitarianism, so will the society's redistributive effort. The authors' empirical results are based on the assumption that the degree of espoused egalitarianism has remained constant over the period considered. Namely, there have not been significant changes in the overall progressivity of the OECD countries between 1985 and 1994 (see Messere 1998). Of course, distributional objectives differ from one country to another and from one government to another. There is, however, some recent individual-country evidence that there could have been a shift in norms, causing government to become less willing to finance transfers and to levy progressive taxes (e.g. in the UK and Finland; see Atkinson 1999), leading to reductions in the extent of redistribution. One could argue, in line with Atkinson (1999), that these kinds of changes have been episodic rather than time-trend, and are therefore rather difficult to justify for example in the context of median voter models. Thus, future research should be focused on the role of the egalitarian objectives of government, which is also an important component of the Mirrlees model.

A key insight of the optimal tax theory is that the different elements of the tax system cannot be determined without at the same time determining the whole optimum tax and expenditure system. The Mirrlees Review notes (2011, p. 2):

> the crucial insight that the tax system needs to be seen as just that—a system. While we address the impact of each tax separately for simplicity of exposition, we focus throughout on the impact of the system as a whole—how taxes fit together and how the system as a whole achieves government's goals.

In other words, it makes it possible to focus on some element of the tax system, but at the same time we should be sure that no proposals can be valid out of the context of the rest of the tax system. Keeping in mind this insight, we now discuss some policy lessons of optimal tax theory.

Several types of low-income support programmes are used in practice in developed countries. Each of them can be justified by a different theory and set of assumptions. The numerical simulations carried out in the Mirrlees model predict that optimal transfer at bottom takes the form of a negative income tax; the optimal income support programme is characterized by a guaranteed income for those without earnings and a positive phasing-out rate of the support as earnings increase. The level of the guaranteed income depends positively on government's distributional preferences, the curvature of utility over consumption, and the shape of the pre-tax income distribution, and negatively on government revenue requirement and the elasticity of substitution between consumption and leisure. The level of the phasing-out or withdrawal marginal rate also depends positively on government's distributional preferences, the shape of the pre-tax income distribution, the curvature of utility over consumption, and government revenue requirements, and negatively on the elasticity of substitution between consumption and leisure.

As is well known, the older literature on optimal income taxation did not provide support for the general presumption that the taxation of income should be progressive throughout, in the sense of increasing marginal tax rates. Surprisingly, numerical examples in most cases give a negative answer to this, with optimal income tax schedules typically being progressive at low levels of income and then regressive from a certain point onwards. Two main exceptions to this general shape have been noticed in the older literature: one is that with a Pareto distribution of skills, Mirrlees (1971) found rather high asymptotic marginal taxes (about 30–60 per cent) for the thick and slowly falling Paretian upper tail, in contrast with fairly low marginal taxes at high incomes (15~20 per cent, asymptotically zero) for the more rapidly falling lognormal (both for elasticities of substitution between consumption and leisure not greater than one). Given that, the results of Diamond (1998) and Saez (2001)—the marginal tax rates are increasing in the upper part of income distribution—are not perhaps that surprising. Another exception is when the supply of labour is positively sloped at all high levels of (net) income (Mirrlees 1971, case (i) on p. 189), in which case not much money needs to be left to the high-income people from their marginal earnings to have them always working more the more able they are, thus making optimal marginal tax rates tend asymptotically to one, so as to exploit these taxpayers' revenue and/or redistributive possibilities.

As mentioned in the introduction, the increasing share of top income earners in total income has been a notable feature of the changes in income inequality in many advanced countries. We also noted above that the cuts in top marginal tax rates have had a crucial role in this evolution. How high should the top marginal tax rate be? In Chapter 4 we provide some answers based on the standard model. How to assess these results for the top marginal tax rate? It is clear that it depends on whether elements left out of the standard model change them. There are good reasons to suspect that the labour market of top income earners deviates from the standard competitive model in a number of important respects. They are not paid their marginal product. For example, as Persson and Sandmo (2005) argue, a 'tournament' model where wages are determined not by productivity, but by one's productivity relative to other workers, would be more relevant for the salaries of top executives. Or, if the economic activity at high incomes is primarily socially unproductive rent-seeking, then it would be plausible to impose higher marginal rates at top income levels than those calculated above. Based on rent-seeking by executives, and how cutting top rates of tax encouraged this rent-seeking, Piketty, Saez, and Stantcheva (2014) provide an alternative model that they call a 'compensation bargaining' model. They argue that with lower tax rates, the CEO has a much greater incentive to put lots of effort into the bargaining process with the company. They, rather than the tax authority, will receive the rewards from being successful. The paper also shows that there is a 'clear correlation between the drop in top marginal tax rates and the surge in top income shares' (p. 232). Furthermore, they have microeconomic evidence that CEOs' pay for firms' performance (such as stock options) outside the CEO's control is more important when tax rates are low. Lockwood, Nathanson, and Weyl (2012, p. 1) in turn argue that 'If higher-paying professions (e.g. finance and management) generate less positive net externalities than lower-paying professions (e.g. public service and education) taxation may enhance efficiency'. In their model, marginal tax rates may be Pigouvian taxes on externality-generating activities. Interestingly, in their model, high elasticities of switching careers, in response to incentives, may support progressive taxation rather than working against it (see also Rothschild and Scheuer 2012). Our numerical examples on top tax rates in Chapter 7 just take into account the externality effect. In fact, the comments made by Arrow (1978) in his critique of Nozick (1974) capture, essentially, all these above cases. It is useful to reiterate the quotation presented in Chapter 2 here:

> There are large gains to social integration above and beyond what the individuals and subgroups could achieve on their own. The owners of scarce personal assets do not have a private use of these assets which is considerable, it is only their value in a large system which makes these assets valuable, hence, there is a surplus created by the existence of society as such which is available for redistribution. (Arrow 1978, pp. 278–9)

Finally, it is somewhat misleading to count corporate mega-salaries as earned or labour income. Robert Solow in turn made an important observation on this in his review of Piketty's book for *The New Republic* (2014): 'It is pretty clear that the class of super-managers belongs socially and politically with the rentiers, not with the larger body of salaried and independent professionals and middle managers'.

Atkinson (2014) in turn emphasizes that marginal tax rates are not only about incentives; they are just as much governed by notions of fairness. This means that we have to consider social objectives other than revenue maximization. Fairness implies that people should keep a reasonable share of what they make. Hence Atkinson (2014) suggests that the marginal tax rate for the rich should be no different from that applied to the incomes of poor. In the UK case this means that the top rate should also be 65 per cent.

The U-shaped pattern is very close to the marginal rate structure commonly observed in many countries. This pattern has sometimes been referred to as a tax structure which sets the floor for poverty and the ceiling to riches on egalitarian grounds. High marginal tax rates at lower income levels are due to the interaction between the various schemes for income support and income taxation at the lower end of the income scale. The U-shape of tax schedules in Saez (2001) was a direct consequence of the U-shaped pattern of distribution ratio. One of the key lessons from our numerical simulations in Chapter 5 is that without assuming constant labour-supply elasticity, as in Diamond (1998) and Saez (2001), it is difficult to find the U-shaped pattern of the marginal income tax rates over the entire distribution of wages. Our numerical simulations in Chapter 5 show that it is either a sufficiently high pre-tax inequality or a combination of sufficiently high pre-tax inequality and sufficiently low revenue requirement that leads to a pattern of optimally increasing marginal tax rates. In particular, Tuomala (2010) found that the utility function quadratic in consumption and with upper bound on consumption necessarily implies a concave budget constraint in the Mirrlees (1971) model. In other words, the marginal tax rates are increasing in income, at least in the utilitarian case. Hence Tuomala's (1990, p. 14) conclusion that 'it is difficult (if at all possible) to find a convincing argument for a progressive marginal tax rate structure throughout' in the Mirrlees model has turned out to be too hasty.

Our numerical results also indicate that it is a sufficiently high inequality aversion (maximin, 'Rawlsian') that leads to a pattern of optimally declining marginal tax rates. This may sound surprising, but we have to remember that a high marginal tax rate as such has no valuable distributional function. Its role is to increase the average tax rates higher up the income scale. It is also worth noting two things related to the maximin case. The declining marginal tax rates are not surprising, due to the fact that social welfare weights are concentrated only on the least well-off. Second, the extent of redistribution is still much larger in the maximin case than in the other social objectives considered. Furthermore, we show that the revenue requirement has a central role in determining the extent of redistribution and the level of the guaranteed minimum income.

There is a tendency to focus on the efficiency costs and to ignore differences in distributional objectives. In their survey in the *Journal of Economic Perspectives*, Mankiw, Weinzierl, and Yagan (2009, p. 148) say explicitly that they regard these differences as of 'secondary importance, and one would not go far wrong in thinking of the social planner as a classic "linear" utilitarian'. In this book we have examined the effect of the several alternative criterion of social preferences. It turns out to be so that the differences between different social objectives are of far from 'secondary importance'.

The substantial growth in top income shares over the past few decades in rich countries, together with the fact that, over the same period, top tax rates in virtually all these countries have been falling rapidly, has led to the obvious question of the appropriate levels of taxation of top incomes. At the same time we have seen a shift in the burden of taxation from the top to further down in the income distribution. In Chapter 4 there was a lot of emphasis on top marginal tax rates. It is true that much of the literature trades on marginal tax rates, but the computational techniques can also be used to say something about average rates. In Chapter 5 we considered how the optimal income tax schedule changes when top income inequality increases. Our numerical results suggest that this shift in tax burden from top to further down cannot be justified in the standard Mirrlees model, which embodies conventional assumptions about inequality aversion and the trade-off between equity and efficiency. In fact, an appropriate response to rising top income inequality is a shift toward a more progressive income tax system.

The Mirrlees model focuses only on intensive-margin response of labour supply. But empirical literature shows that participation labour-supply responses may be most important especially for low incomes. Diamond (1980), Saez (2002), and Laroque (2005) incorporate such extensive labour-supply responses into an optimal income tax model. By introducing fixed job packages (cannot smoothly choose earnings), refundable tax credits such as EITC are desirable in the Saez extensive-margin model because they redistribute more money to those on a low income and save the government money by getting people away from welfare benefits. In the Mirrlees intensive-margin model, the second effect is ruled out. Creating an EITC would always cost government more through intensive responses. It is always preferable to redistribute by giving more money to the lowest income. The extensive model can be extended to allow both intensive and extensive responses, allowing higher types to switch to lower jobs. Hence the general formula for optimal tax is a function of both intensive and extensive margin elasticity.

There are several benefits in the NIT, such as no one being omitted, low administration costs, and no stigma. On the side of costs are efficiency losses from less work. Benefits of the EITC are that it offers more incentive to work and low administration costs. The costs of the EITC are efficiency loss in phase-out range and no coverage of non-workers. On the basis of the existing research literature it is too early for a final verdict on the choice between the EITC and the negative income tax. There are features missing both in Mirrlees (1971) and Saez (2002). In these models the incidence and efficiency losses of taxes and transfers have been analysed in isolation from expenditure side. There is now a relatively large literature that has attempted to explain the role of public provision of private goods or in-kind transfers (such as education, health care, day care, and care of the elderly) as part of a redistributive set of instruments.[1] Blomquist, Christiansen, and Micheletto (2009) show that the negligence on the expenditure side may imply a serious misperception of the effects of marginal tax rates. The reason is that part of the marginal tax may in fact be payment for publicly provided goods and reflects a cost that the consumers should bear in order to face the proper incentives. Hence, part of the marginal tax has the same role as a market price; it conveys information about the real social cost of working more hours. Their main result is that there is a gain in efficiency where public provision of such a service replaces market purchases. Hence, it might very well be that economies with higher marginal tax rates have less severe distortions than economies with lower marginal tax rates.

Jacquet and Van de Gaer (2011) make the interesting finding that the equality of opportunity approach tends to favour the negative income tax against the EITC. This is an important result because it shows that the choice between the EITC and the NIT is not only on the nature of labour-supply margins (extensive or intensive) but very much dependent on social objectives. In other words, it is not solely a question of 'social engineering'.

The effects of taxes and benefits on behaviour that we have considered so far are short-term—for example, to the extent to which a tax credit might encourage more people to take paid work. In addition to these short-term impacts, there may also be long-term effects. But what effect will the EITC have in the long run, perhaps by influencing the decisions people make about education or training? Since it reduces the financial reward from seeking higher wages, one might expect it to reduce the incentive to invest in training. We know little about these effects and they may be more significant than many of those that we do understand much better.

If relative income matters, how does this affect income tax progressivity? Chapter 7 provides three sets of answers to this general question. First, it supports the conclusion in the literature that relativity leads to higher marginal tax rates. Second, by and large, we find support for greater progressivity, defined as the steepness of the rise of the marginal tax rate schedule, as relativity concern increases. Third, none of the papers in the literature, to our knowledge, examines the interplay of relativity and inequality in determining the optimal structure of taxes. Our special analytical cases and more general numerical calculations support the conclusion that higher inequality dampens the positive impact of greater relativity on the level and the progression of marginal tax rates.

Should we adopt the low-income support programme based on either targeting by income (NIT&EITC) or targeting by indicators (tagging and taxing)? Targeted programmes based not only on income information, as in NIT&EITC, but which can use

[1] See e.g. Nichols and Zeckhauser (1982), Blomquist and Christiansen (1995), (1998a), and (1998b), Boadway and Marchand (1995), Cremer-Gahvari (1997), Boadway, Marchand, and Sato (1998), and Pirttilä-Tuomala (2002).

information on characteristics that are not easily manipulable and are related to work ability such as age, disability, or families with young children could help to improve redistribution with lower efficiency costs on the margin. Tagging relaxes incentive constraint by tying the tax rate to immutable qualities. The issue of policy design is not therefore a confrontation between fully universal benefits and pure income testing; rather, the question is that of the appropriate balance of categorical and income tests.

Simulations point to two important features of the solution in tagging problems. First, the gains from the use of categorical information can quite plausibly be significant. Second, and more strikingly, the qualitative pattern of the optimal group-specific schedule may be entirely different across groups: marginal tax rates optimally decrease with income within the richer group, yet within the poorer group they optimally increase with income (over most of the income range, at least). One possible explanation for this is that inter-group transfers may imply group-specific revenue requirements for poorer groups that are very much lower than simulations have conventionally considered in the standard Mirrlees (1971) model, and optimal tax design in such circumstances may involve a generous poll subsidy recovered from the better-off by a pattern of increasing marginal tax rates over much of the income range. The differences in the shape of the ability distributions in different groups may be an equally or even more important source of the different patterns in rates. Our simulations in a single schedule case already suggest this pattern. It is also important to note that optimal marginal tax rates are lower on poorer groups. This deviates from the practice of using higher combined (tax/benefit systems) marginal rates at the phase-out range.

The large body of literature on 'tagging' shows that group-specific tax and transfer schedules improve welfare over the case where the government is restricted to a single schedule over the whole population. The central assumption, however, is that the groupings available to the government are given and fixed. But how many and which types of groups should the government choose to tag? This is the question addressed by Kanbur and Tuomala (2014). Starting with a simple framework and ending with numerical simulations based on data from Finland, they show how groupings should be formed for tagging, and provide a quantitative assessment of how group differences affect the gains from tagging. They also provide a quantitative assessment of the welfare gains from increasing the number of tagged groups. Their results are the first steps in a richer analysis of tagging which expands the question of design to the arena of choice over groups being tagged.

Do policy prescriptions differ if we adopt non-welfarist social objectives? The safest conclusion in Chapter 9—although a provisional one, because our simulations are inevitably only special cases—seems to be that a concern with income poverty does not in itself provide a strong case for marginal tax rates on the bulk of the poor that are substantially lower than expected from the perspective of the welfarist tradition. The reason for this, it seems, is that shifting from the welfarist to the non-welfarist perspective introduces two considerations that point in opposite directions. First, the case for lower marginal tax rates on the poor is strengthened by the prospect of inducing them to raise their own incomes. The non-welfarist view attaches no weight to the leisure that the poor forgo; this underlies the result that a marginal earnings subsidy on the very poorest is optimal when that individual works. Second, the case for lower marginal tax rates on the poor is weakened by the need to support the incomes of the poor, rather than their welfare, which could be 'bought' by allowing them a relatively high amount of leisure: supporting the incomes of the poor calls for relatively high marginal tax rates in the lower part of the income distribution, and the revenue needed for this support requires that sufficiently high average tax rates be imposed on higher incomes. The simulations suggest that these two opposing effects broadly offset one another.

An important simplification in the optimal income tax model with extensive and/or intensive margins is that individuals differ only in skills but not in other characteristics. In Chapter 10 we extend our discussion into a two-dimensional population. The numerical results obtained in the case where people differ not only in skill but also in some other characteristics direct us toward influences that a richer picture of population would have on the optimal income tax schedule. On the basis of numerical results in this setting, we conclude that the tax system is more redistributive compared to those obtained from the one-dimensional case. This may be surprising to those who believe that taking into account different work preferences is an argument for having less redistribution and hence lower levels of income taxation and social security payments. The problem of optimal taxation when people have different preferences raises difficult normative questions. A higher income may be due either to differences in innate productivity levels or to differences in effort. Over the past several decades, the growing body of work in social philosophy, welfare economics, and social choice theory has investigated problems of responsibility. This is often connected with an ideal of equality of opportunity. The key starting point of the literature on equality of opportunity is the idea that inequalities in outcomes can be partitioned into justifiable sources of inequality and unjustifiable sources, but, as pointed out by Kanbur and Wagstaff (2014, p. 4), 'a clean separation may not be possible, certainly empirically and perhaps even conceptually'.

If we see redistribution as a form of insurance, then a relevant distinction can be made between redistribution before and after the 'veil' of ignorance. In the Rawlsian original position, redistribution is carried out between people whose identity is—hypothetically—not yet known. Appeal to such a principle is an appeal to our moral intuition. But where individuals face randomness in their incomes, social insurance may be in the interest of identified individuals. For some reason, Mirrlees (1974) has received less attention than Mirrlees (1971). One reason (e.g. Kaplow 1991) is that government may not be better than the private market in providing such insurance.[2,3] In adverse

[2] For two potential approaches to addressing private insurance provision see Golosov and Tsyvinski (2006) and Chetty and Saez (2010).

[3] The trouble with this is that it assumes a world of perfectly competitive and perfectly clearing markets, but in such a theoretical framework we find none of the contingencies for which the social insurance exists.

selection (e.g. Mirrlees 1971) models, only government can improve redistributive outcomes once abilities (skills) are revealed to individuals. If, in turn, differences in income are a result only of luck and have nothing to do with ability, then the optimal income tax may well involve taxing top incomes at very high marginal rates. Since the after-tax reward falls, this weakens the incentive to work of top income-earning people. But the chances of becoming a top-income individual (which depend only on luck here) are pretty low anyway, so taxing top incomes at a high rate would not really discourage much effort from those hoping to become one of those at the top.

The findings in a model of optimal non-linear income taxation under income uncertainty, where the preferences are modelled along the lines of prospect theory, have potentially important implications. For income-taxation models, the optimality of full insurance around or below the reference point suggests that high marginal tax rates at low incomes may not necessarily be as harmful as is sometimes claimed. In fact, such a system supports organizing a minimum income level through e.g. social assistance.

Since calculations require simplification, the simplicity of the model is not in itself subject to apology. But we should reassess some of the considerations that have been simplified away or might be thought to have been ignored. Some people may choose to work even when they could receive more income support if they did not work. This is not surprising, because a certain amount of work adds interest to life and helps self-respect. People and jobs vary greatly in the extent to which work is intrinsically desirable. Does this imply higher marginal rates and guaranteed income? It may be imposed as a prior constraint that everyone should derive financial gain from working. If this is the case, then solutions to the low-income or basic income design problem which has the property that at the optimum some people choose not to work will be ruled out. The support scheme may then be constrained to offer a level of guaranteed income which on other grounds would be regarded as inadequate.

On top of the income tax, the government has access to other forms to redistribute income—such as commodity taxation, public goods, and public provision of private goods (education, health care, social services). Can the government design a better redistribution system with the help of these additional instruments? Atkinson and Stiglitz (1976) considerably played down the potential role of differentiated commodity tax rates as a redistributive device. Although such preference structure required for this result is not likely to be empirically valid, optimal tax theory is quite often seen to provide a limited role for commodity taxation in redistribution. Much policy advice has similarly argued that the scope of redistribution achieved by differentiated commodity tax rates is relatively minor and similar impacts could be more easily obtained by income-based targeting. In the optimal tax literature, individual behaviour is largely modelled by utility maximization and social welfare is typically based on welfarism, i.e. assessed in terms of individual utilities. It is this kind of analysis that lies behind the policy recommendations in the Mirrlees Review such as the 'strong case for broadening the VAT base and moving towards a uniform rate' (p. 229). Yet most countries continue to use differential commodity tax rates. There are several considerations that support differential goods taxation in the welfarist tradition. Examples include differences in unobserved endowments of some commodities; differences in preferences; differences in the need for particular goods; differences in labour utilization in producing commodities. In the non-welfarist context (e.g. the aim of the tax policy is to minimize poverty), there is no reason to suppose that influencing income is better than affecting the consumption of the commodities. The poverty index depends directly on the consumption of some commodities, and if it is in the interest of the government to promote their consumption, then this also implies that income-based targeting is not necessarily superior to targeting based on consumption goods.

All above results are based on the assumption of perfect competition. Would the existence of imperfect competition change our conclusions on the optimal design of commodity taxation? There are good reasons to believe they could change. As explained by Auerbach and Hines (2003, p.15), the condition for an optimal tax on an imperfectly competitive market 'carries precisely the interpretation . . . for the tax conditions in the presence of externalities. Intuitively, the "externality" in the case of imperfect competition is the outcome of the oligopolistic output selection, resulting in the extra mark-up'. In fact, this observation implies that externalities are much more widespread than what we considered in Chapter 12. It is not just the environmental harmful goods (pollution) or alcohol and tobacco, but also externalities across many industries.

Much of the activities of modern welfare or social state are related to provision of private goods (pensions, education, health care, childcare, care of the elderly, etc.). Redistribution is one, although not the only, reason why these intrinsically private goods are publicly provided, whereas the share of pure public goods is small (general administration, defence, etc.). Introducing additional distortionary policies, which would not be used in a first-best world without asymmetric information, can be useful in a second-best situation if they help mitigate the distortions stemming from the distortionary income taxation. In other words, public provision can be an efficient complement to the tax-transfer system as a way to design a better redistribution system. This is based on the notion that in a second-best world, quantity controls can be welfare-improving. We can find several welfare-theoretic arguments that may conceivably support a role for public provision of private goods. For example, externalities, scale economies, transaction costs, and merit-good arguments provide some reasons for public provision. There are also non-welfarist reasons for public provision or subsidizing, say, health care, education, and housing. As previously noted, the publicly provided goods typically affect people's capability to function in society and the labour market. Amartya Sen's capability approach might be more plausible in this context than maximizing social welfare as the proper objective for the government. It is clear that provision of public goods and publicly provided goods has an important role in guaranteeing many aspects of capabilities. Hence the government should be concerned with the distribution of capabilities. How should we modify the rules of public provision if we take into account not only willingness to pay but also the contribution to capabilities? This is an important research topic for the future.

The literature has also argued that not only public provision but also public production can be an efficient complement to the tax-transfer system as a way to design a better redistribution system. By employing relatively more low-skilled than skilled labour in public production, low-skilled labour becomes scarcer in the private sector, and the relative wage of low-skilled labour in the private sector increases. Because of the reduction in wage inequality, the need to redistribute income by distorting income taxation decreases. These observations may provide one explanation for the large proportions of the public sector and the combination of public production and public provision in some countries, particularly in the Nordic countries. It also implies that a larger public sector may not necessarily hamper efficiency as much as is sometimes thought.

One of the limitations of the standard income tax model is that it does not address intertemporal problems. In an intertemporal setting, capital income taxation becomes relevant. The theoretical case for capital income taxation seems to be fairly strong, as discussed in Chapter 14. It is particularly strong if those with higher earning capacity are more likely to save and will achieve a higher return on any savings they have. This provides a strong case for taxing savings, because savings are an indicator of high earnings capacity. Capital income could be taxed, and with a different rate schedule.

The recent research in behavioural economics has demonstrated that individual decision-making often suffers from various biases. Some people save more for the future than others because they are more patient. Some save more because they have a greater understanding of the options available and the consequences of saving, or not saving. In particular, those with low earnings capacity do not save enough. They may be impatient and have difficulty making appropriate calculations and decisions. In these situations when there is a possible conflict between an individual's long-term preference and his short-term behaviour, the government may want to intervene. If the observed level of saving is a good proxy for earnings capacity, then taxing savings might be a useful way of redistributing. We might then want to subsidize or otherwise encourage them to save. At the margin, by taxing savings, the government could raise revenue and redistribute from those with a higher earning capacity while reducing tax rates on labour supply.

Allowing the wages to be endogenously determined in the OLG model, Pirttilä and Tuomala (2001) and Chapter 14 (14.6) have shown that capital income taxation may be desirable even when preferences are separable across time where future relative wages are sensitive to current savings via the impact of capital stock on the income-earning abilities of future generations, i.e. their effect on capital income. The latter impact seems to have interesting implications: it calls for violation of production efficiency and means that the separability result derived by Ordover and Phelps (1979) does not hold within the present setting. The latter result can also be interpreted as a reservation to the old issue of the optimality of the so-called expenditure taxation.

If savings were only made for life-cycle smoothing purposes, and everyone has the same preferences, then wealth differences for any given cohort will reflect earnings differences. This is not the only way in which people receive capital, however. For instance, some people inherit it. Recent studies show that after a long period in which inheritance was declining, it is now increasing again in significance in many advanced countries. Again we have a fairly strong case for capital income taxation. This is especially the case if inheritances are not taxed. It is important to note in this context that one of the lessons from Piketty (2014) is that the relatively high degree of equality seen after World War II was partly a result of progressive taxation, but even more a result of the destruction of inherited wealth.

The standard argument against taxing the return to saving relies on the assumption that taxing savings creates inefficiencies and cannot help with redistribution. Other arguments against it are related to administration considerations. One is that some of the most important assets are likely to escape taxation, either because their returns are difficult to tax (imputed housing rents, personal businesses, human capital investment) or because there are reasons for preferential treatment (retirement saving). The other is the administrative complexity of taxing all forms of capital income, which was the one reason for the proportional rate adopted in the Nordic dual system. Often many of these reasons against taxing capital or capital income are political excuses to do nothing to minimize tax avoidance. It is clear that international co-operation in fiscal matters makes it easier to implement taxes on capital.

Our main conclusion in Chapter 14 was that neither zero taxation, nor taxing total income, nor the Nordic dual income tax model were supported by the existing optimal capital income tax models. In sum, the difficulty distinguishing in practice between labour and capital income provides support for a so called comprehensive income tax (i.e. taxing the sum of labour and capital income)—or, at least, for taxing capital and labour income at rates that are not too different.

There are many questions that received little or no attention in this book, as well as more generally in the optimal tax literature. For example, we have not raised issues of political economy. There was, however, some brief discussion about the political economy of redistribution in the context of the median voter model and linear progressive taxation. Moreover, there is a brief mention of it in discussing the backing out of social weights from the observed tax system. This is not to say that nowhere else in the book are tax systems more realistic.

Although in Chapter 14 we assume in examining capital income taxation that the economy is a small open economy, it is clear that international and global perspectives have got too little attention in this book, or more generally in public economics. In particular in the context of capital income taxation, these considerations are important both in understanding the present situation and in designing capital tax reforms in future.

When economists are supposed to allocate most of their research time to worrying about persistent unemployment, it may look odd to study income tax in a model that assumes that every individual succeeds in supplying the labour it would like to supply. In standard optimal tax-transfer models, all unemployment is voluntary. In the Mirrlees variant with variable labour supply the optimum is typically characterized by a certain fraction of individuals, at the bottom end, choosing not to work. In extensive-margin approaches, in turn, individuals of any skill level may choose not to participate in the labour market, depending on their preferences for leisure. Moreover, all those who do not supply labour are treated the same, whether they choose not to participate or are unable to do so. It is clear that both approaches provide too simple a picture of the real world. Since unemployment is the major economic problem in Europe, in particular, today, attempts to integrate the conventional optimum tax approach with the unemployment problem are very important. Many tax theorists have clearly become increasingly uneasy about the state of optimum tax theory within the Arrow–Debreu model while the real world exhibits persistent unemployment. In the models of the Arrow–Debreu type, unemployment only appears if labour is in excess supply at a zero wage rate. What is clearly needed is to extend these models to understand redistribution policy during recessions when people want to work, but cannot find jobs.[4] Also, the need to depart from the assumption of perfectly rational behaviour and perfectly functioning markets is undoubtedly a major priority. The complexity of the second-best problem is such that we need simple models in order to be able to illuminate the structure of the solutions. More general formulations often yield results that are hard to interpret. The development of specific models may also turn out to be fruitful when we contemplate departures from the standard competitive model. It also means a bigger role for numerical simulations connected to empirical evidence.

[4] We briefly referred to this research in Chapter 6.

REFERENCES

Aaberge, R. (2000), Characterizations of Lorenz Curves and Income Distributions, Social Choice and Welfare, 17, 639–53.

Aaberge, R. and U. Colombino (2006), Designing Optimal Taxes with a Microeconometric Model of Household Labour Supply, IZA, DP No. 2468.

Aaberge, R. and L. Flood (2008), Evaluation of an In-Work Tax Credit Reform in Sweden: Effects on Labor Supply and Welfare Participation of Single Mothers, IZA, DP No. 3736, September 2008.

Aarbu, K.O. and T.O. Thoresen (2001), Income Responses to Tax Changes—Evidence from the Norwegian Tax Reform, National Tax Journal, 54, 319–38.

Acemoglu, D., M. Golosov, and A. Tsyvinski (2008), Political Economy of Mechanisms, Econometrica, 76 (3), s 619–41.

Acemoglu, D., M. Golosov, and A. Tsyvinski (2010), Dynamic Mirrlees Taxation under Political Economy Constraints, Review of Economic Studies, 77(3), 841–81.

Adler, M. (2012), Well-being and Fair Distribution: A Framework for Policy Analysis, Oxford University Press.

Ahmad, E. and N. Stern (1984), The Theory of Reform and Indian Indirect Taxes, Journal of Public Economics, 25, 259–98.

Aitchison, J. and J.A.C. Brown (1957), The Lognormal Distribution with Special Reference to its Uses in Economics, Cambridge University Press.

Aiyagari, S.R. (1995), Optimal Capital Income Taxation with Incomplete Markets, Borrowing Constraints, and Constant Discounting, Journal of Political Economy, 103, 1158–75.

Akerlof, G. (1978), The Economics of Tagging as Applied to the Optimal Income Tax, Welfare Programs, and Manpower Planning, American Economic Review, 68(1), 8–19.

Albanesi, S. and C. Sleet (2006), Dynamic Optimal Taxation with Private Information, Review of Economic Studies, 73, 1–30.

Alesina, A., A. Ichino, and L. Karabarbounis (2011), Gender-Based Taxation and the Division of Family Chores, American Economic Journal: Economic Policy, 3, 1–40.

Allen, S. (1987), Taxes, Redistribution, and the Minimum Wage: A Theoretical Analysis, Quarterly Journal of Economics, 102, 477–90.

Allingham, M.G. and A. Sandmo (1972), Income Tax Evasion: A Theoretical Analysis, Journal of Public Economics, 1(3), 323–38.

Alpizar, F., F. Carlsson, and O. Johansson-Stenman (2005), How Much Do We Care About Absolute versus Relative Income and Consumption? Journal of Economic Behavior and Organization, 56, 405–21.

Alvi, E. (1997), First-Order Approach to the Principal-Agent Problems: A Generalization, Geneva Papers on Risk and Insurance, 22, 59–65.

Anand, S. and S.M.R. Kanbur (1993), The Kuznets Process and the Inequality–Development relationship, Journal of Development Economics, 40(1), 25–52.

Anderberg, D. (2009), Optimal Policy and the Risk Properties of Human Capital Reconsidered, Journal of Public Economics, 93, 1017–26.

Anderberg, D. and F. Andersson (2003), Investments in Human Capital, Wage Uncertainty, and Public Policy, Journal of Public Economics, 87, 1521–37.

Andrienko, Y., P. Apps, and R. Rees (2014), Optimal Taxation, Inequality and Top Incomes, IZA Discussion Papers 8275, Institute for the Study of Labor (IZA).

Apps, P., N.V. Long, and R. Rees (2013), Optimal Piecewise Linear Income Taxation, Journal of Public Economic Theory, 16(4), 523–45.

Apps, P. and R. Rees (2009), Public Economics and the Household, Cambridge University Press.

Arnott, R. and J.E. Stiglitz (1986), Moral Hazard and Optimal Commodity Taxation, Journal of Public Economics, 29, 1–24.

Arnott, R. (1993), Reflections On Optimal Tax Theory, in Modern Public Finance, eds. J. Quigley and E. Smolensky, Harvard University Press.

Arnott, R. and J. Stiglitz (1988), Randomization with Asymmetric Information, RAND Journal of Economics, 19(3), 344–62.

Aronsson, T. and O. Johansson-Stenman (2011), Positional Concerns in an OLG Model: Optimal Labor and Capital Income Taxation, International Economic Review, 51(4), 1071–95.

Aronsson, T. and Sjögren, T. (2004), Is the Optimal Labor Income Tax Progressive in a Unionized economy? The Scandinavian Journal of Economics, 106, 661–75.

Aronsson, T. and Sjögren, T. (2010), Optimal Income Taxation and Social Norms in the Labor Market, International Tax and Public Finance, 17(1), 67–89.

Arrow, K. (1971), The Utilitarian Approach to the Concept of Equality in Public Expenditure, Quarterly Journal of Economics, 85, 409–15.

Arrow, K. (1973), Some Ordinalist-Utilitarian Notes on Rawls's Theory of Justice, Journal of Philosophy, 70, 245–63.

Arrow, K. (1978), Nozick's Entitlement Theory of Justice, Philosophia, 7, 265–79.

Arrow, K. and T. Scitowsky (eds.) (1969), Readings in Welfare Economics, Allen and Unwin.

Aschauer, A.D. (1990), Is Government Spending Stimulative?, Contemporary Economic Policy, Western Economic Association International, 8(4), 30–46.

Atkinson, A.B. (1970), On the Measurement of Inequality, Journal of Economic Theory, 2, 244–63.

Atkinson, A.B. (1972), La 'Maxi-Min' et l'Imposition Optimale des Revenus, Cahiers du Séminaire d'Econométrie, 1975, 16, 73–86 (French version of University of Essex discussion paper No 47, 'Maxi-min' and optimal income taxation, accepted for publication by the Review of Economic Studies but never resubmitted).

Atkinson, A.B. (1977), Housing Allowances, Income Maintenance and Income Taxation, in The Economics of Public Services, ed. M.S. Feldstein and R.P. Inman, MacMillan.

Atkinson, A.B. (1982), The Theory of the Design of Income Taxation: Review and Prospects, Working Paper 38, London School of Economics.

Atkinson, A.B. (1987), On the Measurement of Poverty, Econometrica, 55(4), 749–64.

Atkinson, A.B. (1990), Public Economics and Economic Public, European Economic Review, 34, 225–48.

Atkinson, A.B. (1992), On Targeting Social Security: The Experience of Western Countries with Family Benefits. Paper presented at the World Bank Conference on Public Expenditure and the Poor: Incidence and Targeting, Washington, DC.

Atkinson, A.B. (1995), Public Economics in Action, The Basic Income/Flat Tax Proposal, The Lindahl Lectures, Oxford University Press.

Atkinson, A.B. (1998), Poverty in Europe, Yrjö Jahansson Lectures, Basil Blackwell.

Atkinson, A.B. (1999), The Distribution of Income in the UK and OECD Countries in the Twentieth Century, Oxford Review of Economic Policy, 15(4), 56–7.

Atkinson, A.B. (2002), Top Incomes in the United Kingdom Over the Twentieth Century, Economics Series Working Papers 2002-W43, University of Oxford, Department of Economics.

Atkinson, A.B. and A. Brandolini (2010), On Analyzing the World Distribution of Income, World Bank Economic Review, 24(1), 1–37.

Atkinson, A.B. (2012), The Mirrlees Review and the State of Public Economics, Journal of Economic Literature, 3(50), 770–80.

Atkinson, A.B. (2014), Public Economics in an Age of Austerity, Schumpeter Lectures, Routledge/Taylor & Francis Group.

Atkinson, A.B. and J. Micklewright (1991), Unemployment Compensation and Labor Market Transitions: A Critical Review, Journal of Economic Literature, 29(4), 1679–727.

Atkinson, A. and T. Piketty (ed.) (2007), Top Incomes Over the Twentieth Century: A Contrast Between Continental European and English-Speaking Countries. Oxford University Press.

Atkinson, A.B. and T. Piketty (eds.) (2010), Top Incomes: A Global Perspective, Oxford University Press.

Atkinson, A., T. Piketty, and E. Saez (2011), Top Incomes in the Long-Run of History, Journal of Economic Literature, 49(1), 3–71.

Atkinson, A, and J.E. Stiglitz (1976), The Design of Tax Structure: Direct Versus Indirect Taxation, Journal of Public Economics, 6(1–2), 55–75.

Atkinson, A., and J.E. Stiglitz (1980), Lectures in Public Economics, McGraw Hill.

Atkinson, A.B. and A. Sandmo (1980), Welfare Implications of the Taxation of Savings, Economic Journal, 90, 529–49.

Atkinson, A.B. and N.H. Stern (1974), Pigou, Taxation and Public Goods, Review of Economic Studies, 41, 119–28.

Atkinson, T. B. Cantillon, E. Marlier, and B. Nolan (2002), Social Indicators. The EU and Social Inclusion, Oxford University Press.

Azariadis, C. (1975), Implicit Contracts and Underemployment Equilibria, Journal of Political Economy 83, 1183–202.

Balestrino, A. (1999), The Desirability of In-Kind Transfers in the Presence of Distortionary Taxes, Journal of Economic Surveys, 13, 333–53.

Baily, M. (1974), Wages and Employment Under Uncertain Demand, Review of Economic Studies, 41, 37–50.

Balle, S., L. Mangiavacchi, L. Piccoli, and A. Spadaro (2015), Tax Evasion and the Optimal Non-linear Labour Income Taxation, DEA Working Papers 68, Universitat de les Illes Balears, Departament d'Economía Aplicada.

Banks, J. and P. Diamond (2010), The Base for Direct Taxation, in Dimensions of Tax Design: The Mirrlees Review, ed. S. Adam, T. Besley, R. Blundell, S. Bond, R. Chote, M. Gammie, P. Johnson, G. Myles, and J. Poterba, Oxford University Press.

Bargain, O., M. Dolls, D. Nuemann, A. Peichl, and S. Siegloch (2011), Tax-benefit Systems in Europe and the US: Between Equity and Efficiency, IZA DP No. 5440.

Bastani, S. (2013), Gender-Based and Couple-Based Taxation, International Tax and Public Finance, 20(4), 653–86.

Bastani, S., S. Blomquist, and L. Micheletto (2009), Public Provision of Private Goods and Optimal Income Taxation Model with Heterogeneity in Needs. Unpublished.

Bastani, S., S. Blomquist, and L. Micheletto (2013), The Welfare Gains of Age Related Optimal Income Taxation, International Economic Review, 54(4), 1219–49.

Bastani, S., S. Blomquist, and J. Pirttilä (2013), How Should Commodities Be Taxed? A Counterargument to the Recommendation in the Mirrlees Review, Working Paper Series, Center for Fiscal Studies 2013:5, Uppsala University, Department of Economics.

Bastani, S., Y. Moberg, and H. Selin (2013), Labor Force Participation Elasticities of Low Income Couples. Theory and Evidence from a Swedish Housing Allowance Reform, mimeo.

Batina, R.G. (1990), Public Goods and Dynamic Efficiency. The Modified Samuelson Rule, Journal of Public Economics, 41, 389–400.

Bennett, J. (1987), The Second-best Lump-sum Taxation of Observable Characteristics, Public Finance/Finances Publiques, 42, 227–35.

Berliant, M. and J.O. Ledyard (2014), Optimal Dynamic Nonlinear Income Taxes with No Commitment, Journal of Public Economic Theory, 16(2), 196–221.

Bernheim, B.D. and A. Rangel (2007), Behavioural Public Economics: Welfare and Policy Analysis with Non-standard Decision-makers, in Behavioural Economics and Its Applications, ed. Peter A. Diamond and Hannu Vartiainen, Princeton University Press.

Bernheim, D.G. and A. Rangel (2008), Behavioural Public Economics: Welfare and Policy Analysis with Non-standard Decision Makers, in Behavioural Economics and Its Applications, ed. P. Diamond and H. Vartiainen, Princeton University Press.

Besley, T. (1988), A Simple Model for Merit Good Arguments, Journal of Public Economics, 35, 371–84.

Besley, T. (1990), Means Testing versus Universal Provision in Poverty Alleviation Programmes, Economica, 57, 119–29.

Besley, T. and S. Coate (1992), Workfare versus Welfare: Incentive Arguments for Work Requirements in Poverty Alleviation Programs, American Economic Review, 82, 249–61.

Besley, T. and S. Coate (1995), The Design of Income Maintenance Programmes, Review of Economic Studies, 62, 187–221.

Besley, T. and R. Kanbur (1988), Food Subsidies and Poverty Alleviation, The Economic Journal, 98, 701–19.

Besley, T. and T. Persson (2013), Taxation and Development, in Handbook of Public Economics, vol. 5, ed. A.J. Auerbach, R. Chetty, M. Feldstein, and E. Saez, Elsevier.

Bevan, D. (2005), On the Shape of the Optimal Tax-transfer Schedules Under Non-welfarist Objectives, mimeo, Oxford University.

Blackorby, C. and D. Donaldson (1988), Cash versus Kind, Self Selection and Efficient Transfers, American Economic Review, 78, 691–700.

Blackorby, C. and C. Brett (2004), Capital Taxation In A Simple Finite-Horizon Olg Model, The Warwick Economics Research Paper Series (TWERPS) 709, University of Warwick, Department of Economics.

Blanchard, O.J. and P. Diamond (1989), The Beveridge Curve, Brookings Papers on Economic Activity, 20(1), 1–76.

Blanchflower, D. and A. Oswald (2004), Well-being over Time in Britain and the USA, Journal of Public Economics, 88, 1359–86.

Blomquist, S. (1993), Interdependent Behaviour and the Effect of Taxes, Journal of Public Economics, 51, 211–18.

Blomquist, S. and V. Christiansen (1995), Public Provision of Private Goods as a Redistributive Device in an Optimum Income Model, Scandinavian Journal of Economics, 97(4), 547–67.

Blomquist, S. and V. Christiansen (1998a), Topping Up or Opting Out? The Optimal Design of Public Provision Schemes, International Economic Review, 39(2), 399–411.

Blomquist, S. and V. Christiansen (1998b), Price Subsidies versus Public Provision, International Tax and Public Finance, 5(3), 283–306.

Blomquist, S. and V. Christiansen (2004), Taxation and Heterogeneous Preferences, CESifo Working Paper 1244.

Blomquist, S., V. Christiansen, and L. Micheletto (2010), Public Provision of Private Goods and Nondistortionary Marginal Tax Rates, American Economic Journal: Economic Policy, 2(May), 1–27.

Blomquist, S. and L. Micheletto (2006), Optimal Redistributive Taxation when Government's and Agents' Preferences Differ, Journal of Public Economics, 90(6), 1215–33.

Blomquist, S. and L. Micheletto (2008), Age Related Optimal Income Taxation, Scandinavian Journal of Economics, 110, 45–71.

Blumkin, T. and E. Sadka (2005a), A Case for Taxing Education, CESifo Working Paper Series 1440, CESifo Group Munich.

Blumkin, T. and E. Sadka (2005b), Income Taxation and Wage Policy: An Application to Minimum Wage, International Tax and Public Finance, 12, 713–22.

Blumkin, T, Y. Margalioth, and E. Sadka (2007), Anti-discrimination Rules versus Income Taxation in the Pursuit of Horizontal Equity, Journal of Public Economics, 91(5–6), 1167–76.

Blumkin, T. and L. Danziger (2014), Deserving Poor and the Desirability of Minimum Wage Rules, CesIfo working paper No. 4721.

Blundell, R. and T. Macurdy (1999), Labor Supply: A Review of Alternative Approaches, in Handbook of Labor Economics, vol. 3, 1st edn, ed. O. Ashenfelter and D. Card, Elsevier.

Boadway, R. (2012), From Optimal Tax Theory to Tax Policy: Retrospective and Prospective Views: The 2009 Munich Lectures, MIT Press.

Boadway, R. and M. Keen (1993), Public Goods, Self-selection and Optimal Income Taxation, International Economic Review, 34, 463–78.

Boadway, R., M. Marchand, and P. Pestieau (1994), Towards a Theory of the Direct–Indirect Tax Mix, Journal of Public Economics, vol. 55(1), 71–88.

Boadway, R. and M. Marchand (1995), The Use of Public Expenditures for Redistributive Purposes, Oxford Economic Papers, 47(1), 45–59.

Boadway, R. and K. Cuff (1999), Monitoring Job Search as an Instrument for Targeting Transfers, International Tax and Public Finance, 6, 317–37.

Boadway, R., K. Cuff, and M. Marchand (2000), Optimal Income Taxation with Quasi-linear Preferences Revisited, Journal of Public Economic Theory, 2(4), 435–60.

Boadway, R., M. Marchand, and P. Pestieau (2000), Redistribution with Unobservable Bequests: A Case for Taxing Capital Income, Scandinavian Journal of Economics, 102(2), 253–67.

Boadway, R., M. Marchand, P. Pestieau, and M. del mar Racionero (2002), Optimal Redistribution with Heterogeneous Preferences for Leisure, Journal of Public Economic Theory, 4, 475–98.

Boadway, R., K. Cuff, and N. Marceau (2003), Redistribution and Employment Policies with Endogenous Unemployment, Journal of Public Economics, 87(11), 2407–30.

Boadway, R. and L. Jacquet (2008), Optimal Marginal and Average Income Taxation under Maximin, Journal of Economic Theory, 143, 425–41.

Boadway, R. and M. Sato (2011), Optimal Income Taxation with Uncertain Earnings: A Synthesis, CESifo Working Paper Series 3654, CESifo Group Munich.

Boadway, R., E. Chamberlain, and C. Emmerson (2010), Taxation of Wealth and Wealth Transfers, in Dimensions of Tax Design: the Mirrlees Review, ed. J. Mirrlees, S. Adam, T. Besley, R. Blundell, S. Bond, R. Chote, M. Gammie, P. Johnson, G. Myles and J. Poterba, Oxford University Press.

Boadway, R. and P. Pestieau (2011), Indirect Taxes for Redistribution: Should Necessity Goods be Favored?, CESifo Working Paper Series 3667, CESifo Group Munich.

Boadway, R. and N.-G Martineau (2013), Normative Analysis with Societal Constraints, CESifo Working Paper Series 4305, CESifo Group Munich.

Boadway, R., M. Marchand, P. Pestieau, and M. del Mar Racionero (2002), Optimal Redistribution with Heterogeneous Preferences for Leisure, Journal of Public Economic Theory, 4, 475–98.

Boadway, R., M. Marchand, and M. Sato (1998), Subsidies versus Public Provision of Private Goods as Instruments for Redistribution, Scandinavian Journal of Economics, 100(39), 545–64.

Boadway, R. and P. Pestieau (2001), A Minimum Wage can be Welfare-improving and Employment-enhancing, European Economic Review, 45, 553–76.

Boadway, R. and P. Pestieau (2003), Indirect Taxation and Redistribution: The Scope of the Atkinson-Stiglitz Theorem, in Imperfect Economics: Essays in Honor of Joseph Stiglitz, ed. R. Kanbur and R. Arnott, MIT Press.

Boadway, R. and P. Pestieau (2006), Tagging and Redistributive Taxation, Annales d'Economie et de Statistique, 83/84, 123–50.

Boadway, R. and F. Gahvari (2006), Optimal Taxation with Consumption Time as a Leisure or Labor Substitute, Journal of Public Economics, 90: 1851–78.

Bonferroni, C. (1930), Elementi di Statistica Generale, Seeber.
Boone, J. and L. Bovenberg (2002), Optimal Labor Taxation and Search, Journal of Public Economics, 85, 53–97.
Boskin, M.J. and E. Sheshinski (1978), Individual Welfare Depends upon Relative Income, Quarterly Journal of Economics, 92, 589–601.
Bossert, W. (1995), Redistribution Mechanisms based on Individual Characteristics, Mathematical Social Sciences, 29(1), 1–17.
Bourguignon, F. and A. Spadaro (2012), Tax-benefit Revealed Social Preferences, Journal of Economic Inequality, 10(1), 75–108.
Bovenberg, A.L. and F. van der Ploeg (1994), Environmental Policy, Public Finance and the Labour Market in a Second-Best World, Journal of Public Economics, 55(3), 349–90.
Bovenberg, L.A. and R.A. de Mooij (1997), Environmental Tax Reform and Endogenous Growth, Journal of Public Economics, 63(2), 207–37.
Bovenberg, A.L. and B. Jacobs (2005), Redistribution and Education Subsidies are Siamese Twins, Journal of Public Economics, 89, 2005–35.
Bowles, S. and Y. Park (2005), Emulation, Inequality, and Work Hours: Was Thorsten Veblen Right? Economic Journal, 115, F397–412.
Bradbury, B. (2004), Targeting Social Assistance, Fiscal Studies, 25, 305–24.
Brett, C. (1997), Notes on Non-Linear Taxation in an OLG Model, mimeo, University of Essex.
Brett, C. (1998), Who Should Be on Workfare? The Use of Work Requirements as Part of the Optimal Tax Mix, Oxford Economic Papers, 50, 607–22.
Brett, C. and J. Weymark (2003), Financing Education using Optimal Redistributive Taxation, Journal of Public Economics, 87, 2549–69.
Brewer, M., E. Saez, and A. Shephard (2008), Means Testing and Tax Rates on Earnings, IFS Working Paper, April 2008.
Brito, D.L. and W.H. Oakland (1977), Some Properties of the Optimal Income-tax, International Economic Review, 18(2), 407–23.
Broome, J. (1978), Trying the Value of Life, Journal of Public Economics, 9, 91–100.
Browning, M. and C. Meghir (1991), The Effects of Male and Female Labour Supply on Commodity Demands, Econometrica, 59(4), 925–51.
Cahuc, P. and G. Laroque (2007), Optimal Taxation and Monopsonistic Labor Market: Does Monopsony Justify the Minimum Wage?, mimeo, CREST-INSEE.
Calmfors, L. (1982), Employment Policies, Wage Formation and Trade Union Behaviour in a Small Open Economy, Scandinavian Journal of Economics, 84(2), 345–72.
Camerer, C. and G. Loewenstein (2004), Behavioral Economics: Past, Present, and Future, in Advances in Behavioral Economics, ed. C.F. Camerer, G. Loewenstein, and M. Rabin, Princeton University Press.
Camerer, C.F., G. Loewenstein, and M. Rabin (eds) (2004), Advances in Behavioral Economics, Princeton University Press.
Carlsson, F., O. Johansson-Stenman, and P. Martinsson (2007), Do You Enjoy Having More Than Others? Survey Evidence of Positional Goods, Economica, 74, 586–98.
Chamley, C. (1986), Optimal Taxation of Capital Income in General Equilibrium with Infinite Lives, Econometrica, 54(3), 607–22.
Champernowne, D.G. (1937), Notes on Income Distribution, Econometrica, Report of Econometric Conference at New College in 1936.
Champernowne, D.G. (1952), The Graduation of Income Distributions, Econometrica, 20, 591–615.
Champernowne, D.G. (1953), A Model of Income Distribution, The Economic Journal, 63(250), 318–51.
Champernowne, D.G. and F.A. Cowell (1999), Economic Inequality and Income Distribution, Cambridge University Press.

Chetty, R. (2006), A New Method of Estimating Risk Aversion, American Economic Review, 96(5), 1821–34.
Chetty, R. (2008), Moral Hazard versus Liquidity and Optimal Unemployment Insurance, Journal of Political Economy, 116, 173–234.
Chetty, R. (2009), Is the Taxable Income Elasticity Sufficient to Calculate Deadweight Loss? The Implications of Evasion and Avoidance, American Economic Journal: Economic Policy, 1, 31–52.
Chetty, R. and E. Saez (2010), Optimal Taxation and Social Insurance with Endogenous Private Insurance, American Economic Journal: Economic Policy, 2, 85–114.
Christiansen, V. (1981), Evaluation of Public Projects under Optimal Taxation, Review of Economic Studies, 48, 447–57.
Christiansen, V. (1984), Which Commodity Taxes should Supplement the Income Tax? Journal of Public Economics, 24, 195–220.
Christiansen, V. (1999), The Marginal Cost of Public Funds under Information Constrained Taxation, Finanz Archiv, 56, 188–201.
Christiansen, V. (2001), Private Provision of Public Goods or Vice Versa, IIPF Congress 2002, Helsinki.
Christiansen, V. (2007), Two Approaches to Determine Public Good Provision under distortionary Taxation, National Tax Journal, 60(1), 25–43.
Christiansen, V. (2012), Optimal Participation Taxes. CESIFO Working Paper No. 3941.
Christiansen, V. and E.S. Jansen (1978), Implicit Social Preferences in the Norwegian System of Social Preferences. Journal of Public Economics, 10, 217–45.
Christiansen, V. and M. Tuomala (2008), On Taxing Capital Income with Income Shifting, International Tax and Public Finance, 15(4), 527–45.
Clark, A.E. and A. Oswald (1996), Satisfaction and Comparison Income, Journal of Public Economics, 61(3), 359–81.
Clark, A., P. Frijters, and M. Shields (2008), Relative Income, Happiness and Utility: An Explanation for Easterlin Paradox and Other Puzzles, Journal of Economic Literature, 46(1), 95–144.
Coate, S. (2000), An Efficiency Approach to the Evaluation of Policy Changes, Economic Journal, 110, 437–55.
Cohen, G.A. (1989), On the Currency of Egalitarian Justice, Ethics, 99(4), 906–44.
Coles, M.G. (2008), Optimal Unemployment Insurance in a Matching Equilibrium, Labour Economics, 15, 537–59.
Colombino, U. (2009), Optimal Income Taxation: Recent Empirical Applications, Rivista Italiana Degli Economisti, 2009(1), 47–70.
Conesa, J., S. Kitao, and D. Krueger (2007), Taxing Capital? Not a Bad Idea After All! NBE, Working Paper No. 12880.
Conesa, J.C., S. Kitao, and D. Krueger (2009), Taxing Capital? Not a Bad Idea After All, American Economic Review, 99, 25–48.
Corlett, W.J. and D.C. Hague (1953), Complementarity and the Excess Burden of Taxation, Review of Economic Studies, 21, 21–30.
Corneo, G., (2002), The Efficient Side of Progressive Income Taxation, European Economic Review, 46(7), 1359–68.
Cowell, F. (1977), Measuring Inequality, Oxford University Press, 3rd edn, 2011.
Cowell, F. (1986), Welfare Benefits and the Economics of Take-up. Working paper No. 89, ESRC Programme on Taxation, Incentives and the Distribution of Income, London School of Economics.
Cowell, F. (1990), Cheating the Government: The Economics of Evasion, MIT Press.
Crawford, I., M. Keen, and S. Smith (2010), Value Added Taxes and Excises, in Dimensions of Tax Design: the Mirrlees Review, ed. J. Mirrlees, S. Adam, T. Besley, R. Blundell, S. Bond, R. Chote, M. Gammie, P. Johnson, G. Myles, and J. Poterba, Oxford University Press.
Creedy, J. (2008), Choosing the Tax Rate in a Linear Income Tax Structure, Australian Journal of Labour Economics, 11(3), 257–76.

Creedy, J. and P. Francois (1993), Voting over Income Tax Progression in a Two-period Model, Journal of Public Economics, 50(2), 291–8.

Cremer, H., P. De Donder, D. Maldonado, and P. Pestieau (2009), Forced Saving, Redistribution and Non-Linear Social Security Scheme, Southern Economic Journal, 76(1), 86–98.

Cremer, H. and F. Gahvari (1995), Tax Evasion and the Optimum General Income Tax, Journal of Public Economics, 60(2), 235–49.

Cremer, H. and F. Gahvari (1995a), Uncertainty and Optimal Taxation: In Defence of Commodity Taxes, Journal of Public Economics, 56, 291–310.

Cremer, H. and F. Gahvari (1995b), Uncertainty, Optimal Taxation and the Direct vs Indirect Taxation Controversy, The Economic Journal, 105, 1165–79.

Cremer, H. and F. Gahvari (1997), In-kind Transfers, Self-selection and Optimal Tax Policy, European Economic Review, 41(1), 97–114.

Cremer, H. and Gahvari F. (1998), On Optimal Taxation of Housing, Journal of Urban Economics, 43, 315–35.

Cremer, H., F. Gahvari, and N. Ladoux (1998), Externalities and Optimal Taxation, Journal of Public Economics, 70(3), 343–64.

Cremer, H. and F. Gahvari (2001), Uncertainty, Commitment, and Optimal Taxation, Journal of Public Economic Theory, 1, 51–70.

Cremer, H., J-M. Lozachmeur, and P. Pestieau (2004), Social Security, Retirement Age and Optimal Income Taxation, Journal of Public Economics, 88(11), 2259–81.

Cremer, H., F. Gahvari, and J-M. Lozachmeur (2010a), Tagging and Income Taxation: Theory and an Application, American Economic Journal, Public Policy, 2(1), 31–50.

Cremer, H., J-M. Lozachmeur, and P. Pestieau (2010b), Collective Annuities and Redistribution, Journal of Public Economic Theory, Association for Public Economic Theory, 12(1), 23–41, 02.

Cremer, H., and P. Pestieau (2006), Wealth Transfer Taxation: A Survey of the Theoretical Literature, in Handbook of the Economics of Giving, Reciprocity and Altruism, vol. 2, ed. Louis-Andre Gerard-Varet, Serge-Christophe Kolm, and Jean Mercier Ythier, North-Holland.

Cremer, H., P. Pestieau, and J-C. Rochet (2001), Direct versus Indirect Taxation: The Design of the Tax Structure Revisited, International Economic Review, 42, 781–99.

Cremer, H., P. Pestieau, and J.C. Rochet (2003), Capital Income Taxation when Inherited Wealth is Not Observable. Journal of Public Economics, 87(11), 2475–90.

Cremer, H. and K. Roeder (2013), Long-term Care Policy, Myopia and Redistribution, Journal of Public Economics, 108(C), 33–43.

Cuff, K. (2000), Optimality of Workfare with Heterogeneous Preferences, Canadian Journal of Economics, 33, 149–74.

Currie, J. and F. Gahvari (2008), Transfers in Cash and In-kind: Theory Meets the Data, Journal of Economic Literature, 46, 333–83.

da Costa, Carlos E. and T. Severo (2008), Education, Preferences for Leisure and the Optimal Income Tax Schedule, Journal of Public Economics, 92(1–2), 113–38.

Dahan. M. and M. Strawczynski (2001), The Optimal Non-linear Income Tax, American Economic Review, 90(3), 681–6.

Dahan, M. and M. Strawczynski (2012), Optimal Asymptotic Income Tax Rates, Journal of Public Economic Theory, 14(5), 737–55.

Dahlby, B. (1998), Progressive Taxation and the Social Marginal Cost of Public Funds, Journal of Public Economics, 67, 105–22.

Dahlby, B. (2008), The Marginal Cost of Public Funds: Theory and Application, MIT Press.

De Vincenti, C. and R. Paladini (2009), Personal Income Tax Design for Italy: Lessons from the Theory, Rivista Italiana degli Economisti, XIV(1), 7–46.

Deaton, A., (1979), Optimally Uniform Commodity Taxes, Economics Letters, 2, 357–61.
Deaton, A. and J. Muellbauer (1980), Economics and Consumer Behaviour, Cambridge University Press.
Deaton, A. (1983), An Explicit Solution to an Optimal Tax Problem, Journal of Public Economics, 20(3), 333–46.
Decoster, A. and E. Schokkaert (1989), Equity and Efficiency of a Reform of Belgian Indirect Taxes, Recherches Economiques de Louvain, 55(2), 155–76.
De Fraja, G. (2002), The Design of Optimal Education Policies, Review of Economic Studies, 69(2), 437–66l.
Diamond, P. (1968), Negative Taxes and the Poverty Problem—A Review Article, National Tax Journal, XXI(3), 288–303.
Diamond, P. (1980), Income Taxation with Fixed Hours of Work, Journal of Public Economics, 13, 101–10.
Diamond, P. (1998), Optimal Income Taxation: An Example with a U-shaped Pattern of Optimal Marginal Tax Rates, American Economic Review, 88(1), 83–95.
Diamond, P.A. (2003), Taxation, Incomplete Markets, and Social Security. The 2000 Munich Lectures, MIT Press.
Diamond, P.A. (2007), Comment on Golosov et al, NBER Macroeconomics Annual 2006, 365–79.
Diamond, P. (2008), Behavioral Economics, Journal of Public Economics, 92(8–9), 1858–62.
Diamond, P. (2009), Taxes and Pensions, Southern Economic Journal, 76(1), 2–15.
Diamond, P. and E. Saez (2011), The Case for a Progressive Tax: From Basic Research to Policy Recommendations, Journal of Economic Perspectives, 25(4), 165–90.
Diamond, P. and J. Spinnewijn (2011), Capital Income Taxes with Heterogeneous Discount Rates, American Economic Journal: Economic Policy, 3, 52–76.
Diamond, P.A. (1965), National Debt in a Neo-classical Growth Model, American Economic Review, 55, 1126–50.
Diamond, P.A. (1975), A Many-person Ramsey Tax Rule, Journal of Public Economics, 4(4), 335–42.
Diamond, P.A., L.J. Helms, and J.A. Mirrlees (1980), Optimal Taxation in a Stochastic Economy: A Cobb-Douglas example, Journal of Public Economics, 14(1), 1–29, August.
Diamond, P.A. and J. Mirrlees (1971), Optimal Taxation and Public Production I: Production Efficiency and II: Tax Rules. American Economic Review, 61, 8–27 and 261–78.
Diamond, P.A. and J. Mirrlees (1978), A Model of Social Insurance with Variable Retirement, Journal of Public Economics, 10(3), 295–336.
Diamond, P. and J. Mirrlees (2000), Adjusting One's Standard of Living: Two Period Models, in Incentives, Organisation, and Public Economics, Papers in Honour of Sir James Mirrlees, ed. P.J. Hammond and G.D. Myles, Oxford University Press.
Diamond, P. and J. Mirrlees (2003), Social Insurance with Variable Retirement and Private Savings, Journal of Public Economics, forthcoming.
Diamond, P.A. and B. Kőszegi (2003), Quasi-hyperbolic Discounting and Retirement. Journal of Public Economics 87, 1839–72.
Diamond, P.A. and J. Spinnewijn (2009), Capital Income Taxes with Heterogeneous Discount Rates, NBER Working paper 15115.
Dilnot, A.W., J. Kay, and C.M. Morris (1984), The Reform of Social Security, Institute for Fiscal Studies, Clarendon Press, Oxford.
Dixit, A.K. and A. Sandmo (1977), Some Simplified Formulae for Optimal Income Taxation, Scandinavian Journal of Economics, 79(4), 417–23.
Domeij, D. and P. Klein (1998), Pre-announced Optimal Tax Reform, mimeo, Stockholm University.
Duesenberry, J.S. (1949), Income, Saving and the Theory of Consumer Behaviour, Harvard University Press.
Eaton, J. and H.S. Rosen (1980), Optimal Redistributive Taxation and Uncertainty, Quarterly Journal of Economics, 95(2), 357–64.

Ebert, U. (1988), Optimal Income Tax Problem: On the Case of Two-dimensional Population, DP A -169, Department of Economics, University of Bonn.
Ebert, U. (1992), A Reexamination of the Optimal Nonlinear Income Tax, Journal of Public Economics, 49, 47–73.
Ebrill, L.P., M.J. Keen, J.-P. Bodin, and V.P. Summers (2001), The Modern VAT, IMF.
Edgeworth, F.Y. (1897), The Pure Theory of Taxation, Economic Journal 7, 46–70, 226–38, and 550–71.
Edwards, J., M. Keen, and M. Tuomala (1994), Income Tax, Commodity Taxes and Public Good Provision: A Brief Guide, FinanzArchiv, 51, 472–97.
Elster J. (1982), Sour Grapes: Utilitarianism and the Genesis of Wants, in Utilitarianism and Beyond, ed. A. Sen and B. Williams, Cambridge University Press.
Engström, P. (2009), Unemployment Benefits as a Means for Optimal Redistribution, Finanzarchiv, 65(1), 21–36.
Eriksson, T. (1999), Executive Compensation and Tournament Theory: Empirical Tests on Danish Data, Journal of Labor Economics, 17(2), 262–80.
Erosa, A. and M. Gervais (2002), Optimal Taxation in Life-Cycle Economies, Journal of Economic Theory, 105(2), 338–69.
Farhi. E. and I. Werning (2010), Progressive Estate Taxation, The Quarterly Journal of Economics, 125(2), 635–73.
Farhi, E. and I. Werning (2012), Capital Taxation: Quantitative Explorations of the Inverse Euler Equation, Journal of Political Economy, 120(3), 1203–303.
Farhi, E., C. Sleet, I. Werning, and S. Yeltekin (2012), Non-linear Capital Taxation Without Commitment, Review of Economic Studies, 79(4), 1469–93.
Feldstein, M. (1972), Distributional Equity and the Optimal Structure of Public Prices, American Economic Review, 62(1/2), 32–6.
Feldstein, M. (1976), On the Theory of Tax Reform, Journal of Public Economics, 6(1–2), 77–104.
Feldstein, M. (1978), The Effect of Unemployment Insurance on Temporary Layoff Unemployment, American Economic Review, 68, 834–46.
Feldstein, M. (1978), The Welfare Cost of Capital Income Taxation, Journal of Political Economy, 86, 29–52.
Feldstein, M. (1995), The Effect of Marginal Tax Rates on Taxable Income: A Panel Study of the 1986 Tax Reform Act, Journal of Political Economy, 103, 551–72.
Feldstein, M. (1999), Tax Avoidance and the Deadweight Loss of the Income Tax, Review of Economics and Statistics, 81(4), 674–80.
Feldstein, M. (2012), The Mirrlees Review, Journal of Economic Literature, 2012, 50(3), 781–90.
Fischer, S. (1980), Dynamic Inconsistency, Cooperation and the Benevolent Dissembling Government, Journal of Economic Dynamics and Control, 2, 93–107.
Fisk, P.R. (1961a), The Graduation of Income Distribution, Econometrica, 29, 171–85.
Fisk, P.R. (1961b), Estimation of Location and Scale Parameters in a Truncated Grouped Sech-Square Distribution, Journal of the American Statistical Association, 56, 692–702.
Fleurbaey, M. (1994), On Fair Compensation, Theory and Decision, 36(3), 277–307.
Fleurbaey, M. (2006), Is Commodity Taxation Unfair?, Journal of Public Economics, 90(10–11), 1765–87.
Fleurbaey, M. (2008), Fairness, Responsibility and Welfare, Oxford University Press.
Fleurbaey, M. and F. Maniquet (1998), Optimal Income Taxation: An Ordinal Approach, mimeo, CORE.
Fleurbaey, M. and F. Maniquet (2011), A Theory of Fairness and Social Welfare, Cambridge University Press.
Foster, J., J. Greer, and E. Thorbecke (1984), A Class of Decomposable Poverty Measures, Econometrica, 52, 761–6.
Frank, R. (1985), Choosing the Right Pond, Oxford University Press.

Frank, R. (1997), The Frame of Reference as a Public Good, Journal of the American Statictical Association, 56, 692–702.

Frey, B. and A. Stutzer (2005), Happiness Research: State and Prospects, Review of Social Economy, 63(2), 207–28.

Fuest, C. and B. Huber (2001), Labor and Capital Taxation, Fiscal Competition and the Distribution of Wealth, Journal of Public Economics, 79, 71–91.

Fullerton, D., A. Leicester, and S. Smith (2010), Environmental Taxes (with Don) in Dimensions of Tax Design: the Mirrlees Review, ed. J. Mirrlees, S. Adam, T. Besley, R. Blundell, S. Bond, R. Chote, M. Gammie, P. Johnson, G. Myles and J. Poterba, Oxford University Press.

Gahvari, F. (2006), On the Marginal Cost of Public Funds and the Optimal Provision of Public Goods, Journal of Public Economics, 90, 1251–62.

Galbraith, J.K. (1958), The Affluent Society, Houghton Mifflin.

Gaube, T. (2000a), Income Taxation and Production Efficiency in a Simple Two-sector Economy, Bonn Econ Discussion papers 14.

Gaube, T. (2000b), When Do Distortionary Taxes Reduce the Optimal Supply of Public Goods? Journal of Public Economics, 76, 151–80.

Gaube, T. (2005), Financing Public Goods with Income Taxation: Provision Rules vs. Provision Level, International Tax and Public Finance, 12(3), 319–34.

Gaube, T. (2007), Optimum Taxation of Each Year's Income, Journal of Public Economic Theory, 9, 127–50.

Gauthier, S. and G. Laroque (2009), Separability and Public Finance, Journal of Public Economics, 93 (11–12), 1168–74.

Gelber, A. and M. Weinzierl (2012), Equalizing Outcomes vs. Equalizing Opportunities: Optimal Taxation when Children's Abilities Depend on Parents' Resources, Harvard Business School Working Papers 13-014, Harvard Business School, revised Mar 2014.

Gervais, M. (2003), On the Optimality of Age-dependent Taxes and the Progressive U.S. Tax System. Unpublished. Available online at http://aix1.uottawa.ca/~vbarham/PT03.pdf.

Golosov, M., N. Kocherlakota, and A. Tsyvinski (2003), Optimal Indirect and Capital Taxation, Review of Economic Studies, 70(3), 569–87.

Golosov, M. and A. Tsyvinski (2006), Designing Optimal Disability Insurance: A Case for Asset Testing, Journal of Political Economy, 114(2), 257–79.

Golosov, M., M. Troshkin, and A. Tsyvinski (2010), Optimal Taxation: Merging Micro and Macro Approaches, Journal of Money, Credit, and Banking, 43(5): 147–74.

Golosov, M., M. Troshkin, and A. Tsyvinski (2011), Optimal Dynamic Taxes, NBER Working Paper 17642, 2011.

Golosov, M., A. Tsyvinski, and I. Werning (2007), New Dynamic Public Finance: A User's Guide, NBER Macroeconomics Annual, 2006, 317–63.

Gordon, R. and J. Slemrod (2000), Are 'Real' Responses to Taxes Simply Income Shifting Between Corporate and Personal Tax Bases? In Does Atlas Shrug? The Economic Consequences of Taxing the Rich, ed. Joel Slemrod, 240–88. Russell Sage Foundation and Harvard University Press.

Gordon, R.H. and W. Kopczuk (2013), The Choice of the Personal Income Tax Base, mimeo, Columbia University.

Gordon, R. and J. Slemrod (1998), Are 'Real' Responses to Taxes Simply Income Shifting between Corporate and Personal Tax Bases? NBER Working Paper 6576.

Gordon, R.H. and J.K. MacKie-Mason (1995), Why Is There Corporate Taxation in a Small Open Economy? The Role of Transfer Pricing and Income Shifting, in The Effects of Taxation on Multinational Corporations, ed. M. Feldstein, J.R. Hines, and R.G. Hubbard, University of Chicago Press.

Gorman, T. (1980), The Demand for Related Goods: A Possible Procedure for Analysing Quality Differentials in the Egg Market, Review of Economic Studies, 47, 843–56.

Goulder, L. (1995), Environmental Taxation and the 'Double Dividend': A Reader's Guide, International Tax and Public Finance, 2(2), 157–83.

Gradus, R.H.J.M. and J.M. Julsing (2001), Comparing Different European Income Tax Policies: Making Work Pay, mimeo, OCFEB, Erasmus University, Rotterdam.

Gruber, J. and E. Saez (2002), The Elasticity of Taxable Income: Evidence and Implications, Journal of Public Economics, 84, 1–32.

Guesnerie, R. (1995), A Contribution to the Pure Theory of Taxation, Cambridge University Press.

Guesnerie, R. and K. Roberts (1984), Effective Policy Tools and Quantity Controls, Econometrica, 52, 59–82.

Guesnerie, R. and K. Roberts (1987), Minimum Wage Legislation as a Second Best Policy, European Economic Review, 31, 490–8.

Guesnerie, R. and Seade, J. (1982), Nonlinear Pricing in a Finite Economy, Journal of Public Economics, 17, 157–79.

Guo, J-T. and A. Krause (2011), Optimal Nonlinear Income Taxation with Habit Formation, Journal of Public Economic Theory, 13, 463–80.

Guo, J-T. and A. Krause (2013), Optimal Nonlinear Taxation of Income and Education Expenditures, Oxford Economic Papers, 65(1), 74–95.

Haavio, M. and K. Kotakorpi (2011), The Political Economy of Sin Taxes, European Economic Review, 55, 575–94.

Hare, P.G. and D.T. Ulph (1979), On Education and Redistribution, Journal of Political Economy, 87, S193–212.

Hare, P. and D. Ulph (1981), Imperfect Capital Markets and the Public Provision of Education, in Contemporary Economic Analysis, ed. M.J. Bowman, Croom Helm.

Harrison, A. (1974), Inequality of Income and the Champernowne Distribution, University of Essex Dept. of Economics, DP No. 54.

Harrison, D. Jr. (1994), The Distributive Effects of Economic Instruments for Environmental Policy, OECD.

Harsanyi, J.C. (1955), Cardinal Welfare, Individualistic Ethics, and Interpersonal Comparisons of Utility, Journal of Political Economy, 63, 309.

Harsanyi, J. (1982), Morality and the Theory of Rational Behaviour, in Utilitarianism and Beyond, ed. A. Sen and B. Williams, Cambridge University Press.

Hellwig, M.F. (2007), A Contribution to the Theory of Optimal Utilitarian Income Taxation, Journal of Public Economics, 91, 1449–77.

Hellwig, M.F. (2009), A Note on Deaton's Theorem on the Undesirability of Nonuniform Excise Taxation, Economics Letters, 105, 186–8.

Hellwig, M.F. (2010), A Generalization of the Atkinson-Stiglitz (1976) Theorem on the Undesirability of Nonuniform Excise Taxation, Economics Letters, 108, 156–8.

Hersoug, T. (1984), Union Wage Responses to Tax Changes, Oxford Economic Papers, 36(1), 37–51.

Hirsch, F. (1976), Social Limits to Growth, Harvard University Press.

Holmström, B. (1979), Moral Hazard and Observability, Bell Journal of Economics, 10, 74–91.

Holzner, C., V. Meier, and M. Werding (2010), Workfare, Monitoring, and Efficiency Wages, Journal of Macroeconomics, 32, 157–68.

Hopkins, E. (2008), Inequality, Happiness and Relative Concerns: What Actually Is Their Relationship? Journal of Economic Inequality, 6(4), s 351–72.

Hosios, A. (1990), On the Efficiency of Matching and Related Models of Search and Unemployment, Review of Economic Studies, 57, 279–98.

Hsu, M. and C.C. Yang (2013), Optimal Linear and Two-bracket Income Taxes with Idiosyncratic Earnings Risk, Journal of Public Economics, 105, 58–71.

Hungerbuhler, M., E. Lehmann, A. Parmentier, and B. Van Der Linden (2006), Optimal Redistributive Taxation in a Search Equilibrium Model, Review of Economic Studies, 73, 743–67.

Hungerbuhler, M. and E. Lehmann (2007), On the Optimality of a Minimum Wage: New Insights from Optimal Tax Theory, mimeo, CREST.

Hungerbuhler, M., E. Lehmann, A. Parmentier, and B. Van Der Linden (2010), A Simple Theory of Optimal Redistributive Taxation with Equilibrium Unemployment, Working Papers 2010-13, Centre de Recherche en Economie et Statistique.

Immervoll, H. and L. Richardson (2011), Redistribution Policy and Inequality Reduction in OECD Countries: What Has Changed in Two Decades?, OECD Social, Employment and Migration Working Papers 122, OECD Publishing.

Immervoll, H. and L. Richardson (2013), Redistribution Policy in Europe and the United States: Is the Great Recession a 'Game Changer' for Working-age Families?, OECD Social, Employment and Migration Working Papers 150, OECD Publishing.

Immonen, R., R. Kanbur, M. Keen, and M. Tuomala (1998), Tagging and Taxing: The Optimal Use of Categorical and Income Information, Economica, 65, 179–92.

İmrohoroğlu, A., S. İmrohoroğlu, and D.H. Joines (2003), Time Inconsistent Preferences and Social Security, Quarterly Journal of Economics, 118(2), 745–84.

Ireland, N. (2001), Optimal Income Tax in the Presence of Status Effects, Journal of Public Economics, 81, 193–212.

Itsumi, K. (1974), Distributional Effects of Linear Income Tax Schedules, Review of Economic Studies, 41, 371–81.

Jacobs, B. and R. Boadway (2014), Optimal Linear Commodity Taxation and Non-Linear Income Taxation, Journal of Public Economics, 117(C), 201–10.

Jacobs, B. and A. Lans Bovenberg (2010), Human Capital and Optimal Positive Taxation of Capital Income, International Tax and Public Finance, 17, 451–78.

Jacobs, B. and A. Lans Bovenberg (2011), Optimal Taxation of Human Capital and the Earnings Function, Journal of Public Economic Theory, 13, 957–71.

Jacobsen Kleven, H. and W. Kopczuk (2011), Transfer Program Complexity and the Take Up of Social Benefits, American Economic Journal: Economic Policy, 3, 54–90.

Jacquet, L., E. Lehmann, and B. Van der Linden (2009), The Optimal Marginal Tax Rates with Both Extensive and Intensive Responses, NHH Working Paper Series 02/09.

Jacquet, L., E. Lehmann, and B. Van der Linden (2011), Optimal Redistributive Taxation with Both Labor Supply and Labor Demand Responses, IZA working Paper no. 5642, April 2011.

Jacquet, L. and D. Van de Gaer (2011), A Comparison of Optimal Tax Policies when Compensation or Responsibility Matter, Journal of Public Economics, 95(11), 1248–62.

Jacquet, L. and B. Van der Linden (2006), The Normative Analysis of Tagging Revisited: Dealing with Stigmatization, FinanzArchiv, 62(2), 168–98.

Jäntti, M., M. Riihelä, R. Sullström, and M. Tuomala (2010), Trends in Top Income Shares in Finland, in Top Incomes: A Global Perspective, ed. A.B. Atkinson and T. Piketty, Oxford University Press.

Jewitt, I. (1988), Justifying the First Order Approach to Principal-agent Problems, Econometrica, 56, 1177–90.

John, A. and R. Pecchenino (1994), An Overlapping Generations Model of Growth and the Environment, The Economic Journal, 104, 1393–410.

Judd, K.L. (1985), Redistributive Taxation in a Simple Perfect Foresight Model, Journal of Public Economics, 28(1), 59–83.

Judd, K.L. and C.-L. Su (2006), Optimal Income Taxation with Multidimensional Taxpayers Types, Computing in Economics and Finance 2006, 471, Society for Computational Economics.

Kakwani, N. (1980), Income Inequality and Poverty, Oxford University Press.

Kahneman, D. and A. Tversky (1979), Prospect Theory: An Analysis of Decision under Risk, Econometrica, 47, 263–81.

Kahneman, D. (2003), Maps of Bounded Rationality: Psychology for Behavioral Economics (Nobel Prize lecture), American Economic Review, 93, 1449–75.

Kaldor, N. (1955), An Expenditure Tax, Allen & Unwin.

Kanbur, R. (1987), Transfers, Targeting and Poverty, Economic Policy, 4, 112–36 and 141–7.

Kanbur, R. and Keen, M. (1989), Poverty, Incentives and Linear Income Taxation, in The Economics of Social Security, ed. Andrew Dilnot and Ian Walker, Clarendon Press.

Kanbur, R., M. Keen, and M. Tuomala (1994a), Optimal Non-linear Income Taxation for the Alleviation of Income-poverty, European Economic Review, 38, 1613–32.

Kanbur, R., M. Keen, and M. Tuomala (1994b), Labour Supply and Targeting in Poverty Alleviation Programs, The World Bank Economic Review, 8, 191–211.

Kanbur, R., J. Pirttilä, and M. Tuomala (2006), Behavioural Public Economics and Non-welfarist Welfare Economics, Journal of Economic Surveys, 20, 849–68.

Kanbur, R., J. Pirttilä, and M. Tuomala (2008), Moral Hazard, Income Taxation and Prospect Theory, Scandinavian Journal of Economics, 110(2), 321–37.

Kanbur, R., J. Pirttilä, M. Tuomala, and T. Ylinen (2015), Optimal Taxation and Public Provision for Poverty Minimization, WIDER Working Paper 2015/054.

Kanbur, R. and Tuomala, M. (1994), Inherent Inequality and the Optimal Graduation of Marginal Tax Rates, Scandinavian Journal of Economics, 96(2), 275–82.

Kanbur R. and M. Tuomala (2006), Incentives, Inequality and the Allocation of Aid when Conditionality Doesn't Work: An Optimal Non-linear Taxation Approach, in Poverty, Inequality and Development: Essays in Honor of Eric Thorbecke, ed. Alain de Janvry and Ravi Kanbur, Kluwer Academic Publishers.

Kanbur, R. and M. Tuomala (2011), Charitable Conservatism, Poverty Radicalism and Inequality Aversion, Journal of Economic Inequality, 9(3), 417–31.

Kanbur, R. and M. Tuomala (2013), Relativity, Inequality, and Optimal Nonlinear Income Taxation, International Economic Review, 54(4), 1199–217.

Kanbur, R. and M. Tuomala (2014), Groupings and the Gains from Tagging, Tampere Economic Working Papers, Net Series no 86, University of Tampere.

Kaplow, L. (1990), Optimal Taxation with Costly Enforcement and Evasion, Journal of Public Economics, 43(2), 221–36.

Kaplow, L. (1991), A Note on Taxation as Social Insurance for Uncertain Labor Income, NBER Working Papers 3708, National Bureau of Economic Research.

Kaplow, L, (2004), On the (Ir)Relevance of Distribution and Labor Supply Distortion to Government Policy, Journal of Economic Perspectives, 18(4), 159–75.

Kaplow, L. (2006), On the Desirability of Commodity Taxation Even When Income Taxation is Not Optimal, Journal of Public Economics, 90, 1235–50.

Kaplow, L. (2008), The Theory of Taxation and Public Economics, Princeton University Press.

Kay, J.A. and M.A. King (1978), The British Tax System, Oxford University Press.

Keane, M. (2011), Labor Supply and Taxes: A Survey, Journal of Economic Literature, 49(4), 961–1075.

Keane, M. and R. Moffitt (1998), A Structural Model of Multiple Welfare Program Participation and Labor Supply, International Economic Review, 39(3), 553–89.

Kesselman, J.R. and I. Garfinkel (1978), Professor Friedman, Meet Lady Rhys-Williams: NIT vs. CIT, Journal of Public Economics, 10(2), 179–216.

King, M.A. (1980), Savings and Taxation, in Public Policy and the Tax System, ed. G.A. Hughes and G.M. Heal, Allen & Unwin.

King, M.A. (1986), A Pigovian Rule for the Optimum Provision of Public Goods, Journal of Public Economics, 90, 183–95.

Kleiber, C. and S. Kotz (2003), Statistical Size Distributions in Economics and Actuarial Sciences, John Wiley.

Kleven, H. and W. Kopczuk (2011), Transfer Program Complexity and the Take Up of Social Benefits, American Economic Journal: Economic Policy, 3, 54–90.

Kleven, H., C. Kreiner, and E. Saez (2009), The Optimal Income Taxation of Couples, Econometrica, 77(2), 537–60.

Kleven, H. and E. Schultz (2012), Estimating Taxable Income Responses using Danish Tax Reforms, LSE Working Paper.

Kleven, H. and C. Schultz (2014), Estimating Taxable Income Responses Using Danish Tax Reforms, American Economic Journal: Economic Policy, 6(4), 271–301.

Kneller, R., M. F. Bleaney, and N. Gemmel (1999), Fiscal Policy and Growth: Evidence From OECD Countries, Journal of Public Economics, 74, 171–90.

Kocherlakota, N. (2005), Zero Expected Wealth Taxes: A Mirrlees Approach to Dynamic Optimal Taxation, Econometrica, 731, 587.

Kocherlakota, N. (2010), The New Dynamic Public Finance, Princeton University Press.

Kolm, S-C. (1996), Modern Theories of Justice, MIT Press.

Konishi, H. (1995), A Pareto-improving Commodity Tax Reform under a Smooth Nonlinear Income Tax, Journal of Public Economics, 56, 413–46.

Kopczuk, W. (2005), Tax Bases, Tax Rates and the Elasticity of Reported Income, Journal of Public Economics, 89(11–12), 2093–119.

Kopczuk, W. (2013), Taxation of Intergenerational Transfers and Wealth, in Handbook of Public Economics, vol. 5, ed. Alan Auerbach, Raj Chetty, Martin Feldstein, and Emmanuel Saez, Elsevier.

Kopczuk, W. and J.B. Slemrod (2002), The Optimal Elasticity of Taxable Income, Journal of Public Economics, 84, 91–112.

Krause, A (2006), Redistributive Taxation and Public Education, Journal of Public Economic Theory, 8, 807–19.

Kreiner, C.T. and N. Verdelin (2012), Optimal Provision of Public Goods: A Synthesis, Scandinavian Journal of Economics, 114, 384–408.

Kremer, M. (2001), Should Taxes be Independent of Age? Unpublished manuscript, Harvard University.

Krusell, P., L.E. Ohanian, J.-V. Ríos-Rull, and G.L. Violante (2000), 'Capital-skill Complementarity and Inequality: A Macroeconomic Analysis', Econometrica, 68, 1029–53.

Kydland, F.E. and E.C. Prescott (1977), Rules Rather than Discretion: The Inconsistency of Optimal Plans, Journal of Political Economy, 3, 473–92.

Laffont, J.-J., E. Maskin, and J.-C. Rochet (1987), Optimal Nonlinear Pricing with Two-Dimensional Characteristics, in Information, Incentives, and Economic Mechanisms, ed. T. Groves, R. Radner, and S. Reiter, University of Minnesota Press.

LaLonde, R.J. (2007), The Case for Wage Insurance, Council on Foreign Relations Special Report No. 30 (New York: Council on Foreign Relations).

Lambert, P.J. (1989), The Distribution and Redistribution of Income: A Mathematical Analysis, Blackwell.

Lambert, P.J. and T.O. Thoresen (2012), The Inequality Effects of a Dual Income Tax System, B.E. Journal of Economic Analysis & Policy, 12(1), 1–17.

Lancaster, K.J. (1971), Consumer Demand: A New Approach, Columbia University Press.

Landais, C., P. Michaillat, and E. Saez (2010), Optimal Unemployment Insurance over the Business Cycle, NBER Working Paper 16526.

Landais, C. (2007), Les Hauts Revenus en France (1998–2006): Unexplosion des Inègalitès? Mimeo, Paris School of Economics.

Landais, C. T., Piketty, and E. Saez (2011), Pour une Révolution Fiscale: Un Impôt sur le Revenu pour le XXIème Siècle, Le Seuil.

Laroque, G. (2005a), Indirect Taxation is Superfluous under Separability and Taste Homogeneity: A Simple Proof, Economics Letters, 87, 141–4.

Laroque, G. (2005b), Income Maintenance and Labor Force Participation, Econometrica, 73, 341–76.

Layard, R. (1980), Human Satisfaction and Public Policy, Economic Journal, 90, 360, 737–50.

Lee, D. and E. Saez (2010), Optimal Minimum Wage Policy in Competitive Labor Markets, Journal of Public Economics, 96, 739–49.

Lehmann, E., A. Parmentier, and B. Van der Linden (2011), Optimal Income Taxation with Endogenous Participation and Search Unemployment, Journal of Public Economics, 95, 1523–37.

Lerner, A.P. (1944), The Economics of Control, Macmillan.

Liebman, J.B. (2001), The Optimal Design of the Earned Income Tax Credit, in Making Work Pay: The Earned Income Tax Credit and Its Impact on America's Families, ed. B.D. Meyer and D. Holtz-Eakin, Russell Sage Foundation Press.

Lindbeck, A,. (1995), Welfare State Disincentives with Endogenous Habits and Norms, Scandinavian Journal of Economics, 97(4), s 477–94.

Lindhe, T., J. Södersten, and A. Öberg (2002), Economic Effects of Taxing Closed Corporations under a Dual Income Tax, Ifo Studies, 48, 575–610.

Lipsey, R.G. and K. Lancaster (1956), The General Theory of the Second Best, Review of Economic Studies, 24, 11–32.

Lockwood, B.B., C. Nathanson, and E. Glen Weyl (2012), Taxation and the Allocation of Talent. Unpublished.

Loewenstein, G., T. O'Donoghue, and M. Rabin (2003), Projection Bias in Predicting Future Utility, Quarterly Journal of Economics, 118(4), 1209–48.

Lollivier S. and J.C. Rochet (1983), Bunching and Second Order Conditions: A Note on Optimal Tax Theory, Journal of Economic Theory, 31(2), 392–400.

Low, H. and D. Maldoom (2004), Optimal Taxation, Prudence and Risk-sharing, Journal of Public Economics, 88, 443–64.

Lozachmeur, J-M. (2006), Optimal Age-Specific Income Taxation, Journal of Public Economic Theory, 8(4), 697–711.

Lundholm, M. and H. Wijkander (2002), Public Production, Relative Wages and the Pareto-efficient Income Tax, mimeo, University of Stockholm.

Luttmer, E.F.P. (2005), Neighbors as Negatives: Relative Earnings and Well-Being, The Quarterly Journal of Economics, 120(3), 963–1002.

Lydall, H.F. (1968), The Structure of Earnings, Oxford: Clarendon Press.

Macurdy, T. and F. McIntyre (2004), Helping Working-poor Families: Advantages of Wage-based Tax Credits over the EITC and Minimum Wages, Employment Policies Institute, Washington, DC.

Maddison, A. (2001), The World Economy: A Millenial Perspective, available at OECD website.

Malinvaud, E. (1972), Lectures on Microeconomic Theory, North Holland.

Mandelbrot, B. (1960), The Pareto-Levy Law and the Distribution of Income, International Economic Review, 1, 79–106.

Mankiw, G.N., M. Weinzierl, and D. Yagan (2009), Optimal Taxation in Theory and Practice, Journal of Economic Perspectives, 23(4), 147–74.

Mankiw, N.G. and M. Weinzierl (2010), The Optimal Taxation of Height: A Case Study of Utilitarian Income Redistribution, American Economic Journal: Economic Policy, 2, 155–76.

Manning, A. (1993), Wage Bargaining and the Phillips Curve: The Identification and Specification of Aggregate Wage Equations, Economic Journal, 103(416), 98–118.

Marceau, N. and R. Boadway (1994), Minimum Wage Legislation and Unemployment Insurance as Instruments for Redistribution, Scandinavian Journal of Economics, 96, 67–81.

McAfee, P. and J. McMillan (1988), Multidimensional Incentive Compatibility and Mechanism Design, Journal of Economic Theory, 46, 335–54.

McCaffery, E.J. and J. Slemrod (2006), Behavioral Public Finance, Russell Sage Press.

McDonald, J.B. (1984), Some Generalized Functions for the Size Distribution of Income Source, Econometrica, 52(3), 647–63.

Meade Committee (1978), The Structure and Reform of Direct Taxation, Allen and Unwin.

Meade Report (1978), The Structure and Reform of Direct Taxation, Report of a Committee chaired by Professor J.E. Meade, George Allen and Unwin.

Meghir, C. and D. Phillips (2010), Labor Supply and Taxes, in Dimensions of Tax Design: the Mirrlees Review, ed. J. Mirrlees, S. Adam, T. Besley, R. Blundell, S. Bond, R. Chote, M. Gammie, P. Johnson, G. Myles and J. Poterba, Oxford University Press.

Messere, K. (ed.) (1998), The Tax System in Industrialized Countries, Oxford University Press.

Micheletto, L. (2008), Redistribution and Optimal Mixed Taxation in the Presence of Consumption Externalities, Journal of Public Economics, Elsevier, 92(10–11), 2262–74.

Mirrlees, J., S. Adam, T. Besley, R. Blundell, S. Bond, R. Chote, M. Gammie, P. Johnson, G. Myles, and J. Poterba (eds.) (2010), Dimensions of Tax Design: The Mirrlees Review, Institute for Fiscal Studies, Oxford University Press.

Mirrlees, J., S. Adam, T. Besley, R. Blundell, S. Bond, R. Chote, M. Gammie, P. Johnson, G. Myles, and J. Poterba (eds.) (2011), Tax by Design: The Mirrlees Review, Oxford University Press.

Mirrlees, J.A. (1971), An Exploration in the Theory of Optimum Income Taxation, Review of Economic Studies, 38, 175–208.

Mirrlees, J.A. (1974), Notes on Welfare Economics, Information and Uncertainty, in Essays in Equilibrium Behaviour under Uncertainty, ed. M. Balch, D. McFadden, and S. Wu, North-Holland.

Mirrlees, J.A. (1975, 1999), The Theory of Moral Hazard and Unobservable Behaviour. Part I, Review of Economic Studies, 66, 3–22.

Mirrlees, J.A. (1976a), Optimal Tax Theory. A Synthesis, Journal of Public Economics, 6, 327–58.

Mirrlees, J.A. (1976b), The Optimal Structure of Authority and Incentives within an Organization, Bell Journal of Economics, 7, 105–31.

Mirrlees, J.A. (1979), Arguments for Public Expenditure, in Contemporary Economic Analysis, ed. M. Artis and R. Nobay, Croom Helm.

Mirrlees, J.A. (1982), Migration and Optimal Income Taxes, Journal of Public Economics, 18(3), 319–41.

Mirrlees, J.A. (1986), The Theory of Optimal Taxation, in Handbook of Mathematical Economics, vol. 3, 2nd edn., ed. K.J. Arrow and M.D. Intriligator, Elsevier.

Mirrlees, J.A. (1990), Taxing Uncertain Incomes, Oxford Economic Papers, 42(1), 34–45.

Mirrlees, J.A. (1994), Optimal Taxation and Government Finance, in Modern Public Finance, ed. J.M. Quigley and E. Smolensky, Harvard University Press.

Mirrlees, J.A. (1997), Information and Incentives: The Economics of Carrots and Sticks, Economic Journal, 107(444), 1311–29.

Mirrlees, J.A. (2002), Optimal Marginal Tax Rates at Low Incomes, mimeo, University of Cambridge.

Mirrlees, J.A. (2005), The Theory of Optimal Taxation, in Handbook of Mathematical Economics, vol. 3, 2nd edn, ed. K.J. Arrow and M.D. Intriligator, North Holland.

Mirrlees, J.A. (2006), Welfare, Incentives, and Taxation, Oxford University Press.

Mitchell, B.R. (2007), International Historical Statistics, Palgrave Macmillan.

Moffitt, R. (1983), An Economic Model of Welfare Stigma, American Economic Review, 73, 1023–35.

Moffitt, R. (2006), Welfare Work Requirement with Paternalistic Government Preferences, Economic Journal, 116, F441–58.

Mortensen, D. and Pissarides, C. (1999), New Developments in Models of Search in the Labor Market, in Handbook of Labor Economics, vol. 3, ed. O. Ashenfelter and D. Card, North-Holland.

Mortensen, D.T. and C.A. Pissarides (2003), Taxes, Subsidies and Equilibrium Labor Market Outcomes, in Designing Inclusion, ed. E.S. Phelps, Cambridge University Press.

Munk, K. (1978), Optimal Taxation and Pure Profit, Scandinavian Journal of Economics, vol. 80(1), 1–19.
Murphy, L. and T. Nagel (2002), The Myth of Ownership, Oxford University Press.
Musgrave, R. (1959), The Theory of Public Finance, McGraw Hill.
Myles, G.D. (1989), Ramsey Tax Rules for Economies with Imperfect Competition, Journal of Public Economics, 38(1), 95–115.
Myles, G.D. (1995), Public Economics, Cambridge University Press.
Myles, G.D. (1997), Depreciation and Intergenerational Altruism in the Private Provision of Public Goods, European Journal of Political Economy, 13, 725–38.
Naito, H. (1999), Re-examination of Uniform Commodity Taxes under a Non-linear Income Tax System and its Implication for Production Efficiency, Journal of Public Economics, 71, 165–88.
Nichols, A.L. and R.J. Zeckhauser (1982), Targetting Transfers through Restrictions on Recipients, American Economic Review, 72, 372–7.
Nielsen, S.B. and Sörensen, P.B. (1997), On the Optimality of the Nordic System of Dual Income Taxation, Journal of Public Economics, 63, 311–29.
Nozick, R. (1974), Anarchy: State and Utopia, Blackwell.
O'Donoghue, T. and M. Rabin (2003), Studying Optimal Paternalism, Illustrated by a Model of Sin Taxes, American Economic Review, 93, 186–91.
OECD (1986), Personal Income Tax Systems Under Changing Economic Conditions, OECD.
Okun, A. (1975), Equality and Efficiency: The Big Tradeoff, Brookings Institution Press.
Ordover, J. and E. Phelps (1979), The Concept of Optimal Taxation in the Overlapping-generations Model of Capital and Wealth, Journal of Public Economics, 12, 1–26.
Oswald, A. (1983), Altruism, Jealousy and the Theory of Optimal Nonlinear Taxation, Journal of Public Economics, 20, 77–87.
Padovano, F. and E. Galli (2002), Comparing the Growth Effects of Marginal vs. Average Tax Rates and Progressivity, European Journal of Political Economy, 18, 529–44.
Pareto, V. (1896, 1897), Cours d'économie politique professé a l'université de Lausanne, Vol. I 1896, Vol. II 1897.
Pareto, V. (1917), Trattato Di Sociologia Generale (4 vols.), The Mind and Society, Vol. III, Vol. IV, Jonathan Cape, 1936.
Park, N.-H. (1991), Steady-state Solutions of Optimal Tax Mixes in an Overlapping Generations Model, Journal of Public Economics, 46, 227–46.
Parsons, D.O. (1996), Imperfect 'Tagging' in Social Insurance Programs, Journal of Public Economics, 62, 183–207.
Pekkarinen, J., K. Takala, and M. Tuomala (1985), The Personal Distribution of Wealth in Finland Report I, no. 49, Department of Economics University of Helsinki.
Pencavel, J. (1986), Labor Supply of Men: A Survey, in Handbook of Labor Economics, vol. 1, 1st edn, ed. O. Ashenfelter and R. Layard, Elsevier.
Persson, M. and S. Sandmo (2005), Taxation and Tournaments, Journal of Public Economic Theory, 7, 543–59.
Pestieau, P. (1974), Optimal Taxation and Discount Rate for Public Investment in a Growth Setting, Journal of Public Economics, 3, 217–35.
Petrongolo, B. and C.A. Pissarides (2001), Looking into the Black Box: A Survey of the Matching Function, Journal of Economic Literature, 38, 390–431.
Phelps, E. (1979), The Concept of Optimal Taxation in the Overlapping-generations Model of Capital and Wealth, Journal of Public Economics, 12, 1–26.
Pigou, A.C. (1947), A Study in Public Finance, Macmillan.
Piketty, T. (1997), La redistribution scale face au chômage, Revue Française d'Economie, 12(1), 157–201.
Piketty, T. (2014), Capital in the Twenty-first Century, Harvard University Press.

Piketty. T. and E. Saez (2003), Income Inequality in the United States, 1913–1998, Quarterly Journal of Economics, 118(1), 1–39.

Piketty, T. and E. Saez (2012), A Theory of Optimal Capital Taxation, NBER Working Papers 17989, National Bureau of Economic Research.

Piketty, T. and E. Saez (2013), Optimal Labor Income Taxation, in Handbook of Public Economics, vol. 5, ed. Alan Auerbach, Raj Chetty, Martin Feldstein, and Emmanuel Saez Elsevier.

Piketty, T, and E. Saez (2013), A Theory of Optimal Inheritance Taxation, Econometrica, 81(5), 1851–86.

Piketty, T., E. Saez, and S. Stantcheva (2014), Optimal Taxation of Top Labor Incomes: A Tale of Three Elasticities, American Economic Journal: Economic Policy, 6(1), 230–71.

Piketty, T. and G. Zucman (2014), Capital is Back: Wealth-Income Ratios in Rich Countries 1700–2010, Quarterly Journal of Economics, 129(3), 1255–310.

Piolatto, A. and M. Rablen (2013), Prospect Theory and Tax Evasion: A Reconsideration of the Yitzhaki Puzzle, IFS Working Papers W13/25.

Pirttilä, J. and H. Selin (2011), Income Shifting within a Dual Income Tax System: Evidence from the Finnish Tax Reform of 1993, Scandinavian Journal of Economics, 113(1), 120–44.

Pirttilä, J. and I. Suoniemi (2014), Public Provision, Commodity Demand and Hours of Work: An Empirical Analysis, Scandinavian Journal of Economics, 116(4), 1044–67.

Pirttilä, J. and S. Tenhunen (2008), Pawns and Queens Revisited: Public Provision of Private Goods when Individuals Make Mistakes, International Tax and Public Finance, 15(5), 599–619.

Pirttilä, J. and M. Tuomala (1997), Income Tax, Commodity Tax and Environmental Policy, International Tax and Public Finance, 4, 379–93.

Pirttilä, J. and M. Tuomala (2001), On Optimal Non-linear Taxation and Public Good Provision in an Overlapping Generations Economy, Journal of Public Economics, 79, 485–501.

Pirttilä, J. and M. Tuomala (2002), Publicly Provided Private Goods and Redistribution: A General Equilibrium Approach, Scandinavian Journal of Economics, 104(1), 173–88.

Pirttilä, J. and M. Tuomala (2004), Poverty Alleviation and Tax Policy, European Economic Review, 48, 1075–90.

Pirttilä, J. and M. Tuomala (2007), Labour Income Uncertainty, Taxation and Public Good Provision, Economic Journal, 117 (March), 567–82.

Pisauro, G. (1991), The Effect of Taxes on Labour in Efficiency Wage Models, Journal of Public Economics, 46(3), 329–45.

Pogge, T.W. (1989), Realizing Rawls, Ithaca: Cornell University Press.

Pollak, R. (1970), Habit Formation and Dynamic Demand Functions, Journal of Political Economy, 78(4), 745–63.

Racionero, M. del Mar (2000), Optimal Redistribution with Unobservable Preferences for an Observable Merit Good, International Tax and Public Finance, 7, 479–501.

Racionero, M. del Mar (2001), Optimal Tax Mix with Merit Goods, Oxford Economic Papers, 53, 628–41.

Ramsey, F.P. (1927), A Contribution to the Theory of Taxation, Economic Journal, 37, 47–61.

Ramsey, F.P. (1928), A Mathematical Theory of Saving, The Economic Journal, 38, 543–59.

Ravallion, M. (2013), The Idea of Antipoverty Policy, Working Paper 19210, http://www.nber.org/papers/w19210.

Ravaska, T., S. Tenhunen, and M. Tuomala (2015), On the Optimal Lifetime Redistribution and Equality of Opportunities, mimeo.

Rawls, J. (1971), Theory of Justice, Harvard University Press.

Rawls, J. (1974), Reply to Alexander and Musgrave, Quarterly Journal of Economics, 88(4), 633–55.

Rawls, J. (1974), Some Reasons for the Maxi-Min Criterion, American Economic Review, Paper and Proceedings, 141–6.

Rawls, J. (1982), Social Unity and Primary Goods, in Utilitarianism and Beyond, ed. A. Sen and B. Williams, Cambridge University Press, 159–85.

Renström, T. (1998), On Optimal Taxation in Overlapping Generations Economies, mimeo, University of Birmingham.

Revesz, J.T. (1986), On Some Advantages of Progressive Indirect Taxation, Public Finance/Finances Publiques, 41, 182–97.

Revesz, J.T. (1989), The Optimal Taxation of Labour Income, Public Finance/Finances Publiques, 44, 433–75.

Revesz, J.T. (2005), The Optimal Tax Mix Reconsidered, Public Finance/Finances Publiques, 1–2/54, 1–21.

Riihelä, M., R. Sullström, and M. Tuomala (2008), Economic Poverty in Finland 1971–2004, Finnish Economic Papers, 21, 57–77.

Riihelä, M., R. Sullström, and M. Tuomala (2013), Top Incomes and Top Tax Rates: Implications for Optimal Taxation of Top Incomes in Finland, Tampere Economic Working Papers, Net Series no 81, University of Tampere.

Riihelä, M., R. Sullström, and Matti Tuomala (2015), Veropolitiikka huipputulojen ja -varallisuuden taustalla – Onko Pikettyn kuvaama kehitys nähtävissä Suomessa? Hyvinvointivaltio 2010-luvulla – mitä kello on lyönyt? Taimio Heikki (toim.).

Roberts, K. (1977), Voting over Income Tax Schedules, Journal of Public Economics, 8(3), 329–40.

Roberts, K. (1984), The Theoretical Limits of Redistribution, Review of Economic Studies, 51(2), 177–95.

Roberts, K. (2000), A Reconsideration of Optimal Income Tax, in Incentives, Organization and Public Economics, Papers in Honour of Sir James Mirrlees, ed. P. Hammond and G. Myles, Oxford University Press.

Rochet, J-C. (1985), The Taxation Principle and Multitime Hamilton-Jacobi Equations, Journal of Mathematical Economics 14 (1985), 113–28.

Rochet, J-C. and P. Choné (1998), Ironing, Sweeping and Multidimensional Screening, Econometrica, 66(4), 783–826.

Røed, K. and S. Strøm (2002), Progressive Taxes and the Labour Market: Is the Tradeoff Between Equality and Efficiency Inevitable?, Journal of Economic Surveys, 16(1), 77–110.

Roemer, J.E. (1998), Equality of Opportunity, Harvard University Press.

Roemer, J.E., R. Aaberge, U. Colombino, J. Fritzell, S. Jenkins, A. Lefranc, I. Marx, M. Page, E. Pommer, and J. Ruiz-Castillo (2003), To What Extent do Fiscal Regimes Equalize Opportunities for Income Acquisition Among Citizens? Journal of Public Economics, 87(3–4), 539–65.

Roemer, J. (2008), Equality of Opportunity, in The New Palgrave Dictionary of Economics, ed. S. Durlauf and L. Blume, Macmillan.

Rogerson, W. (1985), The First-Order Approach to Principal-Agent Problems, Econometrica, 53, 1357–67.

Rogerson, W. (1985), The First-Order Approach to Principal-Agent Problems, Econometrica 53, 1357–67.

Romer, T. (1976), On the Progressivity of the Utilitarian Income Tax, Public Finance, 31, 151–78.

Rothschild, C. and F. Scheuer (2012), Optimal Taxation with Rent-Seeking, http://www.wiwi.uni-frankfurt.de/kolloquium/ws1213_/Scheuer.pdf.

Rothschild, M. and J. Stiglitz (1971), Increasing Risk I: A Definition, Journal of Economic Theory, 2, 225–43.

Rothschild, M. and J. Stiglitz (1976), Equilibrium in Competitive Insurance Markets: An Essay on the Economics of Imperfect Information, Quarterly Journal of Economics, 90, 629–49.

Ryder, H. and G. Heal (1973), Optimal Growth with Intertemporally Dependent Preferences, Review of Economic Studies, 40, 1–33.

Sadka, E. (1976), On Income Distribution, Incentive Effects and Optimal Income Taxation, Review of Economic Studies, 43(2), 261–67.

Sadka, E, (1976), On Progressive Income Taxation, American Economic Review, 66(5), 931–35.

Sadka, E., I. Garfinkel, and K. Moreland (1982), Income Testing and Social Welfare: An Optimal Tax–Transfer Model in Income-Tested Transfers Programs: The Case For and Against in Garfinkel (ed).
Saez, E. (2001), Using Elasticities to Derive Optimal Income Tax Rates, Review of Economic Studies, 68, 205–229.
Saez, E. (2002a), Desirability of Commodity Taxation under Non-linear Income Taxation and Heterogeneous Tastes, Journal of Public Economics, 83, 217–30.
Saez, E. (2002b), Optimal Income Transfer Programs: Intensive vs Extensive Labour Supply Responses, Quarterly Journal of Economics, 117, 1039–73.
Saez, E. (2004), Direct or Indirect Tax Instruments for Redistribution: Short-Run versus Long-Run, Journal of Public Economics, 88(3–4), 503–18.
Saez, E., J. Slemrod, and S.H. Giertz (2012), The Elasticity of Taxable Income with Respect to Marginal Tax Rates: A Critical Review, Journal of Economic Literature, 50(1), 3–50.
Saez, E. and S. Stantcheva (2013), Generalized Social Marginal Welfare Weights for Optimal Tax Theory, NBER Working Paper no. 19777.
Sandmo, A. (1975), Optimal Taxation in the Presence of Externalities, Swedish Journal of Economics, 77, no. 1, 86–98.
Sandmo, A. (1981), Income Tax Evasion, Labour Supply, and the Equity Efficiency Tradeoff, Journal of Public Economics, 16(3), 265–88.
Sandmo, A. (1983), Ex Post Welfare Economics and the Theory of Merit Goods, Economica, 50, 19–33.
Sandmo, A. (1993), Optimal Redistribution when Tastes Differ, Finanz Archiv, 50(2), 149–63.
Sandmo, A. (1998), Redistribution and the Marginal Cost of Public Funds, Journal of Public Economics, 70, 365–82.
Sandmo, A (2005), The Theory of Tax Evasion: A Retrospective View, National Tax Journal, 58, 643–63.
Sandmo, A. (2011), Economics Evolving: A History of Economic,Thought, Princeton University Press.
Sandmo, A. (2012), An Evasive Topic: Theorizing about the Hidden Economy, International Tax and Public Finance, 19(1), 5–24.
Schokkaert, E., D. Van de Gaer, F. Vandenbroucke, and R.I. Luttens (2004), Responsibility-sensitive Egalitarianism and Optimal Linear Income Taxation, Mathematical Social Sciences, 38, 151–82.
Schroyen, F. (1997), Pareto Efficient Income Taxation under Costly Monitoring, Journal of Public Economics, 65(3), 343–66.
Schroyen, F. (2005), An Alternative Way to Model Merit Good Arguments, Journal of Public Economics, 89, 957–66.
Seade, J. (1980), Optimal Non-linear Policies for Non-utilitarian Motives, in Income Distribution: The Limits to Redistribution, ed. D.A. Collard, R. Lecomber, and M. Slater, Scientechnica.
Seade, J. (1982), On the Sign of Optimum Marginal Income Taxation, Review of Economic Studies, 49, 637–43.
Seade, J.K. (1977), On the Shape of Optimal Tax Schedules, Journal of Public Economics, 7, 203–35.
Sen, A. (1970), Collective Choice and Social Welfare, Holden-Day.
Sen, A. (1973), On Economic Inequality, Norton.
Sen, A. (1974), Informational Bases of Alternative Welfare Approaches: Aggregation and Income Distribution, Journal of Public Economics, 3(4), 387–403.
Sen, A. (1976), Poverty: An Ordinal Approach to Measurement, Econometrica, 44, 219–31.
Sen, A. (1980), Equality of What? In Tanner Lectures on Human Values, ed. S. McMurrin, Cambridge University Press.
Sen A. (1982), Choice, Welfare and Measurement, Basil Blackwell.
Sen A. (1984), Resources, Values and Development, Basil Blackwell.
Sen, A. (1985), Commodities and Capabilities, North-Holland.
Sen, A. (2000), Social Justice and the Distribution of Income, in Handbook of Income Distribution, vol. 1, ed. A.B. Atkinson and F. Bourguignon, Elsevier.

Sen, A. (2009), The Idea of Justice, Harvard University Press and Allen Lane.
Shaw, J., J. Slemrod, and J. Whiting (2010), Administration and Compliance, in Dimensions of Tax Design: The Mirrlees Review, ed. S. Adam, T. Besley, R. Blundell, S. Bond, R. Chote, M. Gammie, P. Johnson, G. Myles, and J. Poterba, Oxford University Press.
Sheshinski, E. (1972), The Optimal Linear Income Tax, Review of Economic Studies, 39(3), 297–302.
Sheshinski, E. (1989), Note on the Shape of the Optimum Income Tax Schedule, Journal of Public Economics, 40(2), 201–15.
Sheshinski, E. (2002), Bounded Rationality and Socially Optimal Limits on Choice in a Self-selection Model, mimeo, The Hebrew University of Jerusalem.
Sheshinski, E. (2003), Optimal Policy to Influence Individual Choice Probabilities, mimeo, The Hebrew University of Jerusalem.
Shimer, R. and I. Werning (2005), Liquidity and Insurance for the Unemployed, Federal Reserve Bank of Minneapolis Research Department Staff Report 366.
Sillamaa, M-A., and M.R. Veall (2001), The Effect of Marginal Tax Rates on Taxable Income: A Panel Study of the 1988 Tax Flattening in Canada, Journal of Public Economics, 80, 341–56.
Simula, L. (2010), Optimal Nonlinear Income Tax and Nonlinear Pricing: Optimality Conditions and Comparative Static Properties, Social Choice and Welfare, 35(2), 199–220.
Simula, L. and A. Trannoy (2010), Optimal Income Tax under the Threat of Migration by Top-Income Earners, Journal of Public Economics, 94, 163–73.
Sinn, H.-W. (1996), Social Insurance, Incentives and Uncertainty, International Tax and Public Finance, 3, 259–80.
Slemrod, J. (1992), Do Taxes Matter? Lessons from the 1980's, American Economic Review, 82(2), 250–56.
Slemrod, J. (1996), High Income Families and the Tax Changes of the 1980s: The Anatomy of Behavioral Response, in Empirical Foundations of Household Taxation, ed. Martin Feldstein and James Poterba, University of Chicago Press.
Slemrod, J. (1998), Methodological Issues in Measuring and Interpreting Taxable Income Elasticities, National Tax Journal, 51, 773–88.
Slemrod, J. and J. Bakija (2000), Does Growing Inequality Reduce Tax Progressivity? Should It? NBER Working Papers 7576, National Bureau of Economic Research.
Slemrod, J. and S. Yitzhaki (2001), Integrating Expenditure and Tax Decisions: The Marginal Cost of Funds and the Marginal Benefit of Projects, National Tax Journal, 54, 189–201.
Slemrod, J. and S. Yitzhaki (2002), Tax Avoidance, Evasion and Administration, in Handbook of Public Economics, vol. 3, ed. A. Auerbach and M. Feldstein, North-Holland.
Slemrod, J., S. Yitzhaki, J. Mayshar, and M. Lundholm (1994), The Optimal Two-bracket Linear Income Tax, Journal of Public Economics, 53(2), 269–90.
Slemrod, J. and W. Kopczuk (2002), The Optimal Elasticity of Taxable Income, Journal of Public Economics, 84(1), 91–112.
Smith, A. (2012), The Wealth of Nations, Simon & Brown.
Smith, S. (1992), Taxation and the Environment: A Survey, Fiscal Studies, 13, 21–57.
Solnick, S. and D. Hemenway (2005), Are Positional Concerns Stronger in Some Domains than in Others? American Economic Review, Papers and Proceedings, 45, 147–15.
Solow, R. (2013), Greenspan is Still Trying to Justify His Bad Decisions: What the Maestro Doesn't Understand, New Republic, 16 December.
Solow, R. (2014), Thomas Piketty is Right: Everything You Need to Know about 'Capital in the Twenty-First Century', New Republic, 22 April.
Sørensen, P.B. (1997), Public Finance Solutions to the European Unemployment Problem?, Economic Policy, 12(25), 223–64.

Sørensen, P.B. (1999), Optimal Tax Progressivity in Imperfect Labour Markets, Labour Economics, 6, 435–52.

Spinnewijn, J. (2010), Unemployed but Optimistic: Optimal Insurance Design with Biased Beliefs, mimeo, London School of Economics.

Stantcheva, S. (2011), Optimal Taxation with Adverse Selection in the Labor Market, MIT Working Paper.

Starmer, C. (2000), Developments in Non-expected Utility Theory: The Hunt for a Descriptive Theory of Choice under Risk, Journal of Economic Literature 38, 332–82.

Stephens, E. (2009), Constraints and Policy in Education and Public Budget Limits, PhD thesis, Queen's University.

Stern, N. (1976), On the Specification of Optimum Income Taxation, Journal of Public Economics, 6, 123–62.

Stern, N. (1977), Welfare Weights and the Elasticity of the Marginal Valuation of Income, in Studies in Modern Economic Analysis, ed. M. Artis and R. Nobay, Basil Blackwell.

Stern, N. (1982), Optimum Taxation with Errors in Administration, Journal of Public Economics, 17, 181–211.

Stern, N. (1986), On the Specification of Labour Supply Functions, in Unemployment, Search and Labour Supply, ed. R. Blundell and I. Walker, Cambridge University Press.

Stiglitz, J.E. and P. Dasgupta (1971), Differential Taxation, Public Goods and Economic Efficiency, Review of Economic Studies, 38(114), s151–74.

Stiglitz, J.E. (1982), Self-selection and Pareto-efficient Taxation, Journal of Public Economics, 17, 213–40.

Stiglitz, J.E. (1985), Inequality and Capital Taxation, IMSSS Technical Report 457, Stanford University.

Stiglitz, J.E. (1987), Pareto-efficient and Optimal Taxation and the New New Welfare Economics, in Handbook of Public Economics, Vol II, ed. A. Auerbach and M. Feldstein, Elsevier.

Straub, L. and I. Werning (2014), Positive Long Run Capital Taxation: Chamley-Judd Revisited, NBER Working Papers 20441, National Bureau of Economic Research.

Strawczynski, M. (1998), Social Insurance and the Optimum Piecewise Linear Income Tax, Journal of Public Economics, 69, 371–88.

Tanninen, H. and M. Tuomala (2005), Inherent Inequality and the Extent of Redistribution in OECD Countries, CESifo DICE Report, Ifo Institute for Economic Research at the University of Munich, 3(1), 48–53.

Tanninen, H. and M. Tuomala, (2009), Work Hours, Inequality and Redistribution: Veblen Effects Reconsidered, Tampere Economic Working Papers, Net Series no. 70, University of Tampere.

Tarkiainen, R. and M. Tuomala (1999), Optimal Nonlinear Income Taxation with a Two-Dimensional Population: A Computational Approach, Computational Economics, 13, 1–16.

Tarkiainen, R. and M. Tuomala (2007), On Optimal Income Taxation with Heterogeneous Work Preferences, International Journal of Economic Theory, 3, 35–46.

Tenhunen, S. (2007), Essays on the Theory of Optimal Taxation, Acta Universitatis Tamperensis 1276, Tampere University Press.

Tenhunen, S. and M. Tuomala (2007), Housing Policy and Redistribution, Tampere Economic Working Papers, Net Series no. 53, University of Tampere.

Tenhunen, S. and M. Tuomala (2010), On Optimal Lifetime Redistribution Policy, Journal of Public Economic Theory, vol. 12(1), 171–98.

Thaler, R.H. and C.R. Sunstein (2008), Nudge: Improving Decisions About Health, Wealth, and Happiness (New Haven: Yale University Press).

Thoresen, T.O. and A. Alstadsæter (2010), Shifts in Organizational Form under a Dual Income Tax System, Finanz Archiv, 66(4), 384–418.

Tuomala, M. (1979), Optimal Income Taxation and Uncertainty, mimeo, University of Helsinki.

Tuomala, M. (1984a), On the Optimal Income Taxation: Some Further Numerical Results, Journal of Public Economics, 23, 351–66.
Tuomala, M. (1984b), Optimal Degree of Progressivity under Income Uncertainty, Scandinavian Journal of Economics, 87, 184–93.
Tuomala, M. (1985), Simplified Formulae for Optimal Linear Income Taxation, Scandinavian Journal of Economics, 87(4), 668–72.
Tuomala, M. (1986), On the Optimal Income Taxation and Educational Decisions, Journal of Public Economics, 30, 183–98.
Tuomala, M. (1990), Optimal Income Tax and Redistribution, Oxford University Press.
Tuomala, M. (2010), On Optimal Non-linear Income Taxation: Numerical Results Revisited, International Tax and Public Finance, 17(3), 259–70.
Tuomala, M. and S. Tenhunen (2013), On the Design of an Optimal Non-linear Pension System with Habit Formation, International Tax and Public Finance, 20, 485–512.
Tversky, A. and Kahneman, D. (1992), Advances in Prospect Theory: Cumulative Representation of Uncertainty, Journal of Risk and Uncertainty, 5, 297–323.
Ulph, D. (1977), On the Optimal Income Distribution and Educational Expenditure, Journal of Public Economics, 8, 341–56.
Van de Gaer, D. (1993), Equality of Opportunity and Investments in Human Capital, PhD thesis, KULeuven.
van der Wijks, J. (1939), Inkomens, en Vermogensverdeling, Publications of the Netherlandsisch Economisch Institut, 26, De Erven F, Bohn N.V.
Varian, H. (1980a), Intermediate Microeconomics, 3rd edn, Varian.
Varian, H. (1980b), Redistributive Taxation as Social Insurance, Journal of Public Economics, 14, 49–68.
Viard, A.D. (2001a), Optimal Categorical Transfer Payments: The Welfare Economics of Limited Lump-sum Redistribution, Journal of Public Economic Theory, 3, 483–500.
Viard, A.D. (2001b), Some Results on the Comparative Statics of Optimal Categorical Transfer Payments, Public Finance Review, 29, 148–80.
Vickrey, W.S. (1945), Measuring Marginal Utility by Reactions to Risk, Econometrica, 13, 319–33.
Wane, W. (2001), The Optimal Income Tax when Poverty is a Public 'Bad', Journal of Public Economics, 82(2), 271–99.
Weinzierl, M.C. (2011), The Surprising Power of Age-Dependent Taxes, Review of Economic Studies, 78(4), 1490–518.
Weinzierl, M.C. (2012), Why Do We Redistribute So Much but Tag So Little? The Principle of Equal Sacrifice and Optimal Taxation, Harvard Business School Working Paper, No. 12–64.
Werning, I. (2002), An Elementary Proof of Positive Optimal Marginal Taxes, mimeo.
Werning, I. (2007), Optimal Fiscal Policy with Redistribution, Quarterly Journal of Economics, MIT Press, 122(3), 925–67.
Weymark, J.A. (1986), A Reduced-form Optimal Nonlinear Income Tax Problem, Journal of Public Economics, 30(2), 199–217.
Wildasin, D.E. (1984), On Public Good Provision with Distortionary Taxation, Economic Inquiry, 22(2), 227–43.
Wilson, J.D. (1982), The Optimal Public Employment Policy, Journal of Public Economics, 17, 241–58.
Wilson, J.D. (1991), Optimal Public Good Provision with Limited Lump-Sum Taxation, American Economic Review, 81, 153–66.
Wilson, R. (1993), Nonlinear Pricing, Oxford University Press.
Wilson, R. (1995), Nonlinear Pricing and Mechanism Design, in Handbook of Computational Economics, vol. 1, ed. H.M. Amman, D.A. Kendrick, and J. Rust, Elsevier Science Publisher.
Yitzhaki, S. (1979), Relative Deprivation and the Gini Coefficient, The Quarterly Journal of Economics, 93(2), 321–24.

Yitzhaki, S. (1987), On the Excess Burden of Tax Evasion, Public Finance Review, 15(2), 123–37.
Zoutman, F., B. Jacobs, and E. Jongen (2012a), Optimal Redistributive Taxes and Redistributive Preferences in the Netherlands, mimeo, Erasmus University Rotterdam, CPB Netherlands Bureau for Economic Policy Research.
Zoutman, F., B. Jacobs, and E. Jongen (2012b), Revealed Social Preferences of Dutch Political Parties, mimeo, Erasmus University Rotterdam/CPB Netherlands Bureau for Economic Policy Research.

INDEX

References such as '178–9' indicate (not necessarily continuous) discussion of a topic across a range of pages. Wherever possible in the case of topics with many references, these have either been divided into sub-topics or only the most significant discussions of the topic are listed. Because the entire work is about 'taxation' and 'redistribution', the use of these terms (and certain others which occur constantly throughout the book) as entry points has been restricted. Information will be found under the corresponding detailed topics.

The manufacturer's authorised representative in the EU for product safety is Oxford University Press España S.A. of el Parque Empresarial San Fernando de Henares, Avenida de Castilla, 2 – 28830 Madrid (www.oup.es/en or product.safety@oup.com). OUP España S.A. also acts as importer into Spain of products made by the manufacturer.

www.ingramcontent.com/pod-product-compliance
Ingram Content Group UK Ltd.
Pitfield, Milton Keynes, MK11 3LW, UK
UKHW050950290926
15470UKWH00005B/1742
* 9 7 8 0 1 9 8 7 5 3 4 1 4 *